THE OXFORD HANDBOOK OF
THE HISTORY OF YOUTH CULTURE

THE OXFORD HANDBOOK OF

THE HISTORY OF YOUTH CULTURE

Edited by
JAMES MARTEN

OXFORD
UNIVERSITY PRESS

Oxford University Press is a department of the University of Oxford. It furthers the University's objective of excellence in research, scholarship, and education by publishing worldwide. Oxford is a registered trade mark of Oxford University Press in the UK and certain other countries.

Published in the United States of America by Oxford University Press
198 Madison Avenue, New York, NY 10016, United States of America.

© Oxford University Press 2023

All rights reserved. No part of this publication may be reproduced, stored in a retrieval system, or transmitted, in any form or by any means, without the prior permission in writing of Oxford University Press, or as expressly permitted by law, by license, or under terms agreed with the appropriate reproduction rights organization. Inquiries concerning reproduction outside the scope of the above should be sent to the Rights Department, Oxford University Press, at the address above.

You must not circulate this work in any other form
and you must impose this same condition on any acquirer.

Library of Congress Cataloging-in-Publication Data
Names: Marten, James Alan, author.
Title: The Oxford handbook of the history of youth culture /
edited by James Marten.
Description: New York, NY : Oxford University Press, [2023] |
Series: Oxford handbooks series | Includes index. |
Identifiers: LCCN 2023020445 (print) | LCCN 2023020446 (ebook) |
ISBN 9780190920753 (hardback) | ISBN 9780190920777 (epub) |
ISBN 9780190920784
Subjects: LCSH: Youth. | Teenagers. | Adolescent psychology.
Classification: LCC HQ796.M333 2023 (print) | LCC HQ796 (ebook) |
DDC 305.235/5—dc23/eng/20230601
LC record available at https://lccn.loc.gov/2023020445
LC ebook record available at https://lccn.loc.gov/2023020446

DOI: 10.1093/oxfordhb/9780190920753.001.0001

Printed by Integrated Books International, United States of America

Contents

About the Editor   ix
Contributors   xi

1. Introduction: A Kaleidoscope of Youth Cultures   1
   JAMES MARTEN

PART I: PREMODERN YOUTH CULTURES

2. Monastic and University Education in the Medieval and Early Modern West   21
   ANDREW REEVES

3. Coming of Age in Elite Families, c. 1200–c. 1650   39
   LOUISE J. WILKINSON

4. Contested Territory: Non-Elite Youth and Youth Culture in the Premodern West   59
   ADRIANA BENZAQUÉN

PART II: SHAPING MODERN YOUTH CULTURES

5. Youth Participation in Political Violence: Comparative Cultural Constructions   79
   DAVID M. ROSEN

6. Youth Culture as a Battleground: Atlantic World Slavery and Enslaved Youth in Jamaica   97
   COLLEEN A. VASCONCELLOS

7. A "Tomboy" and a "Lady": Religion, Modernity, and Youth Culture in Twentieth-Century Zanzibar   113
   CORRIE DECKER

8. Industrialization: Youth at Work 131
   James Schmidt

9. Urbanization: Youth Gangs and Street Cultures 149
   Simon Sleight and Jasper Heeks

10. Gender, Agency, and Sex: Postwar European Youth and the
    Generation Gap 169
    David Niget

PART III: SELF-EXPRESSION

11. The Power of Style: Transnational Youth (Sub)Cultures, Socialist
    Habitats, and the Cold War 193
    Juliane Fürst

12. Play Cultures, Social Worlds, and Youth in Familial Settings,
    1700–1905 213
    Mary Clare Martin

13. Youth Culture and Indian Boarding Schools 235
    Kristine Alexander

14. Globalizing the Americas through Twentieth-Century Youth
    Organizations 255
    Elena Jackson Albarrán

15. Youth and Consumer Culture: Entrepreneurial Consumption 275
    Elizabeth Chin

16. Youth Cultures of Activism and Politics 293
    Nazan Maksudyan

17. Sexuality, Youth Cultures, and the Persistence of the
    Double Standard in the Twentieth-Century United States 313
    Nicholas L. Syrett

18. Celebrating Holidays and Instilling Values: Religion, Nationalism,
    and Youth Organization in Twentieth-Century Youth Culture 333
    Dylan Baun

PART IV: REPRESENTATIONS OF YOUTH

19. Youth in the Visual Arts   353
   ANN BARROTT WICKS

20. Transforming Rebellion into Affirmation: A History of Youth
   Literature and Reading Cultures   375
   PAUL RINGEL

21. Youth Culture on Screens Big and Small   395
   HELLE STRANDGAARD JENSEN AND GARY CROSS

22. Paradox and Possibility: Youth Media Culture across the Globe   413
   STUART R. POYNTZ

Index   433

About the Editor

The author, editor, or co-editor of more than twenty books, James Marten taught at Marquette University for thirty-six years, where he is now professor of history emeritus. He was a founder of the Society for the History of Children and Youth (SHCY) and served as the Society's president from 2013 until 2015. He is a former editor of the *Journal of the History of Childhood and Youth*.

Contributors

Elena Jackson Albarrán, Associate Professor in the History and Global and Intercultural Studies Departments, Miami University of Ohio

Kristine Alexander, Associate Professor of History, University of Lethbridge

Dylan Baun, Associate Professor of History, University of Alabama in Huntsville

Adriana Benzaquén, Professor of History, Mount Saint Vincent University

Elizabeth Chin, Editor-in-Chief, *American Anthropologist*

Gary Cross, Distinguished Professor Emeritus of Modern History, Pennsylvania State University

Corrie Decker, Associate Professor of History, University of California, Davis

Juliane Fürst, Head of the Communism and Society Department, Center for Contemporary History, Potsdam, Germany

Jasper Heeks, PhD Candidate, Department of History, King's College London

Helle Strandgaard Jensen, Associate Professor, Aarhus University

Nazan Maksudyan, Researcher, Center Marc Bloch / Freie Universität Berlin

James Marten, Professor Emeritus of History, Marquette University

Mary Clare Martin, Principal Lecturer and Research Lead, Institute of Lifecourse Development, University of Greenwich

David Niget, Assistant Professor of History, University of Angers

Stuart R. Poyntz, Professor and Director of the School of Communication and Co-Director of the Community Engaged Research Initiative (CERi), Simon Fraser University

Andrew Reeves, Associate Professor of History, Middle Georgia State University

Paul Ringel, Professor of History, High Point University

David M. Rosen, Professor of Anthropology, Fairleigh Dickinson University

James Schmidt, Presidential Teaching Professor, Northern Illinois University

xii CONTRIBUTORS

Simon Sleight, Reader in Urban History, Historical Youth Cultures and Australian History, King's College London

Nicholas L. Syrett, Associate Dean and Professor of Women, Gender, and Sexuality Studies, University of Kansas

Colleen A. Vasconcellos, Professor of History, University of West Georgia

Ann Barrott Wicks, Professor of Art History Emerita, Miami University of Ohio

Louise J. Wilkinson, Professor of Medieval Studies, School of Humanities and Heritage, University of Lincoln

CHAPTER 1

INTRODUCTION

A Kaleidoscope of Youth Cultures

JAMES MARTEN

THE phrase "youth culture" brings together two of the easiest and most difficult words to define. We all know what a "youth" is, and we all have at least a sense of what "culture" is, even though it is a fungible kind of word, related to literature, performing arts, and music, of course—but also to ethnicity, belief systems, and socioeconomic class. But the challenges and opportunities that scholars face in writing about youth and culture come from the fact that these words are highly elastic and relative; used together, they create an almost impossible-to-define concept. Yet youth is one of the most fascinating, rewarding, frightening, and fraught passages in a person's life, and the way young people experience and describe that passage—and the way parents and society try to narrow the possibilities of that passage—makes up much of what we know about youth culture.

In his 1985 sociological overview, *Comparative Youth Culture*, Mike Brake writes that sixty or seventy years of scholarship on youth cultures had coalesced around the theme "that if the young are not socialized into conventional political, ethical and moral outlooks, if they are not programmed into regular work habits and labour discipline, then society as it is today cannot continue." These perennial, age-old fears lend urgency to the need to understand youth culture, and they provide hints as to why social scientists—in the fields that developed late in the nineteenth- and early twentieth centuries, such as psychology, sociology, and social work—studied youth culture for decades before historians took it seriously. Brake goes on to write,

> What is central to any examination of youth culture is that it is not some vague structural monolith appealing to those roughly under thirty, but is a complex kaleidoscope

of several subcultures, or different age groups, yet distinctly related to the class position of those in them.

The historians who contributed to this handbook might not use precisely the same language, but they would certainly agree with the notion that there is not one "youth culture." And, although it may stretch the metaphor to say so, youth culture is similar to a kaleidoscope in that it represents multiple communities and values, and that it can be seen differently depending on the perspective from which it is being viewed.[1]

Societies have often focused on youth culture as a series of problems: delinquency, illicit sex, loud music, protest, and countless other forms of behavior often viewed as threats to social order that demand solutions. This reductionism is reflected in the titles found on the shelves of the Library of Congress's HQ subsection in any academic library: *Fitting In, Standing Out*; *Youth Crisis*; *My Son Is an Alien*; *Search for Identity*; *All Grown Up and No Place to Go*; *Lost Youth in the Global City*; *Teenage Wasteland*; *Growing Up Absurd*; *The Vanishing Adolescent*; *Strangers in the House*; *Pathways through Adolescence*; *Not Much, Just Chillin'*; *Re/Constructing "The Adolescent"*; *Goth's Dark Empire*; *Super Girls, Gangstas, Freeters, and Xenomaniacs*.

Although the specifics have varied, the general concerns have not much changed since the early twentieth century. In a recent collaboration with *Scientific American*, the journal *Nature* devoted much of a 2018 issue to "Coming of Age: The Science of Adolescence." Its introduction states that

> It's widely accepted that adolescents are misunderstood. Less well known is how far we still have to go to understand adolescence itself. One problem is that it is hard to characterize: the concept of puberty does not capture the decade or more of transformative physical, neural, cognitive and socio-emotional growth that a young person goes through. Another is that science, medicine, and policy have often focused on childhood and adulthood as the most important phases of human development, glossing over the years in between.

The rest of the issue examines contemporary health and social issues: brain development, generational relationships, use of media, alcohol, obesity, and antisocial behavior.[2]

In some ways historians have followed the lead of psychologists, political scientists, social workers, activists, and policymakers in exploring youth culture through the lenses of pathologies, failures of society, or attempts to solve perceived problems. Yet historians by their very nature do not see themselves as solvers of problems; rather, they step back to study the actions and desires that seem to feed those problems along with the institutions, organizations, and laws intended to control them. In the introduction to their excellent anthology, Joe Austin and Michael Nevin Willard write that "the practices of young people become occasions for moral panic . . . resulting in calls for social renewal and action." Drug use, sex, crime, sexuality and teen pregnancy, and shortcomings in our educational systems have all taken their turns, some several times—as sources of community anxiety and increased supervision and regulation. The more than two dozen essays that Austin and Willard assembled tend to focus more on youth agency than on attempts to control it, highlighting music, art, dress, cars, zines, and other forms of self-expression.[3]

The difference, perhaps, between historians and social scientists examining youth culture is that, while the latter are consciously trying to find solutions to perceived problems (and, of course, there *are* problems that need to be solved), the former are more interested in explaining why particular aspects of youth culture are *perceived* as problems. Historians seek to understand the motivations behind the youth forming those cultures and the adults expressing their anger, fear, or dismay.

In Paula Fass's *Encyclopedia of Children and Childhood: In History and Society*, Austin offers a useful overview of the historiography and history of youth culture. The first line of his entry is instructive: "Culture is among the most complicated words in the English language." He goes on: "It refers to the processes by which . . . traditions and rituals" and "frameworks for understanding experience . . . characteristically shared by a group of people" are "maintained and transformed across time." Some, he points out, are "distinctive from those of their parents and the other adults in their community." Another useful point he makes is that, even if the institutions and concrete evidence of culture do not appear in the historical record, it does not mean that youth culture did not exist. For him—and for many of the authors in this handbook—*behavior* is as much a product and signifier of youth culture as are institutions, organizations, and movements.[4]

Defining a Historical Youth Culture

The essays in this volume explore the development and diversification of youth culture around the world from the medieval period to the present. Although global in scope, this is not a comprehensive history of youth culture. It *does*, however, address a comprehensive set of issues related to youth culture. Throughout, authors distinguish between the histories of *youth* (in other words, the experiences of youth and the conditions in which they live) and the histories of *youth culture* (the cultural and emotional products of youths' interaction with one another and with their larger community or communities). For instance, an essay on youth and work provides an overview of the nature of the work experience, but it emphasizes the ways in which youth responded to work, and the ways in which greater autonomy, access to spending money, and relationships to other youth contributed to the formation of youth culture.

Taken together, the chapters demonstrate that youth culture has developed out of efforts by adults to shape coming of age and the efforts of youth themselves to find their own paths. It encompasses the aspects of "culture" that we are familiar with—art, literature, drama—as well as the less tangible but perhaps more important organizations, associations, customs, and styles that draw youth together and separate them from others. The ways in which youth spend their leisure time has figured prominently in the ways that parents and policymakers have worried about youth culture, even as leisure activities provided structure to that culture, and a significant segment of youth culture has also been almost inseparable from popular culture—music, movies, and television, especially—since at least the 1950s and 1960s. Normal biological, emotional, and intellectual development naturally intersect with youth culture, especially in the contexts of emerging sexuality, mental health issues, and the relationship of youth to authority figures and institutions.

Studying the history of youth culture in any society provides a crucial lens for understanding that society's value systems, educational and economic structures, gender relations, and virtually every facet of cultural expression and human development. This is particularly important during the modern period, which saw the development of economies that required less labor from adolescents while at the same time offering—and requiring, in most places—more opportunities for formal education, both of which encouraged the development of a separate youth culture. Although these conditions emerged first in the United States and then in Western Europe, they gradually expanded to most of the world, although specific forms of youth culture varied greatly by place, ethnicity, and religion, among other factors. Moreover, societies around the world have periodically experienced crises in the behavior of adolescents (the "boy problem" in the United States in the early twentieth century, for instance).

The Search for a Definition of Youth Culture

Humans have for many centuries recognized "youth" as a separate phase of life. It appeared in many early demarcations of the "stages of man," although the exact ages at which it began and ended could vary from the mid-teens to late twenties. But the important point is that virtually all societies recognized some distinct facets of youth, from legal responsibility to the ability to articulate thoughts and feelings to being physically ready and mature enough to consider courtship. As a recent brief survey of adolescence says, one definition is disarmingly simple: the "period of transition between life as a child, and life as an adult." The author goes on to state that puberty has normally been a fairly safe starting point for thinking about adolescence, but a paragraph later he writes that although the teenage years are generally considered identical to adolescence, some researchers consider ages ten to eighteen as more accurate, and the World Health Organization identifies it as ten to nineteen.[5]

Looming large over any study of youth or youth culture is the work of G. Stanley Hall, who earned the first doctorate in psychology in the United States and published *Adolescence* in 1904. This two-volume tome set the stage for much of what we think about adolescence and youth, although thinking about adolescence has become more complex since its publication. His borrowing of the German phrase *Sturm und Drang*—storm and stress—to describe the transformations and tensions that adolescents experience still resonates today. Indeed, many of the essays in this collection could be organized around three of the primary ways in which Hall's work is still found useful: adolescents' changing relationships with their parents and peers, with the former receding in importance and the latter increasing in importance; their increased willingness to take risks, and their emerging sexuality.[6]

One of the issues facing historians of youth culture is the difficulty of separating youth from children in the past. The study of children and youth as a field of history emerged from the 1960s' interest in social history, specifically in family and women's history. The history of children is, at least on the surface, easier to define than the history of youth. Although individual historians often focused on children *or* youth, they were often lumped together, at least partly because of the variable nature of the social construction of both categories and the extremely subjective coming-of-age markers that attended the transition from one to the other. The fields are often combined, as the names of the flagship journal and one of the leading professional associations indicate: the *Journal of the History of Childhood and Youth* and the Society for the History of Children and Youth. But even children's historians understand that they are dealing with a construct that has varied and does so considerably from time to time, place to place, and community to community. By the same token, we rarely write about a culture belonging entirely to children; they lack the agency, independence, and resources to create a truly separate culture.[7]

It may be something of an artificial distinction to try to determine where those categories of age begin and end, and historians have placed more importance on understanding young people's interactions with society no matter their age. Although a brief entry on "Youth Culture" in *Adolescence in America: An Encyclopedia* now seems outdated, the final paragraph of the entry offers an appropriate call for a deeper understanding of youth culture: "Culture is a prevalent and powerful presence in the lives of youth. We cannot understand today's teenagers without attending to, studying and understanding their culture." Youth culture can be found in the internal and external tension created by the push toward adulthood and the pull back toward childhood.[8]

Most studies of youth culture focus on modern history—by its very nature, social science research used living subjects, and historians rely on written sources, which for youth are extraordinarily rare before the nineteenth century. Moreover, suggesting that youth formed a culture suggests that they had the freedom and space in which to create it, and except for the most elite families, that was rarely the case for premodern youth, who were normally integrated tightly into family economies, rarely had any kind of personal privacy, and had no or very little access to institutions devoted to young people. The primary evidence of youth culture from premodern eras often comes out of descriptions of their behavior, including participation in religious rituals and rowdyism among apprentices, rather than of institutions or self-conscious groupings. Schools provided some of that space, as educational opportunities slowly expanded from small academies and cathedral schools to various forms of local and even public education. Apprenticeships and guilds also provided a different kind of social group in which a kind of youth culture could flourish.

Perhaps the key transformations for the development of youth culture were industrialization and urbanization, with their attendant creation of large groups of ethnically and economically homogenous youth, a middle class with smaller families and greater resources, and a selection of pastimes and amusements. Although many factors could speed or slow the development of youth culture, by the twentieth century, many different youth cultures had emerged, along with many different responses to nurturing or controlling them, but the rise of consumerism and mass entertainment opportunities provided even more impetus to the formation of youth culture. Those developments would lead to periodic "scares" about delinquency, sex, and substance abuse. The primary innovation in the study of the history of youth culture over the last twenty years has been its expansion into non-western countries and more securely into gender studies, especially the burgeoning field of girls' history.

Sampling the Historiography of Youth Culture

Because the authors of the chapters in this handbook have provided case studies rather than a comprehensive history of youth culture, it would be well to sample some previous scholarship on youth in general and youth cultures in particular, starting with a few broad studies.

A History of Young People in the West, a two-volume anthology first published in English in 1997, provides eighteen essays on the history of youth, mainly on continental Europe. Like many scholars prior to the twenty-first century (indeed, like many reformers and policymakers), the authors focus primarily on males. None write about "youth culture" as such, but their work shows that it is difficult to avoid youth culture when researching the things that are important to youth and the ways in which society tries to deal with youth. Many of these essays foreshadow the topics that appear in this handbook, including youth in early modern warfare, as sources of menace and disruption, and as members of socioeconomic classes. Some focus on youth exerting agency and some semblance of control over their lives, while others examine efforts to limit their control and to mold them to meet society's needs. Perhaps the most important contribution to our understanding of the history of youth culture is the book's demonstration that youth itself is a social construction, whose parameters and assumptions vary greatly over time and space. The lack of a single definition of either "youth" or "culture" provides historians with a great amount of freedom to explore myriad forms of expression or repression, but it also burdens them with the responsibility of defining for themselves what exactly they mean when they explore youth culture.[9]

A much more tightly organized study is *Youth Culture and Social Change*, edited by a team of scholars interested in the ways in which music, especially, has reflected and influenced protest, rebellion, and even violence in late-twentieth- and early-twenty-first-century Great Britain. The salient feature of the book is its insistence that youth culture matters, and not simply to youth. "In this book we go further than documenting the sounds of dissent," the editors write. "We explore how music worked as a way of making a difference" in issues including labor strife, race relations, student protests, courtship and sex, and gang culture. Each of the essays connects a form of popular music—usually a specific song or band—with a particular time, place, and issue. Its importance to this volume has less to do with its subject matter and more with the weight that it gives to youth culture in general.[10]

Historians who have tried to offer broad overviews of youth and youth culture have usually placed them in tension with the history of childhood or of adult culture. Most of the broadly framed books deal with youth as a period of life rather than with the culture it produces. Joseph Kett's *Rites of Passage: Adolescence in America 1790 to the Present* was the first major effort by an American historian to provide such an overview. He argues that in the late eighteenth and early nineteenth centuries "youth" could mean anyone from the ages of ten to twenty-five; one of the major developments as attitudes about childhood, education, and work changed was the narrowing of that age range. Although Kett spends more time on efforts to shape and control youth than on the creation of a youth culture, his book was a first step toward understanding the history of youth culture in America.[11] Although the term "teenager" is a decidedly modern construct (even as it is also a simple descriptor), Grace Palladino's history of this population associates nearly universal attendance in high school with the building of a "teenage culture" that she describes as "a story of institution building, market expansion, racial desegregation, and family restructuring" after the Second World War.[12] Although not purporting to be a history of youth or of youth culture, a number of the essays in a recent anthology edited by Corrine T. Field and Nicholas L. Syrett touch on issues related to American youth culture, particularly political participation and voting, sexuality, work, and drinking.[13] Finally, David Pomfret's and Richard Ivan Jobs's collection of essays show youth as a "historical force" in the twentieth century, with case studies on such topics as the modernization of rural Japan, male scouting in Mexico and female scouting in Malaya, youth travel, youth displacement, political protest, and popular culture.[14]

The generation that, in America at least, provided the most grist for the study of youth culture was that of the "baby boomers" of the 1940s–1960s; an excellent introduction on their impact on the larger culture and, in the 1960s, the creation of their own is Victor D. Brooks, *Boomers: The Cold War Generation Grows Up*. Although not limited to youth, as such, but providing a deep understanding of the twentieth-century globalization of the contours of youth culture is Paula S. Fass, *Children of a New World: Society, Culture, and Globalization*.[15]

More narrowly conceived histories of youth culture can be divided into several categories of inquiry, which follow.

Delinquency and Control

One of the oldest traditions in the study of youth culture is the history of juvenile delinquency—although the original scholars would not have couched their work in that way, focusing more often on ways of combating the problem rather than on the points of view of the youth themselves. Two recent examples of transnational investigations into delinquent behavior and policy are Jean Trepanier and Xavier Rousseaux, eds., *Youth and Justice in the Western States, 1815-1950: From Punishment to Welfare*, and William S. Bush and David S. Tanenhaus, eds., *Ages of Anxiety: Historical and Transnational Perspectives on Juvenile Justice*. A number of books published over the last twenty years have explored the particular ways in which notions and biases related to race and gender contributed to the behaviors identified as delinquent, including Mary E. Odem, *Delinquent Daughters: Protecting and Policing Adolescent Female Sexuality in the United States, 1885-1920*; Tera Eva Agyepong, *The Criminalization of Black Children: Race, Gender and Delinquency in Chicago's Juvenile Justice System, 1899-1945*; and Jenifer S. Light, *States of Childhood: From the Junior Republic to the American Republic, 1895-1945*.[16]

The efforts by most societies throughout history to raise youth into productive citizens run through many of these essays and throughout the literature; this becomes even more imperative in times of crisis. Just two of several excellent works on this effort are Sayaka Chatani, *Nation-Empire: Ideology and Rural Youth Mobilization in Japan and Its Colonies*, and Sian Edwards, *Youth Movements, Citizenship and the English Countryside: Creating Good Citizens, 1930-1960*.[17] These books and others focus on the work of organizations—village-level youth associations in the far-flung reaches of the Japanese empire, and the Boy Scouts, Girl Guides, and other such organizations in Britain and the West—in obligating youth to their current or future civic duties.

Youth and the Economy

Work is one of the more confusing elements of the history of youth; the major campaigns to set limits on the work of young people attacked "child labor," rather than "youth labor," and the laws that were eventually passed to regulate age in the workplace usually set the point at which employers could legally hire young people squarely in the middle of what would commonly be considered "youth." Yet studies of child labor can tell us a lot about the ways in which work could contribute to the development of youth culture at the local level by creating pride in the ability to do a day's work, a sense of belonging to a community, and a sense of contributing to their families' well-being. One of the most useful books on the legal as well as community facets of child and youth work is James Schmidt, *Industrial Violence and the Legal Origins of Child Labor*.[18] Related to the issue of work is the issue of how youth spend their own money—whether received as allowance or earned as wages. Elizabeth Chin's *Purchasing Power: Black Kids and American Consumer Culture* shows how that agency among older children and youth in underprivileged families is not necessarily governed by acquisitiveness, but by numerous other factors, including the welfare of other family members.[19]

Armed Conflict

One of the confusing elements of studies of children and war is that they virtually always include people we would call "youth," although the word rarely appears in titles. David M. Rosen, one of the contributors to this volume, is perhaps the leading authority on the history of child soldiers—who are usually, of course, youth, and for whom defending their country, protecting their family, or promoting a certain political view can often shape their identity as youth.[20] The experiences of young people on the home front are often difficult to separate from those of younger children, but among the books that investigate the ways in which war can create opportunities for youth—by providing more room for developing their own cultures and contributions, narrowing possibilities by requiring them to work or by depriving them of family and government support, or by causing governments to pay more attention to them—is Nazan Maksudyan, *Ottoman Children & Youth during World War I*. James Marten's *The Children's Civil War* shows the development of proto-youth cultures during the American Civil War through literature, home front hardships, work, and familial sacrifice. Although dated, Victoria Sherrow's *Encyclopedia of Youth and War: Young People as Participants and Victims* provides brief summaries of hundreds of events, policies, and people related to the ways in which youth were forced or chose to engage in war, mainly in the twentieth century (although a few entries extend back into the eighteenth and nineteenth centuries).[21]

Political Awareness and Activism

The essays in Mark Roseman's anthology, *Generations in Conflict: Youth Revolt and Generation Formation in Germany, 1770–1968*, offer a long view of the ways in which conflict between generations shaped class relations and political movements, including Nazism and especially in East Germany.[22] Although youth contributed greatly to the protests that led to the end of apartheid in South Africa, for decades before that the frustration and generational tension sparked the creation of sometimes violent and criminal gangs.[23] More typical accounts of youth activism—one challenging the existing power structure, one being enthusiastically socialized into it—appear, respectively, in Louie Dean Valencia-García, *Antiauthoritarian Youth Culture in Francoist Spain: Clashing with Fascism*, and Anne Luke, *Youth and the Cuban Revolution: Youth and Politics in 1960s*.[24] Perhaps even more central to their nation's political and social development were the youth of Argentina, whose culture helped modernize the nation even as it engaged its authoritarian government; see Valeria Manzano, *The Age of Youth in Argentina: Culture, Politics, & Sexuality from Peron to Videla*.[25] Although we commonly associate the political activism of the 1950s and 1960s with college campuses, Gael Graham pushes that narrative back to the high school years in *Young Activists: American High School Students in the Age of Protest*, and the thirty essays in *Student Revolt, City and Society in Europe* begins in the Middle Ages and runs all the way to the present, covering everything from riots to strikes to protests on issues ranging from town/gown conflicts and curricula to political radicalism and oppression. Sampling activism from every part of Europe through the ages, the book collectively shows the importance of action, resistance, and group formation (even temporary group formation) to the creation of youth culture.[26]

Girlhood

A flurry of recent books on "girlhood" captures the ambiguity of age as a category of analysis, as "girl," "youth," "young girls," and "young women" can all be identifiers of female youth. The title of Sherrie Inness's 1998 anthology *Delinquents and Debutantes: Twentieth-Century American Girls' Culture* suggests the dichotomy that girls faced as they reached sexual maturity and in the ways that historians have analyzed that segment of youth culture.[27] But these books often capture the intersections of sexual coming of age and the transition from economic dependence to at least partial independence in ways that separate the experiences of female youth from male youth. Abosede George's *Making Modern Girls: A History of Girlhood, Labor, and Social Development* is an excellent example of this genre of study and adds the all-important colonial aspect to the issue of "girl-saving."[28] Ann Kordas's recent overview of *Female Adolescent Sexuality in the United States, 1850–1965* covers the typical proscriptive efforts by adults throughout the twentieth century to regulate girls' sexuality, but it emphasizes the ways in which girls reappropriated the message of the larger society in creating their own girls' culture, while Nicholas L. Syrett's *American Child Bride: A History of Minors and Marriage in the United States* tackles the complicated problem of how local and regional attitudes and politics have influenced thinking about the rights of youth and gender relations.[29]

Popular Culture

The study of popular culture often intersects with the study of youth culture, as shown in a recent spate of books on Irish youth in the twentieth century, most recently Eleanor O'Leary's *Youth and Popular Culture in 1950s Ireland*. O'Leary also shows that the study of youth culture can revise common assumptions about a time and place; the films, comics, clubs, and other leisure activities—including illicit ones—are a counterpoint to the traditional narrative of hardship and stifling traditionalism that usually dominates the Irish narrative.[30] Similarly, in *Machines of Youth: America's Car Obsession*, Gary S. Cross tackles a seemingly well-worked subject but makes larger points about how working-class male culture often created a community that revolved around autonomy, masculinity, technical know-how, and rebellion.[31] Devorah Levenson's well-received study of gangs in Guatemala City goes well beyond the usual account of juvenile gang activity to explore poverty, class, and the failure of a revolution to live up to its promise.[32] In *Stalin's Last Generation: Soviet Post-War Youth and the Emergence of Mature Socialism* Juliane Fürst shows how even as the Cold War heated up after the Second World War, the youth who had grown up during the last years of Stalin produced a youth culture that looked to the West for style and popular culture and began to challenge Soviet assumptions and hegemony.[33] Chinese youth culture since the 1960s has been shaped by both local and global currents, argues Paul Clark. While the Cultural Revolution dominated youth culture in the 1960s, by the late 1980s sports and rock music had begun to influence Chinese youth, and by the twenty-first century the Internet became both a source of information about the wider world and an outlet for frustration with their sometimes constrained lives.[34]

Spaces of Their Own

Youth have often developed their own cultures by taking over certain locations and spaces. The young in these books range from the newsboys (actually youth and young men) of David Nasaw's *Children of the City: At Work & at Play*, to the youth claiming places to work, consume, play, court girls, and form gangs in Simon Sleight's *Young People and the Shaping of Public Space in Melbourne, 1870–1914*, to Joe Austin's young graffiti artists in *Taking the Train: How Graffiti Art Became a Crisis in New York City*.[35] Jason Reid examines a more literal physical space in *Get Out of My Room: A History of Teen Bedrooms in America*, which includes, of course, ideas about privacy, sex, and technology.[36]

The Oxford Handbook of the History of Youth Culture

Inspired by and complementing this wide-ranging and flourishing historiography of youth culture, the authors who contributed to this handbook come out of a number of academic disciplines, although all write with a historic sensibility. Their essays address topics from their particular points of reference and methodologies. Although global in scope, it is not comprehensive. Each author highlights a particular place or time but draws comparisons and contrasts with other locations and periods. Their samples might cover a century or a decade, a specific country or a larger region, or young men or women or both. But each essay is representative in that, despite its necessarily limited temporal and geographical coverage, it offers conclusions useful to understanding other times and places.

The essays can be split into multiple approaches, with most essays fitting into more than one category. The handbook itself is organized into several sections.

Just a few chapters deal with premodern youth, when the institutions created by and for youth did not yet exist; the sources are few; and the perceptions of this troublesome phase of life were so different than in our own time. These essays illustrate how historians have tried to identify the elements of youth culture during the pre- and early modern periods, when the concept of adolescence, although recognized as a biological phase, was not clearly seen as a discrete period during which youth created their own spaces, prerogatives, and traditions. Nevertheless, several threads that would emerge in youth culture—and in the ways that scholars have explored youth culture—are evident and will surface in the essays that compose the bulk of the book.

Perhaps the first hint of a youth culture emerged in the monasteries, cathedral schools, and universities of medieval and early modern Europe. The boys and young men attending these schools created a proto-youth culture based on their self-conscious "performance," as Andrew Reeves puts it, of masculine traits and values. Reeves shows that the emergence of the Catholic orders of the thirteenth century, and the Protestant reformation of the sixteenth century, offered youth "countercultures" that rejected established male identities and what they believed to be oppressive Catholic institutions, respectively.

Louise J. Wilkinson's study of youth culture among the European elite from the thirteenth to the mid-seventeenth-centuries describes a phase that sounds a little more like modern youth. Acknowledging that not all historians of the period agree on what "youth" might have meant to people living during this time, she argues that a tiny fraction of the population—males and some females—took on some adult responsibilities; completed training or education in universities, noble households, or royal courts; and had access to economic resources that helped them prepare for adulthood. Most of these youth came from the European economic elite or were headed for membership in the institutional elite. Adriana Benzaquén's examination of non-elite youth in the premodern West shows that male youth (and very few females) defined and enlivened a culture of their own through rowdiness, sexuality, and rebelliousness, despite the persistent efforts of the Church and civil authorities to control them.

The second grouping of essays focuses on external forces acting on youth and on the ways that youth have engaged those forces: sometimes resisting, sometimes accommodating, but usually finding some sort of middle ground. All have contributed to the development of youth culture in their times and places.

Armed conflict is one of only a few human enterprises in which the boundaries separating youth and adulthood are simultaneously blurred and reinforced. In war youth can be victims and soldiers, heroes and villains, observers and actors. David M. Rosen reveals how youth have interacted with armed conflict in all its complexity, as participating in war becomes a form of coming of age, socialization, and opportunity for self-expression. Moreover, in certain conflicts, such as revolutionary movements, youth become symbols of a future for which they are fighting. In any case, Rosen argues, youth mobilization has been a "relative constant in human history."

At face value, the institutions and practices of slavery seem as though they should have quashed any attempt to form a youth culture. Yet, using Jamaica as a case study, Colleen A. Vasconcellos declares that youth culture became a "battleground" in which masters, parents, and youth themselves tried to control lives that, although tightly constrained by violence and law, still represented a chance for youth to use various levels of resistance to create a "culture of survival."

Corrie Decker looks at the ways in which religion—another constant in youthful lives through much of recorded history—can shape a particular kind of youth culture. Although focusing on one place—Zanzibar—and one faith tradition—Islam—her analysis of the tensions caused by modernization, especially in terms of gender roles, can help us understand the process by which youth culture is formed and evolves. As she writes, "religious ideals held singular importance for young people's understanding of themselves and their relationships with family members and friends."

James Schmidt examines another point of continuity through the ages, one that both inhibited and enhanced the development of a youth culture: work. Although youth have worked in nearly every society and every epoch, the extent to which work prepares youth for responsible adulthood, or simply exploits their cheap labor, has been the subject of debate since at least the early nineteenth century. Schmidt studies three distinct periods that demonstrate the widely varying attitudes about work from the points of view of both working youth and reform-minded policymakers in the United States and across the globe.

Urban spaces have always provided conditions and opportunities that encouraged the creation of cultures among the youth living in crowded tenements, attending high schools, or working in shops or on street corners. Simon Sleight and Jasper Heeks explore a particular expression of that youth culture: gangs. Although focusing on the English-speaking world between the middle of the nineteenth and middle of the twentieth centuries, their essay shows the ways in which self-conscious choices about style, a sense of uniqueness, a touch of rebellion, and consumerism merged into this most-talked-about and feared form of youth culture.

Sexuality emerges in a number of chapters, but in David Niget's essay it provides an occasion to study how values and expectations of the larger society can influence youth culture. The "sexual liberation" of the 1960s, which cracked the "moral order" created by the Cold War, reflected youth's efforts to achieve greater autonomy in politics and in all aspects of their lives.

The handbook's third section offers case studies on the ways in which youthful self-expression helps young people create their own cultures. Technology has played an important role in this, but so have political institutions created by adults, which youth have adapted for their own purposes, including patterns and cultures of consumption, sexual mores, and religion.

According to Juliane Fürst, the "power" of style in clothes, hair, music, and entertainment reflected youth interests and politics. Concentrating on the Soviet Union in the twentieth century, she argues that the rise of the Soviet Republic, the Cold War and its aftermath, and the globalization of youth culture shaped the sometimes-subversive youth culture as it grew and evolved under Communism.

Mary Clare Martin expands the parameters of "youth" by investigating the ways in which outdoor activities, imaginative play (such as theatricals), and home-produced magazines and newspapers played important roles in the transition from childhood to youth and then on to adulthood. Focusing on Great Britain between 1700 and 1900, she argues that these processes cut across class and gender lines and show that activities instigated by children and youth complemented those initiated by adults; many took place in familial settings where children and youth of all ages frequently played together.

The boarding schools attended between the mid-nineteenth- through the mid-twentieth-centuries by indigenous children and youth—some voluntarily, most involuntarily—were, in fact, intended to quash native culture. Kristine Alexander shows, however, that indigenous youth in the United States and Canada were often able to resist acculturation by forming their own cultures within the schools, often by sustaining language and other elements of their native cultures, but also through such activities as sports and student journalism and publishing.

Elena Jackson Albarrán casts a wide net throughout Latin America to trace the relationship between national governments and political movements and youth cultures. Although leaders from communist regimes, populist movements, dictatorships, and every other point on the political spectrum tried to employ such organizations as Boy Scouts and Girl Guides, youth exchanges, and others to politicize children and youth into specific ideologies, young people often reshaped those organizations to meet their own ideas and "social goals."

The ways in which youth spend their money has long been recognized as a form of self-expression. Elizabeth Chin explores the ways in which "entrepreneurial selfhood" shapes the choices and aspirations of wealthy Qataris and poor African and Haitian youth. Despite the huge differences in their backgrounds and opportunities, they are connected by the "global reach of neoliberalism and the pressure to develop entrepreneurial selves."

Although focusing partly on the Middle East since the late nineteenth century, Nazan Maksudyan provides a broad view of the ways in which youth cultures have been influenced by and, in turn, shaped political activism. Reformers and repressers alike have sought to mobilize youth to promote particular points of view, from nationalist movements in the early twentieth century to antiestablishment movements in the 1960s to the recent rise of environmental and other groups.

Highlighting the centrality of sexuality to the ways in which youth have always identified themselves and the larger culture has always sought to define them, Nicholas L. Syrett offers a second chapter on sexuality, this time focusing on the United States. Although the century witnessed major changes in courtship patterns and sexual activity leading toward the "sexual liberation" of both sexes, there remains a significant double standard based on gender, particularly in the ways that some males used sexual conquests to enhance their masculinity even as some women pay the social price of premarital sexual activity.

Although in most cultures religion has come to play a smaller role in the development of youth culture, Dylan Baun suggests that in Lebanon and other parts of the Global South, religious-oriented youth organizations promoted religion, nation, and masculinity—central components of male youth culture in the twentieth century.

The ways that youth cultures have been depicted in the arts and media, and the ways in which youth interact with them, provide a fourth and final major area of inquiry for this collection.

Although images of youth are relatively rare in the visual arts—unlike children, who are plentiful—Ann Barrott Wicks explores several themes that surface in depictions of youth in China. Despite the difficulty of identifying them, representations of youth, like children, expressed family priorities, such as "lineage, moral outlook, political view, power, or wealth." As such, rather than being realistic portrayals of youth, they became symbols of aspirations.

Like other commercial art forms, literature has always reflected youth culture and been part of society's efforts to shape its youthful readers. Paul Ringel takes a broad look at American literature for youth from the late eighteenth to the late twentieth centuries. Unlike other popular art forms, he argues, literature did not give up moral instruction to be commercially successful. Even as the plots have expanded to include more adventure and youthful agency, the themes have continued to reinforce the importance of existing institutions and values.

Helle Strandgaard Jensen and Gary Cross show the intersections and divergences in the ways that television and movies have shaped youth identity and created anxiety among adults in the United States and in Scandinavia. They find deep differences in the ways content was created and the ways that youth were involved between the commercially driven model in the United States and the publicly funded processes in Scandinavia.

Stuart R. Poyntz traces youth culture through the production, representation, circulation, and consumption of mainstream and social media, both in the West and, more recently, in emerging societies. Although originating in tightly controlled commercial settings, the expansion of such platforms as YouTube and WeChat offer youth a chance to create their own media culture.

More than two decades ago, Joseph Hawes, a pioneer historian of childhood, declared that "Childhood is where you catch a culture in high relief." Hawes can be paraphrased in a way that provides a wonderful framing device for the essays in this anthology: Youth culture is where you catch a community in high relief. Studying the history of youth culture reveals the values that are—or are not—most important to a society, and how they are passed from one generation to the next. Youth culture often provides a sampling of the ways in which new ideas and technologies—from politics and sexuality to television and social media—might eventually affect an entire community. And youth culture, if observed closely, is a constant reminder of our own coming of age, with all the anxiety and joy and sense of discovery that brings. Despite the countless variations over time and space, youth culture is one thing experienced by all humans.[37]

Notes

1. Mike Brake, *Comparative Youth Culture: The Sociology of Youth Cultures and Youth Subcultures in America, Britain and Canada* (London: Routledge, 1985), ix.
2. "Introduction," to "Coming of Age: The Science of Adolescence," special issue, *Nature* 554, no. 7693 (2018), https://www.nature.com/collections/vbmfnrsssw, accessed March 30, 2021.
3. Joe Austin and Michael Nevin Willard, eds., *Generations of Youth: Youth Cultures and History in Twentieth-Century America* (New York: New York University Press, 1998), 1.
4. Joe Austin, "Youth Culture," in *Encyclopedia of Children and Childhood: In History and Society*, vol. 3, ed. Paula S. Fass (New York: Gale, 2004), 910.
5. Peter K. Smith, *Adolescence: A Very Short Introduction* (Oxford: Oxford University Press, 2016), 1.
6. Smith, *Adolescence*, provides an excellent, brief discussion of Hall; 12–15.
7. For two examples of excellent overviews of children's history in which childhood and youth are blended together, see Colin Heywood, *A History of Childhood*, 2nd ed. (Cambridge: Polity, 2018), and Steven Mintz, *Huck's Raft* (Cambridge, MA: Harvard University Press, 2004).
8. Jacqueline V. Lerner and Richard M. Lerner, eds., *Adolescence in America: An Encyclopedia* (Santa Barbara, CA: ABC Clio, 2001), vol. 2, 810.
9. Giovanni Levi and Jean-Claude Schmitt, *A History of Young People in the West*, 2 vols. (Cambridge, MA: Belknap Press of Harvard University Press, 1997).
10. Keith Gildart, Anna Gough-Yates, Sian Lincoln, Bill Osgerby, Lucy Robinson, John Street, et al., eds., *Youth Culture and Social Change: Making a Difference by Making a Noise* (London: Palgrave Macmillan, 2017), 2.

11. Joseph Kett, *Rites of Passage: Adolescence in America 1790 to the Present* (New York: Basic Books, 1977).
12. Grace Palladino, *Teenagers: An American History* (New York: BasicBooks, 1996), xxi.
13. Corrine T. Field and Nicholas L. Syrett, eds., *Age in America: The Colonial Era to the Present* (New York: New York University Press, 2015).
14. Richard Ivan Jobs and David Pomfret, *Transnational Histories of Youth in the Twentieth Century* (New York: Palgrave Macmillan, 2015).
15. Victor D. Brooks, *Boomers: The Cold War Generation Grows Up* (Chicago: Ivan R. Dee, 2009); and Paula S. Fass, *Children of a New World: Society, Culture, and Globalization* (New York: New York University Press, 2007).
16. Mary E. Odem, *Delinquent Daughters: Protecting and Policing Adolescent Female Sexuality in the United States, 1885–1920* (Chapel Hill: University of North Carolina Press, 1996); Tera Eva Agyepong, *The Criminalization of Black Children: Race, Gender and Delinquency in Chicago's Juvenile Justice System, 1899–1945* (Chapel Hill: University of North Carolina Press, 2018); and Jenifer S. Light, *States of Childhood: From the Junior Republic to the American Republic, 1895–1945* (Cambridge, MA: MIT Press, 2020).
17. Sayaka Chatani, *Nation-Empire: Ideology and Rural Youth Mobilization in Japan and Its Colonies* (Ithaca, NY: Cornell University Press, 2018); Sian Edwards, *Youth Movements, Citizenship and the English Countryside: Creating Good Citizens, 1930–1960* (Cham, Switzerland: Palgrave Macmillan, 2018); and Kristine Alexander, *Guiding Modern Girls: Girlhood, Empire, and Internationalism in the 1920s and 1930s* (Vancouver: University of British Columbia Press, 2017).
18. James Schmidt, *Industrial Violence and the Legal Origins of Child Labor* (New York: Cambridge University Press, 2010).
19. Elizabeth Chin, *Purchasing Power: Black Kids and American Consumer Culture* (Minneapolis: University of Minnesota Press, 2001).
20. David Rosen, *Child Soldiers in the Western Imagination: From Patriots to Victims* (New Brunswick, NJ: Rutgers University Press, 2015); and *Armies of the Young: Child Soldiers in War and Terrorism* (New Brunswick, NJ: Rutgers University Press, 2005).
21. Nazan Maksudyan, *Ottoman Children & Youth during World War I* (New York: Syracuse University Press, 2019); James Marten, *The Children's Civil War* (Chapel Hill: University of North Carolina Press, 1998); Victoria Sherrow, *Encyclopedia of Youth and War: Young People as Participants and Victims* (Phoenix, AZ: Oryx Press, 2000).
22. Mark Roseman, *Generations in Conflict: Youth Revolt and Generation Formation in Germany, 1770–1968* (Cambridge: Cambridge University Press, 1995).
23. Clive Glaser, *Bo-tsotsi: The Youth Gangs of Soweto, 1935–1976* (Oxford: Oxford University Press, 2000).
24. Louie Dean Valencia-García, *Antiauthoritarian Youth Culture in Francoist Spain: Clashing with Fascism* (London: Bloomsbury, 2018); and Anne Luke, *Youth and the Cuban Revolution: Youth and Politics in 1960s Cuba* (Lanham, MD: Lexington Books, 2018).
25. Valeria Manzano, *The Age of Youth in Argentina: Culture, Politics, & Sexuality from Peron to Videla* (Chapel Hill: University of North Carolina Press, 2014).
26. Gael Graham, *Young Activists: American High School Students in the Age of Protest* (DeKalb: Northern Illinois University Press, 2006); Pieter Dhondt and Elizabethanne Boran, eds., *Student Revolt, City and Society in Europe Begin the Middle Ages: From the Middle Ages to the Present* (New York: Routledge, 2018).

27. Sherrie Inness, *Delinquents and Debutantes: Twentieth-Century American Girls' Culture* (New York: New York University Press, 1998).
28. Abosede George, *Making Modern Girls: A History of Girlhood, Labor, and Social Development* (Athens: Ohio University Press, 2014).
29. Ann Kordas, *Female Adolescent Sexuality in the United States, 1850–1965* (Lanham, MD: Lexington Books, 2019), and Nicholas L. Syrett, *American Child Bride: A History of Minors and Marriage in the United States* (Chapel Hill: University of North Carolina Press, 2016).
30. Eleanor O'Leary, *Youth and Popular Culture in 1950s Ireland* (London: Bloomsbury Academic, 2018).
31. Gary S. Cross, *Machines of Youth: America's Car Obsession* (Chicago: University of Chicago Press, 2018).
32. Devorah Levenson, *Adiós Niño: The Gangs of Guatemala City and the Politics of Death* (Durham, NC: Duke University Press, 2013).
33. Juliane Fürst, *Stalin's Last Generation: Soviet Post-War Youth and the Emergence of Mature Socialism* (Oxford: Oxford University Press, 2010).
34. Paul Clark, *Youth Culture in China: From Red Guards to Netizens* (Cambridge: Cambridge University Press, 2012).
35. David Nasaw's *Children of the City: At Work & at Play* (New York: Oxford University Press, 1985); Simon Sleight's *Young People and the Shaping of Public Space in Melbourne, 1870–1914* (London: Routledge, 2013); and Joe Austin, *Taking the Train: How Graffiti Art Became a Crisis in New York City* (New York: Columbia University Press, 2002).
36. Jason Reid, *Get Out of My Room: A History of Teen Bedrooms in America* (Chicago: University of Chicago Press, 2017).
37. Dale Russokoff, "On Campus, It's the Children's Hour," *Washington Post*, November 13, 1998 https://www.washingtonpost.com/archive/politics/1998/11/13/on-campus-its-the-childrens-hour/a3d0ee1f-dac7-4543-80db-a95eb07ce215/, accessed December 19, 2022.

PART I
PREMODERN YOUTH CULTURES

CHAPTER 2

MONASTIC AND UNIVERSITY EDUCATION IN THE MEDIEVAL AND EARLY MODERN WEST

ANDREW REEVES

THE concepts of youth and of youth culture are both often formed in school. This phenomenon is as true of medieval and early modern Western Europe as it is of other times and places. And in the European Middle Ages, school—especially what we might refer to as higher education—was usually the preserve of the Catholic Church. Under its aegis, a youth culture recognizable as such to moderns would emerge within the universities of Europe by the twelfth and thirteenth centuries. This culture was a liminal one, standing between childhood and an adult career, in which the young man formed a masculine identity and a sense of self including both an aggressive self-fashioning and also membership in a nobility, not of the sword, but of letters. This sense of membership in an elite came not only from a mimicry of noble masculinities, but also from a sense of collective access to knowledge beyond that of the general population. With the foundation of the orders of mendicant friars and their arrival in the universities shortly thereafter, young men in the universities would join these orders in an ostentatious rejection of ecclesiastical careerism and sexually predatory masculinity. Centuries later, with the arrival of the Protestant Reformation, young men in parts of Europe would reject the institution of the Catholic Church itself. With youth flocking to the mendicants and then three centuries later to the revolutionary ideals of the Protestant Reformation, the youth culture of the university also generated countercultures.[1]

To understand how this university culture and associated countercultures emerged, we must first note the medieval understanding of youth and where it stood in the life cycle and in the Church's education system as it developed over more than a millennium. We begin with the medieval and early modern understanding of youth, both of which were drawn from the Roman tradition. Childhood, *pueritia* in Latin, was held to end at twelve for girls and fourteen for boys. The next stage of life, adolescence or *adulescentia*, had different ranges depending upon the writer, although most held it to end in one's early twenties. What medieval writers call youth—*iuventus*—was closer to early adulthood as understood my moderns (i.e., one's twenties), the age in which lay nobles had taken up knighthood, and in which clerics had begun their church careers. As such, when we refer to "youth culture," we will be focusing primarily on what medievals called *adulescentia*. Religious thinkers held that by this time children were morally responsible for serious sins, and they could also testify in court and in some jurisdictions inherit property.[2]

Although notions of youth remained relatively constant, the system of education underwent major changes. For the purposes of this chapter, the traditional categories of early Middle Ages, high Middle Ages, and early modern period more or less work to distinguish the shifting of educational institutions and systems. In the early Middle Ages (roughly 500 to 1050), monasteries served as the primary centers of education in Western Europe. Over the course of the later eleventh and twelfth centuries, the cathedral schools of Europe's growing cities came to serve as centers of higher learning that by the thirteenth century had become the universities. These universities would gradually lead to a unified university culture across Western Europe. Finally, the twin forces of both Renaissance Humanism and the Protestant Reformation brought about an end to an international university culture and further cemented a growing trend of national universities. At the same time, university student bodies came to be made up of aristocrats, thus turning university youth culture into a subset of aristocratic youth culture.

Monastic Education: The Early Middle Ages

The constant of medieval youth culture was that it was a liminal space in which young men formed a collective identity as future sociocultural elites. This feature of medieval youth culture went all the way back to education in the late Roman Empire. In his late fourth-century autobiography *Confessions*, St. Augustine of Hippo recounted his rise from the local elite in North Africa to the more rarified atmosphere of Rome and Milan among elites from all over the Empire. He recalled his schooling in terms of acculturation to a "smart set," prone to both violent misbehavior and sexual indulgence, and he laments that with these peers he was ashamed that he "was not as shameless as they were."[3] The violence that accompanied the sexual aggression of this subculture was also foundational, from the beatings children received in the classroom to the games attended by these same young adults.

After the Western Empire's collapse, the schools of Europe's emerging monasteries imported many characteristics of the elite education system—indeed, most early medieval monks came from the ranks of social elites—but although monastic education showed a strong sense of differing stages of life, we see little in the way of a self-conscious youth culture in the early Middle Ages. Thus, other sources are necessary to look for ideals of a monastic youth culture.

Early medieval writers maintained the ancient Roman notion of different life stages with different needs and priorities. An understanding of children with different needs appears in Paul the Deacon's commentary (ca. 786) on the sixth-century Rule of St. Benedict, in which he allows an hour of recreation for children. Medieval monastic writers also had a keen understanding of adolescence as a period of an awakening sex drive—although to monastics this sex drive was a source of temptation. The tenth- and eleventh-century customaries of the Cluniac monasteries thus cautioned that youth should be extensively supervised to prevent same-sex or autoerotic experimentation.

There was a societal ideal of monastic youth—or at least one that survives in the extant sources. This model of monastic youth was a fusion of secular nobility and Christian piety, and that ideal is primarily noble, one of service, but applied to the cloister rather than the battlefield or warrior's hall. The noblewoman Duodha (fl. 824–844) wrote a spiritual guidebook for her son, a lay noble, that explained service as part of Christianity. Although Duodha herself is particularly devout and possibly unrepresentative, her call to "keep strong and true faith" with his monarch woven in with stories of the Old Testament prophets and patriarchs demonstrates the intermingling of Christian and noble values.[4] The young man in the monastery, by contrast, was not a warrior in training but, rather, a spiritual warrior training to fight through a life of prayer. In the domain of the cloister, the ideal of school tied together with noble service appears in the Rule of Benedict, which calls the monastery a "*scola* [school] for the Lord's service." Such a notion melded service, study, and metaphorical warfare, since a *scola* could also refer to a military unit.[5]

Monastic documents tell us of monastic values of youth, but they tell us little of youth *culture* except that it is a period of turning the ideals of the battlefield to those of the divine office. Hagiographies tell us of children and adolescents who distinguished themselves by being more somber than their rambunctious peers. These understandings of childhood and adolescence come not from young people themselves but, rather, from adults, who see characteristics of childhood as an obstacle to the holiness of the life of an adult monk.[6] But the voices of youth themselves are nearly silent.

The Central Middle Ages and the Beginnings of a Youth Culture

By the late eleventh century, a self-conscious sense of youth had begun to emerge. Efforts at Church reform, especially in Northern Europe, led to both the founding of new reforming monasteries and existing monasteries adopting reforms in life and practice. These reforms led to monasteries producing a greater literary output than their early medieval counterparts. These monasteries and their literary production bring more voices to light. The monk Guibert of Nogent (ca. 1055–1124), for example, left behind a rare autobiography. In it, he shows a youth culture among Europe's elites that would not have been alien to that of St. Augustine of Hippo. He writes that after his tutoring, when he entered *adulescentia*, he associated with young men with whom he rejected the asceticism of a monastic education and delighted in behavior he calls "wild and destructive."[7] Much of his (possibly exaggerated) language of repentance later in life is nearly stereotypical, but it shows us a sense of adolescent identity that pushes against the disciplinary constraints of the cloister. When taken together with monastic customaries showing worry about adolescent sexuality and the need to discipline children and adolescents, the reader can discern hints of a sense of youth in a monastic environment pushing against their constraints and seeking to emulate the youth culture of lay aristocrats.

Modern scholars of youth culture have often noted that a recognizable youth culture is dependent on material conditions, and this holds true especially for Europe moving from the early Middle Ages to the central Middle Ages. The growth of cathedral schools in the cities of Western Europe led to an environment in which a self-conscious and assertive clerical youth culture, related to but distinct from that of the knightly class, could take shape. This culture was abetted by the twin motors of Europe's increasing urbanization and the consequent growth of an ecclesiastical bureaucracy that needed educated men to staff it. Thus, the cathedral schools that would eventually become Europe's universities served as an incubator for the Western Church's "bourgeois church officialdom" to fashion its own identity.[8]

Through ecclesiastical institutions, young men began to gain the ability to chart their lives through a process of choice and geographic mobility. Saints' lives like those of Romuald of Ravenna show that as early as the tenth century, the Church provided the opportunity for a knight to pursue the life of a monk rather than the life of a warrior. Over the eleventh and twelfth centuries, the practice of families giving their children to monasteries for a lifetime as a monk (child oblation) gradually came to an end, so that by the twelfth century most monks professed based on their choice to do so in the age that we today call adolescence. Although most careers in the Church still came from family connections and most monks were still of noble families, new possibilities for a self-fashioning became available that had not been available before.

A few words are in order about the cathedral schools and universities that would grow from them and the age and status of their students. Outside of some Italian cities, in most of Western Europe letters were the domain of the Church, and so the boys and young men in primary and advanced schooling were clerics in what we call the "minor" orders; most were expected to be ordained to the priesthood. A child destined for a career in the Church would study in a school or under a private tutor. When he started school, he would receive his first ordination and begin the study of "letters," i.e., Latin, first with the Psalms and then with the ancient Roman poets. He would pursue further study in a cathedral school (or, later, a university) in his teens, arriving in an ecclesiastical career by the time of what contemporaries called *iuventus*. His social rank would be variable: north of the Alps, in schools and universities that looked to the Parisian model, the student could range from the ranks of the prosperous peasants or other commoners to the ranks of the knightly class, although the student would typically not come from the ranks of the very poor or the very great nobles. The cathedral school and university taking in students of varied backgrounds marked a dramatic shift from the monastery, whose members were almost all elites. In universities south of the Alps that looked to Bologna, students more generally came from the ranks of the nobility, might not be ordained to the major orders (subdeacon, deacon, or priest), and were also somewhat older. Although a great deal of scholarship has examined the distinctions between the student in these two types of universities, for our purposes, there were broad similarities between these two university cultures as a social space leading into an adulthood in Church officialdom.

These youth cultures of the schools were male. Although young women—especially elites—would receive an education in their households or in nunneries, the primary school classroom was male as was the classroom of the cathedral school. Men might be able to wander with some institutional and societal sanction, but women were unable to do so outside of the control of men if they were to maintain a sense of sexual "honor." Likewise, young men might be allowed to experiment sexually outside the confines of a marriage, but such an option was not open to women. Nor did the nun's education lead into an ecclesiastical career. What youth culture young women had was distinct from the male youth culture of the schools and universities.

The self-fashioning of the students in these organizations manifested in a sense of geographic as well as social mobility. In his autobiography written around 1130, Peter Abelard recounts students traveling from school to school in Northwestern Europe in search of the best masters, unwilling to be place bound. This mobility was a part of an overall liminality of youth and also stood in direct contrast to the traditional monastic vow of stability. The student standing outside the traditional boundaries of place and space had acquired enough of a presence that it had become a literary topos by the twelfth century. Contemporary "goliardic" poetry, that is, relatively short, rhyming Latin poems, spoke in the voice of the student unbound by social constraints. The twelfth- and thirteenth-century collections of poems today known as the Cambridge Songs and *Carmina Burana* show many examples of the mobile, wandering student: "I'm like a leaf carried about by the wind" says the poem known as "Estuans interius." Scholars in the first half of the twentieth century had read these poems naively as reflecting a community of wandering students. Recent scholarship has been more cautious in reading goliardic literature, rightly noting that the figure of the goliard, the "wandering scholar," is a literary construction—but a literary construction nevertheless suggests a cultural vocabulary that had a place for such a wandering student. These poems present perhaps an idealized portrait of the student's mobility described in Abelard's account of the restless students of his own day. These peregrinations themselves reflected an earlier generation of monastic students like Anselm, who, in the eleventh century, could travel from Italy to Normandy in search of the best master.

This sense of possibility and self-fashioning was heavily tied in with an aggressive masculinity that characterized Europe's knightly class, which furnished many of Europe's students and teachers and which those men of other social classes sought to emulate. This aggression and contest—what anthropologists call *agon*—entailed both intellectual and actual violence. An examination of Peter Abelard's autobiography demonstrates this culture of aggressive competition. As his education and childhood progressed—he does not give precise ages—he says that he "renounced the glory of the knight's life." He preferred, he writes, "the weapons of dialectic."[9] These weapons involved the practice of classroom disputation, in which two students—or a student and a master—would face off in a debate to determine a logical question. As a practice, the disputation had existed in monasteries in earlier centuries. With the twelfth century, it became more aggressive and performative. Rather than the master–student debate meant to help draw out a student's thought processes, the classroom disputation was a public display of one's prowess. The best masters were to be willing to allow any student to challenge them, which created a space for contesting authority. This combative schoolroom environment was often remarked upon by contemporaries. Abelard speaks of being able to best all comers in debate in his student days, although the hagiography of St. Goswin of Anchin recounts the saint besting the cocksure Abelard in the classroom. And William FitzStephen's description of twelfth-century London says that even young boys would play at being scholars holding classroom debates.[10]

The attitude of the arrogant student excited to debate his teacher reflects another element of this student body's *esprit de corps*, namely, a sense of collective access to and command of an advanced body of knowledge. Moralists condemned this cockiness, denouncing "curiosity" as a vice of prideful youth who had gained much knowledge but little wisdom. Bernard of Clairvaux (1090–1153), the Cistercian monk so known for his holiness that he served as an advisor to popes, nobles, and kings, denounced the eagerness of, "green young students . . . and those who are barely able to keep down, so to speak, the first solid food of the faith" to pry into the mysteries of theology and philosophy.[11] The churchman Gerald of Wales (1146–1223) tells the anecdote of a student who had returned from the schools in Paris and was excited to show off his mastery of philosophical logic to his father. He used logic to prove to his father that the six eggs in the house were actually twelve, and, so, writes Gerald, his father ate the six eggs and left "the other six" for his son. This student excitement with learning did not necessarily meet with approval from elders.

From School to University: Identities and Institutions

By the turn of the thirteenth century, these cathedral schools had become institutionalized into universities, particularly in Paris, Oxford, and Bologna, but with more universities emerging in Central and Southern Europe as the Middle Ages went on. The institutions, bound by statutes, solidified many of the protean elements of the twelfth-century culture of the cathedral schools. In some ways the institutionalization of a student enrolling under a particular master curtailed the practice of the student traveling from school to school and master to master as the desire, interest, or need took him. But this institutionalized structure also brought about a more distinct subculture based on rites of passage into the student body that would, in turn, prepare the students to staff the ranks of the Church and the growing legal profession.

The students' professionalizing space gave them a collective sense of identity as students, but within the university they would acquire still more identities. Hazing, one particular rite of passage, was a key element of this.[12] Students in the first year were known as *beani* (from the Old French *bec jaune*, yellow beak) and through the end of the first year were subject to various forms of abuse and pranks, particularly insults (that the *beani* were filthy, stinking, or beast-like), getting pelted with urine or feces, and the like. The *beanus* year would end in a ceremony in which the *beanus* would be fitted with goat horns and covered in a salve made of dung. Then the horns would be struck off, he would be washed, and he would then buy a dinner and drinks for the upperclassmen, at which point the passage was complete. He was no longer a *beanus* but had moved from beast to man. This movement as a rite of passage into a student community also signified the movement from rusticity to an urban, professional social class.

Student identities would emphasize status in terms of mastery of letters, but a commonplace of the student life was also that of struggling poverty. Some commonplaces concerning student poverty are doubtless literary stereotypes. The commonplace of claiming extreme poverty appears especially in letters of poets to patrons in both classical poetry and its medieval pastiches—even when both the poet and his patron came from the ranks of social elites. So, we may well cast a skeptical eye on the model letters that have students writing to their parents with claims of dire poverty—and their parents writing back to them with moralized admonitions against spending their meager incomes on drink. Many of these may indeed be emulations of the model of the client claiming poverty to his literary patron.

In spite of the clear commonplace nature of these letters, other evidence shows that at least some students genuinely struggled as part of a culture of students clinging to the margins. Many students made do with part-time work. Their training as clerics put them in demand as chanters for choirs in liturgical solemnities like major feasts, funerals, and the like, and their literacy made them valuable for Europe's burgeoning book trade. In the thirteenth century, the production of books became commercialized, with an increasing number of books coming not from monasteries or secular churches, but from urban commercial stationers (i.e., the producers and sellers of books). The stationers of Paris and Oxford developed a system of copying books called the *pecia* system, which allowed students to supplement their income through part-time work as copyists.

We see students struggling financially with respect to housing as well. As a thirteenth-century university had no "campus" but, rather, had masters (i.e., instructors) offer instruction in whatever rooms were available, students—whom, we must re-emphasize, were teenagers—were often left to their own devices to find housing. Indeed, a sense of grievance at the seemingly high cost of services, particularly essentials like housing, served to sharpen a student body's sense of identity against that of the community in an antagonistic "town versus gown" relationship.

The dire nature of early student housing led to the eventual institution of the college that would end up furnishing another student identity. These colleges provided room and board and employed their own teaching staff. The most famous of these was Paris's Sorbonne, founded in 1257 by Louis IX's chaplain, Robert of Sorbonne. Walter de Merton, bishop of Rochester, founded Oxford's (and England's) first college in 1264. Originally founded by lay or ecclesiastical elites for "needy" students (the language of foundation charters will speak of helping the poor), they eventually came to serve elites from certain regions. This led to a cliquish sense of a college's collective identity, and this cohesion gained further reinforcement through sets of rules and rituals, some of which reinforced students' identity qua students, such as requirements of consistently speaking Latin not only in the classroom but also in residence.

The other student identity that we see is of membership in the "nation." In the thirteenth century, the student bodies in Paris and Bologna were international in character, and so for the purposes of both student and faculty government, the university classified students according to "nation," that is, their place of origin.[13] This is significant to student identity and culture because it was these national identities that formed the medieval student communities—not their identities as noble or common. The formerly elite and largely noble monastic system of education was now open to young men of theoretically every social background, and more importantly, the students themselves more often identified their role by nation rather than family status. Indeed, students identified closely enough with their nations that fighting would often break out between different nations—and this fighting was part of another element of the formation of student identity: violence.

Student liminality was part of a passage from boy to man—and thus student identity was heavily tied up in reinforcing a masculine identity. This masculinity found expression in both sexual aggression and physical violence, reflecting the aristocratic youth culture of which university culture was an offshoot. It also emulated a culture in which, although the dominant Christian religion proclaimed that sex was reserved for marriage, it was understood that young men would engage in sexual activity prior to marriage. (This was a masculine prerogative: premarital sex was not open to women of "honorable" status.)

Such ideologies of masculinity gained reinforcement in the primary schooling the students received before they went to university. As it had been since the days of the later Roman Empire, a key component of a boy's education was the enforcement of discipline by frequent beating. Even before arriving in university, then, these boys were enculturated into a habitus of violence, and it was in their primary schooling that they would pick up attitudes about sex as well.

Much of the literature that students might have consumed in their schooling before university described nonconsensual sex. As children (*pueri*), they would have studied Ovid's classical poetry as well as works less well known to moderns like *Pamphilus*, a medieval pastiche of a classical Roman comedy. In many of these works, "when the protagonist is young, the rape signifies the onset of manhood."[14] Rape, which is a masculine sexuality of aggression, figured heavily in the literary commonplaces as well, with texts such as the songs of the *Carmina Burana* using rape as a literary device.

This association of manhood and a heteronormative sexuality appears not only in fiction, but also in the works of moralizers. The preacher Jacques de Vitry angrily spoke of schoolmasters who would hold classes on the upper floors of buildings while prostitutes plied their trade on the lower floor. That this sexual activity served as a means of performing masculinity becomes clear in that prostitutes are said to have mocked students who refused to hire sex workers as "sodomites." This heteronormativity appears in the works of other preachers who worried about an apparent lack of interest in sexuality serving as a cover for same-sex desire. The Franciscan friar John of la Rochelle's (df. 1245) sermon to university students on the first Sunday of Advent inveighs against "that hypocrisy concealing the ignominies of the cursed and unspeakable ugliness of the sin against nature under the appearance of sanctity."[15] Mentors and senior churchmen alike would rather see young clerics engaging in fornication—itself a mortal sin!—as evidence that they were not participating in the "vice against nature."

If performative sexuality was one element of a masculine student identity, another was violence. The pugnacity of the university student was proverbial. Both manuals for and sermons to students inveighed against fighting. The French poet Rutebeuf writes satirically of students from all over Christendom engaging in fighting in the city of Paris. Several causes célèbres involving student violence marked the early history of the University of Paris. In February of 1200, fighting broke out between German students who had been drinking and the proprietors of a tavern. This fight turned into a more general riot that left two citizens badly beaten (one close to the point of death), and the city's provost subsequently launched a retaliatory attack on the hostel that lodged students of the German nation. Five students were killed, and the king himself intervened and punished the provost. In 1229, a similar outbreak of violence occurred when during the city's pre-Lent carnival celebrations, a group of students was expelled physically from a tavern after a dispute about a bill, and the next day a mob of students attacked the tavern, and the fighting broke out into a larger citywide riot. When the regent Blanch of Castile allowed the Provost of Paris to retaliate against these students, the faculty of Paris went on a teaching strike. These and other violent episodes were probably exacerbated by the fact that students, as clerics, had the canonical immunities from prosecution in civil courts in addition to often being protected by kings or regional nobles for the value that a university added to town, region, and kingdom.[16]

In addition to this violence, the rules of the university and institutionalization of disputation created a licit atmosphere for rituals of competition. Spectacles of competitive violence marked much of medieval life, from the tournament at the higher end of the socioeconomic ladder to entertainment such as bearbaiting on the street. The disputation moved from a performance within the classroom to a public competition. The more common disputation, the ordinary disputation, took place between two bachelors (i.e., students studying for their master's degree) with students from throughout the university as an audience. But the most popular public disputation by far was the *disputatio de quolibet*. These "quodlibetal" disputations took place in Advent and Lent and were such popular entertainment that members not only of the university, but of the general public whose members attended them. In a quodlibetal disputation, a master would agree to debate any proposition that the audience would propose with only a day's preparation. Students would gather with particular enthusiasm to watch a *disputatio de quolibet* in a raucous atmosphere that Haimeric de Vari, chancellor of the University of Paris in the mid-thirteenth century, compared to a cock fight.

Late Medieval Countercultures: The Friars

The institutionalization of the university and growing ecclesiastical careerism of the student body led to countercultures among students who sought alternatives, particularly with the rise of mendicant friars like the Franciscans and Dominicans, whose orders were founded in 1209 and 1216, respectively. The friars sought to live an ascetic life, following an ideal of "apostolic poverty," owning no property, living by begging, and traveling from place to place to preach repentance of sin. These orders offered a rejection of careerism and the pursuit of wealth. The Franciscans had been founded by St. Francis of Assisi, who had ostentatiously rejected his own family's wealth as a young adult. The rejection of a performative masculine sexuality that marked rites of passage was another key element of the youthful recruits of the mendicant orders' counterculture. The hagiography of Thomas Aquinas, the greatest intellectual of the Middle Ages, tells us that when he resolved as a teenager to join the Dominican Friars, his parents attempted to dissuade him by hiring a prostitute—but the young Thomas fled the scene.

During their first century, these orders recruited heavily from university students to fill their ranks with Western Europe's "best and brightest." Their appeal to these students came at least in part from the offer of a counterculture opposed to both the careerism of this professionalizing student body as well as the excessive indulgence that characterized (or purported to characterize) student life. These orders' aggressive recruiting from student bodies sometimes gained recruits in a first flush of enthusiasm who might not have been suited to an ascetic life. As a result, the orders began to institute a one-year probationary period.

Contemporary sermons show us the orders' countercultural appeal as well: A sermon to Parisian students plays on this excitement with rejecting parental authority in warning them of parents who would try to warn them off joining a mendicant order:

> Be careful, you, young men, and you, masters who have young men to guide! When they send them to Paris, parents say to the masters of their sons: "Don't let our boys go to the Franciscans and Dominicans. They are thieves, and will quickly snatch our sons." They do not say to them, "Don't let them go to the brothel or the tavern."[17]

Such a denunciation also shows a tension between two university youth cultures, one of an aggressive and "misbehaving" masculinity demonstrated in sex and drinking, with another that rejects these conventions.

The orders' recruiting of a university student demonstrated a culture that now allowed a space for young people to choose vocations. Unlike the older monastic orders in which one's life as a monk had been determined by one's family, the university student came to the order as a voluntary recruit, even interviewing with a friar of the order to establish his suitability. These choices might often be opposed by both family and friends, thus lending this decision a feeling of transgression, but a transgression falling well within the framework of medieval Catholic Christianity.

Although the mendicant orders' counterculture urged the students to resist the vices, work by Neslihan Şenocak has shown that both Dominican and Franciscan orders appealed because they offered membership into an elite with access to advanced knowledge that had been such a draw to earlier generations in the cathedral schools. The Dominican order's guides to confessions in some way acknowledge this, listing "glorying in letters" as an expression of the capital vice of pride.[18] And when the Dominican order began preparing a center for undergraduate study in Provence, the order received so many postulants that the provincial chapter ordered that the convents make sure to inform postulants that joining the Dominicans would not necessarily result in enrollment in this institution.

As the mendicants became institutionalized, took professorships in the universities, and became a fixture of life throughout Western Europe, new forms of rebellion within a Christian framework appeared. In the Netherlands, the Brethren of the Common Life began among adult members of the bourgeoisie who sought to live communally in a pursuit of a deeper religious life, but not found an order. They quickly came to attract young people as alternatives to the careerism of the schools, and so we read about young men like Egbert of Beek, who in his studies adopted a posture of ostentatious piety to the point that his own sister denounced him as a "Lollard."

The Early Modern University: Reformations

The transition from medieval to early modern Europe is in many ways an artificial one, and many elements of university youth culture showed little change from their medieval counterparts. The student bodies themselves were less international, as an expansion of the number of universities meant that a young man was more likely to attend university closer to where he had grown up than in the days when Paris served as a magnet for much of Christendom. The rituals of youth life, from the hazing of the *beanus* to the college rules and ceremonies, remained as they had among their medieval counterparts. Italian court records still speak of armed young men from the universities looking for trouble with town residents. Substantial changes, however, were to come about over the sixteenth and seventeenth centuries.

The culture of the early modern university was marked by two stark changes: the Protestant Reformation and the change in the social class—and thus university culture—of the student bodies. In the first place, the university saw the birth of one of the most momentous countercultures of early modern times: the Protestant Reformation. At the same time that the university-born outbreak of rebellion would shake a unified Christendom to the core, the university youth culture was becoming less that of a professional bourgeois and more of an element of noble youth culture. The universities of medieval Europe had been engines of (relative) social mobility, with university students and masters alike coming not only from the middling nobility, but even from the ranks of the peasantry. In early modern times, however, the university's student body became increasingly drawn from a noble background.

In its early days, the Protestant Reformation began as a student counterculture. Its opening salvo had been fired by a university professor, and when Martin Luther threw a collection of canon law texts into a bonfire, he did so to an audience of wildly cheering students. The so-called *Wildwuchs*, or wild growth, that sprang up in the opening years of the Protestant Reformation was a student and youth movement, filled with the excitement of breaking taboos. The smashing of stained glass, outbursts of foul language at previously revered men and institutions of the Church, and the denunciation of such doctrines as purgatory and devilish lies all served to channel a youthful energy that quickly spread from its origin in northern Germany to other parts of Europe. This was not just a student counterculture, but a revolution.

The institutionalization of the Reformation, from student counterculture to establishment, is beyond the scope of this chapter, but at the end of this process, there was a Protestant Europe and a Catholic Europe, and their universities stood divided by confession. This institutional division brought about one major change in university culture in that the international culture of medieval universities, already diminishing by the end of the Middle Ages, nearly vanished. The other great change to university culture to come about in the period of the Reformation and Catholic Reformation was the arrival of the Society of Jesus.

Ignatius Loyola (1491–1556) had originally founded the Society to serve as a meditative order, but it quickly became an order of educators with the goal of reconverting Protestant Europe, converting non-Christians to Catholic Christianity, and also fully catechizing Catholic Europe. This trajectory is not terribly surprising, since Loyola himself and the founding Jesuits had trained in the University of Paris. Their educational goal would require a strong presence in the universities, and so the Jesuits established themselves in universities throughout Catholic Europe. Many Jesuits were initially disgusted at the moral depravity they encountered in university towns. They observed students prone to games of chance, violence, moral laxity, and skepticism of received doctrines that could slide into outright atheism. It seems that the university youth culture of the Middle Ages still flourished in early modern France and Italy—and this culture drove the Jesuits to found their own institutions of higher learning where they believed young men could receive a better education. These secondary and post-secondary schools trained young men in their mid-to-late teens.

This Jesuit education would be part of another early modern trend: the combination of university culture with aristocratic culture. The Jesuits recruited the elites of Europe for their educational institutions. Although elite recruitment had originally occurred as the unplanned result of the Society's reputation for holiness and learning, it soon came to be a strategy. The Jesuits thus had a university culture that became a key component of elite culture in Catholic Europe. Even Protestant students were drawn to the Jesuits' schools, the value of a Jesuit education trumping any confessional considerations. The Jesuit colleges and universities whose students rejected the excesses in sex and violence of the student life were incubators of the aristocracy. When not studying philosophy or theology students in the Jesuit college of Santa Catarina in Parma, for example, learned such noble arts as horsemanship, dancing, and the design of fortifications.

The early modern university, like its medieval predecessor, was almost exclusively male. A women's youth culture as such still did not exist in the domain of education, even though a religious order like that of the Ursulines, approved by the papacy in 1535, allowed a space for women to receive an advanced education, which, after it came under the direction of the Society of Jesus, became an institution for elite women.

An Aristocratic University

In the Middle Ages, universities had taken in students of all socioeconomic backgrounds. Maybe 20 percent had come from the ranks of the "poor." A medieval French knight wrote of how "through clergie [i.e., scholarly training] the son of a poor man becomes a great prelate ... nay, he may become pope, and father and lord of all Christendom."[19] By the time of the eighteenth century, however, only 1 percent of Oxford's students did not come from the ranks of nobles or wealthy commoners. Although an extreme example, Oxford reflected a trend throughout Europe. The university culture was still a liminal one that carried on rites of passage, but it was part of a set of rites of passage of the aristocracy or wealthy commoners.

The universities of northern Italy served one particular element of the aristocratic youth culture of Northern Europe in that some of them still took Protestant students. Thus, for those few Northern European students who would travel to study in Italy's universities, study abroad came to serve as a rite of passage that itself would presage the eighteenth-century aristocratic practice of the "grand tour." And like the later "grand tour," travel to study in university held an element of frisson. To study so close to Rome, the heart of the ideological enemy of Protestant Christianity, held an element of transgression. Young men from Northern Europe likewise were understood to be allowed to indulge in various vices in Italy that might be more constrained in Germany or Britain. This period of debauchery then was part of an aristocratic sense of youthful indulgence that would eventually be left behind with adulthood and an "honorable" marriage (or at least a marriage and a mistress kept discreetely).

The youth culture of the early modern university remained medieval in character. In terms of official institutions and curriculum, but also in terms of the informal student cultures, the greatest change was not university life, but the social status of the university student. No longer did it serve as a rite of passage for young men mingling from all social classes. It was now a life stage for elites of wealth, of birth, or both. And it was still overwhelmingly masculine. As the eighteenth century drew to a close, there was little sense of the coming developments in mass society that would end up throwing open a university education to other social classes in Europe and especially the United States. This all-male preserve would end up open not only to men of differing social classes, but also to young women. In the end, a set of subcultures birthed in the

Middle Ages would eventually open up to people of all social classes in what would amount to a rebirth of the university.

Notes

1. The bibliography on the medieval university is vast. For a good introduction on university culture as youth culture, see especially Ruth Mazo Karras, *From Boys to Men: Formations of Masculinity in Late Medieval Europe* (Philadelphia: University of Pennsylvania Press, 2003), particularly chs. 1 and 3. The definitive books on the university in medieval and early modern times are Hilde de Ridder-Symoens, ed., *A History of the University in Europe: Volume 1, Universities in the Middle Ages* (Cambridge: Cambridge University Press, 1991), and idem, *A History of the University in Europe: Volume 2, Universities in Early Modern Europe (1500–1800)* (Cambridge: Cambridge University Press, 1996).
2. The classic text for the understanding of medieval childhood and its place in the life cycle is Shulamith Shahar, *Childhood in the Middle Ages* (New York: Routledge, 1990).
3. Augustine of Hippo, *Confessions*, ed. and trans. Garry Wills (New York: Penguin, 2002), 44.
4. "... puram et certam ... tene ... fidem," Dhuoda, *Handbook for Her Warrior Son: Liber manualis*, ed. and trans. Marcelle Thiébaux (Cambridge: Cambridge University Press), 3.4, pp. 92–93.
5. Rule of St. Benedict, quoted in C. H. Lawrence, *Medieval Monasticism: Forms of Religious Life in Western Europe in the Middle Ages*, 3rd ed. (London and New York: Routledge, 2014), 29.
6. Modern anthropological studies of youth cultures have also struggled with the issue of whether youth is defined strictly with respect to adulthood. Mary Bucholtz, "Youth and Cultural Practice," *Annual Review of Anthropology* 31 (2002): 525–552; see 526–528.
7. Guibert of Nogent, *Guibert of Nogent: Autobiographie*, ed. and trans. Edmond-René Labande (Paris: Les Belles-Lettres, 1981), translated into English by Paul J. Archambault as *A Monk's Confession: The Memoirs of Guibert of Nogent* (University Park: University of Pennsylvania Press, 1996), 48.
8. The turn of phrase "bourgeois church officialdom" is Peter Moraw's, "Careers of Graduates," in de Ridder-Symoens, *Universities in the Middle Ages*, 244–279; see p. 257.
9. Peter Abelard, *Historia Calamitatum*, in *The Letters of Abelard and Heloise*, trans. and ed. Betty Radice (New York: Penguin, 1974), 57–106; see p. 58.
10. On Abelard and the disputation, see especially Alex J. Novikoff, *The Medieval Culture of Disputation: Pedagogy, Practice, and Performance* (Philadelphia: University of Pennsylvania Press, 2013), 76–82. There are numerous translations of Fitzstephen's description of London available. The Latin original appears in *Vita Sancti Thomæ Cantuarensis archiepiscopi et martyris*, in *Materials for the History of Thomas Becket: Archbishop of Canterbury (Canonized by Pope Alexander III., A. D. 1173)*, ed. James Craigie Robertson, 3 vols. (London: Longman, 1875–1885), 3:1–154, see pp. 2–5.
11. Quoted in Claire M. Waters, *Translating Clergie: Status, Education, and Salvation in Thirteenth-Century Vernacular Texts* (Philadelphia: University of Pennsylvania Press, 2016), 69.
12. Most of our evidence of hazing practices comes from continued efforts of university officials to stifle these activities.

13. It did not correspond to origin by state. Paris's nations, for example, were French, Picard, Norman, and English (which also included Germans and other Central Europeans).
14. Woods, Marjorie Curry, "Rape and the Pedagogical Rhetoric of Sexual Violence," in *Criticism and Dissent in the Middle Ages*, ed. Rita Copeland (Cambridge: Cambridge University Press, 1996): 56–86; see p. 60.
15. John of la Rochelle, first Sunday in Advent, "Erunt signa in sole et Luna et stellis et in terris pressura gentium, pre confusione sonitus maris et fluctuum, arescentibus hominibus pre timore et exspectatione, que superuenient uniuerso orbi," in Jean Désiré Rasolofoarimanana, OFM, "Étude et édition des sermons de l'Avent de Jean de la Rochelle, OMin († 3 février 1245)," *Archivum Franciscanum Historicum* 98 (2005): 41–149, 115–127; see pp. 120–121.
16. On student violence in the University of Paris in the thirteenth and early fourteenth centuries, see especially Hanna Skodah, *Medieval Violence: Physical Brutality in Northern France, 1270–1330* (Oxford: Oxford University Press, 2013), 119–158.
17. Quoted in Neslihan Şenocak, *The Poor and the Perfect: The Rise of Learning in the Franciscan Order, 1209–1310* (Ithaca, NY, and London: Cornell University Press, 2012), 173.
18. See, for example, the guide to confession appearing in London, British Library, MS Additional 30508, fols. 180r.—193r.; see 180rb.
19. Quoted in Şenocak, *Poor and the Perfect*, 178.

Further Reading

Baldwin, John. *The Scholastic Culture of the Middle Ages, 1000–1300*. Lexington, MA: D.C. Heath, 1971.
de Ridder-Symoens, Hilde, ed. *A History of the University in Europe: Volume 1, Universities in the Middle Ages*. Cambridge: Cambridge University Press, 1991.
de Ridder-Symoens, Hilde, ed. *A History of the University in Europe: Volume 2, Universities in Early Modern Europe (1500–1800)*. Cambridge: Cambridge University Press, 1996.
Goldberg, P.J.P., and Felicity Riddy, eds. *Youth in the Middle Ages*. York, UK: York Medieval Press, 2004.
Haskins, Charles Homer. *Studies in Mediaeval Culture*. New York: Frederick Ungar Publishing Co., 1929.
Janin, Hunt. *The University in Medieval Life, 1179–1499*. Jefferson, NC: McFarland & Company, 2008.
Karras, Ruth Mazo. *From Boys to Men: Formations of Masculinity in Late Medieval Europe*. Philadelphia: University of Pennsylvania Press, 2003.
Lawrence, C.H. *Medieval Monasticism: Forms of Religious Life in Western Europe in the Middle Ages*. 3rd ed. London and New York: Routledge, 2014.
Mulchahey, M. Michèlle. *"First the Bow Is Bent in Study . . . ": Dominican Education Before 1350*. Toronto: Pontifical Institute of Mediaeval Studies, 1998.
Novikoff, Alex J. *The Medieval Culture of Disputation: Pedagogy, Practice, and Performance*. Philadelphia: University of Pennsylvania Press, 2013.
O'Malley, John W. *The First Jesuits*. Cambridge, MA: Harvard University Press, 1993.
Orme, Nicholas. *Medieval Schools: From Roman Britain to Renaissance England*. New Haven: Yale University Press, 2006.

Po-Chia Hsia, R. *The World of Catholic Renewal, 1540–1770*. Cambridge: Cambridge University Press, 1998.

Riché, Pierre. *Education and Society in the Barbarian West, Sixth Through Eighth Centuries*. Translated by J.J. Contreni. Columbia: University of South Carolina Press, 1976.

Roest, Bert. *A History of Franciscan Education (c. 1210–1517)*. Leiden: Brill, 2000.

Şenocak, Neslihan. *The Poor and the Perfect: The Rise of Learning in the Franciscan Order, 1209–1310*. Ithaca, NY, and London: Cornell University Press, 2012.

Skodah, Hannah. *Medieval Violence: Physical Brutality in Northern France, 1270–1330*. Oxford: Oxford University Press, 2013.

Woods, Marjorie Curry. "Rape and the Pedagogical Rhetoric of Sexual Violence." In *Criticism and Dissent in the Middle Ages*. Edited by Rita Copeland, 56–86. Cambridge: Cambridge University Press, 1996.

CHAPTER 3

COMING OF AGE IN ELITE FAMILIES, C. 1200–C. 1650

LOUISE J. WILKINSON

A lively and vibrant aristocratic youth culture existed in Western Europe during the medieval and early modern periods. As a time of life for elite adolescents, youth was characterized by their first experiences of responsibility, but also elements of newfound freedom from direct parental control, especially for those who moved away from home to experience life and finish their education in great households and courts, and at schools and universities. For the landed aristocracies of England, France, and Germany, who formed the wealthy echelons of medieval and early modern society, the expectation and, in some cases, realization of access to property and inheritance exercised profound influences on young men and women, as did instruction and training for adulthood, growing authority over the lives of others, and opportunities for social exchanges with their peers.

Admittedly, opinion is divided between those scholars who argue for the existence of a concept of youth at this social level, and those who argue that life during the Middle Ages and the Renaissance was marked by different stages of transition from those that we know today. The former regard youth as a period between the early teens and mid-twenties during which elite adolescents "underwent a distinctive shaping time," which prepared them for the "grown up roles" they assumed in adulthood. The latter contend, instead, that there was "a single developmental phase" that covered "childhood and adolescence." In his study of the lives of premodern, elite teenage girls, John Carmi Parsons identified certain modes or forms of "adult" behavior among young, female aristocrats, such as assuming the role of advisor and mediator to a husband, which began in adolescence and continued into old age. This meant that, "while certain phases of life were acknowledged in theory, their definition in practice may have been fluid, [and] not linked inflexibly to chronological or biological criteria."[1] Despite the potential for such fluidity, in the medieval and early modern periods, young men and women experienced youth, a time of formative life experiences between the onset of puberty and their early twenties, when they were no longer fully children and not quite adults. In youth, they experienced psychological changes, as well as increasing economic and social obligations, which transformed them into grown-ups. Literary works throughout this period readily distinguished between "Children and ladies and maidens, / Servant girls and young damsels," suggesting that writers were sensitive to distinctions of youth, rank, marital and sexual status, and occupation.[2] Youth culture is understood as shared experiences and interests common to young adults. In spite of their growing responsibilities and continuing education, young lords and ladies were allowed, and found, time to interact with one another, form friendships with their social equals, bond through certain rites of passage, enjoy communal leisure pursuits and recreational activities, and undergo courtship and preparations for marriage. These were the key characteristics of elite youth culture as it was enjoyed by young elite men and women, all of which helped to shape the adults who they later became.

Wardship, Property, and Inheritance Rights

Social expectations of the different modes of life followed by elite young men and women were regulated, first and foremost, by the different laws and customs surrounding property rights, inheritance, and the assumption of legal responsibilities that were enforced by parents, guardians, lords, churches, and states. This was one important way in which the frameworks in which aristocratic youth culture operated differed from those of other social classes. In adolescence, many young men and women remained legally under the authority of their parents or other guardians, and presumably these adult figures controlled, at least to a degree, those people with whom elite adolescents socialized. Young people who lost their fathers were placed in wardship, meaning that they passed into the legal authority of another adult. Wardship remained a right that was heavily exploited by the English crown throughout this period, ensuring that the custody of many minors of both sexes, together with the rights to their properties, and to arrange their marriages (a subject to which we shall return later), was sold off or granted away to favored courtiers. In France, the custody of minors frequently passed into the hands of a widowed mother, as was the case in Champagne, or to the firstborn child if they had reached legal maturity. In *The Nibelungenlied*, a Middle High German epic, the reader is introduced to the young, female character, Kriemhild, who was raised by her three brothers after the death of her father, Dancrat.

At the upper end of the social spectrum in Western Europe, experiences of youth were gendered and drew inspiration from religious and medical ideas inherited from the ancient world about the different natures of adult male and female bodies: men were strong, rational beings, while women were weaker and irrational. These beliefs informed provincial customs and legal theories about the ages at which elite boys and girls assumed adult duties and began to exercise meaningful authority over others. For instance, in the late medieval and Renaissance plays known as "interludes," all the main young male characters had servants. The practice of living with, and managing, attendants paved the way for young noblemen to form and preside over their own great households when they passed into adulthood; the wealthiest already had their own households in childhood and adolescence, although final financial accountability usually rested with their parents and guardians. The household accounts of John II of Brabant, King Edward I's prospective son-in-law, who resided at the English court in his teens, document expenditure on this young nobleman's servants, esquires, and valets in the late thirteenth century.

When John II of Brabant returned to his homeland, he did so to rule the duchy, following his father's death at a tournament in 1294. For the landed aristocracies, the expectation and/or assumption of estates accompanied the transition through adolescence, arguably functioning as a form of adult restraint on youth culture, since young people at this social level needed preparing to control landed estates and other financial assets. Yet, customs differed among the regional aristocracies of Western Europe when it came to establishing who was entitled to inherit lands. In medieval Champagne, partible inheritance customs prevailed in lands held by feudal tenure; here estates were divided between all legitimate children, although each sister received half the amount of each brother. If the property was allodial, all daughters received shares equal to those of sons. In some parts of northern France, by contrast, the eldest son was usually the preferred heir. Similar practices to those found here prevailed in England, whereby family estates usually descended to the oldest son, and daughters only inherited in the absence of male heirs in the same generation. An aristocratic family deprived of male heirs, like that of the knight Gurnemanz after his three sons were killed in the German romance *Parzival*, was vulnerable to uncertainties over its future. In *Parzival*, Gurnemanz went so far as to try to lure the eponymous hero of the story into marriage to his daughter Liaze; Liaze, for her part, complied with her father's wishes. In reality, the development of the entail in England in the later Middle Ages enabled some families to ensure that their estates descended only in the male line. In Germany, on the other hand, partible inheritance customs persisted into the early modern era, with nobles and territorial princes apparently preferring to divide their lands between several sons.

Elite experiences of youth and participation in youth culture were also influenced by the ages at which young men and women could inherit property, and these varied considerably in different kingdoms and regional principalities. According to the custom of the county of Champagne in the thirteenth century, for example, orphaned aristocratic heirs were expected to assume legal responsibility for their dead parents' fiefs at the age of fifteen for boys and eleven for girls. Yet, in Lotharingia in the same period, the heirs of ducal vassals remained in wardship until the age of twelve, while in England twenty-one was the legal age of majority for the male heirs to estates held by knight service, and sixteen was the legal age of majority for unmarried heiresses. The marriage of an heiress could also terminate her time in wardship in England.

Coming of Age Through Education and Responsibility

Since issues surrounding access to wealth and its transfer between generations were such distinctive and constant features of aristocratic life between ca. 1200 and ca. 1650, noble families across Western Europe took the future prosperity and maintenance of their heirs and of their non-inheriting offspring into careful consideration. There was a strong social expectation of marriage at this social level (a subject to which we will return later). In the later Middle Ages and in states that remained Catholic after the Reformation, some young aristocratic women joined formal religious communities as novices, while others who were not destined for matrimonial or religious life tended to remain in the households of their kin as damsels or ladies-in-waiting. For younger sons who possessed no rights of inheritance, the Church, royal government, the law, and the military all offered professions or occupations for which they could train. The preparation for, and assumption of, adult responsibilities therefore exerted a heavy influence not only on the construction of youth in medieval, Renaissance, and Reformation elite societies, but also on the settings in which youth culture operated at this social level.

In their teens and early twenties, young aristocrats underwent a final stage of instruction, schooling, and acculturation into the grown-up world of the governing classes. Adolescence was therefore characterized by socialization and social conditioning through education, training, and service. Courtesy books, educational treatises, letters, and literature offered guidance on conduct, and especially on which moral qualities and ideals their young readers should uphold and which they should eschew. The close attention that was paid to both proper and improper modes of comportment in these works reflects, perhaps, what adults were observing as behavioral traits in their own offspring or in other young men and women of noble rank. It is, after all, usually easier to trace how adults in this period responded to youthful actions and tried to shape experiences of youth, than it is to see directly into the lives of medieval and early modern adolescents. The authors of contemporary tracts stressed the importance of young noble men and women maintaining the highest standards of behavior, and their advice offers us welcome glimpses of the expectations surrounding idealized, youthful conduct, and social interactions.

Contemporary writers regarded good manners in the young as essential, since they reflected inner morality and good breeding. The fourteenth-century writer Geoffroi de Charny, for instance, praised chivalric nobles "who conduct themselves properly and pleasantly, as is appropriate for young men, gentle, courteous and well-mannered toward others." In a similar vein, Book I of the thirteenth-century writer Thomasin von Zirclaria's *Der Welsche Gast* counseled young lords and ladies to behave with modesty, adopt a good demeanor, speak well, and respect other people, including strangers. He advised them to reflect upon and model their own behavior on that of good, respectable, established figures at court, the principal social arena in which young aristocrats encountered one another and their elders, in a formal setting. Fine table manners among the young at mealtimes and feasts were also essential; speaking with one's mouth full was frowned upon, as was eating "with both hands." Similarly, boasting, wantonness, too much laughter, and talking in public settings should be avoided. Young women were encouraged to imitate the actions of literary heroines with "fine minds," while young men were to emulate knightly figures like Gawain and King Arthur in contemporary, chivalric romances.[3]

Elite youngsters were repeatedly cautioned in conduct literature against excessive personal grooming and elaborate clothing. Then, as now, the young were seen by their elders to be particularly susceptible to fashionable trends and ornaments, presumably because they appealed to them. De Charny, for example, counseled that, while it was both fitting and appropriate for young men to dress elegantly and fashionably in court settings, presumably in ways that were in keeping with their rank, they should remember God's teaching and avoid the sin of pride. "But," as Geoffroi observed, "one should dress well when in company with other young people and to fit in with them; and it is a fine and good thing to spend one's youth in honest fashion." According to this writer, young aristocratic ladies and damsels were permitted to adopt fine attire and wear jewelry more than men, since it might help them to secure good marriages by attracting suitable husbands. After all, outward appearance and good looks in the young reflected inner virtue and true nobility. On the other hand, contemporary writers cautioned young women against enhancing their appearances and succumbing to vanity. *The Book of the Knight of the Tower*, a late medieval French handbook, advised the knight's daughters "not to put any paint or makeup on your faces which were made in God's image." Nor were they to "pluck" their "eyebrows," "temples or forehead." In a similar vein, Christine de Pisan counseled young women at court to dress in fine, rich, but "simple" and "seemly" clothing "without fripperies."[4]

Since most noble boys were expected to assume knighthood in the Middle Ages, the chivalric aspects of their education in adolescence also placed a strong emphasis on ideal personal qualities and modes of behavior allied to Christian teaching: loyalty, forbearance, honesty, liberality, honor, and a readiness to protect or defend the weak. Ramon Llull's *The Book of the Order of Chivalry*, written between 1274 and 1276, advised young knights to practice, "uphold and defend the Holy Catholic Faith." Spirituality remained an important feature in Renaissance culture for elite young men. The Italian humanist scholar Pier Paolo Vergerio, for instance, considered it "proper for a well-educated youth to respect and practice religion, and to be steeped in religious belief."[5]

Christian instruction also occupied a central place in the upbringing of adolescent girls, albeit with subtle differences from that received by boys. The *Lives* of the teenage Virgin Martyrs, which were popular in medieval and early modern Catholicism, offered models of young, perfect, and pious womanly behavior for young ladies to emulate. All the female saints who featured in the *Gilte Legende*, a Middle English translation of Jacobus de Voragine's *Legenda Aurea*, were born to noble parents, offering young women readily identifiable, if idealized, role models. A perfect, holy maiden, like St. Elizabeth of Hungary, was portrayed in this work as taking off her gold jewelry and placing it all "on the ground" whenever she heard readings from the Gospels in church, or whenever she witnessed the elevation of the host during Mass. Later works for elite girls, like Juan Luis Vives' *The Instruction of a Christian Woman*, written in 1523 for Catherine of Aragon, similarly placed a great emphasis on young women following lives of chastity, honesty, and obedience, since even women of elevated social rank were perceived, like Eve in the Book of Genesis, as the weaker, both physically and mentally, of the two sexes. Young ladies who featured in German medieval romances exhibited similar, idealized, qualities, like the shy, modest maiden Enide in *Erec und Enide*. *The Book of the Knight of the Tower* advised the knight's daughters to be "meek," as well as "courteous and humble." Francesco Barbaro's marriage manual, written in 1415 against the backdrop of Venetian humanism and following the advice of the Spartan Geradatas, advocated that would-be husbands should seek out young virgins as their brides, who exhibited the qualities of "frugality, modesty, and chastity." Similar merits in young women were championed in a marriage song composed around 1555 by Duchess Elisabeth of Brunswick-Calenberg in which the singer congratulated a noble groom on his choice of bride, advising him: "Good friend, this will be to your profit / That you have married this young lady, / She shines with honorable virtues, / God will certainly bless you spiritually."[6]

The emphasis on the need for personal restraint in youth, which was prevalent in literary works addressed to elite audiences, may well have reflected strong, contemporary concerns about inappropriate behavior among the young. In some texts there was an apparent disjuncture between clerical advice that young women should be biddable, deferential, and speak little, and the literary and hagiographic portrayals of youthful, well-born female saints. Many of the young, female saints of the *Gilte Legende* were strong-willed, disobedient, and outspoken in their defense of the Christian faith. Even so, youth was also identified in didactic and romance literature as a life stage when elite boys and girls might be tempted, like their social inferiors, into folly and indecorum, thereby threatening their souls. It is precisely within such literary tropes that we catch glimpses of what contemporary writers regarded as unsavory characteristics of elite youth culture. In a popular medieval allegorical poem, *The Pilgrimage of Human Life*, by Guillaume de Deguileville, Idleness was personified as a young, finely dressed noblewoman, who led the pilgrim toward the seven deadly sins. In the eyes of Zirclaria, idleness itself was "a vice among young people: laziness ill befits youth." Zirclaria also condemned "Shouting and boisterousness" as modes of behavior that were "very much the game of ill-bred youngsters," while warning that "Bad jokes" could lead to "serious consequences."[7]

The potential for youthful rebellion or waywardness, both of which reflected social immaturity, was a concern among the aristocracies of Western Europe, since it potentially undermined their position near the top of a divinely ordained social and moral hierarchy. It was also an issue to which writers paid careful attention, and it strongly hints at the existence of an elite youth culture that was loud, disruptive, rowdy, and characterized by a tendency toward excess. Zirclaria counseled his young, masculine readers that poor behavior in youth could lead to feelings of dishonor and shame for an old man "because he did not wish to do what he should have done when he was able to do it." De Charny, similarly, offered advice on the importance of achieving honor in youth through achievement, or risking the prospect of an old age tarnished by shame and regret. Vergerio cautioned young men against lying, in case this practice carried forward into their more mature years. He also went further, writing that "The young must also be kept within limits" and avoid "excess food and drink and sleeping too much."[8] Too much wine and other forms of alcohol in adolescence posed a threat to health and to an individual's moral judgment.

It was not just young lords who misbehaved. Conduct literature recognized that young damsels and ladies might behave in unseemly and inappropriate ways. Christine de Pisan advised the older lady in charge of a young, noble bride to reprimand "her mistress" if she committed "some fault of the sort young people commit." This author counseled that when young elite young women were "surly and malicious, spiteful and aloof," they should be censured and reprimanded by an older female attendant whose duty it was to teach them good manners.[9] In her memoirs, the seventeenth-century author Lady Ann Fanshawe recalled, perhaps with a hint of rose-tinted nostalgia, how she had personally managed to avoid mischief and immodest words when she was young.

Noble Service, Training, Acculturation, and Play

The social construction of gender gathered apace when aristocratic girls and boys reached adolescence. Across Western Europe, service in noble households offered opportunities for young, unmarried boys and girls to train for their future lives in a range of settings that differed markedly from those of their social inferiors. The practice of sending them away from home allowed them to acquire refinement in the skills they were most likely to need in adulthood as well as the potential for them to begin forging important networks of social connections, which might prove beneficial to them in the future. Many young lords were placed in royal and aristocratic households, where they served as pages until around the age of fourteen and as squires thereafter. In his autobiographically framed poem *Frauendienst* ("The Service of Ladies"), Ulrich von Liechenstein, the son of an Austrian nobleman, recalled how he was sent away from home and served as a page in another domestic establishment between the ages of twelve and sixteen.

Life within a great household allowed young men to polish their manners, learn practical skills in estate and household management, and receive specialist military training appropriate to their rank. Llull advised that a knight should place his son in the service of another knight "and know what it is like to serve a lord, for otherwise he would not understand the nobility of his seigneury when he was a knight."[10] In late medieval Europe, becoming a knight was a major rite of passage for an aristocratic son who was not destined for another career in the Church. The common experience of serving as pages and squires therefore created a unique form of youth culture, peculiar to those of noble status, which functioned as a period of transition leading into knighthood. As De Charny acknowledged, youth for elite boys was associated with physical strength and ability, qualities that made them suited to instruction in knighthood. In medieval England, France, and Germany, military training took place in the mid-to-late teens. Through service as a squire to another knight, an aristocratic son could learn how to care for horses and how to become proficient in different types of armed combat. Riding horses, participating in tournaments, fencing, and hunting, and practicing at the quintain, all provided essential training for the practical side of knighthood and allowed young boys of high birth to mix with one another, experience camaraderie, form friendships with their peers, and undergo male bonding. Contemporary literature recognized the relationships that young, elite men formed with one another as "brothers in arms," while they trained in and practiced the arts of war.[11]

The knighting ceremony was both a solemn and celebratory occasion for the young elite men who went through it, rendering it a key component of aristocratic masculine youth culture. Geoffroi de Charny described how some adolescents chose to enter the order of knighthood "when young, so that they can strive longer without fear and without sparing their bodies or possessions in all the services and conditions which pertain, can and should pertain to knighthood." The order of knighthood was not something that was bestowed easily or lightly, such was the importance attached to it. Chivalric treatises of the later Middle Ages described a lengthy and complex series of rituals, which were firmly tied to Christian religious practice. A young, prospective knight was, first, required to "confess, repent of all his sins, and make sure that he is in a fit state to receive the body of our Lord [the Host]."[12] On the eve of the ceremony, the aspiring knight was expected to bathe in order to cleanse his body of earthly and spiritual impurities. He was then to rest in a new bed, with clean white sheets, after which he was to dress, with the assistance of knights, in white linen clothing, signifying his purity, over which a blood-red tunic was placed, symbolizing his readiness to spill his own blood for the Church and the Christian Faith. Next, he put on black hose, representing the earth to which he would return in death, and a white belt, symbolizing the pure and chaste lifestyle he ought to follow henceforth. Finally, he received a red cloak, denoting humility. The aspiring knight then spent the night in church, keeping vigil. The day of the ceremony itself then began with the young man attending Mass, before the honor of the order of knighthood was conferred, with a ceremonial kiss and dubbing with a sword. The Old French epic, *Girart of Vienne*, written between around 1190 and 1200, described how the fictional character Oliver, the son of Count Renier and one of Girart's nephews, was stripped, dressed, taken off to church to "attend a Mass to pray for help / In gaining fame or earning brave success / Or ruling lands with good and noble sense," before he received knightly attire, comprising a coat of chain mail, a helm, a sword, a shield, a spear, and a "noble steed." Elaborate and lengthy festivals accompanied mass knightings. In *The Nibelungenlied*, four hundred young men were knighted at the same time as Siegfried, the fictional son of King Siegmund, and each received surcoats stitched by young ladies; the ceremony was followed by a vigorous tourney between "The boisterous young knights" and more seasoned warriors, and then, finally, by feasting.[13] The festivities lasted seven days, and horses and new clothes were distributed to all participants. Similar revelry is echoed in late medieval and early modern descriptions of similar, nonfictional events.

In the early modern period, it remained the norm for young male aristocrats to be taught the use of "arms," sometimes in preparation for future royal service and/or military service overseas, although their weapons changed to reflect developments in technology, including the use of guns and gunpowder. The prevalence of a martial ethic among the Italian aristocracy was reflected by the popularity of specialized French and Italian schools of fencing, like the Delian academy in Padua, which was established in 1608, and which attracted well-born students of fencing and riding from across Western Europe. Some elite boys in the medieval and early modern periods sought to prove themselves through feats of arms and military service overseas. In *Girart of Vienne*, Girart's nephew, "Young Aymeri" is described as "a gallant, gay young blade" who traveled first to his uncle's court; he then wished to journey on to that of Charlemagne, in order to enter the emperor's service and gain honor. In *The Nibelungenlied*, Siegfried "travelled throughout foreign lands boldly seeking to test his strength against others," attracting admiration from onlookers for his "amazing feats," as well as "his fame and reputation."[14] Yet, he was still dependent on the services of teachers, who pressed upon him the importance of honorable behavior. In the Old French romance *Robert the Devil*, which circulated in different versions between the thirteenth and eighteenth centuries, the hero, Robert, the initially violent and disruptive son of a noblewoman who had conceived with Satan's assistance, was described in his mid-teens, threatening his teachers, as well as clerics and priests, who came to his father's court.

Just as schools in modern times offered opportunities for youth to form a shared ethos, formal educational settings in medieval and early modern Europe also provided occasions for elite young men to shape their own culture in certain ways. Young, male lay aristocrats were educated in a range of skills in the period between 1200 and 1650, in addition to the arts of war. They often received training and instruction in athletics and usually learned how to be proficient in a range of courtly pursuits and pastimes, such as playing instruments, singing, and painting. Besides this, adolescent boys often built upon their early education in letters and literacy. Writing was often taught separately from reading and more usually performed by clerks in the employment of the aristocracy than by aristocrats themselves. Young, fledgling lords, however, were arguably the best positioned to take advantage of the increased spread of literacy in the sixteenth and seventeenth centuries, since most noble households employed staff to oversee the academic education of the young. Young men who came from the lower ranks of the nobility may also have benefited from the proliferation of schools, especially grammar schools, as well as universities and Inns of Court. As Lawrence Stone, Rosemary O'Day, and Jacqueline Eales have argued, these developments were influenced and informed "by humanist and Renaissance ideas about learning, which advocated that boys should be fully prepared for their future roles as administrators and citizens of the state."[15] Young men were to receive instruction in subjects that prepared them for their adult responsibilities, including the seven liberal arts that comprised both the *trivium*—grammar, logic, and rhetoric (useful for preparing them for public speaking)—and the *quadrivium*—astronomy, arithmetic, geometry, and music. In the early modern period, it also became increasingly common for young aristocratic men to broaden their own, personal horizons, by undertaking foreign travel for personal improvement in civility, culture, and foreign languages. Sir Kenelm Digby, a member of King Charles I of England's court, visited France, Italy, and Spain in his youth, acquiring and refining his linguistic skills.

The educational experiences of young women differed from those of their brothers. In England, France, and Germany, elite girls were often sent away in adolescence to the royal court or placed in other aristocratic establishments, where they served as the attendants, or damsels, of great ladies. Those young women who were destined to become nuns were often sent, instead, to board at schools attached to nunneries in Catholic countries. Yet, for most elite girls, there was a strong social expectation, reflected in works like Christine de Pisan's *The Treasure of the City of Ladies*, that they would marry, become wives, and assume responsibility for running their own and their husbands' great households and estates. Aristocratic young women therefore needed to gain an understanding of the techniques and responsibilities involved in running a household, directing domestic affairs, overseeing servants, and defending or promoting a family's estates and their wider interests. This necessitated some familiarity with property rights, local customs, and the machinery and operation of the law. While away from home, young women were also able to observe, learn from, and participate in political life by engaging, for example, in petitioning, and in acts of personal intercession or mediation. Although the period before marriage might be brief, especially for girls, training often continued in their husbands' households.

Unmarried damsels were frequently placed under the supervision of *magistrissae*, well-born women who essentially served as governesses and regulated those aspects of youth culture with which their young charges were permitted to engage. Young ladies were "schooled" in the essential elements of feminine courtly accomplishments: proper deportment; dancing, singing, and making music; and needlework, sewing, and weaving. The lute and virginals were popular instruments for young well-born women in Tudor and Stuart England. In her memoirs, Lady Ann Fanshawe recalled how her mother had overseen her "working all sorts of fine works with my needle, and learning French, singing, [the lute], the virginals, and dancing."[16] Damsels often performed personal service for the ladies of the household in which they were placed. They were also expected to acquire a familiarity with basic medical knowledge and sometimes continued their early education in reading and writing.

The authors of educational treatises differed in their perceptions of the levels and nature of the literate or "academic" education that was considered appropriate for young ladies. In young female elite society, reading skills in vernacular languages tended to be more prevalent than those in Latin, the language of the Catholic Church. Throughout the later Middle Ages and the early modern periods, young aristocratic women usually owned their own religious books, such as breviaries, psalters, and books of hours, as well as *lais* and romances. During the fifteenth century, like their brothers, they benefited from the circulation of texts written on paper, a cheaper material than parchment, and from the invention of printing. These developments made books more easily and readily available than they had been for previous generations. With the rise of print culture, came the circulation of printed versions of advice books, ballads, plays, and chivalric romances, some of which were targeted at, and appealed to, youthful, aristocratic readers.

Engagement with textual culture allowed elite young men and women to be not only consumers, but also producers, of youth culture. Members of both sexes, at the level of the elite, aspired to write poetry and compose songs. Fifteenth-century Germany was home to several aristocratic women poets, authors, and composers of songs, including Eleonore, Duchess of Austria, and Elisabeth, Countess of Nassau-Saarbrücken. Another fifteenth-century lady, Helene Kottaner, who served as a royal chambermaid, wrote one of the earliest surviving sets of German memoirs in 1439–1440. These elite women presumably received their education in writing in childhood and adolescence. In the early modern period, some aristocratic girls benefited from the arguments put forward by humanist writers that they should receive a higher standard of education than previously. Yet general levels of literacy among young, elite girls still lagged behind those of men, reflecting contemporary expectations of the more limited social roles open to women when they transitioned into adults, even among the aristocracy.

David Cressy has suggested that, whereas 1 per cent of women and 10 per cent of men were capable of signing their own names in England at the beginning of the sixteenth century, 10 per cent of women and 30 per cent of men were able to produce signatures in the mid-1600s. Furthermore, access to formal educational settings and institutions generally remained closed even to well-born and wealthy young women. There were some secondary-level schools that admitted women, such as those girls' schools found in early seventeenth-century London, but these were the exception rather than the rule.

Yet, amid training for adult life, there were still opportunities for play—for adolescent girls and boys to mix, socially, to discuss common interests, and to engage in similar, youthful pastimes, entertainments, and recreational pursuits. Both young men and young women are described attending a fictional betrothal, and its accompanying celebrations, in *The Nibelungenlied*, during which a circle of "young men" stood around the young couple, "cheerfully, thinking about what young people still tend to think about." Hawking, archery, and games such as chess, or those involving dice and cards, provided occasions for social interaction with other adolescents. John, the teenage heir to the duchy of Brabant, lost more than £271 at chess in 1290, a considerable sum that his father-in-law discharged on his behalf, and further money at bowls in 1292–1293. In *The Pilgrimage of Human Life*, Youth herself was depicted as a flighty young woman, who enjoyed hunting and playing games, as well as listening to minstrelsy and songs. St. Elizabeth of Hungary was portrayed in the *Gilte Legende* as "playing with the other maidens of her estate," but avoiding taking too much enjoyment from "games," and reluctantly attending "festivals." An anonymously authored life of St. Katherine of Alexandria that was written in around 1420 similarly noted how this youthful female saint was unusual for an adolescent girl, since "She did not care for plays, or jokes, or idle words, or secular songs, but instead devoted herself entirely to the study of holy scripture." In *The Treasure of the City of Ladies*, Christine de Pisan advised her readers that it was fitting for a young, noble princess to spend some time privately at leisure in company with "the younger women among her servants," since "it is natural for youth to play and laugh." On such occasions, the youngsters were to be left alone to enjoy their pursuits, provided they were not indecorous or uncouth. Ann, Lady Fanshawe, recalled the long hours that she had spent as a young girl in England, in "recreation," riding, running, and skipping: "I was that which we graver people call a hoyting girl."[17]

COURTSHIP PRACTICES AND MARRIAGE

Adolescence for elite men and women was often marked by their first experiences of courtship and marriage, the latter being a formal rite of passage. In the great households and royal courts of Western Europe, male youths and damsels formed friendships, and sometimes these blossomed into affection. Courtship rituals therefore formed a key component of aristocratic youth culture. The degree to which social interactions between young members of the opposite sex were supervised or policed depended on the organization and nature of the individual establishments in which they lived or were placed. Adolescence was a time of potential moral and spiritual danger, as young men and women's bodies came to sexual maturity and were potentially exposed to the temptation of committing carnal sin. It was also the life stage most strongly related to beauty and physical perfection, leading inevitably to magnetism between the sexes. The teenage years were associated with awakening sexual appetites and sexual desire, hence Kim Phillips' belief that "Maidenhood in late medieval England was a stage characterized primarily by a tension between sexuality and virginity." In French satirical literature, "Wantoness" was described as the "customary attendant" of "Youth" and personified as a young noblewoman in Alan of Lille's *Anticlaudianus*. In *The Book of the Knight of the Tower*, the author warned his daughters that in order to maintain her "honor," a woman "must always ensure that she keeps her body clean and undefiled, and refuse the delights of youth and foul pleasures."[18]

The physical attraction that elite young men and women felt toward one another was reflected in contemporary songs. In a songbook produced for the German patroness Ottilia Fenchlerin and completed in 1592, the scribe Caspar Schröder included these lyrics:

> His noble comportment pleases me well,
> He acts just as a young man should,
> He has two brilliantly shining eyes
> And attractively cut hair.
> He struts like a true nobleman,
> He has [beautiful] red lips.
> Oh God, send my greetings to this young man.[19]

The idea of youthful love among the nobility pervaded late medieval art. Scenes of young, amorous, and courting noble couples were common themes that adorned elaborately carved mirror cases, caskets, and writing tablets used in the private apartments of the elite. A pair of ivory mirror cases made in Paris in the third quarter of the fourteenth century incorporates images depicting a young, well-dressed couple, and the progress of love, including the moment when the young man offers his heart to the lady who is the object of his desire. A richly decorated, painted jewel box made in the Upper Rhineland in the second quarter of the fourteenth century is decorated with romance scenes and carries pictures and inscriptions describing the wounding of a male lover's heart, and his surrender to his ladylove. Similarly, an embroidered purse of the early 1300s shows two well-dressed lovers, with the young man offering up a ring.[20] In spite of the prevalence of such imagery in material culture, young ladies at court were advised by Christine de Pisan against becoming too well acquainted or close to men in behavior, conversation, or deed. This author carefully advised the chaperone of a young, married princess to remind her charge of the qualities and wisdom of her husband if the young woman was attracted, instead, to other men at feasts and dances held at court. The chaperone was also to look out for young lords who deliberately paid attention to her young mistress. Not only was she to see them firmly off with quiet, brief, determined words, but she was also to advise the girl of the folly and potential evil in encouraging their attentions. It was essential, in the opinions of their elders, for young ladies as the future bearers of legitimate heirs to great estates to preserve their honor and their sexual reputations.

In medieval canon law, girls were able to consent to marriage at the age of twelve and boys at the age of fourteen. Yet, the married state itself did not necessarily signal the end of youth, since some brides, grooms, and couples married in their teens. In sixteenth-century Germany, Elisabeth, daughter of the duke elector Joachim I of Brandenburg, was fourteen years old on her wedding to Eric I of Brunswick-Calenberg, although in this case her groom was forty years her senior. The Italian writer Barbaro advised his readers that girls were usually ready for marriage at the age of eighteen, following the views of classical authors and philosophers. The will drawn up by Sir William Berland in 1383 made arrangements for the posthumous sale of lands and tenements for the marriages of his daughters Joan and Elizabeth, in the expectation that they would be married before the age of fifteen if they wished to marry.

Since elite marriage was so closely tied to the formation of political alliances and to the transfer of wealth, it was often considered too important a matter to be left to young couples alone, thereby offering another example of the ways in which adults attempted to shape youth. Arranged marriages negotiated between a couple's parents and guardians remained the norm for the medieval and early modern aristocracies of Western Europe, ensuring the persistence of the practice of endogamy. The provision of dowries by the fathers, brothers, and guardians of young brides helped young women to attract marriage partners of suitable wealth and status. Descriptions of marriage negotiations were often presented in literary works in ways that reflected life, such as when the young Lord Giselher was betrothed in *The Nibelungenlied*. In this work, the young bride, a margravine, was first summoned to court. As part of the settlement, lands and castles were bestowed on the bride, while her father Ruediger conferred gold and silver on his daughter. The bride-to-be's youthful embarrassment was described when she was asked if she accepted the groom, Giselher, whom she barely knew, in the presence of her entire father's court.

Royal and aristocratic weddings marked another rite of passage and were usually times of celebration, accompanied by lavish celebrations and festivities in all the courts of Europe. In *Robert the Devil*, the "nuptials" of the hero's parents, a fictional Duke of Normandy and a count's daughter, were described as "a splendid fete, / With counts and great lords in attendance; The Duke lavished silver and gold / On singers, jugglers and tales new told."[21] No fewer than 426 minstrels performed at John of Brabant's marriage to Edward I's daughter, Margaret, in July 1290, which also saw plenty of music and dancing. The chronicle of Geoffrey Le Baker of Swinbrook described how the weddings of Roger Mortimer's daughters at Hereford to the heir of John Hastings and the Earl Marshal's son were accompanied by a celebratory tournament in 1327, which was attended by King Edward III of England and his mother, Queen Isabella.

Yet, not all marriages were arranged in accordance with the wishes of the bride or groom's families. The existence of young, wealthy heiresses, for instance, placed these youthful women in danger of abduction from ambitious male suitors who wanted to secure their lands, in both literature and life. In Eilhart's rendition of the medieval Tristan story, for instance, Count Riole of Nantes went to war after more peaceful modes of courtship failed, and forcibly tried to take Havelin's daughter as a bride. Similarly, in *Robert the Devil*, a seneschal resorted first to warfare, and later to subterfuge, when his attempts to court the emperor's daughter were rebuffed by the girl's father. The count's and seneschal's behavior highlights contemporary perceptions of the vulnerability of elite maidens, especially, in a patriarchal society and the limits on their personal agency or freedom of action.

Even so, abductions were the exception, rather than the norm. Love matches were also relatively rare and tended to be frowned upon by parents, lords, and wider kin. Margery Paston, a young gentlewoman, endured an examination by the bishop of Norwich into the validity of her marriage to Richard Calle in 1469, after she married, secretly, a man below her status in direct opposition to her family's wishes. Margery's refusal to turn her back on the husband whom she had married for love was seen by her natal kin as an act of extreme obstinacy and disobedience, two of the more troublesome characteristics of youth.

Although the personal feelings of the young bride and groom were seldom given priority over more material considerations in arranged marriages, affection was not necessarily discouraged. On the contrary, arranged matches that led to love, respect, and warmth between young brides and grooms were welcomed. In a letter written by John Paston II to his mother in 1477 about his brother's mooted marriage to Margery Brews, he commented favorably on the bride's "person, her youth, her family, [and] the love on both sides." Loveless unions involving young couples were often presented negatively in medieval romances, including the German renditions of the Tristan story, where suspicious and jealous husbands either locked away or placed their beautiful young brides under strict surveillance. Admittedly, some marriages ultimately proved so displeasing to at least one of the partners involved that they prompted requests for annulments from the Church to dissolve the union, like that which John de Warenne, earl of Surrey, sought in an unsuccessful attempt to end his marriage to his young wife, Joan of Bar, in the early fourteenth century. Love affairs, especially on the part of unhappily married young brides, were roundly condemned in contemporary conduct literature. Christine de Pisan advised a chaperone who was faced with a "young high-born lady who wants to plunge into a foolish love affair" to speak sternly with her mistress and convey the evils, dangers, and harm that were likely to result from her imprudent actions.[22] A love affair by a young, married woman could bring absolute disgrace upon the young bride and ruin her reputation forever. Yet, the sexual double standards of the time saw elite young men take mistresses and father illegitimate children before and after their marriages, like the men of the Medici family in Renaissance Florence.

Contemporary conduct literature recognized that relationships between the sexes—and especially between young married couples—needed careful guidance and management in order to inspire true love and affection. Zirclaria, for example, warned young noblemen that love could not be bought with wealth or material gifts. Instead, tender feelings should be reciprocal: "One should give one's heart in exchange for another heart; one should desire fidelity by being faithful; one should secure constancy and truth with constancy." Christine de Pisan tasked the older, well-born female attendant of a young, married princess with the responsibility of encouraging and cultivating affection between the young bride and her groom through the use of loving words and terms of endearment in their conversations and messages. The language and contents of the letters exchanged in the late 1590s between the teenage Charlotte Brabantine (d. 1631) of Orange-Nassau and her slightly older sister Elisabeth (d. 1642), Duchess of Bouillon, bear all the hallmarks of girlish "inexperience and uncertainties" as these two youthful women turned to one another for mutual support as they entered married life and young motherhood.[23]

Young Aristocrats as Participants in Youth Culture

Property rights, educational settings, recreational activities, courtship rituals, and marriage all shaped adolescence and allowed young lords and ladies to participate in an aristocratic youth culture based upon shared interests and pursuits throughout the medieval and early modern periods. As a life stage, aristocratic "youth" was characterized by physical perfection, but also by moral tugs between virtuous and overly boisterous, playful behavior, which could sometimes lead to rebelliousness against their elders. In these respects, elite youth was like that of boys and girls of lesser social status. Yet, the aristocracy's access to wealth and privilege set them apart from other members of society; it also gave their parents, lords, and guardians a vested interest in framing and shaping their experiences of youth, and in ensuring that strategies were in place to govern adolescents, and to maintain and protect distinctions of noble rank. Even so, the youthful identities of these fledgling lords and ladies found outward expression and a common culture through the ways that they enthusiastically embraced contemporary modes and trends in adornment and clothing and collectively underwent training for their adult lives and roles. Within the courts and great households of the elite, young noblemen and women had plenty of opportunities to socialize and pass time in one another's company, be it at the chessboard, or while hunting, hawking, tourneying, dancing, singing, or celebrating their own and other people's nuptials.

Notes

1. Elizabeth S. Cohen and Margaret Reeves, "Introduction," in *The Youth of Early Modern Women*, ed. Elizabeth S. Cohen and Margaret Reeves (Amsterdam: University of Amsterdam Press, 2018), 11–32, at p. 11; Fiona Harris Stoertz, "Young Women in France, and England, 1050–1300," *Journal of Women's History* 12, no. 4 (2001): 22–46, at 35; John Carmi Parsons, "The Medieval Aristocratic Teenaged Female: Adolescent or Adult?," in *The Pre-Modern Teenager: Youth in Society, 1150–1650*, ed. Konrad Eisenbichler (Toronto: Centre for Reformation and Renaissance Studies, 2002), 311–22, at p. 318.
2. *Robert the Devil*, trans. Samuel N. Rosenberg (Philadelphia: Pennsylvania State University Press, 2018), 123.
3. Geoffroi de Charny, *The Book of Chivalry of Geoffroi de Charny: Text, Context, and Translation*, trans. Richard W. Kaeuper and Elspeth Kennedy (Philadelphia: University of Pennsylvania Press, 1996), 84–5 (cap. 3); Thomasin von Zirclaria, *Der Welsche Gast (The Italian Guest)*, ed. and trans. Marion Gibbs and Winder McConnell, Medieval German Texts in Bilingual Editions IV (Kalamazoo, MI: Medieval Institute Publications, 2009), 62, 68.
4. *The Book of Chivalry of Geoffroi de Charny*, 190–191 (cap. 42); *Women of the English Nobility and Gentry, 1066–1500*, trans. Jennifer Ward (Manchester, UK: Manchester University Press, 1995), 52n35; Christine de Pisan, *The Treasure of the City of Ladies, or the Book of Three Virtues*, trans. Sarah Lawson (Harmondsworth, UK: Penguin, 1985), 110n2.
5. Ramon Llull, *The Book of the Order of Chivalry*, trans. Noel Fallows (Woodbridge, UK: Boydell Press, 2013), 44 (book 2, cap. 2); Pier Paolo Vergerio, "The Character and Studies Befitting a Freeborn Youth," in *Humanist Educational Treatises*, ed. and trans. Craig W. Kallendorf (Cambridge, MA: Harvard University Press, 2002), 2–46, at 24–25.
6. *Women of the Gilte Legende: A Selection of Middle English Saints Lives*, ed. Larissa Tracy (Cambridge: D. S. Brewer, 2003), 57; *Women of the English Nobility and Gentry*, 52n35; Francesco Barbaro, *The Wealth of Wives: A Fifteenth-Century Marriage Manual*, trans. Margaret L. King, Medieval and Renaissance Texts and Studies 485 (Toronto: Iter Academic Press, 2015), 77; *Late-Medieval German Women's Poetry: Secular and Religious Songs*, trans. Albrecht Classen (Cambridge: D. S. Brewer, 2004), 91n12(3).
7. Zirclaria, *Der Welsche Gast*, 57, 59, 63.
8. Ibid., 57; Vergerio, "The Character and Studies Befitting a Freeborn Youth," 22–23.
9. Christine de Pisan, *The Treasure of the City of Ladies*, 88–89n23.
10. Llull, *The Book of the Order of Chivalry*, 42 (book 1, cap. 12).
11. Sean McGlynn, "Pueri sunt pueri: Machismo, Chivalry, and the Aggressive Pastimes of the Medieval, Male Youth," *Historical Reflections* 42, no. 1 (2016): 88–100, at p. 96.
12. *The Book of Chivalry of Geoffroi de Charny*, 166–167, 170–171 (cap. 36).
13. "Girart of Vienne," in *Heroes of the French Epic: Translations from the Chansons de Geste*, trans. Michael Newth (Woodbridge, UK: Boydell Press, 2005), 281–471, at pp. 369–370; *The Nibelungenlied, with The Klage*, trans. William Whobrey (Indianapolis: Hackett Publishing, 2018), 5.

14. "Girart of Vienne," 334–338; *The Nibelungenlied*, 3–4.
15. Jacqueline Eales, *Women in Early Modern England, 1500-1700* (London: UCL Press, 1998), 35.
16. *The Memoirs of Ann, Lady Fanshawe* (London: John Lane, 1907), 22.
17. *The Nibelungenlied*, 137; *Women of the Gilte Legende*, 56–57; *Chaste Passions: Medieval English Virgin Martyr Legends*, trans. Karen A. Winstead (Ithaca, NY: Cornell University Press, 2000), 132; Christine de Pisan, *The Treasure of the City of Ladies*, 89n23; *The Memoirs of Ann, Lady Fanshawe* (London: John Lane, 1907), 22.
18. Kim M. Phillips, *Medieval Maidens: Young Women and Gender in England, 1270-1540* (Manchester, UK: Manchester Medieval Press, 2003), 7; Alan of Lille, *Anticlaudianus or the Good and Perfect Man*, trans. James J. Sheridan (Toronto: Pontifical Institute of Medieval Studies, 1973), 176; *Women of the English Nobility and Gentry*, 53n35.
19. *Late-Medieval German Women's Poetry*, 36n5(2).
20. New York, Metropolitan Museum of Art 41.100.160; The MET Cloisters L.2010.36; The MET Cloisters 50.141; 64.101.1364.
21. *Robert the Devil*, 9.
22. *Women of the English Nobility and Gentry*, 39n22; Christine de Pisan, *The Treasure of the City of Ladies*, 95n25.
23. Zirclaria, *Der Welsche Gast*, 71; Jane Couchman, "'Is it possible that my sister [...] has had a baby?': The Early Years of Marriage as a Transition from Girlhood to Womanhood in the Letters of Three Generations of Orange-Nassau Women," in *The Youth of Early Modern Women*, 195–214, at p. 196.

Further Reading

Barbaro, Francesco. *The Wealth of Wives*. Translated by Margaret L. King. Medieval and Renaissance Texts and Studies 485. Toronto: Iter Academic Press, 2015.
Charny, Geoffroi de. *The Book of Chivalry of Geoffroi de Charny: Text, Context, and Translation*. Translated by Richard W. Kaeuper and Elspeth Kennedy. Philadephia: University of Pennsylvania Press, 1996.
Cohen, Elizabeth S., and Margaret Reeves, eds. *The Youth of Early Modern Women*. Amsterdam: University of Amsterdam Press, 2018.
Humanist Educational Treatises. Edited and translated by Craig W. Kallendorf. Cambridge, MA: Harvard University Press, 2002.
Karras, Ruth Mazzo. *From Boys to Men: Formations of Masculinity in Late Medieval Europe*. Philadelphia: University of Pennsylvania Press, 2003.
Late-Medieval German Women's Poetry: Secular and Religious Songs. Translated by Albrecht Classen. Cambridge: D. S. Brewer, 2004.
McGlynn, Sean. "Pueri sunt pueri: Machismo, Chivalry and the Aggressive Pastimes of the Medieval, Male Youth." *Historical Reflections* 42, no. 1 (2016): 88–100.
The Nibelungenlied, with The Klage. Translated by William Whobrey. Indianapolis: Hackett Publishing, 2018.
Parsons, John Carmi. "The Medieval Aristocratic Teenaged Female: Adolescent or Adult?" In *The Pre-Modern Teenager: Youth in Society, 1150-1650*. Edited by Konrad Eisenbichler, 311–22. Toronto: Centre for Reformation and Renaissance Studies, 2002.

Phillips, Kim M. *Medieval Maidens: Young Women and Gender in England, 1270–1540*. Manchester, UK: Manchester University Press, 2003.

Pisan, Christine de. *The Treasure of the City of Ladies, or the Book of Three Virtues*. Translated by Sarah Lawson. Harmondsworth, UK: Penguin, 1985.

Stoertz, Fiona Harris. "Young Women in France and England, 1050–1300." *Journal of Women's History* 12, no. 4 (2001): 22–46.

von Zirclaria, Thomasin. *Der Welsche Gast (The Italian Guest)*. Edited and translated by Marion Gibbs and Winder McConnell. Medieval German Texts in Bilingual Editions 4. Kalamazoo, MI: Medieval Institute Publications, 2009.

Women of the English Nobility and Gentry, 1066–1500. Translated by Jennifer Ward. Manchester, UK: Manchester University Press, 1995.

Women of the Gilte Legende: A Selection of Middle English Saints Lives. Edited by Larissa Tracy. Cambridge: D. S. Brewer, 2003.

CHAPTER 4

CONTESTED TERRITORY

Non-Elite Youth and Youth Culture in the Premodern West

ADRIANA BENZAQUÉN

WHETHER non-elite youth in premodern Western societies had a culture of their own is an open question. The first task is thus to determine if they did, what traces this culture may have left, and what its main characteristics and functions were. "Youth culture" here refers to the many ways in which young people found meaning in and made meaning out of their lives, while "non-elite youth" designates young men and women who grew up in working families; in late medieval and early modern Europe, most of them were the children of peasants, artisans, and day laborers. Youth, as a distinctive group or an identity experienced by young people themselves and recognized by the community, had imprecise and shifting boundaries. Physically, its beginning was marked by sexual maturation; socially and culturally, it was associated with leaving the parental home. Youth ended with marriage and economic autonomy. Because in many regions these events occurred considerably late, youth comprised what today are two separate life stages: adolescence, beginning around the ages of twelve to fourteen, and young adulthood, from the early- to the mid-twenties, and for some even the late twenties or early thirties. Youth lasted a long time, and young people, like children, made up a large proportion of the population.

The status of youth was ambiguous. First, if childhood was indisputably a state of dependence and adulthood represented the attainment of independence, then youth was in the middle, neither completely subordinated nor completely autonomous. Youth entailed both dependence and independence, in different circumstances and at different times. For non-elite young men and women, the ambiguities intrinsic to the time of youth were complicated by their social rank. In European and colonial societies, power was withheld from all young people—even those who would come to exercise it later in their lives, namely, elite men—but working youth endured forms of subjection that were specific to their condition. At the same time, in some respects working youth enjoyed more freedom, as a group, than their better-off counterparts. Second, if marriage and the establishment of a separate household usually indicated the threshold between youth and adulthood, how did this affect the many people who never married, who married at a very young age, or who continued to live with their or their spouses' parents after marriage? The point at which lifelong bachelors and spinsters would reach the status of full adulthood, and how a teenage wife would be perceived and treated, varied according to sociocultural and individual contexts. A further level of complexity is added when we factor in gender as it impinged on the definition of, and boundaries between, childhood, youth, and adulthood, and consider how the experiences of young women overlapped with or diverged from those of young men.

Just as the status of youth was ambiguous, the culture of non-elite youth in the premodern West was, and remains, contested territory. It was contested at the time, between youth and the rest of society—especially the authorities, both religious and secular—and also between male and female youth, who claimed or were assigned very different roles and ways of participating in it. It continues to be contested territory among historians, whose interest in premodern youth culture has ebbed and flowed in recent decades and whose interpretations of it have been ambivalent. Indeed, some historians have rejected altogether the very idea of a premodern youth culture. Any attempt to explore premodern, non-elite youth culture must grapple with the problem of scarcity of evidence. By definition, non-elite young people lacked, or had little, formal education, yet many of them experienced more autonomy than elite youth in several areas of their lives, including leisure time spent with peers, the chance to leave home and have adventures, some sexual freedom, and some say over their future occupations and the choice of a spouse—and it is there that historians must look for traces of their culture. But what sources can historians use to reconstruct the culture of a group that was largely illiterate? Parish registers and service or apprenticeship contracts are helpful to understand the everyday setting of youthful lives, but their impersonal character limits their value for an inquiry into the meaning young people created out of their lives. Traces of youth's voices are found in court records about young men and women who got in trouble with the law, were victims of a crime, or testified as witnesses, and of their activities in the decrees and regulations the authorities issued when they tried to suppress them. Toward the end of the early modern period, the number of literary, printed, and personal sources bearing on the study of non-elite youth culture increases. The availability or scarcity of sources affects not just what we can know about youth culture but also how we can make sense of it.

Youth Culture and the Tasks of Youth

The times and spaces available to non-elite boys and girls to develop and experience their own culture were framed by the two tasks most of them had to accomplish during their youth: acquire the skills that would allow them to earn a living and set up a household in the future and find the spouse with whom they would run that household and start a family. These tasks both limited their access to literate, elite culture and provided opportunities for them to spend time together in more or less structured settings. While some young people remained at home and learned from their parents, many others left the parental home during their teenage years.

Most adolescent girls, and many boys, left home to enter into service. In Northwestern Europe and parts of Central and Eastern Europe, service in another household was a common experience of youth, while in the south young people worked as servants when their families were very poor or if they had lost one or both parents. This type of service, known as life-cycle service, shaped the experiences of young men and women in a number of ways. It was integral to the protracted youth and late marriages that characterized the family system in many parts of Europe at this time, and while, by deferring entry into adulthood, it kept young people in a "state of semi-dependence," as Michael Mitterauer observes, it also loosened ties with their families and produced "a higher degree of self responsibility."[1] Life-cycle service had many benefits, for the young women and men involved, their families, and the community. It was a means for young people to make a living, thus easing the economic burden on their families, and it also included an element of training. Because young servants were provided room and board, and sometimes clothes, they could save their wages until they were ready to marry or set up on their own. Servants were generally hired on an annual basis, and many of them changed positions after a year or two. In England, annual hiring fairs in the countryside facilitated the process, as prospective servants and employers would be seeking one another at a common time and place. Masters and mistresses were expected to act, to some degree, as surrogate parents, but most young servants remained in contact with their families. If they were literate, like the three daughters of George and Sarah Trent, who served Edward and Mary Clarke at their estate in Somerset in the 1690s, they could keep in touch with their parents through the regular exchange of letters. Servants might also come to a parent's assistance when needed, like Phil Woodman, the Clarkes' footboy, who upon hearing that his poor mother was ill in London asked his master to send her part of his saved wages.[2]

While young servants received some training that prepared them for their future responsibilities as adults, adolescent boys were placed as apprentices with a master for the express purpose of learning the master's trade. Apprenticeship contracts bound boys to masters for terms ranging from two or three to ten or twelve years. The master promised to teach the skills of the trade and supply food, drink, lodging, light, fire, clothes and shoes, medical care, and occasionally a small wage. In return, the apprentice promised to serve the master faithfully, further his business and keep his secrets, and not go out at night, run away, gamble, fornicate, or marry during the term of the contract. Some masters undertook to offer, besides the skills pertaining to the trade, instruction in religion, reading, writing, and arithmetic. In premodern towns, male apprentices were a visible group with a shared identity and similar aspirations. Upon completion of the apprenticeship, they would become journeymen working for a master for a wage and eventually attain the status of masters within the guild system. Few girls were given the advantage of an apprenticeship, for which parents or guardians had to pay a fee, but those who did were bound to a mistress or might be taught by the master's wife. Even then, only a tiny minority of trained young women were permitted to become members of a guild. Orphans and very poor children could be placed as apprentices by charitable organizations or political authorities, like the siblings Jane and Nicholas Turner, who were placed with Edward Clarke in September 1681, Jane to be instructed in housewifery and Nicholas in husbandry "or such other profession."[3] Apprenticeships for orphans and poor children frequently started at a younger age, freeing the authorities from financial responsibility for their well-being while ensuring they would be able to support themselves in later life.

For non-elite youth, growing up often involved mobility. For daring young men, the opportunities for travel and adventure were boundless. The journeymen who spent years traveling, after completing their training, not only perfected their skills working for other masters but also got to see their own and other countries and met other journeymen along the way. Younger boys whose families could not support them took to the roads to eke out a living. Thomas Platter, born in 1499 to a poor rural family in the Valais, trekked to Germany hoping to study—his family wanted him to become a priest but lacked the funds to send him to school—and survived by begging, singing in the streets, taking odd jobs, and stealing.[4] Young men flocked to bustling commercial centers like London and Amsterdam. If they were unhappy or restless on land, they might go to sea, like Edward Barlow, who became an apprentice seaman in the English navy in 1659, at the age of seventeen, and later rose to become chief mate.[5] Barely a year after Nicholas Turner became his parish apprentice in husbandry, Edward Clarke let the boy bind himself anew to the merchant John Wheddon as an apprentice sailor for nine years. For Nicholas, the excitement of life at sea may have been even more enticing than the potential material returns of his new apprenticeship.[6] Between the late fifteenth century and the end of the seventeenth century, hundreds of thousands of European boys and young men crossed the Atlantic, Indian, and Pacific oceans as eager, indifferent, or unwilling participants in the exploration of new lands and settlement of colonies overseas. Portuguese boys accompanied the Jesuits to Brazil and helped them in their missionary work. The Dutch East India and West India Companies, in desperate need of young men for their ships and colonies, recruited orphans and other boys whose families were unable to care for them. In the seventeenth century, young men migrated from England to the Chesapeake region or the Caribbean as indentured servants, bound to serve a master for several years in exchange for room and board and the cost of their passage. The rewards of migration could be substantial, especially for those who had little or nothing to begin with, yet the risks were exceedingly high. Shipwrecks, the stresses and dangers of an unfamiliar and often hostile environment, and diseases such as malaria and dysentery cost numerous lives.[7] The growing size of armies afforded another outlet for restless or troublesome young men, who enlisted voluntarily or were forcibly recruited into military service in droves.

Although, for practical reasons, working girls were not as closely supervised as girls growing up in elite families, their access to space and use of time were more restricted than young men's. For young women, mobility commonly took the form of traveling to another village, a town, or a city to enter into service. Very few European girls and young women went overseas in this period, but concerns about racial mixing in the colonies spurred attempts to facilitate their emigration to be available as wives for European men. The eight hundred or so French girls who arrived in New France in the second half of the seventeenth century were known as *filles du roi* because the king paid for their voyage and gave them a dowry and trousseau. Like the young women similarly sponsored by the Portuguese government and the Dutch East India Company, most of the *filles du roi* were poor orphans.[8]

Where life-cycle service was common, young people married in their mid-to-late twenties. The experience they gained and the wages they saved during their youth allowed them to establish a separate household following marriage. Whereas among the elites arranged marriages were the norm, young women and men of the lower ranks often took the initiative in choosing a spouse. Moreover, young women who contributed their own dowry to a marriage could expect to enter it on a more equal footing than those who depended on their fathers—or, in their absence, their brothers, an employer, or a charitable institution—to provide a dowry for them. Young people could meet possible partners in public spaces, such as the household where they lived and worked, fairs and markets, and village or town festivals. Love and physical attraction were critical, but they also took into account whether the potential bride or groom would be able to fulfill the economic, parental, social, and religious responsibilities attached to the roles of wife and husband in their community. Although they treasured their right to choose, most young people sought the approval of family and friends to corroborate the appropriateness of their choice and ensure cordial relations in the future. And even where young men and women were relatively free to interact, like in England, clandestine relationships could cause considerable concern. Mary Clarke and her steward John Spreat went to great lengths to thwart the relationship between Spreat's brother Gabriel and Nan Trent, one of Mary's servants, which in their view could never lead to an acceptable marriage. When Gabriel was sent to London, Nan fell ill with a "Love sick distemper."[9] Where parents took a more active role in choosing their child's spouse, like in Italy, some young people engaged in secret courtships or went as far as refusing to marry the person their parents had chosen for them.[10]

The long time that normally elapsed between sexual maturation and marriage, whether for men only, as in some southern regions where women married early, or for both sexes, as in Northern Europe, created problems that had to be dealt with at the communal, familial, and individual levels. For the medieval Church, all sexual activity outside marriage was sinful, a position upheld by both Catholics and Protestants after the Reformations. Young people were required to refrain from sex until marriage. Secular authorities and ordinary people evinced a more flexible and undoubtedly more realistic attitude toward premarital sex. Still, a double standard shaped attitudes toward youth and sex. In general, it was presumed that young men would become sexually active before marriage, while for young women honor was closely associated with virginity. Indeed, girls had less freedom and mobility than boys because as they physically matured their sexual reputation was of paramount concern. In Southern Europe, prostitution was tolerated as a necessary evil. The work of some young women as prostitutes, in many cases in regulated municipal brothels, made it possible to satisfy male sexual urges while protecting the honor of respectable women. Where both women and men married late, traditional custom admitted a range of heterosexual acts between unmarried people, especially when they were openly courting and after they were betrothed. Young couples might be permitted to spend time together, alone, with other couples or under the eyes of adults, and in some places they could share a bed for the night and experiment with sexual intimacy as long as they abstained from intercourse. By channeling youth's sexual needs into sanctioned and non-procreative forms, communities sought to prevent the birth of illegitimate children that would tax the public purse.

Following a promise of marriage or betrothal, couples might begin to have sexual intercourse without compromising the young woman's virtue, as in the story of William and Susan, an apprentice and a servant, related in an English chapbook:

> So being night they went to bed,
> not making any strife,
> He did obtain her Maiden-head,
> before she was his Wife
> But afterwards they Married were,
> As Lovers ought to do,
> And now they live at hearts content,
> and long may they do so.[11]

That many brides were pregnant at the time of their marriage is revealed by the large (but regionally variable) number of records of baptisms or births occurring eight months or less later. An unmarried pregnant woman taken to court on charges of fornication might claim that she had consented to sex only after being promised marriage; in turn, a man could falsely promise marriage to a girl to convince her to have sex, only to abandon her later. In cases of pregnancy out of wedlock, marriage was usually the preferred solution, for the woman and her family—as it would restore her reputation—and for the community—as it would release it from any obligation toward the child. The pregnant woman or her father, mother, or guardian might sue an unwilling father to force him to do the right thing. The alternative was to pursue some kind of financial compensation. When in 1625 Neeltje Jorisdochter sued Jacob Porret, a medical student at Leiden, for having impregnated her daughter Maritje, the university's academic court did not grant her demand that Porret marry her daughter but awarded her 200 guilders for the loss of Maritje's honor, the midwife's fee, and an alimony of 60 guilders a year.[12]

Youth Culture and Youth Groups

The culture of non-elite, working youth in premodern Europe has been a subject of scholarly debate since the 1970s. The debate hinges on two issues. The first is the different ways in which historians understand the idea of a youth culture. For instance, when Barbara Hanawalt and Ilana Ben-Amos deny the existence of a youth culture in late medieval and early modern England, what they have in mind is the kind of youth culture that developed in the nineteenth and twentieth centuries, one that has its own values, styles, and organizations, that is entirely separate from adult culture, and where all youth share a cohesive identity and are influenced chiefly by their peers. In contrast, Paul Griffiths contends that a youth culture need not be completely distinct and separate from adults'; in his view, English working youth were "creative proposers of cultural and social options" distinguished by "a different sense of place and time, and an alleged preference for play and leisure."[13]

Historians' disagreements about youth culture also hinge on the sources on which they base their studies. As premodern, non-elite youth culture was predominantly oral and nonliterate, to reconstruct it we must rely on written accounts produced by educated adults. The study of youth culture gained momentum with the publication of Natalie Zemon Davis's seminal article "The Reasons of Misrule." Davis mined court records and municipal archives and drew on nineteenth- and twentieth-century folklorists to depict the irreverent festive organizations of young men in late medieval and early modern France, known as Abbeys of Youth or of Misrule, among other names. The rural Abbeys, which gathered together the unmarried men of a village under the leadership of an elected Abbot, were in charge of organizing festivals and had jurisdiction over courtship and marriage. In urban areas there were also festive organizations of young men, but instead of a single Abbey, French towns and cities hosted many Abbeys or fraternities that grouped young men by neighborhood, social rank, or profession.[14] However tantalizing, the picture of joyful Abbeys, fraternities, or *Knabenschaften* (boys' societies) offered by Davis and other historians of youth groups, in France and elsewhere in Europe, is based on fragmentary evidence and consequently raises questions about their representativeness as manifestations of youth culture. Most relevant to the topic of this chapter is the question of their social composition. While it seems clear that among these groups' members were the sons of wealthy men (nobles, merchants) and students (in university towns), whether young men from the lower classes participated as well is less certain. Some historians, like Robert Trexler and Davis herself, assume that working and poor young men were integrated in the youth groups as a matter of course, but note that the groups' elected leaders were usually members of the elites; others suppose that, in the cities, non-elite young men formed their own groups or joined confraternities on the basis of neighborhood or occupation.[15]

Although it may not be possible to ascertain the precise extent of working youth's participation in structured youth groups, that they congregated in informal and transient groups is much better documented. Joining such a group could be a matter of survival. When Thomas Platter left his home in the Valais, he traveled with a group of around ten boys, led by a young man, Antony Schalbetter, whose brave character earned him their obedience and gave them a measure of security against strangers and other dangers they might encounter on the roads.[16] The informal youth group's importance lay primarily in the areas of recreation and sociability. In villages and towns, young men spent much of their free time together, in casual groups that met at night, after their work was done, and on Sundays and holidays to walk in the fields, streets, or churchyards, to make their presence felt in public spaces, markets, and fairs, and to chat, jest, sing, and play games. The streets at night were a favored space for urban male youth, a space of freedom they claimed as their own, where they could be rowdy and noisy. But when they could afford it, in cold weather and in Northern Europe above all, they also frequented alehouses and taverns, where they ate and drank (often excessively), and played cards, dice, and other games.

Young men were major actors in the Christian and agricultural festivals and rituals that were central to premodern popular culture as a whole. In some contexts, the festivals were organized by the youth groups, while in others youth participated along with the entire community. Among the festivals dominated by youth were Carnival (in England, Shrove Tuesday) and other celebrations typified by reversal and misrule, or the "world-turned-upside down." Young people donned masks and disguises, cross-dressed, and mocked the elders and the authorities in rites that, as Robert Muchembled remarks, "vigorously contested the established order, social hierarchy, and values of their age."[17] During festivals, male youths competed in games between teams of married and unmarried men of the same village or of young men from different parishes or neighborhoods in the cities. Ball games and other sports allowed young men to display their skill and strength and could sometimes turn violent and brutal. Young men's hot-bloodedness and desire to show off made them enthusiastic partakers in the Venetian battles for bridges (*guerre dei pugni* or *battagliole sui ponti*), where artisans, servants, and other workers fought for personal honor, with sticks in the sixteenth century and with fists in the seventeenth, while supplying entertainment to throngs of spectators.[18]

Youth's involvement in festivals and rituals also conveyed the crucial role of sexuality and courtship during this life stage. On May Day, celebrated throughout Europe and associated with spring and fertility, young men planted bushes, branches, or bunches of flowers in front of girls' houses. Like competitive games, dancing was a common aspect of many festivals. On May Day, young people danced around the maypole, and they organized dances at other times of the year too. During festive occasions male youths also passed judgment on other people's behavior. Depending on the kind of tree or flower they planted before a girl's house on May Day, they would be honoring or insulting her reputation. At weddings, they would demand the payment of a fee, which signaled the right they collectively claimed to the girls of their village or town. Their most powerful, because most humiliating, weapon was the noisy, discordant mock serenade called *charivari* in France, *mattinata* in Italy, *Katzenmuzik* in Germany, *ketelmuziek* in the Dutch Republic, and rough music in England. The charivari was a ritual of public derision and ridicule against people perceived as having transgressed the accepted sexual and marital norms: widows and widowers who remarried (particularly when there was a significant age gap between bride and groom), wives who ruled over or beat their husbands, and cuckolds. Historians have interpreted the charivari as a form of popular justice, with the young men's organization acting as the voice of the community to punish transgressions that would not be prosecuted officially by the authorities. In England, however, rough music was not the exclusive preserve or right of the youth group but part of the broader popular culture, shared by different ages and by both men and women.[19]

Although judicial records and official measures (usually condemnatory) provide a glimpse into the activities of the male youth groups, they may in other respects skew our understanding of premodern youth culture. For instance, Maurice Aymard states that the hierarchical structure of the Abbeys of Youth and the "discontinuous nature and occasional brutality" of their activities were "hardly conducive" to the formation of close, intimate friendships between their members.[20] But this may be a case of overinterpreting the (lack of) evidence. That illiterate youth have not left written accounts of intense and emotional friendships should not be taken to mean that such friendships did not exist among them. Likewise, the pervasive assumption, in much of the scholarly literature on premodern youth culture, that "youth" equals "male youth" both reflects and reproduces young men's overwhelming presence in the records on which these studies rely. Even if no traces of female youth groups comparable to the male Abbeys of Youth or nocturnal gangs have been found, the history of non-elite youth culture cannot be limited to groups from which girls were excluded and activities in which they took no part or played a minor role. Scattered references to working girls' culture occur in the writings of elite women and men, like Dorothy Osborne's 1653 letter describing the "great many young wenches" she saw during walks in a common near her house, who would "sitt in the shade singing of ballads" as they looked after sheep and cows, and Samuel Pepys's recollection of milkmaids dancing together in London on May Day, 1667. Bernard Capp proposes that just as games or fights allowed young men to display their daring, for young women dancing was the means to exhibit their skill and grace.[21]

Because girls and young women spent more time in the household than young men, even when working, and worries about virginity restricted their freedom, their culture must perforce be located mainly in the domestic realm. Eleanor Hubbard claims that young women did have a nocturnal culture of their own, but unlike young men's, it unfolded in the household while parents and masters (or mistresses) slept. An example is the secret meeting, in 1617, in the room of Joan Symonds, the daughter of a Levant Company merchant living in London, that included, besides Joan herself and her sweetheart James (her father's apprentice), several female and male servants, all of whom drank posset, talked, and laughed while Joan and James courted and kissed. The prevalent practice of bedsharing, moreover, encouraged intimate conversations, gossip, and sharing of secrets. Girls would treasure these "moments of youth culture" all the more because they were "fleeting and hushed."[22] Historians of Germany and France have identified one form of rural sociability in which young women were the main actors: the spinning rooms or spinning bees (*Spinnstube* or *veillées*), informal gatherings, especially on winter nights, where girls spun, chatted, laughed, sang songs, and told stories and jokes.[23] The spinning bees combined work and recreation but were not necessarily limited to young women: married and older women could be present and kept a watchful eye over them, while young men would visit and court them.

Responding to Youth Culture

For many historians, youth groups were not just a central element of premodern youth culture, but they also performed a major integrating and disciplining function for young men of the lower ranks in traditional societies, where there were no, or very few, institutional settings devoted to their socialization. Young men were granted jurisdiction over public and private morals because the norms they enforced were widely shared, and their boisterous behavior was tolerated because it stemmed from youthful exuberance and playfulness. Youth groups made possible the smooth transition from one generation to the next, while unruliness and excess were the price the community willingly paid for keeping young men in a subordinate position until the attainment of full adulthood.[24] In the early modern period, however, the customary tolerance of youth's disruptive and rowdy behavior gave way to fear and suspicion and to resolute efforts, on the part of the religious and political authorities, to curb the activities of youth groups. Criticisms of "disorderly youth" were not new, at least among reforming sectors within the educated elites, and some scholars have noted local measures against youth culture and youth groups in the late Middle Ages, mainly in urban areas and in times of crisis, like the moral panics instigated by Bernardino of Siena and by Savonarola in Florence, but there was an intensification of such measures as a consequence of the religious Reformations of the sixteenth century and the rise of centralized power. The renewed emphasis on godliness and discipline made youth a target, while the increase in the power of the state, both locally and nationally, allowed for long-standing complaints about youth to be more effectively translated into repressive actions. Spiritual and political rulers throughout Europe undertook campaigns to control, Christianize, restrict, or ban the behavior and activities of the young, as demonstrated in numerous edicts, decrees, statutes, and ordinances against various aspects of youth culture issued in the sixteenth and seventeenth centuries. The crackdown on youth has also been linked to worsening economic conditions paired with population growth, which resulted in guilds imposing restrictions on the admission of new members.

Just as youth, by reacting to or resisting the conditions under which they lived, whether individually or collectively, were striving to make meaning out of their experiences, outsiders viewed youth culture as a problem and sought to contain it, redefine it, or channel it into acceptable forms. The contested idea of "disorderly youth" can be explored through three themes: rebelliousness, illicit sexuality, and violence, which refer both to young people's behavior and to outsiders' perception of and responses to their behavior. To begin with, youthful rebelliousness was manifested as conflicts between young people and the adults they were bound to serve and obey. Court records reveal that many servants and apprentices were unhappy in their positions and many masters and mistresses were neglectful or abusive. In *The Unlucky Citizen* (1673), Francis Kirkman, born in 1632, recounted how, as the youngest of three apprentices to a scrivener in London, he was ordered to do "petty services" like cleaning shoes, sweeping the shop, and fetching beer or coals, and he had to "humour and please the maid" because otherwise she would "tell tales of me to my mistress, who would not let me live a quiet hour." When he told his father about his misery, his master beat him. Like many others, Kirkman ended up breaking his contract and running away.[25] The growing number of journeymen excluded from guild membership and forced to work for a master for a wage begrudged the prolongation of their state of dependence. But even when they were well treated, according to the standards of the time, working youth often resented the subjection they lived under and wanted more freedom and independence, which made them appear ungrateful in their employers' eyes. When Phil Woodman quit Mary Clarke's service because "he Could not Confine himselfe to be soe much within dore," she was displeased because had she known he would leave so soon she would not have taken the trouble of bringing him down from London to Somerset.[26] Young people who were not living under the rule of a master were the ones who raised most concern, and they could be liable to diverse punishments including whipping, imprisonment, exile, being forced to enter into service or apprenticeship, and transportation to the colonies as indentured servants. In 1549, the city council of Malmø decreed that "all girls who are self-supporting should enter into service again" or suffer banishment.[27] For the Portuguese, Spanish, English, Dutch, and French authorities, shipping destitute or troublesome "masterless" boys overseas was a means to relieve urban tensions at home while meeting the needs of their rising empires.

The escalating concern about illicit (non-marital) sexuality in the early modern period may also be seen as part of the contest around young people's behavior as an expression of their own culture or a challenge to authority. Religious reformers railed against fornication and any activity or occasion that might enable it, like nocturnal walks or meetings, dances, May Day celebrations, and spinning bees. If young men or women were brought to court on fornication charges, they could be punished with a fine, some form of public humiliation, a whipping, or banishment. To put an end to indecency and immorality, in many towns the municipal brothels were closed down. But even though youthful sexuality in general came under attack, the double standard endured, and the hardening attitude toward illicit sex meant, in practice, stricter controls placed on women and harsher responses to pregnancies out of wedlock and illegitimate children. Young women whose behavior contravened community norms, who walked around at night, visited or worked in alehouses, or kept male company were compromising their reputation and putting their safety at risk. For disgraced young women, the consequences could be dire. Many vagrants in early modern England were unmarried pregnant girls who "took to the roads by choice to hide a pregnancy" or were driven out by their parents, their masters, or the parish authorities.[28]

The importance of female sexual honor, both within youth culture and in society at large, underlies a phenomenon that seems inconceivable to us: that young women who claimed in court to have been raped might not only continue to have sexual relations with their rapist but also deem marriage to him the best possible outcome. It also explains why some unmarried pregnant women took an extreme course and committed infanticide, a crime that was punished more severely in the early modern era than before. The double standard, according to which any sexual activity stained a woman's reputation and character, made female servants and apprentices vulnerable because it blurred the line between willingness and seduction, acquiescence and assault. Young girls living away from family and friends were easy prey. If they were poor, as so many of them were, or came from broken homes, they might put up with the sexual advances of their masters, their masters' sons, or other men, hoping they would achieve a desirable end: economic rewards or security, a favorable marriage, or simply love and attention. The degree to which young women exploited (or thought they were exploiting) their sexuality for their own purposes or fell victim to harassment and abuse may be impossible to discern. For the many teenage boys (*fanciulli*) who had sex with older male youths (*giovanni*) or adult men in fifteenth-century Florence, the line between consent and coercion was blurred as well. Michael Rocke, who has examined the records of the Office of the Night, the agency in charge of prosecuting homosexual activity in the city, found that sexual relations between Florentine men and boys "varied widely, from rape to prostitution, from casual encounters to affairs that could last for years."[29]

Finally, male youth groups and gangs provoked fears and suspicion because of the violence that was latent or overt in their behavior. Young men's pranks and mischief repeatedly turned into attacks on property (throwing snowballs and rocks, smashing windows, stealing fruit), cruelty against animals (cats, cocks, dogs, horses), fights among themselves or battles with rival groups, and physical assaults on older people, foreigners, Jews, and authority figures. Episodes of ritualized violence were a habitual occurrence during popular festivals and charivaris, like the sacks of brothels by the London apprentices on Shrove Tuesday.[30] Young men, acting alone or in groups, were frequently behind the sexual violence of which so many young women, and in some places (like Florence) boys, were victims. Young, humble women who were out at night or had a reputation for being "loose" might become the targets of individual or collective rape—even though the alarming rate of rapes committed by male youth groups Jacques Rossiaud discovered in fifteenth-century Dijon seems to have been exceptional.[31] To rein in youthful violence, early modern communities implemented a variety of measures, such as curfews, edicts against nocturnal noise, roaming the streets, alehouses, and other disreputable establishments, and banning popular festivals and charivaris. The introduction of streetlighting in major cities like Amsterdam, Paris, and London, starting in the late seventeenth century, had as one of its goals the reduction or elimination of nocturnal violence.[32]

While the proliferation of measures against youth across Europe and its colonies is evidence of a concerted effort to reshape or suppress youth culture, the effect of such measures was limited, as the unruly behavior of youth persisted, and the youth groups and the festivals and rituals they controlled survived. This suggests that the measures were not consistently enforced and that the common people continued to tolerate youthful disorder. In the conflict between youth culture and authority, the rest of the community often sided with youth, silently or overtly.

Recent historians' responses to the culture of premodern non-elite youth, and to the authorities' campaign against it, have been as ambivalent as the responses of premodern adults. Was (male) youth culture an expression of joy, vitality, creativity, and freedom, inherently benign, even utopian or revolutionary, or was it inherently violent, aggressive, and cruel? Was the violence peripheral or exceptional, as some historians insist, or was it inseparable from, in Norbert Schindler's words, the "symbolic bravado that accompanied rites of virility: acts of provocation and retaliation, stoicism during ordeals, the ability to prove one's valor?"[33] Indeed, it is possible to see premodern youth culture as in essence hyper-masculine and misogynist, and young women's negligible role in its public manifestations as a deliberate segregation. Thus, young male servants and apprentices balked at being placed under the supervision of their masters' wives, daughters, or older female maids, and journeymen frustrated in their aspiration to become masters lobbied the guilds to keep women out.[34] When the young Florentine boys mobilized as "shock troops" by Savonarola in the 1490s actively supported the friar's moralizing reforms and his anti-sodomy crusade, aimed primarily at older youth—Savonarola taught the boys "how to reprimand men who propositioned them for sex, beginning with individual admonition and proceeding to collective ridicule and denunciation to the authorities"[35]—was this a case of impressionable children "co-opted" into participation in a homophobic moral panic, or the boys' attempt to protect themselves against abuse, using the resources available to them? More generally, was the fight against youth culture a confrontation between gloomy puritans and young people who just wanted to have fun, or was it, at least in part, an effort to restrain male youths' unruliness for their victims' benefit?

The campaign against youth culture was not, and could not be, wholly negative and repressive: something else had to be offered in its place. If the traditional youth groups had indeed played a crucial socializing function, they could not be merely eradicated but would have to be replaced by other, adult-controlled organizations that could promote civil behavior and meet young people's need for play and recreation in culturally appropriate ways. The purpose of the youth confraternities instituted in fifteenth-century Florence, which included boys from different social backgrounds, was to ensure that their members would spend their leisure time engaged in wholesome and pious activities: religious devotions, processions, music, and dramatic performances (as an alternative to popular festivals and rituals). Charitable associations for poor girls and orphans, like the Conservatory of Santa Caterina in sixteenth-century Rome, founded by the Jesuits, had both a protective and a socializing mission: in this case, to prevent very poor girls and daughters of prostitutes from becoming prostitutes themselves, while providing them with more fitting formative and cultural experiences. Protestant reformers also realized that to discipline youth they had to create spaces and institutions where young people could spend time together, like the special meeting for youth established by Cotton Mather in Boston in the 1680s.[36]

Two other, related developments contributed to the transformation of non-elite youth culture in the early modern period: the spread of literacy and the growth of the urban middle classes. Rising literacy, among the population as a whole but especially among men living in urban areas of Northwestern, Protestant Europe, gave many young people access to print culture and a path to upward mobility. Literacy, together with the self-examination promoted by the Protestant Reformation, inspired the writing of diaries and autobiographies, some of which, like Thomas Platter's, dwelled on the youth years and the writer's escape from poverty into the middle classes (after his wandering youth, Platter went on to become a printer, teacher, and scholar). Some literate, godly young people used writing to reflect on their spiritual turmoil as they struggled to overcome the temptations of youth. In the seventeenth century, more young people in Northwestern Europe became consumers of what Peter Burke calls "'chap-book culture,' the culture of the semi-literate, who had gone to school but not for long."[37] Some scholars have argued that this printed, non-elite youth culture—didactic literature, stories, plays, ballads, and jest-books addressed to apprentices and servants or featuring them as main characters—fostered a common identity among readers.[38] It was, however, a culture produced for youth rather than created by young people themselves.

Notes

1. Michael Mitterauer, "Servants and Youth," *Continuity and Change* 5, no. 1 (1990): 29–30.
2. Ann Kussmaul, *Servants in Husbandry in Early Modern England* (Cambridge: Cambridge University Press, 1981); Mary Clarke to Edward Clarke, October 5, 1696, and May 26, 1700, Somerset Archives and Local Studies (SALS) DD/SF 7/1/31; Chipley account book, SALS DD/SF 9/1/5.
3. Apprenticeship indentures, September 12, 1681, SALS DD/SF 16/12/5-7.
4. Emmanuel Le Roy Ladurie, *The Beggar and the Professor: A Sixteenth-Century Family Saga*, trans. Arthur Goldhammer (Chicago: University of Chicago Press, 1997), 16–23.
5. David Booy, ed., *Personal Disclosures: An Anthology of Self-Writings from the Seventeenth Century* (Aldershot, UK: Ashgate, 2002), 216.
6. Apprenticeship indenture, August 24, 1682, SALS DD/SF 16/12/7.
7. Isabel dos Guimarães Sá, "Up and Out: Children in Portugal and the Empire (1500–1800)," in *Raising an Empire: Children in Early Modern Iberia and Colonial Latin America*, ed. Ondina E. González and Bianca Premo (Albuquerque: University of New Mexico Press, 2007), 32; Benjamin B. Roberts, "On *Not* Becoming Delinquent: Raising Adolescent Boys in the Dutch Republic, 1600–1750," in *Becoming Delinquent: British and European Youth, 1650–1950*, ed. Pamela Cox and Heather Shore (Aldershot, UK: Ashgate, 2002), 44; Meaghan N. Duff, "Adventurers Across the Atlantic: English Migration to the New World, 1580–1780," in *The Atlantic World: Essays on Slavery, Migration, and Imagination*, ed. Wim Klooster and Alfred Padula (Upper Saddle River, NJ: Pearson, 2005), 77–90.
8. Merry E. Wiesner-Hanks, *Women and Gender in Early Modern Europe*, 4th ed. (Cambridge: Cambridge University Press, 2019), 345–349.
9. Mary Clarke to John Spreat, February 24, 1698, SALS DD/SF 7/1/29.
10. Roni Weinstein, "'Thus Will *Giovani* Do': Jewish Youth Sub-Culture in Early Modern Italy," in *The Premodern Teenager: Youth in Society 1150–1650*, ed. Konrad Eisenbichler (Toronto: Centre for Reformation and Renaissance Studies, 2002), 56–57.
11. Margaret Spufford, *Small Books and Pleasant Histories: Popular Fiction and Its Readership in Seventeenth-Century England* (Athens: University of Georgia Press, 1981), 167.
12. Benjamin B. Roberts, *Sex and Drugs Before Rock'n'Roll: Youth Culture and Masculinity During Holland's Golden Age* (Amsterdam: Amsterdam University Press, 2012), 165.
13. Barbara Hanawalt, *Growing Up in Medieval London: The Experience of Childhood in History* (Oxford: Oxford University Press, 1993), 11–12, 125, 137; Ilana Krausman Ben-Amos, *Adolescence and Youth in Early Modern England* (New Haven, CT: Yale University Press, 1994), 176, 183, 205–206; Paul Griffiths, *Youth and Authority: Formative Experiences in England, 1560–1640* (Oxford: Clarendon Press, 1996), 120, 122–123.
14. Natalie Zemon Davis, "The Reasons of Misrule: Youth Groups and Charivaris in Sixteenth-Century France," *Past and Present* 50 (February 1971): 41–75.
15. Richard C. Trexler, "Ritual in Florence: Adolescence and Salvation in the Renaissance," in *The Pursuit of Holiness in Late Medieval and Renaissance Religion*, ed. Charles Trinkaus and Heiko A. Oberman (Leiden: E.J. Brill, 1974), 202–203; Jacques Rossiaud, "Fraternités de jeunesse et niveaux de culture dans les villes du Sud-Est à la fin du Moyen Age," *Cahiers d'histoire* 21 (1976): 67–102; Bernard Capp, "English Youth Groups and *The Pinder of Wakefield*," *Past and Present* 76 (August 1977): 127–133; Norbert Schindler, "Guardians of Disorder: Rituals of Youthful Culture at the Dawn of the Modern Age," in *A History of*

Young People in the West, vol. 1: *Ancient and Medieval Rites of Passage*, ed. G. Levi and J.-C. Schmitt (Cambridge: Harvard University Press, 1997), 240–282.
16. Le Roy Ladurie, *The Beggar and the Professor*, 19.
17. Robert Muchembled, *Popular Culture and Elite Culture in France, 1400–1750* (Baton Rouge: Louisiana University Press, 1985), 56.
18. Robert C. Davis, *The War of the Fists: Popular Culture and Public Violence in Late Renaissance Venice* (New York: Oxford University Press, 1994).
19. Martin Ingram, "Ridings, Rough Music and the 'Reform of Popular Culture' in Early Modern England," *Past and Present* 105 (November 1984): 79–113; Griffiths, *Youth and Authority*, 169–174.
20. Maurice Aymard, "Friends and Neighbors," in *A History of Private Life*, vol. 3: *Passions of the Renaissance*, ed. Roger Chartier, trans. Arthur Goldhammer (Cambridge: Belknap Press of Harvard University Press, 1989), 484.
21. Dorothy Osborne, *Letters to Sir William Temple, 1652–54*, ed. Kenneth Parker (Aldershot, UK: Ashgate, 2002), 103; Bernard Capp, *When Gossips Meet: Women, Family, and Neighbourhood in Early Modern England* (Oxford: Oxford University Press, 2003), 350–351, 340.
22. Eleanor Hubbard, "A Room of Their Own: Young Women, Courtship, and the Night in Early Modern England," in *The Youth of Early Modern Women*, ed. E. S. Cohen and M. Reeves (Amsterdam: Amsterdam University Press, 2018), 297–299, 311.
23. Hans Medick, "Village Spinning Bees: Sexual Culture and Free Time Among Rural Youth in Early Modern Germany," in *Interest and Emotion: Essays on the Study of Family and Kinship*, ed. H. Medick and David Warren Sabean (Cambridge: Cambridge University Press, 1984), 317–339; Andreas Gestrich, "Protestant Religion, the State and the Suppression of Traditional Youth Culture in Southwest Germany," *History of European Ideas* 11 (1989): 629–635.
24. Davis, "The Reasons of Misrule," 54–55; Roger Thompson, *Sex in Middlesex: Popular Mores in a Massachusetts County, 1649–1699* (Amherst: University of Massachusetts Press, 1986), 199; Norbert Schindler, *Rebellion, Community and Custom in Early Modern Germany*, trans. Pamela E. Selwyn (Cambridge: Cambridge University Press, 2002), 13; Robert Muchembled, *A History of Violence: From the End of the Middle Ages to the Present*, trans. Jean Birrell (Cambridge: Polity, 2012), 57–58.
25. Booy, ed., *Personal Disclosures*, 189–192.
26. Mary Clarke to Edward Clarke, March 17, 1701, SALS DD/SF 7/1/57.
27. Monica Chojnacka and Merry E. Wiesner-Hanks, eds., *Ages of Woman, Ages of Man: Sources in European Social History, 1400–1750* (London: Longman, 2002), 51.
28. A.L. Beier, *Masterless Men: The Vagrancy Problem in England 1560–1640* (London: Methuen, 1985), 52–53.
29. Michael Rocke, *Forbidden Friendships: Homosexuality and Male Culture in Renaissance Florence* (Oxford: Oxford University Press, 1996), 161–162.
30. Paul S. Seaver, "Apprentice Riots in Early Modern London," in *Violence, Politics, and Gender in Early Modern England*, ed. Joseph P. Ward (New York: Palgrave Macmillan, 2008), 17–39.
31. Jacques Rossiaud, "Prostitution, jeunesse et société dans les villes du Sud-Est au XVe siècle," *Annales: Economies, sociétés, civilisations* 31, no. 2 (1976): 289–325.
32. Craig Koslofsky, *Evening's Empire: A History of the Night in Early Modern Europe* (Cambridge: Cambridge University Press, 2011), 159.
33. Schindler, "Guardians of Disorder," 275.

34. Merry E. Wiesner, "*Wandervogels* and Women: Journeymen's Concepts of Masculinity in Early Modern Germany," *Journal of Social History* 24, no. 4 (summer 1991): 767-782.
35. Rocke, *Forbidden Friendships*, 210-211.
36. Konrad Eisenbichler, *The Boys of the Archangel Raphael: A Youth Confraternity in Florence, 1411-1785* (Toronto: University of Toronto Press, 1998); Alessandra Franco, "Malleable Youth: Forging Female Education in Early Modern Rome," in *The Youth of Early Modern Women*, 217-234; Cotton Mather, *Diary of Cotton Mather, 1681-1708* (Boston: Massachusetts Historical Society, 1911), 67-68; Roger Thompson, "Adolescent Culture in Colonial Massachusetts," *Journal of Family History* 9, no. 2 (Summer 1984): 138.
37. Peter Burke, *Popular Culture in Early Modern Europe* (New York: New York University Press, 1978), 63.
38. Tim Reinke-Williams, "Misogyny, Jest-Books and Male Youth Culture in Seventeenth-Century England," *Gender and History* 21, no. 2 (August 2009): 324-339; Edel Lamb, "Youth Culture," in *The Ashgate Research Companion to Popular Culture in Early Modern England*, ed. Andrew Hadfield, Matthew Dimmock, and Abigail Shinn (Farnham, UK: Ashgate, 2014), 31-42.

Further Reading

Ben-Amos, Ilana Krausman. *Adolescence and Youth in Early Modern England*. New Haven, CT: Yale University Press, 1994.

Cohen, Elizabeth S., and Margaret Reeves, eds. *The Youth of Early Modern Women*. Amsterdam: Amsterdam University Press, 2018.

Davis, Natalie Zemon. "The Reasons of Misrule: Youth Groups and Charivaris in Sixteenth-Century France." *Past and Present* 50 (February 1971): 41-75.

Eisenbichler, Konrad, ed. *The Premodern Teenager: Youth in Society 1150-1650*. Toronto: Centre for Reformation and Renaissance Studies, 2002.

Griffiths, Paul. *Youth and Authority: Formative Experiences in England, 1560-1640*. Oxford: Clarendon Press, 1996.

Levi, Giovanni, and Jean-Claude Schmitt, eds. *A History of Young People in the West*. Vol. 1. *Ancient and Medieval Rites of Passage*. Translated by Camille Naish. Cambridge, MA: Harvard University Press, 1997.

Mitterauer, Michael. *A History of Youth*. Translated by Graeme Dunphy. Oxford: Blackwell, (1986) 1992.

Muchembled, Robert. *Popular Culture and Elite Culture in France, 1400-1750*. Translated by Lydia Cochrane. Baton Rouge: Louisiana University Press, (1978) 1985.

Roberts, Benjamin B. *Sex and Drugs Before Rock'n'Roll: Youth Culture and Masculinity During Holland's Golden Age*. Amsterdam: Amsterdam University Press, 2012.

PART II

SHAPING MODERN YOUTH CULTURES

CHAPTER 5

YOUTH PARTICIPATION IN POLITICAL VIOLENCE

Comparative Cultural Constructions

DAVID M. ROSEN

YOUNG people across the globe channel their energy and vitality into conflicts, large and small, and youth are often found at the core of organized political violence. Both history and ethnography teach us that there is nothing particularly new about this. Young people have been involved in organized political violence—war, revolution, resistance, terrorism—in virtually all known societies, from the relatively small war parties organized by hunting and gathering societies, to the mass armies recruited by warring nation-states in the last centuries, to current-day conflicts that involve a volatile mix of state armies and nonstate actors. What varies dramatically from instance to instance is how this involvement is understood—culturally, politically, and socially. Equally important is that, largely beginning in the twentieth century, war and revolution began to be carried out, at least partially, not just *by young fighters* but in the *name* of youth. Within these revolutionary movements, youth began to be imagined as a distinct category of persons, often with its own distinct set of abilities and values, with a special role to play in revolutionary violence and social change. At the same time the ephemeral quality of youth, its transitory nature, subverts the ability of young people to play more than a supporting role in revolution.

Who Is a Child? Who Is a Youth?

The considerable variation in human societies means that there are numerous cross-cultural and historical differences in the ways age and the idea of youth are understood and, accordingly, the ways in which youth participation in conflict is understood. While the biological processes of human growth and development are substantially uniform across the globe, the cultural processes associated with them are not. Concepts such as "child" or "youth" in one society may lack conceptual equivalents in another, and even where similarities exist, the assumption of equivalence may be misleading, glossing over significant and powerful distinctions among the ways it is understood within each society. There may be marked differences as to who is considered a youth, but also different understandings of the rights, duties, privileges, and responsibilities linked to different age categories. In some societies—particularly complex societies that have many distinctions based on ethnicity, social class, and gender—there may be many youth cultures. Youth cultures are best understood as subcultures or co-cultures, which, although they may exhibit distinctive values and behaviors, also share values with and participate in the institutions of the larger societies. There are two keys to understanding this: first, how young people understand themselves in society and the ways in which they help shape and define youth culture through their own agency and participation, and second, how the larger society consciously or unconsciously works to shape youth culture. The overall need for the energy of youth generates multiple and often-contradictory understandings, ranging from situations in which youth participation serves as a proxy for the establishment of a new social order to conflicts in which the participation and sacrifice of youth are understood as representing the highest virtues of the existing society.

This chapter examines the way the mobilization of youth for political conflict is mediated through culture, the particular constellation of norms and values that inform, shape, and justify young people's participation in conflict and violence, and how that constellation is in turn shaped by young people themselves. Using historical examples, it pays special attention to conflicts in which youth and the specific qualities of youth are explicitly articulated and invoked as essential elements of the conflict. The examples are necessarily selective and come from a range of preindustrial and contemporary societies, including the hunter-gatherer communities of the Great Plains of the United States, the pastoral Masai and Samburu of East Africa, and more recent conflicts in Europe and Africa. I do not provide a general theory or complete survey of youth mobilization but intend to demonstrate the rich variety of ways in which youth are culturally implicated in violent conflict.

Youth and Political Violence in the Preindustrial World

In many preindustrial societies, much of the early socialization of children and youth, especially boys, was socialization for participation in violence. For boys, the boundaries between childhood, youth, and manhood were fluid, and the valorization of war was integral to adult and youth culture alike. Socialization for risk-taking and mistrust were frequently central elements of youth culture. For many youth the enhancement of their personal status and their hopes of achievement and recognition as adults were linked to their success at war. There was little actual formal training of youth for war; rather, their preparation for violence and their acquisition of the skills of war were developed through participating in the routines of daily life and were usually supported by adults.

Young people sought many opportunities to participate, regardless of the risk involved, even if this was sometimes discouraged or prohibited by adults. Black Elk (1863–1950), the famous Lakota holy man, was only thirteen when he determined that it was time for him to become a Sioux Warrior. His participation in youth culture was his basic training for battle. "I was thirteen years old," said Black Elk, "and not very big for my age, but I thought I should have to be a man anyway. We boys had practiced endurance, and we were all good riders, and I could shoot straight with either a bow or a gun."[1] Black Elk's family and band had just decided to join with his cousin Crazy Horse to continue to fight against white incursions in the Black Hills. Black Elk's aunt had given him a revolver and told him that he was a man, but an uncle convinced him not to go. Black Elk believed his uncle may have thought that he was too young. Yet Black Elk's close friend Iron Hawk, a fourteen-year-old who described himself as a "big boy," did go into battle with Crazy Horse. Whatever power of persuasion Black Elk's uncle may have had at that moment, it had no lasting effect. Shortly after his uncle's intervention, in June 1876, Black Elk, still age thirteen, fought at the Battle of the Little Big Horn, and there he was cheered on by his mother, who, "Gave me a big tremolo . . . when she saw my first scalp."[2] In reflecting on the lives of the Sioux, Black Elk valorized the traditional Sioux age categories. "When we were living in the power of the circle, in the way we should," says Black Elk, "boys were men at twelve or thirteen years of age."[3]

The Crow warrior Two Leggings (1844–1923) tells a similar story. He was fourteen years old in 1858, and he wanted to join a war party against the Piegans (Blackfoot) to recover some stolen horses. His brother had forbidden him to go, but Two Leggings's strategy was to continually trail the war party until they relented and let him join. Two Leggings described the war party as consisting of six experienced warriors, two younger men, and himself. The experienced warriors told the younger ones to remain behind when they crawled out in the dark to spy out the Piegans for the attack. The two young men agreed. Two Leggings claims he tried to persuade them to crawl out with him, but they said they were "too young for real fighting." But Two Leggings persisted. "I was a man now," he said, "and wanted to see what kind of people these Piegans were."[4]

Black Elk's and Two Leggings's descriptions of their self-recruitment are consistent with the settled ethnographies of these societies. War was highly valorized in many of the Native American societies of the Great Plains, and certainly powerful cultural values shaped and channeled the lives of the young. But within this framework individuals—even children—were free to shape their lives with only minimal direct control by figures in authority.[5] Adults could be persuasive but not authoritative. The boundaries between childhood and adulthood were fluid. There appears to have been no bureaucratically fixed concept of youth or adolescence at play here. At the core of such analyses lies the contingency and fluidity of age, a factor often rendered invisible or seemingly inconceivable to observers in the modern world with its strict chronological and bureaucratic renderings of time.

The cultural and social landscape of the preindustrial world was marked not by unity but by its diversity. In the popular imagination, youth and youth cultures or subcultures are usually associated with the rise of industrialized society, but specific youth subcultures have emerged and persisted in many types of societies. In societies that made distinct demarcations between childhood and adulthood, these distinctions were often connected to violence and war. A notable example is the traditional societies of Maa-speaking peoples, such as the Masai and Samburu of Kenya and Tanzania, which organized individuals, primarily males, into age sets and age grades. These were broad age-based collectivities (age sets) that moved together through culturally prescribed stages of life (age grades): warrior, junior elder, and elder. Beginning at about age fourteen, youngsters were socially and ritually transformed and placed into specifically named aggregates of warriors (*moran*) and remained in these cohorts for about fifteen years. Throughout this period, they had a separate social identity marked by distinctive behavior, dress, and custom. Forbidden to marry and regarded as wild and irresponsible, they occupied a liminal space between childhood and adulthood and functioned as a coveted, privileged, often subversive, and highly self-conscious youth subculture.[6]

This distinctive youth culture was intimately connected to local political violence; its prime goal was carrying out raids against neighboring enemies to gain control of land and resources. The members of the age sets were bound together by a warrior ethos and were expected to show unflinching courage and to share food with one another in a generous and egalitarian manner. They were deeply emerged in an ethos of honor, prestige, and avoidance of shame. Yet at the same time warriors were highly sensitive to issues of personal status and to the behaviors of others who violated these rules; such violations could be easily perceived as personal affronts and lead to conflict and violence.

The warrior culture has powerful attractions. Warriors have few economic responsibilities. Their distinctive dress and robust physical appearance were believed to appeal to young women, and warriors spend a great deal of time in local gatherings of youth, in dance, and flirtatious and sexual relations. The glamour and prestige accorded to warriors, and the heightened sense of their physical prowess, make the warrior age set the envy of the young and old. Young boys clamor and push their elders to open up possibilities for transition into this world and elders point to the warriors as the epitome of cultural distinctiveness.

THE LIMITATIONS OF YOUTH AND POWER

The relationship between the Maa-speaking warriors and the elders raises the issue of the power of youth and provides a cautionary note: the existence of a distinctive youth culture is not synonymous with significant youth political power. In societies with age sets and age grades, the power of youth is part of an enduring and repeating pattern of generational change. Its temporal limitations are normative: youth power and youth self-consciousness are part of a society's continual need to maintain a more or less permanent group of warriors. The complicated relationship between youth and adults during and between periods of collective political violence and war signals the severe limitations on the ability of youth—even youth with a high degree of self-consciousness—to act as an independent force. This is not to say that youth lack agency—their agency is obvious—but it does indicate that the power of the youth is temporally limited, contingent, and ultimately subordinate to adults.

For young Maa warriors, and probably for young warriors in many other societies, it is possible that nothing else in their lives will equal the kind of personal prestige that accompanies this life. Even though Maa warriors are widely celebrated, they are politically powerless and under the authority and control of elders. They are denied access to the key resources of Maasai society during the entire period of their youth until they transition into elderhood.[7] At the same time that elders celebrate this distinctive subculture, they clearly manage it for their own interests. The pleasures of warriorhood are eclipsed by its subordinate position in society. As warriors age, they increasingly realize their poverty and lack of society-wide power, and they see the linkages between these and adulthood, marriage, the creation of families, and the ownership of cattle, none of which are allowable for warriors. This leads to an undercurrent of opposition to elders that must remain controlled and suppressed. The important point is that for Masai and Samburu warriors, the celebration of youth culture by children, youth, and elders deflects attention from its inherent powerlessness. The more that young people are committed to the warrior ethos, the less likely they are to challenge the authority of elders. In a trade-off between power and prestige, veneration of youth culture by the society masks youth's political weakness.

In the Maa case, youth culture and youth power are continuously created and recreated and institutionalized as part of the life cycle of every member of society. More commonly, youth power is not institutionalized but emerges during exceptional moments in the history of society. During these moments youth may obtain and assert considerable power—sometimes demanding power in the name of youth. But as a general rule, a generation that seizes power as "youth" or in the name of youth does not transfer that power to succeeding generations of young people. Instead, the conditions of war or revolutionary violence often soften, but not eliminate, most of the peacetime social and legal norms and distinctions that serve as pillars of ordinary civil life. Instead, social hierarchies are temporarily suspended, and taken-for-granted ideas about the relationship of gender, status, and age to authority situationally refashioned by circumstance. For adolescents, already straddling the boundaries between childhood and adulthood, purely chronological designations of the boundaries between childhood and adulthood become dysfunctional and meaningless. At these moments, youth may emerge as a vital social and cultural force, but the history of youth mobilization, even where political power is seized in the name of youth, shows that it rarely results in sustained political power.

Youth in the American Revolution

The vitality of youth culture was sharply evident during the American Revolution, when armies, militias, and partisan groups were filled with youngsters. Colonial militias had played a significant role in the emerging youth culture in colonial America. Organized in opposition to dominant Puritan values, youth culture began to take shape around militia training days, which afforded young people the opportunity to congregate, and to the alarm of many adults, enabled youngsters to meet, smoke, carouse, and swagger.[8] The desire for autonomy and independence and the rejection of authority and patriarchal values and organized religion were significant drivers of youth culture. The political ethos of the American Revolution was mirrored in a personal ethos of freedom—not only from authoritative government, but also from the hierarchical structures of family life. In his autobiography *Private Yankee Doodle*, Joseph Plumb Martin describes his urge to enlist and how he frequented the "rendezvous" where many of his "young associates" would join up. Of his decision to enlist at age fifteen, he said, "I had obtained my heart's desire."[9]

The statistics reflect that large numbers of youngsters found their freedom and identity in enlistment. Between 30 and 40 percent of adolescent males participated in armed conflict between 1740 and 1781.[10] Local militias were often organized at college campuses, which were themselves cauldrons of revolutionary thinking.[11] Teenagers played a major role in American resistance to British rule. Between 1765 and 1770, there were at least 150 anti-British riots in the American colonies, and the rioting mobs were filled with teenage apprentices and youthful laborers.[12] The Continental Army had no fixed policy as to who could serve as soldiers,[13] and with half the American population under age sixteen, it is not surprising that the Continental Army was filled with boys of every age.[14] The army itself was composed largely of men and boys drawn from the poor, the young, the marginal, and the unfree.[15] Caroline Cox's recent analysis of pension applications and memoirs of former Revolutionary soldiers reveals the pervasive presence of boy soldiers under age sixteen in the American Revolution.[16] Many were between thirteen and fifteen, and some were as young as nine or ten.[17] The records of the many regiments camped at Valley Forge with Washington during the winter of 1777–1778 show that there were many youngsters in regiments from all over the country, with large percentages of youngers between twelve and seventeen.[18] Baron Ludwig von Closen, an aide-de-camp of General Rochembeau, who commanded seven thousand French troops allied with the Continental Army, stated, "I admire the American troops tremendously! It is incredible that men of every age, even children of fifteen, of whites and blacks, almost naked, unpaid, and rather poorly fed, can march so well, and withstand fire so steadfastly.[19]

Youth in the American Civil War

Available data on the ages of soldiers during the U.S. Civil War also point to startling mixtures of children, youth, and adults on the front lines. By the beginning of the war the foundation for the recruitment of youth had already been laid down by an emerging youth culture. In the era preceding the Civil War youth were bound up with political parties, and young people were sometimes seen as the most violent of political partisans. Youth-focused political parties, marching clubs, lectures, and numerous other events provided a framework for both political and adolescent courtship and flirting.[20] Politics and youth culture were inextricably entwined. The fervent patriotic clamor of youth was sometimes criticized but rarely thwarted. As early as 1861, Herman Melville raised his skeptical voice against the chorus of hosannas surrounding young boys' eagerness to march off to the Civil War. In his poem "The March into Virginia Ending in the First Manassas," he writes, "All wars are boyish, and are fought by boys, the champions and enthusiasts of the state."[21] But whatever these concerns may have been, there is little doubt that youth culture had primed them for war.

Beyond this, youngsters often had practical reasons for signing up. Many sought to escape poverty or the drudgery of factory labor. Luther Ladd, age seventeen, who grew up on a farm in New Hampshire before obtaining work at the mills in Lowell, Massachusetts, left the mills to go to war. Sixteen-year-old Joseph Darrow enlisted after his parents agreed that it was more economically feasible for him to go instead of his father, who was a steady breadwinner. Twelve-year-old Clarence MacKenzie grew up in poverty and attended mission Sunday schools before enlisting.[22] What bound all these boys together was a youth culture that emboldened them, combined with real-life challenges that had already drawn them into adult responsibilities. There were immediate economic incentives, including military salaries and signing bonuses that often went to poor families. The fact that the military itself was hierarchical did not deter them because it gave such boys the possibility of meaning in lives that were already marked by drudgery.

Many boys came directly from orphanages, juvenile delinquency facilities, and reform schools, which for the most part meant children from minorities and the poor. Here a combination of patriotism, the opportunity for personal freedom, and the fact that these facilities could pocket the signing bonuses of youngsters who enlisted provided great incentives for both the institutions and the boys. It appears that the majority of boys were seventeen or eighteen years of age, but some were between fourteen and sixteen. Boys who were disciplinary problems were encouraged to enlist regardless of their age. In one Michigan reform school, five of the ten most frequently punished boys—all between ages fourteen and eighteen—were sent into the military. During the course of the war, 162 boys of the Massachusetts Nautical Reform School enlisted in the army or navy. The Providence Reform School developed a special relationship with army recruiters to promote the enlistment of boys seeking their liberty.[23] In sum, a combination of a youth culture that valued risk-taking, economic incentives, patriotism, and the desire for liberty and freedom sent a river of children and youth into the military.

Clearly not all youth joined the military; the vast majority stayed at home. Moreover, there was no single youth culture, and the many tens of thousands drawn from cities, towns, and the countryside into war were divided by race, class, and ethnicity. But the numbers were still great. In 2006, Pizzaro, Silver, and Prause examined the full medical records of recruits from 303 randomly selected companies of the Union Army.[24] Assuming the random sample is representative of all recruits across the armed forces, then approximately 420,000 of the 2.1 million soldiers in the Union forces were between ages nine and seventeen.

Fighting in the Name of Youth

While children and youth bearing arms were common in the nineteenth century, a striking feature of twentieth-century conflict is the degree to which revolutions and wars have been fought, at least partly, in the name of or on behalf of youth. Wars of revolution and national liberation were central drivers of social change in the twentieth century, and revolutionary leaders such as Vladimir Lenin clearly envisioned youth as a revolutionary force.[25] The Russian Revolution, the Chinese Revolution, the Cuban Revolution, the Mexican Revolution, and others all held out the promise that the revolutions were created to bring a greater future for young people. At the heart of revolutionary movements is the rejection of an old social order. Revolutionary movements equated youth with the future—positioning them as agents of social change and a revolutionary political category.

In the Soviet Union, the consolidation of communist party power involved nurturing a culture for children and youth that stood in opposition to Western values. Soviets officially viewed children as independent, powerful agents of revolutionary change, in sharp contrast to Western concepts of children as vulnerable, innocent, dependent, and weak.[26] The independence and heroism of youth was a significant theme during World War II. Youth fighters and youth martyrs played a big role in the Soviet struggle against Nazi Germany. Powerful stories of the sacrifices of children and youth fighters resonated throughout the Soviet Union during the war. The most famous is that of Zoya Kosmodemyanskaya, widely regarded as the Joan of Arc of the Soviet Union. Zoya was a teenage schoolgirl when she joined a Soviet partisan unit in October 1941. Captured and executed by the Germans, she was celebrated as a Soviet martyr and was the first female to be awarded the title Hero of the Soviet Union during World War II.[27]

Children and youth were similarly venerated in revolutionary movements across the globe. In Cuba, for example, radical youth played an important role both prior to and during the Cuban Revolution. Much of the discourse of the revolution involved both the creation of youth as a specific social category and the celebration of the role of youth in the success of the revolution. But as the successful revolution planted its roots in Cuban society and began the long process of building a new society, the energy and agency of youth increasingly became subject to state domination. The revolutionary leadership, as Ann Lukes tells us, moved away from its direct identification with youth and adopted a more remote and paternal attitude.[28] In South Africa, where youth played an important role in the struggle against apartheid, youth were largely ignored and politically demobilized in the post-apartheid era.[29] Schoolgirls and peasant women who fought in the Eritrean People's Liberation Front temporarily enjoyed rough equality with male fighters during the war, but after independence they were pressed back into extremely conservative gender roles and barred from the benefits of full citizenship. Thus, while participation in war, even for schoolgirls, was not a wholly negative experience, it clearly did not lead to empowered youth.[30] Children and youth who served in the Liberation Front of Mozambique's (FRELIMO) *Destacemento Feminino*, or Female Detachment, saw their participation in combat as empowering and liberating, and they continued to see it this way as adults. Many of these youngsters interpreted their war experiences as having freed them both from colonial rule and from male structures of dominance in "traditional" Mozambique society. They saw their participation in combat and other revolutionary acts as threshold events that led to becoming full citizens in the political life of Mozambique. The revolution may not have brought youth to power, but it clearly had an important impact on individuals.[31]

Youth in Service to the State: Hitler Youth and the Mobilization for War

One of the most striking examples of the mobilization of youth for collective violence in Western history is the emergence of the *HitlerJugund* or Hitler Youth in Germany. National Socialism came to power as the party of youth. The Nazi Party itself celebrated the young, and youth was a key element of its vitality and strength. The mobilization of the Hitler Youth was built upon a cultural foundation of youth self-consciousness that began with the German youth movement at the beginning of the twentieth century. As originally conceived, the German youth movement was a movement "of youth, by youth and for youth."[32] In its earliest form, the German youth movement was known as the *Wandervogel* (literally "wandering bird"), which was characterized by the embrace of hiking, rambling, and immersion in the countryside. Its members were between the ages of twelve and nineteen. As a youth movement, it sought to radically distance itself from adult society, disdaining any involvement in ordinary politics, local or national. Nevertheless, as a cultural movement, it absorbed the political ethos of its time. It was a *völkisch* or racial-nationalistic movement that was romantic, nationalistic, and xenophobic, with little interest in social democracy. Its values were rooted in the German Protestant middle class. It was generally anti-Semitic, though some local groups admitted a small number of Jews.[33]

The importance of the *Wandervogel* movement waned after the German defeat in World War I, and it was superseded by the *Bunde* or *Bündische Jugend*, which absorbed the *Wandervogel* and other youth movements under its larger organizational umbrella. The *Bunde* was more militaristic and hierarchically organized than the more free-spirited *Wandervogel*. Its internal culture shifted toward more competitive activities and even war games. Group singing shifted away from folk songs toward military songs. In the end, "the soldier supplanted the strolling scholar as the ideal type."[34] But despite its strengthened *volkisch* and military ethos, the *Bunde* remained distant from state politics, and its focus was on the group experience and individual expression. It existed outside the domain of state power.

When Hitler and the Nazis came to power in 1933, a radical mobilization of youth began. The party publicly scorned the older generation and blamed it for Germany's defeat in World War I. Hitler himself was obsessed with the idea of youth as a potent political force. When the Nazi Party began to organize the Hitler Youth, its key support came from a very different demographic than earlier youth movements in Germany, which had been largely a middle-class phenomenon. The Hitler youth originated among the working class, the unemployed, and lower-middle-class families who had become impoverished during the economic crisis that gripped Germany in the post–World War I era. As the Nazis solidified their power in Germany, the independent German youth movements were outlawed, and virtually all German youth—both boys and girls of all social classes and backgrounds—were mandatorily recruited into the Hitler Youth. As all German youth were essentially conscripted into the Hitler Youth, there was no longer space for autonomous youth culture. Youth were now mobilized into the service of the state in the framework of a highly militaristic organization that worshiped militarism and the Nazi cause. Military service for youth was widely propagated as an ideal in popular culture, including in documentaries and feature films. The Hitler Youth became the ideological training ground for recruitment of all youth into all German military forces, but the relationship between the Hitler Youth the Nazi SS (*Schutzstaffel* or Protective Force) was especially intense. The SS was the Nazi Party's elite paramilitary force. It was also one of the most criminal elements of the Nazi regime, infamous for its brutality and its enthusiastic participation in the wholesale murder of civilians, especially Jews. A powerful organizational relationship was created—a virtual generational alliance—between the Hitler Youth and the SS, an organization that the Hitler Youth idealized and emulated. Thus, by passion, ideology, design, and circumstance the Hitler Youth served as a junior SS.[35]

The defeat of the German military at Stalingrad in 1943 was a turning point in the relationship between the Hitler Youth and the SS. As Germany reeled from its defeats, recruitment of youth increased across the armed forces. By 1943, youth began to be recruited as *Flakhelferin* (auxiliaries) to man aircraft batteries and assist in other activities. The American anthropologist Karl Schlesier was a fifteen-year-old high school student in Germany when he and eleven of his schoolmates became part of the two hundred thousand boys between ages fifteen and sixteen who were called up in 1943. The *Flakhelferin* were part of the Flieger HJ, the air division of the Hitler Youth. Many died at the flak guns during air raids, others engaged in ground combat during the Allied invasion of Germany, and many were killed or captured.[36] By the endgame of the war in 1945, the true logic of Nazi fanaticism prevailed, as barely trained children and youth battled experienced soldiers to the death. Even in these final moments, the national leader of the Hitler Youth, Arthur Axman, raised a Hitler Youth division and compared this final German battle to the heroism of Sparta, rallying the youngsters and urging them on to total victory or defeat.[37] Many Hitler Youth demonstrated near-apocalyptic fanaticism, but the final days of battle also involved large numbers of youngsters press-ganged into the slaughter by the SS.[38]

The totalitarian nature of the German state under Nazism did not completely prevent the emergence of an oppositional youth culture outside the framework of the Hitler Youth. This included various largely urban groups such as "swing" and "jazz" groups in Hamburg, the Mueten in Leipzig, and the Edelweiss Pirates in Cologne. These groups were characterized by their sometimes hidden and sometimes open hostility to the Hitler Youth, the Nazi regime, and especially the regimentation of daily life. The key motivation of most of these groups was less political than it was the creation of a youth counterculture that stressed personal fulfillment, individual autonomy, and escape from the rigidity of life under Nazi rule. The Edelweiss Pirates, among the most politically oriented of these groups, began with a core of boys between ages twelve and eighteen. They first modeled themselves on the *Wandervogel* movement, adopting distinctive styles of dress and appearance, and taking long country hikes to escape the Nazi regime. But the boundaries between personal freedom and political opposition blurred as the war continued, and members began to engage in more overt actions against the state. Open defiance proved fatal, and several of the Edelweiss Pirate leaders were publicly executed in Cologne in 1944.[39] It is clear, however, that a sizable minority of young people across Nazi Germany attempted to create *a youth counterculture* to subvert the ethos of the regime. All these groups, however, were brutally suppressed.[40]

The role of children and youth in Nazi Germany is notable because of the levels of commitment and fanatic devotion many children and youth retained for the Nazi cause, which was always a radical populist movement that held the German people in thrall. It was youngsters, often fanatical youngsters, who largely provided the Nazi movement's cultural resonance. Looking at the actual circumstances of children and youth participation in the Nazi agenda, we are left with a sense of both fascination and repulsion at the virtually unparalleled embrace of collective violence by children and youth in modern history. Among the masses of children and youth who were incorporated into the Hitler Youth, doubtless some were victims of force, pressure, or exploitation. But what is more striking is the collective participation of the German people—children, youth, and adults—in the mad spectacle of power and violence that characterized Nazi Germany during peace and war. The Nazification of children and adults began as a peacetime project between 1933 and 1939, and the early Nazi conquests and victories in war only cemented popular support and devotion to Hitler. Only as Germany began to lose the war and Germans began to pay the price for a decade of Nazi rule did Hitler's star begin to fade. Whatever autonomy or agency the Hitler Youth exhibited, they were among the principal agents of the Nazi regime and functioned within the framework of state power.

Jewish Youth Movements in the Holocaust: Organizing Against State Power

In an almost ironic way, while the Hitler Youth thrived in the hothouse of authoritarian state power, it was the absence of political power that gave rise to Jewish youth movements in the twentieth century and marked their transformation into resistance movements during World War II and the Holocaust. The prewar Jewish youth movements that formed the core of Jewish resistance to the German invasion of Eastern Europe and the destruction of their Jewish communities were completely outside the umbrella of state power, either because they were indifferent to it (in the case of Zionist youth) or excluded from it (in the case of Jewish socialists and communists). However, it was not just the absence of state power but the near-collapse of independent leadership of the Jewish communities under German occupation and destruction that created a political vacuum that was filled by Jewish youth.

Jewish resistance began to take shape from the moment Germany invaded Poland and long before substantial anti-German armed partisan movements began to emerge in Eastern Europe. The young people within the Jewish community—not the adult leadership, which often had fled, been co-opted, or otherwise tried to bargain with or stave off German oppression—took up the challenge of organizing against the German plans of extermination and envisioned the possibility of armed resistance. The majority of these youthful resisters were members of the Zionist, socialist, and communist youth organizations that were an important part of Jewish life in Poland and other parts of Eastern Europe in the years between the two world wars. These groups had experience in combating the rising tide of anti-Semitism prior to the outbreak of World War II and adapted themselves for battle against the Germans.

Zionist, socialist, and communist youth movements had developed throughout Eastern Europe between World War I and World War II, especially in Poland, Lithuania, Byelorussia, and Ukraine. They were usually associated with adult political parties or political movements and brought Jewish youngsters together for social, cultural, and political activities. They were strong, coherent, and highly ideological movements that often used scouting as a model for their basic structure. They recruited youngsters from about thirteen to eighteen years old and sometimes created groups for even younger children. These movements became an important part of Jewish communal life. In addition to providing a social setting in which to solidify and strengthen Jewish identity, the movements were a response to the growing external threat of anti-Semitism, especially in Eastern Europe.

Zionist-socialist youth such a *Hashomer Hatzair* ("Young Guard") or *Dror* ("Freedom") were a minority in prewar Poland and distanced themselves from the Jewish mainstream. The adults saw these young people, who created a quasi-communal way of life and who intended to move to Israel and live in socialist collectives, as childish, nonconforming eccentrics and kooks. But with their strong and coherent utopian ideologies, their dreams of an alternative future, these organizations provided young people a vision around which to organize resistance. The youth groups had long functioned as surrogate forms of family and kinship for their members, relationships that were strengthened during the occupation. There was an increasing move toward communal living, and many young people left their families to live with friends in the movement. The intimacy and trust built over the years enabled local chapters to convert themselves into clandestine cells of resistance that could take advantage of resources of the organizations such as meeting places and mimeograph machines to create an underground press.

The Zionist-socialist groups were part of a larger system of organized youth political subcultures. In contrast to the Zionist-socialists, the nationalist-Zionist youth movements such as *Betar* were militaristic—organized as military and ideological training grounds for a Jewish legion in Palestine. Socialist but non-Zionist Jewish youth movements included *Tzukunft* (Future), the youth movement of the social democratic General Jewish Labour Bund in Poland. Jews were also an important component of the Communist Union of the Polish Youth, the youth wing of the Polish Communist Party until it was dissolved in 1938.[41] But it was the *Bund* and *Tzukunft* that attracted the most Jewish interest. It remained an independent noncommunist social democratic party that supported strengthening Jewish identity within Poland as part of a broader socialist movement. Most of *Tzukunft* members were young workers, which meant that *Tzukunft* had important ties to the youth sections of trade unions that worked to protect young workers' rights. Like *Betar*, *Tzukunft* organized a militia, *Tzukunft-Sturem*, which provided protection for its meetings and rallies against the rising threat of anti-Semitic pogroms in 1930s Poland.[42]

The youth movements' success was due not solely to their rebelliousness, but also to their sense that resisting the Germans was, in essence, a realization of their values. When Germany invaded Poland, the youth movements were uniquely positioned for resistance. At the beginning, resistance did not mean engaging in armed conflict. Indeed, the ability of these groups to engage in any form of armed conflict was severely hampered by the lack of arms, ammunition, weapons training, and the fact that any attack on Germans and their allies would inevitably lead to massive and deadly retaliation against the ghettoized Jewish community.

The youth groups worked to help their members and others survive, and they fought passivity and depression in the oppressive conditions in the ghettos. They attempted to create an alternative cultural and educational environment that would preserve the prewar ideals of the youth movements. The youth groups worked to fashion a culture of resistance that would overcome the isolation and oppression ever present in ghetto life and to sustain a hope for the continuity of Jewish life through resistance to German control.

While the particular trajectory was different for each ghetto and community, at least at the beginning this involved very little armed resistance. Most of the activity of these groups was focused on sustaining a vibrant Jewish counterculture. However, armed resistance was never far from people's minds, and children and youth played a key role in preparation for armed conflict, serving as couriers, helping manufacture crude weapons, smuggling weapons and weapon components into ghettos, and distributing resistance publications. Young resisters did not necessarily regard themselves as children. They often referred to themselves as "youth," a term normally used in Hebrew, Yiddish, and Polish to describe young people from about thirteen to twenty-one years of age. Sometimes, they described themselves as children but saw little conflict between the life of the child and the serious business of resistance. Indeed, youth sustained much of the political life of the Warsaw Ghetto in Poland. "It is no exaggeration," said one observer, to state that the only environment in which political movement still pulsates with life, in which the will to act has not utterly failed and in which action takes place, is that of the youth. Nobody but the youth publishes and distributes illegal publications nowadays; nobody else engages in political and idealistic activity in Jewish society on a large scale.[43]

The underground newspaper *Neged Hazerem* (Against the Current), published in the Warsaw Ghetto by the *Hashomer Hatzair* youth movement, illustrates how some children and youth imagined themselves politically: "We the children, aged 13 to 18, will be the ones to lead the Jewish masses to a different future, a better future."[44] These words speak to the imagined empowerment of youth in that time and place and to the self-confidence of the Jewish resisters. They were written on the threshold of the annihilation of the Jewish community of Warsaw. For most of these youngsters there would be no Jewish future in Europe or anywhere else, for as heroic as these resistance units were, most members of Jewish youth movements did not survive the destruction of the ghettos. As Yehuda Bauer put it, ghetto resistance mostly offered "a different type of death."[45]

THE POWER OF YOUTH

History shows that the mobilization and participation of youth in war and revolution has remained a relative constant in human history. Comparative and historical analysis also shows that the emergence of distinctive youth subcultures or co-cultures that celebrate and emphasize the distinct qualities of youth—including energy, vitality, and risk-taking—contribute to this process of mobilizing youth participation in conflicts. Youth-powered subcultures often provide a powerful framework for self-mobilization for participation in conflict. Although the diversity of cultural logics and ethical imperatives that drive youth cannot be ignored, it is plain that youth frequently have seized the opportunities to empower themselves.

In many societies, youth cultures harbor some oppositional elements to the adult world, but in more modern times they have sometimes blossomed into or embraced utopian and dystopian alternatives to the entire existing social order. In contemporary revolutionary moments this has led to the idea of making war and revolution in the name of youth. In these new contexts, the emphasis on youth is a way to signal and legitimize the hope for new and radical social change. But while the promise of youth is frequently harnessed to goals of radical change, the evidence shows that these are generally short-lived moments. All social change ultimately becomes institutionalized, and the appeal to youth and its promise of a new social order inevitably fades. Youth may serve as a powerful political symbol, but given its temporal limitations as a social category, it remains ephemeral as a base of political power. Real power, it seems, always lies elsewhere.

Notes

1. John Niehardt, *Black Elk Speaks: Being the Life of a Holy Man of the Oglala Sioux* (Albany: SUNY Press, 2004), 43.
2. Ibid., 89.
3. Ibid., 156.
4. Peter Nabakov, *Two Leggings: The Making of a Crow Warrior* (New York: Thomas Crowell, 1967).
5. Robert Lowie, *The Crow Indians* (Lincoln: University of Nebraska Press, 2004), 218.
6. Paul Spencer, *Youth and Experiences of Ageing Among Maa: Models of Society Evoked by the Maa* (Berlin: De Gruyter: 2014), 17.
7. Ibid., 31.
8. Steven Mintz, *Huck's Raft: A History of American Childhood* (Cambridge: Harvard University Press, 2004), 29.
9. Joseph Plumb Martin, *Private Yankee Doodle* (Fort Washington, PA: Eastern National, 2002).
10. Harold E. Selesky, *War and Society in Colonial America* (New Haven, CT: Yale University Press, 1990).
11. Mintz, *Huck's Raft*, 69.
12. Ibid., 62.
13. Charles Royster, *A Revolutionary People at War: The Continental Army and American Character, 1775-1783* (Chapel Hill: University of North Carolina Press, 1996), 34.
14. Mintz, *Huck's Raft*, 62.
15. Ibid., 63n2.
16. Caroline Cox, "Boy Soldiers of the American Revolution: The Effects of War on Society," in *Children and Youth in a New Nation*, ed. James Marten (New York: New York University Press, 2009), 18.
17. Cox, Caroline, *Boy Soldiers of the American Revolution* (Chapel Hill: University of North Carolina Press, 2016), 7-8.
18. Harold Selesky, "A Demographic Survey of the Continental Army That Wintered at Valley Forge, Pennsylvania, 1777-1778," National Park Service, Washington, DC, 1987, http://www.nps.gov/vafo/historyculture/demographic-survey.htm.
19. Evelyn M. Acomb, ed., *The Revolutionary Journal of Baron von Closen, 1780-1783* (Chapel Hill: University of North Carolina Press, 2012), 102.
20. Jon Grinspan, "America's 'Violent Little Partisans,'" *The Atlantic*, May 5, 2016. https://www.theatlantic.com/politics/archive/2016/05/violent-little-partisans/481641/; Jon Grinspan, "Young Men for War: The Wide Awakes and Lincoln's 1860 Campaign," *Journal of American* 96, no. 2 (2009): 357-378; *The Virgin Vote: How Young Americans Made Democracy Social, Politics Personal, and Voting Popular in the Nineteenth Century* (Chapel Hill: University of North Carolina Press, 2016).
21. Herman Melville, "The March into Virginia Ending in the First Manassas," in *American War Poetry: An Anthology*, ed. Lorrie Goldensohn (New York: Columbia University Press, 2006), 65-66.
22. *Life of Luther C. Ladd, Who Fell in Baltimore, April 19, 1861 Exclaiming All Hail to the Stars and Stripes* (Concord, NH: P. B. Cogswell, 1862), 18; Bernhard J. Nadal, *The Christian Boy-Soldier: The Funeral Sermon of Joseph E. Darrow Preached in Sands Street Methodist Episcopal Church, Brooklyn, on the 27th of October, 1861* (New York: Steam, 1862), 9;

Anonymous, *The Little Drummer Boy, Clarence McKenzie: The Child of the 13th Regiment New York State Militia and the Child of the Mission Sunday School* (New York: Reformed Protestant Dutch Church, 1861), 124.
23. Dennis Thavenet, "The Michigan Reform School and the Civil War: Officers and Inmates Mobilized for the Union Cause," *Michigan Historical Review* 13, no. 1 (1987): 21–46; *Report Made to the Senate Relative to the Enlistment of Boys from the Reform School into the Army of the United States* (Providence, RI: Hiram H. Thomas, 1865), 1–4; M.L. Elbridge, "History of the Massachusetts Nautical Reform School," in *Transactions of the National Congress on Penitentiary and Reformatory Discipline*, Cincinnati, 1870, ed. Enoch C. Wines (Albany: Weed Parson, 1871), 350–358.
24. Judith Pizzaro, Roxanne Cohen Silver, and JoAnn Prause, "Physical and Mental Health Costs of Traumatic War Experiences Among Civil War Veterans," *Archives of General Psychiatry* 63, no 2 (2006): 193–200. Avaiablle at https://jamanetwork.com/journals/jamapsychiatry/fullarticle/209288.
25. Vladimir Lenin, *On Youth* (Moscow: Progress Publishers, 1967).
26. Lisa Kirschenbaum, *Small Comrades: Revolutionizing Childhood in Soviet Russia: 1917–1932* (London: RouteledgeFalmer, 2001), 5.
27. Nina Tumarkin, *The Living and the Dead: The Rise and Fall of the Cult of World War II in Russia* (New York: Basic Books, 1994), 77.
28. Ann Lukes, *Youth and the Cuban Revolution: Youth Culture and Politics in 1960's Cuba* (New York: Lexington Books, 2018), 22.
29. Clive Glaser, "Youth and Generation in South African History," *Safundi* 19, no. 2 (2018) 117–138, 131.
30. Virginia Bernal, "Equality to Die For? Women Guerilla Fighters and Eritrea's Cultural Revolution," *PoLar: Political and Legal Anthropology Review* 28, no. 2 (2000): 72–73.
31. Harry West, "Girls with Guns: Narrating the Experience of War of Frelimo's 'Female Detachment,'" *Anthropological Quarterly* 73, no. 4 (2000), 180–194.
32. R.H.S. Crossman, "Introduction," in Walter Laqueur, *Young Germany: A History of the German Youth Movement* (London: Routledge, 1962), xxi–xxiv.
33. Walter Laqueur, *Young Germany: A History of the German Youth Movement* (London: Routledge, 1962), 3–5.
34. Jean-Denis Lepage, *Hitler Youth: 1922–1945* (Jefferson, NC: McFarland & Co., 2008) 13.
35. Guido Knopp, *Hitler's Children* (Stroud, UK: Sutton, 2004), 4, 193.
36. Karl H. Schlesier, *Flakhelfer to Grenadier: Memoir of a Boy Soldier, 1943–1945* (Lexington, KY: K. H. Schlesier, 2011), 12.
37. Anthony Beever, *Fall of Berlin* (New York: Penguin, 2002), 181.
38. Ian Kershaw, *The End: The Defiance and Destruction of Hitler's Germany, 1944–1945* (New York: Penguin, 2011), 311.
39. Frank MacDonough, *Opposition and Resistance in Nazi Germany* (Cambridge: Cambridge University Press, 2001).
40. Daniel Horn, "Youth Resistance in the Third Reich: A Social Portrait," *Journal of Social History* 7, no.1 (1973): 26–50.
41. Henryk Cimek, "Jews in the Polish Communist Movement," *Polityka i Społeczeństwo* [Studies in Politics and Society] 9 (2012):42–57. Available at https://bazhum.muzhp.pl/media/files/Polityka_i_Spoleczenstwo/Polityka_i_Spoleczenstwo-r2012-t-n9/Polityka_i_Spoleczenstwo-r2012-t-n9-s42-57/Polityka_i_Spoleczenstwo-r2012-t-n9-s42-57.pdf

42. Roni Gechtman, "Tsukunf," *YIVO Encyclopedia of Jews in Eastern Europe*, 2010, https://yivoencyclopedia.org/article.aspx/Tsukunft.
43. Joseph Kernish, *To Live with Honor and Die with Honor: Selected Documents from the Warsaw Ghetto Archives "O.S" [Oneg Shabbat]* (Jerusalem: Yad Vashem, 1986), 516–517.
44. Israel Gutman, "Youth Movements and the Underground and the Ghetto Revolts," in *Jewish Resistance During the Holocaust*, ed. Mei Grubsztein (Jerusalem: Yad Vashem, 1971), 264
45. Yehuda Bauer. *Rethinking the Holocaust* (New Haven, CT: Yale University Press, 2001), 136.

Further Reading

Atran, Scott. *Talking to the Enemy: Religion, Brotherhood, and the (Un)Making of Terrorists.* New York: Ecco, 2011.

Best, Amy, ed. *Representing Youth: Methodological Issues in Critical Youth Studies.* New York: New York University Press. 2007.

Bucholtz, Mary. "Youth and Cultural Practice." *Annual Review of Anthropology* 31 (2002): 525–552.

Cornell, Richard. *Revolutionary Vanguard: The Early Year of the Communist Youth International, 1914–1924.* Toronto: University of Toronto Press, 1982.

Drumble, Mark A., and Jastine C. Barrett. *Research Handbook on Child Soldiers.* Northhampton, MA: Elgar, 2019.

Durham, Deborah. 2004. "Disappearing Youth: Youth as a Social Shifter in Botswana." *American Ethnologist* 31, no. 4: 589–605.

Ember, Carol, and Melvin Ember. "Resource Unpredictability, Mistrust, and War: A Cross-Cultural Study." *Journal of Conflict Resolution* 36, no 2 (1992): 242–262.

Glowacki, Luke, and Richard W. Wrangham. "The Role of Rewards in Motivating Participation in Simple Warfare." *Human Nature* 24, no. 4 (2013): 444–460.

Hoffman, Danny. "Culture by Other Means: An Africanist Anthropology of Political Violence and War." In *A Companion to the Anthropology of Africa*, ed. Roy Richard Grinker, Stephen C. Lubkemann, Christopher B. Steine, and Euclides Gonçalves (Hoboken, NJ: Wiley, 2019), 173–198

Korbin, Jill E. "Children, Childhoods, and Violence." *Annual Review of Anthropology* 32 (2003): 431–446.

Kucherenko, Olga. *Little Soldiers: How Soviet Children Went to War, 1941–1945* (Oxford: Oxford University Press: 2011).

Levine, Robert A. "Ethnographic Studies of Childhood: A Historical Overview." *American Anthropologist* 109, no. 2 (2007): 247–260.

Rosen, David M. *Child Soldiers in the Western Imagination: From Patriots to Victims* (New Brunswick: Rutgers University Press, 2015).

Vigh, Henri. *Navigating Terrains of War: Youth and Soldiering in Guinea Bissau* (New York: Berghahn, 2006).

CHAPTER 6

YOUTH CULTURE AS A BATTLEGROUND

Atlantic World Slavery and Enslaved Youth in Jamaica

COLLEEN A. VASCONCELLOS

ONE summer day in late June or early July of 1791, a boy named Brutus escaped from his plantation in Black River, a small town named after the waterway that ran through the sugar parish of St. Elizabeth, Jamaica. Not long after he was found to be missing, an advertisement appeared in the Kingston *Royal Gazette* with an interesting description: Brutus "calls himself a Creole, but is supposed to be from Africa, as he talks both the Eboe and Coromantee languages very fluently." Unfortunately, neither his age, destination, nor his outcome appear in this advertisement or any other that survived after its publication.[1]

Though this advertisement is sparse, as most were during this period, it speaks volumes about Brutus, the environment in which he lived, and the nature of youth culture on the island. Although the name of the estate from which he fled is unknown, Brutus's life was undoubtedly one of backbreaking labor and harsh punishment, leading to what sociologist Orlando Patterson called "social death." Sugar estates were notorious for their draconian conditions, and Brutus's refusal to accept that this was the life he was forced to live gives insight into his spirit. Brutus had been sold at least once before running away, or the advertiser would have been clear as to whether he was Creole or African born. Brutus himself identified as Creole, and he should be taken at his word. What stands out, however, is that he was multilingual, speaking at least three languages if one were to count English among them. Although he likely heard any number of African languages and dialects within his community, his parents could have come from both the Bight of Biafra and the Gold Coast, and he grew up speaking these languages at home. Or, as historian Douglas B. Chambers suggests, perhaps Brutus was born in Africa and learned another West African language after arriving in Jamaica.[2]

The complexities that appear in just one short runaway advertisement exemplify the diverse cultural environment that helped shape youth culture within the slave villages of Jamaica and the wider Atlantic World. Given the fact that Brutus escaped during one of the peak years of the trans-Atlantic slave trade, Africa was very much alive on any given plantation in the Atlantic World, and the boy would have grown up around a plethora of West African cultural traditions, practices, and beliefs. Traditionally, scholars have argued that the horrors of the slave trade, alienation from natal kin, and isolation from those who were culturally similar destroyed any possibility of a vibrant African culture within an increasingly creolized slave community. However, more recent historiographical trends set by scholars like Joseph E. Holloway, Kwasi Konadu, and Stephanie E. Smallwood argue otherwise, opening the door for a more nuanced consideration of the nature of youth culture within the plantation complex.

No matter their geographical location or time period, enslaved children and youth like Brutus lived in an environment designed to reinforce their status as chattel by the very nature of their work. Their lives were not completely their own, and enslaved youth throughout the Atlantic World matured within an environment that defined their childhoods as a means of production. As historian Wilma King established in her groundbreaking study *Stolen Childhood* (1995), children's experiences in the antebellum South forced them to grow into adulthood well before their time. Their life outside the workforce failed to prepare children for a life of enslavement, and they suffered a "stolen childhood" as a result.[3] Needless to say, youth culture within the enslaved community was defined by a set of norms, values, and practices outside of those experienced by other youth of the period. Yet, while enslaved children experienced a life surrounded by harsh labor, brutality, and death, Brutus's escape in 1791 proposes that their values and practices prioritized survival.

Using enslaved children and youth in eighteenth- and nineteenth-century Jamaica as a case study illustrates how youth culture came to mean different things to different groups as each struggled to maintain control of a life enslaved. In fact, youth culture was a battleground of sorts within the Jamaican plantation complex with three groups at play: the planter class, enslaved parents, and enslaved youth themselves. As planters faced increased abolitionist threats to the slave trade and later slavery itself, their increased reliance upon enslaved youth in a changing economy had profound influence in shaping youth culture among the enslaved. Meanwhile, enslaved parents struggled to raise their children within a system that refused to acknowledge or protect their childhoods. Subsequently, enslaved youth grew up in an environment where most agreed that they were important players within the plantation complex. While planters saw youth as an investment that could lead them out of an impending economic collapse, enslaved children provided an opportunity to protect and preserve African cultural identity within the enslaved community. Caught in the middle of that struggle was youth culture itself, as both sides envisioned enslaved youth as a way to survive.

How then did enslaved youth define and perceive youth culture? This is difficult to say, as source material is elusive. Most enslaved individuals were illiterate, and only a few published accounts exist. There are few first-hand accounts like those penned by Mary Prince, Frederick Douglass, and Olaudah Equiano, but they were written and published when these individuals were adults. When one combines the complexities of history and memory with the biases of the abolitionists who helped facilitate the publication of their stories, validity becomes a concern. Nonetheless, although the majority of the source material available is from the planter point of view, actions speak louder than words as enslaved youth reacted to their enslavement through various acts of resistance, self-harm, and outright rebellion, giving insight into how this environment helped to shape youth culture within the plantation complex. Despite a historiography that often characterizes enslaved life as one of social death and stolen childhoods, ultimately how enslaved youth fought for survival as they coped with the hardships of slavery and the realization that they were slaves is explored.

Categorizing youth culture within the plantation complex is a difficult task, largely because there are so many variables. When one considers the different systems of slavery that existed throughout the Atlantic World, one child's experience in the antebellum South significantly differed from that experienced by the child enslaved in Saint-Domingue. The adolescent laboring in the sugar fields of Jamaica had a much different life than the young laundress who washed clothes day in and day out in colonial Cuba. Despite these variables, there is a shared experience that allows for the construction of a collective history that predictably mirrored that of the adults enslaved alongside them. Like adults, enslaved youth were expected to work twelve- to fifteen-hour days in the fields, or even longer hours as domestics or apprentices to enslaved artisans. When their work was slow or imperfect, they were flogged or put in various contraptions designed to torture and humiliate, just like enslaved adults. No matter their age, the enslaved from Maryland to Brazil lived in an environment that commodified and dehumanized them for economic gain.

Moreover, as historians Deborah Gray White and Wilma King have both shown in their work on enslaved children in the American South, early childhood development within the American system was devoid of any gender-specific socialization or work expectations. The same is true for the Caribbean system, where preteen boys and girls performed the same tasks, wore the same clothing, and even played the same games. Instead, any grouping within the plantation system was categorized by age and task. As historian Marie Jenkins Schwartz argues, planters were acutely aware that the formative years of early childhood were crucial to child development, which led plantation managers to take an active role in setting age-specific tasks while also attempting to foster loyalty and subservience through a paternalistic agenda.[4]

Therefore, as enslaved children transitioned from nursery to field, from child to adult, labor expectations and pressures from above set a specific tone for the daily tasks they performed in a constant effort to reinforce their status as chattel and force them to accept the reality of their situation from the start. Furthermore, those tasks were designed to progressively socialize and acclimate them to their lives as slaves so that they could work at the same capacity as adults when they reached adolescence. Even before they entered the fields themselves as laborers by age five, enslaved children under the age of five toiled in the hot sun while strapped to their mothers' backs. Those who spent their early childhoods in plantation nurseries watched their community leave long before sunup and return long after sundown exhausted from the day's labors. After entering the children's gang at age five or six, enslaved children picked grass, tended livestock, carried cane husks from the boiling houses to the trash, and performed other light tasks around the estate. At age eight or nine, they transitioned to the second gang, where they performed more strenuous labor in the fields. There they were expected to harvest sugar cane and other cash crops, boil cane juice into molasses, and begin learning the refining process. Although this was a gang comprised of preteens and teenagers, they were expected to perform the same work at the same pace as the adults who toiled beside them in the first gang. By the time they joined the first gang at the age of fifteen or sixteen, they had already been performing first gang tasks for at least six years.[5]

Such an oppressive system, combined with a lack of archival sources, makes it difficult to ascertain how the enslaved community defined childhood and its stages. However, it is clear from the system described earlier that the plantocracy designated the enslaved boys and girls aged fifteen and younger as children. Nonetheless, enslaved children and youth lived a life not unlike that of enslaved adults, and the tasks required of the second gang make that abundantly clear. Furthermore, this planter-imposed definition evolved and changed as a direct result of growing abolitionist sentiment, the changing nature of the plantation economy, and the changing nature of work on Jamaica's estates. While some planters classified all enslaved children not yet working on their estates as *infants* or *children*, *boys* and *girls* labored in the children's and second gangs. By the late eighteenth century, planters and estate managers added new stages to enslaved youth through the increased usage of labels like *man-boy* and *woman-girl* in order to distinguish prepubescent fourteen- and fifteen-year-olds about to transition to the first gang. Further still, girls as young as twelve were added to the lists of breeding wenches, which added an entirely new labor expectation to an already long list. Therefore, within the plantation complex, a very subjective definition of childhood and youth evolved alongside the very nature of slavery itself, with plantation labor and economic need serving as the catalyst.[6]

It becomes clear fairly quickly that Jamaican planters only valued childhood and youth as an economic investment, and that had a profound impact on the development of youth culture within the enslaved community. Only by looking at the place of youth and youth culture within that community can that be fully understood. Although the villages were located in the center of the plantation, so as to minimize the amount of time the enslaved spent traveling to and from the fields, they were also within sight of the overseer's residence and the great house, serving as a powerful reminder that someone was always watching.[7] Still, at its core, the slave village itself was the very ethos of youth culture, responsible not only for its development, but also its very survival. There, enslaved youth resided with their kinship groups, some in nuclear or matrifocal family units, others in extended family units, while others still simply tried to coexist as best as they could in the same space as the others assigned to their dwelling. Amid the four walls of a small thatched hut and a few personal belongings, enslaved parents and children alike struggled to find stability and strength in an otherwise unstable life.

That struggle would have a profound impact on the development and very nature of youth culture within the enslaved community. Separated from long established natal kinship networks, West Africans and Creoles alike developed new strategies of coping by identifying themselves with those who shared similar experiences of capture, sale, and enslavement. They not only survived through adaptation, but also by reorganizing and redefining their kinship groups. Enslaved youth were no different, as is evidenced in the attachment that sixteen-year-old Prince felt toward Philippa, an enslaved woman who adopted Prince in his infancy on Cornwall Estate in the Jamaican parish of Westmoreland. When Philippa was ill and confined to Cornwall's hospital in February of 1816, Prince spent every free moment he had by her side.[8] For Prince, Philippa was the only mother he had ever known, and his vigil by her bedside suggests a deep bond. As West Africans young and old sought to find a place within the slave villages, youth culture took root through the stability that relationships like these provided.

For many, that stability was short-lived, as enslaved youth often faced the trauma of being separated from their families by sale or even death. Although the Jamaican Assembly passed a law in 1735 stipulating that families sold for debt could not be separated, that law made no provision to prevent the separation of families sold for profit. When Lord William Montagu, 5th Duke of Manchester, completed his tenure as governor of the island and relocated to England in 1827, he manumitted an enslaved woman named Catherine Gray but sold her two children to a Miss Rennall for sixty pounds. The Jamaican Assembly did not pass a law preventing the separation of families until 1832, just one year before the Emancipation Act of 1833.[9]

Furthermore, the plantocracy failed to consider the complex nature of kinship within the enslaved community, as is evidenced in an 1818 law that specifically defined family as "a man and his wife, his, her, or their, children." Therefore, unrecognized familial units were unprotected by the law and separated. In 1821, a ten-year-old boy named Henry who worked with his grandmother Betsy Newell as a domestic at King's House in Spanish Town was sold away from her without warning. Archival sources do not give any information as to the nature of their relationship, nor do they indicate what happened to Henry after he was sold. The loss of the only family he had likely ever known, as well as the stability of his life at King's House, must have been devastating. Therefore, even from an early age, the enslaved understood that kinship was not immune to planter interference. Still, kinship was an important component of the development of youth culture within the enslaved community, as it was the basis of their very identity outside their status as slaves.[10]

As anthropologist Douglas V. Armstrong has argued, while the planter class owned the land and the enslaved men, women, and youth who labored upon it, they also understood the significance that this space held for the Africans and Creoles living there.[11] Calculating as it may be in their intentions, planters did allow for some degree of cultural freedom within the slave villages through the mid-eighteenth century. This period also experienced a peak in the number of Africans imported into the region, which was essential to the maintenance and reinvention of a multiplicity of African cultural traditions and beliefs throughout the Atlantic World, albeit in varying degrees. This vibrant cultural landscape had a profound influence on the development of youth culture within the plantation complex, and while one could not possibly tackle the thousands of variations in one book chapter, the slave villages of Jamaica provide for an excellent case study.

Despite the absence of written accounts by freedmen and women, archival sources do indicate that some specific West African cultural practices were transferred to enslaved youth, beginning with the very process of choosing their names. While some received traditional West African day names like Cudjoe and Phibbah, as was customary in Akan, Ga, and Ewe cultures, where children were named after the day of their birth, others received modified names like Friday or January, reflecting English influence and cultural reinvention. The 1817 Jamaican Registry of the Returns of Slaves lists two Creole women of African parentage on two different Westmoreland estates who named their children Eboe and Fantee, while a twenty-eight-year-old Creole woman named Banda is listed under the returns for the parish of St. George. Names like these not only passed down West African naming practices to other generations, but they also gave enslaved youth an education about their past and identity outside of their identity as slaves by connecting them to the West African ethnic groups of their ancestors. Plantation registries and inventories throughout the Atlantic World are peppered with Creole children, often of Creole parentage, with both traditional and modified West African names, or variations thereof, signifying the perseverance of West African naming practices. The persistence of these African cultural traditions not only helped to maintain youth culture's roots to its past; it also helped to reinforce the spirit of survival that came to define that culture's very character.[12]

But what of the struggle between planter and parent? Historian Trevor Burnard argues that the enslaved were seldom allowed the right to name themselves or their children, maintaining instead that many of the names given to the enslaved are less the continuation of African cultural identities and more an indication of what whites thought of their slaves. Although there is wide usage of traditional English names like John and Betsy, some planters chose historical names like Shakespeare and Brutus or geographical names like Bristol, Oxford, and Cambridge. According to Bernard, "this determined effort to rename their slaves ... [was] part of the transformative process whereby Africans became their property." What better way to solidify ownership of a child than by controlling the very naming process itself? Therefore, while some enslaved children's names assisted them in developing an identity apart from their English owners or fellow slaves, other names served as constant reminders that they were slaves first and children second.[13]

Using the extensive diaries of Jamaican planter Thomas Thistlewood as an example, Burnard does add that many enslaved went by another name at home. Throughout his diaries, Thistlewood noted the "country names" of the slaves he discussed like Ogo and Owaria, while also stating several times that he himself named his slaves. This practice not only suggests a dual identity among enslaved youth, but it also speaks to the struggle between planter and parent over the control of youth culture in the plantation complex. Political scientist James C. Scott's theoretical framework on resistance is an important aid in unraveling how this tradition relates to the development and sustenance of youth culture within the enslaved community. In his book *Domination and the Arts of Resistance* (1990), Scott outlines the complexities of coded public behavior through the presence of public and hidden transcripts. Therefore, in a system of institutionalized slavery, the enslaved maintained a public transcript for the benefit of the plantocracy that reinforced stereotypical characterizations of enslaved life, while a hidden transcript allowed the enslaved to resist acculturation by reinventing and maintaining their African cultural identity in private. This hidden transcript was reinforced by enslaved parents, who attempted to sustain or reinvent their national identities as well as circumvent and undermine the destructive process of slavery by transferring West African cultural practices and traditions to enslaved youth. The presence of "country names" like those described by Thistlewood certainly attests to that, as does the persistence of West African kinship networks and languages within the slave villages.[14]

This brings the discussion back to Brutus, who fled his estate in June or July of 1791 for parts unknown. In his runaway advertisement, his owner noted that he spoke at least two West African languages. However, as enslaved Creoles came to outnumber enslaved Africans in the years following the abolition of the slave trade in 1807, children like Brutus became more exceptional than ordinary. Since the enslaved community lacked a common language and daily life required a greater usage of European languages, the various dialects and languages spoken in the slave villages combined to create region-specific lingua franca in many areas of the Atlantic World. While the planter class heard nothing more than "gibberish," this new patois allowed for privacy and the preservation of West African words and phrases that might otherwise be lost.[15] From Haitian Creole to Jamaican patois to the Gullah-Geechee dialects of the coastal South, these languages are still heard and spoken fluently today. Therefore, what started as hidden transcripts created a space for youth to use the more commonly spoken language on the island, a dialect that became more functionable for them. Once again, the idea of survival through adaptation and reinvention is put into practice, as the usage of the island's patois eventually superseded the assimilation of English-only vernacular.

Enslaved parents continued this approach in their cultural transference of folklore traditions. While folklore continued as a tool to teach children respect, caution, courage, perseverance, and morality, enslaved parents reinvented those traditions to educate a new generation of children that was born into slavery. Therefore, youth culture within the enslaved community was shaped by stories of the past that were intertwined with lessons for surviving the present and future. For instance, the Jamaican riddle that asked children to guess what resembled a "guinea ship full of people who came out with red coats & black heads" not only taught children about the slave trade but also enhanced memory and language skills; the answer, "ackee," is derived from the Twi word *ankye*, which is a black-seeded fruit inside a large red pod that was brought to Jamaica by a West African slaver in 1788.[16]

Fables featuring animals taught moral lessons through song and story. Jamaican planter Thomas Thistlewood related one tale told to him in 1751 by a Coromantee enslaved woman about a monster called Cokroyamkou who waited in the shadows to eat children after they fell asleep. Another story Thistlewood recounted, featuring an old woman who refused to give her grandchild meat unless he could say her name, is incredibly similar to a Ga fable featuring a hippo and a tortoise; while the moral of the story remained the same, the characters changed to reflect a new environment where food was scarce. Stories like these—known as Anancy stories in the Caribbean and Brer Rabbit stories in North America—helped create and shape a youth culture defined by self-sufficiency and survival.[17]

In a diary entry for June 19, 1765, the ever-observant Thomas Thistlewood noted the purchase of ten Africans, four of whom were children below the ages of fifteen. Because Thistlewood was one of those rare planters who occasionally spoke to those he enslaved about their culture, his diaries are a treasure trove of information about the nature of African cultural identity among the enslaved. In his diaries he described Chub, a boy about thirteen, who had "3 perpindicular scars down each Cheek," and Damsel, a girl of about the same age, who had "3 long strokes down each Cheek... her belly full of Country Marks, & an Arch between her Breasts." These scars fascinated planters throughout the Atlantic World, many of whom understood that besides being "highly ornamental... they are said to indicate free birth and honourable parentage."[18]

What planters called "country marks," however, were actually given to African youth as an initiation into adulthood. Famed abolitionist Olaudah Equiano, who was kidnapped as a boy from his village of Isseke in present-day Nigeria, stated that marks such as these were only given to relatives and descendants of the elders and leaders of the community in Igbo society. While this was a significant component of West African youth culture, rituals such as these failed to survive in the youth culture of the slave villages across the Atlantic. In his work on scarification practices in the African diaspora, Paul Lovejoy connects the loss of this cultural tradition to Orlando Patterson's arguments concerning social death and the enslaved community. These marks coincided with certain tasks and rites performed by West African youth in an initiation into adulthood that occurred shortly after puberty. Aside from a lack of free time to perform these rituals, the responsibilities and rights they signified could not be accomplished by enslaved youth in the Americas.[19]

Lovejoy also suggests that scarification rituals disappeared as a form of resistance, as they always appeared as identifiers in runaway advertisements. While the disappearance of these marks created some anonymity for the enslaved, it also removed a form of cultural expression and a connection to the past for enslaved youth. The absence of direct markers like these that connected to West African cultures within the slave villages limits our knowledge of how enslaved youth participated in these aspects of cultural expression. While it is clear that enslaved youth lived in a diverse cultural environment, how that environment shaped their own self-perception can only be conjectured. Furthermore, the failure of these marks to survive the Atlantic crossing speaks to the changing nature of youth culture within the plantation complex. While survival was a large part of youth culture itself, it was limited to the confines of the environment in which these children lived.[20]

Still, there is evidence of enslaved youth attempting to take control of their own lives through various acts of resistance and revolt. When William Sells, a Jamaican physician, tried to separate two unrelated African children in his household who had been shipmates on the voyage to Jamaica and, as such, considered themselves to be siblings, they made it clear to him that they would not be separated from each other, and the children were sold together to a buyer living in Spanish Town.[21] Not only did these children actively resist their separation by sale; they also succeeded in negotiating a joint sale in order to keep their reinvented family together.

Not all enslaved youth were as lucky, and runaway advertisements listed in newspapers and broadsides throughout the Atlantic World contain the names of enslaved youth who "absconded" from their estates in response to shared experiences. One runaway advertisement that appeared in the Kingston *Royal Gazette* listed the description of a boy named John who was believed to be "lurking around" Spanish Town in March of 1782 in search of his mother, who lived there as a slave after being sold at public auction a few months earlier. Another girl named Harriet, who fled the horrible conditions of the St. George Workhouse in June of 1823, was listed as having "scars on her back and stomach from flogging." While John refused to be separated from his mother, Harriet attempted to flee the harsh punishment she likely received on a daily basis. Although most Jamaican enslaved youth progressed through their childhood without any chance of freedom, instances like these suggest that many attempted to take control of the situation themselves.[22]

What becomes obvious after spending any amount of time in the archives is that planters underestimated the tenacity of the enslaved youth on their estates, as is evidenced by the events and instances of survival put into practice as discussed earlier. Through instances like these, it becomes apparent that while youth culture can be defined in a very literal sense through an examination of African cultural identity within the enslaved community, the agency of enslaved youth within that culture and community as a whole must also be included. While the paternalism of the period created a belief that the enslaved should be content and happy because "in the language of a poet, *the sun always shines* ... They are carefully attended without expense, and they are provided with every comfort which their condition requires," such a utopia did not exist.[23]

In fact, enslaved youth throughout the Atlantic World lived in an environment comparable to any impoverished underdeveloped nation today. While most played a part in the growth of their household economy by working in their house gardens and provision grounds in the evenings or accompanying enslaved women to the town markets, some resorted to theft in an effort to find food for their household. In April of 1789, a boy named Drake appeared before the St. Ann Slave Court for stealing a steer "with Force and Arms" from Joseph Price with another boy named Quashy. In November of 1823, a boy named James was brought to trial for stealing a "she Goat the Value of forty shillings," in an attempt to provide milk for his family. Others stole expensive items of clothing or furniture, which they likely intended to sell at the town markets. In these instances, what the planter class characterized as "crime" was actually agency, clearly indicating that some enslaved youth imagined themselves as family providers not unlike the adults in their household. Their actions reinforce not only the sense of community that ran so prevalently through the nature of youth culture within the slave villages, but also its inherent sense of survival as well.[24]

While one can only surmise how enslaved youth's experiences shaped or obstructed their psychological development, the island's slave court records are peppered with instances of enslaved youth acting out their frustrations. While some turned to alcohol, others appeared before the slave courts for "making use of abusive language" toward free and white residents. Other instances were more violent. Port Royal Slave Courts sentenced a girl named Jemima to three months hard labor for setting fire to a building in January of 1819, while another unnamed girl received just one day of hard labor—on account of her "extreme youth"—for throwing dirt and filth on individuals in town. Then there is the case of a girl named Bessie, who, along with her sister Kitty, was found guilty and sentenced to transportation off the island by the St. Ann Slave Court in July of 1797 for poisoning their mistress's tea with arsenic. Such behavior certainly indicates that enslaved youth were capable of resisting their situation as strongly as adults, and this is not unique to the island of Jamaica.[25]

Yet, where historians see agency and resistance, planters saw primitive behavior and savagery. In 1798, Reverend Rees of Kingston preached a sermon on the advantages of the religious socialization of children "both to themselves and to the community." Quoting Proverbs 22:6, Rees argued that every slave owner in Jamaica should take complete responsibility in raising the slave children on their estates and to "Train up a child in the way he should go." By teaching them labor skills as well as educating them in the ways of Christian morality and chastity, enslaved youth could lead Jamaican planters to a future of labor security in an environment increasingly hostile toward chattel slavery. Christian education would guarantee a docile, civilized labor force in the future. Otherwise, Rev. Rees reasoned, enslaved children would simply grow to imitate their uncivilized parents.[26]

Terrified to live among "ignorant savages" who failed to understand their subordinate place in society, those planters who had once allowed for a degree of cultural freedom within the enslaved community now saw African cultural identity as a threat to the profitability of their estates. Consequently, youth culture also came under attack as planters attempted to control the "savagery" of the island's youth by impressing a program of religious instruction that stressed a Protestant work ethic as well as loyalty and subservience. By 1826, the entire Jamaican enslaved population was baptized, and from that point on enslaved children were baptized at their birth.[27] By teaching the enslaved population that theft, unruly behavior, alcohol consumption, and promiscuity were mortal sins, planters and estate managers hoped that Christianization would acculturate enslaved youth into more docile, manageable subjects. In doing so, they attempted to manipulate and reshape an established youth culture within the slave villages.

While the planter class seemed to declare war on African cultural identity, there is further evidence of the persistence of that dual identity explored earlier. On Cornwall Estate in Westmoreland, for example, the enslaved community produced "Eboe drums" for each child's baptism and continued to educate their children as they had before by teaching them "Nancy stories," proverbs, and riddles. Furthermore, there are numerous instances where missionaries began to baptize the enslaved en masse. "'It was like driving cattle to a pond,'" missionary Hope Masterton Waddell wrote, quoting a convert, "'I heard something about God,' said another, 'but thought the parson in the long gown was he.'" Waddell's complaints about the insincerities of mass baptism go further to allege that the enslaved came forward for baptism largely at their owners' urging. Furthermore, while some men of the cloth saw their work as a progression toward bringing salvation to the godless, others saw it as a means of increasing revenue for the parish, the rectory, and for themselves. Therefore, baptism and Sunday worship did not necessarily mean that the enslaved youth abandoned their own traditions and beliefs for Christianity. While the planter class envisioned themselves one step closer toward a more prolific and fertile enslaved population, enslaved youth and adults alike saw Sunday worship as less time in the fields. In other words, the public transcript merely adjusted to the times.[28]

Enslaved parents and youth could not plan for the instillation of parish and estate schools, however, and youth culture faced serious interference as Jamaican planters intensified their acculturation programs in an effort to take a more direct approach at the socialization and education of enslaved youth. Feeling pressure from increased petitions before Parliament calling for the end of slavery, Jamaican planters feared a situation that mirrored the economic devastation that accompanied their neighbors in the newly independent Haiti. Anglican cleric and fervent opponent of abolition George Wilson Bridges spoke for many when he wrote that "children, from the most tender age, are permitted to indulge the basest instincts of their nature; their mind... is a waste."[29]

Therefore, the planter class took preventive action, removing enslaved youth from their communities' influence. By teaching them English morals and values, to properly speak and read the English language, "to obey their master, and to be content in the situation in which Providence has placed them," the transition to freedom may not be as disastrous as most planters feared. Once again, planters and estate managers attempted to manipulate and reshape an established youth culture, this time by removing it from the slave villages into a more controlled environment. Despite cries from skeptics who argued that education went beyond the purpose and need of slavery, advocates argued that education would beat abolitionists at their own game by teaching children to become good workers who knew their place. Although there is no quantitative estimate of the number of schools or the number of enslaved youth educated on the island before the abolition of slavery in 1834, George Baille, a Jamaican planter, noted before the House of Lords in 1832 that there was hardly a town in Jamaica that did not have a school.[30]

On the eve of abolition, Jamaican planters convinced themselves that the enslaved youth on their estates benefited from their religious education. When Reverend John Jenkins, a Wesleyan missionary, arrived in Jamaica in 1830, he "expected to find at my arrival an ignorant, depressed, and miserable set of people, whose knowledge was as little as their condition was destitute," but was pleased to find children who sang hymns, quoted scripture, and met the standards he had set for them in his own mind.[31] One may never know whether they did this of their own free will or at the urging of their owners, but it was enough to convince Jenkins that the savages he had only heard about were now a civilized group of laborers.

How these children perceived themselves is more difficult to discern. While their acts of violence and disobedience suggest how some children related to their situation and the situation of those around them, their voices largely remain silent. Although some West African cultural practices and beliefs—such as naming practices, folklore traditions, and language—were transferred to enslaved youth, what these children retained and passed on to their own children is unknown. Therefore, it may be impossible to fully know how enslaved youth saw themselves connecting with the diverse cultural landscape of the island.

Despite moderate planter interference and manipulation, enslaved parents gained many opportunities to raise their children on their own terms until the educational conditioning of enslaved youth challenged the traditions and beliefs practiced within the slave villages. Therefore, as enslaved youth grew up in an environment that became increasingly more English, Christianization and socialization created obstacles for the cultural transference of African cultural beliefs and among Jamaican children. As a result, enslaved parents fought a losing battle not only to maintain control of their children, but also of how their children connected to the culture and history of their ancestors. Consequently, by the early nineteenth century, both English and West African cultural traditions and beliefs influenced and shaped youth culture within the enslaved community, ultimately leading to the creation of a "Jamaican" cultural identity.

Whether Jamaica's planters truly believed that they had succeeded in their goals is irrelevant. What is important, however, is that they had come to view youth culture itself as a viable economic investment. Enslaved youth were no longer just a means of production; they were moral commodities. Yet, both the plantocracy and enslaved parents envisioned enslaved youth as a means of protecting a way of life that was in crisis, and that struggle continued into the apprenticeship period. As Jamaican planters and estate managers placed increased responsibility on enslaved youth to lead them toward the economic stability and profitability they needed during their time of imagined crisis, enslaved youth attempted to negotiate their place within the plantation complex through acts of violence, theft, self-destruction, and even murder. No matter how hard they tried, enslaved youth could never truly escape the traumas they faced on a daily basis. Therefore, at its core, youth culture within the enslaved community was a culture of survival.

Notes

1. National Library of Jamaica, *The Royal Gazette* (Kingston), June 4–11, 1791. The National Library of Jamaica will be abbreviated as NLJ in all subsequent footnotes.
2. Orlando Patterson, *Slavery and Social Death* (Cambridge, MA: Harvard University Press, 1982); and Douglas B. Chambers, "The Links of a Legacy: Figuring the Slave Trade to Jamaica," in *Caribbean Culture: Soundings on Kamau Brathwaite*, ed. Annie Paul (Kingston, Jamaica: University of the West Indies Press, 2007), 287–288.
3. Wilma King, *Stolen Childhood: Slave Youth in Nineteenth-Century America* (Bloomington: Indiana University Press, 1995).
4. Deborah Gray White, *Ar'n't I a Woman?: Female Slaves in the Plantation South* (New York: W.W. Norton & Company, 1985), 92–94; King, *Stolen Childhood*, 21; and Marie Jenkins Schwartz, *Born in Bondage: Growing Up Enslaved in the Antebellum South* (Boston: Harvard University Press, 2000), 76–78.
5. Colleen Vasconcellos, *Slavery, Childhood, and Abolition in Jamaica* (Athens: University of Georgia Press, 2015), 25–33.
6. Ibid., 31.
7. Barry Higman, "A Report on Excavations at Montpelier and Roehampton," *Jamaica Journal* 8 (1974): 41; and Douglas V. Armstrong and Kenneth G. Kelly, "Settlement Patterns and the Origins of African Jamaican Society: Seville Plantation, St. Ann's Bay, Jamaica," *Ethnohistory* 47 (2000): 378–379.
8. Matthew Lewis, *Journal of a West Indian Proprietor Kept During a Residence in the Island of Jamaica*, ed. Judith Terry (London: John Murray, 1834; reprint, Oxford: Oxford University Press, 1999), 109. Page citations are to the reprint edition.

9. Jamaica Archives, Laws of Jamaica, 8 George II, c. 5 (1735). The Jamaican Archives will be abbreviated as JA in all subsequent notes; NLJ, Duke of Manchester Accounts, 1823–1827, MS 1768; and Great Britain, Parliament, The Agency Anti-Slavery Committee, *The Condition of the Slave, Not Preferable to That of the British Peasant, from the Evidence Before the Parliamentary Committees on Colonial Slavery* (London: W. Johnston, 1833), 2.
10. JA, Laws of Jamaica, 8 George II, c. 5 (1818); and West Indies and Special Collections, UWI-Mona, Journals of the Assembly of Jamaica, vol. 13, f. 580, MR 3721. The West Indies and Special Collection will be abbreviated as WISC in all subsequent notes.
11. Douglas V. Armstrong and Mark L. Fleischman, "House-Yard Burials of Enslaved Laborers in Eighteenth-Century Jamaica," *International Journal of Historical Archaeology* 7 (2003): 41.
12. Vasconcellos, *Slavery, Childhood, and Abolition in Jamaica*, 63; and JA, Registry of the Returns of Slaves, Westmoreland, 1817, 1B/11/7/9; and ibid., St. George, 1817, 1B/11/7/22.
13. Trevor Burnard, "Slave Naming Patterns: Onomastics and the Taxonomy of Race in Eighteenth-Century Jamaica," *Journal of Interdisciplinary History* 31 (2001): 326, 329.
14. Ibid., 335; and James C. Scott, *Domination and the Arts of Resistance: Hidden Transcripts* (New Haven, CT: Yale University Press, 1990).
15. Edward Long, *The History of Jamaica, or, A General Survey of the Antient [sic] and Modern State of That Island*, vol. 2 (London: T. Lowndes, 1770), 278; and Lady Maria Nugent, *Lady Nugent's Journal*, ed. Philip Wright (London: Issued for Private Circulation, 1839; reprint, Kingston: Institute of Jamaica, 1966), 76. Page citations are to the reprint edition.
16. Abdou Moumouni, *Education in Africa* (London: Andre Deutsch, 1968), 20–21; Michael Omolewa, "Traditional African Modes of Education: Their Relevance in the Modern World," *International Review of Education* 53 (2007): 593–612; Olive Senior, *A–Z of Jamaican Heritage*, 3rd ed. (Kingston, Jamaica: Heinemann Educational Books and The Gleaner Company, 1985), 1; and Vasconcellos, *Slavery, Childhood, and Abolition in Jamaica*, 66.
17. WISC, Thomas Thistlewood Diaries, May 16, 1751, Monson 31/2; and NLJ, "Anancy Stories," Lily Perkins Collection, MS 2019.
18. WISC, Thomas Thistlewood Diaries, June 19, 1765, Monson 31/16; and Edwards, *History of Jamaica*, vol. 2, 152.
19. Olaudah Equiano, *The Interesting Narrative of the Life of Olaudah Equiano, Written by Himself*, ed. Robert J. Allison (New York: W. Durell, 1791; reprint, Boston: Bedford Books, 1995), 34–45; page citations are to the reprint edition; Paul Lovejoy, "Scarification and the Loss of History in the African Diaspora," in *Activating the Past: History and Memory in the Black Atlantic World*, ed. Andrew Apter and Lauren Derby (Cambridge: Cambridge University Press, 2009), 100; and Vasconcellos, *Slavery, Childhood, and Abolition in Jamaica*, 71.
20. Lovejoy, "Scarification and the Loss of History in the African Diaspora," 100, 103.
21. William Sells, *Remarks on the Condition of the Slaves in the Island of Jamaica* (London: Hughes, 1825), 28.
22. NLJ, *The Royal Gazette* (Kingston), February 23, 1782, March 2, 1782, and June 14–21, 1823.
23. Jesse Foot, *A Defense of the Planters of the West Indies* (London: J. Debrett, 1792), 32.
24. JA, St. George Slave Court, 1822–1831; JA, Port Royal Summary Slave Trials, 1819–1834, 2/19/30; and NLJ, St. Ann Slave Court, 1787–1814, MS 273.
25. WISC, Thomas Thistlewood Diaries; JA, Port Royal Summary Slave Trials, 1819–1834, 2/19/30; and NLJ, St. Ann Slave Court, 1787–1814, MS 273.

26. NLJ, *Columbian Magazine* 2 (1798): 532, C652.
27. JA, Register of Baptisms, Marriages, Burials, St. Catherine (St. Dorothy and St. John), 1693–1836, 1B/11/8/3/22; JA, Baptisms of Slaves, Hanover, 1817–1834, 1B/11/8/7/1; JA, Baptisms, Manchester, 1827–1833, 1B/11/8/10/3; JA, Baptisms, Portland, 1804–1826, 1B/11/8/12/1; and JA, Slave Baptisms, St. Ann, 1817–1826, 1B/11/8/2/3.
28. Lewis, *Journal of a West Indian Proprietor*, 80, 155–159, 253–261; Hope Masterton Waddell, *Twenty-nine Years in the West Indies and Central Africa, 1829-1858* (London: Nelson, 1863), 23; Henry de la Beche, *Notes on the Present Condition of the Negroes* (London: T. Cadell, 1825), 27; and Richard Bickell, *The West Indies as They Are; or a Real Picture of Slavery: But More Particularly as It Exists in the Island of Jamaica* (London: J. Hatchard and Son, 1825), 91.
29. George Wilson Bridges, *Annals of Jamaica*, vol. 2 (London: J. Murray, 1828), 430.
30. Robert Hibbert, *Facts Verified on Oath, in Contradiction of the Report of the Rev. Thomas Cooper, Concerning the General Condition of the Slaves in Jamaica* (London: John Murray, 1824), 3; T. Bunn, *An Essay on the Abolition of Slavery Throughout the British Dominions, Without Injury to the Master or His Property, With the Least Possible Injury to the Slave, Without Revolution, and Without Loss to the Revenue* (Frome, UK: Printed for the author by W.P. Penny, 1833), 11–13; and Legion, *A Second Letter from Legion to His Grace* (London: S. Bagster, 1833), 39.
31. George Jackson, *A Memoir of Rev. John Jenkins, Late a Wesleyan Missionary in the Island of Jamaica* (London: n.p., 1832), 87.

Further Reading

Bush, Barbara. "African Caribbean Slave Mothers and Children: Traumas of Dislocation and Enslavement Across the Atlantic World." *Caribbean Quarterly* 56, nos. 1–2 (2010): 69–94.

Campbell, Gwyn, Suzanne Miers, and Joseph C. Miller, eds. *Children in Slavery Through the Ages*. Athens: Ohio University Press, 2009.

Campbell, Gwyn, Suzanne Miers, and Joseph C. Miller, eds. *Child Slaves in the Modern World*. Athens: Ohio University Press, 2011.

Diptee, Audra. "Imperial Ideas, Colonial Realities: Enslaved Children in Jamaica, 1775–1834." In *Children in Colonial America*. Edited by James Martin, 48–60. New York: New York University Press, 2007.

"The Hardships of an Enslaved Childhood." In *Memories of the Enslaved: Voices from the Slave Narratives*. Edited by Spencer R. Crew, Lonnie G. Bunch III, and Clement A. Price, 37–72. Santa Barbara, CA: Praeger, 2015.

Jones, Cecily. "'If this be living I'd rather be dead:' Enslaved Youth, Agency and Resistance on an Eighteenth Century Jamaican Estate." *The History of the Family* 12, no. 2 (2007): 92–103.

King, Wilma. *Stolen Childhood: Slave Youth in Nineteenth-Century America*. Bloomington: Indiana University Press, 1998.

Schwartz, Marie Jenkins. *Born in Bondage: Growing Up Enslaved in the Antebellum South*. Cambridge, MA: Harvard University Press, 2000.

Thompson, Alvin O. "Enslaved Children in Berbice, with Special Reference to the Government Slaves, 1803–1831." In *In the Shadow of the Plantation: Caribbean History and Legacy*. Edited by Alvin O. Thompson, 163–195. Kingston, Jamaica: Ian Randle Publications, 2002.

Vasconcellos, Colleen A. "From Chattel to Breeding Wenches: Girlhood in a Jamaican Slave Community." In *Girlhood: A Global History*. Edited by Jennifer Hillman Helgren and Colleen A. Vasconcellos, 325–343. New Brunswick, NJ: Rutgers University Press, 2010.

Vasconcellos, Colleen A. *Slavery, Childhood, and Abolition in Jamaica, 1788–1838*. Athens: University of Georgia Press, 2015.

Zelizer, Viviana. *Pricing the Priceless Child: The Changing Social Value of Children*. 2nd edition. Princeton, NJ: Princeton University Press, 1994.

CHAPTER 7

A "TOMBOY" AND A "LADY"

Religion, Modernity, and Youth Culture in Twentieth-Century Zanzibar

CORRIE DECKER

OFTEN modern youth culture is associated with growing secularism, but religion remained a significant factor in youth cultures that emerged during the twentieth century, and it continues to do so in the twenty-first century. In many places around the world, religious ideals held singular importance for young people's understanding of themselves and their relationships with family members and friends. This is certainly the case in many Muslim societies. From debates over the role of girls' education in the late nineteenth century to the Arab Spring of the 2010s, issues related to gender and sexuality have been at the heart of cultural transformations among Muslim youth. The tensions between Islamic ideals and modernizing youth cultures came to a head during the early and middle decades of the twentieth century, a time when many Islamic territories gained independence from European colonialism, the United States became a superpower, and the push toward modernization permeated economic, political, social, and cultural debates across the globe. By the 1960s, the "sexual revolution" and the "women's liberation" movement brought earlier cultural shifts into sharp focus. Religion shaped young people's ideas about gender and sexuality as these topics moved into the realm of public discourse and political activism. These changes were earth-shattering to Muslims who practiced forms of seclusion or veiling and to any religious community who placed a high value on female virginity before marriage. Young Muslims grappled with their desire to embrace and create new cultural ideals around gender and sexuality, on the one hand, and their need to protect their reputations and those of their families, on the other.

One woman who reconciled these tensions was Muna, who came of age in the Zanzibar Islands of East Africa during the late 1950s and 1960s. At that time, the islands were governed by both an Omani sultanate established in the early nineteenth century and the British protectorate administration that ruled between 1890 and 1963. Young people like Muna balanced the enticement of new youth cultures introduced alongside European colonialism with Islamic community values. Muna reconciled these tensions by walking a fine line between adolescence and adulthood, femininity and masculinity, and respectability and mischievousness. She was a self-professed "tomboy" who resisted fulfilling the role of a proper Muslim "lady" as long as possible. If growing up meant abiding by religious codes that strictly controlled her behavior, then she would remain immature as long as possible. At the same time, Muna's desire to maintain her respectability and that of her family meant she could not remain a "tomboy" forever. Muna's story of coming of age was one of simultaneous precocity and arrested development, a tension that reveals the schisms between pervasive religious ideals and the changing attitudes of youth in late colonial Zanzibar, as in many other twentieth-century Muslim communities. Muna's girlhood also serves as a useful vector for exploring young Zanzibaris' relationships with parents, siblings, teachers, friends, and lovers and highlights how Muslim girls both upheld and subverted religious ideals in navigating the volatile path toward adulthood in Zanzibar. Muslim adolescents rewrote the rules on morality, sexuality, and gender to suit changing trends in youth culture even as they invented new ways to honor the religious mores of their parents and grandparents.[1]

Youth Culture at the Crossroads of Religious Expectations and Modern Influences

Modern youth often encountered religion initially through families, institutions, and authority figures—basically, as a set of rules. Religious authorities placed much emphasis on the proper rearing of children and their transition to young adulthood, marriage, and parenthood. The first modern schools were built by religious authorities long before governments took responsibility for the secular education of their citizens and subjects. At the same time, young people created social worlds of their own among age-mates at schools, churches, mosques, synagogues, and other institutions. Teenagers and young adults placed their own spin on religious messages about their development and maturation and adapted them to the political, social, or cultural ideals of their generations.

During the nineteenth and twentieth centuries, religious organizations emphasized the importance of recruiting young people to their particular cause and keeping them devoted to their faith. The establishment of the Young Men's Christian Association (YMCA) in London in 1844 and the Young Women's Christian Association (YWCA) the following decade revitalized young Britons' excitement over Christian social life. These organizations expanded to other parts of the world in the 1800s and 1900s, where local youth formed their own chapters of the YMCA and YWCA and launched other Christian youth programs modeled after them. Islamic organizations also sought to instill a sense of morality among young people both within their own communities and globally. The popularity of Muslim "brotherhoods" across the Islamic world over the past few centuries has facilitated young men's socialization and integration into networks based on trade, politics, and religious practice. In the nineteenth and twentieth centuries, Islamic modernists in Iran, Turkey, Egypt, India, and East and West Africa sought to implement educational reforms to prepare young people for a world being transformed rapidly by European imperialism and Westernization. Though the Young Men's Muslim Association (YMMA), established in Egypt in 1927, was the Islamic equivalent to the YMCA, it aimed to counter the influence of Christian missionaries. Egyptian scholars concerned about youth developed a specialized field of adolescent psychology after the Second World War. Historian Omnia El Shakry explains how one scholar concerned about young people's "extreme religiosity" attributed this phenomenon to "the conflicts youth experienced between self and society" during adolescence. Youth cultures across the nineteenth- and twentieth-century world continued to place a high value on religion.[2]

Young people were both the advocates and targets of global religious "civilizing missions" during the 1800s and 1900s. Christian missionary groups recruited young men and women to convert, colonize, and "civilize" other people around the world. Historically, European and American missions directed their efforts toward those most vulnerable and susceptible to their message—enslaved people, children and youth, women, and the poor.

In Africa, the arrival of Christian missionaries in the 1800s contributed to generational tensions, the emergence of new youth cultures, and moral campaigns to divert young people's attention away from "dangerous" customs and undesirable elements of Westernization. Young Africans gravitated to missions or churches where they formed their own social enclaves independent from their parents and grandparents. Upwardly mobile "modern" Girls and young women in Africa laid claim to new forms of Christian respectability in the 1920s and 1930s. Histories of youth, music, and popular culture in Africa also demonstrate how Christianity has been used to control young people's cultural expressions. In colonial Zimbabwe, missionaries suppressed the traditional musical cultures of youth and sought to replace them with European-style "tea parties" and "wedding celebrations." Catholic missionaries in the Belgian Congo resorted to Westerns and other popular films to recruit wayward youth into their churches. European churches in Africa that catered to White settler communities and their descendants encouraged segregated socialization and courtship. Young people engaged with these interventions selectively, taking advantage of those that came with new opportunities and ignoring or rejecting others that did not suit them.[3]

Globally, religious interventions often concentrated on young people's sexuality, and the sexual and social behaviors of unmarried girls and young women in particular. People practicing versions of Judaism, Christianity, and Islam shaped youth cultures by imprinting onto the bodies of girls the abstract values of honor and respectability in order to ensure female virginity before marriage. "Runaway daughters" in nineteenth-century Latin America had to negotiate between Catholic ideals of honor, their own or their lovers' romantic yearnings, and strict parental control. In some Jewish communities in the United States and elsewhere, girls brought shame to their families by merely touching a stranger of the opposite sex. The behavior of Muslim girls in the Middle East and North Africa also had the potential to either bring shame or uphold the honor of their families. Protecting and controlling female sexuality was a primary means to maintain moral order and enforce religious, cultural, or political norms, especially during times of conflict or upheaval.

Adolescents and young adults navigated conflicting and confusing messages about their religion and culture. As historians Mona Russell and Beth Baron have argued, modernist Muslims in Egypt encouraged girls and women to acquire more advanced secular and religious education and take on greater responsibilities as a wife, mother, *and* citizen amid the rise of Egyptian nationalism in the early twentieth century. Women's education and professional advancement was also a prominent feature of Islamic modernist movements in Iran, Turkey, India, North Africa, East Africa, and other parts of the Islamic world. For many young people, Islamic modernist ideas about gender raised more questions than it answered. Were young women expected to work outside the home? How would this conflict with their primary commitment to their families? What did this mean for modern masculinity? During the 1930s and 1940s, male students at the American University of Beirut in Lebanon expressed anxiety over tackling such difficult questions about changing gender roles in Muslim society. Historian Betty Anderson pointed out that while male students lauded the ideals of "modern" womanhood, they made derogatory remarks against their ambitious female counterparts, the actual modern women attending the university. Muslim youth contended with increasingly contradictory messages regarding gender and sexuality during the twentieth century.[4]

Debates about the role of religion in youth culture have not disappeared in the twenty-first century. There has been an explosion of research and popular writings about Muslim youth cultures in the 2000s. Sunaina Marr Maira's *Missing: Youth, Citizenship, and Empire After 9/11* (2009) examines the experiences of South Asian Muslim youth living in the United States who faced stigmatization after 9/11. Several recent works, such as Albana Dwonch's *Palestinian Youth Activism in the Internet Age* (2019), investigate the importance of social media in reshaping the political and religious cultures of youth. Richard A. Stevick's *Growing Up Amish* (2014) and Ibrahim

Abraham's *Evangelical Youth Culture* (2017) point to concerns about the fading impact of religion on youth in conservative Christian communities. Religious groups have published instructional books and self-reflective studies that discuss the difficulties of maintaining religious influence over youth or that offer advice about how to recruit young people into churches, mosques, and synagogues. While many people perceive these changes in youth culture as recent challenges that threaten the viability of their faith communities, religious leaders have expressed anxiety about the secularization of youth for at least the past two centuries.

Some youth cultures have helped to reconnect religious ideologies with politics locally and globally. The number of young Americans engaged in international missionary work has skyrocketed since 2000, and American churches send tens of thousands of young people on missions to Africa, Latin America, and Asia every year. Amy Stambach's *Faith in Schools* (2009) examines the growing influence of young American evangelical missionaries in pushing for abstinence-only sex education to prevent the spread of HIV in East Africa. American evangelicals have been at the forefront of changing religious youth cultures in Uganda, where President Museveni and others have preached anti-homosexuality to young Christians claiming this is an "un-African" practice imported from the West. Worried that they are losing their hold over youth cultures in the United States, many American religious groups have ramped up their international outreach in places where young people take religious norms around gender and sexuality more seriously.

Young people everywhere have been adept at balancing competing religious and cultural value systems with their own ambitions and desires. Austere theological prohibitions around sex and gender sought to guide young people into forms of adulthood contained within the heteronormative, procreative family. However, what young people were told to do, what they said they would do, and what they actual did often diverged quite drastically. When it came to gendered expectations and prohibitions against premarital sex or same-sex romance, the primary issue for many young people was not their actions per se, but whether or not these actions became known. The fear of exposure was at least as great if not greater than the fear of transgression. This was the case with regard to Islamic prohibitions against premarital sex among boys and girls in colonial Zanzibar. Young Zanzibaris certainly broke the rules, but they went to great lengths to avoid being caught.

A Young Woman's Scandal in Nineteenth-Century Zanzibar

The Zanzibar Islands of East Africa became the center of a scandal in the late nineteenth century when the daughter of the sultan, Princess Salme, brought shame to her family when she ran off with her Christian German lover. The Zanzibar Islands were deeply connected to the broader Islamic world through trade and Arab colonialism long before they became part of the British Empire in 1890. The Omani Sultanate ruling the islands in Princess Salme's time instilled a strict regime of respectability governing the behavior of Muslim girls and young women, especially those in elite families. Born in 1844, Salme had a life of relative freedom compared with that afforded to most elite Muslim girls in Zanzibar. She became acquainted with the foreign diplomats and traders who worked with her father and her brothers, who ruled after their father died in 1856. Sometime in her late teens, Salme met a German merchant and, soon after, escaped to Germany where she married him and converted to Christianity. For many decades afterward, the ruling family refused to speak with her and cut off all financial support to which she had been entitled previously. To this day, Zanzibaris recount the story of Princess Salme as a warning to young girls about the dangers of damaging the *heshima* (respectability) of their families.

Rumor has it that Salme left secretly because she was pregnant, though she claimed it was because their "union would have been out of the question" in Zanzibar. In her memoirs about growing up an "Arabian Princess" in Zanzibar, which were first published in German in 1886, Salme wrote about her "happy attachment" to the "young German" in direct contrast to the "dark days of dissention and strife" in her family. She admitted that her "friendship" with her future husband "grew into deep mutual love" after she spied on his dinner parties from the roof of her house, which happened to overlook his rooftop. She does not explain how they got to know each other face to face without her family knowing.[5]

Princess Salme's account highlights two important ways in which religious ideals around gender and sexuality shaped youth culture in nineteenth-century Zanzibar. First, young elite women were expected to remain chaste and in seclusion, even when they had important public roles and unusual freedoms like Salme had. Second, girls and young women discovered ways to circumvent these rules and develop relationships of their own, often in secret. Young women acted on their own passions within and sometimes beyond the social and physical boundaries imposed on them. One hundred years after Princess Salme's scandal, Muna also disobeyed certain religious codes in order to carve out her own future, but she did so without overtly defying religious morality itself. She envisioned new opportunities for other girls and young women within her cohort and, as she grew older, recognized her influence over the emerging culture of the next generation of youth in East Africa. Many of the same religious ideals of gender prevalent in Salme's time shaped Muslim youth cultures in twentieth-century Zanzibar, but new youth cultures emerged with the introduction of Western schooling, new economic and professional opportunities under British colonialism, and the shift toward nationalism in the 1960s.

Muslim Youth Culture in Zanzibar After Salme

Young people growing up in colonial Zanzibar encountered contradictory messages. One the one hand, Omani elite culture was still the ideal that many young Muslim Zanzibaris emulated; on the other hand, young people were drawn to global fashions and more liberal sexual mores they learned about from talking to schoolmates, reading magazines, and going to the movies. More and more, the regime of respectability imposed by ruling Arab elites seemed out of touch with modern youth culture in Zanzibar, but young people were never fully free from the control of parents, religious leaders, and schoolteachers.

Zanzibar Town was a small town divided between the wealthy Stone Town, the seat of the Omani Sultanate and the British colonial administration, on the one side, and the ever-sprawling "Other Side" of town called Ng'ambo, separated physically from Stone Town by a creek until the 1950s. The division between Stone Town and Ng'ambo represented ethnic and class cleavages, with Ng'ambo referred to as the poorer, "African" side of town and Stone Town the area where Arab and South Asian elites lived. Children and youth were highly visible in the streets and public spaces of both areas of town and often stayed outside playing until late in the evening. Many boys and girls underwent some form of an initiation rite marking their transition to young adulthood. Female initiation (*ukungwi*) involved one-on-one instruction and, for some, participation in communal dances known as *unyago*. Depending on their social position and economic means, initiated girls were expected to prepare for marriage or remain secluded from public view until marriage—or both. Male initiation, called *jando*, usually centered around circumcision and sometimes also included participation in communal dances and other ceremonies. Young men usually waited until they were financially stable to marry. These practices were more common in the early twentieth century than in the time of Muna's childhood, and participation in at least the communal initiation ceremonies had faded by the 1950s. Some versions of the one-on-one instruction for girls still occurred into the twenty-first century.

Young people in Zanzibar Town would split their days between religious study, schoolwork, play, and time with family. Most boys and girls living in Stone Town attended Quranic schools for religious instruction and government or private schools for academic instruction. The colonial government schools also included lessons in Islamic studies. People of all ages went with their families to public Maulidi celebrations of the Prophet Muhammad's birthday or to Eid al-Fitr ceremonies to mark the end of Ramadan.

Youth cultures were different in the rural areas of the islands, where the routines of agricultural life took precedence over socialization with age-mates. From an early age, boys and girls worked with their parents on spice plantations, in the markets, or at home. Some children received Quranic education at their local mosque or at the home of a teacher living in their neighborhood. Children sometimes did chores for their Quranic teachers to help offset the cost of their education. In hard times, like those many experienced during the 1940s and 1950s, fathers sent their children to work as domestic servants in the homes of relatives, bosses, or acquaintances. Desperate parents handed their children over to employers based in Zanzibar Town or Wete in Pemba, cities far away from their villages. Others went against established Islamic norms to marry off their daughters before they reached puberty so that they could collect the bridewealth or dower. Whether or not she had started menstruating, a girl sent to live with her husband (or future husband) was expected to perform domestic labor in her new home under the supervision of her mother-in-law. Technically, husbands were not to consummate marriages with wives until they reached puberty, but people did not monitor these relationships closely. Many boys from the villages also did domestic work for wealthier families, though they received small salaries for their labor. Some sought out opportunities to attend the government schools, while others looked for part-time jobs in town to either help families back home or accrue cash to start their own households.

There was a vibrant public life for young people in the urban areas of the islands. In Zanzibar Town, some children and youth sold cheap food or other goods in the open markets, girls often accompanying their mothers or aunts. Boys had more freedoms than girls. Many boys spent their days and nights playing cards (sometimes gambling), playing marbles, going swimming, stealing, or sneaking off to drink alcohol. Older boys and young men also went to the movies, played football (soccer), went dancing at nightclubs, and, if you believe the colonial reports, frequented brothels. Starting in the 1910s, British colonial officials became concerned about the "town boys" wreaking havoc in the streets of Zanzibar Town. While there were certainly homeless or food-insecure children of poor families who came to town in search of opportunities, many of the children whom officials assumed lived on the streets had homes in or near town. After the British colonial administration passed the Compulsory Education Act of 1921, boys found roaming about Stone Town were arrested and sent to school. Other boys around town who were excluded from the schools for ethnic, geographic, or financial reasons found themselves in juvenile courts facing charges of theft, trespassing, or other petty crimes.

Girls in Zanzibar Town also helped to shape urban youth culture, but daily life changed drastically as they approached the age of puberty. While younger girls played in the streets with boys, post-pubescent "respectable" girls and unmarried young women did not mingle publicly with boys or men other than their male relatives. One Zanzibari woman recalled that she could play freely with anyone in the neighborhood as a small girl because everyone was considered "a brother or sister." Once she reached puberty, though, she had to stay indoors and do chores like cooking, washing clothes, and looking after younger siblings, while the boys "could go out and do what they wanted."[6] The practice of separating girls from boys at puberty was common across the Islamic world. Huda Shaarawi, who grew up in Egypt in the 1880s and 1890s, spent most of her childhood playing with boys from her neighborhood until about the age of eleven when she was told to stay only with girls and women. Shaarawi wrote, "Being separated from the companions of my childhood was a painful experience. Their ways left a mark on me."[7] Muslim girls had to think more seriously about their future as wives and mothers as they approached puberty.

Young Zanzibaris were serious about preparing for marriage. In Zanzibar, first marriages were usually arranged between parents and interested suitors, but young people of the twentieth century increasingly pressured their parents to accept their chosen partners. Elders ensured that the husband was the wife's equal in social status, thus fulfilling the Islamic principle of *kafā'a*. Grooms typically offered gifts to the bride's family and paid a dower to the bride herself. Though the dower technically belonged to the bride, fathers or other male guardians often claimed this gift as a sort of insurance against divorce.[8] In cities like Istanbul, the payment of the dower, also known as dowry or *mehr*, became less important after 1900, when young Muslims began to make their own decisions about marriage.[9] As occurred in Turkey and Egypt, the guardian or "guarantor" who attested to the legality of the marriage took on greater importance in Zanzibar during the twentieth century.[10] The guardian not only ensured that the marriage was an appropriate match approved by the bride's male elders but also that the bride was physically and mentally prepared for marriage. In East Africa and elsewhere, desperate young couples who did not have the consent of the bride's parents to marry appealed to a qadi (Islamic judge) to stand in for the bride's male guardian.

New age-of-consent laws across the world generated much debate about when young people should get married during the late nineteenth and twentieth centuries. In many regions of the Middle East, South Asia, and Africa, the average ages of marriage for brides rose throughout the course of the twentieth century. Both shari'a and secular legal codes introduced new laws or reinforced older ones that girls either had to reach a certain chronological age or attain puberty before marriage or before the consummation of a marriage. At the same time, young men and women were choosing to delay marriage in order to pursue higher education or professional opportunities. In Istanbul, the average age of brides at first marriage rose from around twenty in 1905 to about twenty-three by the late 1930s. In Turkey, after the turn of the century many people considered only mature, responsible women suitable for wifehood and motherhood, giving young women greater influence over decisions about their marriages.[11] Similarly, many Zanzibari women who were among the first generations of girls to attend Western-style schools starting in the late 1920s dreamed of becoming teachers or nurses before becoming wives and mothers.

Even where early marriage was common, vibrant female youth cultures thrived. Historian Ruby Lal argues for a deeper understanding of girlhood subjectivity in nineteenth-century India, where the "child marriage" debate presumed that Hindu girls were devoid of a childhood or youth. She foregrounds the concept of "playfulness" in order to locate girls' "social and sexual interaction without asserting authority" and to recognize "forms of self-expression and literary creativity that are not dependent on masculinist definitions of fulfillment."[12] Imperialist and Islamophobic narratives criticizing non-Western practices of "child marriage" fail to see how young people viewed religious ideals as integral to their cultures and subcultures rather than as the impositions of oppressive religious authorities. Like their Indian counterparts, girls and young women in Zanzibar created their own social worlds both within and outside religious and cultural institutions. Despite strict sex segregation and tendencies toward early marriage, girls found ways to flirt, date, and arrange marriages clandestinely, all the while maintaining their respectability and upholding the honorable reputations of their families. Islam has been and still is a foundational feature of Zanzibari society. Girls, boys, young women, and young men understood their relationships and social experiences through the gendered religious values of respectability and honor. At the same time, they did not adhere to static definitions of respectability, and they often challenged, subverted, or ignored religious codes of conduct.

Youth Culture in Muna's World

Born in 1943 and married in December 1963, the same month that Zanzibar became independent from Britain, Muna came of age among a generation of young revolutionaries and nationalists. Her story demonstrates poignantly how changes in religion and politics shaped youth culture in late colonial Zanzibar, and how young people of this era recognized their valuable role in redefining the culture of the islands.

Muna grew up in Ng'ambo, the "Other Side" of Zanzibar Town. Her parents were upwardly mobile Zanzibaris who sometimes had to contend with ethnic and class discrimination. They believed in protecting their good reputation, but they were willing to break rules they deemed unjust. From an early age, Muna learned that she did not fit in; she was a "tomboy." While other girls wore dresses, she wore trousers and shorts to the chagrin of her status-conscious neighbors. She dreamed of going to school like her brothers, but her father at first would not allow it. Eventually, with the help of her aunt, one of the first Zanzibari women to attend college, Muna convinced her father to send her to school. By her own admission, she was an "incorrigible" student at the Ng'ambo Girls' Primary School. Schoolgirls were generally quiet and obedient, but Muna made fun of teachers, acted out in class, and cheated to get out of doing the homework she did not like. The lessons at the girls' school were meant to mold girls into good Muslim wives and mothers. Many girls loved domestic science subjects, even if they—like Muna—envisioned their adult selves working outside the home.[13]

Zanzibari girls cared a lot about their appearance; thus, growing up was awkward for girls like Muna who did not act or look like the other girls in their classes. In Stone Town, the wealthy section of Zanzibar Town where Muna attended secondary school, clothing and jewelry were markers of social class. Given that "respectable" girls past the age of puberty covered themselves fully while in public, the girls' school was one of the only public places where girls could show off their wealth and sense of fashion to their peers. That is, until the mid-1940s when an incident of jewelry theft at the girls' secondary school prompted authorities to introduce a school uniform.[14] Fortunately for Muna, whose family did not have the means to buy her expensive clothing and jewelry, the school uniform was introduced before she entered the school. Still, she hated the school uniform, which was a blouse and skirt, because she could never look "smart" in it like the girls with more typically feminine physiques. She was older than most of her classmates because she started school at the age of eight, two or three years after others first enrolled. She was also naturally tall, the tallest girl in class. "All bones, tall, and no meat, no flesh at all," she lamented, "nobody could tell whether I was a girl or boy." Even after puberty she remained tall and thin and thus looked different from her "buxom" classmates. Outside the school, however, Muna blended in with the other girls. When they ventured outside, post-pubescent girls maintained respectability by wearing a headscarf (hijab) and long robe, called a *buibui*. The *buibui* became a fashionable status symbol among young urban women who grew up in the 1920s. Muna and her classmates wore the *buibui* over their school uniforms while traveling between home and school. "When you went outdoors from home and school," she explained, "you were properly covered like a Muslim young lady irrespective of whether you were a tomboy like me."

Often the class clown, Muna made friends in school despite her unusual appearance and subversion of gender norms. Whenever they dramatized Arabic lessons in class, she "was always the boy or the man." She would dress up in the boys' clothes while her classmates "would put on the high heels and . . . dresses" to look like their teachers. She would strut around and in a deep voice recite the Arabic sentences they learned for male speakers, "I am the father" or "I am working." She played the same roles in English class dramas. Given that girls played both female and male roles in the school dramatizations, it is likely that Muna was not the only girl who enjoyed dressing up as a man. Gender play offered "practice" in heteronormative family relations while also allowing schoolgirls to make fun of stereotypes about gender and age.

Muslim girls from big families developed close relationships with both brothers and sisters. For the first ten years of her life, Muna was the only girl among six kids in the family. She idolized her big brothers, the oldest of whom was six years older. At home, she liked to play school with them, and she always made them pretend to be the students while she acted as the teacher. Later, they switched roles as her brothers helped Muna with her "serious studies" in school. They tutored her in preparation for exams and told her about life in college. She did so well on school exams that she skipped two grades (Standard IV and Standard VIII). Muna said she was smarter than the other girls in her class because she was a bit older than them, but she had also learned a lot at home. Her brothers were her role models, and Muna never imagined herself becoming a woman who spent her days grinding millet, cooking, or washing clothes. For her and many other girls, academic lessons offered respite from these "hateful" domestic responsibilities.

Schooling also offered a chance to make new friends with girls of similar ages. Muna and her classmates would laugh together at the pictures in textbooks and play jokes like hiding the eraser from their teacher. While in primary school, they also became friends with the young, female teachers and teachers-in-training who did their practice teaching at Ng'ambo school. They would offer food or gifts to student teachers so that they would become their "very personal friends." Most of the teachers-in-training were teenagers, some only a few years older than the girls in primary school. At that time, teachers were recruited for training after Standard VII (usually between the ages of fourteen and sixteen), though by the time Muna entered the Teacher Training course, most of them had finished Form IV and were around age eighteen. Some of the regular class teachers were teenagers as well and most were very young. In colonial Zanzibar, all unmarried girls and women beyond puberty were in a sense, "teenagers." The Swahili term *mwari*, which means a pubescent girl who has reached puberty but who has not yet married, was used interchangeably to mean "adolescent girl" and "unmarried woman." Older students and younger teachers bonded over the fact that they were both *wari* (pl. of *mwari*) as well as the fact that they were among the first generations of girls to receive a Western education in Zanzibar.

Whether or not they attended school, Zanzibari girls had to navigate the fine line between maintaining respectability and pursuing their romantic interests. Once they reached puberty, girls' families took on the enormous responsibility of protecting their daughters' *heshima* (honor or respectability) by preserving her virginity before marriage. Maintaining a daughter's *heshima*, by extension, preserved the honor of the family and, especially, of the girl's father. Muna discovered her own ways to circumvent the rules of *heshima*. She admitted, "I was all crazy with this idea of having a boyfriend and running away properly dressed in this *buibui* and ending up on some beach somewhere." In her fantasy and, it turned out, her reality, the *buibui* gave her the freedom to sneak off with her lover without being spotted. Or so she thought; her brothers soon discovered her secret. Often, friends and siblings were well aware of such transgressions, and Muna was by no means the only schoolgirl to behave badly. Many other girls got into trouble for reading "lurid magazines" and skipping class to meet up with boys or men.[15] Though pubescent girls were not allowed to mingle with boys in public, girls and boys—and women and men, for that matter—knew how to create the illusion of *heshima* while fulfilling illicit desires.

Young romances developed in populated public spaces as well as on secluded beaches. Schools, public religious festivals, and other social gatherings offered chances for subtle flirtations, the passing of love notes, and brief exchanges under the cover of a crowd. Young love also blossomed in Zanzibar's movie theaters. Historian Laura Fair explains:

> Cinema seating was assigned, and occasionally, a young couple would be so bold as to purchase their tickets ahead of time, thus assuring adjacent seats even if they arrived

separately. One trick was for a young man to make an advanced booking for himself, his girlfriend, and her friends. When she approached the ticket window, the agent, who was well aware of the plan, could let her know which seat to take to sit closest to her man. Sitting in the dark during a film was as intimate as most youngsters would ever get with a member of the opposite sex prior to marriage. Part of the thrill of such a romance was the risk (despite one's own fervent hope to the contrary) of being caught.[16]

Though people took extreme measures to conceal forbidden relationships, young romances were often open secrets. Even when these relationships were obvious to the people around them—friends, siblings, and ticket agents—they were not spoken about publicly. "In those days it was the greatest taboo to have a boyfriend," Muna explained, "so ... nobody told anybody else." In many ways, the exposure of the secret was more damaging to a family's *heshima* than the secret itself. The worst way the secret could become public was if the girl became pregnant. Pregnancy was proof that she had become "spoilt" (Sw. -*haribikwa*) or had lost her virginity before marriage. This was one of the most serious marks of shame damaging the reputation of a girl's family as it meant the parents did not do their part to protect their unmarried daughter.

When Muna's brothers found out about her affair, they told her parents. She was in love with a man her father knew well; in fact, he was her father's cousin by marriage. When he learned about the relationship, Muna's father called the man over and said to him, "*Bwana* [Sir], you be careful with my girl, eh. I don't want you to get her into trouble." That was enough to scare him into ending things, but Muna threatened to go out with someone else unless he agreed to marry her. They got married a couple of years later, right after she earned her teaching certificate.

Muna was clearly adept at the art of persuasion, but by the early 1960s young Zanzibaris were starting to assert their right to choose their own marriage partners. Not all parents would have been as understanding as Muna's, but parents did accept relationships in cases where they might have envisioned the match anyway. Most first marriages in colonial Zanzibar were arranged by the parents of the bride and groom, and extended family were fair game. Fatma Baraka, a Zanzibari woman a few years older than Muna, said, "if a boy wants to marry a girl, he must approach her parents first because he must not see her." It was "not possible" for a girl to love someone else, and she was supposed to feel lucky to get married. If she loved someone else, it was her "personal secret" that amounted to nothing else. Usually, the only way to pursue such an illegitimate relationship was to run away together, as Princess Salme had done in the 1860s. It was fortuitous that Muna fell in love with a man her family accepted as a good marriage partner for her. As long as the secret of their affair stayed within the family, they could plan the wedding without damage to Muna's or the family's honor.

Many Zanzibaris considered marriage the end of a girl's youth, the time at which she transitioned from a *mwari* into a *bibi* (Mrs.). Like other gendered expectations, Muna resisted the notion that marriage, or even motherhood, ended her youth.

She finished the teacher training course in 1962, got married the following year, and started teaching in the girls' secondary school. Much later, in 1978, she got a scholarship to attend Makerere University in Uganda. By that time, she was a married woman in her mid-thirties with six children. She had been teaching for about fifteen years. By every Islamic and cultural standard in Zanzibar, she was well beyond her youth. "In Swahili territory you were done with" by the age of 35, Muna joked, and "usually your husband takes on a second wife before you are that old." Yet it was not until she arrived at Makerere that she recognized herself as an adult woman. She realized then that she could no longer "play the tomboy.... There's a time when you have to accept that now ... you have girls to model for, so I went to the university a properly-behaved old teacher.... I had to act like a lady, middle-aged and all that." Perhaps the recognition that she was a role model for the next generation of girls or the responsibility of balancing marriage, motherhood, and a career yanked Muna abruptly out of her youth. Muna's sudden maturation in the late 1970s also reflects broader historical changes in Zanzibar's youth culture.

Muna's experiences of coming of age spanned the closing years of British colonialism, the violent Zanzibar Revolution of 1964 that overthrew the Omani Sultanate, and the first decade and a half of Tanzanian independence. On the one hand, Muna's maturation occurred rapidly. She recounted in horror how the revolution, which started on the night of January 11, 1964, began just days after she got married and moved in with her husband. "Everything went upside down," she said. This alone seemed to mark a sudden end to her cheerful youth. On the other hand, Muna's refusal to grow up, to become a "lady" and a "properly-behaved old teacher" until her mid-thirties, suggests she imagined a parallel between what she considered the arrested development of Zanzibar and that of her generation who came of age in uncertain times. She married, had children, and worked as a teacher during the same years that the Revolutionary Government came to power and Zanzibar joined the mainland (Tanganyika) to form the nation of Tanzania. By the time she attended Makerere University, Tanzania was starting to move away from its revolutionary-era socialist agenda.

The 1960s and 1970s were times of drastic changes in Zanzibari youth culture. Some young married and unmarried women traded in their *buibuis* for jeans and T-shirts. When the new government implemented co-education, girls and boys of all ages began socializing openly at school. Coed youth clubs and government-run camps also brought young women and men together in very public ways. New youth cultures challenged the Islamic ideals of respectability implemented by the Arab elite no longer in power. Some young women were afraid of these changes, while others embraced new professional and social opportunities. Fatma recalled being shocked to see "women wearing lipstick in offices." These changes were visceral. As Andrew Ivaska (2011) has shown for Dar es Salaam on the mainland, transformations in youth culture reflected the massive shift in politics where nationalism became the new morality.

ZANZIBAR'S YOUTH CULTURES OVER TIME

Looking at the one hundred years between the time of Princess Salme's coming of age to that of Muna's youth, several trends demonstrate the changing role of religion in Zanzibar's youth culture. Religious and cultural codes of conduct dictating the behavior of young people, especially girls and unmarried women, in the Arab elite families of Stone Town influenced the principles by which many Zanzibaris interpreted the respectability of youth. At the same time, these codes of conduct did not prevent young people from carving out their own ideas about gender, sexuality, and respectability. Salme both abided by these rules and found ways around them to pursue her "friendship" with her future husband. Colonial sex-segregated schooling, introduced to girls in Stone Town in the late 1920s and expanded across the islands over the following three decades, created new venues for playing with gender and gender roles even while the curriculum sought to train girls to become "good wives and wise mothers."[17] Girls and young women pursued academic and professional interests beyond the domestic training designed to ensure the girls' *heshima*. By the early 1960s, many young Zanzibari women were training to become teachers and nurses and some aspired to work in government offices or private companies. Those with the family support to do so pursued higher education or training before getting married and having children, and many continued to work while married. The realm of possibility was already expanding for girls and young women before the Revolutionary Government began requiring young people to join the ruling party's youth groups and participate in public life after independence.

The lives of boys and young men also adapted to the spread of Western education and the eventual rise of nationalism. Many families sent their boys to government schools so that they could qualify for a government job amid shrinking opportunities in other areas of the Zanzibari economy. Boys had always been economic assets, for example, as laborers on clove plantations working alongside their parents, but now they had a greater responsibility to reach their potential as earners of more lucrative government salaries. On rare occasions, boys and girls found ways to meet and socialize with youth of the opposite sex outside of home and school in the early twentieth century, but their life choices were largely dictated by parents and grandparents. Boys and young men discovered new avenues for work and coed socialization by the 1950s and early 1960s. Movie theaters, nightclubs, and public festivals presented fleeting chances to flirt with girls, but boys and young men also orchestrated elaborate schemes for meeting young lovers—both male and female. After the revolution, some boys and young men asserted their newfound independence by arranging their own marriages or dating openly while others engaged in campaigns to assert moralistic codes over girls and young women whose actions appeared to threaten their positions in Zanzibar's old and new patriarchies.

By the time of the Zanzibar Revolution, Islam was no longer the only, or even the primary, factor in shaping youth culture. Some people attribute this shift to the "time of politics" (*wakati wa siasa*), and others to Westernization or globalization, but the apparent fading of *heshima* meant that some young people felt less obliged to keep their affairs secret or distance themselves from youth of the opposite sex in public. Since the late 1990s, there has been a reversal in this trend with an "Islamic revival" among young Zanzibaris who are reshaping the dynamic between religion, politics, and social behavior.[18] The *buibui* and the veil have come back in fashion among girls and young women. Religion is not merely a set of values that adults impose on young people; to young Zanzibaris, religion has also been a tool for reinventing their own cultures.

The 1960s appeared to usher in dramatic changes to Zanzibar's youth culture, but young people like Salme and Muna had already been pushing the boundaries of "respectable" behavior long before this time. It was not youth culture that transformed so much as the public acknowledgment of youth culture. After the revolution, parents and elders were forced to face young people's illicit romantic attachments, refusals to embrace gender norms, and the realization of other forbidden fantasies. For the first time, youth culture was out in the open.

Understanding the role of religion in modern youth culture requires a deep engagement with young people's personal experiences as well as the discourses that sought to circumscribe young people's actions. Muna's story says so much more than the archival record can about how she and her peers navigated the expectations for Muslim girls in colonial Zanzibar. Muna both yielded to and resisted the pressures placed on her. Even as a young person, she felt in charge of her life. She persuaded her father to first send her to school, she played the role of the head of household in the dramatizations, she pretended to be a teacher to her older brothers at home, and she made the decision to get married to her sweetheart. She used the word "tomboy" to describe herself in her youth not merely to convey her androgynous appearance, but to articulate her sense of power over herself. In the gendered language of Islamic respectability in Zanzibar, she expressed her sense of self-possession by claiming more senior positions than she occupied within the existing hierarchies of gender, age, and education—the father, the teacher, and the one who arranged her own marriage. Muna explained, "Boys were very careful whom they married, you didn't just get married to anyone. When they came to ask for your hand . . ., they knew what girl they're marrying." "You see I sit here smoking," Muna said with a smile directed toward her husband. "He doesn't like it. . . . He comes saying, 'Hey, since 9, this is your third one.' But somebody has emptied it. He comes through and I've done six." Muna eventually grew into a respectable "lady," but she never lost the "incorrigible" spirit of her youth. She never stopped being a "tomboy."

Notes

1. Muna (pseudonym), interview with the author, Zanzibar Town, January 27, 2005.
2. Mansoor Moaddel, *Islamic Modernism, Nationalism, and Fundamentalism: Episode and Discourse* (Chicago: University of Chicago Press, 2005), 210; Omnia El Shakry, *The Arabic*

Freud: Psychoanalysis and Islam in Modern Egypt (Princeton, NJ: Princeton University Press, 2017), 80.
3. Mhoze Chikowero, *African Music, Power, and Being in Colonial Zimbabwe* (Bloomington: Indiana University Press, 2015), 100; Ch. Didier Gondola, *Tropical Cowboys: Westerns, Violence, and Masculinity in Kinshasa* (Bloomington: Indiana University Press, 2016), 13.
4. Beth Baron, *Egypt as a Woman: Nationalism, Gender, and Politics* (Berkeley: University of California Press, 2007); Mona Russell, *Creating the New Egyptian Woman: Consumerism, Education, and National Identity, 1863–1922* (New York: Palgrave Macmillan, 2004); Betty S. Anderson, *The American University of Beirut: Arab Nationalism and Liberal Education* (Austin: University of Texas Press, 2011), 101–104.
5. Emily Ruete (Sayyida Salme), *Memoirs of an Arabian Princess*. Translated by Lionel Strachey. New York: Doubleday, Page and Co., 1907, University of Pennsylvania Digital Archive, A Celebration of Women Writers, http://digital.library.upenn.edu/women/ruete/arabian/arabian.html#XIX, accessed August 1, 2019.
6. Arafat Salim Mzee, interview with author, Zanzibar Town, July 14, 2012.
7. Huda Shaarawi, *Harem Years: The Memoirs of an Egyptian Feminist, 1879–1947*, trans., ed., and intro. Margot Badran (New York: The Feminist Press at the City University of New York, 1987), 52.
8. Elke E. Stockreiter, *Islamic Law, Gender, and Social Change in Post-Abolition Zanzibar* (New York: Cambridge University Press, 2015).
9. Alan Duben and Cem Behar, *Istanbul Households: Marriage, Family and Fertility, 1880–1940* (New York: Cambridge University Press, 1991), 112–113.
10. Amira El Azhary Sonbol, "Adults and Minors in Ottoman *Shari'a* Courts and Modern Law," in *Women, the Family, and Divorce Laws in Islamic History*, ed. Sonbol (Syracuse, NY: Syracuse University Press, 1996), 250.
11. Duben and Behar, *Istanbul Households*, 122–127.
12. Ruby Lal, *Coming of Age in Nineteenth-Century India: The Girl-Child and the Art of Playfulness* (New York: Cambridge University Press, 2013), 39.
13. Unless otherwise noted, this section is drawn from the following interviews with the author in Zanzibar Town: Muna (pseudonym), January 27, 2005; Mama Asha (pseudonym), December 13, 2004; Arafat Salim Mzee, July 14, 2012; Inaya H. Yahya, February 8, 2005; and Fatma Baraka, December 20, 2008.
14. Zanzibar National Archives (ZNA) AD 21/3, English translation of article titled, "Bangles Lost in the Arab Girls' School," in the *Zanzibari, Gazeti la Kiswahili*, November 15, 1943.
15. United Kingdom National Archives (UKNA) 850/42/2, Immorality Case, Zanzibar, 1934; ZNA AD 21/8 Secondary School Pupils, 1960–1961.
16. Laura Fair, *Reel Pleasures: Cinema Audiences and Entrepreneurs in Twentieth-Century Urban Tanzania* (Athens: Ohio University Press, 2018), 133.
17. ZNA BA 5/3, Education Department Annual Report for 1928, 26.
18. Simon Turner, "'These Young Men Show No Respect for Local Customs'—Globalisation and Islamic Revival in Zanzibar," *Journal of Religion in Africa* 39, Fasc. 3 (2009), 237–261.

Further Reading

Abraham, Ibrahim. *Evangelical Youth Culture: Alternative Music and Extreme Sports Subcultures*. London: Bloomsbury Academic Press, 2017.

Bastian, Misty L. "Young Converts: Christian Missions, Gender and Youth in Onitsha, Nigeria 1880–1929," *Anthropological Quarterly* 73, no. 3 (2000) 145–158.

Decker, Corrie. *Mobilizing Zanzibari Women: The Struggle for Respectability and Self-Reliance in Colonial East Africa*. New York: Palgrave Macmillan, 2014.

Duff, Sarah. *Changing Childhoods in the Cape Colony: Dutch Reformed Church Evangelicalism and Colonial Childhood, 1860–1895*. New York: Palgrave Macmillan, 2015.

Dwonch, Albana S. *Palestinian Youth Activism in the Internet Age: Online and Offline Social Networks After the Arab Spring*. London: Bloomsbury Academic, 2019.

Fair, Laura. *Pastimes and Politics: Culture, Community, and Identity in Post-Abolition Urban Zanzibar, 1890–1945*. Athens: Ohio University Press, 2001.

Ivaska, Andrew. *Cultured States: Youth, Gender, and Modern Style in 1960s Dar es Salaam*. Durham, NC: Duke University Press, 2011.

Lal, Ruby. *Coming of Age in Nineteenth-Century India: The Girl-Child and the Art of Playfulness*. New York: Cambridge University Press, 2013.

Maira, Sunaina Marr. *Missing: Youth, Citizenship, and Empire after 9/11*. Durham, NC: Duke University Press, 2009.

Ruete, Emily (Sayyida Salme). *Memoirs of an Arabian Princess*. Translated by Lionel Strachey. New York: Doubleday, Page and Co., 1907, University of Pennsylvania Digital Archive, A Celebration of Women Writers, http://digital.library.upenn.edu/women/ruete/arabian/arabian.html#XIX.

Scott, Joan Wallach. *The Politics of the Veil* (Princeton, NJ: Princeton University Press, 2007).

Shaarawi, Huda. *Harem Years: The Memoirs of an Egyptian Feminist, 1879–1947.* Translated, edited, and introduced by Margot Badran. New York: The Feminist Press at the City University of New York, 1987.

Sloan, Kathryn A. *Runaway Daughters: Seduction, Elopement, and Honor in Nineteenth-Century Mexico*. Albuquerque, NM: University of New Mexico Press, 2008.

Stambach, Amy. *Faith in Schools: Religion, Education, and American Evangelicals in East Africa*. Palo Alto, CA: Stanford University Press, 2009.

Stevick, Richard A. *Growing Up Amish: The Rumspringa Years*. Second Edition. Baltimore: The Johns Hopkins University Press, 2014.

Stockreiter, Elke E. *Islamic Law, Gender and Social Change in Post-Abolition Zanzibar*. New York: Cambridge University Press, 2015.

CHAPTER 8

INDUSTRIALIZATION
Youth at Work

JAMES SCHMIDT

WHEN Professor Harold Hill arrived in River City in 1912, he quickly discovered a key to unlock the fears of the Iowa rubes he hoped to fleece. A recently erected pool hall would do the trick, for it conjured up visions of youth frittering away their chore time and their suppertime, too. Drawing upon notions of youth and work stretching far back in Western culture, the good doctor recited a piece of conventional wisdom, albeit in a more syncopated fashion than it was intoned from the Sunday pulpit: "the idle brain is the devil's playground." In this pleasure palace, youngsters would think of nothing more than getting the ball in the pocket, never mind household chores. Eventually, it would all lead down the road to slang, cigarettes, dancing, and "libertine men and scarlet women." The nadir of it all? Ragtime, race-tinged music "That'll grab your son, your daughter/With the arms of a jungle animal instinct! Mass-staria!"

  Prof. Hill, of course, was a product of nostalgia and imagination, cooked up by Iowan Meredith Willson, but Willson's imaginary bandleader captured key elements of youth culture about work. The author chose his time period well, for 1912 represents a moment of transition in the history of youth and work, a time when progressive reformers did worry about youth hanging out in pool halls and sent incorrigibles to industrial schools for doing so. Beyond specific concerns about illicit amusement, Willson's fictional account (*The Music Man*) centers our attention on a central problem in the history and historiography of youth culture. As child labor reformers succeeded in erecting a legal preserve where younger people could not labor, they created a conundrum. If young people were not supposed to work for wages but adults were, when and how did the transition occur? By the early twentieth century in the industrialized and industrializing worlds, the answer to that question appeared to lie along two paths: a period of regulated wage work for some, and more importantly, compulsory attendance at school for all. The latter of those solutions created problems of its own, for it fostered an increasingly separate youth culture that could lead in the opposite direction of purposeful employment.

It would be only a mild overstatement to assert that the history of *youth* at work remains to be written. For decades, historians have followed, consciously or not, the lead of child labor reformers. Histories of youthful labor tend be subsumed into the general history of child labor reform, or into the history of labor. Thomas Dublin's classic account of the young women who labored in the Lowell mills considers "*women* at work," even though many of these "women" would have been legally prevented from working there a century later. Accounts of child labor usually take their subject to be "the child," even if some attention is paid to older young people. Some of the best accounts of youthful labor come from the history of slavery. Marie Jenkins Schwarz, for instance, pays careful attention to stages of life and work. Simple keyword searching in *The Journal of the History of Childhood and Youth* confirms that these trends continue. As of summer 2019, "child labor" produces eighty-three results, while "youth labor" produces one, in an article about socializing young people in revolutionary-era Vietnam. "Young workers" yields fifteen, most in book reviews and articles that concern "child labor."[1]

The complex relationships embedded in the youth culture of work during the modern era will be examined. The history of youthful work looks different if we focus on people who are coming of age and entering the world of work, even if they might be defined as "children" by labor law. Since the beginning of the industrial era, young people have gained employment on their own terms, both to assist family economies and to gain independence from those households. Learning to work and earning a wage became markers of adulthood, and young people across the industrializing world shaped labor markets and workplaces by their participation. As reformers pushed the legal age of labor upward, they came into conflict with young people's economic activities. At the same time, as education, play, and consumption became signs of childhood, older people worried about whether young people would enter a life of economic contribution. Ironically, reformers moved both to prevent young people from working and to force them to labor in institutional settings such as industrial schools. This legacy has persisted into the twentieth and twenty-first centuries as young people continue to face a culture that delegitimizes their economic activities yet expects them to prepare for usefulness in the future.

These ideas will be explored in three areas. First, the focus will be on the early nineteenth century, pairing a brief look at early wage work and child labor reform in Europe and America with a closer examination of the experience of working girls in Lowell, Massachusetts. *The Lowell Offering*, a classic source, provides an avenue to explore how young workers in the industrializing Northeastern United States embraced producer values centered on the dignity of labor. Theirs was a youth culture of work not yet fully separated from that of the working class itself. Second, the late nineteenth and early twentieth centuries will be addressed. It will survey the successful efforts to restrain and then delegitimize wage work for younger people with a more in-depth examination of youthful work in industrial and reform institutions. The actions that landed youth in this system, their activities inside the walls, and their adventures after leaving the institution reveal a strain of youth culture that did not fully accept the rationalized toil offered by those who founded and ran industrial and reform schools. Finally, the youth culture of work in recent years will be explored briefly. Here, the main focus will be on the United Nations. On the one hand, the UN has provided a center of child labor reform; on the other, *Voices of Youth*, a website associated with the United Nations Children's Emergency Relief Fund (UNICEF) shows how contemporary youth across the globe interact with the world of work. Their voices leave a record of youthful work culture in the postindustrial West and the industrializing Global South.

It is customary in treatments of child labor to note that children have always worked. This rudimentary point is true to a degree. Certainly, we do not mean that children or youth in elite households work, in the past or in the present. At the other end of the spectrum, it seems almost redundant to argue that young people in bound labor relationships worked. What is usually meant is that young people came of age in productive households. In Europe and Euro-America before industrialization, large majorities of the population lived in agrarian households, and young people did chores from at least age seven. Boys eventually took on more work in the fields, and girls customarily handled dairy operations. Before textile industrialization, girls also learned to spin, and possibly weave, from an early age. Sewing, cooking, and other customary household labor took them through marriage into adulthood. Beyond the domestic hearth, boys and young men served in bound apprenticeships, learning a craft as they grew. Girls and young women might work in domestic service, or in nascent industries such as cottons, linens, and woolens. By the eighteenth century, a particularly adventurous and highly dangerous avenue for young men lay in the whaling trade. These occupations frequently involved bound or semi-bound labor, and the largest portion of working youth toiled in slavery. What made most of this labor different from what followed is that it occurred in a household, even if that household was a slave household. Wage work did occur, but the cash nexus awaited full-scale industrialization.

These avenues of employment brought youth into contact with larger cultures of work, but they did not establish a youth culture of work, save in areas such as whaling or craft apprenticeship. In the early modern era, at least in the West, the Christian ideal prescribed work as a Christian duty and idleness a sin. Often called the Protestant Ethic after Max Weber's famous appellation, these ideas predated the Reformation-era sects that would ensconce them in the Western psyche. During the fourteenth century, Geoffrey Chaucer recited many of these ancient and medieval proverbs in *The Tale of Melibee*. Starting in the wake of the Black Death, the crown in England began to outlaw unemployment with increasingly harsh vagrancy laws. Still, the Puritan Reformation and its related Calvinistic sects on the Continent brought the duty of work to the forefront of Western culture, and young people were no exception.[2]

At the dawn of the industrial era, it would have been logical to predict that young people would work, that they would continue to do so, and that their labors would be seen as a cultural good. The first happened, but the second two did not, and historians have been trying to explain why that occurred ever since. Some have looked to economic change for both the rise and fall of child labor, although others have placed more emphasis on social and cultural factors. Viviana Zelizer famously drew a distinction between the economic value of children in working households and their emotional worth in middle-class abodes. Although such dichotomies overdraw the lines of demarcation, the household was the critical nexus. Wage work outside of domestic discipline grew rapidly during the eighteenth and early nineteenth centuries. As it increased, it generated plainly visible economic exploitation of young people in an era when humanitarian sentiment was on the rise.

The social and economic changes of the nineteenth century industrializing world combined with the cultural shifts wrought by child labor reform to create semiautonomous worlds of child and youth culture, especially as those cultures related to work. Increasingly, legal restriction and cultural opprobrium barred younger children from working for wages at all, or at most under controlled conditions. Youth, on the other hand, could enter the labor market, and the older they got, the more they were expected to do so. This divide created new worlds of youthful work culture, as young people took part in growing consumer markets for the goods and service their wages bought.

In Britain and the United States, the rapid rise of youthful wage work after 1800 produced a reform zeal that would have momentous consequences for young people. In Britain, this movement produced the first national child labor law, the 1833 Factory Act. It contained most of the fundamental principles of all child labor laws to come: a ban under a certain age; limitations in age brackets; certificates to work; regulations on time of labor, including a ban on night work; and provisions for schooling. In the United States, regulation proceeded in a piecemeal fashion because of its federal structure. Passed in the 1820s, the earliest regulation of child labor laws formed part of compulsory school attendance, but the first full-fledged child labor law appeared in Massachusetts in 1836. Over the next century, reformers across the West worked to tighten the reins on youthful employment and eventually secured fourteen as the age of banned wage work in most areas. Simultaneously, emancipation altered the lives of young people in slavery, though many would continue to work outside their households in apprenticeships or domestic service long after the onset of freedom.

Reformers did more than change the law of work for young people; they changed the culture. A barrage of editorials, pamphlets, and poetry popularized dreary government reports on child labor. In "The Cry of the Children" (1843), English poet Elizabeth Barrett Browning painted word pictures that would last for the next century.

Drawing on a recently published report, she voiced the agony of youthful work: "For, all day, we drag our burden tiring, / Through the coal-dark, underground— / Or, all day, we drive the wheels of iron / In the factories, round and round."[3] In the decades that followed, reformers turned the Protestant Ethic on its head. Although extreme, the baldest statement of the new culture came from U.S. child labor reformers. Speaking to an Alabama audience in 1902, Edgar Gardner Murphy asserted "amongst the most distinctive rights of the little child is the divine right to do nothing."[4] A decade later, fellow National Child Labor Committee founder Alexander McKelway penned a "Declaration of Dependence by the Children of America." By that time, a broader children's rights movement had emerged, and McKelway delineated how it applied to the world of work. In his voice, children called for

> freedom from toil for daily bread; the right to play and to dream; the right to the normal sleep of the night season; the right to an education, that we may have equality of opportunity for developing all that there is in us of mind and heart.

In all, McKelway's children declared themselves to be "helpless and dependent."[5]

By the turn of the twentieth century, reformer writers had bifurcated child labor from adult work. In forging a new definition of childhood, reformers left unclear where youth work and youth culture fit into the emerging social order of industrial capitalism. The scholarly literature on these developments has largely been the story of brave reformers battling against those who would prevent progressive change. In the United States at least, this theme runs though accounts of child labor reform from Walter Trattner and Jeremy Felt's classic work through Hugh Hindman's comprehensive history to John Fliter's recent account of federal child labor reform.

The historical and historiographical dichotomy between adult work and child labor ignored the realities of working households, but it particularly disregarded the experience of working youth, those who had passed the universally recognized age of "child labor" but who had achieved neither the age of legal majority nor the cultural markers of adulthood such as marriage. Often overlooked by historians, young workers created their own understandings of work, generating a youth culture of labor. An especially clear window into their world appears in *The Lowell Offering*, a publication produced by young female textile operatives in Lowell, Massachusetts, in the 1840s. By that time, cotton and woolen mills had sprung up throughout the Northeastern United States, and they had attracted a generation of young, unmarried women. These factory girls worked for several years before marriage, sending their wages home or keeping them to spend in the burgeoning markets created by the consumer revolution of the eighteenth century. In the classic study of their story, Thomas Dublin found that factory records revealed these women as mostly in their teens and twenties, and they were normatively in their teens when they left home. As such, they give voice to an important slice of youthful work culture at the dawn of the industrial era. Writing for themselves, these young workers offered a vision of youth employment different from the image being established by the Mrs. Brownings of the world. They drew upon the artisan republicanism of their era, an ideology that prized economic production, treasured personal independence, and extolled the dignity of labor.

It could be said that the *Offering's* authors downplayed the harsh conditions of a textile mill and overlooked the degradation of wage work, but an early issue of the magazine sketched "The Pleasures of Factory Life." The repetitiveness of the work left operatives free to contemplate weightier matters, and the steady wage helped them support infirm parents or fund the education of a sibling. The move to the mill broadened horizons by bringing them into contact with other girls from the region and with new ideas via the lyceum lecture. Their guardians in the mill towns looked out for their health, physical and moral, and the spinning rooms themselves were cheerfully decorated. Like so many such defenses of mill life, this one commenced as response to a visitor (real or hypothetical) who had decried the conditions she found. The onlooker had been, according to the author, "a lady whom fortune had placed above labor." The magazine's editors helpfully corrected her: "Indolence, or idleness, is not *above* labor, but *below* it."[6]

Another entry exemplified the choices young women faced in the labor market. An operative who signed as Matilda recounted how she and her friend, Ann, came to the mills. Having grown up together, both took jobs as schoolmistresses, one of the few other paths of employment open to young women. Still young, Matilda found that many of her scholars were her senior, but she won them over. Conversing with a cousin who worked in the mills, Matilda resolved to go herself, overcoming her own professed prejudices against factory girls. Arriving in Lowell proved to be a sound economic move. "I found my task much less perplexing as a factory girl, and my pay much more satisfactory," she recalled. She recruited her friend to join her, and they enjoyed the comparative advantage of a steady wage and access to the educational opportunities that Lowell afforded. After three years, Ann returned home to Maine, eventually to wed there. When Matilda visited for the nuptials, she had to pass as a schoolmarm to avoid the disdain of the locals. "By this title I passed off pretty well among the aristocrats of the place, and was often compelled to hear my avocation slandered and my associates misrepresented," she noted. "I could not endure such bondage, and resolved to return where I could enjoy a dearly-loved freedom."[7]

It might appear that the magazine defended the power of industrialists at the cost of workers, but it became a beacon for labor rights. Even before its appearance, the Lowell operatives had organized and gone on strike in 1836 after owners cut wages. Their rallying cry echoed the political rhetoric of the day, calling for liberty, abhorring slavery. The writers in *The Offering* built these themes into a broader vision of rights, for workers, for women, and for women workers. An 1841 piece presented the dream of "A New Society," a vision that would still stand as progressive in some respects today. The writer envisioned equal education and equal pay for women. Such equality would enable women to "maintain proper independence of character, and virtuous deportment." Drawing on Jacksonian labor language, she resolved that "as the laborer is worthy of his hire, the price for labor shall be sufficient to enable working-people to pay a proper attention to scientific and literary pursuits." Perhaps most radically, this new society would not attend to anyone who did not spend at least some time in manual labor or work for the public good. Reflecting the leveling tone of other Jacksonian radicals, a final resolution maintained "that industry, virtue and knowledge, (not wealth and titles) shall be the standard of respectability for this society."[8]

The factory girls at Lowell demonstrate a work culture of youth unlike the dark imagery presented by child labor reformers. As Jon Grinspan has shown in *The Virgin Vote*, young people in the nineteenth century led the way to the expansion of democracy. The Lowell operatives were no exception. Indeed, they were early adopters. They developed a political consciousness seen only rarely in U.S. history. That consciousness came from their understandings of work and from their interactions with the wider work culture of their day. Historians would do well to think more about such examples of young people and labor. Even if the Lowell operatives are exceptional, they show us that young people were not simple, exploited victims of industrial capitalism. Certainly, younger children followed the lead of their parents, but anyone who had worked for any amount of time developed their own ideas about what that work meant to themselves, and to the broader society. If we understand "culture" as the deep values that structure society, the Lowell operatives advanced their own culture about work, but by definition, it was one that drew on the work culture of the emergent industrial working class. In the antebellum period, child labor reformers and education activists were only beginning to split childhood from adulthood. The young women of Lowell proffered a work culture that prized regulated toil, dignified production, and mental advancement. The keen consciousness of Lowell faded as industrialization progressed, but young workers perforce interacted with the work cultures of their day.

As child labor reformers worried about young people working too hard in factories, they simultaneously fretted that they did not work hard enough in school. By the early nineteenth century, juvenile delinquency had been identified as a social problem in the United States and Europe. The solution lay down various paths, but a common palliative was the reform school. In the United States, the first of such institutions opened in 1825: the New York House of Refuge. By the turn of the twentieth century, most states had a range of reform schools, industrial schools, homes for wayward youth, and reformatories that incarcerated young people and trained them in the habits of industry. After the rise of the juvenile court movement, inmate populations rose. Until their demise in the later part of the twentieth century, industrial and reform schools represented another place where youth created youth culture about work. Inside these institutions, reformers sought to instill a middle-class ethic that prized steadiness and thrift but to punish the spontaneous enjoyment that dominated the youth culture of the streets.

Scholarly attention to industrial and reform schools has a long history and, of late, has witnessed a renaissance of sorts. Earlier works often focused on matters of class and social control; more recent accounts have turned attention to matters of race and gender. Karin Zipf's gripping investigation of Samarcand Manor in North Carolina shows how the reform school's attempts to mold young Southern women sparked arson and other forms of resistance.[9] The school morphed into a center for scientific racism, a theme also at the center of Miroslava Chávez-García's *States of Delinquency*. This resurgence in research on industrial and reform schools has deepened our understanding of such institutions, but necessarily the work experiences of young people in such places is not a focus. Looking at reform schools through the lens of labor history allows us to see young people coming of age and encountering cultural expectations about their future economic lives.

Young people landed in industrial schools for a variety of reasons and via a variety of routes. Some committed crimes, especially minor property crimes. Girls frequently found themselves committed for breaches of sexual propriety. As historians have shown, working families also used commitments to relieve economically stressed households. Many older inmates asked for continued commitments because they had nowhere else to turn. The greatest source of incarcerated youth in most states, however, was a general charge of incorrigibility, essentially an equivalent of the twenty-first-century diagnosis of "behavioral disorders." Many young people simply did not accept the disciplined path that ran through the school system into a life of self-directed toil. Colloquially, such people would be called "lazy," but laziness is the expression of a set of cultural values about work. Youth who chose not to follow the time and work discipline of industrial capitalism expressed ideas about work that reflected a preindustrial outlook. Work was not an end in itself; it was only a means to an end. When that end was achieved, work could cease. If that end could be achieved another way, say by stealing, then the outcome was the same. In this view, idleness was a virtue, not a vice, and one to be achieved as often as possible.

Life inside the walls meant training for capitalist work culture. Most institutions divided the day in half. One part of the population attended school in the morning and worked in the afternoon, while the other did the opposite. As in the outside school system, silence was the rule, and breaches of the rules were met with the ruler. Work in industrial schools broke into two kinds: institutional work and actual training. Although most schools employed considerable staff, inmate work also kept the place going from day to day. Such duties included meal preparation, laundering clothes, cleaning rooms, gardening, tending furnaces, and more elaborate projects such as decorating the facility. Industrial schools promoted industry not solely through daily housekeeping; they also served as carceral counterparts to vocational training centers on the outside. For the most part, job training in such places split along gendered lines. For girls, much training involved an extension of the household chores that kept the place running. Beyond domestic service, the most common type of training involved clerical work, but some schools trained girls for factory work. While girls' work followed along lines laid down by gender conventions, boys' work varied more. It is worth noting that because many institutions were sex segregated, boys performed far more "women's work" than they would have at home. Still, boys worked in shops that would fit them for common jobs on the outside. Such training was critical to their overall success, according to managers, because they needed a way to find stable employment once they achieved parole or came of age.

Although all of this might seem like prison labor, industrial schools tried to follow the educational trends of their day. A good example comes from the use of the "Sloyd" method at the New York House of Refuge. Sloyd teaching used woodworking to develop both handicraft skills and advanced cognitive functions. The House of Refuge adopted Sloyd as an entry point for new inmates, especially younger ones. Generally, they were assigned to the "Art and Sloyd" Department before graduating to more advanced skills. In this fashion, managers hoped to encourage both steady work habits and actual marketable abilities.

Whether it was dedicated handicraft training such as Sloyd or simple work that echoed apprenticeship, young people worked in ways that mirrored occupations in the outside world. By the early twentieth century, annual reports regularly featured cheerful pictures of young people hard at work in handicrafts. Many of these young workers would have been legally prevented from working in similar activities on the outside. Ironically, these activities created visual images that grated against those being generated by child labor reformers such as Lewis Hine. As the official photographer for the National Child Labor Committee, Hine traveled around the country capturing images of young people working in oppressive conditions. Some of his most famous photos portrayed girls at spindles in textile mills and dust-covered "breaker boys" picking coal. Hines' images could be read in multiple ways, however, for they also depicted young people, especially young men, coming of age in a world of labor that affirmed the producer values of their families and peers. The images that decorated the annual reports of industrial and reform schools augmented this latter reading. Managers and boards were keen to show that their institutions succeeded in creating reliable working-class laborers, an outcome best demonstrated by showing a group of boys cheerfully at work in a carpentry shop.

These cultural products of industrial schools illustrated the liminality of young people and the tensions inherent in youth culture at the turn of the twentieth century. At that moment in time, reform rhetoric had not yet settled on an upper limit for the "divine right to do nothing." Compulsory attendance laws continued to inch upward, as did child labor restriction. Yet the "adult" labor market easily absorbed anyone old enough to work. The massive immigrant stream, which contained millions of potential young workers, strained the lines between rhetoric and reality even more. As a group of mostly immigrant young people told Chicago reformer Helen Todd in 1913, factory work was more appealing than the oppressive authority of the schoolrooms where youthful workers legally belonged.

Images of toiling young people purported to show that industrial schools effectively trained their charges, but did they? Superintendents and their critics often argued vociferously about recidivism rates, and whether any "reform" transpired inside the walls. For girls, such debates focused more on character—sexual propriety—than on labor. Intelligence that a girl had been working in a saloon or seen associating with people in or near a red-light district was enough to call into question the effectiveness of an administration's approach. For boys, character issues, such as tobacco use, also played a part. Boys caught breaking and entering called into question just how much they had adopted capitalist values.

Much of the effectiveness of reform was judged by success in the labor market. States typically employed agents to seek spots for parolees and inmates who had completed their time. For girls, this frequently meant placement as domestic servants, but it could also mean factory work. Inmates from the Indiana Industrial School for Girls worked at a furniture factory in Indianapolis after receiving training in chair caning at the institution. More commonly, agents found spots for girls in private homes. Sometimes these positions worked out quite successfully, leading to a relatively smooth transition to adult life. In others, girls smoked, drank, and caroused their way back inside the walls. Such failures clashed with the values of those who kept watch in industrial schools, many of whom were members of women's clubs and other female reform organizations. By the turn of the twentieth century, middle-class women in these organizations voiced a feminist critique of industrial school training and parole placements. For them, girls on the inside should acquire the skills necessary for independent living on the outside, even if these were confined mostly to traditional domestic duties.

For boys, work on the outside meant work in shops and factories. A particularly detailed account of these activities comes from parole reports at California's Preston School of Industry during 1912. During that year, parole agent H.E. Kellington submitted accounts that outlined his efforts to find work for parolees. His notes on an inmate named Christen are typical. Writing on February 27, 1912, he informed Superintendent Charles H. Dunton that he had just completed a "strenuous day" in which he had called on a man with a job prospect for Christen. Turned down there, he "got busy" and went to a union hiring hall to put in an application. Having missed the proper authority, he sought a friend who worked as an architect in Oakland, California. The friend referred him to the foreman at a large, unionized firm, and there, he secured a job for Christen, but his work was not done. Next, Kellington "hunted up a good private boarding place in a Catholic Family" and then procured the tools needed for Christen's work.[10]

Kellington's reports provide an on-the-ground record of youthful work culture in the heart of the Progressive Era. In his position, Kellington drove all around central California, inquiring about jobs, securing places to live, and checking up on former inmates. A richly detailed view of working-class life, his reports are also filled with ethnic, racial, and class stereotypes typical of the era. For instance, he found the home of Joe Bastile "very good for an Italian." Other boys simply turned out to be no good, in his eyes. Louis Garrett, for example, had "stolen a lot of gum," been caught smoking cigarettes, and given another boy a black eye. He tried to behave, but he had spells where he backslid. Garrett's father chalked up such behavior to the fact that Louis's "head had been run over with a beer wagon when he was small boy and [he] has been that way since." For Louis's part, the boy "begged to be left in his home as he has been trying to do better lately."[11]

Kellington's reports aligned with what other superintendents, managers, and other state agents tracked at other institutions. During investigations, the matter of successful work versus recidivism turned up time after time. Minnie L. Jenner, state agent at the Indiana Industrial School for Girls, estimated that about one-third of parolees returned from work assignments. It was not always the fault of the girls, she disclosed. Often, their employers were to blame because "more is expected of the girls than they can do."[12] But sometimes it *was* their fault. Dr. Mary A. Spink, physician at the Indiana institution, had convinced her own mother to take inmate Agnes Prentice as a domestic. Agnes worked satisfactorily, but "my mother had to send her back. She would run out at night; climb out the window and slip away," Spink recalled. In this case, the youthful work culture that landed Agnes and her cohorts in the industrial school in the first place undercut efforts to keep her out of it. Ironically, wage work provided the means to economic independence that subverted the institutional control exerted by the growing system of law meant to control youthful work habits.[13]

Agnes likely slipped out to carouse the locale, but other inmates violated the terms of their parole by actively seeking work on their own. In 1903, Grace Davis Lozee won her parole and returned to her home in Elkhart, Indiana, to care for a sick grandmother. She was supposed to stay with her family, but she had never gotten along with her father. So, she took off and headed to "a private boarding house of good name there in town, because I was told by a party that I could wait table there for my board, because the college girls boarded there and some of the girls waited on table." Once in Elkhart, she got a new lead on employment: "There was a newly married couple, and the husband was hard of hearing; I heard they wanted a girl, and I went there and staid [sic] until I was married." By the time she recounted this story in 1905, Grace, at age twenty, was working as a "public stenographer," though she felt little at the school had prepared her for the role.[14]

Grace's narrative provides a particularly multifaceted window into work, industrial school life, and girls' culture in the early twentieth century. Grace had been a participant in a riot that brought the school to a standstill for a few days in 1901. She could have easily become one of the "fallen girls" that critics cited as evidence of the schools' failure, but she did not. In some ways, she and the school seem to have succeeded despite themselves. If the goal was proper behavior, steady employment, and secure domesticity, the institution did eventually accomplish its ends. But Grace's own actions played a large part in that outcome as well. She was supposed to stay at home, but she sought her own fortunes, even if they were in the confines of a small Indiana town. She desired to work, and she evinced a keen sense of her own worth in the labor market. Within the terms of her time, she wrote her own story.

These narratives of life in and out of reform schools should challenge historians to rethink how we understand youthful labor and the tensions between youth labor and youth culture. The literature on this issue has been dominated by accounts of child labor reform, while the stories of industrial and reform schools have been seen as an element of juvenile delinquency. We have tended to focus on efforts to *restrict* youthful wage work in this area without paying enough attention to efforts to *encourage* it. These two narrative lines are much closer than we commonly think. Industrial and reform schools aimed to correct what would now be called "behavioral disorders," but they did so by, through, and for work. Their success was gauged by post-institutional behavior, criminal and otherwise, but also by success in the labor market.

It would be easy to think that these two literatures simply follow one after the other, based on the age of the young people involved, but the story is muddier than that. As child labor reformers pushed the age of employment regulation and restriction upward, juvenile delinquency advocates pushed the age of commitment downward. The Iowa Juvenile Home, which opened in 1920, is an example of this latter trend, for it welcomed both boys and girls of quite tender ages. Inmate populations in reform schools centered on the mid-teens, but they often contained inmates as young as ten or even younger. Josephine Stafford, for instance, came to the Indiana Industrial School for girls when she was eight and stayed until age twenty. Although she represents an extreme case, most institutions contained inmates who would have been prevented from working for wages under their state's child labor statutes. Inside the walls, they did work, protected by a veil of institutional domesticity. In this microcosm, reformers resolved the paradoxes their efforts had produced in the outside world, but once released young people found their own way into the world of work and adulthood. There, they discovered alternatives to the rationalized toil offered by institutions. Immigrant work cultures often held vestiges of preindustrial values, and the instability of the labor market for youth augured against steady work.

More importantly, youth culture itself represented a kind of alternate vision of economic life. The cheap amusements of the industrializing city offered a place for young people to congregate outside of school and factory. As leisure took hold of American culture, youth led the way. A century after Lowell, dignified toil during laboring hours and mental advancement after work had faded as cultural referents for many young people. Viewed from the standpoint of youth, "incorrigibility" itself represented a worldview borne of incipient economic independence combined with social and cultural rewards for seeing leisure as the goal of work.

This youthful perspective on work and consumption was not confined to the United States. Scholars who have studied child labor and youthful work around the globe have noticed common patterns regarding young people and work, and older morality-based narratives are giving way to a more nuanced picture of child and youthful labor. Recent work on British industrialization notes how young people found pride in their work and gained economic independence. Similarly, the experience of young people in Brazil's labor courts in the twentieth century shows that young workers had a keen sense of their rights as laborers. Historians of Africa have also found that young people were economic actors, as both producers and consumers. These stories do not a neatly fit the chronology of industrialization, but they do reveal common patterns in that process. The transition to capitalism called forth new labor markets for youth and efforts to regulate those activities. Although often toiling in exploitative conditions, young people, especially older youth, embraced industrial labor, often becoming the vanguard of the transformations that wrought the modern economy and its accompanying cultural expressions.[15]

By the early decades of the twentieth century, most industrialized nations had begun to restrict the activities of young people in the labor market. Across the next century, youthful labor would become a global issue, one increasingly focused on the Global South. That story played out in a legal and cultural context increasingly established by international organizations. In 1924, the still-young League of Nations adopted the Geneva Declaration of the Rights of the Child. Its fourth principle encapsulated the twin pillars of youth and work that arose in previous eras: "The child must be put in a position to earn a livelihood, and must be protected against every form of exploitation." Thirty-five years later, the United Nations adopted a fuller version of the statement, and the difference in the section pertaining to labor is telling. By this time, child labor restriction had become an accepted norm, and the new declaration reflected this new reality:

> The child shall not be admitted to employment before an appropriate minimum age; he shall in no case be caused or permitted to engage in any occupation or employment which would prejudice his health or education, or interfere with his physical, mental or moral development.

Gone was the notion that young people possessed a right to a livelihood. Of course, this does not mean that young people the world over did not work or seek to work in the 1950s, but as a statement of principles, youthful labor had come to focus on what young people should *not* do rather than what they should do. In 1989, the UN adopted its most comprehensive statement on children's rights, the United Nations Convention of the Rights of the Child. Article 32 addressed employment and read as a precis of the previous two centuries of child labor reform. Appropriately following the article that asserted a right to rest, leisure, and play, the child labor article recognized

> the right of the child to be protected from economic exploitation and from performing any work that is likely to be hazardous or to interfere with the child's education, or to be harmful to the child's health or physical, mental, spiritual, moral or social development.

To realize this right, the convention urged member states to establish minimum employment ages and regulate hours and conditions.[16]

If international principles focused on restriction, the expansion of manufacturing in the Global South violated them. As the West deindustrialized, young people in Asia, Africa, and Latin America followed the paths of their historical peers and found wage work outside their households in burgeoning urban environments. A new international child labor reform movement arose to restrict these economic transformations. Sometimes lost in these far-flung shifts were the voices of youth themselves. One small window into the culture of global youth on work comes from *Voices of Youth*, an online publication associated with UNICEF (the United Nations International Children's Emergency Fund). Aimed at young people age thirteen or older, *Voices of Youth* "seeks to create a space that will help young people develop into active global citizens equipped to communicate and collaborate effectively to make a positive difference in their countries and communities." Written by young people, its articles span a wide range of topics, including education, culture, environment, health, personal growth, and others. For our purposes, one section in particular is important: employment. In the cacophony of voices that is modern culture, these young people articulated youthful outlooks and priorities—"hopes and dreams" might not be too strong—about their current economic situations and future working lives. In 2019, the publication's home page for employment tackled a question that would have not been surprising to managers of industrial schools a century earlier: "What skills do young people need in today's job market?" Ironically, the text focused on paths young people might take to avoid youth *unemployment*, a social problem with growing visibility in the early twenty-first century. [17]

The contributions of young authors in *Voices* provide an impressionistic view of how contemporary youth understand labor and interact with its culture. Reflecting on an issue salient in many professional settings, "Indianleewrites" offered advice on how to overcome imposter syndrome, counseling readers to "try using an affirmation to put yourself back in control." Citing high levels of youth unemployment, Krzystof Rentflejsz explored the dissatisfaction of European Union youth with an education that did not prepare them for the labor market they faced as young adults. A native of Warsaw, Poland, Rentflejsz called for reforming outdated high school curricula and for more cooperative ventures with potential employers. A short post by "Dia.Mxnte" decried workplace discrimination against teens, noting that "older employees feel as if they can treat them any kind of way." Penned mostly by young people on the cusp of adulthood, the entries contain a common fear of failure to find work. As Aida Serna wrote from Mexico, "I am just one human of the thousands that have recently graduated and are unable to find a job." [18]

The 1989 UN Convention defined "the child" as anyone under the age of eighteen. By its definition many of the young women who worked in the Lowell mills and extolled the dignity of their labors would be rendered as children. Yet others would not. And such is the conundrum of youth and employment. With labor laws that allow employment before the end of childhood, an educational system that prepares people for the world of work, but a culture that emphasizes rest, leisure, and play, youth face the future with uncertainty. That uncertainty is reflected in another corner of the UN, where "youth" was defined as the age cohort between fifteen and twenty-four. Here the UN acknowledged that societies understand youth differently, but that the interplay between education and employment was central. Youth constituted the time between the end of compulsory education and the beginning of gainful employment. Such a definition necessarily reflected the Western middle-class values that drive the UN, for it ignored the fact that many working-class young people begin employment while still under the aegis of compulsory education laws.

The definitional fluidity that surrounds youth and youth culture, particularly for employment, has continued to influence how historians understand the scholarly problems of their field. In the 2008 inaugural issue of *The Journal of the History of Childhood and Youth*, Paula Fass called for globalization in the study of youth culture and drew attention to the matter of employment. Access to consumer goods, she pointed out, can be liberating for many of the world's young people. Her views are worth quoting at some length because, more than a decade later, they still pertain to our understanding of this matter:

> Americans have developed a historical aversion to the work of children because starting in the late nineteenth century, reformers in the West made child labor into a taboo. By defining childhood as an ideal and as something to be freed from economic calculation and its contamination, child labor became a form of exploitation. We substituted schooling for work as the only legitimate form of socialization. But labor can also provide the means to expand the autonomy of choices, as it has for women in the recent past, for example.[19]

Her words recall a lesson about the Lowell Mills in the U.S. survey course. Students read a group of documents and usually conclude that the "women" employed there were being liberated. When the ages of these "women" are revealed, the conversation usually changes considerably. Such is the power of the cultural construction that Fass describes.

To liberate scholarly inquiry from that construction, historians will need to pay more attention to the culture of youthful employment. Older youth come of age in societies with fraught understandings of their incipient labors, and historians need to attend to these contextual matters. This is not to argue that scholars should draw a bright line between "childhood" and "youth" where employment is concerned. Far from it. To understand youthful labor, historians need more work on the jobs that young people do. Miriam Forman-Brunell's *Babysitter: An American History* provides one example of this kind of work. Sociologist Yasemin Besen-Cassino also looks carefully at recent youth labor in *Consuming Work: Youth Labor in America*.

More attention might also be paid to the interactions of employment and education. For instance, much more work could be done on the history of vocational training, in industrial schools, by unions, and through the school system. *Industrious in Their Stations*, a study of urban working youth in early America, by Sharon Braslaw

Sundue suggests ways to investigate this interplay as does Stephen Lassonde's *Learning to Forget*. Admittedly, sources for such endeavors can be hard to find. As numerous studies have shown, the story of youthful work can often be found in the law, both in actual case law and in administrative records. Sometimes the most private details are in the public sphere.

Attention to youthful employment and the culture of youthful labor requires framing questions differently. Historians will certainly want to continue to explore the exploitation of children in capitalist and non-capitalist societies, but they also can benefit from investigating how older young people came to understand work, both waged and non-waged. Such projects will likely stretch beyond the usual age boundaries of youth and into early adulthood, requiring more attention to how adulthood itself has been constructed as Corinne Field has recently done in *The Struggle for Equal Adulthood*. They will require further development of age as a category of analysis, along lines followed by the authors in Field and Nicholas Syrett's *Age in America*. They will need more work on how young people interacted with the larger culture of employment. In all, these projects will help the history of youth culture and labor grow beyond its infancy.

Notes

1. Thomas L. Dublin, *Women at Work: The Transformation of Work and Community in Lowell, Massachusetts, 1826–1860* (New York: Columbia University Press, 1979); Marie Jenkins Schwartz, *Born in Bondage: Growing Up Enslaved in the Antebellum South* (Cambridge, MA: Harvard University Press, 2001).
2. Max Weber, *The Protestant Ethic and the Spirit of Capitalism* (New York: Routledge, [1905] 2001); Geoffrey Chaucer, *The Canterbury Tales*, Penguin Classics (New York: Penguin, 2003), 185.
3. Elizabeth Barrett Browning, "The Cry of the Children," 1843, https://www.poetryfoundation.org/poems/43725/the-cry-of-the-children, accessed July 3, 2019.
4. Edgar Gardner Murphy, *The Case Against Child Labor*, Alabama Child Labor Committee pamphlet, 1902, Rare Books Room, Wilson Library, University of North Carolina-Chapel Hill, 6.
5. Alexander J. McKelway, "The Declaration of Dependence by the Children of America," National Child Labor Committee pamphlet, 1913.
6. "The Pleasures of Factory Life," *The Lowell Offering*, December, 1840, 25.
7. Matilda, "Ann and Myself," *The Lowell Offering*, 1841, 76–78.
8. Tabitha, "A New Society," *The Lowell Offering*, 1841, 191–192.
9. Karin Lorene Zipf, *Bad Girls at Samarcand: Sexuality and Sterilization in a Southern Juvenile Reformatory* (Baton Rouge: Louisiana State University Press, 2016).
10. H.E. Kellington to Charles H. Dunton, February 27, 1912, Preston School of Industry, Superintendent's Correspondence, 1912, Folder 1; California Youth Authority Collection, California State Archives, Sacramento, California.
11. Kellington to Dunton, February 15, 1912, ibid.

12. "Investigation of Charges Against Emily E. Rhoades, Superintendent Indiana Industrial School for Girls and Woman's Prison, December 4–8, 1905, Volume I," Indiana Department of Corrections, Confidential Investigation Reports, 1905, Indiana State Archives, 107.
13. Ibid., 605.
14. Ibid., 785.
15. Nigel Goose and Katrina Honeyman, eds. *Childhood and Child Labour in Industrial England, 1750–1914* (Farnham, UK: Ashgate, 2013); José Pacheco Dos Santos Jr., "The Right to Claim: Children and Youth Workers in Labor Court at the Time of the Civil-Military Dictatorship (Southwestern Bahia, Brazil)," *The Journal of the History of Childhood and Youth*, 6 (Fall 2013): 482–501; Jack Lord, "Child Labor in the Gold Coast: The Economics of Work, Education, and the Family in Late-Colonial African Childhoods, c. 1940–57," *The Journal of the History of Childhood and Youth* 4 (Winter 2011): 88–115.
16. Geneva Declaration of the Rights of the Child of 1924, adopted Sept. 26, 1924, League of Nations O.J. Spec. Supp. 21, at 43 (1924), http://hrlibrary.umn.edu/instree/childrights.html, accessed July 3, 2019; Declaration of the Rights of the Child, G.A. res. 1386 (XIV), 14 U.N. GAOR Supp. (No. 16) at 19, U.N. Doc. A/4354 (1959), http://hrlibrary.umn.edu/instree/k1drc.htm, accessed July 3, 2019; Convention on the Rights of the Child, G.A. res. 44/25, annex, 44 U.N. GAOR Supp. (No. 49) at 167, U.N. Doc. A/44/49 (1989), *entered into force* Sept. 2, 1990, http://hrlibrary.umn.edu/instree/k2crc.htm, accessed July 3, 2019.
17. https://www.voicesofyouth.org/faq, accessed July 3, 2019; https://www.voicesofyouth.org/topic/employment, accessed July 3, 2019.
18. https://www.voicesofyouth.org/blog/overcoming-imposter-syndrome-your-work, accessed July 3, 2019; https://www.voicesofyouth.org/blog/education-and-labour-market-mismatches-what-can-be-done, accessed July 3, 2019; https://www.voicesofyouth.org/blog/discrimination-towards-teens, accessed July 3, 2019; https://www.voicesofyouth.org/blog/crowd-thousands, accessed July 3, 2019.
19. Paula Fass, "The World Is at Our Door: Why Historians of Children and Childhood Should Open Up," *The Journal of the History of Childhood and Youth* 1 (Winter 2008): 25–26.

Further Reading

Besen-Cassino, Yasemin. *Consuming Work: Youth Labor in America*. Philadelphia: Temple University Press, 2014.

Chavez-Garcia, Miroslava. *States of Delinquency: Race and Science in the Making of California's Juvenile Justice System*. Berkeley: University of California Press, 2012.

Dos Santos Jr., José Pacheco. "The Right to Claim: Children and Youth Workers in Labor Court at the Time of the Civil-Military Dictatorship (Southwestern Bahia, Brazil)." *The Journal of the History of Childhood and Youth* 6 (Fall 2013): 482–501.

Dublin, Thomas L. *Women at Work: The Transformation of Work and Community in Lowell, Massachusetts, 1826–1860*. New York: Columbia University Press, 1979.

Field, Corinne T. *The Struggle for Equal Adulthood: Gender, Race, Age, and the Fight for Citizenship in Antebellum America*. Chapel Hill: University of North Carolina Press, 2014.

Field, Corinne T., and Nicholas L. Syrett, eds. *Age in America: The Colonial Era to the Present*. New York: New York University Press, 2015.

Fliter, John A. *Child Labor in America: The Epic Legal Struggle to Protect Children.* Lawrence: University Press of Kansas, 2018.
Forman-Brunell, Miriam. *Babysitter: An American History.* New York: New York University Press, 2009.
Goose, Nigel, and Katrina Honeyman, eds. *Childhood and Child Labour in Industrial England, 1750–1914.* Farnham, UK: Ashgate, 2013.
Grinspan, Jon. *The Virgin Vote: How Young Americans Made Democracy Social, Politics Personal, and Voting Popular in the Nineteenth Century.* Chapel Hill: University of North Carolina Press, 2016.
Hindman, Hugh D. *Child Labor: An American History.* New York: Routledge, 2002.
Jenkins Schwartz, Marie. *Born in Bondage: Growing Up Enslaved in the Antebellum South.* Cambridge, MA: Harvard University Press, 2001.
Lassonde, Stephen. *Learning to Forget: Schooling and Family Life in New Haven's Working Class, 1870–1940.* New Haven, CT: Yale University Press, 2005.
Lord, Jack. "Child Labor in the Gold Coast: The Economics of Work, Education, and the Family in Late-Colonial African Childhoods, c. 1940–57." *The Journal of the History of Childhood and Youth* 4 (Winter 2011): 88–115.
Schmidt, James. D. *Industrial Violence and the Legal Origins of Child Labor.* New York: Cambridge University Press, 2010.
Sundue, Sharon Braslaw. *Industrious in Their Stations: Young People at Work in Urban America, 1720–1810.* Charlottesville: University of Virginia Press, 2009.
Tanenhaus, David S. *The Constitutional Rights of Children: In re Gault and Juvenile Justice.* Lawrence: University of Press of Kansas, 2011.
Zelizer, Viviana A. *Pricing the Priceless Child: The Changing Social Value of Children.* New York: Basic Books, 1985.
Zipf, Karin Lorene. *Bad Girls at Samarcand: Sexuality and Sterilization in a Southern Juvenile Reformatory.* Baton Rouge: Louisiana State University Press, 2016.

CHAPTER 9

URBANIZATION

Youth Gangs and Street Cultures

SIMON SLEIGHT AND JASPER HEEKS

CITY streets have long hosted groups of young people labeled as gangs. Unique to no single period or place, gangs nonetheless proliferated in the modern era, seemingly synonymous with rapid urban growth. For the late nineteenth century, the almost simultaneous emergence of recognized gang cultures in multiple city settings is especially striking. In February 1870, newspapers in Melbourne first noted the public outrages of "larrikins," bands of mostly male working-class youths with a liking for showy attire, affray, and petty theft. Across the Pacific, groups of "hoodlums" troubled the San Francisco press from April 1871, charged initially with disrupting the picnicking activities of polite society. The following October, several of Manchester's "scuttlers"—lads aged in this instance from twelve to sixteen—were brought before the court for public disorder and fined for hurling stones during pitched battles along the city's Rochdale Road. To the south, Birmingham's "slogging gang" attracted similar public attention just six months later, while in 1874 the term "cornermen" was first applied to criminal factions in both Dublin and Liverpool. Back in the southern hemisphere (and indicative of a transnational circuit of gang reportage), journalists in South Africa were also anxious by this time about local varieties of Australian larrikins, said to be using foul language and upsetting women about town.[1] The popularizing of further collective nouns would follow, alongside more detailed analysis of gang members' cultural repertoires—their appearances, speech, and practices—and speculation on cultural similarities and differences. Writing after his round-the-world tour in 1895, for instance, American author Mark Twain opined that "Novelties are rare in cities which represent the most advanced civilization of the modern day" and contended that an array of impulsive youth—including larrikins, "loafers," "roughs," "toughs," and "bummers"—were essentially alike.[2]

Encompassing multiple urban communities for the period circa 1850–1930, the international phenomenon of youth gangs and the fashioning of associated youth cultures are addressed in what follows. A number of interwoven aims are pursued: to outline the urban contexts and territorial configurations sponsoring the efflorescence of gangs; to scrutinize the values, interests, and activities that gang cultures yielded; to ponder global patterns and cleavages; to furnish a detailed case study of the cultural dynamics and international influence of Australian larrikin gangs; to reflect on pertinent approaches and sources for historians new to the theme; and to broach non-criminal aspects of associational street-based youth cultures. Mark Twain's thesis is also tested—did similarities in the nature of gangs around the world outweigh any differences in the period concerned?

Following literary theorist Raymond Williams, for the purposes of our analysis we eschew notions of "culture" that privilege cultivated learning or high artistic forms. Instead, we define culture as "ordinary": a lived expression of everyday meaning, not the preserve of elites. "Youth culture" hence applies here to those rough and respectable cultural pursuits adopted, adapted, and generated by young people, a group encompassing those regarded as youthful within their shifting social worlds. Grounding our discussion within the specific urban settings we wish to explore, the deployment of "street cultures" within our chapter title is deliberate, referencing those public modes of being and activities that characterize our case study groups—urban youth gangs—and relate in one way or another to conditions of city living for the period concerned. As Williams further insists, "culture and production are related."[3] We agree. It follows that one should not regard culture as free-floating and seek instead to identify the influence of tethers—factors such as work and housing—in constraining and widening the scope of cultural practices. We begin in this vein by outlining as concisely as possible the commonalities and specificities of the urban environments in which, from around 1850 to 1930, so many gangs appeared and were sustained.

Urbanization and Urban Conditions

Rapid urbanization stimulated youth gangs and their street cultures. In 1899, American statistician Adna Weber published his detailed international survey on *The Growth of Cities in the Nineteenth Century*. The evidence presented was stark. Whereas in 1851 Britain alone hosted more than 10 percent of its population in cities of more than one hundred thousand inhabitants in size, by the early 1890s it had been joined in that category by seventeen other nations, of which eight—including Britain—hosted more than 20 percent of their citizens in cities similarly defined. The vast majority of these rapidly urbanizing countries were Western (also counting the Australian colonies as a single group). Retaining the one hundred thousand figure as a minimum criterion, a later team of demographers calculated that by 1925 around 20 percent of the global population was urban: a surge that again masked an unequal distribution given that 39.9 percent of those residing in "developed" nations were city dwellers, compared with just 9.3 percent of people in countries deemed "less developed."[4]

Behind the numbers were human stories, and the tramping of feet. Seeking financial betterment and yearlong employment, people moved en masse from rural areas and smaller towns toward cities. In turn they started families, further boosting the urban population and giving it a notably youthful face. As a case in point, in 1870 one contemporary observer noted that the boom city of Melbourne was "perspiring juvenile humanity."[5] More than two-fifths of the city's population was fourteen years of age or younger at this time, a proportion echoed in many British conurbations, in bigger American cities, and selectively beyond.[6]

City-born youth found themselves in the vanguard of an accelerating modernity, surrounded by an increasing range of urban pleasures and pitfalls, and subject to the amplified concerns of "child-savers" who perceived city living as harmful and sponsored schemes of removal to rural areas. Urban living conditions were indeed often harsh, with crowded and unhealthy accommodation around points of arrival and high population densities wherever rent was relatively low. For city youth, work insecurity was also especially common, and youthful solidarities sometimes cohered around types of work enjoyed to a greater or a lesser extent—newsboys fraternized with one another, for instance, so too did young women employed in canning factories. Unless formally apprenticed to a trade, during times of employment repetitive tasks and poor pay were norms across an array of jobs from light manufacturing and shop work to street selling. Deskilling, or the breaking up of work-related processes into discrete tasks overseen by individuals, could sponsor frustration. In *Hooligans or Rebels? An Oral History of Working-Class Childhood and Youth, 1889–1939* (1981), Stephen Humphries found that the desire to escape a "life of monotonous and low-paid labour" was highly significant in sponsoring gang membership. His conclusions were based on hundreds of interviews gathered across Britain. Frederic Thrasher's fieldwork in 1920s Chicago led him to identify a broader range of drivers. Here the stated determination to escape sometimes violent family life was coupled with an intention to form meaningful bonds within a context of educational inefficiency, religious formalism, political indifference, poor pay and monotony in work, unemployment, and "lack of opportunity for wholesome recreation." Deteriorating housing and sanitary conditions exacerbated these stimuli for gang membership, Thrasher found.[7]

With their paid labor concluded, or without employment, urban youth could socialize at home (most likely with siblings and parents in crowded rental properties) or look to a wider range of long-standing and emergent city spaces for amusement. Their public presence boosted due to the slow enforcement of compulsory schooling legislation in the late nineteenth century, young people's socializing frequently took place in streets, parks, and markets, or else—for Western youth—in such spaces as low theaters, billiard saloons, and early forms of cinema promising cheap entry.

Some social commentators identified excitement and the promise of city attractions such as these as causal factors for urban growth.[8] A number then went on to link the conditions of modern urban life to crime and youthful "deviancy," a word popularized and given a specific urban edge in the early twentieth century. For American sociologist Louis Wirth, writing in the 1930s, the heterogeneity and concentration of life in large cities led to frequent but impersonal contact, to status confusion, and to an emphasis on outward appearance. Individual dysfunction and social malady followed all too easily, Wirth argued: lacking the common ground of smaller-scale village or town life, ethical systems were in flux and anonymity could sponsor alienation. Out of earshot of these discussions, young people fashioned their own cultural responses to the opportunities and hardships of urban life in cities ranging from Liverpool to Lagos, and from San Francisco to Trinidad, and historians debate whether economic want or disposable (albeit limited) income and free time nurtured gang formation.[9] To understand the resultant street cultures, we next need to consider the granularities of space and of territory, deploying illustrative evidence of cultural practices as we proceed.

The Territories of Youth

Urbanization and its accompanying spatial and population changes helped generate youth cultures informed and defined by their urban territory. Thrasher most famously presented the notion that cities are seedbeds for gang formation in his classic work, *The Gang: A Study of 1,313 Gangs in Chicago* (1927). Thrasher's qualitative comparative analysis and taxonomy represented the culmination of eight years' observation and interaction. Although the project was parochial, frequently imprecise, and particularly reflective of contemporary political and academic currents, Thrasher vividly described youthful imagination, collaboration, and organization as part of the first forensic study of juvenile gang development and gang life. For Thrasher, gangs were a phenomenon of adolescence and he defined them as follows:

> The gang is an interstitial group originally formed spontaneously, and then integrated through conflict. It is characterized by the following types of behavior: meeting face to face, milling, movement through space as a unit, conflict, and planning. The result of this collective behavior is the development of tradition, unreflective internal structure, esprit de corps, solidarity, morale, group awareness, and attachment to a local territory.[10]

Urbanization and urban spatial dynamics played crucial roles in Thrasher's natural history of gangs. He drew on the contemporary urban ecology theory of Chicago sociologists Robert Park and Ernest Burgess, who conceived of the city as a dynamic organic ecosystem with discernible patterns. The effects of Chicago's rapid urbanization, industrialization, and experience of multiple waves of immigration were identified as generating fertile conditions for gangs. First, a changing urban landscape encouraged gangs to emerge in the interstices of the growing city, and Thrasher stressed the impact that the built environment had on structuring the possibilities of outdoor activity. Second, Thrasher considered gangs not merely as products of the city, but of a specific and clearly defined part of the metropolis, the "zone of transition." This zone was a poor, deteriorating, and unsightly area of industry and transitory populations set between the central business district and more stable residential wards. For Thrasher, youth gangs and other collectivities were a natural response from the city's new arrivals to the social dislocations caused by urban life. High population density and overcrowding forced large numbers of young people to socialize on the streets and form their own micro-societies.[11]

Urban growth provided opportunities for juvenile gangs. Throwing stones was a popular amusement for youth across the world, but in late nineteenth-century Birmingham, "[s]logging each other in gangs became the new self-organized distraction, pastime, even sport."[12] For Philip Gooderson, Birmingham was "maturing and expanding," and slogging gangs were an example of "Young Brum" "exploring its new streets, its new social space."[13] For Melbourne at a similar time, Simon Sleight examines the interstitial, in-between possibilities for gangs in an urban landscape replete with vacant lots, laneways, and building sites. On the corner of Fitzroy and Gertrude Streets to the north of the city center, for example, Melbourne's larrikins hauled around leftover blocks of stone from the construction of the adjacent Granite Terrace in 1858 to form a stage. Here city youth would act out and sing scenes from popular theater with the aid of an old songbook published in London. The many spaces between the slabs of stone became "a favourite playground for boys of more than one generation," observed "A Fitzroy Boy" in 1896, his anecdotes substantiated by records of complaints from local residents regarding "young hopefuls" occupying the location for large portions of the day, swearing and enjoying outdoor suppers of pilfered crayfish and alcohol.[14]

As in suburban Melbourne, the coalescence of gangs and associated street cultures into territorial configurations was a universal phenomenon. The connection between gangs and place is most evident in their names: "Bengal Tigers" (Bengal Street, Manchester), "Calton Entry" (Calton, Glasgow), "Millers' Point push" (Sydney), and "Cordova Street gang" (Vancouver)—to note just a few. Scholarship on late-Victorian British gangs, drawing on demographic information in court and police reports and geographical associations found in witness statements, has further emphasized the significance of territory. Heather Shore argues that territory was a new defining feature of London gangs and the commentary surrounding them. In Manchester and Birmingham, moreover, territorial ties were found to have superseded those based on ethnicity, religion, or trade. The founding of football teams also promoted stronger links with "turf." Gangs often displayed intense local pride and rivalries were fierce. Territory was staunchly defended, and even the slightest infringement, regarded as a deliberate provocation, was met with violence. In Manchester's Ancoats neighborhood, youths would travel in small groups to deter attack, but dozens could be rallied to maintain gang honor. Elsewhere, rivalries were spawned in the densely packed slums of towns in Trinidad; "amalaita" gang conflicts in Durban were distinctly spatial and had rural antecedents in the territorial nature of cattle herding; and hostilities between gangs of boys in Mumbai—brought to the fore each year during the Muharram Islamic festival—intensified and became more territorial in the 1880s and 1890s.[15]

The urban "youthscape"—the overlapping, underlying, and competing terrain produced by young people—featured key sites for gangs.[16] Street corners, public houses, rum shops, and temples held strategic significance. Certain open spaces were designated as battlegrounds to which multiple groups would venture for skirmishes. Music halls played host to hostilities and rowdy behavior, while vacant ground—as we saw in Melbourne—was the perfect spot to while away time free from adult supervision. Gangs' claims on urban territory brought them into conflict with adults and the authorities. Juanita De Barros positions "centipede" (*santapee*) gangs at the center of struggles for urban space in Georgetown, British Guiana, in the early twentieth century. Centipedes' distinct use of streets, bridges, and parks for recreation, festivity, and to support their livelihoods contributed to intra-class and racial tensions in an expanding city and clashed with elite designs and perceptions of public space. De Barros reveals the military influences on gangs, who had organized structures with captains and colonels. In 1924, for instance, the "Peppersauce Team" fought the "Berlin Team," whose name may have alluded to Berlin's "enemy" status during the First World War. In a similar vein, scuttlers in north west England re-enacted battles from the Franco-Prussian War and Russo-Turkish conflict in the 1870s, and dance societies in Tanzanian coastal towns performed the "bom," which mimicked German military drill.[17]

Intersecting with territorial and topographical configurations of youth culture, urban contours of race and racism also strongly influenced gang cultures. In the barrack ranges of Port of Spain in Trinidad in the latter half of the nineteenth century, the inequality of a racist plantation society caused young people to form gangs (bands) for drinking, gambling, and fighting. More than just mirrors of circumstance, though, these gang members were social actors who constructed a defiant subculture and used the annual Carnival to ridicule and undermine their economic and political oppressors through masquerade and song. Similarly, amalaita gangs of African houseboys in early twentieth-century Durban adapted Zulu rural cultural and organizational forms in response to racial oppression and economic hardship. Drawing on oral histories, Paul La Hausse interprets amalaita gangs as aggressive and defensive forms of migrant association that served to reinforce the rural roots of members faced with the new conditions of town life. Alongside the amalaita, the *isihabahaba* were another youth subculture of domestic workers in Durban that exhibited wariness toward their new urban context and sought alternative forms of social security. The isihabahaba used vocabulary associated with cattle herding power relations, appropriated female styles of dress, and participated in homosexual practices possibly in order to avoid sexual contact with the small numbers of urban Black women, who were referred to as prostitutes.[18]

African youth in Durban made themselves known physically and sonically in the city's streets. Within a context of conflict between young migrant workers and white residents over private and public spaces, and new regimes of etiquette and discipline, amalaita occupied and ran through the streets at night, performed the *ingoma* Zulu dance, and announced themselves by playing harmonicas. Stick-fighting traditions were transferred from the countryside, and amalaita engaged in ritualized fights and demonstrations. Groups of youths also carried sticks as weapons and used them to attack trespassers and Black police officers, who were targets for gangs' socioeconomic frustrations. Public space was thus a platform for presentations of youthful resistance. Lynette Finch interprets Australian larrikin gangs' visible use of the street as a means of demonstrating their opposition to middle-class morals and commercial interests during a time in which previously multifunctional public spaces were remade into open boulevards for shopping and strolling.[19] Street-based defiance and display were hence also integral to larrikinism.

Common Threads?

As youth gangs held the streets and defended their turf, there was a vital aesthetic element to their identity. Gang members across the world were intensely fashion conscious. Hoodlums were known as swaggering felonious dandies, Parisian "apaches" sported colorful shirts and silk scarves; amalaita added beads and bracelets to their big trousers and heeled boots; and writer Clarence Rook's 1899 London hooligan composite, Alf, was similarly sharply dressed and streetwise. Outfits were produced from accessible materials and items (often tailored by female relatives or girlfriends), bought through payment plans, or pilfered. Youths were dressed to kill, and clothing could double as a weapon. Scuttlers' thick belts, for instance, were wrapped round the wrist and whirled at opponents. Large ornate buckles would inflict serious damage to the head and would be taken as spoils of war. With donkey fringes and Mohican haircuts, the younger generation stood out in the crowd and set themselves apart from their elders. Uniforms also served as collective symbols of gang identity. Variations in fabric and color existed between groups: velvet and plaid caps either side of the Thames in turn-of-the-century London, or black or red ribbons in Durban a decade later. In the 1920s, street gangs in Tokyo would target university students, and the leader of the "Rabbits" gang wore a Keio University cap and pin taken from victims along with his gang tattoo. Tokyo schoolboys were also warned not to mimic gang styles to avoid being mistaken for rivals and attacked.[20] Many gang members took great pride in their sartorial sense, which signaled status and toughness and grabbed public attention.

Journalists dissected gang members' ensembles, cartoonists exaggerated and satirized appearances, and police and press notices spread stylistic details far and wide. Chris Brickell notes the influence of international print culture and imported identities on young people in New Zealand, for instance, while according to David Ambaras, Japanese *yotamono* youths derived gang names and slang from American films in the early twentieth century, with groups called the "Indians" or "Apaches." Derogatory Native American imagery traveled widely in popular culture from the late nineteenth century onward, and the label "apache" was applied in Paris and St. Petersburg. Yotamono also modeled themselves on the people with whom they shared the streets: actors, gamblers, hawkers, and construction workers. The cinema and historical novels gave new life to images of Japanese folk heroes, which provided inspiration for the yotamono just as British and Irish outlaw traditions had done for Australian larrikins fifty years earlier. Melissa Bellanta also emphasizes the global influences of the popular stage and of touring troupes on the modes of self-presentation of poor urban youth and calls for the greater use of theatrical sources by historians. For instance, female larrikins modeled themselves on the mannerisms and costumes of burlesque characters, and male larrikins attending theaters in Brisbane, Melbourne, and Sydney were avid fans of the imposing and macho "coons" depicted in American blackface minstrelsy.[21] Young people asserted themselves visibly in the city, their territorial claims reinforced by their sartorial choices.

Genus Larrikin

While British and American popular culture would inspire street gangs worldwide from the nineteenth century onward, influences did not always fan out from "core" to "periphery." A detailed consideration of Australian larrikin gangs, introduced earlier, demonstrates this amply, taking us inside a street-based culture ripe with meaning and helping us understand the international influence of rowdy Australian youth.

By attacking the police and Chinese communities, abusing pedestrians and dressing flamboyantly, larrikins generated intense, sustained, and often sensational social commentary across the Australian colonies. Foreign travelers and emigrants in Melbourne, and later Sydney, were compelled to comment on larrikins, who were an urban presence with a bad reputation. One visitor from Bulawayo, for instance, was relieved not to have fallen foul of any larrikin gangs (or "pushes" in the local parlance) in Melbourne, despite hearing dreadful stories about them prior to arrival.[22]

The intricacies of larrikin gang culture are borne out in investigative writings composed by the police or by journalists. A series of articles published in January 1882 by the Melbourne newspaper *The Argus* is especially useful in this regard, and unusual in that the unnamed reporter attempted through close observation to understand rather than merely sensationalize his subjects. The fourth piece in the series saw the reporter set out on a Saturday afternoon to gather information on larrikin customs. After observing a slanging match between groups of larrikins on the flanks of the Yarra River—featuring volleys of expletives "the publication of which would disgrace any newspaper"—the journalist continued on foot to take in scenes of raffish young people bathing in the Corporation Baths and parading the streets of suburban Hotham prior to nightfall. There the writer encountered larrikins in twos and threes, sporting "their well-known swagger" as well as dark and tight-fitting "Tommy Dodd" jackets accessorized with braiding and buttons (and inspired by a British swell character and comic stage song). Flared tweed trousers with striking patterns, heeled boots with steel caps and mock lacing, gaudy neckwear, felt hats with broad velvet bands, precisely cut oiled hair, and silver, brass, or engraved bone rings encompassing fingers and neckties completed an arresting ensemble.

Continuing his observations of larrikin youth culture, in inner-suburban Carlton, the peripatetic *Argus* journalist next observed bands of young men on vacant allotments, boasting about fighting with policemen, performing a dance routine featuring steps recently acquired, and singing with the aid of a concertina. By 8:00 p.m. the writer had reached Melbourne's city center. In front of a theater he observed dozens of larrikins chewing tobacco, expectorating, and flirting with larrikin girls, while outside a nearby pub he watched larrikins denigrating passersby with ribald observations and pithy insults, treading on women's dresses, and knocking off the hats of any pedestrians who objected. At Mace's boxing saloon, farther along the street, a revolving stage featured youth demonstrating boxing and dancing, watched by a rowdy audience. Come 11:00 p.m. and the unflagging journalist studied larrikins and larrikinesses disputing the ownership of a stolen purse beneath a veranda at the Eastern Market, before thirty minutes later a fight erupted between two couples, which ended in torn clothing. He concluded his article with an encouragement to readers to go beyond the newspapers' court reports in seeking to understand larrikin culture, noting that no charges had been issued—let alone any arrests made—pertaining to anything he had seen.[23] That much of the noisy and antisocial behavior so carefully noted was not in fact illegal went unremarked.

As a result of the summarizing and recirculating of articles such as this, journalists in different cities writing on the cultural expressions of gangs became very well informed about larrikins, presenting news of the latest incidents and offering international comparisons for the benefit of their readers. Looking abroad helped journalists to define local and national identities and shape transnational categories of youth. The transoceanic circulation of people and information enabled the subject of larrikins go global, and after 1870 firsthand encounters and news coverage spread talk of Australian larrikins rapidly. Exchanges within and beyond the British empire took news of Australian larrikins to each inhabited continent, and with mention made of "the world's worst juveniles" in Argentina, France, the Netherlands, and Germany.

A close analysis of overseas responses to Australian larrikins from the late nineteenth century uncovers some of the extended conversations about urban youth gangs and their associated street cultures.

Cities were characterized by their street gangs, and vice versa. In 1908, an article in *Pearson's Weekly* (London) listed eleven slang terms for youthful ruffians used across the world: "hooligan," "larrikin," "hoodlum," "apache," "santapee," "copperhead" (New Orleans), "lazzaro" (Naples), "budmash" (Calcutta), "peaky blinder" (Birmingham), "tough" or "Bowery Boy" (New York), and "scorpion" (Gibraltar). Later that same year, a more detailed comparison between cities was made in the *Mexican Herald*. According to an article on "Rowdies and Hooligans," as lawless youths troubled residents in Melbourne, London, and New York, groups of similar young men on street corners were not to be found in Mexican cities and towns, owing to the swift and efficient actions of the police.[24] The same writer also detailed the insults offered to women in the streets and parks of Madrid, noted the progress made by the police of Buenos Aires in making their city safer, and took considerable pride in overturning the tag of "barbarous Mexico" with pointed comments directed toward "boastful communities" overseas.

In Britain, press coverage of Australian larrikin gang culture in the 1870s reassured the public that local miscreants, though troublesome, were not as bad as their colonial cousins. For example, a roving Cumbrian reporter composed the following from Melbourne in 1872: "The curse of Australia is its youthful population, or 'larrikins.' They are wholly uneducated, and for rowdiness and independence beat anything Europe can produce, either the London street boy or Parisian gamin."[25] Larrikins' infamy in Britain was assured when a letter from cricketer Lord Harris—one of the most influential figures in the game at the time, known for his decency and sportsmanship—recounted the moment he was "struck by some 'larrikin' with a stick" as spectators rioted in Sydney in 1879.[26] The vituperation towards larrikins soon escalated. Larrikin opportunism as police were diverted from city beats by Ned Kelly's bushrangers led the Melbourne correspondent at the *Globe* to describe the larrikin as "the most obnoxious kind of ruffian in the world. He is as brutal as he is cowardly, foul-tongued, and skulking."[27] Within a year, writer and politician James Inglis had gone further and called the Sydney larrikin "the most detestable creature on the earth's surface."[28]

Such striking depictions of antisocial behavior informed the impression of larrikins in Britain and prepared the ground for use of the term to designate local youths. Echoing the description provided by the correspondent at the *Globe*, an article in the *Portsmouth Evening News* referred to the groups of "cowardly brutes" that had committed an unprovoked assault in London as "ruffians of the Larrikin class."[29] While there were localized complaints of unruliness nationwide over the coming years, larrikins were also associated with an apparent increase in juvenile gang activity in London. In October 1881, a week after the *Pall Mall Gazette* compared the street-fighting gangs of Clerkenwell and Islington to larrikins and hoodlums, the *Spectator* referenced the larrikins who "make the streets of Islington impassable on Sunday evenings" as it again implored the Home Secretary to deal with the deteriorating situation.[30]

The phrase "London larrikins"—used to describe socialist-associated mob disorder in 1886—was later deployed as part of the panic over territorial street gangs in the aftermath of the 1888 Regent's Park murder, a stabbing committed by one of the "Tottenham Court Road Lads." This was a full decade before the adoption of the term "hooligan" by the press to label the city's gangs in August 1898.[31] The influence of the so-called periphery of empire on the core was underscored by comments made by the Lord Mayor of London in January 1889. After two gang members were charged with assault, the Lord Mayor regretted to say that the larrikin element had made its way from Australia into the metropolis.[32] In the 1890s, "London larrikin" gangs regularly occupied urban space, fought one another, and terrorized other citizens. Activities came to a head in 1898 after a sequence of court appearances and incidents across the capital, but most notably in south London. Here, the exploits of the notorious "Hooligan" gang captured the national imagination and a new youth descriptor was born.

Britain was not the only place where the influence of Australian larrikin culture was felt. Numerous and detailed reports were reprinted in New Zealand, and "larrikin" quickly entered popular usage there in 1871. Larrikin gangs in New Zealand also distinguished themselves from others with their clothing, bad language, and violence, and historian Chris Brickell considers larrikinism a new mode of youthful self-expression and autonomy in an increasingly unsettled and class-conscious society. Cultural influences came from Australia, and Brickell notes how larrikin masculinity in New Zealand was informed by Ned Kelly's frontier rebelliousness. Boys in 1894 role-played the outlaw in Auckland's Albert Park, and a new generation of larrikins was inspired by the world's first feature film, *The Story of the Kelly Gang* (1906).[33] Larrikins in Melbourne had long been inspired by Kelly's violent escapades, following the unfolding chase, capture, and execution of their folk hero from the late 1870s, and the reception of the subsequent film foreshadowed further associations between early cinema and gang-related activities.

Just as with their counterparts across the Tasman Sea, there would be reaction to New Zealand larrikins elsewhere in the British Empire. In 1882, a reader responded to an editorial in the *Ceylon Observer* and defended the good people of New Zealand, who were being tarnished by the exploits of their youngsters. In Cape Town in 1888 it was also recognized that "the larrikin" was not now solely an Australian product as the city was "becoming infected with the same plague."[34] There the "Woodstock Lads" would congregate, throw stones, and take possession of the streets at night. Residents implored the police to protect them from the tyranny of wild colonial boys, described in correspondence as "Our Larrikins." In several southern African cities, and also in Mauritius, gangs of white and Black youths vexed adults by making music, playing dangerously, and wearing respectable clothes that, in the minds of their detractors, hardly suited their raucous behavior.

Approaches to Urban Youth Gangs and Street Cultures

Since the early 1970s, youth gangs and their cultural practices have often been understood globally with recourse to the hugely influential sociological work of Stanley Cohen. In *Folk Devils and Moral Panics: The Creation of the Mods and Rockers* (1973), Cohen popularized the term "moral panic" and applied it to the representation of contemporary British youth. The first page of his opening chapter summarized his overarching thesis and merits quoting at some length:

> Societies appear to be subject, every now and then, to periods of moral panic. A condition, episode, person or group of persons emerges to become defined as a threat to societal values and interests; its nature is presented in a stylized and stereotypical fashion by the mass media; the moral barricades are manned by editors, bishops, politicians and other right-thinking people; socially-accredited experts pronounce their diagnoses and solutions; ways of coping are evolved or (more often) resorted to; the condition then disappears, submerges or deteriorates and becomes more visible. Sometimes the object of the panic is quite novel and at other times it is something which has been in existence long enough, but suddenly appears in the limelight.[35]

Cohen went on to argue that "over reporting" by media outlets was a common response to perceived youthful deviancy. Exaggeration of the severity of an incident, the numbers involved, and any associated violence was commonplace, he maintained, and sensationalist language and melodramatic flourishes heightened a sense of fear.[36]

Holding Cohen's ideas in mind for the late nineteenth century, perhaps it is no coincidence that the rapid emergence of youth gangs globally occurred at just the same historical moment in which printing presses the world over ran hot, with many more newspapers than ever before coming into existence, each with an editor hungry for eye-catching copy and jostling to become a leading social authority. Contemporaries at the time perceived a link, too. Statistician Adna Weber commented in 1899 on "the blaze of an Argus-eyed press" in probably exaggerating urban viciousness and criminality,[37] while in Melbourne references were made in parliamentary debates during 1874 to "a sort of mania" among newspaper editors concerning larrikins.[38]

As foreshadowed by these commentators, caution should be urged with deploying the "moral panic" concept as the natural point of entry for understanding youth cultures. Students writing on gangs often push the idea too far, picking up on the use of "creation" in Cohen's book title to determine that gangs are (and were) media myths.

Instead, it is more productive to approach the real-world cultural practices of youthful gang members and the reportage on their behavior as occurring within a repeating circuit. Hence, we find seventeen-year-old bootmaker Richard Turvey, noted by a Melbourne paper as proclaiming himself "King of the Richmond Larrikins" in 1871, and John-Joseph Hillier, dubbed by the *Salford Reporter* as "King of the Scuttlers" in 1894, subsequently appearing on local streets wearing a jersey bearing the moniker stitched in capitals.[39]

If the notion of "moral panic" as a mode of analyzing youthful gang cultures requires prudence, then the merits and shortcomings of other conceptual apparatus also warrant consideration. Spatial approaches, advocated earlier, offer an opportunity to ground gang activities with a finely understood urban terrain, but if applied bluntly they can underemphasize change through time in favor of geographical factors. Linked to space, factors of scale also command careful thought. Those commencing research need to weigh up the relative merits of pursuing a detailed case study of individuals involved in gangs, an assessment of a particular group or city, a national comparison, or an international survey. More complex is the researcher's stance on semiology versus materiality as framing devices for understanding youth cultures. The former approach—advanced most prominently by Roland Barthes and applied to British youth in Dick Hebdige's influential *Subculture: The Theory of Style* (1979)—reads surface signs in order to infer meaning. For Hebdige, this entailed interpreting outré style as a form resistance to the dominant political system. The latter methodology—preferred by Bellanta and Sleight, among others—seeks to locate such facets as appearance within the material contexts of production and advocates determining how clothes were manufactured or purchased, for instance, as well as where and when they were worn.[40]

Also deserving of consideration in analyzing the cultural expressions of youth gangs is the interplay of gang activities with a range of social demarcations, among them relative age, race, class, and gender. Traditionally, scholars of gangs have been very slow to address adequately the last of these factors, especially regarding young women's connection to gang life. Seen as add-ons, absentees, or mere victims, generations of (mostly male) scholars afforded girls only background positions. Recent attempts to rescue young women from such condescension have started to redress this imbalance. The active role of young women as gang members and gang leaders has been brought to light. In New Zealand, female larrikins were an ever-growing and confident street presence as the nineteenth century drew to a close, and one well-known leader and her gang met with disapproval at a Sunday night dance in the rural town of Te Aroha in 1891. Women were also central to centipedism in British Guiana after 1895. The "Tigress of Tiger Bay" and "Daisy the Centipede Queen" were prominent gang members, and De Barros reveals that the epithet "santapee" could mean a "brawling woman" or "foul-mouthed prostitute." In Trinidad, women were not only influential in encouraging male members of carnival bands in the second half of the nineteenth century but also formed all-female fighting gangs, such as the

"Mourcelines" and "Don't care dams."[41] The exploits of sisters Alice Sugar, Piti Belle Lily, and others earned them immortality in calypso legend—an example of a nontraditional historical source useful for recovering marginal experiences.

Given the more restrictive societal codes endured by women historically, participation in gang activities, and particularly in instances of fighting or assault, casts the young women involved as especially rebellious. This is all the more so when one further considers the constraints on women in accessing some of the city spaces that nurtured gang life, such as hotel saloons. Problems of classification in historical sources have also been raised by Melissa Bellanta. She notes the tendency of Australian commentators, and later historians more widely, to dismiss rowdy female youth appearing in public as "prostitutes," a slur that has helped prevent these young women from receiving their due. Police preferences for arresting male gang members—based presumably on the assumption that they presented a greater physical threat—also underplay the street presence of female gang members in associated records, Bellanta observes.[42] Further research on the histories of gangs around the world is needed to determine parallel or conflicting trends.

For historians, accounting for the disappearance, or abeyance, of a phenomenon is far more difficult than charting its rise, given the relative lack of contemporary coverage. Individual motivations for leaving gang life have been broached, however, with marriage identified as a key point of transition.[43] It is also highly probable that comparatively few youthful gang members historically have been "full-time," usually mixing their evening or weekend socializing with forms of work. Alterations in the apportioning of time by force of circumstance or by choice could hence see an individual drift out of gang life, where permitted. Incarceration for extended periods could elicit the same effect, with such penalties also inviting scholars to consider the impact of wider social forces. Within all societies phases of judicial repression (often including the handing down of "exemplary sentences" to deter further comparable offending) have impacted on the activities of youth gangs. Physical punishment of offenders—strongly advocated in the nineteenth century—has also intersected in complex ways with gang membership. Waves of social reform warrant further consideration, too; from the establishment of youth clubs to the opening of urban playgrounds, progressively minded intervention has exerted a periodic influence. The shifting sands of economic opportunity probably also play a role, though as noted earlier, historians diverge on the effects of squalor and plenty.

Perhaps more significant in explaining the ebbing of gangs like the larrikins following the First World War is the slower transition of young people from earners to learners in the West during the early twentieth century, a change that reduced the opportunities for the development of workplace associational cultures while simultaneously increasing the number of school-based gangs. And finally, one must also consider the interruptions occasioned by armed conflict. What role did the second South African War (1899–1902), for example, play in drawing into the military male gang member volunteers from the swathe of participating nations?

BEYOND CRIMINALIZATION

Although we are attempting here to outline factors of potential significance for understanding the cultural expressions of youth gangs globally, it is important also to emphasize the specificity of historical settings, and to note that only fine-grained archival research can unlock the dynamics of individual gang culture and membership. We also wish to stress—contrary to much of the scholarship on youth gangs in history—that far from all youthful street cultures were inherently or continuously criminal, and hence that for most of the time members of youth gangs were not breaking the law. Early writing by sociologist Paul Corrigan noted the prevalence of "doing nothing" within street-corner culture, for instance—periods of time filled with anticipation, discussion, joking, mischief, boredom, and giving rise to "weird ideas" about future activities, such as smashing milk bottles.[44] Corrigan's case studies were fourteen- and fifteen-year-old boys in early 1970s Sunderland, but the same experiences can be said to hold true in earlier times—in 1870s Melbourne, for example, or in Salford and Manchester at a similar moment.

Young people found a range of means to cope with urban life during the period addressed here, and many street cultures exhibited practical and ingenious components. David Trotman regards the gangs formed by new immigrants to Trinidad in the late nineteenth century, for example, as fraternities or sororities that acted as "oases of friendship for newcomers to strange and alienating situations."[45] Bonds were formed and based on ethnicity, Caribbean island of birth, old plantation, or current neighborhood or yard. Carnival was an opportunity for gang members and other residents to air discontent in an imaginative and subversive fashion. The masquerades, sexual displays and cross-dressing of the "jamette" carnival (1860–1899) were used to ridicule the middle and upper classes, briefly inverting power dynamics.[46] For Timothy Gilfoyle, writing on street children in New York at the same time, an independent "street kid ideology" flourished, informed by juvenile experiences in the city. Pickpocketing was just one element of this subculture, which also displayed moral and artistic facets. In 1871, for instance, street boys founded the Grand Duke's Opera House. This cellar theater's audience, staff, and actors were mostly newsboys and bootblacks, creating and enjoying something for themselves. In addition, the youths fostered their own slang, pivotal to their livelihood, and complex and tricky to comprehend for the uninitiated.[47] Creativity was hence a major part of historical youth street cultures.

The criminalization of those street cultures has been influenced historically by the age, gender, race, and class of participants, and has fallen subject to powerful forms of representation. As a case in point, newspaper boys in Rio de Janeiro often socialized at kiosks in the city from the 1870s to 1920s, settings where the authorities regularly harassed them. In July 1893, six young men and children were arrested for vagrancy and *capoeiragem* at a cafe kiosk. The youths claimed they were misidentified, caught up in the renewed campaign against *capoeira*—a stylized martial art and form of cultural expression among the young predominantly Black urban poor, with origins in West and Central African dance traditions. In the opinion of journalists, public officials, and the upper class from the mid-nineteenth century onward, *capoeira* was a dangerous threat to society, particularly in the form of gangs, known as *maltas* or *badernas*, which wielded razors and clubs. For historian Maya Talmon-Chvaicer, however, official and news reports were affected by prejudice and contrasted starkly with *capoeiras*' own perceptions. Many members of the public and participants, she argued, enjoyed watching the scenes as *capoeiras* danced and leaped in front of processions and humiliated the authorities with their games.[48]

The types of sources consulted can also often influence associations between street cultures and crime. Autobiographies and other "ego texts" like diaries provide different insights than more numerous police or court records, for example. This is not at all to dismiss the usefulness of the judicial material, with case files able to reveal much about private lives and period speech, but it is important to evaluate provenance carefully. Alternative methodologies, such as anthropological analysis and reading "against the grain" are also fruitful.[49] Through his cultural history of African martial arts across the Atlantic, T.J. Desch-Obi believes scholars' very use of "gang" to describe *capoeira maltas* makes them "complicit in the criminalization of these cultural practices" because the "imprecision and cultural baggage of the term invites misunderstanding."[50] Desch-Obi has in mind with these comments late-twentieth century street gangs involved in drug trafficking: criminal fraternities that all too easily come to mind as soon as the word "gang" is deployed. Historians, it is argued, must be open, self-reflexive, and critical in selecting methods and tease out understandings through detailed research.

Transurban Phenomena

Modern urban youth gangs and associated street cultures originated in the second half of the nineteenth century. Well before the arrival of "the teenager" as a phenomenon in the mid-twentieth century (together with well-known, and heavily studied, rebellious youth subcultures of that era), an array of gangs claimed public attention. They came to prominence in a rapidly urbanizing world of demographically youthful cities. Crowded living arrangements and often-menial work were widespread. Within these contexts, gangs arose for multiple reasons—popping up like mushrooms in steamy paddocks, as one Melbourne journalist put it in 1910—and cohered around territory and flashy aspects of self-presentation.[51] Many places that hosted youth gangs were also port cities, awash with international trends and commerce, and all of the cities discussed here were increasingly restless hubs yielding pleasures and perils in varying measures. Mark Twain pushed his assessment too far in arguing that gang members the world over were like-for-like, but there was certainly an equivalence encompassing underlying social conditions, stylistic elements, and modes of behavior. Local inflections were based, in particular, on different religious and ethnic blends.

Balancing the activities, and where possible the experiences, of youthful participants with the recorded reactions of adults, an international overview of juvenile street cultures has been offered. Cognizant of the shape and shortcomings of archival evidence on youth gangs and the conceptual approaches that we have outlined, youthful gang cultures have been shown to be multifaceted, and creative as well as destructive. For historians new to the theme, a rich and deepening body of secondary scholarship can scaffold ongoing research, and we warmly recommend breaking out of national boundaries by testing insights on one historical setting in another. The contours of such a transnational—or, more accurately, a *transurban*—evaluation have been sketched with regard to the global import of Australian larrikins, and this type of analysis promises to yield exciting new understandings.[52] Young people across the world responded to the possibilities and challenges of urbanization by making their own entertainment and taking action. Youth fashioned spaces for themselves and gave new meanings to developing urban geographies. In varying degrees, juvenile street cultures embodied play, politics, pugilism, and public display as young people were inspired by—and left marks on—the world around them.

Notes

1. "The Town and Suburbs," *Herald* (Melbourne), February 3, 1870, 2; "The Remedy. How to Circumvent the 'Hoodlums,'" *Daily Alta California*, April 19, 1871, 2; "Mimic Warfare in Rochdale Road," *Manchester Evening News*, October 24, 1871, 2; "Riot in Birmingham by the 'Slogging Gang,'" *Birmingham Daily Post*, April 8, 1872, 5; *Irish Times*, February 5, 1874, 5; "Murders and Suicides," *Globe* (London), August 5, 1874, 4; "Miscellaneous News," *Cape Mercantile Advertiser*, September 15, 1873, 3.
2. M. Twain, *Following the Equator: A Journey Around the World* (Hartford, CT: The American Publishing Company, 1897), 363.
3. R. Williams, "Culture Is Ordinary," in *Resources of Hope: Culture, Democracy, Socialism* (London: Verso, 1989), 8.
4. A. F. Weber, *The Growth of Cities in the Nineteenth Century: A Study in Statistics* (New York and London: Macmillan and P. S. King and Son, 1899), 144–145; United Nations Population Division, *Orders of Magnitude of the World's Urban Population in History* (New York: United Nations Population Division 1977), 27, 37, 30, accessed Aug. 13, 2019, https://population.un.org/wup/Archive/.
5. Marcus Clarke, cited in S. Sleight, *Young People and the Shaping of Public Space in Melbourne, 1870–1914* (Farnham and Burlington, UK: Ashgate, 2013), 31.
6. Weber, *The Growth of Cities*, 280–282 and 31–32; P. Horn, *The Victorian Town Child* (Stroud, Sutton, UK: 1999), Appendix 1.
7. R. H. Tawney, "The Economics of Boy Labour," *The Economic Journal*, 19, no. 76 (1909): 517–537; S. Humphries, *Hooligans or Rebels? An Oral History of Working-Class Childhood and Youth, 1889–1939* (Oxford: Basil Blackwell, (1981] 1984, 177; F. Thrasher, *The Gang: A*

Study of 1,313 Gangs in Chicago (Chicago and London: University of Chicago Press, [1927] 1963), 31, 37.
8. E.g., William Lecky (1896), cited in Weber, *The Growth of Cities*, 222.
9. L. Wirth, "Urbanism as a Way of Life," *American Journal of Sociology*, 44, no. 1 (1938): 1–24; A. Davies, "Histories of Hooliganism," in *Mischief, Morality and Mobs: Essays in Honour of Geoffrey Pearson*, ed. Dick Hobbs (New York and London: Routledge, 2017), 93–94.
10. Thrasher, *The Gang*, 57.
11. Ibid.
12. P. Gooderson, "'Noisy and Dangerous Boys': The Slogging Gang Phenomenon in Late Nineteenth-Century Birmingham," *Midland History* 38, no. 1 (2013): 65.
13. Ibid., 78.
14. S. Sleight, "Interstitial Acts: Urban Space and the Larrikin Repertoire in Late-Victorian Melbourne," *Australian Historical Studies* 40, no. 2 (2009): 232–250; Sleight, *Young People*, 131–170; "The First Use of the Word Larrikin," *Argus* (Melbourne), August 4, 1896, 7.
15. H. Shore, *London's Criminal Underworlds: A Social and Cultural History* (Basingstoke, UK: Palgrave Macmillan, 2015), 141–166; A. Davies, *The Gangs of Manchester: The Story of the Scuttlers, Britain's First Youth Cult* (Preston, UK: Milo Books, 2008); Gooderson, "'Noisy and Dangerous Boys,'"; B. Brereton, *Race Relations in Colonial Trinidad 1870–1900* (Cambridge: Cambridge University Press, 1979); D. Trotman, *Crime in Trinidad: Conflict and Control in a Plantation Society, 1838–1900* (Knoxville: University of Tennessee Press, 1986); P. La Hausse, "'The Cows of Nongoloza': Youth, Crime and Amalaita Gangs in Durban, 1900–1936," *Journal of Southern African Studies* 16, no. 1 (1990): 88; J. Masselos, "Change and Custom in the Format of the Bombay Mohurrum During the Nineteenth and Twentieth Centuries," *South Asia: Journal of South Asian Studies* 5, no. 2 (1982): 47–67.
16. Sleight, *Young People*, 50–86.
17. J. De Barros, *Order and Place in a Colonial City: Patterns of Struggle and Resistance in Georgetown, British Guiana, 1889–1924* (Montreal and London: McGill-Queen's University Press, 2002), 93–95; Davies, *Gangs of Manchester*, 39, 77; J. Iliffe, *A Modern History of Tanganyika* (Cambridge: Cambridge University Press, 1979), 238–239.
18. Brereton, *Race Relations in Colonial Trinidad*, 166–175; Trotman, *Crime in Trinidad*, 167–169; La Hausse, "'The Cows of Nongoloza,'" 79–111; 101.
19. La Hausse, "'The Cows of Nongoloza,'" 91–95, 100; L. Finch, "On the Streets: Working Class Youth Culture in the Nineteenth Century," in *Youth Subcultures: Theory, History and the Australian Experience*, ed. Rob White (Hobart, Australia: ACYS, [1993] 2006), 67.
20. M. Bellanta and S. Sleight, "The Leary Larrikin: Street Style in Colonial Australia," *Cultural and Social History* 11, no. 2 (2014): 263–283; Davies, *Gangs of Manchester*; D. Ambaras, *Bad Youth: Juvenile Delinquency and the Politics of Everyday Life in Modern Japan* (Berkeley, CA; London: University of California Press, 2006), 145.
21. M. Perrot, "Dans la France de la Belle Époque, les 'Apaches,' premières bandes de jeunes," in *Les Marginaux et les exclus dans l'histoire*, Cahiers Jussieu no. 5, Université de Paris 7 (Paris: Union Générale d'Éditions, 1979), 387–407; J. Neuberger, *Hooliganism: Crime, Culture and Power in St Petersburg* (Berkeley: University of California Press, 1993), 226–227; M. Bellanta, "Poor Urban Youth and Popular Theatricals: The Case of Late-19th-Century Australia," in *A World of Popular Entertainments*, ed. G. Arrigih and V. Emeljanow (Newcastle-upon-Tyne, UK: Cambridge Scholars Press, 2012), 233–243; M. Bellanta, "The Larrikin's Hop: Larrikinism and Late Colonial Popular Theatre," *Australasian Drama Studies* 52 (2008): 131–147; M. Bellanta, "Leary Kin: Australian Larrikins and the Blackface

Minstrel Dandy," *Journal of Social History* 42, no. 3 (2009): 677–695; M. Bellanta, "The Larrikin Girl," *Journal of Australian Studies* 34, no. 4 (2010): 499–512.
22. "A Bulawayan Abroad," *Bulawayo Chronicle*, June 12, 1901, 4.
23. "Larrikinism," *Argus* (Melbourne), January 31, 1882, 4.
24. "Hooligans in Other Lands," *Pearson's Weekly*, November 5, 1908, 364; "Rowdies and Hooligans," *Mexican Herald*, September 8, 1909, 1.
25. "Victoria," *Carlisle Patriot*, August 2, 1872, 7.
26. "English Cricketers in Australia," *Daily Telegraph*, April 1, 1879, 5.
27. "Australian News," *Globe* (London), July 29, 1879, 6.
28. J. Inglis, *Our Australian Cousins* (London: Macmillan & Co., 1880), 175.
29. "Ruffianly Behaviour," *Portsmouth Evening News*, July 15, 1880, 2.
30. "The Reverse of the Medal," *Pall Mall Gazette*, October 1, 1881, 1; "The Spread of Ruffianism," *Spectator*, October 8, 1881, 1273.
31. G. Pearson, *Hooligan: A History of Respectable Fears* (London: Macmillan, 1983).
32. "Lord Mayor on London 'Larrikins,'" *Sheffield Daily Telegraph*, January 16, 1889, 2.
33. C. Brickell, *Teenagers: The Rise of Youth Culture in New Zealand* (Auckland, NZ: Auckland University Press, 2017), 74, 104, and 107.
34. "Editorials. Prospects for Ceylon Colonists in New Zealand: A Darkly-Shaded Picture," *Ceylon Observer*, September 6, 1882, 759; "A Ceylon Colonist on Life in New Zealand," *Ceylon Observer*, December 16, 1882, 1104; *Cape Times*, September 29, 1888, 2.
35. S. Cohen, *Folk Devils and Moral Panics: The Creation of the Mods and Rockers* (St. Albans, UK: Paladin, 1973), 9.
36. Cohen, *Folk Devils and Moral Panics*, 31.
37. Weber, *The Growth of Cities*, 407.
38. Sleight, *Young People*, 138.
39. Ibid., 149; A. Davies, "Youth Gangs, Masculinity and Violence in Late Victorian Manchester and Salford," *Journal of Social History* 32, no. 2 (1998): 362.
40. D. Hebdige, *Subculture: The Theory of Style* (London: Methuen, 1979); Bellanta and Sleight, "The Leary Larrikin."
41. Brickell, *Teenagers*, 105; De Barros, *Order and Place*, 86; Trotman, *Crime in Trinidad*, 181.
42. Bellanta, "The Larrikin Girl."
43. Humphries, *Hooligans or Rebels?*, 179; Thrasher, *The Gang*, 30, 36, 242; La Hausse, "'The Cows of Nongoloza.'"
44. P. Corrigan, "Doing Nothing," in *Resistance Through Rituals: Youth Subcultures in Post-war Britain*, ed. S. Hall and T. Jefferson (London: Hutchinson & Co, 1976), 103–105.
45. Trotman, *Crime in Trinidad*, 168.
46. H. Liverpool, *Rituals of Power and Rebellion: The Carnival Tradition in Trinidad and Tobago 1763-1962* (Chicago; London: Research Associates School Times, 2001).
47. T. J. Gilfoyle, "Street-Rats and Gutter-Snipes: Child Pickpockets and Street Culture in New York City, 1850–1900," *Journal of Social History* 37, no. 4 (2004): 853–882.
48. P. Acerbi, *Street Occupations: Urban Vending in Rio de Janeiro, 1850–1925* (Austin: University of Texas Press, 2017), 105–107; T. Holloway, *Policing Rio de Janeiro: Repression and Resistance in a 19th-century City* (Stanford, CA: Stanford University Press, 1993), 223–228; M. Talmon-Chvaicer, "The Criminalization of Capoeira in Nineteenth-Century Brazil," *Hispanic American Historical Review* 82, no. 3 (2002): 525–547.
49. A. Stoler, *Along the Archival Grain: Thinking Through Colonial Ontologies* (Princeton, NJ: Princeton University Press, 2009).

50. T.J. Desch-Obi, *Fighting for Honor: The History of African Martial Art Traditions in the Atlantic World* (Columbia: University of South Carolina Press, 2008), 294n38,59.
51. "'Pushes.' Larrikinism a Lost Art," *Argus* (Melbourne), March 19, 1910, 21.
52. R. Roger, "Reflections: Putting the 'Trans' into Transnational Urban History," in *Cities Beyond Borders: Comparative and Transnational Approaches to Urban History*, ed. N. Kenny and R. Madgin (Farnham: Ashgate, 2015), 207–216.

Further Reading

Ambaras, David. *Bad Youth: Juvenile Delinquency and the Politics of Everyday Life in Modern Japan*. Berkeley: University of California Press, 2006.

Bellanta, Melissa. *Larrikins: A History*. St. Lucia: University of Queensland Press, 2012.

Bellanta, Melissa, and Simon Sleight. "The Leary Larrikin: Street Style in Colonial Australia." *Cultural and Social History* 11, no. 2 (2014): 263–283.

Brickell, Chris. *Teenagers: The Rise of Youth Culture in New Zealand*. Auckland, NZ: Auckland University Press, 2017.

Cohen, Stanley. *Folk Devils and Moral Panics: The Creation of the Mods and Rockers*. St. Albans, UK: Paladin, 1973.

Davies, Andrew. "Histories of Hooliganism." In *Mischief, Morality and Mobs: Essays in Honour of Geoffrey Pearson*. Edited by Dick Hobbs, 85–101. New York and London: Routledge, 2017.

Humphries, Stephen. *Hooligans or Rebels? An Oral History of Working-Class Childhood and Youth, 1889–1939*. Oxford: Basil Blackwell, (1981) 1984.

La Hausse, Paul. "'The Cows of Nongoloza': Youth, Crime and Amalaita Gangs in Durban, 1900–1936." *Journal of Southern African Studies* 16, no. 1 (1990): 79–111.

Sleight, Simon. *Young People and the Shaping of Public Space in Melbourne, 1870–1914*. Farnham and Burlington, UK: Ashgate, 2013.

Trotman, David. *Crime in Trinidad: Conflict and Control in a Plantation Society, 1838–1900*. Knoxville: University of Tennessee Press, 1986.

Weber, Adna Ferrin. *The Growth of Cities in the Nineteenth Century: A Study in Statistics*. New York and London: Macmillan and P. S. King and Son, 1899.

CHAPTER 10

GENDER, AGENCY, AND SEX

Postwar European Youth and the Generation Gap

DAVID NIGET

YOUTH SEXUAL CULTURE: BETWEEN NORMS AND SUBVERSIONS

AFTER the Second World War—as "the youth" came onto the social scene, embodying a desire for the "rejuvenation" of Western political cultures—boys' sexuality gradually became the object of regulations, whereas that of girls was, more than ever before, the subject of multiple moral panics.[1] Policies around sexual majority, which established legal limits and laws governing the age of consent and marriage, were reshaped after the war in many countries, extending protections to young people of age to have sexual relations. In France, the age of sexual majority was raised from thirteen to fifteen in 1945. In Canada, the age of criminal responsibility was raised from sixteen to eighteen in 1942, allowing juvenile courts to intervene in the sexual behavior of young people. Throughout the West, the field of psychology supported a juvenile justice system that increasingly focused on sexuality, detecting in it an etiology of youth deviancies.

At the same time, youth culture was sexualized. Reading materials, music, consumption, and leisure activities all indicated preoccupations with sex. Although certain developments were already nascent during the interwar period, the experience of sexuality changed for the young after the Second World War, with new rituals, new codes, and a new culture. Sexuality, into which the youth had previously been inducted by socially defined rites that were marked especially by religious morality, became more of a private practice, with each young person realizing him- or herself through the formation of a sexual identity located at the intersection of collective culture and individual subjectivity. As a generational marker, sexuality tended to become a matter of power and the subject of controversies, conflicts, and negotiations within families, youth socialization institutions (schools, reformatories, and so on), and the public space. The sexuality of the young was politicized, becoming, during the "Global Sixties," a symbol of youth revolt against the social norms of the adult world. But sexuality is not merely a mirror of political culture, reflecting the gradual emancipation of youth; it is a tool of this political emancipation, operating through a new sexual culture. A "sexual revolution" was underway, with forms of knowledge, discourses, and representations of sexuality at its heart, and new rights for the young on the horizon: the right to choose what to do with one's sexualized body, as well as the right to claim amorous affects as constitutive of one's social identity (a "right to love"). Examining social practices, however, reveals that this revolution varied greatly according to social class, gender, race, and sexual orientation.[2] The "liberation" of mores primarily benefited the dominant and strengthened the hegemony of virility, before being potentially subverted by sexually dominated social groups—women and homosexuals.

The sexual identities of the young were constructed in a highly gendered way, with a double standard that placed virility in a dominant position while femininity was associated with passivity. Virility is not the same as masculinity, and although the term "virility" has often been used either to praise masculinity or deplore the loss of it, it in fact indicates to what extent masculinity is a cultural construction rather than a biological attribute. Historical anthropology points to three major indicators of virility: physical strength and the courage to use it, the desire to dominate and an attraction to power, and finally, sexual potency, including the ability to procreate and to seduce.[3] These models of virility have played an important role in the injunctions made to boys to construct themselves as men. Institutions of socialization, including the family, the school, and the army, have had a determining role in this, distilling the codes of virility specific to a given society and time period. Same-sex peer groups represent the social milieu par excellence where virility is constructed—here, such construction is rendered more effective by the fact that virility is developed under the reciprocal gaze of alter egos. This social environment contributes to instituting a virile ethos that is internalized as constitutive of an identity, a private subjectivity, and, thus, is considered ontological (one is a man "by essence") or "natural." To the extent that this construction, as arbitrary and violent as it may be, comes with social privileges created by masculine domination over women, calling it into question is especially complicated.

George Mosse traces the long history of virility—at once agonistic and warlike and sober and controlled—from the "masculine ideal" of the Enlightenment to the fascist virilism of the Nazis.[4] And although between 1945 and 1975, masculine identity became more fluid, shaped by a polyphonic "youth culture" that combined caricatures of virility with subversive counter-models, surges of virility continued to impose a highly normalizing gender stereotype. The Cold War heightened uncertainty around a supposed "crisis of virility," a social anxiety that led experts on the psyche to focus on adolescents.[5]

For girls, the idea of "the eternal feminine" served to naturalize the relationship between sex and gender and was indicative of a form of social control over women's bodies. Governance of female bodies is the keystone of patriarchal societies. Although as early as the beginning of the twentieth century, radical feminists such as Madeleine Pelletier and Emma Goldman denounced this illusion, it was the publication of Simone de Beauvoir's *The Second Sex* in 1949 that rang out like a thunderclap. de Beauvoir's writing made apparent the relations of domination produced by the sexual order, in which the feminine is constructed as inferior by the social and political structure and by a system of cultural representations that is especially effective because it is internalized by women through their socialization. Her chapters on "the girl" and "sexual initiation" resonated with many young female readers. It was not only the elite who read this philosopher; her work reached many middle-class and working-class adolescents during the 1950s, a fact reflected both in her personal correspondence and in the archives of youth welfare institutions.

Indeed, the 1950s saw the invention of a new category in writings and representations: the *"fille amoureuse"* [girl in love].[6] Signaling a new relation to sexuality, this social representation created an interstice within morality, which, until the interwar period, had distinguished between respectable girls on the one hand and "easy girls" on the other. Thereafter, prenuptial sexuality became acceptable—transgressing the ritual of a girl losing her virginity on her wedding night—but only if the relationship was (or was claimed to be) based on love. Representations of the "girl in love" pervaded the social body, especially within cultural representations: popular novels intended for the youth, cinema, and youth magazines, following the U.S.-American model.[7]

YOUTH, POPULAR CULTURES, AND SEXUALITIES

Perhaps paradoxically, within the institution of the family—the site of sexual and social reproduction—sexuality was discussed little. The sexual education of children was for a long time something unspoken, at least until the 1970s, although this should be qualified: "informal" education did not necessarily take place through words, but through a number of behaviors observable within the family. Thus, a lack of privacy in working-class housing allowed the young to become familiar with sexuality. Prior to children and young adults being granted a certain privacy in the 1960s, shared bedrooms and beds remained common in poor households, and constituted sites of learning that were observed, inventoried, and decried by social workers who entered the homes of families receiving state assistance to map their habits and morals.[8]

Similarly, the elements of popular culture—festive occasions, songs, and humor—that filled certain moments of family life did not seek to shelter children from sex. Moreover, there was a certain tolerance for boys' sexual practices, such as the practice of collective masturbation, which was evoked in the files of the Juvenile Court of Montreal as a rather banal occurrence. Such tolerance was highly gendered, for in working-class milieux, pubescent girls were sheltered from sexuality in the name of family respectability, which constituted a patrimony to be preserved.[9]

Whereas girls were sometimes warned by their mothers or sisters about the dangers of sexuality—in particular the risk of unwanted pregnancy—boys were, however, generally kept in the dark. There were some exceptions to this: in large cities, where prostitution was commonplace, some fathers or brothers would inform boys of the perils of venereal disease or the risks of "going with girls"—warnings that did not amount to an interdiction. Girls, on the other hand, were kept far from the world of prostitution and were threatened with being sent "to the convent" if they showed signs of moral weakness. Gradually, beginning in the 1960s, mothers began to take on the role of informing their children about sex, as noted in the 1972 Simon Report, the first study of sexuality among the French to discuss the topic of sexual education.[10]

Since the nineteenth century, educators have denounced the nefarious influences of reading on the minds of adolescents, who were feared to be "suggestible." Literature, and novels in particular, has often been vilified as subversive. Girls were considered more vulnerable in this respect than boys. Parents and teachers feared that girls would abscond to a world of romantic reverie, far from their duties as future wives. After the war, this fear remained, heightened by the literary resurgence of young authors such as Sartre, de Beauvoir, and Camus in France, Moravia and Morante in Italy, and Böll in Germany. In the archives of social workers, there is evidence of an aversion to existentialism and to sexual liberation, seen as corrupting the youth. In 1955, a Belgian case worker wrote that "Our girls are all more or less affected by this wave of pessimism and somber independence."[11] They stressed the influence of the young Françoise Sagan, whose first novel, *Bonjour tristesse* (*Hello Sadness*) became a media sensation in 1954 due to its frank description of sexuality. In the 1960s, Albertine Sarrazin published *L'Astragale*, the story of her escape from the reform school of Doullens.[12] The book was a massive literary and commercial success and could be found on the nightstands of many middle- and working-class girls. Like Jean Genet, Sarrazin transcended her carceral experience to turn it into a story of sexual modernity, describing her heterosexual and homosexual loves, and proudly proclaiming her prostitution as part of her bohemian lifestyle.

Beyond literature, the best way for the youth to learn about sex and sexuality in the postwar years was through images—postcards and drawings exchanged among peers.

In the accounts given by young people interrogated by the justice system, there are mentions of pornography, which became common thanks to the commercial distribution of photographs and films beginning in the late nineteenth century. Obscene photographs circulated in the form of postcards or albums, which the young might steal or borrow from an older friend. A police constable searched the bedroom of a 16-year-old boy in Montreal in 1950 and found "indecent images" and a "still picture projector." A young girl was arrested in the street in 1966 with a young male friend in possession of pornographic images stolen from her father, which were scrupulously registered in the records of the Juvenile Court. Some popular publications—including youth magazines, which were widespread beginning in the 1940s—contained comic strips that, though not pornographic, evoked sex. These included the comic strip *Tarzan*, a major success in the 1950s. In France, however, increasingly strict laws prohibited the distribution of indecent printed material: the law of July 16, 1949, regulated publications intended for the young and censored books and periodicals. In spite of these restrictions, the 1950s and 1960s saw the development of erotic or pornographic illustrated magazines, a media form through which a large segment of the youth came into contact with sexuality. Such material was considered dangerous by social workers, who associated it with "precocious" sexuality, as in the case of Marie, sent for observation to the Bon Pasteur convent in Angers in 1951: "Since the age of fourteen, she has regularly gone out with young men, has declared on multiple occasions that she is engaged, and has kept up impassioned correspondences. She reads many bad novels and highly questionable magazines," the nun who was her caseworker explained. These magazines were described as "pornographic" by the social worker at the juvenile court and were said to feed the girl's imagination.[13] Such moral panics around the suggestibility of the young—and girls in particular—were widespread in the Western world.[14] Moral regulation also progressed in the English-speaking world; external control was internalized by individuals themselves, with adolescence considered a strategic moment for the inculcation of modesty.

Even though they were disreputable, these "obscene" publications conveyed a relatively normalized representation of sexual acts, which centered on masculine desire, masculine pleasure, and for the most part came out of a heterosexual and sometimes racialized culture of sexuality, with, in particular, images of highly stereotypical, sexualized "Oriental" women, and Black men presented as virile and savage. Erotic magazines contained images—"pinups" intended to be hung on adolescent boys' walls—of women as fantasies: sometimes objects, sometimes sexual dominatrices. Pornographic films, even before the introduction of the "X" rating in 1975, were forbidden to minors, who could thus only see them by sneaking in. Similarly, in television, in France, the "white square" was invented in 1961, signaling to parents to keep their children away from the family television set during certain shows judged too violent or sexual.

On the other hand, there were few or no gay images to be seen before the 1970s. Gay erotic publications remained secret, and the first gay and lesbian magazines of the 1950s, such as *One* and *The Ladder* in the United States and *Futur* and *Arcadie* in France, did not include pornography.[15] Young gay men had to look to the world of sports, to soccer or body-building magazines, or, more rarely, to nudist magazines, to nourish their fantasies. Male nudity remained far rarer and more taboo than female nudity, and images of the male sex organ, especially if erect, were limited to pornography.

SEXUAL EDUCATION: SCHOOL, SCIENCE, AND IGNORANCE

After 1945, experts, demographers, psychiatrists, and psychologists began promoting a new position on sexual education: in order to guarantee public health and ensure that the young would grow up in conformity with gender norms, they had to be led out of ignorance. As early as 1947, the French national education system recommended adding sexual education courses to school curricula—a recommendation that went unimplemented. The Louis François Report advocated providing scientific "sexual information" along with instruction in sexual morality to promote marital sex and self-control. The Report points to the moral threats perceived by educational and political elites during the Glorious Thirty, within the context of the reactionary moral crisis around the dissolution of traditional mores, non-reproductive sex, and homosexuality that defined the Cold War era in the West.[16]

Somewhat paradoxically, the mixing of the sexes and co-education in schools came to be seen as a solution that would guarantee the hegemony of heterosexuality. Although the mingling of the sexes continued to fuel moral fears within Catholic institutions, where a deeply misogynist culture was more tolerant of homosexual experiences than of precocious heterosexual ones, pedagogues increasingly praised co-education as a way of regulating relations between the sexes and reinforcing differentiated gender identities. Thus, Marguerite Chardon, a feminist activist and the honorary director of a primary school, said in 1966:

> Boys must accept themselves as boys and develop their normal virility without conceitedness or brutality, by focusing on protecting the weak, fighting against injustice, and altruism ... Girls must accept themselves, develop their maternal instincts and their psychological intuition... Both must be convinced of their mutual equality at the social and legal levels: they are different and complementary from a biological point of view, but each is as human as the other. Simple and fraternal relations between the youth of both sexes helps combat certain deviations: coquettishness, vanity, obsessions.[17]

A pacified virility began to be promoted, one far from any physical violence or affective passion: a new form of civic, responsible, moral, and reasoned masculinity.

Similarly, girls were invited to cultivate their "natural" inclinations toward gentleness and passivity, and to take on a social role as mediators and pacifiers of customs and habits.

Because to a certain extent schools avoided teaching the young about sexuality, other sites took on this task during the Glorious Thirty. Here, note first an explosion of popular scientific publications on the subject of sexuality during the 1960s and 1970s. Magazines, encyclopedias, manuals, guides, and testimonies proliferated, oscillating between relatively conservative or traditional views and more progressive positions based on the work of gynecologists, psychoanalysts, and sexologists. The distribution of reports on sexuality—the Kinsey Report and the Masters & Johnson Report in the United States and the Simon Report in France—was decisive.[18] The role of the work of the German psychoanalyst Wilhelm Reich and the philosopher Herbert Marcuse in more political student circles must also be emphasized.

In addition, the media, whose modalities and audiences were becoming more diverse, took an interest in "youth issues," and sexuality in particular. The idea that sexuality was no longer a "private" matter gained acceptance, and sex became the object of increasing mediatization. In 1967, Ménie Grégoire addressed the issue of sexual education on his radio show and received thousands of letters in response from young people and parents.[19] The national television station ORTF dedicated several programs to youth sexuality in the late 1960s. In 1968, the German sexual education film *Helga, Vom Werden des Menschichen Lebens* (*Helga - On the Origins of Human Life*), produced by the German Federal Center for Health Education, sold five million tickets in Germany and in France, and over forty million worldwide.

In February 1971, two students kissed in a high school in Corbeil-Essonnes, breaking the school's rules. Their parents were notified, and the students were punished. Following this incident, several high school students formed the Comité d'action pour la libération de la sexualité (Action Committee for the Liberation of Sexuality) and sought the advice of Dr. Jean Carpentier, a general physician known for his free-thinking opinions. Together, they drafted a protest tract, which was intended to serve as a manifesto for sexual education for high school students and against interdictions, taboos, and the hypocrisy of adults regarding sexuality. They focused on anatomy as well as pleasure, desire, and orgasms. Carpentier emphasized above all that with regard to sexuality, "notions of 'normal' and 'abnormal' have absolutely no basis.... The greatest freedom must guide the variety of our choices. There is only one danger: repressing our desires." The tract was published in its entirety in the newspaper *Le Monde* on February 11 and 12, 1973. The debates and criticism it sparked were vigorous. Along with other political figures, one senator denounced "a tract that presents itself in the guise of sexual education, but is no more than a vulgar pornographic text likely to affect and shock the minds of young men and women."[20] Carpentier was suspended from the Conseil national de l'ordre des médecins (National Board of Doctors) for one year. But the text circulated throughout high schools, provoking feverish debates within the context of the controversy surrounding the legalization of abortion.[21] More and more teachers and administrators within the national education system declared themselves in favor of real sexual education, which would not separate biology from affectivity, or the reproductive function from eroticism, but would consider human sexuality in all its complexity. Finally, beginning in September 1973, the national education system integrated "information on matters of procreation" into its curriculum as part of biology courses, and left the (perilous) responsibility of organizing extracurricular sessions on "leading a love life" to heads of schools.

FLIRTATION: A SENTIMENTAL EDUCATION

In the postwar period, adolescent seduction was distinguished by the practice of "flirting." In France, the English word "flirt" was used; this usage had existed since the late nineteenth century and can be found in Proust's writing, but it became widespread after 1945. In using this word, postwar Francophone youth invoked an American imaginary, which was seen as synonymous with sexual modernity and with less formal and freer relations of seduction. In French, the term explicitly refers to a love relationship, and not mere banter. The verb gave rise to a noun: "*avoir un flirt avec*" [to have a flirt with] meant to go out with someone. Boys also used gendered expressions such as "*emballer une fille*" [to bag a girl] or, more rarely, "*draguer*" [pick up], verbs that, in French, are connected with the vocabulary of conquest.

Sites of seduction became more diverse. Cinema, then in its heyday, was feared by respectable society, both for the images of desirable and desiring bodies it depicted and for the physical proximity provided by darkened movie theaters, where bodies grazed against each other and intertwined. Cafes, previously reserved for adult men, became open to young people—boys and accompanied girls—who gathered around jukeboxes or pinball machines. The latter were sexualized objects, both in terms of the erotic images painted on them and the position boys adopted when playing. Carnivals, where boys displayed their strength and skills as they laughed and bantered, remained reliable sites for adolescent seduction. The ballroom gradually gave way to "surprise parties" (referred to as "*sur'pat*" in French) and other types of teenage parties ("*boums*" and "*surboums*"), which were held far from the prying eyes of adults and had their own specific customs. The sound of bebop filled the basements of Saint-Germain-des-Prés in Paris and the first nightclubs in the provinces, mesmerizing older youth and providing the backdrop for nocturnal episodes, stories of which filled the juvenile courts of cities.[22]

Kissing on the mouth, which was long considered obscene, before being popularized by movies and photographs, became an essential ritual and a generational marker that could be clearly displayed in the street (as in Doisneau's 1950 photograph "Le baiser de l'hôtel de ville" ["The Kiss by the Hôtel de Ville"] for *Life* magazine). Initially chaste, during the 1950s, kissing became "deep," increasingly done "with tongue."

The exchange of bodily fluids, and more or less brazen penetration with the tongue, made such kissing a metaphor of the sexual act: a somewhat technical erotic act that required peer initiation and prefigured sexual relations. But far from being strictly intimate, kissing could be done in the presence of friends, as boys would often go in groups to pick up girls. It attested to a kind of virtuosity in seduction and became a source of pride for a boy. Considered "romantic," it was nevertheless one of the gestures highlighting dominance over female bodies.

The "flirt" was a form of sentimental education, a preliminary but also autonomous stage between childlike innocence and reproductive sexuality. Flirting, as a specifically adolescent practice, was also supposed to keep at bay the risks associated with seduction: first and foremost, the risk of sex itself, which could lead to an unwanted pregnancy, because contraception remained inaccessible to most young people until the 1970s. Though it appeared light and insouciant, flirting allowed for a full range of erotic daring, the quintessence of a desire that must remain fantasmatic.[23] Flirting was also supposed to rebalance gender relations within practices of seduction, and to fluidify the sexual roles held by boys and girls. Thus, according to the new codes, girls could be more forward than before. They had to give their consent for a relationship to be established, while at the same time demonstrating their respectability by presenting themselves as "girls in love." Despite the prevalence of such matrimonial representations, more and more young women displayed a desire to seduce without thereby becoming attached. Marie, placed in a child guidance institution in Angers, stood out for her fickleness, which disturbed the psychologists: "Coquette. Has amused herself with various boys; does not seem to be more deeply attached to any one of them over the others."[24]

For many boys, the excitement of an encounter and the casualness sought in the "game of love and chance" could give rise to a somewhat disquieting doubt regarding the superficial nature of a relationship. The reticence of some boys to act as enterprising pickup artists was met with disapproval from their peers and suspicion from adults: were they not virile enough? "Hegemonic masculinity," the source of numerous social privileges, came at a price for boys themselves. In contrast, some boys styled themselves collectors of pickups. Flirting thus became a rite of passage whereby ignorant boys became adolescents confident in their masculinity and sure of their ability to seduce girls. Female resistance was not seen as a true refusal but, rather, as a way of behaving that would demonstrate a girl's virtue while also attracting men. This ambiguity, based on long-standing gender stereotypes, sometimes provided justification for the use of force, causing the anthropological script of the abduction of young women to re-emerge.[25] In the postwar years, the backseats of cars were sometimes the settings of such everyday dramas.[26]

For girls, the game of seduction was not only about romance. Through the 1960s, going out with a young man—often older and therefore already working—was a way for girls to gain a form of material independence from their families. In reform schools, many girls justified their so-called precocious sexual habits by a need or desire for social emancipation.

The racial question was already present in 1960s France: young North African, African, and West Indian men testified to the difficulties they encountered when going out with young white women. These included not only dirty looks in the street and the social judgment directed at mixed-race couples, but also a number of racial stereotypes held by young women after the Algerian War, associating foreigners, and "Arabs" in particular, with a form of sexual savagery that did not fit with the new codes of supposedly temperate white virility.[27]

Young Gays and Lesbians: Invisible Loves and New Scripts

"Male friendship" has been the source of a powerful imaginary in society, one nourished by an abundant literature. For a long time, and without shocking anyone, the bonds of friendship between boys appeared as intense relationships, closer to love than to camaraderie. Roger Peyrefitte won the Prix Renaudot in 1944 for *Les amitiés particulières* (*Special Friendships*), which explicitly described the young loves of two boys aged twelve and fourteen in a Catholic boarding school. But during the second half of the twentieth century, juvenile homosexuality became an object of suspicion. The psychologist Paul Le Moal, an expert on "maladjusted" children, thought that about 17 percent of adolescent boys had homosexual relations.[28] The historian Régis Revenin found that 20 percent of boys at the Savigny Child Guidance Institute (in the Parisian suburbs) between 1945 and 1972 had had exclusively homosexual relations. More common were boys who said they had had both homosexual and heterosexual relations, but this number decreased during the 1960s, as if the imperative to choose a "sexual orientation" was becoming increasingly strong.[29] Thus, as Georges Chauncey has pointed out in his history of gay New York, during the first half of the twentieth century, sexual identities could be fluid. During the first half of the twentieth century, however, individuals were assigned a sexuality corresponding to their gender, and social representations gradually came to define any breach of heteronormativity as transgressive.[30]

Foucault has pointed out the paradox of power that both stigmatizes and produces: the response to such arbitrary designations was the open assertion of homosexuality, at first muted and then gradually becoming more audible, among the young in particular. In 1949, the seventeen-year-old Florimond explained to his caseworker: "homosexuality [*pédérastie*] is normal, it's not a crime or an offense." According to him, homosexuals "don't do any harm to society." And, he added, "I take pleasure in sleeping with a man. I like it when a man kisses me on the mouth." In 1964, an adolescent boy who had broken with his family and run away to Paris declared, "We, the fags [*pédés*], we are normal people and we will never change."[31] Such openly declared positions were nevertheless met with strong social condemnation in postwar France, and young gay men were mostly shunned by their families. Others lived out their identity in secret, admitting it to themselves but hiding it from their friends and family and the world; "coming out" did not become an activist gesture until the 1970s.

For young homosexuals, the ideal love seems to have evolved similarly to that of young heterosexuals: the age gap within couples narrowed, and young gay men sought a "friend" rather than a father figure or a middle-aged man. Racial homogamy was also a requirement: the ideal lover for a white adolescent was also white (or possibly North African, because they were thought to be sensual); Blacks and Asians were not part of the ideal picture. The model of virility remained that of traditional masculinity, subtly subverting the figure of the working man, the hoodlum, the soldier, or sailor, but rejecting any effeminacy: a caricature that, according to young men, discredited all homosexuals. During these years of initial, fairly elitist gay activism, there was still gender conformity, respect for the orthodoxy of the masculine and of virility, which would provide a form of respectability for homosexuals. Thus, the young, "modern" gay man would free himself of all the attributes of the "*tante*" [queer], a caricature that emerged out of the Belle Époque, when homosexuality could only be openly expressed in the world of nightlife and show business. Johnny Hallyday, James Dean, and Marlon Brando were the new gay icons, fantasies boys shared with girls.

In spite of certain homologies, gay seduction scenarios were quite far from the regulated codes of heterosexual encounters. There was no danger of pregnancy. No distance ritualized by sexual alterity. No double-edged system of domination. No moral discussion on "propriety" serving as an education in heterosexuality. Homosexual pickups blended fraternity and seduction within a virile in-group that seemed to facilitate relations. Sexuality played an important role in this context, a role that no doubt increased when, after the war, gay sociability came to center around the category of an exclusive sexual orientation and the practices linked to it. Sexual relations were often direct and furtive, so as not to attract attention. Public urinals, still quite common in postwar France, were iconic pickup spots. There, young men would meet, masturbate each other, and make dates for later in parks or other public spaces sheltered from view. Glances exchanged in public places were strategic, allowing one to be recognized by another without compromising oneself in case of error. Familiarity with pickup sites and neighborhoods was thus essential.

As Régis Revenin notes, "there was no pre-conceived model for homosexual encounters,"[32] and gay pickup culture had to be invented. Scripts varied according to circumstances, bringing into play relations of dominance more subtle than those in heterosexual practices. One could just as easily initiate a pickup as be picked up, as long as one's virility wasn't called into question. Many young gay men didn't want to be "treated like girls"—as objects of desire—and wished to preserve the attributes of power they considered corollaries of their gender. On the face of it, violence was less common than within heterosexual relations: lack of consent was more often taken seriously, in part because until 1982 homosexual relations with minors remained a felony offense, but also because, among men, a form of civil contract was respected. This did not rule out the social violence of male prostitution, which often involved young men. The factor of race was combined with that of class when it was a matter of young North African male prostitutes, who were viewed through an outdated orientalist lens that was revived during the years of decolonization.

In the archives, lesbian love affairs are mentioned less frequently and with less candidness. Social control authorities were less likely to be alerted to female homosexuality, a far more discreet social phenomenon, than to "pederasty." Adolescent female friendships appear to have included the possibility of real or fantasized sexuality, as long as this remained secret. Under certain conditions, such "sexuality in the meantime," which allowed girls to preserve their virtue until they reached marriage age, was tolerated.[33] Girls themselves very rarely claimed to be "lesbians" or homosexuals, and they engaged in different sexual practices depending on their encounters. Nevertheless, the tightening of sexual assignations during the postwar years restricted the moment of youth as a time for experimenting with gender fluidity. Experts and psychiatrists such as Dr. Le Moal at the Chevilly-Larue Child Guidance Center in the Parisian suburbs took an interest in lesbian cases. Although records of them are rare, remarks about girls' "ambiguous" sexual behavior and their open or "latent" "homosexuality" do exist. The diagnoses were uncertain and emphasized the physiological etiology of this type of behavior: hormonal problems indicated by a low voice and small breasts.[34] Psychological problems were also invoked to explain lesbian sexuality as a form of refuge: trauma following a rape, excessive narcissism, or anxiety about future heterosexual life. Reform boarding schools run by the nuns of Bon-Pasteur were sites of fears about "special friendships," and intimacy between girls and time spent in pairs were prevented. Albertine Sarrazin evoked such transgressions in her journal: "Endless lustful stories with girls, love letters spotted in passing by the threatening eye of the old mole; kisses on the lips or ambiguous caresses, sleeping two to a bed."[35] Monique Wittig also described the youthful freedom of amorous girls becoming aware of themselves and their lesbian desire while under the iron rule of nuns in boarding schools in her novel *The Opoponax*, which won the Prix Médicis in 1964. Living a secluded life in convents and residential homes gave some girls the opportunity to have homosexual experiences, and, more rarely, to declare themselves homosexual. Although some young women explained their attractions as games or provocation, others seem to have fully accepted their sexual identity. Nicole, placed in a child guidance center in Saint-Servais near Namur (Belgium), was thus noted for her "homosexual tendencies" and the fact that she "tries to dress like a boy." In her file, Nicole drew herself in the style of a boy, with short hair and bell-bottom pants. During a psychological test, she explained "that the historical figure she identifies with is Joan of Arc.... As for the choice of sex, she expresses a certain ambivalence, then finally states that she would rather be a boy than a girl, since boys are stronger, smarter, and more free."[36] A lesbian ethos, one that would no longer seek to emulate the boys, was still to be invented, a task lesbian activists would take up in the 1970s.

"First Times": Trying Out Sexuality

Although in the twentieth century, one's "first time" has been the focus of adolescent sexual biographies—to the point of becoming a fetishized event—it is relatively difficult to reach an agreement about what this expression, with its powerful imaginary, actually corresponds to, for there are multiple "first times." Does it mean one's first sexual arousal, at a time when the body is still a foreign, desiring object? One's first sexual act, often autoerotic? First sexual relations with another person, either following a conjugal script or transgressive, polyamorous, and marked as experimental? Entry into sexual life is much more complex than its sometimes-stereotypical narration would imply.

Masturbation holds a particular place among forms of initiation into male sexuality. Decried since the eighteenth century, both because it reignited the intransigent moralism that came out of the Counter-Reformation and because it appeared as an intolerable waste of oneself within a nascent capitalist modernity, onanism remained tainted with shame and justified a range of repressive practices by adults against the young.[37] Despite such condemnations, masturbation remained an important rite of passage: the first intimate sexual experience, the movement of a body exploring sexual desire. Between peers, however, there was no such taboo: "jerking off" [*la branlette*] was a good topic of conversation and an inexhaustible source of jokes among adolescent boys. Group masturbation was a common practice among the working classes and was treated with some indulgence by adults. It was a ritual of camaraderie, sometimes performed by gangs in public spaces, as if to mark their territory. In the postwar period, however, it became a source of increasing disquiet on the part of doctors, social workers, and magistrates, because it was thought to presage homosexual practices.

Female masturbation, which was more secretive and was not the subject of initiation stories, was less common. The Simon Report (1972) indicates that 20 percent of women, versus 75 percent of men, said they masturbated. It is nevertheless present in the archives of reform schools: in the evenings, nuns monitored the dormitories to make sure that girls' hands were above the covers, but the interdiction against keeping one's hands beneath the covers was transgressed by many girls and, during episodes of uprising, masturbation was even used as an obscene gesture that the insurgents directed at their jailors.

Oral sex was another way of entering into sexuality, less risky than coitus, with its possibility of unwanted maternity. It was long associated with prostitutes and deemed unworthy of ordinary conjugality. In the 1960s it appeared among young heterosexuals as a form of sexuality-in-the-meantime, similar to mutual masturbation. Though sometimes considered with disgust by some young women, who refused to subject themselves to this rarely reciprocated and specifically male form of sexual touch (cunnilingus was absent from the discussion of the time), it rapidly became widespread, as attested by the hit song, "Les Sucettes" ("Lollipops"), written by Serge Gainsbourg for the young singer France Gall in 1966.

First coitus was the indicator commonly used during the Glorious Thirty by demographers, early sexologists, doctors, and social workers to designate entry into sexuality. According to the social surveys carried out at the Ministry of Justice's child guidance center at Savigny, the median age at which boys born after the war had their first sexual relations was 15.2 years for gay boys and 16.8 years for heterosexual boys. Over 50 percent of the boys in the study had their first sexual experience with a girl their age, though for 37 percent it was with an older woman—another phenomenon that became less common, despite the fantasies it continued to arouse, including the character played by Delphine Seyrig in François Truffaut's *Baisers volés* (*Stolen Kisses*) (1968). Similarly, among young gay men at the Savigny center, sexual initiation by an older man, though still significant (30 percent), was less frequent than experiences with boys of the same age.[38] Working-class boys, more numerous in this type of institution, were more precocious than middle-class boys, who were kept longer in institutions of control such as boarding schools. Social, and thus sexual, age was not the same for everyone.

For boys, performing this first sexual act was imperative to their virility. It was important for a boy to "pop his cherry" [*être dépucelé*] to be a man, whereas femininity was much more associated with a girl's first period and with fertility, and girls had to be extremely careful sexually, because virginity before marriage was still prized, at least in the discourse. Although girls were required to be in love before "giving themselves" to a man, no such affective investment was required of boys. Boys' peers often encouraged them to "do the deed," with "buddies" acting as "guardians of the virile order."[39]

Thus, for boys, sexual performance alone was the source of satisfaction, rather than their feelings toward their partner. According to the Simon Report, 68 percent of young men under thirty years old found satisfaction in their first time, versus only 45 percent of young women, some of whom also declared they took satisfaction in the pleasure they gave to their partner.[40] Even the famous "sexual liberation" of the "68 years" was primarily masculine and was associated first and foremost with the virile desire to experience sexual pleasure without sentimentalism, most often in ignorance of women's desire and pleasure.

Sexual Risks: Health, Rights, and Consent

The postwar years saw the emergence of a new culture of risk associated with sexuality. Although some dangers subsided, others appeared, redefining the contours of the licit and the illicit for the young. The 1950s–1970s—the period between the end of the scourge of syphilis and beginning of the "AIDS years"—were a time when one no longer died from sex, and when entry into sexuality could occur far from the shadow cast by disease. But this in no way meant a time of sexual carefreeness or golden years of sexual freedom for the young: contraception was the great preoccupation of the time. The figure of the girl-mother loomed near, as did that of the young couple who had parental responsibility foisted on them and were compelled by their families to get married. Although fear of unwanted pregnancy was omnipresent in the testimony of girls, and of some boys, the practice of contraception was not widespread during the period between 1945 and 1970. It was initially forbidden, as was, following a 1920 law, any communication, even educational or preventative, judged to be "anti-conception." And even if the young, like adults, practiced an ordinary form of contraception by avoiding "risky" sexual practices, accidents were common; indeed, the practice of "coitus interruptus" requires knowledge and control of one's body, as well as a form of experience that the young did not always have.

As for condoms, they had a bad reputation among the young: they were associated with prostitution and required getting the approval of a pharmacist. In addition, in the inexperienced hands of boys, they did not constitute a technique girls could rely on. Chemical contraception appeared in the late 1950s, offering women the possibility, and responsibility, of protecting themselves without having to count on the vigilance of their male partners or negotiating sexual practices that did not include the danger of pregnancy. Despite the proactive push for birth control policies in France by the Maternité Heureuse (Happy Motherhood) and Planning Familial (Family Planning) movements, and despite some Catholic intellectuals and doctors in Belgium being converted to "the pill,"[41] contraception remained out of reach for most young people. In France, the pill was only truly legalized in 1967 with the Neuwirth Law, and through the early 1970s it remained largely inaccessible to young women. In 1971, high school students declared in the magazine *Actuel* that it was impossible to get, "unless your dad is a pharmacist, your buddy is a doctor, or your mom is super understanding."

Communication about sexuality and procreation was mostly addressed to young women, who were supposed to be more responsible than boys, and were thus made to feel culpable at the same time that they were led believe that sexual fulfillment necessarily led to maternity. In contrast, during the Glorious Thirty, paternity was not seen as a project one chose. Within boys' representations, the experience of sexuality was not closely connected to awareness of their fertility but was, rather, seen as a symbol of their achievement of virility.

Located at the threshold of the public and the private, sexuality was the target of many attempts at control, with families and legal authorities finding arrangements to ensure social reproduction and the preservation of mores.[42] As for the young, they strove to determine their own sexual lives more autonomously, in keeping with the codes established by their peers. Thus, in the postwar years, the line between exploring one's sexuality and the repression of behaviors deemed immoral was fine and constantly renegotiated.

In France, the age of sexual majority—the age after which one could freely consent to sex and before which consent was impossible—was defined by law. It was set at eleven years in 1832, and thirteen years in 1863. Initially, the law did not distinguish between sexual orientations, but a Vichy-era law changed this: after 1942, homosexual relations were forbidden for minors (anyone under twenty-one), regardless of consent and even when both individuals were minors. The ordinance of July 2, 1945, raised the age of sexual majority to fifteen years for heterosexual relations and maintained a distinction from homosexual relations, where the age of majority remained twenty-one. This latter measure stayed in place until it was abrogated by the Socialist government in 1982.

Even more important than the question of consent was the imperative for authorities and some families to preserve the moral and social order, which sometimes implied a form of authoritarian intervention into the sexuality of the young. Thus, several categories of offenses in the French penal code were in fact "victimless crimes," which punished consensual sexual behaviors by the young. For example, "indecent exposure" consisted in having sexual relations in a visible public space (city parks, cars, movie theaters, etc.), even if any exposure that occurred was unintended. "Debauching a minor" consisted in initiating supposedly "pure and innocent" minors into practices thought to corrupt them, but these practices were not defined. Anyone of age who had sexual relations with a minor could be charged with this crime, including when the difference of age was minimal, as was the case in many adolescent couples. In addition, many homosexual couples, where the age gap was more significant, were specifically targeted by this form of repression. Finally, "corruption of a minor" was in reality not a sexual crime but simply meant taking a minor away from his or her family. Parents who were opposed to their child's relationship often invoked this offense, especially in cases where a minor had run away.

French civil law also allowed for the regulation of juvenile sexuality, with the provision for "paternal correction," which gave fathers—and, in certain conditions, mothers—the right to confine their children simply for being undisciplined. Paternal correction was mostly applied to girls and after 1945 was administered by juvenile court judges, who worked closely with fathers worried about their daughters' sexual reputations. The juvenile justice system, established in France in 1945 following an international model, took an increasingly close interest in the sexuality of both girls and boys. Police forces in North America and Europe established youth squads, one of whose stated objectives was to monitor the morality of the young.[43] Sexuality was among the "youth problems" that alarmed political authorities in the postwar era, and its regulation was seen as central to maintaining the fabric of citizenship.[44] The sciences of the mind, including the triumphant field of psychology, were called to the bedside of "maladjusted" youth and contributed to unveiling their private and intimate lives within youth welfare institutions. Thus, youth sexuality was exposed. Beginning in 1960, as customs and habits were becoming freer and the youth began to proclaim a desire for social and sexual emancipation, legislation became increasingly intransigent. Birth control was on the agenda everywhere, but its legalization had to be wrested from conservative powers. The repression of abortion meant many working-class girls came under the scrutiny of the justice system and were turned into media figures whom the feminist movement latched onto. In 1960, the Gaullist representative Paul Mirguet introduced a vote on the penal code to classify homosexuality as a "social evil." In the midst of the "Global Sixties," in an atmosphere of racial fear linked to the Algerian conflict, the gap between sexual norms and sexual practices had never been so wide for the young, and two sexually suspect populations were particular objects of suspicion: "bad girls" and young gay men.

In contrast to these arbitrary interventions into youth sexuality, the legal system rarely got involved in situations of sexual violence. The question of girls' consent, for example, was rarely taken seriously, including when girls were below the age of consent.[45] Cases involving sex offenses by minor boys against minor girls were usually dropped or dismissed. Paradoxically, many girls accused of indecent exposure were found guilty, although examination of the facts showed that they were the victims of sexual assault. According to members of the judicial system, this was a way of protecting them without having to establish the guilt of their aggressors.

As peer groups took on greater importance in boys' entry into sexuality during the postwar years, gang rape became a public issue, although here, it is sometimes difficult to distinguish between actual social practices and alarmist media representations. According to the press, the practice of "bagging a goose" [*lever . . . une bécasse*], an "easy girl," was done in "a square, the woods . . . the basement of a project high-rise."[46] In interrogations by the legal system, boys described these gang rapes using terms such as "*complots*" [plots], "*rodéos*" [rodeos], "*barlus*," or "*montages de galères*" (the latter two of which are untranslatable). The boys recounted how the gang imposed certain sexual behaviors, which it was necessary to perform in order not to lose face; how one had to "share" one's girlfriend with one's friends; how boys who were still chaste with their girlfriends would set their sights on a sexual prey, whom they would portray as debauched in order to justify their acts. The practice, which may have been specific to large cities, was linked to the phenomenon of gangs, and in certain cases had a racial dimension, as in New York City, where young African American and Puerto Rican men confronted one another. As bearers of a racialized masculinity, they justified their acts of violence against girls as a way of defending their sexual reputations.[47]

Thus, those who committed rape never considered it the crime that it legally was, seeing it instead as an act of male bonding, a mark of virility. As for girls, they rarely turned to the justice system, because their chances of success were so slim and the risks of having their reputation ruined by a public investigation so great. Some teenage girls internalized their status as prey to such an extent that in their memory an experience of violence became an experience of love, as Annie Ernaux recounts with clinical detachment in her autobiographical novel *Mémoire de fille* (*A Girl's Story*). The foundations of a veritable rape culture were in place, excusing perpetrators on the pretext of a virile ritual and trapping victims in forced consent. However, social tolerance for such "offensive virility" diminished. The feminist movement was the main driver of the 1970s campaign to criminalize rape, which intersected with the demand to legalize abortion. During the Bobigny trial in 1972, the feminist lawyer Gisèle Halimi defended a sixteen-year-old girl named Marie-Claire who was raped by a boy in her high school and then denounced by him for having had an abortion. Although the prosecutor cast doubt on the girl's honesty—she was suspected of having consented because she never went to the police—the judges acquitted her, opening the way for a wider debate about the sexual abuse of women.

A Youth "Sexual Revolution"?

The Glorious Thirty redrew the map of youth sexuality, while at the same time preserving some of its forms. Thus, the term "sexual revolution" to describe the 1950s–1970s must be used cautiously.

The boundaries of intimacy shifted under the influence of the sciences, politics, and a new culture of sexuality. Postwar youth policies tended to establish a "biopolitics" of sexuality and, more broadly, to govern youth sexuality on the basis of new knowledge. Youth sexuality was uncovered, studied, and made the subject of scientific debate and demonstrations. Sexuality was mediatized in a proliferation of communication taken up by mass culture, which the youth both consumed and transmitted. This profusion of representations stood in stark contrast to the difficulty of gaining acceptance for the establishment of real sexual education among families and within youth socialization institutions, and for recognition of the young as agents in their own sexual lives.

Sexual practices did evolve, however, shaping a new sexual culture for the young. There was a palpable loosening of norms, with greater sexual freedom visible in the practice of flirting and the gradual emergence of gay culture among the young. These elements contributed to creating a specific cultural space for the youth and, ultimately, a global culture of sexual modernity that tended to valorize individual freedom and its corollary, individual responsibility, in the form of sexual citizenship. But this "sexual liberation" went along with a certain rigidification of sexual identities: the fluidity of sexual practices decreased as it became necessary to choose one's "sexual orientation" very early on, and it remained difficult to affirm a gay, or, especially, a lesbian identity.

Finally, sexuality was associated with a series of interdictions, deviances, and conflicts, which indicated a still-pervasive moral unease around youth sexuality, at the same time that sexuality and procreation were beginning to be dissociated from one another. The game of seduction, even if it was reshaped by codes of flirting that doubtless gave girls more room to maneuver and appeared to value the notion of mutual consent, remained dominated by male privilege in terms of initiation and choice. Until the 1970s, insistence, harassment, violence, and sexual predation were considered normal, and thus legitimate, behaviors of male seduction. What changed, however, was that during the 1950s to 1970s, sexuality was called into question by new efforts to temper male sexual domination of women. These struggles largely contributed to reshaping the definition of virility in relation to sexuality, contesting domination, violence, and heteronormativity, while at the same time transforming the relationship between sex and politics. Slowly, and in the face of adversity, girls' will to challenge male domination and to claim their right to choose what to do with their bodies ("our bodies, ourselves") changed the social relations that sexuality reflects. Within this struggle, culture—that is, knowledge, communication, and representations around sexuality—played a determining role.

In the 2020s, hegemonic masculinity is once again being called into question by the #MeToo movement, and a new queer youth is taking shape, auguring the birth of a new culture of sexuality. Now, more than ever, sex is political and structures the power relations between generations.

Translated from the French by Daniela Ginsburg.

Notes

1. Richard Ivan Jobs, *Riding the New Wave: Youth and the Rejuvenation after the Second World War* (Stanford: Stanford University Press, 2009), chap. 5.
2. Sarah Fishman, *From Vichy to the Sexual Revolution: Gender and Family Life in Postwar France* (New York: Oxford University Press, 2017).
3. Arnaud Baubérot, "On ne naît pas viril, on le devient," in *Histoire de la virilité, t.3: La virilité en crise? XXe–XXIe siècle*, ed. Alain Corbin, Jean-Jacques Courtine and Georges Vigarello (Paris: Seuil, 2011), 159–184.
4. George L. Mosse, *The Image of Man: The Creation of Modern Masculinity* (New York: Oxford University Press, 2010), chap. IX.
5. Mary Louise Adams, *The Trouble with Normal: Postwar Youth and the Making of Heterosexuality* (Toronto: University of Toronto Press, 1997).
6. Anne-Claire Rebreyend, "Les 'filles amoureuses': une nouvelle catégorie des années 1950," in *Les jeunes et la sexualité: initiations, interdits, identités (XIXe–XXIe siècle)*, ed. Véronique Blanchard, Régis Revenin, and Jean-Jacques Yvorel (Paris: Autrement, 2010), 299–309.
7. Kelly Schrum, *Some Wore Bobby Sox: The Emergence of Teenage Girls' Culture, 1920–1945* (London: Palgrave Macmillan, 2006).
8. Karen W. Tice, *Tales of Wayward Girls and Immoral Women: Case Records and the Professionalization of Social Work* (Urbana: University of Illinois Press, 1998).
9. Judy Giles, "'Playing Hard to Get.' Working-Class Women, Sexuality and Respectability in Britain, 1918–1940," *Women's History Review* 1, no. 2 (1992): 239–255.
10. Pierre Simon, *Rapport sur le comportement sexuel des Français* (Paris: R. Julliard; P. Charron, 1972), 134.
11. M.-L. Martino (Sœur Marie-Irma), *Évolution de nos méthodes, 1946–1955* (Saint-Servais, France: Établissement d'éducation de l'État), 1955.

12. Albertine Sarrazin, *L'Astragale* (Paris: J.-J. Pauvert, 1965).
13. Bibliothèque et Archives Nationales du Québec (BANQ), Archives of the Court of Social Welfare, TL484; Archives du Bon-Pasteur d'Angers. Dossier d'observation 57/1951.
14. Mary Louise Adams, "Youth Corruptibility, and English-Canadian Postwar Campaigns against Indecency, 1948–1955," *Journal of the History of Sexuality* 6, no. 1 (1995): 89–117; Regina Kunzel, "Pulp Fictions and Problem Girls: Reading and Rewriting Single Pregnancy in the Postwar United States," *The American Historical Review* 100, no. 5 (1995): 1465–1487.
15. Julian Jackson, *Living in Arcadia: Homosexuality, Politics, and Morality in France from the Liberation to AIDS* (Chicago: University of Chicago Press, 2009).
16. Tarah Brookfield, *Cold War Comforts: Canadian Women, Child Safety, and Global Insecurity, 1945–1975* (Waterloo, Canada: Wilfrid Laurier University Press, 2012).
17. Marguerite Chardon, "Les différents plans de l'éducation sexuelle," *Cahiers pédagogiques* 59 (1966): 5.
18. Janine Mossuz-Lavau, *Les Lois de l'amour: Les Politiques de la sexualité en France, de 1950 à nos jours* (Paris: Payot, 2002).
19. Anne-Marie Sohn, *Age tendre et tête de bois. Histoire des jeunes des années 1960* (Paris: Fayard, 2012).
20. Mr Paul Pelleray, center-right Senator for the Département of Orne, "L'inculpation d'un professeur de philosophie pour outrage aux bonnes mœurs soulève des protestations", *Le Monde*, December 7, 1972; "L'affaire du tract du docteur Carpentier; le texte", *Le Monde*, February 11-12, 1973.
21. Bibia Pavard, Florence Rochefort, and Michelle Zancarini-Fournel, *Les lois Veil. Les événements fondateurs: Contraception 1974, IVG 1975* (Paris: Armand Colin, 2012).
22. Véronique Blanchard, *Vagabondes, voleuses, vicieuses: adolescentes sous contrôle, de la Libération à la libération sexuelle* (Paris: Éd. François Bourin, 2019), 64–70.
23. Fabienne Casta-Rosaz, *Histoire du flirt. Les jeux de l'innocence et de la perversité* (Paris: Grasset, 1999).
24. Archives du Bon-Pasteur d'Angers. Dossier d'observation 57/1951.
25. Françoise Héritier, *Masculin/féminin II: Dissoudre la hiérarchie* (Paris: Odile Jacob, 2012).
26. Beth L. Bailey, *From Front Porch to Back Seat: Courtship in Twentieth-Century America* (Baltimore: The Johns Hopkins University Press, 1989).
27. Todd Shepard, *Sex, France, and Arab Men, 1962–1979* (Chicago: University of Chicago Press, 2018), Chap. 1.
28. Paul Le Moal, *Pour une authentique éducation sexuelle* (Lyons, France: E. Vitte, 1960).
29. Régis Revenin, *Une histoire des garçons et des filles. Amour, genre et sexualité dans la France d'après-guerre* (Paris: Vendémiaire, 2015), 158–160.
30. George Chauncey, *Gay New York: Gender, Urban Culture, and the Making of the Gay Male World, 1890–1940* (New York: Basic Books, 1995).
31. Revenin, *Une histoire des garçons et des filles*, 167–168.
32. Ibid., 199.
33. Laura Di Spurio, *Du côté des jeunes filles: discours, (contre-)modèles et histoires de l'adolescence féminine (Belgique, 1919–1965)* (Bruxelles: Éditions de l'Université de Bruxelles, 2019).
34. Véronique Blanchard et Mathias Gardet, *La parole est aux accusés: Histoires d'une jeunesse sous surveillance 1950–1960* (Paris: Textuel, 2020), 88–99.
35. Albertine Sarrazin, *Journal de Fresnes. Le Passe-peine* (Paris: Julliard, 1976), 106.
36. Institution d'Observation de l'État de Saint-Servais (Belgique). Dossier A2265, 1967.

37. Thomas Walter Laqueur, *Solitary Sex: A Cultural History of Masturbation* (New York: Zone Books, 2004).
38. Revenin, *Une histoire des garçons et des filles*, 214.
39. Georges Falconnet and Nadine Lefaucheur, *La fabrication des mâles* (Paris: Seuil, 1975), 168.
40. Simon, *Rapport sur le comportement sexuel des Français*, 216.
41. Wannes Dupont, "The Case for Contraception. Medicine, Morality and Sexology at the Catholic University of Leuven (1930–1968)," *Histoire, Médecine et Santé* 13 (2018): 49–65.
42. David Niget, "La régulation socio-judiciaire de la sexualité juvénile à Montréal dans le premier XXe siècle," in *Les jeunes et la sexualité: initiations, interdits, identités (XIXe–XXIe siècle)*, ed. Véronique Blanchard, Régis Revenin, and Jean-Jacques Yvorel (Paris: Autrement, 2010), 87–98.
43. Tamara Gene Myers, *Youth Squad: Policing Children in the Twentieth Century* (Montreal: McGill-Queen's University Press, 2019); Louise A. Jackson, *Policing Youth: Britain, 1945–70* (Manchester, UK: Manchester University Press, 2014).
44. Abigail Wills, "Delinquency, Masculinity and Citizenship in England 1950–1970," *Past & Present* 187, no. 1 (2005): 157–85.
45. Sonja Matter, "'She Doesn't Look Like a Child': Girls and Age of Consent Regulations in Austria (1950–1970)," *The Journal of the History of Childhood and Youth* 10, no. 1 (2017): 104–122.
46. "Le syndrome du 'barlu,'" *L'Express*, September 12, 1966.
47. Anne Campbell, *Girls in the Gang: Report from New York City* (Cambridge, MA: Blackwell Publishers, 1986); Eric C. Schneider, *Vampires, Dragons, and Egyptian Kings: Youth Gangs in Postwar New York* (Princeton, NJ: Princeton University Press, 1999).

Further Reading

Bailey, Beth L. *From Front Porch to Back Seat: Courtship in Twentieth Century America*. Baltimore: The Johns Hopkins University Press, 1989.

Bantigny, Ludivine. *Le plus bel âge? Jeunes et jeunesse en France de l'aube des "Trente Glorieuses" à la guerre d'Algérie*. Paris: Fayard, 2007.

Blanchard, Véronique. *Vagabondes, voleuses, vicieuses: adolescentes sous contrôle, de la Libération à la libération sexuelle*. Paris: Éd. François Bourin, 2019.

Blanchard, Véronique, and David Niget. *Mauvaises filles: incorrigibles et rebelles*. Paris: Textuel, 2016.

Blanchard, Véronique, Régis Revenin, and Jean-Jacques Yvorel. *Les jeunes et la sexualité: initiations, interdits, identités (XIXe–XXIe siècle)*. Paris: Autrement, 2010.

Connell, Raewyn. *Masculinities*. Berkeley: University of California Press, 2005.

Cox, Pamela. *Gender, Justice and Welfare: Bad Girls in Britain, 1900–1950*. Basingstoke, UK: Palgrave MacMillan, 2002.

Di Spurio, Laura. *Le Temps de l'Amour: jeunesse et sexualité en Belgique francophone (1945–1968)*. Bruxelles: Le Cri, 2012.

Fishman, Sarah. *From Vichy to the Sexual Revolution: Gender and Family Life in Postwar France*. New York: Oxford University Press, 2017.

Inness, Sherrie. *Delinquents and Debutantes: Twentieth-Century American Girls' Cultures.* New York: NYU Press, 1998.

Jackson, Julian. *Living in Arcadia: Homosexuality, Politics, and Morality in France from the Liberation to AIDS.* Chicago: University of Chicago Press, 2009.

Jackson, Louise A. *Policing Youth: Britain, 1945-70.* Manchester, UK: Manchester University Press, 2014.

Jobs, Richard. *Riding the New Wave: Youth and the Rejuvenation of France after the Second World War.* Stanford: Stanford University Press, 2007.

Meis Knupfer, Anne. *Reform and Resistance. Gender, Delinquency, and America's First Juvenile Court,* New York: Routledge, 2001.

Myers, Tamara Gene. *Youth Squad: Policing Children in the Twentieth Century.* Montreal: McGill-Queen's University Press, 2019.

Revenin, Régis. *Une histoire des garçons et des filles. Amour, genre et sexualité dans la France d'après-guerre.* Paris: Vendémiaire, 2015.

Sangster, Joan. *Girl Trouble: Female Delinquency in English Canada.* Toronto: Between the Lines, 2002.

Schneider, Eric C. *Vampires, Dragons, and Egyptian Kings. Youth Gangs in Postwar New York.* Princeton: Princeton University Press, 1999.

Schrum, Kelly. *Some Wore Bobby Sox: The Emergence of Teenage Girls' Culture, 1920-1945.* Palgrave Macmillan, 2006.

Shepard, Todd. *Sex, France, and Arab Men, 1962-1979.* Chicago: University of Chicago Press, 2018.

PART III
SELF-EXPRESSION

CHAPTER 11

THE POWER OF STYLE

Transnational Youth (Sub)Cultures, Socialist Habitats, and the Cold War

JULIANE FÜRST

FOR many centuries style used to be a matter of class. Exterior markers of fashion were used to distinguish between different social and professional groups in line with the ordering principle of society at large. In the twentieth century style became the domain of youth. Indeed, the concepts of youth, youth culture, and youth style arose together. Before the nineteenth century youth was a subcategory of class. The way you were young depended first and foremost on your social standing. Youth as a specific state of adolescence was only afforded to a privileged few, notably the aristocracy. With the rise of the middle class in the nineteenth century the category of youth was significantly extended. The concept of a "youthful style" as a constituent of youth culture made its first shy appearances, most notably among students and pupils. By the turn of the century a roughly defined fashion style was an accepted concomitant of youth-specific movements such as the Wandervogel in Germany. In the case of more conservative groups such as Boy Scouts, Boys Brigade, or student fraternities this style could come in the form of a uniform. In the left-wing movements imitation of working class or peasant attire was common. Yet it was only with the rise of "youth" as a category across the social spectrum and hence the independent access of young people to financial resources that "youth style" became a major factor in creating youth identity and youth culture. Style became a marker of generations. Youth became synonymous with progress (or the fear thereof). And hence youth style soon became a cipher for social, cultural, and political messages.[1]

Youth style was both a result and a driver of increased globalization during the twentieth century. It is customary to view style, and especially youth style, through the prism of the Western world, and here in particular of the United States, which seemed to be propelling (and selling) so much of what was emblematic of youth culture in that century. The rise of the United States as a political and economic powerhouse in this time did indeed drive the creation of a global mass culture all over the world, and youth culture occupied a more and more important place in this mass culture. Yet the "West" is only one part of the twentieth-century story of youth style. Although undoubtedly indebted to Western music, Western products, and Western ideas of what it meant to be young, modern youth cultures in non-Western parts of the world were interesting hybrids, combining both imported elements and indigenous factors, thus subtly changing both the style and the meaning of style in their respective locations. Youth cultures everywhere were complicated entanglements between hegemonic and subcultural, traditional, and avant-garde forces. This constant making and remaking of local variations can be observed even in the Western world, but it is thrown into sharp focus in places where the West was considered an ideological enemy: the socialist East.

Youth style is framed as a transnational project that demonstrates the growing interconnectedness of young people all over the world and highlights geographical and political particularities. Highlighting their inter- and transnational contexts focuses on subcultural youth styles in the Soviet Union (looking at both their radical proponents and its wider following). The tension between, and co-existence and mutual fertilization of, global and local factors in creating "style" are emphasized. The Soviet lens reveals that there is no such thing as a single, definitive prototype of youth style, but that style is a never-ending negotiation between different intellectual, emotional, and physical forces that incorporate imported and local elements. Tracing the history of youth cultural style from the revolution to Perestroika will reveal youth style as a globally interconnected phenomenon with translations, mutations, and adaptations existing simultaneously.

DEFINING SOCIALIST YOUTH STYLE IN ONE COUNTRY

The long period of warfare that started with the First World War in 1914 and ended with the Civil War and the victory of the Bolsheviks in 1921 brought to a halt much of the bourgeois youth culture that had started to develop in Russia during the last two decades of Tsarist rule. Much prewar youth cultural style was based on Western models and included a Russian version of the Scouts, which was strongly sponsored by aristocratic adults, and more youth-led initiatives such as student corps in the Baltic regions on the conservative side of the spectrum and radical revolutionary student circles at the other.[2] The vast majority of the country, however, who toiled as peasants or lived in the vast periphery, knew youth culture only in the form of traditional rites of passage, mostly linked to courtship and marriage. Youth as a modern concept beyond biological adolescence was meaningless to most people under Tsarist rule.

Although bourgeois youth culture was on hold and/or in decline, the war both created and stifled youth culture and youth style. With the rise of the Bolshevik party, youth as a societal force unexpectedly saw itself elevated into hitherto unknown political, ideological, and cultural heights. The Bolsheviks had "youth" written onto their banners as a synonym for enthusiasm, radicalism, and utopian vision. They did not consider themselves a party *for* youth. Despite the middle age of their leaders, the Bolsheviks considered themselves a party *of* youth. The Bolshevik cause was a young cause, and the Bolsheviks believed that it was the young who were to champion their cause and make its utopian ideals a reality. As such, the outer markers and symbols of the communists created the first Soviet youth style: leather jackets, military boots, worker caps, coarse language, and disregard for manners, which were considered bourgeois. This extended to love and life as well. Young people in the revolutionary period lived in communal settings, shared their material resources, and tried to make their private lives align with the needs of the Soviet project.[3] Alexandra Kollontai's pronouncement on sex as a glass of water that was consumed when needed was very popular among revolutionary youth. Young women seriously challenged gender norms by adopting not only the communist rhetoric of gender equality but its (mainly masculine) style markers, essentially painting the young Soviet person in androgynous ways, whose gender-specific markers were played down, and his or her visible and invisible ideological markers were emphasized. In the wake of (usually short-lived) European revolutions after the First World War, communist style crept into youthful style elsewhere in the world, but in this respect the newly created Soviet Union for once led the way, and the flow of information went from East to West. As the first and only socialist state in the interwar period, the style of its youth became synonymous with revolutionary progress and modernity. The shiny faces and bodies of Soviet girls and boys were projected both into and outside of the country to herald the bright future.

This did not mean that the marriage of Bolshevik and youth style was always a happy one. The same spontaneity and radicalism that Bolsheviks found so promising in youth led to friction as soon as the revolution settled and started to create its own establishment. Youthful disappointment in what felt like an unfinished revolution in the 1920s led first to schisms in the radical youth–Bolshevik alliance. The same markers that once signaled support for the Soviet cause could now also be read as the silent protest of discontented enthusiasts. The poet Sergei Esenin, whose elegiac, nature-infused poetry infused many young Soviet spirits, initiated a suicide craze when he took his own life at the Hotel Astoria in Leningrad in 1925. Vladimir Mayakovsky, the poet who more than anyone embodied to contemporaries the new youthful

Sovietness, followed in 1930 with a gunshot through his heart, symbolically ending the period of revolutionary youth style. Suicide and melancholy had no place in the new Soviet world, where hands and minds were needed to build up a country rather than to reflect on the self and its inner emotions, except if they were productive. Joyfulness, optimism, and a stern look toward the future became the hallmarks of Stalinist policy, not only but especially for youth.

In the meantime, however, Soviet youth style was challenged from a very different corner: the West. European, and later American, influence remained a thorn in the Soviet youth program for the entirety of its existence. At all times, even during the height of the Cold War, there were ways into the isolated Soviet Union. During the New Economic Policy Western imports were legal and privately financed, especially, but not exclusively, in the film sector. As Europe and North America celebrated the tough but exciting postwar period, bits of the hedonism of the golden 1920s also spilled over into the Soviet Union, forcing for the first time the question of what Soviet youth culture and style could or could not include. Flappers and foxtrotters became a much derided but widespread phenomenon; their raison d'être did not seem to serve any political goals. The increasingly global—indeed, long before people traveled widely in person— youth style led to their popularity. Mary Pickford and Douglas Fairbanks were major film stars in the USSR and in the United States, and Josephine Baker was as famous in Moscow as she was in Paris. Their sense of fashion, music, and entertainment contributed to Soviet youth culture as much as the increasing employment of youthful sentiments pushed through Soviet policies. Young people danced the tango *and* arrived in droves to construct the steel city of Magnitogorsk, becoming literate and Soviet on the way. But just as the laissez-faire commerce and agricultural production existed uneasily with state-owned factories employing the vast share of the working class, the coexistence of contradictory youth styles caused tension and ultimately moral panic.[4] At the end of the 1920s Stalin launched both a cultural revolution against "bourgeois leftovers" and his campaign to collectivize the peasantry, employing in this endeavor predominantly young agitators and volunteers. A young Lev Kopelev was among those sent to the countryside to eradicate the remnants of the old order; he later recalled both the esprit de corps this assignment created and the horrors he witnessed. In the case of Kopelev, who became a prominent dissident in the 1960s and 1970s, the latter began to sow doubt about the righteousness not only of his youthful actions but of the system he served overall.[5]

Interestingly, though Stalin made no concessions on the economic front, cultural policy of the 1930s was not so clear-cut. It was made increasingly clear that youth was neither expected to toady to Western influences nor to exhibit hedonistic behavior, and also that the avant-garde position of youth in radical politics was not supported by the new Stalinist order. The Komsomol congress of 1936 closed the question about whether the organization was to be slim and radical or broad and educational once and for all with a decision for the latter. The new Komsomol, however, was inclusive in other ways too. Dancing the tango and foxtrot was not incompatible anymore with being a Komsomol member or a good Soviet youth. Swing jazz, a feature in major Soviet motion pictures such as the hugely popular *Happy Guys* (*Veselye rebiata*), decisively shaped the youth style of the times. Liubov Orlova, who looked a lot like Mary Pickford, first epitomized the Soviet film star complete with fans, fan culture, and promotional articles and materials. A very successful project that socialized Soviet youngsters to theater, classical literature, and classical music shaped the outlook and character of the Soviet intelligentsia for decades to come. Unbelievably, all of this happened in and survived the most brutal years of Soviet history: the collectivization campaign that ended in mass famine, and the show trials and purges that culminated in the witch hunts of 1937–1938. One famous primary source, *The Diary of Nina Kosterina*, demonstrates the ability of youth to accommodate these different forces in their culture and style. Motivated by grand and lofty ideas of justice and equality, Nina, a strong-willed, independently-minded young girl in late-1930s Moscow, who loved literature, both Soviet and foreign, also occupied herself with personal love affairs. She desperately wanted to be a good communist but sometimes had doubts about the actions of her fellow students and teachers. Her father's arrest threw her into despair over her internal dilemma of loyalty. But as war broke out and the Germans rapidly advanced toward Moscow, she volunteered for the partisan forces, both out of a sense of Sovietness and out of a hope to save her father.

Style and (at) War

One of the unintended consequences of modern wars, and certainly the two world wars of the twentieth century, is the fact that they put in motion massive transnational exchanges, not only in the military and political fields, but also in the cultural sphere. Large parts of the Soviet Union came under German or Romanian occupation. Even more important, millions of Soviet soldiers found themselves in Central Europe, rubbing shoulders with their Western allies. It was inevitable that both material items and cultural knowledge were exchanged in this global event, which lasted for much longer than merely the years of war but found its logical continuation in the Cold War.

The most obvious global "winner" of the wartime cultural exchange was jazz and a new form of dancing, swing, which along with the lindy hop included jazz dance forms such as the jive, the balboa, the collegiate shag, and the boogie-woogie. Jazz as a music and dance form did not come from anywhere, of course, but had made its European, and Soviet, debut already in the 1920s, especially in Paris, which became a mecca for Black American jazz artists. The Soviet Union had responded to the trend by setting up its own jazz bands, first and foremost sponsoring Leonid Utesov and his band, who starred in high-profile films. During the war the Lvov orchestra of Eddie Rosner became another star on the Soviet jazz horizon, connecting the Soviet scene with the Polish, Central European, and American ones. Both orchestras played extensively for the Red Army during and shortly after the war, with Rosner and his authentically Western swinging style becoming absolute stars of the era.[6] At the same time Allied servicemen—for example, sailors passing through the port of Archangelsk delivering Lend-Lease items—brought all kinds of items into Soviet territories, including American jazz records and the knowledge of how to move and groove to this music. Jazz made it not only to the Allied powers. Germany and Italy also knew hot rhythms, and the resulting youth styles, that became known as *Swingjugend* or *Swing Heinis* and resulted in several hundred arrests when their secret parties became known to the Gestapo.[7]

The front lines were drawn consciously and subconsciously: jazz embodied freedom, spontaneity, and unruliness, though the authorities considered its stylistic expressions to be rebellious, dangerous, and against the hegemonic order. (The jazz lover and historian Eric Hobsbawm devoted a whole book to extolling the revolutionary potential of jazz musicians.) This was true for the so-called French Zazous, who loved jazz and hated the German occupiers. It was true for the Austrian *Swing Heinis* who rebelled against the military uniformity of Nazi youth culture. But it was also true of the Los Angeles zoot-suiters, who were mainly Latino, and pushed not only borders of style with their extremely wide trousers and long jackets, but also challenged the racism they experienced in their everyday life.[8] It was true for the British Teddy Boys, who imitated the style of a world that was financially and socially out of their reach. Stylistic nonconformism was a game with symbolic markers that hid under an apolitical facade very political messages and was indeed perceived as such by the establishment, which reacted with what Stanley Cohen later called "moral panics."[9] British sociologists have interpreted subcultural style as part of the struggle between classes, though the American interpretation has centered on the psychological implications of such stylistic challenges to the status quo.[10] Yet all agree that the politics of style addressed fundamental questions and tensions simmering in societies. And because youth were politically less powerful than their elders, the fields of fashion, language, music taste, and dancing became their preferred battlefields.

For contemporaries, however, and certainly in the Soviet Union, jazz had mainly American connotations. It was not surprising that as soon as the wartime alliance fell apart, jazz in the Soviet Union became one of the first casualties of the emerging Cold War. Stalin banned jazz in 1946, supposedly confiscating all saxophones, in order to take the characteristic kick out of jazz tunes. Eddie Rosner found himself in the Gulag, while Utesov was now heading the State Variety Orchestra rather than the State Jazz Orchestra. Perceived as American and Jewish, jazz became a victim of the anti-Western and antisemitic, anti-cosmopolitan campaigns. At the same time the policies were enacted unevenly and left many loopholes, as the writer John Steinbeck and the photographer Robert Capa discovered on their 1947 tour through the Soviet Union, where they were entertained by the Tbilisi State Jazz Orchestra and followed everywhere by the tunes of "Moonlight Serenade," the "Chattanooga Choo-Choo," and "In the Mood."[11] Indeed, they only saw (and heard) the tip of an iceberg.

Jazz and swing created the first true subculture in the Soviet Union, the so-called *stiliagi*. *Stiliaga*—the singular to *stiliagi*—is actually an extremely broad (and ascribed) term, coined by a 1948 article in the satirical journal *Krokodil*, which described a young Soviet man devoted to his fashionable appearance and exotic way of dancing. The phenomenon of "over-stylish" youth was not new to the postwar Soviet Union and had made appearances in documents and newspaper articles already in the 1930s and early 1940s. Even then it was seen as problematic when youngsters liked to give themselves English names for addressing each other. A *Komsomol'skaia pravda* article from 1946 depicted in an accompanying cartoon what was undoubtedly a zoot-suiter and his "dressed up doll."[12] The article did not elaborate on the transnational aspect but decried the "superficiality" and "stupidity" of the two young factory workers. The cartoon that accompanied the 1948 *stiliaga* article showed that now the trousers were already tighter, the tie and socks more colorful, and the slang more part of the show. It is difficult to say how much impact it had at the time, because *stiliagi* themselves did not use the term until much later, preferring to call themselves *chuvaki*, a term derived from the jazz scene. Later evidence points to a return to a more understated, black-and-white theme in fashion, possibly under the influence of the new Italian cinema.[13]

Stalin preferred to keep silent about the phenomenon, making *stiliagi* a word-of-mouth subculture, predominant in the big cities and with a heavy (but not exclusive) representation of youngsters from well-connected and privileged homes, who had better access to Western goods. It was not, however, a subculture of the intelligentsia, with much evidence indicating that it was popular in factories and schools and universities.[14] After Stalin's death Khrushchev changed media policy, tackling wayward youth in scathing editorials and articles—with the effect that the now much publicized *stiliaga* became media celebrities and found many more imitators. Authorities and youth alike now had a label, which was meant to be derogatory by officials who bestowed it onto a youth said to be full of style but devoid of thought. Yet in the ears and words of youth it soon transformed itself into a badge of honor in the internal lingo. The last *stiliagi* were active well into the 1960s when their style had become more Mod-like (as in the British Mods, who wore colorful rockabilly jackets and chequered shirts) and their music rock 'n' roll rather than jazz. Sometimes they were the older brothers of later hippies. The Khrushchvite media campaign threw out a couple of other terms such as "parasites" and "do-nothings" (*tuneadtsy*). The term *stiliagi* rose from its Cinderella slumber in the Brezhnev period, when Perestroika saw a revival among glam rock youth. *Stiliagi* were now already one of many styles of youth that late socialism accommodated, more or less willingly. They coexisted with hippies, punks, breakers, weightlifters, and football hooligans.[15] True fame, however, came only with a blockbuster Russian film. *Stiliagi*, released in 2008, which couched the first Soviet subculture into a colorful and fast-paced love story, obscured rather than enlightened its historical reality.

In reality, the original *stiliagi*, who seem to have formed in the immediate postwar years, were a relatively small and not-much-noticeable band of young men (except to the attentive visitor of Moscow's and Leningrad's main streets), who nonetheless had an important signaling function: they showed that, even in Stalin's Soviet Union, style could be used to negotiate identity on a field that was much less policed and repressed than the spoken or written word. They were truly nonconformists, as they not only broke norms but consciously intended to do so. The question of whether they counted as dissidents is more ambiguous. The article on them in *Krokodil* made it clear that they were unwanted, yet subjectively the existing testimony does not indicate that many of them considered themselves non-Soviet, let alone anti-Soviet.[16] Yet, because their choice of communication was their style, clues to their political character have to be sought on this level rather than in their rare verbal pronouncements.

The *stiliaga* was a true worshiper of style in its meaning as a *Gesamtkunstwerk*. He created a homology between his looks, his music, and his words, almost all of which were American infused, even though there were traces of Russian criminal underground culture visible too. At the center of his universe was undoubtedly jazz, which arrived in the Soviet Union in the form of trophy records brought back by returning Red Army soldiers. But alongside music the *stiliaga* was keen on the external attributes that accompanied this music: the snazzy, tight trousers of the jazz musicians; the black-and-white color scheme of their concert attire; the thickly soled shoes that became fashionable in the early 1950s; the slang and argot, which in the Soviet version was constituted from a mixture of Yiddish and the language of the criminal underworld. *Stiliagi* loved colorful socks, cinematic hairstyles, a certain walk down Broadway, as both Moscow and Leningrad *stiliagi* christened their main drag, Western-style coats, and in general everything that distinguished them from the gray masses.[17]

Western observers were much keener to cast the jazz-loving, style-seeking nonconformists into an oppositional framework. The *stiliagi*'s worship of jazz had a number of elements that could be read as more than fashion and taste choices. Frederick Starr, the foremost chronicler of Soviet jazz, concluded that "Jazz with its emphasis on individuality and personal expression, became the lingua franca of dissident Soviet youth, the argot of jazz their verbal medium."[18] He found that this became more and more true as jazz developed into bop. It was here that true individualism became apparent. As part of the contemporary U.S. embassy staff, Starr was much aware that there was an active propaganda angle to the story. The staff's fascination with the *stiliagi* and their fondness for jazz had resulted in the creation of a special music program on Voice of America called "Jazz Hour" and later "Music USA" and moderated by Willi Conover. This program, iconic among youth, inspired many subsequent careers. Conover spoke slowly and with a "special English" script. His voice epitomized the longing Soviet youngsters felt for the fabled other: what Alexei Yurchak has called the "imaginary West"[19]: "For us, the people of the Soviet Union, who loved jazz," stated an article published in an Azeri jazz magazine in 2013, "Conover and his Music USA were 'a window to America'; a window which was open constantly and for a long time."[20] Soon Conover brought not only American music into the East but East European music to its audiences. He frequently invited Soviet, Polish, Czech, and other jazz musicians from behind the Iron Curtain onto his program and gave them both volume and credibility as "authentic," in other words, American certified. The Czech jazz accordion player Jan Zappner remembered about the Jazz Hour,

> There it was, "The A Train," and the great voice of Willis Conover. I will never forget that feeling of sweet conspiracy. While the barracks, the country, indeed, the whole socialist camp was asleep, I . . . found out that over the trenches of the Cold War there was normal life, with great music.

Conover himself was both a jazz aficionado and a firm believer in the righteousness of the American cause. He told *Time Magazine* in 1966, "Jazz tells more about America than any American can realize. It bespeaks vitality, strength, social mobility; it's a free music with its own discipline, but not an imposed, inhibiting discipline."[21] The Soviet side came to a similar conclusion about the impact of jazz, declaring in an internal top-secret document that "today youngsters listen to jazz and tomorrow they will betray their fatherland."

Yet it was not as black and white as the American and Soviet authorities imagined it to be. In the process of translating Western youth culture some interesting local quirks emerged, and some fascinating mutations ensured adaptation to local conditions. There was first of all the fact that all "Western-ness," including the *stiliaga* style, arrived through loopholes, which could close at any moment. Radio broadcasts were frequently disturbed by meddling with the frequencies. Foreign visitors to the Soviet Union under Stalin were few and far between. Much of what was known about the West was hence a mélange of a few material items, a bit of knowledge, and a lot of imagination. The "imaginary West" with its many gaps between the beacons of information left room for much fantasizing and exoticizing. When the *stiliagi* renamed Moscow's Gorky Street and Leningrad's Nevsky Prospekt "Broadway," they only knew of the bit that housed glamorous theaters but little of its uptown and downtown existence in New York. When they listened to their favorite radio host Willis Conover, they did not know the battles he fought in Washington, D.C., against the second-class treatment of the Black musicians he championed. At the same time, jazz and its style were a much more serious business for them than for many of their Western peers. Official disapproval and real repression (cutting off trousers and hair, beatings and public shaming via meetings and newspapers) and the constant material deficits they faced required hard and persistent commitment among the devoted followers of style seeking.

Another peculiarity of a youth subculture in a socialist habitat was that its members embraced a variety of Western products indiscriminately. The quality of the style marker was not anymore determined by its distinction from the mainstream or by its refined character, but first and foremost by the fact that it came from the West, full stop. That is not to say that the *stiliagi* looked less sartorial than their Saville Row–clothed Teddy Boy peers—certainly not when measuring the relative distance to the "normal" crowd in the respective countries—but it allowed for strange bedfellows, because identification came from the definition of non-Sovietness. *Stiliagi* embraced, for instance, both Louis Armstrong and Glen Miller as well as Johnny Weismüller and his fictional incarnation Tarzan. Tarzan and his swept-back hair were prominent models for a while as were, of course, all items connected to the American military. The son of the second Belorussian party secretary starts his memoirs of being a *stiliaga* with a description of his Studebaker coat, an item that underlined his privileged access to things Western and furthered his swagger as he traversed the "grayness" of the late-Stalinist landscape.[22] For youngsters like him and other dwellers of big towns an important influence were foreign tourists and diplomats whose appearance in the centers of bigger Soviet towns told style-conscious youngsters how to dress. *Stiliaga* interrogated by the police and the Komsomol give evidence to what revealed the lengths and pain to which they went to observe the changing details of fashion, acquire the necessary materials, and translate the fashion requirements into a Soviet reality of scarcity. For instance, a young Moscovite, Arkadii Bairon, told his interrogators that, inspired by Fellini's films, he slept with a hairnet, while his friends plaited their hair every night. He also informed them about the precise distance between buttons on a Reglan coat.[23] He is echoed these days by other voices appearing in memoirs of the *stiliaga* crowd. Jazz musician Alexei Kozlov muses as much about his socks as about the music he loved and that shaped his career, and author Vasilii Aksenov recalls how his style journey started with a Norwegian reindeer sweater making an appearance in the film *Sun Valley Serenade*, shown in the USSR as part of "trophy film" captured in Berlin with German dubbing (the same was indeed true for *Tarzan*, which also reached Soviet audiences in its German version).[24] What united all *stiliagi*—and *stiliagi* with the French Zazous, the British Teddy Boys, and American zoot-suiters— was a quest to be different, to be more refined than the gray and downtrodden masses around them, and to break a few norms of decency on the way.

What these rules were, exactly, depended very much on young people's location. In Britain it was often rules of class, as argued by several authors in the Birmingham School, who coined the term "resistance through ritual." In the United States it was often a question of race, as in the case of the Los Angeles Latino zoot-suiters but also for the Harlem jazz lovers and swing dancers. In the Soviet Union of the 1940s and 1950s, neither class nor race helps to explain why *stiliagi* and the Soviet system came to antagonize each other. Most *stiliagi* deny having had any kind of political motivation at all. As a group they never made any overtly political pronouncement, nor did they try to change the system. Rather, if anything, they made bypassing the system their sport. Apoliticalness was their creed. But that, of course, was highly oppositional. In the Soviet project you were supposed to self-improve, not live for fun. The individual, and particularly the young individual, was meant to be part of the system, not to put his or her energy into circumventing it. Just as in the case of the Western moral panics, the chasm that opened between young subculturals on the one hand and the establishment and authorities on the other was widened the more this chasm was discussed.

Bradley Gorsky argues that the cult writer Aksenov "learned" his vocabulary of dissent from his experience as a *stiliaga* and the subsequent official campaign degrading them in the press and elsewhere.[25] The us-versus-them paradigm was not only created by subcultural youth, but, as in the West, by the hegemonic forces threatened by the existence of difference.

There were other factors that gave *stiliagi* a decidedly socialist twist, in the sense of living within a socialist state where they represented the third generation of youngsters to come of age and where continuity, not revolution, was the order of the day. Fastidious obsession with fashion was a trait more commonly associated with women, who, in East and West, were not only allowed but indeed expected to be concerned about their appearance. And it was exactly here where the true rebelliousness of *stiliagi* became apparent. The "appropriation" of this "female" trait by young men, especially in a world that had just emerged from a global war and venerated a military style of masculinity, was an affront against hegemonic notions of gender. Youngsters concerned about their long hair, fashionable buttons, and thickly soled shoes were not paying respect to the heroes of the war, let alone showing an inclination to follow them into action. Rather, their openly transnational style was a negation of the world at war and a rejection of the dichotomy emerging under the aegis of Cold War culture. Their style was also showing up their Soviet habitat specifically: to be dandy-like and stylish in an economy of shortages and low-quality production was an affront, particularly because it explicitly challenged the ideological socialist underpinning that style did not matter, though content did. The *stiliagi* turned this on its head: all that mattered was style; the content was only a means for achieving it. Ironically, this meant that style became content, the mere act of being stylish was an ideological expression. That was as true for the Soviet *stiliagi* as it was for the English Teddy Boys, who rebelled against their class-ridden society by appropriating upper-class style to their working-class neighborhoods.

Style and/or Peace

The marriage, or indeed overlap, between style and ideological message emerges even more clearly when jumping ten years forward in Soviet history into the late 1960s. By 1967 Nikita Khrushchev had been ousted as Soviet leader, yet it was not clear yet what kind of politics his successor Leonid Brezhnev would pursue. Clearly, however, the course of reforms, which Khrushchev had followed with sometimes more and sometimes less ambition, was coming to an end—a fear that was confirmed to the country's intelligentsia, the part of society most involved in the so-called Thaw culture of the previous years, in 1968 when Soviet troops marched into Prague and ended the experiment of "socialism with a human face." 1967, however, was also the year that Soviet hippies declared as their year of birth (on what grounds exactly is not quite clear anymore). They were a logical consequence of the enthusiasm for the Beatles and their music that had started to sweep the country a few years earlier. Via the music came knowledge about the bands. And via the bands came interest in this new thing from across the ocean called hippies. 1967 was also the year *Pravda* reported for the first time about American hippies and yippies, singling out Abbie Hoffmann's stunt at the New York Stock Exchange of throwing money from the gallery.[26] It was not an unfavorable report at all. The press was impressed by their resistance against the capitalist system and their anti-materialism. A longer piece in the following year by the journal *Around the World* (*Vokrug Sveta*) was even more apt in capturing the adventurous, melancholic, yet rebellious spirit of the American flower children. The article "Travel into the Hippieland" became the bible for many aspiring Soviet hippies then and in the following decade. The moralistic conclusions about how the movement was doomed without a proper ideological foundation went unheard among many young readers, who lapped up the freedom and nonconformism inherent in people who lived and slept anywhere they wanted and rejected the norms of their elders, teachers, and other authorities.

The hippie movement was the first Soviet youth culture that was not only consciously transnational—that had been true already for the *stiliagi*—but indeed defined itself as international. They saw themselves not only as influenced from abroad, but indeed also as one part of a big, global community. The disappearance in the future of national borders (and along with them war, national differences, and social boundaries) was part of the creed. And in many ways hippies achieved their utopian vision, if not fully, to no small extent. Hippies became a global movement, which was held together by a few simple markers, most of which were markers of style. Hippies everywhere wore their hair long and flowing, a quintessential requirement that chimed even better with the creed insofar as hair grew at no cost and was hence free from materialistic concerns. They loved colorful, free flowing clothing that did not distinguish between male and female attire. They identified with the naturalness, ease, and delicacy of flowers. They shunned displays of wealth and refused to conform to the ambitions and norms of the postwar period, which had championed domesticity, the nuclear family, and economic success. Their main symbol, the peace sign, became an absolutely global phenomenon, even outliving the movement itself.[27] Hippies' decisive break with the norms of the establishment was at the heart of hippies everywhere and certainly in the Soviet case as well, even if the socialist habitat required some tweaking.

The early Soviet hippie communities were as-good-as-they-could-manage imitations of their Western peers. While in the west of the country, where there was a certain amount of contact with Poland—which had already in the 1960s a flourishing hippie community, or even with a nonsocialist country such as Finland, whose television could be watched from Soviet Estonia—young people looked more "hippyish" than in the rest of the country, the signposting of hippie style was clear all across the country: hair, flowers, jeans, and rock music, and sometimes nudity, sometimes drugs. There were many invocations of Western hippies, freedom, and America.[28]

Surviving documents show that the essence of these communities had the same matters at heart as the San Francisco and Greenwich Village originals. Here as there, the exterior style was an expression of a more serious inner style, which included a desire to live in greater harmony with other people and nature, escape the strict conformity of postwar morals, and live in greater freedom, be it personal or indeed political. The program drawn up by one of the earliest hippies in the Western Ukrainian town of Lviv could easily have been drawn up in an American commune, if maybe using a slightly different vocabulary:

> To be oneself.
> To love those close to you.
> Nature has to become your home
> No difference—he or she—all are the same.
> Destroy all barriers that hinder people from talking to each other.
> Make love is the message of today.
> Love flowers and do not make politics out of this.
> Ideology and religion are for idiots.
> Let sacred laughter and sacred wailing ring out.[29]

The reason for this success in hippie homogeneity lies in the fact that hippie youth culture was very much a product of a generational shift. Those born after the Second World War were less encumbered by a belief in military virtues and more eager to explore their individual and spiritual selves than their nation's collective prowess. This was true in both East and West, augmented in the East by the fact that hippies recruited themselves from a generation with no conscious memory of Stalinism. International hippie homogeneity was, however, also testimony to the fact that the consumption of certain material items and cultural products had become global, if still experiencing a time lag when traveling across the Iron Curtain. Hence, as the hippie movement was winding down in the United States, it was only just on the rise in the Soviet Union, where it reached its full bloom somewhere in the mid-1970s. Bell-bottom jeans became trendy in the West in the mid-1960s but only really made their way into the USSR in the early 1970s, as the young Muscovite David Gurevich, a self-declared connoisseur of style, remembers. In early 1969 he bought a pair of jeans from an African student, in which he was first very disappointed due to their shape. Only a year later he realized that he had been ahead of the curve.[30]

Music held a special role as a transnational transmission belt. Music traveled fast through the ethers of shortwave radio. Almost every Soviet youngster of the seventies seems to have listened to the BBC, Deutsche Welle, Voice of America, or Radio Liberty, all of which had more or less extensive music sections. Records took longer, but if people were well connected, a Beatles album could cover the distance between London and Moscow within a week.[31] The rise of the so-called *magnitofon*, a reel-to-reel tape player, allowed for the first time easy and home-based recording (previously Soviet youngsters had relied on X-ray plates on which music could be engraved, so-called music on bones). The Beatles, whose 1967 *Sgt. Pepper's Lonely Hearts Club Band*, was their most hippyish album, with songs such as "Lucy in the Sky with Diamonds," "A Day in the Life," and "Within You Without You," representing pure psychedelia. Soviet youngsters did not fail to notice that the Beatles had changed their image. Their nice-boy-from-next-door style had given way to shoulder-length hair and mustaches. In the early 1970s that was the style often imitated by the Moscow crowd, despite the fact that such an exterior led to frequent arrests by citizen's patrols and local police. Another significant motor spreading hippie creed and style (and making the two inseparable) was the universal success of *Jesus Christ Superstar*, whose 1970 soundtrack circulated widely in the USSR and which spawned a great many imitations of homemade rock operas. Here the merger of style and message became even more pronounced: the similarity between the plight of the band of young idealists around their guru, Jesus, and the situation of hippies in conservative societies just rang too true. In the Soviet Union the fact that the Orthodox Church was also persecuted and was in the underground heightened the alliance between Soviet hippiedom and Christianity. One of the imitation rock operas was written by a young Aleksandr Ogorodnikov, whose Christian Seminar was soon to become one of the main loci of the Orthodox Underground.[32] Other hippyish spiritual pursuits such as yoga, Buddhism, Hare Krishna, and even Islam, Kabbalah, and Ecumenism, were also sought out by Soviet hippies, but ultimately homegrown Orthodoxy trumped them all, indicating the limits of hippie globality and internationalism.

Although the Vietnam war and the Western hippie protests against the military gave the movement from the very beginning an international cause around which to rally, Soviet hippies found it harder to connect to the political side of their American idols. Already the anti–Vietnam War cause was a bit diminished in the ears and eyes of Soviet youngsters who desired distance from the Soviet system, not agreement. Yet initially protest against the war was nonetheless taken in as part of the Soviet hippie canon, not least because the Moscow hippie leader Iura Burakov, alias Solntse, hoped to carve out a place for his hippies within the permitted public sphere by organizing a demonstration against the war, which was to go from Moscow University to the American embassy.[33] Although content-wise entirely within the Soviet ideological parameters, the mere fact of a spontaneous demonstration organized without party permission was enough to arrest all those who assembled—according to Radio Liberty, 3,000 young people. This shocking event—in the Soviet Union even the eight people protesting the 1968 invasion into Prague on Red Square were a scandal—signaled the end of a relatively laissez-faire approach toward the hippie phenomenon. It also spelled the end of overt political action on the part of Soviet hippies, even though some voices raised the pacifist cause in 1979 when the Soviet Union invaded Afghanistan.[34]

This almost complete withdrawal from the political arena meant that "style" became the most potent marker for Soviet hippies, while their American counterparts soon atomized into their different political manifestations, which ranged from radical left-wing revolutionary activity to feminism, from ecological engagement to right-wing rejection to state intervention. Soviet hippies were spared this fate, because the hostility and repression from above kept them unified, and their reluctance to engage politically plastered over differences they might have had but did not articulate. This gave them lots of time to perfect and think about their style, which soon became both an art form and a commentary on late Soviet life. The first fascination of Soviet hippies was American blue jeans. Yet one bought not only a piece of durable clothing. They were difficult to obtain and cost a fortune, a month's salary in the early 1970s. It is thus not surprising that Soviet hippies soon turned to making their own garments: this fits better with Soviet reality, and it was also more in the hippie spirit of *samodelka*, "do-it-yourself" in an uncommercial way. Soviet hippie style, especially in Moscow, became the product of some very skilled and talented tailors, who imbued Soviet hippies with a plethora of messages, which by choice or by need they did not articulate verbally.

One of the most provocative of these messages was the androgynization of the hippie body. The exaggerated bellbottoms that became so typical for the Moscow hippies together with their slender youth gave both men and women a very distinctive, yet not gender-specific shape. Both sexes wore their hair long and adorned themselves with hairbands, little ornaments, and paintings, usually of flowers, on their clothing. All this was extremely subversive vis-à-vis the reigning gender norms coined by a military-inspired masculinity and a femininity that stressed propriety. Indeed, proper dress had been a hallmark of Soviet socialization ever since the 1930s, when some older models of revolutionary, anti-bourgeois dress had been decidedly abandoned in favor of a style of neat correctness. The hippies' decision to shun "proper" and "neat" clothes and replace them with items that were manipulated, painted, and often purposefully disheveled was a slap in the face of this decades-old campaign to make the Soviet Union respectable. Indeed, the very fact that not in style, but in spirit, hippies were reminiscent of a more revolutionary era in Soviet history accentuated the norm breaking: the nonchalance hippies displayed toward materialism was a sharp reminder of how much official Soviet material norms and practices had deviated from their revolutionary ideal.

At the same time, the hippie dress style fit neatly with the realities of late socialism. To create clothing that was extravagant but did not rely on expensive or rare ingredients suited an economy that experienced more and more deficits and where choice was not part of the consumer experience. Expressing belief in a visual rather than verbal way was far less dangerous, because the visual was always ambiguous and the verbal was soon judged as anti-Soviet and hence criminal. The mere fact that hippies imitated an American style was of course an immensely political statement, but it was not the same as writing about one's love for the West. The patchwork of self-tailored clothing was highly individual and to a certain extent a form of resistance against Soviet collectivism, but it also was just a variation of a widespread Soviet practice of tailoring at home or in small ateliers. And, last but not least, long hair took a long time to grow, but it came absolutely free and was a resource that replenished itself.

Hippie style and late socialism meshed well on some level, precisely because the socialist framework prevented the commercialization of the subculture, and the back-to-nature and anti-materialist aspects of hippie style flourished well in a society where crafty skills were commonplace and distinction was frowned upon but easily achieved. It turned out that in the last decade of the Soviet Union late socialism provided a fertile soil for a number of further subcultural styles, which joined the long-lived hippies and whose common enmity of the Soviet system meant a relatively peaceful coexistence among each other. In the mid-1980s punk swept over the Soviet Union, leaving its traces especially forcefully in Leningrad and Siberia.[35] Even more than the anti-materialist hippie style, the trashy preferences of the punks seemed to be made for a socialist realism whose economy increasingly unraveled in the eighties, exposing a wrecked infrastructure, a crippling problem of alcoholism within society, and a thoroughly alienated youth. It was not only provincial youngsters who found punk an appropriate style for their mood and life situation. The whole country went kind of "punk," meaning it embraced a style of trash, nihilism, and hopelessness that was only punctured by a brief spike of activity when Gorbachev introduced his glasnost and perestroika reforms. The Soviet punks were not only in style nonconformist, but verbally extremely provocative, indeed to such an extent that one has to conclude that here the relationship of "style carrying message" had been inverted into "the message representing style." Punk music bands such as Grazhdanskaia Oborona (Civil Defense) goaded the system with the most anti-communist symbolism that was available: fascist insignia. In 1987 they played a set at a Novosibirsk concert under the heading "Adolf Hitler." Swastikas and other Nazi emblems were widely sported at their concerts. And yet, it is hard to call them straightforwardly fascist. Just as fifteen years earlier the English language had become a cipher for otherness and cool style, irrespective of the meaning of the words in question, now Nazi references only stood in as symbols of full alienation, underlining the industrial noise of the music and deliberately improper appearance of the band and its followers.[36] Another example of the extreme "stylification" of youth cultural slang was the Mitki in Leningrad, who were actually not so young anymore, but whose deadpan, nihilist, and satirical style commanded a huge following among young people not only in Leningrad but also from further afield. The Mitki perfectly encapsulated the *Gesamtkunstwerk* of late-socialist alternative cultures, which was constantly riffing off (playing with) the special condition of late-Soviet reality by imitating yet mocking them. They accepted these realities, but in their acceptance, they protested them. They relied on clothing (in the Mitki case this was simply a striped Soviet sailor shirt, which perfectly embodied the described imitation with mockery), art (simple but humorous drawings depicting the absurdities of late Soviet life), and fame (the information and dissemination mechanisms of the underground were at the height of their functionality in the 1980s). Shinkarev, one of the Mitki founders, conceded the extent to which the alienation and protest culture of the youth scene required the Soviet system as the "other," invoking the near productivity of an "atmosphere of healthy anxiety, and a certain danger."[37]

In reality there were, of course, two layers of "other" that defined postwar Soviet youth style in the subcultural sphere. There was the youthful desire to be "non-Soviet," thus making the Soviet mainstream the counter-image against which one's own style could be curated and defined. But for the Soviet Union, the West, and in particular, the United States, were the "others." Socialism in the postwar years was increasingly as non-capitalist and non-imperialist, especially when from the 1960s onward the USSR stepped up its international involvement in second- and third-world countries. To be Soviet always meant to be non-Western, and thus to be non-Soviet automatically acquired a sense of "Western-ness." Youth subcultures and Soviet authorities were in surprising agreement about this automatic geographical link with nonconformism. The Cold War made any youth subculture by definition "Western" and thus almost every socialist youth subculture tended to orient itself toward the "West," or at least toward its material and cultural products. The Cold War determined the style parameters of youth subcultural style, and increasingly of Soviet youth style overall. The humble American jeans could hardly have become such a cult item without the multitude of statements its possession and wearing made vis-à-vis Soviet system. Even in the Soviet Union's dying days, when the Iron Curtain had already been breached in a number of places, wearing jeans was a statement of latent anti-Sovietness. When one looks at pictures of the 1991 putsch it almost seems as if this were not a confrontation of two different political sides but a battle of styles: on the one side were the uniforms of the young recruits, and on the other a sea of jeans worn by the mostly young protesters.

There was no immediate change in how subcultural style was defined after 1991, when the Soviet Union ceased to exist and with it the Cold War. A combination of new permissiveness, economic hardship, and pent-up energy made for a super vibrant youth scene, which lived through a number of transformations and phenomena in rocket speed, including several conservative youth cultures inspired by religion and nationalism. It became clear very quickly, however, that the old, simple binaries that had shaped youth subcultures hitherto, socialist norms and Western imagination, were no longer the parameters between which style developed. Socialist norms were not valid anymore, and the West had been transformed from an imaginary utopia into a very hard commercial reality. Style, however, had not lost its power or its capability of making political statements, as the scandal surrounding the activist group Pussy Riot demonstrated.[38] Although the performance of a "punk prayer" in the Christ the Savior Cathedral was primarily designed as a political message, all the contributing attributes were elements of style: the performance of the "prayer" in the newly reconstructed Orthodox church as such, the reference to punk as a former counter-style, and the identical dress in colorful tights and balaclavas and short dresses. Even the group's English name Pussy Riot was a nod back at former times when English was the forbidden language of the ideological enemy and a cipher for nonconformism.

Notes

1. Much has been written about the "meaning of style," first and foremost by Dick Hebdige, *Subculture: The Meaning of Style. New Accents* (London: Routledge, 1988). See also Heike Jenss, *Fashioning Memory: Vintage Style and Youth Culture* (London: Bloomsbury, 2015), and Andy Bennett, "Subcultures or Neo-Tribes? Rethinking the Relationship between Youth, Style and Musical taste," *Sociology* 33, no. 3 (1999): 599–617.
2. Susan K. Morrissey, *Heralds of Revolution: Russian Students and the Mythologies of Radicalism* (New York, Oxford: Oxford University Press, 1998); V. Kudriashov, *Istoriia, Teoriia I Praktika Skautizma: Organizatsionnye Voprosy*: Dokumenty i Materialy (Arkhangel'sk, Russia: PGPU, 1992).
3. Andy Willimott, *Living the Revolution: Urban Communes & Soviet Socialism, 1917–1932* (Oxford: Oxford University Press, 2019). See also Orlando Figes and B. I. Kolonitskii, *Interpreting the Russian Revolution: The Language and Symbols of 1917* (New Haven, CT; London: Yale University Press, 1999); Matthias Neumann, "Youth, It's Your Turn": Generations and the Fate of the Russian Revolution," *Journal of Social History* 46, no. 2 (2012): 273; Isabel A. Tirado, "The Socialist Youth Movement in Revolutionary Russia," *The Russian Review* 46 (1987): 135.
4. Anne E. Gorsuch, "Soviet Youth and the Politics of Popular Culture during NEP," *Social History* 17, no. 2 (1992): 189–201.
5. Lev Kopelev, *The Education of a True Believer* (London: Wildwood House, 1981).
6. S. Frederick Starr, *Red and Hot: The Fate of Jazz in the Soviet Union, 1917–1980* (New York, Oxford: Oxford University Press, 1983).
7. Michael H. Kater, *Different Drummers: Jazz in the Culture of Nazi Germany* (New York: Oxford University Press, 1992).
8. Luis Alvarez, *The Power of the Zoot: Youth Culture and Resistance during World War II* (Berkeley: University of California Press, 2009).
9. Stanley Cohen, *Folk Devils and Moral Panics: The Creation of the Mods and Rockers* (Oxford: Routledge, 1980).
10. Stuart Hall and Tony Jefferson, *Resistance through Rituals: Youth Subcultures in Post-War Britain*, 2nd ed. (London: Routledge, 2006); Ken Gelder, *Subcultures: Cultural Histories and Social Practice* (London: Routledge, 2007); Chris Jenks, *Subculture: The Fragmentation of the Social* (London: SAGE, 2005); Shane Blackman, "Youth Subcultural Theory: A Critical Engagement with the Concept, Its Origins and Politics, from the Chicago School to Postmodernism," *Journal of Youth Studies* 8, no. 1 (2005): 1–20.
11. John Steinbeck and Robert Capa, *A Russian Journal* (London: Penguin Classics, 2000).
12. *Komsomol'skaia pravda*, 'Zolotaia Koronka' (May 18, 1946): 3.
13. RGASPI M-f.1, op. 46, d. 175, ll. 91–92.
14. Mark Edele, "Strange Young Men in Stalin's Moscow: The Birth and Life of the Stiliagi, 1945–1953," *Jahrbücher für Geschichte Osteuropas* 50, no. 1 (2002): 37–61.
15. Hilary Pilkington, *Russia's Youth and Its Culture: A Nation's Constructors and Constructed* (London: Routledge, 1994).
16. D. Beliaev, 'Stiliagi', *Krokodil*, 7 (1949): 10.
17. Juliane Fürst, *Stalin's Last Generation: Soviet Post-War Youth and the Emergence of Mature Socialism* (Oxford: Oxford University Press, 2010).
18. S. Frederick Starr, *Red and Hot: The Fate of Jazz in the Soviet Union 1917–1991* (Oxford: Oxford University Press, 2004).

19. Alexei Yurchak, *Everything Was Forever, until It Was No More: The Last Soviet Generation* (Princeton, NJ: Princeton University Press, 2006).
20. "Sounds and Waves of Freedom. Jazz Hour" with Willis Conover. *Jazz Dünasyi* 16 (April), 2013, https://web.archive.org/web/20151227042059/http://jazzdunyasi.jazz.az/content/view/211/55/lang,en/.
21. Simon Scott, Willis Conover, *The Voice of Jazz behind the Iron Curtain*, NPR Opinion, July 25, 2015, https://text.npr.org/426029637.
22. Vladimir Gusarov, *Moi otets ubyl Mikhoelsa* (Frankfurt am Main: Posev), 90
23. Fürst, *Stalin's*, 225.
24. Ibid.
25. Bradley Gorski, "Manufacturing Dissent: Stiliagi, Vasilii Aksenov, and the Dilemma of Self-Interpretation," *Russian Literature* 96–98 (2018): 77–104.
26. Iurii Zhukov, "Khippi i drugie," *Pravda* June 5, 1967, 4.
27. Barry Miles, *Peace: 50 Years of Protest* (Pleasantville, NY: Readers Digest Association, 2008). See also Timothy Miller, *The Hippies and American Values*, 2nd ed. (Knoxville: University of Tennessee, 2011).
28. On Soviet hippies see Juliane Fürst, *Flowers through Concrete: Explorations in Soviet Hippieland* (Oxford: Oxford University Press, 2021); S. I. Zhuk, *Rock and Roll in the Rocket City: The West, Identity, and Ideology in Soviet Dniepropetrovsk, 1960–1985* (Washington, DC: Woodrow Wilson Center, 2010); Mark Allen Svede, "All You Need Is Lovebeads: Latvia's Hippies Dress for Success," in *Style and Socialism. Modernity and Material Culture in Post-War Eastern Europe*, ed. Susan Reid and David Crowley (Oxford: Berg, 2000), 189–2008.; William Jay Risch, "Soviet 'Flower Children.' Hippies and the Youth Counter-Culture in 1970s L'viv," *Journal of Contemporary History* 40, no. 3 (2005): 565–584.
29. "Vypiska iz zapisnoi knizhki Eres'ko," TsDahOU, f. 7, op. 20, d. 609, l. 12.
30. David Gurevich, *From Lenin to Lennon: A Memoir of Russia in the Sixties* (New York: Harcourt Brace Jovanovich, 1991).
31. Interview with Zaborovskii cited by Juliane Fürst, *Flowers through Concrete*.
32. A. Shchipkov, *Sobornyj Dvor* (Moscow: Mediasoiuz, 2003).
33. Fürst, *Flowers through Concrete*, 83–93.
34. OSA (Open Society Archive) 300-85-9: 128/40.
35. Juliane Fürst and Josie McLellan, *Dropping Out of Socialism: The Creation of Alternative Spheres in the Soviet Bloc* (Lanham, MD: Lexington Books, 2017).
36. Yngvar B. Steinholt, "Siberian Punk Shall Emerge Here: Egor Letov and Grazhdanskaia Oborona," *Popular Music* 31, no. 3 (2012): 401–415.
37. Alexandar Mihailovic, *The Mitki* (Madison: The University of Wisconsin Press), 7.
38. Fabrizio Fenghi, *It Will Be Fun and Terrifying: Nationalism and Protest in Post-Soviet Russia* (Madison: University of Wisconsin Press, 2020); Eliot Borenstein, *Pussy Riot: Speaking Punk to Power* (London: Bloomsbury Academic, 2020); Masha Gessen, *Words Will Break Cement: The Passion of Pussy Riot* (London: Riverhead Books, 2014).

Further Reading

Cohen, Stanley. *Folk Devils and Moral Panics: The Creation of the Mods and Rockers*. Oxford: Routledge, 1980.
Fürst, Juliane. *Flowers through Concrete: Explorations in Soviet Hippieland*. Oxford: Oxford University Press, 2021.

Fürst, Juliane. *Stalin's Last Generation: Soviet Post-War Youth and the Emergence of Mature Socialism*. Oxford: Oxford University Press, 2010.

Fürst, Juliane, and Josie McLellan. *Dropping out of Socialism: The Creation of Alternative Spheres in the Soviet Bloc*. Bristol, UK: Lexington Books, 2017.

Gorsuch, Anne. *Youth in Revolutionary Russia: Enthusiasts, Bohemians, Delinquents*. Indianapolis: Indiana University Press, 2000.

Hall, Stuart, and Tony Jefferson. *Resistance through Rituals: Youth Subcultures in Post-War Britain*. 2nd ed. London: Routledge, 2006.

Hebdige, Dick. *Subculture: The Meaning of Style*. New Accents. London: Routledge, 1988.

Pilkington, Hilary. *Russia's Youth and Its Culture: A Nation's Constructors and Constructed*. London: Routledge, 1994.

Woodward, Leslie. *How the Beatles Rocked the Kremlin: The Untold Story of a Noisy Revolution*. London: Bloomsbury, 2013.

Yurchak, Alexei. *Everything Was Forever, until It Was No More: The Last Soviet Generation*. Princeton: Princeton University Press, 2006.

CHAPTER 12

PLAY CULTURES, SOCIAL WORLDS, AND YOUTH IN FAMILIAL SETTINGS, 1700–1905

MARY CLARE MARTIN

BETWEEN 1902 and 1905, four sisters, Kitty, Nellie, Winnie, and Peggy, daughters of Colonel Edward Kenyon, then living in Middlecot, Hampshire, co-produced a magazine, *The Bee-Hive*, with their extended family of cousins. As the editor explained in Summer 1903, "The little Bee-Hives make up the Big Bee-Hive."[1] This youth-led manuscript illustrates a familial play culture that was inclusive of all age groups, enabling the youngest to participate, and to "critisise" older siblings and adults. The youngest Kenyon sister, Peggy, aged eight in 1902, was a frequent author. A few adults contributed, and Aunt Rhoeta, who lived on the Isle of Wight, was on the editorial team. *The Bee-Hive* drew on earlier models of youth-produced magazines, which were replicated later in the twentieth century, and indicates how play can be a fertile ground for studying the transition between childhood and adulthood.

Sources about play cultures, social worlds, and youth in relation to outdoor play, imaginative play, and juvenile periodicals are often fragmentary. There might seem to be a clear trajectory from child-focused activities to more public or adult-facing activities involving youth. These continuities can be characterized as "play cultures" that provide insights into youthful social worlds and the ways these changed within familial contexts. These "social worlds," however, might also include adults. While this complicates the notion of children's cultures, it also justifies the concept of youth culture in familial settings by demonstrating how practices of outdoor play, drama, and writing could be inclusive of all age groups at different levels. Adults (especially fathers), including governesses and tutors, were involved in teaching and supervising games for outdoor play, not only for youth but also as participants. They thus demonstrated Lev Vygotsky's concept of "scaffolding" and theories of the transition to adulthood.[2] "Scaffolding" or the "zone of proximal development" is characterized as a process by which the older person, including siblings or friends, supports the learning of the younger one. This contrasts with theorists' definitions of play as activity that is only self-generated, with no external engagement by adults.[3]

The chronological scope here is ambitious, and examples to substantiate different aspects of these life stages to support the overall arguments have not always survived. Nevertheless, the model illustrated by Kenneth Grahame in *The Golden Age*, of a world of "Olympians" (adults) inhabiting a different world from the young, and of little emotional connection across the generations, because of adults' lack of interest in children's pursuits, bears little resemblance to the complex webs of interactions that will be documented.[4]

The phenomenon of youth culture, mainly focused on males, has usually been associated with the Swinging Sixties, Mods and Rockers, rival gangs, the "rise of the teenager," and the development of commercial youth culture over the twentieth century. Many scholars associate the emergence of the concept of adolescence in the early twentieth century with the publication of Stanley Hall's *Adolescence* in 1904 and the development of secondary schooling. Yet, the life stage of "*adolescentia*" (for fourteen- to twenty-one-year-olds) was recognized in the ancient world and was known in the Middle Ages. Early modernists have long acknowledged the rituals of misrule among young people and debated whether there was a distinction between youth and adolescence.[5]

Although young people, especially elites, spent much of their time in the family home, few scholars have considered how play cultures might develop into youthful pursuits that spanned the transition to adulthood. A number of historians have acknowledged the significance of sibling relationships, however, and their neglect.[6] Frequently, play has been treated in an object-related and antiquarian fashion, focusing on the history of toys, rather than considering what it might reveal about family relationships or child development. A related perspective focuses on youth as consumers. The themes selected here reflect Brian Sutton-Smith's emphasis on the significance of social play rather than play with objects, and they facilitate analysis of play cultures regardless of social status. The play cultures created and developed by youth in familial contexts in England, Scotland, Wales, and Ireland between 1700 and 1900 will be explored. The *longue duree* includes the period of the "First Industrial Revolution," from 1700, when London was already a major city, to 1900, when one-quarter of the globe was associated with the British Empire.[7]

The eighteenth century has been perceived as a major period of change in attitudes toward the young, owing to the ideas of John Locke and Jean-Jacques Rousseau. Other scholars have focused on the nineteenth century, particularly on concepts of "adolescence" and "girlhood," arguing for a recognition of more autonomy for youth in their late teens by the late nineteenth century. Culture can be defined as membership of a group with specific interests and shared meanings. That different families, especially with large numbers of siblings, developed their own systems of shared understandings and practices, relates to the concept of "social worlds."[8]

How far did the process of transition to adulthood change over the eighteenth and nineteenth centuries? Estimates include "youth," as identified by Lord Chesterfield, as the age of nine until about the mid-twenties, or from seven to the mid-twenties, in relation to the Poor Law. Neither sex could inherit until the age of twenty-one, but they were frequently expected to start work in their teens, even in the upper and middle classes, in a condition of semi-dependence. Fourteen has also been regarded as the age of adulthood. Peter Borsay noted that eighteenth-century young people, especially elite girls, were represented as socializing with their parents from about twelve, and that childhood became "compressed."[9]

The age of schooling impacted on the transition to adulthood. Despite the increasing tendency from about 1760 onward to send elite boys to boarding school, especially from overseas locations, contact with home and family members continued. Moreover, many boys from the professional and middle classes attended secondary day schools rather than boarding schools. Day schools for the laboring poor existed in increasing numbers from 1800 particularly, so that by 1858, every child's name was estimated to be on the books of a school. There was no compulsory school age until 1880 (ages five to ten), and this was targeted at working-class children. In their Oxfordshire village of Lark Rise, Flora Thompson recalled that there were no girls aged over twelve, as they had all gone into service. In industrial or urban areas there was less reason to leave home for work, and three-generation family clusters might develop. Girls from the middling sort and especially elites were more likely to remain at home, and the latter to have more leisure, while middling sort girls might be working in the family business.[10]

The number and spacing of siblings clearly had an impact on the experience of familial youth culture. The average household size in Britain remained relatively constant from the late seventeenth century until the early twentieth, at 4.75. The eighteenth-century household was likely to include servants and apprentices as well as kin. While family size dipped in the aristocracy in the early eighteenth century, from 1750 to 1800 it increased to its largest size over the previous two hundred years. In working-class families, there were averages of six to eight children, depending on occupation. The average number of children per family shifted from 6.16 in 1860–1899 to 4.13 in 1890–1899. By the 1870s the "large sprawling families" (or "long families") of early-nineteenth-century elites had been replaced by about six children. In some cases, due to parental or child death, there was only one child. Some people were never regarded as fully adult if they were not householders; indeed, Carol Dyhouse argues that women were never perceived as fully adult by Stanley Hall and others in 1900.[11]

Thus, while variable according to gender and class, youth will be considered to extend from seven to the mid-twenties.

Youth, Play, and Memory

Despite the neglect of play by historians, many or most autobiographies or memoirs have sections including childhood and youthful play. Issues about the fallibility of memory have been well rehearsed, and autobiographies were clearly written with reference to the time period in which they were produced. But protagonists' reflections on their younger selves can be significant, as can absences, and the recurrence of specific memories or themes. Some memoirs had no reference to play or youth culture and emphasized solitariness as well as peer culture. Furthermore, play was often disapproved of by adults, or regarded retrospectively as a sign of childishness, or worse (such as Sabbath breaking), to which studiousness was preferred. Adriana Benzaquén concluded from the letters of the Clarke family from the 1690s that they do not represent the "authentic self" of the individual, but they do illustrate webs of relationships. These are particularly significant for the purposes of this study in mapping the interactions of siblings and other peers. Letters from adults with observations about children provide the detail of everyday occupations, as do adults' journals and journals by youth, even if edited. Magazines produced by the young (in this case, *The Bee-Hive*) have been cross-referenced with unpublished memoirs. The rich seam of working-class autobiography, mainly collected in the nineteenth century, was anticipated by religious autobiographies from the eighteenth century, such as the *Lives of the Early Methodist Preachers* (1837–1838).[12] The source material has been taken from a wide range of social classes and regions, both urban and rural. The subjects here include children and youth from the royalty and aristocracy as well as the lesser gentry and the professions, the middling sort, and laboring poor. After an exploration of family cultures, this chapter will focus on outdoor play, imaginative play and theatricals, and juvenile writing, especially magazines, with reference to the themes of youth as producers, the transition from childhood play cultures to youthful independence, and the complexity of gender relations.

Family Cultures and Sibling Relationships

Despite claims and demographic evidence that most eighteenth-century youth lived in large families, most histories relate to the mid-to-late nineteenth century, reflecting the stereotype of the children accommodated in separate wings of the house with nannies and governesses. Not all children had a peer group, whether of siblings or friends. Solitude could be a temporary condition, caused by health issues. Some memoirs emphasize adolescent pursuits such as drinking, gaming, womanizing, and "bad company" with the peer group. Others mention mixing with adults from a young age. Some aristocratic young women such as Lady Sarah Cadogan were married in their early teens (to the nineteen-year-old future Earl of Richmond, in 1718). Yet the Princess Royal was unmarried at twenty-two in 1783. Due particularly to the increase in family size from the 1750s, many children had large numbers of cousins. Discipline in such large families could be sibling imposed and harsh. Indeed, not all sibling relationships were collaborative, nor did all siblings feel affinity with one another. The memoir of Frances Margaret Kenyon indicates that she found her sisters rather distant and controlling. Indeed, some children's main playmates were servants.[13]

Whereas in the seventeenth century, "tomboy" referred to a boy, the term for a boylike girl in the eighteenth was "hoyden." Thus, Lord Orrery wrote in 1733, though affectionately, "Betty is . . . a veritable Miss Hoyden."[14] While Dyhouse argued that natural exuberance in a boy was regarded as "hoydenism" in a girl, Abate indicated that tomboyishness became an acceptable characteristic for girls from the mid-nineteenth century onward, a theme that occurs in accounts of future suffragists and missionary wives. The aristocratic Lucy Lyttelton recalled that "At twelve years old I was a heedless tomboy of a child," though she later regretted her "sinfulness."[15]

Outdoor Play, Skill, and Inventiveness

Familial play cultures frequently encompassed a wide age range of young people, including not only youth, but also older siblings and friends. Many of these groupings may have been initiated by adults but were then developed autonomously by children and youth. While John Locke and Jean-Jacques Rousseau recommended outdoor activities as essential for a healthy upbringing, few eighteenth-century accounts of outdoor family activities exist, with the image of the "tomboy" and the promotion of health for "healthy bouncing girls" being associated with the late nineteenth. Muscular Christianity is usually associated with schools or voluntary organizations rather than home life. Some authors have challenged arguments about the gendering of childhood. Although working-class girls were more restricted than boys, and more likely to have to help with chores or childcare, country laboring girls might play outside when they had time.[16]

How much space did children have to play outside? Pamela Horn maintained that, despite poverty, Victorian laboring children living in the country still had a better, healthier environment with space to play than town children. Some accounts emphasize the space available in the countryside, for gentry, middling sorts, and laboring families. Rebecca Brewin, daughter of a hosier, draper, and Methodist preacher, and future missionary's wife, from Mountsorrel, went for rambles looking for wildflowers or blackberries in the woods or countryside in the 1850s. Louise Jermy missed the fields and river after moving to London. In cold weather, the affluent might play games indoors. In the 1690s, the Clarke girls requested that battledores be bought for them to play with in cold weather, while in winter Mabel Hunt's family played "Hare and Hounds" indoors as well as outside.[17]

While children of the middle classes and elites were likely to be accompanied by servants on walks, male youth especially might have considerable freedom to move across town, like ten-year-old John Pocock or fifteen-year-old Dickie Doyle. Location was significant. Fanny Burney, aged seventeen, walked alone in the countryside from 6:00 to 7:00 a.m. on holiday in 1768 but felt unable to do so in town settings. Gardens large and small were also sources of pleasure, for both sexes, and many youth from mercantile, professional, and gentry backgrounds could roam freely in large private grounds, able to develop their own play cultures free from adults. Margaret Nevinson, a Leicester clergyman's daughter, recalled of the 1860s and 1870s that "We had plenty of room for play in our garden and the disused stables; we quarrelled and fought to our hearts' content, disturbing none."[18]

Frideswide's Catholic family in the 1880s had to become more decorous soon after early childhood. For some, being outdoors was not considered desirable. The niece of the future author Charlotte Yonge described her ambivalence: whereas in childhood, she enjoyed scrambling about with her cousin George, in "girlhood" (from age fifteen upward), she saw being outdoors as "dawdling." In cold weather, walking three times around the gravel path (approximately a mile) was seen as enough exercise. In Lark Rise in the 1880s, children as young as two might be turned outside to play on their own. Indeed, elder girls went to service aged twelve and were represented as too grown up to play, a reminder that laboring girls might go straight from childhood to adulthood without an adolescence. Images of working-class children playing in urban streets have become commonplace. Girls, however, were often described as standing by, supervising, rather than playing, or else working indoors.[19] The following activities will now be considered riding, boating, swimming, skating, and cricket, with reference to the themes of youth as producers, the transition from childhood play cultures to youthful independence, and the complexity of gender relations.

Riding was a skill taught in childhood that could facilitate independence. Learning might start young; seven-year-old Henry Solly, a timber merchant's son, was given a pony and was given an errand to ride from Essex to Hackney (about three miles) on his own in 1820. Moreover, this was not limited to elites. Matthias Joyce, one of the early Methodist preachers, born in 1754 in Dublin, fell from a horse in full gallop aged about eleven. Riding could be taught to both sexes in elite families. In 1832, Prince George, Duke of Cambridge, noted how a girl aged nine to ten rode confidently on a big horse, while he had been rather fearful. In 1862 "Grandpapa" had promised an Exmoor pony to Angie Acland, an Oxford professor's daughter, aged thirteen, who had been able to ride for four years. Youth might go riding without adults, including disabled young people. Thus, in Scotland, in 1860s, a special saddle was made for Lady Victoria Campbell, who was lame, so she could ride with her seven siblings. Hunting, very important to country dwellers, was another potentially mixed-age, mixed-gender, and cross-class activity, though one led by adults. In 1843, all the house party at Minto, in Scotland, including the youth, went hunting, except for three women, aged seventeen upward. Mabel Hunt's clerical father insisted his daughters join the Meet in the 1880s.[20]

Sea bathing became fashionable in the eighteenth century as a perceived cure for many health problems, though not necessarily for enjoyment. In 1755, Dr. Johnson distinguished between bathing for medicinal purposes and swimming for pleasure. While Orme and Allen argue that before 1719, virtually the whole female sex was excluded, young children, both male and female, might swim if taken by adults. Queeney Thrale, whose mother was an enthusiastic swimmer, was taught to swim by her father with a frog in a large basin, and she was swimming in the sea aged eleven. Emily, Duchess of Leinster, promoted sea bathing all year round, and in the 1780s, her offspring went bathing at Black Rock in Ireland twice a day. Francis Place, son of a London debt collector, whose father forbade him to swim, was pushed into the river by a man who said that most boys about eleven years of age could swim. But elites as well as the laboring poor might swim for pleasure. The disabled Anna Gurney, aged eight, insisted on being carried down to the beach at Cromer so she could swim with her cousins. In the 1860s, Oundle British school children went bathing in the river Nen during their school lunchtime. The diarist Rev. Henry Kilvert watched youth swimming in the sea in the 1870s.[21]

Gender had an impact on elite girls' participation. Whereas Sarah Richardson, a judge's daughter, mentioned only boys bathing in the Thames during family holidays with cousins in the 1830s, Frances Balfour, of the aristocratic Argyll family in Scotland, recalled sea bathing as recommended, and "pleasurable," in the mid-nineteenth century. She also remembered, however, that they were hampered by wearing bathing dresses resembling long nightgowns. Nevinson and Acland, the only girls in families of brothers, recorded frustration at the limitations posed by their gender. Twelve-year-old Angie Acland, writing on holiday in 1862, wished she could swim more than once a week, like the other youth.[22] "One of the sorrows of my childhood," wrote Margaret Nevinson,

> was that boys were allowed to swim in river and canal. I was told that "little ladies" must not bathe in fresh water but only in the sea. I felt this deeply as I was an enthusiastic swimmer and hardly remember the time when I could not float like a cork on the water.[23]

Louisa Grey loved her daily swim in the special seawater bathing pool that her family shared with Queen Victoria's children at Osborne on the Isle of Wight. For elites, there could be a transition to independent, self-organized activity by youth. When the Hunts moved to Feering, Essex, their two older cousins (Christopher and Elizabeth) organized bicycling picnics in Essex to get to the coast at Mersea or Maldon, where they could swim.[24]

Boating could also foster independence as well as pleasure, for girls as well as boys. William Hickey, aged fifteen, used to sail on the Thames near his father's house in Twickenham, in the 1760s. Francis Place spent much of his leisure time rowing in a barge. Sarah Richardson, a judge's daughter, recalled the enjoyment of brothers and cousins in bathing and boating, and girls in boating on their holidays in the 1830s. Frideswide noted how, when they moved to Kidlington (near Oxford), the boys camped out and the girls picnicked and went boating. In 1844, seventeen-year-old Agnes Cotton, daughter of a governor of the Bank of England, was acting as "Man Friday" for her younger brother Arthur, "paddling about the last day or two with him alternately in the little boat [their elder brother . . .] gave Harry and in the little canoe."[25]

Access to skating depended on availability of equipment, the acquisition of which also depended on personal initiative; in this as in other activities, youth might develop the skills necessary to create or acquire play objects. Francis Place wanted to skate when he was twelve years old, so he dug for iron and lead in an underwater ruin with his schoolfellows, which he sold to buy skates. Victorian country laboring boys had skates that were usually homemade, but that still allowed them to enjoy the activity. Funds were limited for the clergy families. Margaret Nevinson recalled how, on one occasion, when her brother was carrying their shared skates, he dropped the blade of one of them, and they both knew they could not buy another.[26] Neither said anything to the adults, providing an example of youthful peer group solidarity.

Like riding, skating might start young and include both sexes. In 1842, Arthur Cotton was beginning to learn at the age of nine. The aristocratic Lucy Lyttelton went sliding with "the boys" when she was thirteen.[27] Although Louisa Grey (born in 1855), who remembered skating, might be considered to model propriety, being in the queen's household, it was not universally accepted for young elite women. Gulielma Lister, from an Essex Quaker family, reported of the 1880s how "all the Wildsmith sisters were beautiful skaters . . . and this at a time when it was thought very advanced for girls to skate."[28]

Toy boats linked outdoor play and imaginative play with the development of a skill. The favorite sports of Thomas Arnold, the future headmaster, included sailing rival fleets of ships with his few childhood playmates. Ellen Weeton recalled that, when the weather was fine, they played her brother's amusements in the garden; this included sailing ships in the rain tub. Older boys could be producers as well as consumers, across the social spectrum. Francis Place learned the use of tools in a carpenter's shop, in the 1780s, aged about twelve, making many models of sailing boats, which were sold for him by adults, his father and the sculptor, Flaxman, in a shop at the Strand.

Henry Solly was taught to make boats in the carpenter's shop on his father's estate and sailed boats (Nelson's fleet) on ponds from when he was a small boy until he was older (age thirteen) at school in 1830. Thus, sailing toy boats, which seems to have been a particularly gendered activity, perhaps because they depended on equipment, also illustrates a transition from childish play to youthful production. Adults might help youth from working-class backgrounds learn to fish, but girls could also participate. Rebecca Brewin often spent Saturday afternoons on fishing trips with her brothers, while Katharine Chorley, of Alderley Edge, was shown how to make a fishing rod and to fish by a stable hand.[29]

The mid-nineteenth-century public school is usually associated with the rise of organized sport for the upper- and middle-class young, yet children played competitive games in the eighteenth century in a family context. Eighteenth-century paintings depicted girls and boys playing cricket. Exercise was considered important for both the male and female children of George III, who played cricket, hockey, and other games. Indeed, by the mid-eighteenth century there were all-female cricket matches. By the 1830s, the whole mission community at Paihia in New Zealand—all ages, Pakeha and indigenous people alike—played a cricket match. Nineteenth-century elite girls participated in team games. In 1854, Lucy Lyttelton (aged thirteen), played cricket with the boys at Hagley. Mabel Hunt, fifth sister in her family, recalled how her clerical father was always ready to coach them and taught them to play cricket and not fear the hard ball.[30]

Country boys could be inventive producers, making cricket bats in the 1860s. In the Buckinghamshire village of Haddenham the young carpentry apprentice Walter Rose added to his pocket money by making cricket bats in his spare time. Urban girls and boys played cricket in the streets in the nineteenth century. Yet family members and servants might send mixed messages. Margaret Nevinson "took part in all [her five brothers'] sports, and became a good cricketer, tree-climber, etc." But, once when she broke her finger on a hard cricket ball, she was told "It served me right for being a Tom Boy—little ladies should not play cricket."[31] But games organized by adults might be tedious and dull, as in the case of Frideswide's mother's birthday croquet party. The youth demonstrated "resistance" by falling in the pond and getting soaked.[32]

Thus, outdoor play encompassed activities that extended across the age range. Close analysis of specific aspects of youthful play, such as organized games, shows how their experiences across gender and social class were more varied and also more similar than is frequently suggested. The *longue duree* calls into question the practice of limiting the focus on the late nineteenth century as a key period for girls to have more freedom physically. Young people had roles as producers of equipment, which enabled working-class boys to alleviate class divides. Whereas specific skills such as riding and skating might be taught, or activities such as bathing carefully managed, youth were able to demonstrate autonomy in many activities. Yet, anecdotes highlight the role of adults as well as older siblings in imparting skill.

Drama at Home: Imaginative Play and Theatricals

Whereas psychologists would consider socio-dramatic play as an essential aspect of child development, dramatic activities were woven into the fabric of different households far down the social scale. Family games like "dumb crambo" or charades, which involved answering questions through mime, might be played by all-age family groups. Disapproval of imaginative play and the theater by different religious groups, notably Methodists, and Evangelicals, was communicated to some young people. Charlotte Yonge's only youthful friends near her home, the Shipleys, did not approve of imaginary play, as it was not "real." Even as late as 1900, the Streatfeilds were not allowed to dress up during Lent.[33]

Although historians might assume a transition from children's imaginative play to older children performing in public, the reality was far more complex. The very young might attend the theater and be co-opted into public performances by adults. Gleadle has argued that juveniles "playing at soldiers" in the early 1800s saw this as an apprenticeship for their future military activity. Cultures of imaginative play developed into more formal presentation of theatricals, and the co-opting or voluntary engagement of the young. Some practices occurred across the age range, some were organized by adults, but some by young people. In contrast with Abigail Williams' typology of reading, recitation, and performing, these processes connected imaginative play, reading, recitation, and performance, both domestic and public, in ways which were not necessarily age-specific.[34]

Religious play was one of the most common themes across the period. Indeed, biographies sometimes interpreted early religious play as indicative of later genius. Many memoirs, across social classes, describe children, male and female, "acting the preacher." While many did so very seriously, some were mocking. Children also played at funerals, from the early eighteenth to the early twentieth century. In the 1750s, the young Hannah More used to "make a carriage of a chair, and then to call her sisters to ride with her to London, to see bishops and booksellers." She wrote "supposititious letters to depraved characters to reclaim them from their errors, and letters in return expressive of contrition, and resolutions of amendment."[35] Reading plays aloud was a family as well as a solitary activity, undertaken not only by the higher classes but also by the middling sort and even the poor. One of the Clarkes asked for a copy of *Don Quixote* in the 1690s. The Harris family, who lived in the cathedral close in Salisbury, read Shakespeare plays together in the 1760s, while Harriet Martineau, aged about nine, loved reading them on her own in the drawing room. In the 1840s, Joseph Ashby, the farm laborer, knew some speeches from Shakespeare, and his brother would teach him in bed at night the set pieces taught at school, making a tent from an old blanket.

Newsboys paid 6d for copies of *Hamlet* and *Macbeth*. Alice Foley's father forced her to act the part of Desdemona.[36]

The public theater was very popular in the eighteenth century, and as early as 1712 parents took children as young as four years old. The children of the Duke of Kildare, aged seven upward, went to the pantomime, which was universally popular, titled *A Trip to the Dargil*, in Dublin near Christmas in 1762.[37] The creativity of the young could result in self-generated performance. Georgiana, the future Duchess of Devonshire, loved to compose poems and stories to perform after dinner, "and entertain her family with playlets featuring dramatic heroines in need of rescue."[38] In 1767 [Lady Bute's] youngest daughter, a child of ten years of age, "shew'd us the beginning of a french Novel, wrote by herself, & inform'd us She was going to write a play: that the plan was fixt (sic) & was to be taken from a Roman Story."[39] Lord Pigot's "natural" daughter, aged about nine or ten, performed extracts and songs from popular plays for as many as fifty people in 1767. Thomas Arnold, the future headmaster of Rugby, wrote a tragedy around 1800, when he was only six, about Percy, Earl of Northumberland. Charlotte Yonge wrote plays for the Moberlys, children of the headmaster of Winchester, aged sixteen, in the 1830s, customizing the parts for the characters.[40]

As indicated earlier, children and young people included classical allusions in their play as well as their amateur theatricals. The future colonial administrator, Thomas Macaulay, played imaginary classical games, though these would seem to have been beyond the capacities of his siblings. Thomas Arnold acted the battles of the Greek heroes. The Solly children of Rotherhithe acted a play of "Alexander the Robber" (Alexander the Great) on Twelfth Night, 1831. By the early nineteenth century, the young (especially boys) had toy theaters that provided further opportunities for experimentation, using a range of storylines, and for elder siblings to help younger ones. Girls also performed historical scenarios, Frances Balfour stringing Blondin across her sickbed and re-enacting a duel with her brother. In the 1880s, the Baptist Tom Moore enacted Fenimore Cooper's *The Last of the Mohicans* in the castle grounds at Reigate, and the exclusive (male) Boomerang Club played Red Indians. Victorian country boys played at fox hunting, would make their own stilts, and would act the beginnings of several stories.[41]

Formal performances in public were related more to status than to age. In the late seventeenth century, royal and court youth performed in dramas, such as *Calisto*. By 1722, nine-year-old Lady Caroline Lennox was acting in a play staged in a private theater at the Royal Mint, watched by royalty: *The Arrival of the Indian Emperor in Mexico*. *Tableaux vivants*, which might involve royal children from eleven months upward as well as youth, were organized, for example in 1769. By the end of the nineteenth century, children across social classes might be co-opted to participate in patriotic tableaux.[42]

Youth were frequently involved in performing with and for adults. Williams described private theatricals by gentry and aristocracy but also mentioned that cross-dressing was a concern both for the Clarkes (in the 1690s) and the Harrises in the 1760s. In 1768, Fanny Burney participated in theatricals with guests of all ages when staying with her friends such as Mr. Crisp at Chesington. Fitzjames Stephen's only appearance on a stage, as Toby Trumpkin, occurred at Christmas, 1844, when he was staying with family friends at Warrington. Charades at the Mintos' castle might involve all ages; for example, in December 1856, the game included three adults and one youth, Nina Minto's eleven-year-old boy.[43] These examples illustrate the difficulty of disassociating the activities of young people from those of adults.

Young people might also organize theatricals themselves. From 1768 onward, young women of the musical Harris family in Salisbury organized amateur theatricals with others, led by Gertrude, aged eighteen, and including Louisa, aged thirteen. These were held in grand private homes, such as the chapel in the Harrises' home. The Austen family sometimes held private theatricals, as in the novel *Mansfield Park*, but with the barn as the theater. Plays produced by the elite young could be performed in distinctly public places. In 1831 and 1832, the schoolboy Frederick Young, son of a Limehouse shipowner and MP, "acted female parts in theatricals at the 'Bow Brewhouse (Mr Drane's),'" before a large audience. His friend and business colleague Joseph Dawson acted as Lydia Languish and Frederick as her servant Lucy, in dresses especially made by dressmakers. Charles Dickens's children acted in plays such as *The Frozen Deep*, at home and in a private audience with the Queen in 1857. John Kitto, from a much poorer background, was inspired by the ubiquitous printed playbills to organize a play with other youth. They charged eight to ten pins and bought a feast with the profits, thus foreshadowing the "penny gaffs" held at street corners in working-class areas from the 1840s.[44]

Performance might develop directly from youthful imaginative play. Clergy daughters from the mid-nineteenth century produced entertainments for the parish and for public consumption. In 1860, at Pradoe in Shropshire, the Kenyon family home, a performance of "Blue Beard" was held, acted by adults and mainly children, with the program appearing in children's handwriting. Clergy daughter Margaret Nevinson produced little plays and *tableaux vivants* with two girlfriends at their country house, "B-Hall," in Leicestershire. In one, they acted a scene in which a young girl joined a convent, the path later taken by one of the girls. Frideswide, however, described the tedious aspects of home theatricals organized by their mother in the 1870s. On one occasion they rebelled and went to the village in historical costume and started making speeches to the village children.[45] Such resistance was the exception rather than the norm, however.

Thus, aspects of youthful imaginative play suffused life in country houses and homes further down the social scale and included dramatic performances by adults. Self-generated imaginative play might result in productions, both dramatic and written, for adults in their households or even wider communities. Inevitably, these processes were refracted by class and gender, although there were similarities across social strata.

Juvenile Writing and Periodicals: Play as Apprenticeship

Youthful cultures of reading and writing could develop, regardless of adult attitudes. Fanny Burney, who published *Evelina* when she was eighteen, was encouraged by her father's friend, Mr. Crisp ("Daddy Crisp"), and literary friends. John Kitto was asked to write a story for a friend, and illustrate it as well, for a small fee. Writing for publication was possible. The young men in the Gurneys' circle in Norwich contributed articles to *The Cabinet*, a local Jacobin magazine. Harriet Martineau and Charlotte Yonge published in juvenile magazines as teenagers. Catherine Marsh submitted an article to *The Youth's Companion* when she was seventeen, but it was rejected.[46]

Christine Alexander has described the culture of family magazines in the nineteenth century as "Play and apprenticeship." She analyzed the literary productions of later well-known authors in the context of youthful play and as preparation for their future roles as authors, using concepts such as "serious play," "family play," and "communal play." The culture of producing homemade magazines has been characterized as a form of female empowerment, but boys were often involved, even as initiators. Indeed, they were also produced by boys' schools, for the working class as well as the middle classes, into the twentieth century.[47] The earliest known examples of family magazines were the stories written by the Burney family in the 1750s. *The Loiterer*, to which other siblings contributed, was started by Jane Austen's brother at Oxford. The Bronte family's *Glasstown* was based around toy soldiers brought home by their father in the late eighteenth century. Other famous child authors and productions included Lewis Carroll (Charles Dodgson), and the Woolf family's *Hyde Park Gate News*, which Virginia Woolf edited in the early 1890s between the ages of nine and thirteen. Alexander emphasized the power wielded by females as editors, while noting the role of, say the young Lewis Carroll in organizing his siblings. Sibling hierarchy was evident in the Stephen family: the younger brother Adrian was squashed when he tried to start a new paper, the *Talland Gazette*. This "communal play" with siblings has frequently been identified not only as part of their youth culture, but also as the source of these authors' later creativity. Many other families besides the future famous produced their own magazines, however. The "Boomerang Club," composed of the Moore boys' siblings and friends, produced a monthly magazine of prose and verse in the 1880s.[48]

The Bee-Hive provides more detailed insights into how such magazines might function across the age range and with extended family. Produced and edited by a family of four sisters (the Kenyons, born 1886–1894, whose father was a career military officer), and their extended family of cousins and some adults from 1902 to 1905, it provides insights into family dynamics and shows how the skills of the youngest could be developed in collaboration with older siblings. The first editor was Kitty (Katharine), who was sixteen. The four sisters all contributed, though Peggy (aged eight) comes across as the most enthusiastic. The magazine also included contributions by members of other households from their extended family: the Fairfax Taylors, who attended Oxford High School, the De Butts family, who lived in Albury, near Guildford, and Aunt Rhoeta (De Butts), who lived on the Isle of Wight. The magazine had all the expected features, such as letters pages, editorials, and puzzles. Contributors were encouraged to write "critisisms" (sic) of other articles. The first edition was handwritten (in the same handwriting) but later versions were typewritten. They also had themed issues, such as "Cats," which allowed contributors to write at their own levels. The news pages allowed the youngest to add their interests (about new baby Freddy's baptism in the Isle of Wight in 1902), juxtaposed with accounts of school, and their adult elder brother Herbert's report back from India. The magazines also illustrate how writing competence was not dependent on "age." Peggy, the youngest, was a more frequent contributor than her elder sister Winifred. The content also provided insights into the lives of older cousins.[49]

CONCLUSION

Specific forms of youth culture that were generated in familial environments, across different social classes and genders, have been identified. Outdoor games, whether free-flowing or with rules, might be introduced or facilitated by adults or older siblings but practiced by young people independently. Youth (mainly boys, and often from poorer backgrounds) made their own resources such as skates, and toy boats. While elite girls recorded the constraints of their gender in relation, to, say, swimming, many girls, from different social classes, did engage in outdoor play and learned the skills of independence associated with riding and boating.

Imaginative play could develop into family-produced or publicly performed theatricals produced by the young. That these flourished within an environment of adult play reading and charades does not negate their identity as the creations of youth. Juvenile magazines might include the whole age range of a family and be sufficiently inclusive of the youngest to make this a collective endeavor. Indeed, in *The Bee-Hive*, younger members were invited to "critisise" older ones, thus developing their own writing capacity, and giving the young a voice within hierarchical family structures. This therefore extends the understanding of youth culture as a collaboration across age groups, and a means for the youngest to develop, rather than as an exclusive, narrowly age-related category.

Clearly, a short discussion cannot capture the complexities of change over time, or class and gender differences. Childhood would seem to have ended more abruptly in the eighteenth century, even for the middle and upper classes, than in the nineteenth, as a result of early marriage, socializing with adults, or leaving home for apprenticeships. Nevertheless, given that much sociability for the elites occurred at home, the distinctions between "childhood," "youth," and "adulthood" were rarely consistent. The complexity of sibling dynamics is also demonstrated. Girls with many brothers might participate in boys' games. Conversely, families with solid cohorts of girls might be encouraged to play boys' games on their own. Whereas a focus on the acquisition of toys may emphasize a deficit model of class difference or disadvantage, to consider children and young people as producers opens up a much wider range of play experiences for investigation. This discussion thus develops and contributes to definitions and interpretations of play cultures, social worlds, and youth for the eighteenth and nineteenth centuries. Despite limited examples of youthful protests, the continual, perhaps surprising, existence of "scaffolding" by adults rejects the idea that youth culture is, by definition, opposed to that of the adult world (assuming there is one). Moreover, it also nuances the frequent assertion of the gendering of childhood and youth.

Notes

1. *The Bee-Hive, 1902–1905*, manuscript magazine, ed. Katharine Kenyon, author's possession. *The Bee-Hive*. Summer Number 1903, end page.
2. Michael Wyness, *Childhood and Society*, 2nd ed. (Basingstoke, UK: Palgrave Macmillan, 2012), 179–185, 204–213; David Wood, *How Children Think and Learn*, 2nd edn. (Oxford: Blackwell, 1988, 2001 reprint), 26–37, 40–43, 97–103.
3. Wyness, *Childhood and Society*, 179–185, 204–213.
4. Kenneth Grahame, *The Golden Age* (London: J. Lane, 1895), 1–2.
5. Jon Savage, *Teenage: The Creation of Youth Culture* (London: Faber and Faber, 2021); Carol Dyhouse, *Girls Growing Up in Late Victorian and Edwardian England* (London: Routledge, 2013), Chapter 4; John Gillis, *Youth and History: Tradition and Change in European Age Relations, 1770–Present* (rev. expanded student ed., New York and London: Academic Press, 1982); Nicholas Orme, *Medieval Children* (London: Yale University Press, 2001), 6–8; Natalie Zemon-Davis, "The Reasons of Misrule: Youth Groups and Charivari in Sixteenth-Century France," *Past and Present* 50 (Feb. 1971): 41–75.
6. For works including siblings, see Amy Harris, *Siblinghood and Social Relations in Georgian England: Share and Share Alike* (Manchester, UK: Manchester University Press, 2012), 18; Ginger Frost, *Victorian Childhoods* (Westport and London: Praeger, 2008), 27; Leonore Davidoff, *Thicker than Water: Siblings in British History, 1750–1914* (Oxford: Oxford University Press, 2012); Rosamund Bayne-Powell, *The English Child in the Eighteenth Century* (London: John Murray, 1939), 175–224.
7. For play, objects, and consumerism, see Kathryn Gleadle, "'Playing at Soldiers': British Loyalism and Juvenile Identities during the Napoleonic Wars," *Journal of Eighteenth Century Studies* 38 (2015): 335–345; Dennis Dennisoff, *The Nineteenth-Century Child and Consumer Culture* (Farnham, UK: Ashgate, 2008); Brian Sutton-Smith (1986, 26) cited in William A. Corsaro, *The Sociology of Childhood*, 3rd ed. (London, Sage, 1997), 139; Troy Bickham, "Preparing for an Imperial Inheritance: Children, Play and Empire in Eighteenth-Century Britain," *Journal of British Studies* 60 (2021): 658–688.
8. Hugh Cunningham, *Children and Childhood in Western Society since 1500*, 2nd ed. (London: Longman, 2005), 55–65; Bickham, "Preparing for an Imperial Inheritance, 60, 2021, 658–688. Hilary Marland, *Health and Girlhood in Britain, 1870–1914* (Basingstoke,

UK: Palgrave, 2013), 5-6 and passim; Stuart Hall, "Introduction" in *Representation: Cultural Representations and Signifying Practices*, ed. Stuart Hall (London: The Open University, 2012), 1-2

9. Harris, *Siblinghood*, 30-31; Anna Davin, "What Is a Child?," in *Childhood in Question*, ed. Stephen Hussey and Anthony Fletcher (Manchester, UK: Manchester University Press), 15-36; Peter Borsay, "Children, Adolescents and Fashionable Society in Eighteenth-Century England," in *Fashioning Childhood in the Eighteenth Century*, ed. Anja Muller (Aldershot, UK: Ashgate, 2008), 53-65. K. Gleadle, "The Juvenile Enlightenment: British Children and Youth during the French Revolution," *Past and Present* 233 (2016): 144-145, 143-184.

10. Henry French and Mark Rothery, *Man's Estate: Landed Gentry Masculinities, 1600-1900* (Oxford: Oxford University Press, 2012), 43-83; W. B. Stephens, *Education in Britain, 1750-1914* (Basingstoke, UK: Macmillan, 1998), 1-35. Flora Thompson, *Lark Rise to Candleford* (Harmondsworth, UK: Penguin, 2008), 19, 155-167; Michael Anderson, "What is New about the Modern Family?" in *Time, Family and Community*, ed. Michael Drake (London: Open University Press, 1994), 78, 69-70; Margaret Hunt, *The Middling Sort: Commerce, Gender and the Family in England, 1680-1780* (Berkeley: University of California Press, 1998), 125-146; Davidoff, *Thicker than Water*, 79-83, 103-107.

11. Alison Mackinnon, "Was There a Victorian Demographic Transition?," in *The Victorian World*, ed. Martin Hewitt (London: Routledge, 2013), 125. Randolph Trumbach, *The Rise of the Egalitarian Family: Aristocratic Kinship and Family Relations in Eighteenth-Century England* (New York: London Academic Press, 1978), 170. Peter Laslett, "Mean Household Size in England since the Sixteenth Century," in *Household and Family in Past Time*, ed. Richard Wall (Cambridge: Cambridge University Press, 1972), 126, 139; Jane Humphries, *Childhood and Child Labour in the British Industrial Revolution, 1750-1850* (Cambridge: Cambridge University Press, 2010), 56-57.

12. Thomas Jackson, ed., *Lives of the Early Methodist Preachers, Chiefly Written by Themselves*, 6 vols (London, 1837-1864); Adriana Benzaquén, "'Pray Lett None See This Impertinent Epistle': Children's Letters and Children in Letters at the Turn of the Eighteenth Century," in *Literary Cultures and Eighteenth-Century Childhoods*, ed. Andrew O' Malley (Basingstoke, UK: Palgrave Macmillan, 2018), 200-257.

13. Stella Tillyard, *Aristocrats: The Illustrated Companion* (London: Seven Dials, 2000), 29, 44; Flora Fraser, *Princesses: The Six Daughters of George III* (London: Bloomsbury, 2004), 31-32; Frost, *Victorian Childhoods*, 2; Jackson, ed., *Lives of the Early Methodist Preachers*, III,17: IV, 110, 153, 170, 174, 237; Bayne-Powell, *English Child*, 21; Frances Margaret Taylor, *Memories, 1894-1979*, Vol. I (1969), author's possession; Katharine Chorley, *Manchester Made Them: Some Reminiscences* (London: Faber and Faber, 1950), 195.

14. Countess of Cork and Orrery, ed., *The Orrery Papers: Selected from a collection of papers chiefly made by John, 5th Earl of Orrery. With portraits.* (London, Duckworth & Co, 1903), 122; Lord Orrery to Tom Southerne, Marston, UK, November 7, 1733.

15. Michelle Abate, *Tomboys: A Literary and Cultural History* (Philadelphia: Temple University Press, 2008), v, xv; Dyhouse, *Girls Growing Up*, 46-47; John Bailey, ed., *The Diary of Lady Frederick Cavendish* (London: John Murray, 1927), 11; Sheila Fletcher, *Victorian Girls: Lord Lyttelton's Daughters* (London: Phoenix, 2004), 64; Margaret Wynne Nevinson, *Life's Fitful Fever: A Volume of Memories* (London: A & C Black, 1926) 5-6, 13.

16. Bayne-Powell, *English Child*, 21-22; Marland, *Health and Girlhood*, 6-8; Dyhouse, *Girls Growing Up*, 39-40; Anthony Fletcher, *Growing Up in England, 1600-1914* (Yale

University Press, 2008); Bickham, "Preparing for an Imperial Inheritance," 667–677; Maeve O'Riordan, "Childhood in the Country House: Munster, 1850–1914," in *Historical Perspectives on Parenthood and Childhood in Ireland*, ed. Mary Hatfield, Jutta Kruse, and Rhona Nic Congaill (Dublin: Arlen House, 2018), 45–70; Pamela Horn, *The Victorian Country Child* (Kineton, UK: Roundwood Press, 1974), 150–152.

17. Benzaquén, "Pray Lett None," 211; Robert Brewin, *Memoirs of Mrs Rebecca Wakefield: Missionary in East Africa*, 3rd ed. (London: Andrew Crombie, 1888), 8; Mabel Hunt, *Eighty Years through Peace and War* (Lowestoft, UK: The Borough Press; Saxmundham, UK: H.G. Crisp, 1959), 6. Louise Jermy, *The Memories of a Working Woman, etc* (Norwich: Goose & Co, 1934); Horn, *Victorian Country Child*, 150–152.

18. Nevinson, *Life's Fitful Fever*, 12–13, Fanny Burney, *Fanny Burney's Diary: A Selection from the Diary and Letters*, ed. John Wain (London: Folio Society, 1961), 20–21. Wed August 10th 1768; Edward Hall, ed., *Miss Weeton: Journal of a Governess, 1807–1811* (London: Oxford University Press, 1936, 1937), 15–16; Richard Doyle, *Richard Doyle's Journal 1840, Introduction and Notes by Christopher Wheeler* (Edinburgh: John Bartholomew and Sons; in association with London: British Museum Publications, Ltd, 1980); Tom Pocock, ed., *Travels of a London Schoolboy, 1826–1830: John Pocock's Diary of Life in London and Voyages to Cape Town and Australia* (London: Historical Publications, 1996), 16–19.

19. M. W. F. Stapleton [Frideswide, O.S.B], *Reminiscences, Life Story of a Catholic Victorian Family* (East Bergholt, UK: Abbey Press, 1938), 18; Christabel Coleridge, *Charlotte Yonge: Her Life and Letters* (London, New York: Macmillan & Co, 1903), 90, 125; Anna Davin, *Growing Up Poor: Home, School and Street in London 1870-1914* (London: Rivers Oram Press, 1996), Vol. 66, 63–68; Dyhouse, *Girls Growing Up*, 119; Thompson, *Lark Rise*, 41–42;.

20. Jackson, *Early Methodist Preachers*, IV, 229; Edgar Sheppard, *George, Duke of Cambridge: A Memoir of His Private Life Based on the Journals and Correspondence of His Royal Highness, Vol 1, 1819–1871* (New York: Longmans Green & Co, 1906), 21; Bodleian Library, Oxford, MS Acland, d. 106, f. 90, Sarah Angelina Acland to Sarah Acland, 1862; Brian Fitzgerald, *Emily, Duchess of Leinster, 1731–1814: A Study of Her Life and Times* (London and New York: Staples Press, 1949), 62; Henry Solly, "These Eighty Years," or, the Story of an Unfinished Life (London: Simpkin & Marshall, 1893), 25, 43, 30; John Evans, ed., *The Victorian Elliots in Peace and War: Lord and Lady Minto, Their Family and Household between 1816 and 1901* (Stroud, UK: Amberley, 2012), 142; Hunt, *Eighty Years*), 6, 181; Nevinson, *Life's Fitful Fever*, 19, 12–13; Mary Clare Martin, "Disabled Children and Domestic Spaces in Britain, 1800–1900," in *Children, Spaces and Identity*, ed. Margaret Romero et al. (Oxford: Oxbow Books, 2015), 142–143.

21. Julia Allen, *Swimming with Dr Johnson and Mrs Thrale* (Cambridge: Lutterworth Press, 2012), 235, 224; A. Hayward, ed., *Autobiography of Mrs Thrale*, 2nd ed. (London: Longman, Green, Longman, and Roberts, 1861), Vol. II, 444; Nicholas Orme, *Early British Swimming, 55 BC–1719 AD, with the First Swimming Treatise Published in English, 1595* (Exeter, UK: University of Exeter, 1983), 107; Allan Brodie, "Towns of 'Health and Mirth': The First Seaside Resorts, 1730–1769," in *Resorts and Ports: European Seaside Towns since 1700*, ed. Peter Borsay and John Walton (Bristol, UK, and Buffalo: Channel View Publications, 2011), 18–19, 54; Fitzgerald, *Emily, Duchess of Leinster*, 129; Tillyard, *Aristocrats*, 237; Mary Thale, ed., *Autobiography of Francis Place, Edited with an Introduction and Notes by Mary Thale* (London, Cambridge University Press, 1972), 52, 53, 59; John Burnett, *Destiny*

Obscure: Autobiographies of Childhood, Education and Family from the 1820s to the 1920s (London: Allen Lane, 1982) 86; Irina Stickland, *The Voices of Children 1700-1914* (Oxford, Basil Blackwell, 1973), 175-177; Martin, "Disabled Children," 142-143.

22. Bodleian Library, Oxford, MS Acland, d. 106, fol. 89, Sarah Angelina Acland to Sarah Acland, Aug. 26, 1862, Portland; Frances Balfour, *Ne Obliviscaris: Dinna Forget, An Autobiography with Portraits* (London: Hodder and Stoughton, 1930), 29-30; "Reminiscences of Sarah Selwyn, 1809-1907" (typescript), 10-11, ENZB - 1961 - Selwyn, Sarah H. Reminiscences, 1809-1867. - [TEXT] p. 1–77 (auckland.ac.nz), accessed April 17, 2022.
23. Nevinson, *Life's Fitful Fever*, 5.
24. Elizabeth Longford, ed., *Louisa Lady in Waiting: The Personal Diaries and Albums of Louisa, Lady in Waiting to Queen Victoria and Queen Alexandra* (London: Jonathan Cape, 1979), 14; Hunt, *Eighty Years*, 17.
25. Bodleian Library, Oxford, MS Acland, d. 184, f. 154, (date unavailable), Sarah Acland to William Charles Cotton (likely to be 1841–1848); Peter Quennell, ed., *Memoirs of William Hickey* (London: Century Publishing, 1984), 16-17; Thale, *Place Autobiography*, 52-54; Selwyn, "Reminiscences," 10; Frideswide, *Reminiscences*, 67; Horn, *Victorian Country Child*, 150-152.
26. Ning de Coninck Smith, "Geography and the Environment," in *A Cultural History of Childhood and Family in the Age of Empire*, ed. Colin Heywood (London: Bloomsbury, 2010), 87; Horn, *Victorian Country Child*, 152; Thale, *Place Autobiography*, 48; Nevinson, *Life's Fitful Fever*, 27.
27. Bailey, ed., *Diary*, 15, 113; Bodleian Library, Oxford, MS Acland, d. 189, f. 102, Agnes Cotton to William Charles Cotton, Jan. 30, 1842.
28. Longford, ed., *Louisa, Lady in Waiting*, 14; Waltham Forest Archives, Walthamstow, UK, L96, Gulielma Lister and Isabella Lister, "Memories of Old Leytonstone," 4.
29. Dyhouse, *Girls Growing Up*, 42; Burnett, *Destiny Obscure*, 66; Brewin, *Memoirs of Mrs Rebecca Wakefield*, 8; Fletcher, *Victorian Girls*, 14; Horn, *Victorian Country Child*, 151; Chorley, *Manchester Made Them*, 195; Hall, *Ellen Weeton's Journal*, 14-16; Thale, *Place Autobiography*, 54, 47; Solly, *These Eighty Years*, 25, 41, 43; Arthur Penrhyn Stanley, *The Life and Correspondence of Thomas Arnold, D.D.*, 6th ed. (London, Ward Lock & Bowden, Ltd, New York and Melbourne), 2.
30. Harris, *Siblinghood*, 32; Jill Shefrin, *Such Constant Affectionate Care: Lady Charlotte Finch-Royal Governess and the Children of George III* (Los Angeles: CotsenOccasional Press, 2003), 64; Mary Clare Martin, "Play, Missionaries and the Colonial Encounter, 1800-1870," in *Creating Religious Childhoods in Anglo-World and British Colonial Contexts*, ed. Hugh Morrison and Mary Clare Martin (London, Routledge, 2017), 74, 61-85; Bailey, *Diary*, 22, Aug. 26, 1854. Allen, *Swimming with Dr Johnson and Mrs Thrale*, 107-109; Hunt, *Eighty Years*, 6.
31. Nevinson, *Life's Fitful Fever*, 5-6, 13.
32. Martin, "Disabled Children," 142-143; Frideswide, *Reminiscences*, 40-43; Horn, *Victorian Country Child*, 151-152; Frost, *Victorian Childhoods*, 82.
33. Evans, ed., *Victorian Elliots*, 141; Coleridge, *Charlotte Yonge*, 95; Midori Yamaguchi, *Daughters of the Anglican Clergy* (Basingstoke, UK: Palgrave Macmillan, 2014), 37.
34. Gleadle, "Playing at Soldiers," 336, 344; Abigail Williams, *The Social Life of Books: Reading in the Eighteenth-Century Home* (London: Yale University Press, 2017), 169-182.
35. William Roberts, *The Life and Correspondence of Mrs Hannah More* (London: Thomas Seeley, 1835), 14; Mary Clare Martin, "Childhood, Youth and Denominational Identity: Church, Chapel and Home in the Long Eighteenth Century," in *Childhood, Youth and Religious*

Minorities in Early Modern Europe, ed. Tali Berner and Lucy Underwood (Houndmills, UK: Palgrave, 2019), 141; Martin, "Disabled Children," 138–142; Nicholas Blundell, *The Great Diurnal of Nicholas Blundell of Little Crosby, Lancashire. Vol 1, 1712–1719, Transcribed and Annotated by Frank Tyrer*, ed. for the Record Society by J. J. Bagley (Liverpool, UK: Record Society of Lancashire and Cheshire, 1968), 29.

36. Harriet Martineau, *Harriet Martineau's Autobiography* (London: Smith, Elder & Co, 1877), Vol. I, 70; Benzaquén, "Pray Lett None", 211; Williams, *Social Life*, 182–190; Donald Burrows and Rosemary Dunhill, eds., *Music and Theatre in Handel's World: The Family Papers of James Harris, 1732–1780* (Oxford: Oxford University Press, 2002); Jonathan Rose, *The Intellectual Life of the British Working Classes* (New Haven and London: Yale University Press, 2002), 122; Mabel Ashby, *Joseph Ashby of Tysoe* (Cambridge, The University Press, 1961), 21.
37. Blundell, *Great Diurnal*, II, 1712, 30; Bayne-Powell, *English Child*, 118, 120; Fitzgerald, *Emily, Duchess of Leinster*, 109–110.
38. Amanda Foreman, *Georgiana, Duchess of Devonshire* (London: HarperCollins, 1999), 9.
39. J. A. Home, ed., *Letters and Journals of Mary, Lady Mary Coke*, Vol. I (Bath, UK, Kingsmead Bookshops, 1970), March 12, 1767, note).
40. Home, *Letters of Mary, Lady Coke*, 199; Stanley, *Life of Thomas Arnold*, 2; Coleridge, *Charlotte Yonge*, 130–131.
41. Rachel Bryant-Davies, "Fun from the Classics: Puzzling Antiquity in *The Boy's Own Paper*," in *Pasts at Play: Childhood Encounters with History in British History, 1750–1914*, ed. Rachel Bryant-Davies and Barbara Gribling (Manchester, UK: Manchester University Press, 2020), 96–122; Catherine Hall, *Macaulay, Father and Son: Architects of Imperial Britain* (London and New Haven: Yale University Press, 2012), 95–96; Stanley, *Life of Thomas Arnold*, 2; Waltham Forest Archives, Walthamstow, UK, Solly Letters, W96/SOL, 1/15, Elizabeth Solly to Neal Solly; Balfour, *Ne Obliviscaris*, 141; Sylvia Legge, *Affectionate Cousins: T. Sturge Moore and Maria Appia* (Oxford, New York, Toronto, and Melbourne: Oxford University Press, 1980), 37; Horn, *Victorian Country Child*, 151; *Richard Doyle's Journal*, 61, 130.
42. James Anderson Winn, *Queen Anne, Patron of the Arts* (Oxford: Oxford University Press, 2014), 7–10, 34; Tillyard, *Aristocrats*, 29–30; Home, ed., *Letters of Lady Mary Coke*, 1766, 101; Fraser, *Princesses*, 17–18; Ashby, *Joseph Ashby*, 21.
43. Williams, *Social Life*, 194–196; Leslie Stephen, *The Life of Sir James Fitzjames Stephen, Bart., K.C.S.I., a Judge of the High Court of Justice* (London: Smith & Elder, 1895), 85; *Letters and Diaries of Nina, Countess of Minto. (A selection)*. Ed. The Hon Arthur D. Elliot (Printed privately, 1920), 136; Wain, *Fanny Burney's Diary*, 10, 37; Desmond McCarthy and Agatha Russell, *Lady John Russell: A Memoir, with Selections from Her Diaries and Correspondence* (London, Methuen & Co, 1910), 5.
44. Burrows and Dunhill, eds., *Music and Theatre in Handel's World*, 531; Cambridge University Library, Royal Commonwealth Society Library, Letters and Papers of Frederick Young, 54/1, 1831, 1832, ff. 15–16; Valerie Sanders, *The Tragi-Comedy of Victorian Fatherhood* (Cambridge: Cambridge University Press, 2009), 58; David Cecil, *A Portrait of Jane Austen* London: Book Associates Club, 1978), 55–56; John E. Ryland, *Memoir of John Kitto, Compiled Chiefly from His Letters and Journals* (Edinburgh: William Oliphant, 1956), 13–14; John Springhall, *Youth, Popular Culture and Moral Panics: Penny Gaffs to Gangsta-Rap* (Basingstoke, UK: Macmillan, 1998).
45. Yamaguchi, *Daughters*, 87–89; Bailey, ed., *Diary*, 46; Nevinson, *Life's Fitful Fever*, 33; Handwritten flyer for "Blue Beard," 1861, Kenyon papers box, possession of the Rt. Rev. G. H. Thompson; *Letters of Lady Minto*, 169; Frideswide, *Reminiscences*, 37, 68.

46. Wain, *Fanny Burney's Diary*, 10, 37; Ryland, *Memoir*, 13; Gleadle, "The Juvenile Enlightenment": 159; Coleridge, *Charlotte Yonge*, 149; L. E. O'Rourke, *The Life and Friendships of Catherine Marsh* (London: Longmans Green & Co, 1917), 10; Martineau, *Autobiography*, 71.
47. Christine Alexander, "Play and Apprenticeship: The Culture of Family Magazines," in *The Child Writer from Austen to Woolf*, ed. Christine Alexander and Juliet McMaster (Cambridge: Cambridge University Press, 2005), 42; Kathryn Gleadle, "Magazine Culture, Girlhood Communities, and Educational Reform in Britain," *English Historical Review* 134 (2019): 1169–1195; Magazines of Woolwich Polytechnic, Day Schools, 1905-1906, 1923, GB 2121/WP/30/5/1-3. University of Greenwich Archives, London.
48. Patricia Crown, "Stories for Cecilia Burney Written by Her Sisters and Illustrated by Edward F. Burney and Other Hands: A Manuscript for, by and about Children," *British Journal for Eighteenth-Century Studies*, 29 (2006): 399–411; Alexander, "Play as Apprenticeship," 42; Legge, *Affectionate Cousins*, 37.
49. Gleadle, "Magazine Cultures"; *The Bee-Hive.*, author's possession. Christmas number, (1902), 4, 16, 24: Spring number (1903), 3: Summer number (1903), 9 (spelt correctly).

FURTHER READING

Alexander, Christine, and Juliet McMaster, eds. *The Child Writer from Austen to Woolf*. Cambridge: Cambridge University Press, 2005.
Bayne-Powell, Rosamund. *The English Child in the Eighteenth Century*. London: John Murray, 1939.
Benzaquén, Adriana. " 'Pray Lett None See This Impertinent Epistle'; Children's Letters and Children in Letters." In *Literary Cultures and Eighteenth-Century Childhoods*. Edited by Andrew O' Malley, 200–257. Basingstoke, UK: Palgrave Macmillan, 2018.
Bickham, Troy. "Preparing for an Imperial Inheritance: Children, Play and Empire in Eighteenth-Century Britain." *Journal of British Studies* 60 (2021): 658–688.
Frost, Ginger. *Victorian Childhoods*. Westport and London: Praeger, 2008.
Gleadle, Kathryn. "Magazine Culture, Girlhood Communities, and Educational Reform in Britain." *English Historical Review* 134 (2019): 1169–1195.
Gleadle, Kathryn. "Playing at Soldiers": British Loyalism and Juvenile Identities during the Napoleonic Wars. *Journal of Eighteenth Century Studies* 38 (2015): 335–345.
Hamlett, Jane. *Material Relations: Domestic Interiors and Middle-Class Families in England, 1850-1910*. Manchester, UK: Manchester University Press, 2010.
Hamlett, Jane. " 'Tiresome Trips Downstairs': Middle-Class Domestic Space and Family Relationships in England, 1850-1910." In *The Politics of Domestic Authority in Britain since 1800*. Edited by Lucy Delap, Ben Griffin, and Abigail Wills, 111–131. Basingstoke, UK: Palgrave Macmillan, 2009.
Harris, Amy. *Siblinghood and Social Relations in Georgian England: Share and Share Alike*. Manchester, UK: Manchester University Press, 2012.
Horn, Pamela. *The Victorian Country Child*. Kineton, UK: The Roundwood Press, 1974.
Martin, Mary Clare. "Disabled Children and Domestic Living Spaces in Britain, 1800-1900." In *Children, Spaces and Identity* edited by Margaret Romero, Eva Alarcón García, Gonzalo Aranda Jiménez, 136–154. Oxford: Oxbow Books, 2015.

Martin, Mary Clare. "Play, Missionaries and the Colonial Encounter, 1800–1870." In *Creating Religious Childhoods in Anglo-World and British Colonial Contexts, 1800–1950*, edited by Hugh Morrison and Mary Clare Martin, 64–85. London: Routledge, 2017.

Sanders, Valerie. *The Brother-Sister Culture in Nineteenth-Century Literature*. Basingstoke, UK: Palgrave Macmillan, 2002.

Williams, Abigail. *The Social Life of Books: Reading Together in the Eighteenth-Century Home*. London: Yale University Press, 2017.

CHAPTER 13

YOUTH CULTURE AND INDIAN BOARDING SCHOOLS

KRISTINE ALEXANDER

THE modern idea of youth as a particular kind of "trouble"—a problem to be solved through law, the state, and the efforts of religious and charitable bodies—was a product, it is now widely understood, of urbanization and industrial capitalism. Over the past several centuries, youth—not-yet-adults who are also no longer children—have also played important material and symbolic roles in settler colonial projects, where Indigenous populations were seen as standing in the way of hoped-for white national futures characterized by private property, social order, and capital accumulation. The creation myths of settler states, which often center on narratives about "youthful" white nations "coming of age" through revolution or armed conflict, depend on the erasure of Indigenous presence. This erasure is a violent discursive and material process that, in the territories currently known as Canada and the United States, has sought over the past several centuries to solve the so-called Indian problem by focusing—through abduction, attempts at religious conversion, and resocialization in total institutions like boarding schools—on Indigenous children and youth. At government-funded and government-run boarding schools—designed specifically to sever the ties of language, kin, and community—students responded to the social and material constraints of institutional life by producing forms of youth culture that were characterized by solidarity and creativity.

The History and Historiography of Indian Boarding Schools

The Indian boarding school, according to Ojibwe historian Brenda J. Child, is a particularly powerful metaphor—a symbol of settler colonialism "at its most genocidal."[1] Often associated with family separation, overcrowding, abuse, disease, and death, these institutions used imposing architecture, physical labor, and rigid disciplinary regimes to try to remake Indigenous youngsters in cultural, social, religious, linguistic, bodily, and emotional terms. At the same time, however, as Child—an Ojibwe historian whose grandparents attended the off-reservation Carlisle and Flandreau boarding schools in Pennsylvania and South Dakota in the early twentieth century—reminds us, "the history of Indian education ... [is] far more multifaceted and untidy than a simple story of federal policy and assimilationist practice."[2] Since the late 1980s, scholars in Canada and the United States have highlighted the limits of the pedagogical policies and practices of settler states by focusing on resistance, resilience, and the persistence of language, culture, and intergenerational family ties.[3] These studies also make it clear that despite its considerable material and symbolic power, the Indian boarding school was not a monolithic entity that shaped the lives of Indigenous youth in uniform ways. Not every Indigenous youth attended boarding school in the nineteenth and twentieth centuries, and although the biggest schools in Canada and the United States shared a number of important features, local cultures could—and did—vary widely.

A rich body of nation-based and local studies highlights subtle differences in institutions and experiences across time and space, but it is also worth emphasizing the significant commonalities and continuities that shaped the lives and cultures of Indigenous boarding school students in Canada and the United States between the late nineteenth and mid-twentieth centuries. The Carlisle Indian Industrial School in Carlisle, Pennsylvania, founded in 1879 by U.S. army officer Captain Richard Henry Pratt, established a prototype for assimilative, federally supported Indigenous schooling that was emulated by politicians, bureaucrats, and educators across Canada and the United States.[4] By the 1880s, both countries had opened multiple militarized boarding schools whose ultimate goals were the assimilation and absorption of Indigenous populations into the settler body politic. These carceral institutions, part of a broader state apparatus whose agenda included Indigenous territorial and cultural dispossession, were part of what sociologist Andrew Woolford has called "a complicated experiment in the forcible transformation of multiple Indigenous peoples so that they would no longer exist as an obstacle (real or perceived) to settler colonial domination."[5]

Indigenous boarding schools in Canada and the United States therefore need to be understood as an outcome of the permanent migration of millions of European (and especially Anglo) colonizers to North America, the Antipodes, and other parts of the world between the late eighteenth and early- to mid-twentieth centuries. The American and Canadian settler nation-states, which followed the Spanish, French, and British empires in North America, sought—in ways that were regionally varied and always contested—to erase and displace Indigenous populations in order to control land and resources. Young people, because of their perceived malleability, were at the heart of many of these attempts, and Indian policy as it developed on both sides of the forty-ninth parallel reflected the widespread settler belief that it was only possible to make lasting and significant changes to Indigenous cultures and lifeways by intervening in the early stages of life.

Indigenous boys and girls attended state-supported boarding schools in Canada and the United States from the late nineteenth century and into the twentieth, but these institutions were not the first ones through which non-Indigenous newcomers had sought to educate and "civilize" the Indigenous young people on whose lands they had settled. Christian missionaries had begun enrolling Indigenous students in day and boarding schools (some racially segregated, some integrated) in the seventeenth century, and starting in the early nineteenth century, churches and settler governments also established a small number of industrial or "manual labor" schools that sought to train Indigenous workers in agriculture and domestic service while freeing up land for white settlement. These institutions, according to Rebecca Swartz, "constructed settler colonialism as a humanitarian intervention" and emphasized the redemptive and pedagogical power of physical labor.[6] The development of industrial education for Indigenous youth in early- to mid-nineteenth-century North America took place against a backdrop of hardening racial thinking, in which white people across the Anglo world came increasingly to understand racial difference as fixed and rooted in biology rather than culture. But the question of how exactly settler thinking about race shaped Indian boarding schools is a complicated one: different administrators and teachers held different beliefs, and the shift from cultural to biological understandings of racial difference did not take place in a linear or uniform way.

One thing, however, is clear: from the 1880s on, the Canadian and U.S. governments saw boarding schools *and* industrial education as potentially powerful solutions to the ongoing "problem" of Indigenous presence and resistance. As Laura Briggs has written, the removal of young people from their parents—what she calls "child taking"—is "a counterinsurgency tactic [that] has been used to respond to demands for rights, refuge, and respect by communities of color and impoverished communities, an effort to induce hopelessness, despair, grief, and shame."[7] It is no coincidence that the development and spread of Indian boarding schools occurred in the wake of multiple violent conflicts between Indigenous peoples and the Canadian and American nation-states, as westward expansion and European immigration engulfed more and more Indigenous land. In 1881, Congress declared that school attendance for Indigenous children was compulsory and authorized the U.S. Indian Bureau to withhold rations and clothing from parents who refused to send their children to school.

In Canada, the federal Department of Indian Affairs encouraged and often coerced Indigenous parents to send their children to state-funded and church-run residential schools instead of integrated public schools, eventually making attendance at residential schools compulsory in 1920.

In gender-segregated and age-graded dormitories, classrooms, and spaces of work—such as school laundries, carpentry and printing shops, and fields where students labored to grow and harvest their food—Indigenous boarding school students navigated complex social relationships with non-Indigenous adults and with young people and adults (staff members and occasionally teachers) from different Indigenous communities. During the school week, the Indigenous children and youth who lived, studied, and labored at these institutions—following Pratt's model—spent half their time in the classroom (learning from what Frederick Hoxie has called a "curriculum of low expectations") and half their time working.[8] Officially touted as "civilizing" vocational training, the student labor at the heart of the half-day system was both a source of income for the school and a critical part of each institution's infrastructure. While learning English and performing unwaged and unfree labor, Indigenous students were also taught to regard their cultures, families, and home communities with feelings of shame and disgust.[9]

Agency and resistance are central to the youth cultures that developed in Indian boarding schools, but they are also concepts that need to be approached with caution. Focusing on agency, as many social historians and child and youth studies scholars have done over the past few decades, has allowed researchers to demonstrate the historical significance of people who had previously been understood as passive, powerless, or silent.[10] Over the past several years, however, a growing number of historians have begun to critique this approach for its implicit and generally unquestioned reliance on modern, Western, Enlightenment-based understandings of selfhood, action, autonomy, and rational choice.[11] The stakes involved in this work are particularly high in settler societies, where colonialism remains an ongoing process. In the Canadian context, for example, Robin Jarvis Brownlie and Mary Ellen Kelm have been sharply critical of studies that they claim "go beyond the argument for the recognition of Native agency to . . . us[ing] evidence of Native resilience and strength to soften, and at times to deny, the impact of colonialism, and thus, implicitly, to absolve its perpetrators."[12] Instead of simply looking for agency in Indian boarding schools, Woolford suggests that scholars should "imagine colonialism as a series of nets that operate to constrain agency but are also prone to snags and openings that enable agentic resistance."[13] These nets work on different levels, from the macro (fields like science and the law) to the meso (government and welfare institutions) and micro (individual schools and teachers), and together they form a type of mesh, which "expands and contracts across time and differentially across space."[14]

Historians interested in the peer cultures that developed at late nineteenth- and twentieth-century Indian boarding schools have often focused on moments when this settler colonial mesh expanded or opened slightly. They have done so by analyzing government documents, institutional records, the popular press and school newspapers, correspondence, photographs, published memoirs, oral history interviews, and the words of the more than six thousand former students who testified before the Truth and Reconciliation Commission of Canada. This broad and disparate body of evidence needs to be read carefully and critically, both along and against the grain. Reckoning with silences and absences is crucial, not least as a way to make space for the traumatic intergenerational effects of these institutions and the fact that thousands of Indigenous youngsters died while attending them. The purposeful destruction of evidence is also part of this story: during the 1930s and 1940s, for example, more than fifteen tons of records relating to residential schools and Indigenous young people in Canada were destroyed, and the destruction of government files relating to education, health, and Indian Affairs continued throughout the twentieth century.[15]

Domination, Resistance, and English Language and Literacy

Unsurprisingly, many of the documents produced by settler educators, missionaries, and bureaucrats—those pieces of evidence that have survived government culls—reflect a desire to demonstrate that boarding schools were succeeding in their quest to completely remake Indigenous students' bodies, hearts, and minds. Juxtaposing these sources with students' writing, oral history accounts, and memoirs, however, produces a far richer picture of the Indigenous youth cultures that emerged in these carceral and genocidal institutions. We know, for example, that despite strict "English-only" rules and the constant threat of harsh punishment, many students continued to think, dream, and speak (or whisper) to each other in their own languages throughout their time at school. Unsurprisingly, this fact—a recurring thread in Indigenous memoirs and oral history accounts—does not appear in the pages of late nineteenth- and early twentieth-century boarding school newspapers, which were printed by student workers and distributed to the school community, government authorities, and paid subscribers. As Jane Griffith has written, this silence "may exemplify how school newspapers carefully created an English-only fantasy for readers, but it may also attest to the success of students' secrecy, since newspapers may not have reported that students still knew Indigenous languages because schools were unaware."[16]

Language and literacy were central to boarding schools' efforts to destroy Indigenous lifeways *and* to Indigenous youth cultures based on persistence and resistance. Although literacy education was frequently discussed in official records as a kind of zero-sum game in which "savage" Indigenous languages were to be suppressed and replaced by "civilized" English, the reality was not that simple. As Albert Yava, a Hopi-Tewa interpreter and author who spent five years of his youth at Chilocco

Indian Industrial School in Oklahoma in the early twentieth century, told anthropologist Harold Courlander, "We wanted to cope with a new culture without giving up on our old one."[17] While speaking and writing in English in accordance with school rules, some students devised creative ways to maintain their own languages and build relationships with each other. Parker McKenzie, who attended the Rainy Mountain Boarding School in Oklahoma in the early twentieth century, wooed his future wife, fellow student Nettie Odlety, by composing letters in phonetically written Kiowa. This practice effectively thwarted teachers' efforts to discourage Indigenous language use *and* contact between male and female adolescents. It also inspired McKenzie to create, in later years, what would become the first written syllabary of the Kiowa language.[18]

For some Indigenous youngsters, learning English could also be a way to participate in the pleasures of North American popular and consumer culture. Theodore Fontaine, a member of Sagkeeng First Nation who attended Canadian government-supported and church-run residential schools in Fort Alexander and Winnipeg between 1948 and 1960, recalled watching his older brothers—who had left for school several years before him—enjoy Dell and Marvel comic books while they were home on the summer holidays. His brothers read their comics out loud, translating the dialogue into Ojibway, and their mother would say, "in Ojibway, 'When you go to school, you will be able to read comics.'" "In my mind," Fontaine writes in his memoir, "this would be the greatest benefit of my schooling, and Mom and even Dad used this to fuel my desire whenever the subject of school came up."[19] However, it soon became clear that this was "the first and probably only positive reason why I should go to residential school": the promise of fun held out by his brothers' comics, Fontaine reveals, was quickly overshadowed by the sexual abuse and physical violence he experienced at the hands of school staff.[20]

The "Printer's Power": Industrial Training and Public Displays

Reading and writing in English, of course, were only part of the total cultural transformation that Indian boarding schools hoped to effect. Manual work was also central to the boarding school experience, and the spaces, practices, and social relations of unfree student labor shaped the development of Indigenous youth cultures at these institutions between the late nineteenth and mid-twentieth centuries. Officially touted as industrial or vocational training to prepare students for future careers in agricultural work, domestic service, and trades, student labor at Indian boarding schools actually served three purposes: teaching students employable skills and self-sufficiency, demonstrating each school's success to outsiders, and offsetting costs.[21] Students grew and prepared the food they ate, sewed their own uniforms, cleaned and maintained school buildings, and manufactured goods that were sold to local settler communities.

In addition to chores like laundry, cooking, and agricultural work, many boarding schools had printing shops, which were staffed by a select group of male students. In these settings, Indigenous students laid type, inked metal, and operated the schools' printing presses, which were often secondhand pieces donated by the owners of local newspapers. In addition to school newspapers, students also printed letterhead, attendance registers, and receipt books for the schools as well as stationery and Sunday school materials that were sold to local settler businesses, churches, and farmers. Looking closely at the experiences of printers and other student workers can provide particularly valuable insights about Indigenous youth culture.

Boarding school printers, many of whom were also strong students and exceptional athletes, were regularly singled out in school newspapers, their mastery of the English language and the modern technologies of mass production held up as evidence of the effectiveness of assimilatory schooling. Some of the material featured in student-printed boarding school newspapers (chosen, of course, by the papers' settler adult editors) encouraged young Indigenous printers to see themselves as part of an elite and powerful guild. The May 19, 1899, edition of the *Indian Helper*, one of a number of different papers printed at Carlisle (this one was aimed at students), included "The Song of the Printer," a popular poem by Philadelphia printer Thomas MacKellar. Asking "O' where is the man with such simple tools / Can govern the world as I?," the poem suggested that, in the modern world, even kings were ultimately unable to "rival the printer's power."[22] These words celebrated mass-produced print (and by extension, written—as opposed to oral—communication) as a superior and particularly powerful medium, the keys to which were held by a select group of sophisticated and technologically advanced workers.

In addition to being praised in school papers and administrative reports, Indigenous student printers and their efficiency, discipline, and technological aptitude were also highlighted—especially in the late nineteenth and early twentieth centuries—in parades and public displays. Accounts of these high-profile events by journalists and former students make it clear that these are also spaces where scholars can find evidence of boarding school youth culture and a growing sense of pan-Indigenous identity and pride. The boys who printed the *Indian Leader*, the paper produced by Haskell Institute, for example, laid type and operated their school's printing press alongside girls operating sewing machines on a float in the Lawrence, Kansas, Fourth of July parade in 1902.[23] Ten years earlier, in October 1892, a group of more than three hundred students from Carlisle (including printers and the school's renowned marching band) had traveled to New York City and Chicago, where they joined thousands of other non-Indigenous young people in a parade celebrating the quadricentennial of Christopher Columbus's "discovery" of the New World.[24] Carlisle students marched in ten "platoons" behind their school banner, which was emblazoned with the words "Into Civilization and Citizenship." The first platoon, in which students performed the transformative "civilizational" power of English language and literacy by carrying schoolbooks and slates, was followed by groups representing different trades. The printers led the way, with boys carrying both pieces of printing equipment (galleys, cases, and the like) and the paper products of their labor.

Newspapers from across New York state and Chicago raved about the neat appearances and impressive discipline of the Carlisle youths, often explicitly framing the students' performance and achievements in terms of colonialism and conquest. The *Jamestown Journal* praised Captain Pratt's practice "of 'arming' Indians" with "implements of industry instead of guns," and the *New York World* summed up the parade by stating that "the Indian boys and girls from Carlisle School did better than all the others. Let them enjoy that triumph over the children of the men whose fathers drove their fathers from the land that Columbus discovered."[25] The Chicago *Inter Ocean* interpreted the event more crudely, as evidence of boarding schools' ability to convert, transform, and prepare Indigenous peoples for modern life: presenting "a fine appearance" and met with "great applause," the paper stated, the Carlisle students "marched like veterans and exemplified what civilization can do and has done for the savage denizens of the Far West."[26]

Canadian and U.S. boarding schools also sent Indigenous students, as representatives of this supposed forward movement from "savagery" toward "civilization," to the Chicago World's Fair in 1893. Whereas the fair's various "Indian Villages," which also displayed human subjects, were performances of salvage ethnography designed to highlight "primitive" cultures "in decline," the live exhibits of boarding school students sponsored by the Canadian and U.S. governments were meant to do the exact opposite: to demonstrate that arming Indigenous youth with the implements of Anglo-American literacy and industry could successfully transform them into modern, useful, assimilated citizens. At the same time, however, the Indigenous students who performed at the fair responded by engaging with and occasionally critiquing American culture and the settler structures of authority that shaped their experiences. Whereas Carlisle had its own display in Chicago—which was organized by Pratt and included both military drill and samples of student work—the U.S. Bureau of Indian Affairs sponsored a separate model boarding school, at which Indigenous students in their teens and early twenties from seven different institutions lived, studied, and worked in front of paying visitors. The Canadian Department of Indian Affairs also built a mock classroom and workrooms on the fairgrounds, where male and female students worked on written assignments and demonstrated their skills in trades like sewing, blacksmithing, and printing. Indigenous youth from eight different Canadian residential schools traveled to Chicago to participate in this exhibit, which functioned both to promote an image of efficient and modern young Indigenous workers and to obscure the deprivation and violence that characterized many Indigenous youngsters' experiences of boarding school life.

For some students, traveling to Chicago and exploring the kaleidoscopic sights and sounds of the fairground were moments when the settler colonial mesh expanded slightly. Young Indigenous people arrived from Canada by train and stayed in government-arranged lodgings in the densely populated southeast Chicago neighborhood of Kensington. Maurice Sanderson, a student printer from Rupert's Land Indian Industrial School in Manitoba, wrote about his journey and initial impressions of Chicago in a letter to his friend and fellow student Arthur Cochrane. Published in the school newspaper *The Aurora* ("A Monthly Record of Our Work and of Indian Education and Progress") in September 1893, Sanderson's account described eating at a restaurant near his boarding house, sharing a bedroom "without books" with a boy from Battleford Industrial School, seeing crowds of people "swarming in the streets," and exploring the fairgrounds. He recounted seeing the "mummy of an Egyptian princess and some idols carved out of stone and wood" as well as the "Indian Exhibits" in the Manufactures Building, which displayed products made by industrial school students like himself. He explained that at the side of the product exhibit, "with a rope round it, is where the children work."[27]

Sanderson's letter, which also noted the disappointingly small size of the printing press he and his peers were expected to operate in Chicago, appeared on the same page as stories about the seventeenth-century English mathematician and physicist Isaac Newton and Garnet Wolseley, the Anglo-Irish army officer whose global imperial career had included leading British troops against the Métis-led Red River Resistance in Manitoba in 1870. Although students physically produced each copy of *The Aurora*, editorial control remained firmly in the hands of the school's principal. The Indigenous voices that were occasionally represented in boarding school papers were highly mediated, and it is worth pausing to wonder about the youthful perspectives that—for various reasons—never appeared in these pages.

In November 1893, a month after publishing Maurice Sanderson's letter, *The Aurora* published a second account of the World's Fair by another Rupert's Land student named Phoebe Kakasoo. Addressing the wife of the school's principal, Kakasoo began by asking the older white woman to excuse any mistakes the letter might contain. She wrote that she had been collecting souvenir cards (which she intended to "take...home" to share with her classmates), described a particularly spectacular fireworks display (which sounded, she wrote, "just like thunderings"), and indicated that her experience of the fair was shaped by both spectacular sights and a lack of spending money: "we went to see the animals yesterday; we couldn't get in, because we have to pay 50 cents if we go in, so we didn't go in. I just saw lions from outside in a big iron cage, five of them."[28] Kakasoo's time in Chicago was also clearly shaped by the performance of gendered domestic tasks like sewing before paying visitors and the surveillance of Charles de Cazes, the federal Indian agent who was in charge of the Canadian residential school display. She worked afternoon shifts at the fair each day, before and after which she made the seven-mile journey from her Kensington lodgings to the fairgrounds. Describing de Cazes as "pretty cross," Kakasoo wrote that although she had been "scared when I first saw him," de Cazes generally reserved his scoldings for another Indigenous student named Isaiah.[29]

As Jane Griffith reminds us, boarding school newspapers "contain institution-imposed narratives *as well as* the possibility of a veiled poetry of resistance."[30] The letters by Maurice Sanderson and Phoebe Kakasoo that were published in *The Aurora* do both of these things, combining a sense of wonder at settler spectacles of progress and modernity with subtle critiques of the conditions under which they were expected to labor. The fact that not every Indigenous student was equally impressed with the fair's offerings is shown especially clearly in the case of Gilbert Bear, who had traveled to Chicago from Battleford Industrial School in Canada's North-West Territories. A strong student and football player who was also in charge of the school's printing shop, Bear's technical prowess had earned him praise from the federal Department of Indian Affairs and from local professionals, with the editor of the *Saskatchewan Herald* calling him "the smartest boy he had ever seen in learning the art of type setting."[31] Bear spent three months in Chicago as part of the Canadian Department of Indian Affairs boarding school display, where he worked with boys from other prairie Indigenous communities—including Maurice Sanderson—operating a printing press.

In addition to performing cultural assimilation and capitalist efficiency in front of paying visitors, Bear and his fellow Indigenous student printers spent their days producing copies of a souvenir pamphlet entitled *The Canadian Indian: The Work of a Few Years Among the Indians of Manitoba and the North-West*. The pamphlet could be purchased by fairgoers at an "Indian Teepee" in the Canadian Department of Manufactures Building.[32] Likely written by Indian agent Charles de Cazes, the pamphlet lauded Indian residential schools as evidence that "the Canadian people have to a large extent succeeded in giving the aboriginal tribes their civilization with its advantages, in return for the lands they have received from them."[33] *The Canadian Indian* also gave voice to settler fears that Indigenous students might "regress" after leaving school, stating

> there yet remains for serious consideration whether pupils should be allowed to return to their reserves, to there run the risk of relapsing into the condition from which they have been taken ... or trusted to hold their own as citizens among white members of the community.[34]

How must it have felt to be the Indigenous student printers who had to reproduce these justifications of racist policies thousands of times over in front of the watchful eyes of de Cazes and the crowds who flocked to the fair?

Small glimpses of possible answers to this question are visible in archival records related to Gilbert Bear's time in Chicago. A robust, skilled, and promising young man, his very existence seemed to demonstrate that family separation and assimilatory schooling could successfully strengthen and modernize Indigenous bodies, minds, and characters. Indian Affairs annual reports noted that Bear "performed some very excellent work" and "conducted himself in a most becoming manner" at the fair, and a story about his trip, published in the *Battleford Herald*, was picked up by other newspapers across the Canadian prairies.[35] Although the reporter who interviewed Bear described him as "lucky," the paper also stated that when asked if he had enjoyed his time at the World's Fair, Bear had responded simply: "No; too hot and too many people."[36] These seven words raise important and mostly unanswerable questions about Bear's understanding of the Columbian Exposition, his feelings about being on display (and about his experiences of residential schooling more generally), and the types of peer relationships he may or may not have developed with other boarding school students. They are also a powerful reminder that Indigenous students' priorities, cultures, and senses of self were never fully transformed by the institutions that sought to shape them.

"Bloomer Stories": Modern Girls, Mischief, and Memory

Further evidence of boarding school youth cultures can be found in the work of K. Tsianina Lomawaima, a scholar whose father attended Chilocco Indian Agricultural School in Oklahoma in the 1920s and 1930s. Known as the U.S. government's flagship agricultural industrial school, Chilocco—like other Indian boarding schools across Canada and the United States—was home to a distinctive student culture that, Lomawaima notes, was "influenced but not determined by the bounds of federal control."[37] Her interviews with men and women who attended Chilocco between 1910 and 1940 revealed that students were often united against school authority—and that strict institutional regimes of surveillance and discipline actually mobilized acts of resistance and a modern "pan-tribal 'Indian' identit[y]."[38]

During the 1920s and 1930s, young women at Chilocco—like their Indigenous and settler counterparts across North America—had to contend with surveillance and behavioral interventions from adults who worried about the social consequences that might follow if fun-loving modern girls chose autonomy and pleasure over selflessness and domesticity. These efforts to regulate girls' behavior in order to control individual and collective futures were particularly charged in settler colonial contexts, in which—as Sara De Leeuw has written—the bodies of young Indigenous women "were sites where the material and ideological converged."[39] At early twentieth-century Indian boarding schools, anxieties about gender and generation intersected with settler understandings of Indigenous bodies as uncivilized, unclean, and prone to disease. These institutions' attempts to physically and morally remake Indigenous girls by focusing on clothing, posture, hairstyles, and hygiene were also, in ways that have yet to be fully reckoned with, about taking young people's labor power away from their families and harnessing it to projects of settler state-building and capitalism. The formal and informal education girls received at boarding schools, Lomawaima writes, functioned as "training in dispossession under the guise of domesticity, developing a habitus shaped by the messages of obedience and one's proper place."[40] The lack of bodily autonomy experienced by boarding school students, in other words, was part of a much broader attack on Indigenous sovereignty across North America.

At Chilocco, the ideological and material makings of the settler colonial mesh loosened somewhat on Saturday nights, which alternated between student dances and movie screenings organized by the school's administrators. It was in these moments of engagement with popular culture and socializing with the opposite sex that Indigenous students' lives most resembled those of their non-Indigenous counterparts, and Chilocco's Saturday night dances were highly anticipated—if brief—respites from regimentation, work, and gender segregation. For female students in particular, they were also opportunities to abandon their drab uniforms and savor the pleasures of dressing up in what many called their "home clothes"—the outfits they had brought with them to school, and which normally remained under lock and key. At the same time, however, dances were strictly chaperoned, and school authorities still tried to maintain some control over female students' bodies by forcing them to wear shapeless, bulky school-issued bloomers underneath their dresses. Many former students remembered having to show their bloomers to female teachers before being allowed to leave their dormitories, and one woman recalled that in the late 1920s an "old matron" had explained to her that bloomers were necessary to prevent girls from "arousing the boys' passions . . . and I didn't know, I hardly knew what that meant, you know."[41]

Memories of girls removing, altering, and hiding their school-issued bloomers on the way to dances—what Lomawaima calls "bloomer stories"—are a common thread that weaves throughout accounts by former students at Chilocco from the first few decades of the twentieth century. Recalled with fondness and told (and retold) to friends, family, and fellow alumni, bloomer stories are celebrations of youthful humor, solidarity, ingenuity, and cooperation—defining features of the "Indian" school culture that flourished despite an institutional emphasis on assimilation. Former students' memories of sharing risks, outwitting teachers and matrons, and protecting one another possess a powerful "symbolic resonance" that, Lomawaima writes, reveals multiple instances of "student triumph over a uniform(ed) existence."[42]

Physical Culture and Team Sports

Physical culture and organized sports also loom large in the memories of many former boarding school students and were similarly central to the formation of an Indigenous youth culture characterized by solidarity and pride in the midst of racism and rigid discipline. At Indian boarding schools across North America, exercise and sports were part of a broader institutional ethos that assaulted the physical sovereignty of Indigenous youth through food, clothing, and Euro-American hygiene practices. Intended to produce colonized bodies that were productive and docile, military-style drill and team sports figured prominently in press coverage and public discussions of the effectiveness of assimilatory schooling from the late nineteenth and into the mid-twentieth centuries. Lauded as evidence of the successful transformation and modernization of malleable Indigenous young people, the public face of boarding school sports increased these institutions' visibility while obscuring the fact that for many young people, attending these schools actually resulted in hunger, disease, and death. Public sporting events, like the hours of supervised practice that preceded them, were moments when the genocidal intentions of boarding schools clashed with the resistant bodies and spirits of Indigenous youth.

Military-style marching and drill, as introduced at Carlisle and adopted at boarding schools across North America in the late nineteenth and early twentieth centuries, were intended to produce obedient, efficient, and disciplined bodies. They were also, however, exercises through which Indigenous students could occasionally articulate visions of identity and pride that did not quite fit with the official assimilative vision of these institutions. At Indian residential schools in Canada, Indigenous boys initially practiced drill through school-sponsored cadet groups. Although the residential school cadet movement was phased out in the early 1920s, marching and drill continued to shape students' daily lives through school-run Boy Scout and Girl Guide groups, which were funded by the federal Department of Indian Affairs.[43] Like their counterparts who performed in parades and exhibitions across the United States, Indigenous Scouts and Guides at Canadian residential schools were often praised for the enthusiasm, efficiency, and apparent ease with which they marched and drilled at public displays. A report by Sidney Rogers, principal of the Mohawk Institute Indian Residential School in Brantford, Ontario, in the 1920s, enthusiastically described the achievements of the school's Girl Guide group by noting their prize-winning needlework and their participation in a citywide parade: "the drill display by our troop," he wrote, "was second to none."[44] Beating non-Indigenous students in marching competitions was a point of pride for students, as well; Marguerite Beaver, a student at the Mohawk Institute between 1940 and 1948, recalled that

> Another thing we really liked—they had the Brownies and the Girl Guides ... we used to look forward to that. And Lady Baden Powell come down there and we all went to the Tutela Park and the ones from the Mohawk Institute—I'll never forget, oh we were so proud—we won everything—the inspections for the Brownies and the Girl Guides, out of all the troops in Brantford.[45]

According to Andrew Woolford, "tactile, social, aural, physical, and other pleasures"—things like school dances, Girl Guides, and sports—"were made available in limited quantities to seduce Indigenous students to the [boarding] school environment."[46] Although boarding school students' lives played out in material and ideological conditions that were not of their own making, many of them also used these attempted institutional seductions to carve out small spaces of sovereignty and create a sense of collective pride. When Alice Littlefield interviewed men and women who had attended Mount Pleasant Indian Industrial School in Michigan in the 1920s and early 1930s, she found that team sports—along with pranks and subversions similar to the "bloomer stories" recounted by Chilocco alumni—were remembered as sources of "autonomy and ... positive identity in the midst of a society which devalued ... [Indigenous students'] heritage."[47] In several cases, she found that photographs of Mount Pleasant's football and basketball teams (which played against and often beat teams from nearby public high schools) were the only material objects that former students had kept from their schooldays. Although officially intended as training for assimilation and settler-style sportsmanship, students also turned sports and athletic prowess into "symbol[s] of Indian identity and Indian pride."[48]

Indigenous young people used sports and spectatorship, in other words, to negotiate and reimagine identity and culture in the carceral and genocidal setting of the Indian boarding school. These negotiations and reimaginings often involved challenging racial hierarchies by literally beating white youth "at their own games." In chronological terms, this phenomenon began with the high-profile athletic programs that were established by several American boarding schools in the late nineteenth century. Between the 1890s and its closure in 1918, for example, Carlisle was home to a nationally known and highly successful football team. Originally intended to demonstrate the effectiveness of the school's assimilative programs, the Carlisle Indians (the team's official name) regularly defeated non-Indigenous teams from colleges and universities including Harvard and the Universities of Chicago, Minnesota, and Pennsylvania.[49] Glenn "Pop" Warner, a legendary figure in American football and the coach of the Carlisle team during its most successful years, commented on this phenomenon in a series of retrospective articles that were published in *Collier's Weekly* in 1931. Using language marked by racism and paternalism as well as a sense of respect, Warner wrote that "Carlisle had no traditions, but what the Indians did have was a very real race pride and a fierce determination to show the palefaces what they could do when the odds were even."[50]

The football team from Haskell Institute, the Haskell Indians, was similarly proud and determined and also excelled against college teams including Notre Dame, Nebraska, Kansas, and Michigan State.[51] The team traveled widely in the 1920s, attracting large crowds as well as media coverage that praised their achievements in sometimes racist terms. After Haskell players defeated the Los Angeles Athletic Club football team in front of thousands of spectators in California, for instance, the *Los Angeles Times* reported that they had "scalp[ed]" their opponents in an "attractive and spicy massacre."[52] Back in Kansas, the team's success inspired a record-breaking fundraising effort, the outcome of which was what Brenda Child has called "the first football stadium in the country funded completely by Indian donations."[53] The 10,500-seat Haskell Stadium opened to great fanfare in October 1926. These celebrations, touted as a "homecoming" for current and former students and their families, included a football game (at which Haskell beat Bucknell), a parade, a display of gymnastics and physical culture by female students, and a powwow featuring representatives from more than seventy-five different tribes.[54] This event, which provided clear evidence of the persistence of Indigenous cultures (including physical practices like dancing that the settler state had sought to destroy and replace with so-called rational recreation), was not uncontested. Expressing a widely held concern that "malleable" boarding school students might "backslide" if allowed prolonged contact with their communities of origin, one Bureau of Indian Affairs official complained that the stadium opening celebration was "a most decisive backward step."[55]

While high-profile intercollegiate sports declined at U.S. Indian boarding schools in the late 1930s (the result of a shift in federal policy that emphasized intramural sports and encouraged more Indigenous students to attend public schools), playing on and supporting school sports teams remained important to many Indigenous youth during the mid-twentieth century. In an interview with historian John Bloom, Jeff McLeod, who attended Flandreau school in South Dakota in the 1950s, emphasized the drawbacks of the school's limited curriculum and emphasis on manual labor. He also spoke about sports. Although not a member of Flandreau's football team (he refused to try out because doing so would have required him to cut his hair), McLeod described the team—and especially its victories over various non-Indigenous opponents—as a source of pride for the entire school:

> I think that's the only thing we felt that we were equal on. That the only thing that they see us as being equal were—we played them and we beat them. You get the impression . . . they already got us beat just by looking at us. But then we end up beating them and they see how good we are, it . . . makes them think of more respect for us, you know?[56]

Institutional Failures, Student Cultures, and Indigenous Critique

Indian boarding schools, created to eliminate Indigenous cultures and facilitate the absorption of Indigenous youth into the settler body politic, failed to achieve their goals. Carceral institutions designed to cement the transformation of Canada and the United States into "white men's countries," they ultimately proved unable to destroy Indigenous languages, lifeways, and family ties.[57] Much of this failure can be explained with reference to fact that boarding school students responded to the material and ideological constraints of institutional life by investing in and supporting a shared student culture characterized by withholding (and sometimes sharing), mischief, possibility, sharp observation, and pride.

The former students whose memories feature in this chapter are the ones who survived, and it is important to consider football victories and bloomer stories alongside the reality that Indian boarding schools were also spaces characterized by racism, abuse, and death. Simplistic claims about agency and victimization are inadequate here, and scholars must take seriously the ethical implications involved in studying the development of youth culture in settings characterized by genocide and trauma. At the same time, however, tracing Indigenous youth cultures through archival documents, oral history, and memoirs brings the failure of the complicated experiment of Indian boarding schools into sharp relief, and using a life course lens further reveals that numerous former students returned to their communities where they fought for Indigenous sovereignty and rights. In the 1960s and 1970s, Indigenous youth on both sides of the Canada–U.S. border combined counterculture with organized activism through their involvement in the Red Power movement.[58] The relationships between these different generations of modern Indigenous adolescents and young adults have yet to be fully examined, but it is clear that between the late nineteenth and mid-twentieth centuries, Indigenous boarding school students created forms of youth culture that allowed them—in the face of racist policies, surveillance, and discipline—to carve out meaningful spaces for resistance, solidarity, and critique.

Notes

1. Brenda J. Child, "The Boarding School as Metaphor," *Journal of American Indian Education* 57, no. 1 (2018): 38.
2. Brenda J. Child, "The Boarding School as Metaphor," *Journal of American Indian Education* 57, no. 1 (2018): 40.
3. Significant nation-based and locally focused works include John S. Milloy, *A National Crime: The Canadian Government and the Residential School System, 1870 to 1986* (Winnipeg: University of Manitoba Press, 1999); J.R. Miller, *Shingwauk's Vision: A History of Residential Schools* (Toronto: University of Toronto Press, 1996); David Wallace Adams, *Education for Extinction: American Indians and the Boarding School Experience, 1875–1928* (Lawrence: University Press of Kansas, 1995); K. Tsianina Lomawaima, *They Called It Prairie Light: The Story of Chilocco Indian School* (Lincoln: University of Nebraska Press, 1995); Celia Haig-Brown, *Resistance and Renewal: Surviving the Indian Residential School* (Vancouver: Arsenal Pulp Press, 1988).
4. Jacqueline Fear-Segal, *White Man's Club: Schools, Race, and the Struggle of Indian Acculturation* (Lincoln: University of Nebraska Press, 2007), Prologue and chap. 3.
5. Andrew Woolford, *This Benevolent Experiment: Indigenous Boarding Schools, Genocide, and Redress in Canada and the United States* (Lincoln: University of Nebraska Press, 2015), 3.
6. Rebecca Swartz, *Education and Empire: Children, Race and Humanitarianism in the British Settler Colonies, 1833–1880* (Chamf: Palgrave Macmillan, 2019), 132.
7. Laura Briggs, *Taking Children: A History of American Terror* (Berkeley: University of California Press, 2020), 33.

8. Frederick Hoxie, *A Final Promise: The Campaign to Assimilate the Indians, 1880-1920* (Lincoln & London: University of Nebraska Press, 2001), 196.
9. Mary Jane Logan McCallum, *Indigenous Women, Work, and History 1940-1980* (Winnipeg: University of Manitoba Press, 2014), 30; Karen Vallgårda, Kristine Alexander, & Stephanie Olsen, "Emotions and the Global Politics of Childhood," in *Childhood, Youth, and Emotions in Modern History*, ed. Stephanie Olsen (Basingstoke, UK: Palgrave, 2015), 24-25.
10. Mona Gleason, "Agency, Experience, and the Challenge of Historical Experience" (Keynote address at "The History of Experience and Agency: A Critical Intervention" conference, University of Tampere, Finland, March 8-12, 2021); Kristine Alexander, "Agency and Emotion Work," *Jeunesse: Young People, Texts, Cultures* 7, no. 2 (2015): 121.
11. Mary Jo Maynes, "Age as a Category of Historical Analysis: History, Agency, and Narratives of Childhood," *Journal of the History of Childhood and Youth* 1, no. 1 (2008): 114-124; Kristine Alexander, "Agency and Emotion Work," *Jeunesse: Young People, Texts, Cultures* 7, no. 2 (2015): 120-128; Mona Gleason, "Avoiding the Agency Trap: Caveats for Historians of Children, Youth, and Education," *History of Education* 45, no. 4 (2016): 446-459; Susan A. Miller, "Assent as Agency in the Early Years of the American Revolution," *Journal of the History of Childhood and Youth* 9, no. 1 (Winter 2016): 48-65; Lynn M. Thomas, "Historicizing Agency," *Gender & History* 28, no. 2 (August 2016): 324-339; Karen Vallgårda, Kristine Alexander, & Stephanie Olsen, "Against Agency," *Commentaries* section of the Society for the History of Children & Youth (SHCY) website, October 2018, https://www.shcy.org/features/commentaries/against-agency/; Ishita Pande, "Is the History of Childhood Ready for the World? A Response to 'The Kids Aren't All Right,'" *American Historical Review* 125, no. 4 (October 2020): 1300-1305.
12. Robin Brownlie & Mary-Ellen Kelm, "Desperately Seeking Absolution: Native Agency as Colonialist Alibi?," *Canadian Historical Review* 75, no. 4 (December 1994): 545. Further important discussion of the limits of the concept of agency in the context of Indian residential schools in Canada can be found in Crystal Gail Fraser, "T'aih k'iighe' tth'aih zhit diidich'ùh (By Strength, We Are Still Here): Indigenous Northerners Confronting Hierarchies and Power at Day and Residential Schools in Nanhkak Thak (the Inuvik Region, Northwest Territories), 1959 to 1982." PhD dissertation, University of Alberta, 2019.
13. Andrew Woolford, "Discipline, Territory, and the Colonial Mesh: Indigenous Boarding Schools in the United States and Canada," in *Colonial Genocide in Indigenous North America*, ed. Andrew Woolford, Jeff Benvenuto, & Alexander Laban Hinton (Durham & London: Duke University Press, 2014), 31.
14. Woolford, "Discipline, Territory, and the Colonial Mesh," 32.
15. *Honouring the Truth, Reconciling for the Future: Summary of the Final Report of the Truth and Reconciliation Commission of Canada* (Winnipeg: Truth & Reconciliation Commission of Canada, 2015), 89-90.
16. Jane Griffith, *Words Have a Past: The English Language, Colonialism, and the Newspapers of Indian Boarding Schools* (Toronto: University of Toronto Press, 2019), 98.
17. Quoted in Jennifer Bess, "More than a Food Fight: Intellectual Traditions and Cultural Continuity in Chilocco's *Indian School Journal*, 1902-1918," *American Indian Quarterly* 37, nos. 1-2 (Winter/Spring 2013): 78.
18. Clyde Ellis, *To Change Them Forever: Indian Education at the Rainy Mountain Boarding School, 1893-1920* (Norman: University of Oklahoma Press, 1996), 104.

19. Theodore Fontaine, *Broken Circle: The Dark Legacy of Indian Residential Schools: A Memoir* (Victoria: Heritage House Press, 2010), 24–25.
20. Fontaine, *Broken Circle*, 49.
21. Griffith, *Words Have a Past*, 25.
22. Quoted in Amelia V. Katanski, *Learning to Write "Indian": The Boarding-School Experience and American Indian Literature* (Norman: University of Oklahoma Press, 2005), 49.
23. Griffith, *Words Have a Past*, 40.
24. Ibid., 40–41.
25. Quoted in *Annual Report of the Carlisle Indian School 1892–1893*, 17, http://carlisleindian.dickinson.edu/documents/annual-report-carlisle-indian-school-1892-1893 (accessed March 15, 2021).
26. Ibid., 21–22.
27. *The Aurora* 1, no. 10 (October 1893): 2. Thanks to Jane Griffith for sharing digital copies of *The Aurora* with me.
28. *The Aurora* 1, no. 11 (November 1893): 2.
29. Ibid.
30. Griffith, *Words Have a Past*, 1.
31. Ibid., 61–62.
32. Paige Raibmon, *Authentic Indians: Episodes of Encounter from the Late Nineteenth-Century Northwest Coast* (Durham, NC, & London: Duke University Press, 2005), 31.
33. Quoted in ibid., 41–42.
34. *The Aurora* II, no. 17 (May 1894): 1.
35. Quoted in Griffith, *Words Have a Past*, 43.
36. Quoted ibid., 43.
37. Lomawaima, *They Called It Prairie Light*, xi.
38. Ibid., xiii.
39. Sara De Leeuw, "Intimate Colonialisms: The Material and Experienced Places of British Columbia's Residential Schools," *The Canadian Geographer* 51, no. 3 (2007): 352.
40. Lomawaima, *They Called It Prairie Light*, 86.
41. Ibid., 95.
42. Ibid., 98.
43. Kristine Alexander, *Guiding Modern Girls: Girlhood, Empire, and Internationalism in the 1920s and 1930s* (Vancouver: UBC Press, 2017); Mary Jane McCallum, "To Make Good Canadians: Girl Guiding at Indian Residential Schools.", MA Thesis, Trent University (2002).
44. Quoted in Elizabeth Graham, ed., *The Mush Hole: Life at Two Indian Residential Schools* (Waterloo, Ontario: Heffle Publishing, 1997), 145.
45. Ibid., 386.
46. Andrew Woolford, "Discipline, Territory, and the Colonial Mesh," 39.
47. Alice Littlefield, "The B.I.A. Boarding School: Theories of Resistance and Social Reproduction," *Humanity & Society* 13, no. 4 (1989): 437.
48. Ibid., 438.
49. Joseph B. Oxendine, *American Indian Sports Heritage* (Champaign, IL: Human Kinetics Books, 1988), 191.
50. Quoted in John Bloom, *To Show What an Indian Can Do: Sports at Native American Boarding Schools* (Minneapolis: University of Minnesota Press, 2000), 19.

51. Brenda J. Child, *Boarding School Seasons: American Indian Families, 1900–1940* (Lincoln & London: University of Nebraska Press, 1998), 4.
52. "Haskell Indians Scalp Mercury Team, 12-10," *Los Angeles Times*, December 20, 1925, 23.
53. Child, *Boarding School Seasons*, 4; John Bloom, "'Show What an Indian Can Do': Sports, Memory, and Ethnic Identity at Federal Indian Boarding Schools," *Journal of American Indian Education* 35, no. 3 (Spring 1996): 35.
54. John Bloom, *To Show What an Indian Can Do*, 48.
55. Ibid., 40.
56. Quoted in ibid., 51.
57. Marilyn Lake & Henry Reynolds, *Drawing the Global Color Line: White Men's Countries and the International Challenge of Racial Equality* (Cambridge: Cambridge University Press, 2008).
58. Scott Rutherford, *Canada's Other Red Scare: Indigenous Protest and Colonial Encounters During the Global Sixties* (Montreal & Kingston: McGill-Queen's University Press, 2020); Bradley G. Shreve, *Red Power Rising: The National Indian Youth Council and the Origins of Native Activism* (Norman: University of Oklahoma Press, 2011).

Further Reading

Adams, David Wallace. *Education for Extinction: American Indians and the Boarding School Experience, 1875–1928*. Lawrence: University Press of Kansas, 1995.

Alexander, Kristine. *Guiding Modern Girls: Girlhood, Colonialism, and Empire in the 1920s and 1930s*. Vancouver: UBC Press, 2017.

Bloom, John. *To Show What an Indian Can Do: Sports at Native American Boarding Schools*. Minneapolis: University of Minnesota Press 2000.

Child, Brenda J. *Boarding School Seasons: American Indian Families, 1900–1940*. Lincoln & London: University of Nebraska Press, 1998.

Fear-Segal, Jacqueline. *White Man's Club: Schools, Race, and the Struggle of Indian Acculturation*. Lincoln & London: University of Nebraska Press, 2007.

Forsyth, Janice, & Michael Heine. "'The Only Good Thing That Happened at School': Colonizing Narratives of Sport in the Indian School Bulletin." *British Journal of Canadian Studies* 30, no. 2 (2017): 201–225.

Griffith, Jane. *Words Have a Past: The English Language, Colonialism, and the Newspapers of Indian Boarding Schools*. Toronto: University of Toronto Press, 2019.

Littlefield, Alice. "The B.I.A. Boarding School: Theories of Resistance and Social Reproduction." *Humanity & Society* 13, no. 4 (1989): 428–441.

Lomawaima, K. Tsianina. *They Called It Prairie Light: The Story of Chilocco Indian School*. Lincoln & London: University of Nebraska Press, 1995.

McCallum, Mary Jane Logan. "'I Would Like the Girls at Home': Domestic Labour and the Age of Discharge at Canadian Indian Residential Schools." In *Colonization and Domestic Service: Historical and Contemporary Perspectives*. Edited by Claire Lowry & Victoria Haskins, 191–209. New York: Routledge, 2014.

Miller, J.R. *Shingwauk's Vision: A History of Residential Schools*. Toronto: University of Toronto Press, 1996.

Milloy, John S. *A National Crime: The Canadian Government and the Residential School System, 1870 to 1986*. Winnipeg: University of Manitoba Press, 1999.

Te Hiwi, Braden. "'Unlike Their Playmates of Civilization, the Indian Children's Recreation Must Be Cultivated and Developed': The Administration of Physical Education at Pelican Lake Indian Residential School, 1926–1944." *Historical Studies in Education/Revue d'histoire de l'éducation* 29, no. 1 (2017): 99–118.

Te Hiwi, Braden, & Janice Forsyth. "'A Rink at This School Is Almost as Essential as a Classroom': Hockey and Discipline at Pelican Lake Indian Residential School, 1945–1951." *Canadian Journal of History* 52, no. 1 (2017): 80–108.

Woolford, Andrew. *This Benevolent Experiment: Indigenous Boarding Schools, Genocide, and Redress in Canada and the United States*. Lincoln: University of Nebraska Press, 2015.

CHAPTER 14

GLOBALIZING THE AMERICAS THROUGH TWENTIETH-CENTURY YOUTH ORGANIZATIONS

ELENA JACKSON ALBARRÁN

THE twentieth century offered unprecedented opportunities for youth around the world to explore and consolidate their social identities through involvement in social, political, cultural, and ethnic groups, and Latin America proved no exception. Children and youth in a modernizing world found spaces of belonging in organizations that were state-sponsored, religious, private, or international in scope. As mass media outlets increasingly honed their products for age-specific consuming markets, children saw their activities and affinities reflected in the pages of magazines, publications, and television. But youth organizations also could become platforms for state posturing, and vehicles for trotting out nationalist rhetoric and nation-building ideas. Though distinct national contexts offer rich histories in their own right, some regional trends emerge. Moving in a roughly chronological fashion through the century, some specific youth organizations active in Latin American countries in four historical moments are examined. Though the youth activities profiled here ranged across the ideological spectrum, they shared a political tendency to organize youth culture to align with prevailing ideas of ideal citizenship.[1] In many cases, youth organizations had levels tiered by age categories, with children as young as seven participating in a cultural phenomenon modeled by young men that mirrored their future, older selves. Such a tiered structure allowed for long-term generational formation that aimed to produce, as its outcome, an ideal citizen. While the life spans of many institutions transcend the temporal boundaries of the period-specific categories, they have been allocated to the twentieth-century moment in which they were most influential.

Nationalism and Race: Boy Scouts and Girl Guides (1907–1930s)

At the dawn of the twentieth century, many Latin American republics sought to shake off the mantle of coloniality that had plagued their first century of independence, and they began to orchestrate an unsteady balance between European-based models of modernization and distinctly local constructions of national identity. The popularity of the Boy Scouts, and to a lesser degree the Girl Guides, provides an instructive metaphor for this tension. The British organization founded by General Robert Baden-Powell in 1907 took the world by storm in short order; within a generation, the ranks of the International Boy Scout Association swelled to more than three million registered members. Baden-Powell himself visited South America in 1909, precipitating the formal inauguration of chapters in Chile (1909) and Argentina (1912), where ad hoc Boy Scouts had already begun to come together following the global craze, with the organization reaching its golden age in the 1920s. The Boy Scouts allowed for politicians with military backgrounds to channel their nation-making projects through the organization and allowed young people an unprecedented stage for public visibility and adult-sanctioned extracurricular activity. In particular, the widespread practice across Latin America (documented since 1910) of a nation's president serving as honorary president of the national Scout organization affirmed the civilizing potential that could be tapped. In some countries with aspirations to modernize according to European lines, like Chile and Argentina, the British model was transplanted intact; in other countries with more sensitive racial politics, like revolutionary Mexico, the Boy Scouts offered at best a loose organizing principle around which troop members enacted expressions of local cultural realities.

Late nineteenth- and early twentieth-century Argentina found itself in a moment of national reinvention, having solicited and welcomed unprecedented waves of European immigrants as a labor force to support the export-based model of agriculture and shipping industrialization to support the burgeoning beef, hide, and wool industries. The influx of Italian, Spanish, French, and British populations bolstered the economy but created challenges for the state project of constructing cultural nationalism; the organizational structure—and British cultural cache—of the Boy Scouts offered a welcome solution. The first Scout Day commemoration in 1928 marked a clear moment of claiming the Boy Scouts for national purposes. Argentine President Marcelo Torcuato de Alvear, a former military officer and minister of war, presided over the ceremonies in his dual capacity as the national Scout president. Noting the opportunities to foment the public visibility of a unified, respectful corps of youth, officials expanded Scout Day to Scout Week in 1932, filling it out with excursions, parades, athletic tournaments, professional and skill demonstrations, and other incentives for young members. The recruiting power of the spectacle also drew critics, primarily from the Catholic Church, which accused the Boy Scouts organization of "de-Christianizing" the nation's youth, a euphemistic critique of the secular state's claim to the hearts and minds of its youth. Liberalism reached its zenith in early twentieth-century Latin America, and the intentional, if fraught, separation of church and state meant competition between these entities for young people's fealty.

Likewise, the Argentine Boy Scouts organization offered opportunities for the accelerated assimilation of immigrants into the national culture, which opened avenues for military recruitment and other forms of citizenship practice. Argentina's cosmopolitan populace used the Boy Scout structure to consolidate cultural ties among second-generation children. British, German, French, Belgian, Polish, the United States, Syrian, and Armenian enclaves sponsored so-called "ethnic companies" of Boy Scouts until the practice was banned in 1941, when the nationalization of the organization required full integration and conformity with national guidelines. Under the new mandate, Scouts learned a prescribed set of national heroes and a singular official historical narrative, thus assuaging politicians' concerns that children of immigrants would not acquire a love of their adopted country. In this way, the Boy Scouts of Argentina transitioned to a vehicle for the assimilation of immigrants, in a moment in which anxieties about national identity were escalating.

In Chile, Boy Scouts offered thousands of young men the chance to engage with their peers from around the world, both in spirit and in physical reunions. Over the course of the 1920s, Chile sent delegations to international jamborees and conferences in England, France, Denmark, and Switzerland. Chilean and Argentine scouts marched to their shared borderlands to camp together, a peaceful gesture of fraternity that went far to ameliorate past territorial conflict in the region. Brazilian Scouts stepped in to lend a hand after Chile suffered an earthquake, and the Chilean scouts sent them a statue as a goodwill acknowledgment of their solidarity. In 1928, there were thirteen thousand members of the Scout Association, and after suffering a dip following the economic crisis of 1930, those numbers recovered to eighteen thousand by 1943—Girl Guides comprised approximately one-third of the membership throughout that time span. But the social reality of Boy Scouts as an upper-middle-class organization belies the robust numbers. Despite efforts to recruit the "proletarian child" into Scout ranks, the prohibitive cost of the required uniforms and the annual membership dues proved a consistent deterrent to many and ensured the elitist profile of the organization. The indigenous population of Chile remained marginalized from participation as well; although official Scout ceremonies paid occasional lip service to an antiquated "Arawak" heritage as the primeval source of their strength and bravery, virtually nothing was done to extend Boy Scout opportunities to the native Mapuche population. Finally, as in the Argentine case, families from across the ideological spectrum discouraged their children from participating in the Boy Scouts. The strongest opposition came from the religious sector, which actively mobilized Catholic youth into militant alternative organizations; the most popular was La Cruzada Eucarística de los Niños, founded in 1922, which boasted thirty-five thousand young crusaders by 1930, a number that far outstripped the popularity of the Boy Scouts. The Junior Red Cross offered the greatest competition among elementary school girls, with a stunning membership of seventy-five thousand cadets by 1936. The political left countered the Boy Scouts' perceived fascist tendencies (state-aligned militarism, embedded imperialist rhetoric, and aesthetic nods to Nazism) with communist and anarchist youth organizations, which, although rising in popularity in the 1930s, still represented only a small minority. The Girl Guides officially became autonomous from the Association of Boy Scouts of Chile in 1953, consolidating the two groups' respective gendered orientation.

In the case of Mexico, the Corps of Mexican Explorers (later Tribes of Mexican Explorers, and often called Boy Scouts) came together in 1917 under the direction of German-born Mexican citizen Federico Clarck, inspired by but never officially incorporated into the Boy Scouts. At that moment, Mexico was in the final throes of its social revolution from below, the outcome of which yielded two decades of concerted state effort to construct a new national identity that validated the mestizo and indigenous heritage common to the majority of Mexicans. The Boy Scouts grappled with a troubled relationship with indigeneity; on one hand, the smart European-style uniform and glossy Scout-themed magazine *Tihui* offered the promise of membership in a globalized modern club. On the other hand, the national structure of the organization intentionally promoted indigenous knowledge (especially about nature) and relied heavily on Aztec motifs and naming conventions to designate categories within the ranks: for example, "tribe" members were called *tequihua* ("explorer" in Nahuatl). To further complicate matters, many rural indigenous boys urgently wanted to tap into the national vogue more readily available to their urban peers and cobbled together their own "tribes," imposing upon their mothers to hand-fashion simulacra of the official uniforms. Though the Mexican Boy Scouts' structure held the possibility of promoting meaningful interlocutions between rural and urban, and indigenous and mestizo members, such bridge-building expressions unfortunately remained an unrealized potential. The Boy Scout brand of cultural nationalism remained confined largely to rhetorical flourishes and empty symbolism.

In all of the cases mentioned here, the Boy Scouts promoted patriotism in the most literal way: it encouraged young people to become intimately familiar with their nation's topography through hiking, camping, and excursions and in that way fostered a love of country tangibly connected to the land. Though most national Associations of Boy Scouts started out as gender-equitable, with a steady minority of girls' troops represented among the ranks, increasingly the Boy Scouts oriented toward militarized, conquest-style expeditions into "untamed" nature, while the Girl

Guides (or equivalent) tended their activities toward charity, domestic skills, and less-adventurous pursuits. Such a divide, paired with the presidential patronage of the Boy Scouts, underscored the expectation that boys belonged in the political sphere, while girls best served the nation's interest from home.

Scouts enjoyed a new modern identity, crafted though it often was by cultural nationalist interests, distinct from their traditionally assigned roles in the classroom and at home. They forged friendships in new physical spaces like campsites and mountaintops, and parades and charity drives. The formation of chapters by county, region, or state added another layer to their growing sense of belonging to a collective, one that was only enhanced for those fortunate enough to travel internationally to the annual Boy Scout Jamboree. One can imagine the wonder felt by twelve-year-old Mexican Scout Teodoro Albarrán in 1937 as he helped his troop pitch their tent between the Washington Monument and the Pan American Union building on the Washington, D.C., mall alongside thousands of fellow Scouts from around the world. The Mexicans proudly signaled their national heritage by adorning their campsite with sarapes, colorful woven regional blankets that at home might have signaled a sleepy, even backward, rural identity. The Scouts organization became a space for children to negotiate the identities prescribed for them as they circulated in different social and geographical contexts.

INTERNATIONALISM AND EMPIRE: PAN-AMERICAN EXCHANGES (1933–1948)

President Franklin D. Roosevelt declared a new era in hemispheric foreign policy in a 1933 speech in which he unveiled the Good Neighbor Policy, promising a noninterventionist approach toward the republics to the south. The Pan American Union, established in 1890, with its headquarters in Washington D.C., redoubled its efforts to bridge cultural divides and heal political wounds. For the next decade and a half, the hemisphere buzzed with a veritable frenzy of earnest, if lopsided, collaborations between and among the common citizens of the Americas. Pan American Union director L.S. Rowe immediately identified schoolchildren as the best cultural diplomats for a freshly branded amicable future and dispatched a memo to all Latin American ministers of education urging them to organize their youth to engage in expressions of solidarity. Pan American Day (April 14), a holiday first conceptualized in 1930 to commemorate the anniversary of the founding of the Pan American Union, became a focal point for orchestrating children's expressions of hemispheric solidarity, and Lowe assigned the Division of Intellectual Cooperation to be the regional clearinghouse of all materials related to the new holiday's celebration.

The enthusiasm for Pan Americanism spawned a staggering number of extracurricular language and cultural clubs from primary school through higher education, though not surprisingly the vast majority of youth activity bringing together "the two Americas" took place on the Anglo side. The Pan American League of Miami, Florida, founded in 1920, led the way in formalizing club activities; junior high and high school members absorbed the customs, language, and culture of each Latin American republic through book discussions, films, maps, and invited lectures in an earnest effort to best promote the Good Neighbor Policy. Spanish language classes and clubs in schools across the United States celebrated Pan American Day by staging allegorical parades, with students dressed in (what they considered to be) "typical" costumes from each of the twenty-one countries; others held cultural fairs in which they displayed elaborately crafted dioramas of Latin American nations' natural resources, primary exports, flora, and fauna. Still others learned and performed songs in Spanish or prepared traditional menus. Pan American clubs took up pen-pal correspondence with their southern peers, trying out their studied Spanish to convey quotidian details of life in the United States.

The Lancaster Chapter No. 14 of Georgia's Pan American Student Forum was active but representative: in January 1933 alone, members held a "hot tamale supper," sang Spanish songs, made Mexican candy, invited guests to a Mexican restaurant, attended the movie *Flying down to Rio*, collected stamps to trade with a partner school in Mexico City, assembled a pressed flower collection to exchange, curated a display case of items collected, and kept an active bulletin board, all while maintaining "lively correspondence" with their Latin American counterparts.[2] By 1940, the Pan American Student Forum had sixty-three chapters in the state of Georgia, many actively engaged in such ongoing accumulation of knowledge about Latin America. The Division of Intellectual Cooperation fomented the initiative demonstrated by young people, churning out Spanish, English, and Portuguese versions of ancillary educational and curricular materials about endless facets of Latin American culture, politics, and life. The generation growing up in the United States during the Good Neighbor years enjoyed unprecedented (and unmatched since) interest in and engagement with Latin American peers.

Pan American League director J. Harold Matteson yearned to see parallel club systems in the southern republics but approached educational officials tactfully:

> I do not ask that you associate yourself with the movement in the United States, but to proceed along lines that meet with your approval and that of your government....
> I hope you will feel that the youth of to-day, must tomorrow shoulder the burdens of government, and in preparation for to-morrow, let us train them in the principles of love, fellowship and understanding.[3]

On the Latin American side, however, Pan Americanism enjoyed a lukewarm reception, with a few notable exceptions. Schoolchildren's commemorations of Pan American Day were often stilted and formulaic and usually consisted of a flagpole ceremony featuring a boilerplate speech and perhaps a chorus or two. Occasionally a child was selected to read a message of solidarity. The Uruguayan education minister's 1938 attempt to inspire a Pan American essay contest among the elementary school population sputtered along for years without generating meaningful participation. While Pan Americanism in the United States relied heavily on the allure of the exotic, it was more difficult to sell this dimension to Latin American students, many of whom dressed in typical Western fashion in their daily lives and didn't see the United States as having a distinct or unfamiliar culture that drove them to learn more.

The disparity in enthusiasm for Pan Americanism across the republics of the hemisphere can best be illustrated by a graphic included in the Pan American League's promotional pamphlet. In it, a map of the hemisphere shows Miami as the regional hub, from which lines of communication radiate out to indicate other Pan American activity centers. A heavy thicket of lines spread north from Miami, reaching principal and midsize cities alike across the United States. But a very few lines spindle downward, not even one per Latin American nation. Notably, all lines of communication flow through Miami—the suggested pluralism of "Pan" Americanism does not seem to promote inter-American dialogue and discourse so much as centralization from a U.S. perspective. Washington D.C.'s official Pan American Day celebration in 1938 drew eight hundred students from area schools, who assembled in the Pan American Union building, where they listened to a radio broadcast salutation from a single Argentine student. Such a ration provides an apt metaphor for organized Pan Americanism in the Good Neighbor regime.

Some Pan American initiatives for children succeeded. The practice of naming sister schools after another republic, launched in the 1920s but taken up in earnest in the 1930s, forged long-term links that provided a natural justification for students to invest in learning about the history, culture, heroes, and politics of their namesake. Some schools organized especially noteworthy exchanges between their student populations in the 1930s and 1940s. For example, in 1940, elementary students of the Colégio México in Brazil compiled a beautiful album for their school's eponymous friends on the occasion of their mutually celebrated independence month of September. It contained beautifully hand-drawn—or sometimes laboriously traced—renderings of toucans, pineapples, and patriots from Brazil, sprinkled through with cutouts from children's pages from the weekly newspaper and color picture postcards of Ipanema and Sugarloaf. On one page, the official school photographs of fourth-graders are pasted in a frame around a drawing of uniformed schoolchildren caressing the Brazilian flag, accompanied by a hand-lettered verse:

> Mexican friends! In order to see you,
> Off we go as smiling portraits!
> To the noble sons of the impudent Morelos,
> We, sons of the country of Tiradentes![4]

Albums such as these, and the comparative social studies and natural history curricula that must have accompanied their production, not only allowed students to engage in a sustained study of another culture but also promoted the construction of a civic sense of self closely tied to place.

U.S.-led Pan-American fervor might have characterized many youth exchanges in the Good Neighbor era, but many Latin Americans envisioned a version of hemispheric brotherhood organized along racial lines, leading to alternative organized activities for children that excluded the United States. In 1934, Mexico's first lady Aída S. de Rodríguez wrote a letter addressing the attendees of the Second Inter-American Conference of Education, convened in Santiago, Chile, in which she reiterated Mexican children's invitation to their Latin American peers to adopt the practice of pledging allegiance to the Flag of the Americas. Her rationale for this initiative was to forge a distinctly Latin American brand of generational solidarity, quietly nestled within U.S.-led Pan Americanism. She firmly believed that once children cultivated this "germ of love" for the region of the Americas in their hearts, alongside their already-presumed passion for their respective countries, then the adults in their lives would quickly follow suit.[5] She subtly suggested that the racial bonds between Latin Americans, due to their shared Indo-European mixed heritage, might be stronger than friendships forged with the Anglo neighbors to the north. Following Mexican students' lead, young people in the Americas celebrated Día de la Raza (Day of the [Mestizo] Race) more readily than Pan American Day. This episode represents a short-lived effort by Latin American politicians and intellectuals to lay claim to the future of the hemisphere on their own terms, and they saw children's organized participation in civic gestures as central to laying that foundation. It also reflects the tension between growing sentiments of nationalism, and the discourses and institutions of integration that were already set in motion to globalize Latin America. In all of these overlapping conversations—nationalism, regionalism, internationalism—the organization of children and youth proved vital as projections of political strength and potential.

In 1948, as the end of World War II gave way to the new world order of the Cold War, the Pan American Union became the Organization of American States, and as such the multilateral rhetoric that prevailed during the previous decade reverted to alliance-based discourse, with the United States firmly at the head. Children and youth in the Americas who had organized under the auspices of Pan-American solidarity did not suddenly lose interest, and pen pal correspondences and student exchanges continued over the Cold War period. But the official Washington cultural apparatus increasingly began to treat the countries to the south as suspect—youth's verve could easily tip over into radicalization, and the potential for volatility seemed great. George Kennan, counselor to the State Department, traveled to the region in 1950 and came away with a stridently negative opinion of Latin Americans' capacity for stability and self-rule; in a secret memo, his tone negates the decades of good-neighborliness:

> It is important for us to keep before ourselves and the Latin American people at all times the thesis that we are a great power; that we are by and large much less in need of them than they are in need of us ... that the danger of a failure to exhaust the possibilities of our mutual relationship is always greater to them than to us ...[6]

In this framework, children represented less the future of a transnational utopia, and more a hemispheric danger in the form of manifold individual conduits for Communist propaganda. And indeed, as we will see, Latin American nation-states sought to corral the kinetic force of youth during the early Cold War period.

POPULISM ACROSS THE IDEOLOGICAL SPECTRUM: ARGENTINA AND CUBA (1940S–1960S)

The rise of Cold War global posturing created ideal conditions for personalist-style populist politics to loom in Latin America, with the goal of strengthening nationalism from the top. Highly organized initiatives from Juan Perón's Argentina in the 1940s–1950s and Fidel Castro's Cuba in the 1960s conscripted youth into the service of the state, with the explicit goal of citizen formation along political and ideological goals.

In Argentina, the labor-oriented populist government of Juan Perón (1946–1955) and his charismatic wife Eva Perón (endearingly called Evita) fostered a loyal cadre of children and young people that bolstered Perón's mass-based political style by pandering to the proletariat with a nod to fascism. Perón premised his legitimacy heavily on electoral politics and invested an enormous amount in recruiting children into the party to ensure his longevity. Foreign observers who witnessed the 1946 revolution that brought Perón to power marveled that "almost overnight, it looked as if the country had been taken by an army of white pinafores," uniformed schoolchildren turning up in the streets and on the newsreels to protagonize the new government of the people.[7] The strategies employed by Perón invited comparisons to Nazi Germany, which extended from the style of youth-oriented politicking to the racial discourses that lurked in the corners. Compared with its South American neighbors, Argentina's racial composition looked relatively "white," due to the high index of European immigrants, and social engineers sought to maintain this racial advantage. Arturo Rossi, president of the Association of Biotypology, Eugenics, and Social Medicine (a private association with direct ties to Italian fascism) observed a lower fertility rate among white Argentines, expressing alarm that a mixed racial composition could imperil state-driven cultural nationalism. The pervasive strain of racism silently informed discourses about, organizations for, and the public display of children in state-sponsored forums to assuage fears of a racially degenerate national citizenry.

The motto "Perón delivers" (*Perón cumple*) cultivated the public's expectation of government magnanimity, much of which came in the form of welfare, recreational, and institutional benevolence for Argentine children. Such programs were lavish and comprehensive, thanks to the first lady's charity, the Eva Perón Foundation (Fundación Eva Perón, or FEP). Thousands of children came together for high-profile soccer championships (named Campeonatas Evita, or CE, lest the source of patronage go unacknowledged), which featured opportunities to rub elbows with celebrity athletes. The CE allowed poor children from the provinces to participate in well-organized, well-funded, fun events that became an annual highlight for their families and had no small part in shoring up populist support for Perón. In 1954, the sport tournament had expanded to co-ed participation across ten events and involved nearly 216,000 children, all funded by the FEP with subsidies from Congress. While promoting children's recreation was the ostensible function of the tournaments, the Ministry of Public Health was also on hand to provide free medical assessments to the children, belying the event's eugenicist tinge.

Perhaps the most elaborate display of the Perón state's paternalist protection over its child citizens was the construction of La Ciudad Infantil in 1949. The Eva Perón Foundation constructed this "children's city," with a capacity for 450 residents, as a boarding school and respite center where parents down on their luck could leave their children—short- or long-term—for care, education, and recreation while they got back on their feet. Copious publicity ensured that Argentines far and wide were aware of the nation's marginalized children drawn into the sphere of Evita's smiling benevolence. Far from the grim nineteenth-century orphanage model, the Ciudad Infantil was a fantasy brought to life, one that Evita spun to great effect. The ultramodern facilities in Buenos Aires occupied two city blocks, including buildings scaled to a child's stature, and were supplemented by a seaside resort for residents in the summer.

Peronist children's clubs emerged, creating pockets of national community clustered around the central figures of Perón and Evita. Although centralized attempts to create a formal club structure within the public school system fell flat, other children's clubs maintained visibility and vitality through publicity in the official magazines *Mundo Peronista* and *Mundo Infantil*. Clubs were incentivized by the possibility of seeing their organization's activities celebrated in print circulation and eagerly submitted reports of their events and sentiments full of Peronist adulation. The children's club Club Pibes de Perón y Evita submitted their reflections on the meaning of the October 17 holiday—Peronist Loyalty Day—through letters, poems, drawings, and photos. Nine-year-old Lidia Inés López, born on the exact day of the labor demonstration in 1945 that marked the start of Peronism, marveled that her birthday fell on this auspicious date: "What a joy to count my years alongside those of justice, love, and loyalty to Perón and Evita!" Osvaldo M. Fernández contributed an earnest verse:

> I am a very small child
> I want to sing my stanza
> I would like to be at your side
> Present, my General.
> I would like to be grown
> To give my faithful life to you
> I would like to be your soldier
> Present, my General.

Osvaldo followed this formal style with a heartfelt parenthetical addendum: "(I want my General to know that I love him very much.")[8] Through public venues like the magazines, Argentine youth saw opportunities to align their emerging identities with the highest level of political power.

The Peronist political machine of the 1940s and 1950s was decidedly oriented toward children's culture as a populist bulwark, and the long-term strategy paid off: Perón loyalists grew into an umbrella organization called the Brigades of the Peronist Youth, which became staunch public advocates for the authoritarian-tinged labor-oriented politics in the 1970s. In effect, the Peronist Youth channeled the spiritual affinity that children growing up in the 1950s had for the Colonel and Evita into more explicitly political mobilization. State sponsorship of youth organizations sought to redirect the globalizing allure of teen culture to a tightly articulated nationalist structure, through which increasingly authoritarian political directives could be infused. Militant adherents to the Brigades of the Peronist Youth retained their loyalty to Perón, long after Evita's death in 1952 and his fall from power and exile shortly thereafter in 1955. They helped to maintain the constructed image of Perón as a national savior over the course of a generation, stoking a collective historical memory that brought him back to power (briefly) in 1973–1974. In some ways, this provides evidence that Perón's astute investment in the nation's youth worked, at least to his own political advantage in the short term.

While youth, tied to the institutions of school, Boy Scouts, and sports leagues, might have been easily drafted into the nation's service, for some, the propaganda wore off as they transitioned into young adulthood: not all Argentine youth fell under Peronism's sway. Students at the Universidad de La Plata, exercising their right to non-compulsory attendance, learned to vote with their feet, boycotting classes taught by professors with demonstrated fascist or pro-Nazi tendencies; facing attrition, several of these professors lost faculty appointments. The global university-age identity that emerged as a distinct social group brought such student-based expressions critical of the establishment in the 1950s, and this resonated sharply with some individuals seeking a break from state-engineered tracks to social citizenship. As a restless young man growing up in Perón's Argentina, Ernesto "Che" Guevara was disinclined to fall into step with the masses of his peers that congregated in the Plaza de Mayo to celebrate the material concessions that the president offered his people in exchange for their loyalty at the ballot box. He set out on an existential quest across the hemisphere, fatefully coinciding with an exiled Fidel Castro in Mexico in 1955. Comparing notes on their mutual observations of social and economic malaise over cortados in Mexico City's Café La Habana, they charted a course for the Cuban Revolution, a feat of heady anti-imperialism that they implausibly managed to pull off in January 1959 under the nose of the United States.

The Cold War transformed Argentina's political climate, and as Peronist politics fell out of favor in the Western hemisphere as being too conciliatory toward the working class, allegiance to Perón changed from being status quo, to a more radicalized culture of contestation (described more fully later). Youth were at the forefront of the left-wing political agitation, under a Peronist banner, against the establishment. They gained their political consciousness generally by tapping into the 1960s global wave of generational discontent, and specifically through touchstone youth-oriented moments, such as the 1973 "Festival of Liberation" rock concert that furnished an aesthetic and soundtrack to accompany young people's changing expressions of masculine authority so closely tied to conventional authority structures. The contestatory politics of youth culture emerging against the rock-and-roll scrim did not have a singular effect on Argentine's young people; for some, it galvanized the political tendencies already established through the Peronist Youth organization and lent a fresh urgency to their claims against political abuses of power. But to others, it provided a nihilistic justification to "drop out" of political activism altogether and join in the global malaise that swept up many of their generation.

As in Peronist Argentina, a captive youth was vital to the success of the Cuban Revolution, which stood alone in the hemisphere as a socialist state in the 1960s. One of the first institutions to be established by the triumphant revolutionary government in 1960 was the Revolutionary Youth Work Brigades (Brigadas Juveniles de Trabajo Revolucionarias, or BJTR), which sought avenues to explicitly inspire in children and youth support of, and love for, the revolution. As an initiation rite, to prove their physical worth and spiritual devotion to the regime, youth from across the island left their families for the eastern Sierra Maestra mountains—the site of Castro's guerrilla training—to summit the precipitous Turquino Peak five times before gaining recognition by the BJTR.

As part of the nationalizing sweep of institutions that the revolution ushered in, through the state school system children aged six to fourteen joined the Communist Pioneers (Pioneros Comunistas), a socialization structure inspired by the Soviet model of youth organization that strove to guarantee (through no small measure of coercion) continuous upcoming generations of Guevara's socialist ideal of the New Man (*Hombre Nuevo*). Membership was not obligatory, but it might as well have been: from the organization's founding in 1968 to the present, membership estimates hover above 90 percent. Following the daily chant, "Pioneers for Communism: We will be like Ché!" and smartly dressed in a blue and white uniform with a red ascot, young Cuban Pioneers learned to value the collective over the individual. Every October 28, uniformed Pioneers embarked on La Jornada Ideológica Camilo-Che, an annual pilgrimage of bearing flowers to the sea to honor two of the revolution's most conspicuous fallen heroes, a civic ritual that transferred Afro-Cuban religious practices of sending offerings to Yemayá (deity of water) into a strictly secular nationalist act. Team-based classroom competitions for cleanliness, civic behavior, verbatim recitations of texts by independence patriot José Martí, and demonstrations of ideological purity earned merits (badges, certificates, or other formal recognition) in order to stimulate conformist behaviors among a generation in training.

Unlike Argentina, where young people tended to grow wary of state-sponsored organizations as they aged out of them, the density of the communist bureaucratic structure in Cuba incentivized ongoing loyalty to the state as a pathway for upward political mobility. Older teens and university-aged youth joined the Union of Communist Youth, or Unión de Jóvenes Comunistas (UJC), where their fidelity to the revolution could be put to the test. The revolutionary government integrated the UJC into the state in 1965. UJC members rallied under the mantra "Study, Work, Weapon" (*Estudio, Trabajo, Fusil*) behind a logo bearing the profiles, set with resolve, of aspirational communist idols Julio Antonio Mella, Camilo Cienfuegos, and Che Guevara. In the heady 1960s, Cubans exalted their lone and improbable anti-imperialist stance in the hemisphere, and the ranks of the UJC swelled with enthusiastic youth eager to help construct an alternate paradigm to the capitalist model of development. Within five years of its founding, the UJC had become an important centralized organizing force for youth in the university, high school, and middle school; those laboring in technical fields and the agrarian sector; and for those in the professional corps of athletes and in the armed forces. They worked in a variety of capacities, often as interns in their respective sectors training the estimated 1.35 million primary school children in sports techniques, nutritional choices, and hygienic practices, the socialist lifestyle adjustments that supplemented the national curriculum. It was Castro's vision to accelerate the pace of human development with the assistance of this young cadre, to quickly and efficiently meet the needs of all Cubans on the island, and then export this revolutionary success to the rest of the Americas, as he proclaimed in a ceremony fêting the UJC in 1965:

> From today's children there will not be any counterrevolutionaries tomorrow, because they will not be educated in that corrupt demoralizing world, but in this new, revolutionary, and promising world. . . . That is why, you comrades of the youth movement, the generation which made socialism, will receive the torch to carry forward to communism.[9]

Internationalism was an important facet of organizing young people after 1959. The conspicuous global visibility of strong, healthy, and talented Cuban youth became one of Castro's preferred strategies to project the successes of the revolution abroad. Cuba made a point of participating in international initiatives organized around art, music, and cultural expression, especially to signal solidarity with the Third World. In particular, the nationalization of sports through the creation of the Ministry of Sport (Instituto Nacional de Deportes, Educación Física y Recreación, or INDER) reversed the trend established prior to 1959 of professional athletes pursuing their career opportunities in the United States. Local primary school teachers identified children with athletic promise from an early age—as early as fourth grade—from which point they entered specialized sports training facilities run by the INDER at the municipal, then provincial, and ultimately national level, to eventually become professional athletes. Children following the sports track enjoyed special benefits—such as exceptions to national food ration quotas and exemption from mandatory military service—highlighting the privileged status conferred to them by the revolution for their exceptional physical aptitudes. At the 1968 Olympics in Mexico City, under the world's watchful eye, Cuban athletes vindicated the revolution's socialist investment in its national institutions when they took home fourteen medals. But state favoritism did not sit well with all Cuban youth groomed for athletic success and, consequently, for communism. Eighteen-year-old Juan Pablo Vega Romero, a scholarship student and lightweight wrestler, defected from his sports delegation trip to Miami in 1966. Though he acknowledged being the beneficiary of preferential treatment, he admitted that many of Cuba's young athletes adhered to the regime more out of fear than fealty. Vega Romero attributed his departure to the strong punitive actions of the Communist Party, restrictions on intellectual freedom, demonstrated favoritism, and perhaps most significant, the fact that he "didn't like Castro."[10]

Militants of the UJC projected the revolution's ideals to the peers of their generation, impeccably embodying the self-abnegating New Man ideology in public deeds, but their ubiquity also allowed them to double as direct conduits for reporting nonconformist behavior to revolutionary authorities, effectively squelching the emergence of any alternative or contestatory youth-based movements on the island. In one instance, the Cuban government assigned a team of ten UJC members as research assistants to the famed United States anthropologist couple Oscar Lewis and Ruth Behar Lewis—tacit supporters of the Cuban Revolution, it should be noted—in their ethnographic research on the changing conditions of Cuba's urban poor under the regime from 1969 to 1972. After writing up their field notes, the UJC members conveyed direct surveillance of the Lewis's activities to government intelligence officials, opening up their nuanced assessment of the revolution's claims to success to the scrutiny of Cuban authorities, in a move that could lead to sedition charges for their informants. The UJC team members also played a role in surreptitiously recruiting informants for the Lewis's studies that would ensure a pro-revolutionary perspective. As the revolution became increasingly vigilant over the ideological conformity of the Cuban population as the Cold War waged on, UJC membership became more of an act of self-preservation than one of jubilant altruism. This can be demonstrated by the fact that in 2010, arguably the peak of Cuban dissatisfaction with the revolution, the UJC held the largest-ever public meeting of its organization, at which yet another generation of fresh-faced youth came before the same panel of aged revolutionaries to be told, yet again, that the future of the revolution was in their hands. And yet over the course of six decades, power had never yet changed hands.

Contesting Bureaucratic Authority: Militant Youth Organizations in the Southern Cone (1968–1990)

In Latin America, the Cold War fears of communist infiltration permitted the rise—with the approval and support of the CIA—of right-wing authoritarian regimes that both promised to suppress the pink tide and guaranteed a friendly business climate for foreign capitalist interests. In the context of these tensions, Che Guevara's death in 1967 galvanized anti-imperialist tendencies among youth the world over. University students were the protagonists of the global unrest of 1968, calling into question the established structures of authority in new public venues, and appearing en masse as a vital force for social change. Even as political elements of the Cuban Revolution co-opted the image of the martyred Che for the purposes of an increasingly totalitarian left, his posthumous iconoclasm inspired guerrilla-style resistance in much of the rest of the Americas, particularly in the region known as the Southern Cone (Argentina, Brazil, Chile, and Uruguay). Young people, largely from the educated middle and working classes, composed the growing militant, often covert, leftist organizations that sought to subvert the bureaucratic authoritarian regimes that characterized the latter Cold War years. Student movements forged alliances, previously considered unlikely, with the labor union sector, evidence of the political necessity of cross-class solidarity in increasingly authoritarian times. Through underground networks, coded exchanges, and transnational links, young people maintained the culture of resistance in the most challenging circumstances and also bore the brunt of state retaliation—or proactive punitive measures—often for the sheer fact of their age.

One of the most outrageous instances of violent state response to the perceived threat of rebelling youth took place in Mexico in 1968. Although Mexico maintained a reputation as a democracy during the Cold War, the claim was dubious at best. The official ruling of the Institutional Revolutionary Party (Partido Revolucionario Institucional, or PRI) had claimed every election since its foundation in 1929, and by the 1960s a generation of high school and university students had grown weary of the hackneyed promises that the revolution would deliver democracy and prosperity to its citizens. In particular, they rankled against the unjust political imprisonment of an outspoken and popular union leader, Demetrio Vallejo, and the heavy-handed presence of riot police that repressed student public demonstrations and gatherings. Young teens from the local prep schools joined forces with their college-aged peers from the hemisphere's largest public university, the Universidad Nacional Autónoma de México, and the older-generation union members to form the National Strike Council (Consejo Nacional de Huelga, or CNH), to stage an impressively well-organized series of demands before the national government. In the months leading up to October 1968, Mexico was slated to host the first-ever Olympics to be held in the so-called Third World, and the visibility of waves student demonstrations shutting down traffic in the capital's main thoroughfares concerned PRI officials. Ever concerned with hemispheric security, the U.S. State Department kept a close eye on the evolving situation in Mexico; an internal memo from September 1968 affirmed the Mexican government's "forceful shutdown" of organized student actions, making particular note of the composition of the CNH student leadership, "[nine] of whom have visited Cuba."[11] On the fateful night of October 2, the Mexican military and paramilitary special forces gunned down a congregation of student demonstrators at a peaceful rally held in the working-class neighborhood plaza of Tlatelolco, and they issued a draconian censorship of press investigations into the episode. Despite the officially recognized death toll of forty students, estimated casualties from the Massacre of Tlatelolco run into the hundreds. Thousands more languished in the state penitentiary to keep them out of the view of the world's cameras, which, indeed, captured Mexico City at its most modern and civilized during the XIX Olympic Games. The student-led left experienced continued state repression through the early 1970s as Mexico surged ahead with a public façade of democratic transparency that belied the country's ongoing social tensions and widening generational divide.

But Mexico's Dirty War against its organized youth seemed tame compared with its South American neighbors. In 1970s Argentina, the aforementioned Peronist Youth had so successfully rehabilitated an idealized version of the former populist leader that they brought the aged Perón back to the presidency for a brief moment in 1973–1974. The militant left-wing group the Montoneros morphed out of the Peronist Youth in 1967, identifying themselves as a Christian socialist nationalist movement. Though the radicalized Montoneros did not represent the majority of organized youth, their seven thousand members were able to take a few high-profile actions ostensibly in defense of Peronism—including a 1975 arms raid and a 1976 bombing of security police headquarters—before the group's dissolution in 1979. But Perón's death in office precipitated an untidy political devolution that turned Argentina over to the hands of a military junta that lasted from 1976 to 1983. This dictatorship waged the country's infamous Dirty War against its own civilian population, determined to root out potential communist subversives that would threaten Western Christian democratic social order, with the costly price tag of some twenty thousand to thirty thousand souls "disappeared" by the state apparatus. The high visibility of the targeted acts by leftist militant groups like the Montoneros served the state's purpose in justifying an all-out assault against the nation's youth: it was enough to have a Che-like shaggy hairstyle, wear (communist) red, have a beard, or carry an invitation to a youth-based meeting to become victims of unspeakable state violence. To cope, many young people turned to organizations to find protections from, and a way to resist, the increasing totalitarian assault from above.

In Chile, a military coup deposed the popularly elected Chilean democratic socialist president Salvador Allende, establishing the hemisphere's most brutal authoritarian regime under dictator Augusto Pinochet from 1973 to 1990. The military regime quickly identified university students as the dangerous class of Chileans that posed the most immediate threat to national security, and 1973 commenced a sweep to "purify" institutions of higher education to purge them of dissidents. Thousands of Chileans, mostly young people, died or disappeared in the decade and a half that followed, and an estimated thirty thousand suffered heinous physical and psychological torture at the hands of the secret police, the Dirección Nacional de Inteligencia (DINA). Rather than inspiring formal student organization in protest, as we saw in the Mexican case, the sheer magnitude of state terrorism in Chile had a deadening effect on youth mobilization. Informants for the secret police infiltrated university communities, contributing to a climate of mistrust. University enrollments plummeted.

The binary Cold War worldview, and the government's draconian position, forced some middle-class Chilean youth into covert action in the leftist underground. The Revolutionary Left Movement (Movimiento Izquierdo Revolucionario, or MIR) was the most radical option, with roots in the communist wave of the 1930s, but newly awakened to the struggles that emerged in the 1960s, and redoubled its revolutionary imperative with the coup in 1973. Though groups like the MIR attracted those most willing to follow the guerrilla path of opposition to the military regime, any hint of affiliation with such an organization guaranteed one would become a target of state violence. Many others sought more covert avenues to contest the regime from within an established institution: the Catholic Church. Within the relative safety of the Church hierarchy, many Chileans found ways to mobilize; the National Committee to Aid Refugees (CONAR) provided such a network of safe houses, soup kitchens (*ollas comunes*), and conduits for conveying information. Nevertheless, young people's leadership in opposition to the dictatorship could not outweigh the hegemonic forces that kept it in place. DINA disproportionately sought out, detained, and tortured young people at more than eleven hundred clandestine sites around the country, depleting an entire generation. With the return to democracy in 1990, energy for continued student activism and resistance flagged, and young people gave over to the neoliberal wave that washed over Chile.

But in recent years, an unforeseen legacy of the dictatorship in Chile has been a reinvigorated student protest culture. University students of today recognize that the power that made their predecessors the target of the regime's repressive force is one that they still wield. They have determined to mobilize against the injustices that continue to plague their society, and particularly the issues that affect them as young people. Many of them are children of those that struggled to confront the dictatorship, and they see a chance to vindicate their parents in a new, globalized climate. They have drawn strength from new, important advances in intersectional activism and see their destinies tied to the uplift of the indigenous populations, working-class members, un- and underemployed sectors, and others. The first awakening came in 2006, with the March of the Penguins protest by secondary school students, so called because of their conspicuous black and white school uniforms, against the privatization of the education system. For two months, students went on strike, occupied buildings, and cultivated a collective community to care for each other as they took turns in their encampments. At one point, the demonstrations incited by the student movement ballooned to nearly one million participants, expanding to accommodate family members, trade unionists, and reformists from other sectors of education. Evoking poignant sensory memories of the not-too-distant dictatorship, their protests were eventually met with tear gas and riot police. Though temporarily quelled, the student protests have continued over the following decade, needling the neoliberal tendencies of Chile's presidential administrations and urging for better quality, access, and equity in educational conditions for Chile's youth. Notably, one of the most vociferous and visible young leaders in the 2011 protests, Camila Vallejo, emerged from the student movement to gain a seat in Congress as a member of the Chilean Communist Party.

Over the course of the twentieth century, clubs and organizations for children and youth in the Americas have shifted in and out of the purview of the state. The global phenomenon of youth organizations, very often orchestrated by political leaders with quite explicit social engineering goals, nevertheless offered new spaces of socialization for young people that resulted in the creation of meaningful cultural generational bonds. In some instances, youth organizations seemed like the perfect laboratories for the top-down construction—and display—of an ideal citizenry as part of nation-building projects. But in other cases, Latin American regimes did not last long enough to reap the intended rewards, and young people inevitably formed ideas, social connections, and political sensibilities of their own, because of or despite the cultural opportunities afforded them through organized social networks.

Children and youth's visibility in such organizations should be read with a critical eye; their participation in a state-sponsored club does not necessarily signal ideological complicity, nor does it guarantee lifelong adhesion to a political party or cause. To many young citizens and, in ways often lost to history, their brief affiliation with a social cohort offered a temporary material benefit: a uniform, a photo op, an overnight excursion, a soccer game, a rock concert. Such fleeting perks likely had a lasting impact on young people regardless of the more strategic motives of the ruling political forces.

Notes

1. For more on Latin American youth culture in the twentieth century, see Valeria Manzano, *The Age of Youth in Argentina: Culture, Politics & Sexuality from Perón to Videla* (Chapel Hill: University of North Carolina Press, 2014); Elena Jackson Albarrán, *Seen and Heard*

in Mexico: Children and Revolutionary Cultural Nationalism (Lincoln: University of Nebraska Press, 2015); Mariano Ben Plotkin, *Mañana es San Perón: A Cultural History of Perón's Argentina*, trans. Keith Zahniser (Wilmington, DE: Scholarly Resources, 2003); Denise F. Blum, *Cuban Youth and Revolutionary Values: Educating the New Socialist Citizen* (Austin: University of Texas Press, 2011).
2. *Revista Escolar Panamericana* (Atlanta, GA) 2, no. 7 (April 1934): 3-6.
3. Pan American League, clubes estudiantiles. Archivo General de la Nación (Uruguay), Fondo Ministerio de Instrucción Pública, Año 1939, Caja 357 Carpeta 575.
4. José María Morelos and Joaquim José da Silva Xavier (Tiradentes) were independence heroes of Mexico and Brazil, respectively. Translation by the author. Homenagem do Colegio México do Brasil á Escola Brasil do México, 1940. Archivo Histórico Genaro Estrada de la Secretaría de Relaciones Históricos, III-737-27.
5. *Segunda Conferencia Interamericana de Educación*, vol. 1, *Memoria General, Actas, y Documentos* (Santiago: Imp. Universitaria, 1935): 348-351.
6. U.S. Department of State, "Memorandum by the Counselor of the Department (Kennan) to the Secretary of State," March 29, 1950, in *Foreign Relations of the United States, 1950, 2: The United Nations, The Western Hemisphere*, pp. 598-624 (Washington, DC: GPO, 1976).
7. Ruth and Leonard Greenup, *Revolution Before Breakfast: Argentina, 1941-1946* (Chapel Hill: University of North Carolina Press, 1947): 189-190.
8. *Mundo Peronista* 4, no. 83 (April 1, 1955): 33.
9. Live speech by Fidel Castro at opening ceremonies of the national athletic games, at Havana's Pedro Marrero Stadium, October 22, 1965, Castro Speech Database, available from http://lanic.utexas.edu/la/cb/cuba/castro.html.
10. "'I Didn't Like Castro,' Cuban Athlete Says," *The Miami Herald*, June 15, 1966, p. 20.
11. U.S. Department of State Telegram, American Embassy of Mexico to Secretary of State, September 1968.

Further Reading

Acha, Omar. *Los muchachos peronistas: Orígenes de la Juventud Peronista (1945-1955)*. Buenos Aires: Planeta, 2011.

Albarrán, Elena Jackson. "Boy Scouts Under the Aztec Sun: Mexican Youth and the Transnational Construction of Identity, 1917-1940." In *Transnational Histories of Youth in the Twentieth Century*. Edited by Richard Ivan Jobs and David M. Pomfret, 45-69. London, New York: Palgrave Macmillan, 2015.

Albarrán, Elena Jackson. *Seen and Heard in Mexico: Children and Revolutionary Cultural Nationalism*. Lincoln: University of Nebraska Press, 2015.

Bisso, Andrés. "Ser hoy bueno, mañana mejor. Las conmemoraciones del 'Día' y la 'Semana del Scout' en Argentina (1928-1941)." In *Infancias y juventudes en el siglo XX. Política, instituciones estatales y sociabilidades*. Edited by M. Paula Bontempo and Andrés Bisso, pp. 119-161. Buenos Aires: Teseo Press, 2019.

Blum, Denise F. *Cuban Youth and Revolutionary Values: Educating the New Socialist Citizen*. Austin: University of Texas Press, 2011.

Gould, Jeffrey L. "AHR Forum: Solidarity Under Siege: The Latin American Left, 1968." *American Historical Review* (April 2009): 348-375.

Guerra, Lillian. "Former Slum Dwellers, the Communist Youth, and the Lewis Project in Cuba, 1969–1971." *Cuban Studies* 43 (2015): 67–89.

Manzano, Valeria. *The Age of Youth in Argentina: Culture, Politics & Sexuality from Perón to Videla*. Chapel Hill: University of North Carolina Press, 2014.

Pettavino, Paula J., and Geralyn Pye. *Sport in Cuba: The Diamond in the Rough*. Pittsburgh: University of Pittsburgh Press, 1994.

Plotkin, Mariano Ben. *Mañana es San Perón: A Cultural History of Perón's Argentina*. Translated by Keith Zahniser. Wilmington, DE: Scholarly Resources, 2003.

Rojas Flores, Jorge. *Los Boy Scouts en Chile, 1909–1953*. Santiago: Dirección de Bibliotecas, Archivos, y Museos, 2006.

Stepan, Nancy Leys. *The Hour of Eugenics: Race, Gender, and Nation in Latin America*. Ithaca: Cornell University Press, 1991.

CHAPTER 15

....

YOUTH AND CONSUMER CULTURE

Entrepreneurial Consumption

....

ELIZABETH CHIN

CONSUMPTION, for youth globally, has emerged as a deeply important arena of identity making, communication, experience, and participation in society more broadly. Throughout the twentieth century, youth in Western, educated, industrialized, rich, and democratic (WEIRD) populations have become increasingly defined by their status as consumers. More than lifestyle and brand loyalty, consumption has become, as Livermon argues, "one of the primary vectors through which participation, citizenship, and human dignity are forged in a contemporary globalizing world."[1] Meanwhile, neoliberal economic policy has shrunk government safety nets, reduced investment in education, and given birth to the so-called gig economy. These conditions have expanded and intensified the imperative that people become entrepreneurs, curating an identity that is part mission, part worldview, and part personality. This pressure to create an entrepreneurial self operates as forcefully among the economic elites as it does among the world's poor. The peculiar conjuncture of consumer culture with the entrepreneurial self is perhaps especially evident among youth and has reshaped youth consumer cultures across the board. Youth have been redefined nearly exclusively as consumers in WEIRD contexts, simultaneously subjected to pressures and demands to perform entrepreneurial selfhood for nearly the whole of their lives. Through specific case studies, some of the contours of what might be called "entrepreneurial consumer culture" emerge: the highly gendered entrepreneurial consumer culture evident in the shopping, beauty-focused YouTube channels and Instagram feeds of female youth in WEIRD contexts; the luxury consumer culture of rich Qatari youth; and the entrepreneurial scrappiness of poor rural Haitians and poor slum-dwelling Africans as they create fashion and fashionability in a context where virtually everything they buy is from the global trade in secondhand goods.

As consumption becomes the primary vector through which both citizenship and identity are funneled, it has become increasingly important to every aspect of daily living. Discussing "consumer lives" rather than "consumer cultures" is a way of recognizing the centrality of consumption for youth. In recent decades, as consumption has become an extraordinarily powerful social force of its own, identity and even social citizenship are increasingly consumption based, and it is increasingly difficult to draw clear lines between branding, marketing, labor, production, and consumption. Consumption, then, is not just about fashion and beauty; schooling, migration, and the transition to adulthood are, increasingly, also characterized by consumer pressures and entrepreneurial strategies. Furthermore, consumer culture has never been relevant only for those with economic resources. Poverty and immiseration are deeply bound with consumption.

The twentieth century saw the transformation of young people into economic and cultural consumers nearly exclusively, a trend that was especially dominant in WEIRD contexts and among the middle classes and economic elites. The institution of labor laws, establishment of compulsory schooling, and growth of media helped lay the ground for distinctive youth cultures of consumption. Often associated with the urban, the modern, and the rejection of "tradition," youth consumer practices and cultures have often been framed as threats to the larger (and older) milieu. Any number of youth consumer waves have been thought by at least some to presage the end of the world as "we" know it: rock and roll, comic books, the bikini, punk. I want to pay attention to the ways in which consumption is newly inflected for Euro-American youth while also avoiding presenting their worlds as constituting the world in its entirety. Consumption works, in part, by commodifying a thing, opening it up to becoming a product for sale. What and how youth consume, for their part, have become embedded in their sense of self and identity making, processes that take shape in specific cultural and historical contexts that bring them to life.

WEIRD Consumers

A quick tracing of Barbie's place in the world of youth consumption helps to illustrate key transformations in the consumer context in which youth enact consumption in WEIRD sites. Since her inception Barbie has been a model for how to consume—providing narratives and accessories for various kinds of idealized, "dream house" living based on a post-WWII suburban, U.S. model—and a medium through which children and youth exercise consumption. Yet, youth are hardly automatons, and their consumer lives often take up Barbie in off-kilter ways. Dilemmas around class, race, and sexuality, while overtly skirted (so to speak) in Barbie's world, have frequently been subjects of intense scrutiny in youth consumer lives.

The first Barbie television advertisement aired in 1959. The commercial was ground-breaking because it directly addressed young consumers, the first televised advertisement to take this strategy. The Barbie doll was originally aimed at twelve-year-old girls, but by the 1980s, twelve-year-old girls were classed as "tweens" and no longer Barbie's target market: both young people themselves and their engagement with consumption had changed markedly in this time. In the early 2000s, Barbie was briefly upstaged by Bratz, an "urban" (read ethnically diverse and hip) fashion doll line. Bratz, for their part, sought to cash in on the burgeoning youth consumer scene centering around hip-hop music, fashion, and lifestyle. Today, some fifteen years after the introduction of YouTube, the greatest threat to Barbie is not another doll. Barbie's previous threats have come from dolls of similar size and shape, but today Barbie is facing off with a toy where the doll is not the point at all. The L.O.L. Surprise! line of toys was created to tap into the popularity of unboxing, a practice that was birthed in the world of social media. The arc of Barbie's history thus covers the advent of treating youth themselves as consumers, running straight through to today's transformations of youth into consumers fashioning entrepreneurial selves. Youth consumer culture and social media have become deeply entwined, as seen in aspects of entrepreneurial consumption among female youth in WEIRD contexts.

In the realm of entrepreneurial consumption, female youth overwhelmingly focus on fashion, beauty, and shopping, while males dominate in the spheres of gaming, electronics reviews, and car reviews. In a recent *New York Times* article focused on young women and their fashion choices, each discussed the ways in which their curated self-presentation on their Instagram feeds interacted with their decisions of what to wear. Their day-to-day sartorial choices are managed with an eye toward how they will be consumed by imagined and real social media audiences. This, in turn, is facilitated by the speed and low prices achieved in current instantiations of fast fashion. Mia Grantham, one interviewee, is an English high school student who has about fifteen hundred Instagram followers. She has an Instagram routine where the first post of an outfit is a photo she takes in her bedroom. Later she posts pictures of herself in that outfit while she is out with friends. This curated presentation of self is fueled by entrepreneurial consumption—strategies aimed at pleasing followers, amassing views, and collecting likes. Her feed is carefully crafted to show her fashion style and savvy, while also serving as a model for her followers. In the marketing world, she would be categorized as a nanoinfluencer, that is, someone with between one thousand and ten thousand followers. She said: "I wouldn't really want someone seeing me in a dress more than once. People might think I didn't have style if I wore the same thing over and over. Style is about changing for whatever the situation you are in and for different events."[2] The degree to which this version of her consumer life is specifically created as a commodity that must conform to particular formats is evident in that she also has a private Instagram that allows her to be more "real."

Regardless of the number of followers, the youth curating these types of feeds must engage in what Duffy and Hund call "commodification through intimacy," forging relationships with their followers that conform to expectations that girls be nice.[3] Female youth must present as feminized nice girl on the one hand, and masculinized entrepreneurial self on the other. In creating self as brand this version of entrepreneurial self requires deployment of feminized emotional affect designed to create emotional connections with followers mixed with more masculine-coded entrepreneurial strategies. Shopping for these youth involves brick-and-mortar stores less and less. They have their preferred sites and apps and are up front about wanting to spend as little as possible, especially since they plan to wear most items only a very few times. They are savvy about cycling through clothes, selling what they no longer want on sites like Depop so they can earn money to buy other things. Part of what makes youth consumption in these spaces novel is the elision and melding of consumption, work, and merchandising: for the most successful vloggers, being a consumer is a job, and your brand is your identity. But even for those like Mia who have relatively few followers and are not (yet) working to monetize their feeds, techniques of the entrepreneurial self are prominent in shaping their consumer lives even as their consumer lives shape their living more generally. Developing consistent and identifiable visual style for photos, fashion, and makeup requires a nonstop, self-conscious curation and presentation of a carefully managed version of the self. The aim of all this work is often voiced as "doing what you love," intimating that this isn't work at all; it's vocation.

This theme of doing what you love is common, as well, among many self-identified nerds, geeks, and cosplay fans where an "increasing number of fans have come to view social media as something more than just as a way to entertain themselves, engage with brands, and communicate with other consumers."[4] Like the young women discussed earlier, these people also work to get their channels up and running, posting blog entries and DIY videos, and selling things on Etsy; the promise is that by monetizing what was once a hobby, they might be able to end up "doing what they love." The commonality across these interest areas is the forwarding of an entrepreneurial self, coupled with blurring and blending between consumption and production, leisure and work, self and brand.

This particular blend of consumption and entrepreneurialism may be generationally distinct, arising at least in part from the precarity experienced by many youth in the wake of the great recession that began in 2008. Faced with increasingly insecure working situations, the dream among this specific group of geeks, nerds, and cosplay aficionados is that their consumer passions might be fruitfully refashioned as a way to make a living. "Doing what you love" becomes shorthand for twenty-first-century entrepreneurial consumption. The expansion of the imperative to be entrepreneurial in an existential way shows up in diverse contexts. An entrepreneurial mindset is increasingly associated with a bright future both for the individual and the economy.

This mindset, in turn, is evidenced in qualities like happiness, non-depressiveness, and gratefulness, and these are abundantly evident in the feeds and comment sections of hosts of influencers, from the nano to the mega.[5] For these youth, consumption is about demonstrating and performing aspects of the entrepreneurial self, connecting consumer culture and neoliberal capitalism in a never-ending flow like a mobius strip.

For youth like Mia, consumption becomes a project—part of the technology of what Brockling calls "the entrepreneurial self"—an instantiation of the self that has emerged out of the neoliberal moment and is based on innovation, happiness, and risk-taking. In genres like haul videos, where (mostly) young women show off their shopping acumen by scoring good deals on clothes and makeup at MAC, Abercrombie, and Victoria's Secret—there is also a subgenre enthusiastically focused on the Dollar Store—putting their consumption out for audiences is a way to entrepreneurialize their consumption.

Unlike many fashion bloggers who buy online, video haulers are all about brick and mortar. Here, shopping savvy is more important than showing style and lifestyle. Yet creating self-as-brand remains just as important, and developing a signature visual style and presentation persona and creating relationships with an audience are crucial to success. Typically, items come from MAC, Victoria's Secret, Forever 21, and Abercrombie, among others. By one estimate, by 2011 more than 250,000 of these videos had been uploaded to YouTube.[6] Beauty vlogs, too, are consumption oriented, although not usually focused on shopping. Featuring makeup tutorials and reviews of products, beauty blogs offer advice, demonstrate techniques, and make recommendations. On the one hand, makers of haul videos and beauty vlogs are putting their consumption on display, sharing it with others. On the other hand, there may well be money-making aspects to the video or channel: product placement and monetization of views are just two ways a vlogger can generate income. In addition, as a vlogger moves up the influencer ranks from nano to mega, they may generate a host of other relationships with sponsors, be sent free merchandise, and become a celebrity in their own right.

Youth, Consumption, and Malls

In the United States, malls have long been sites for youth consumption and identity making. Indeed, season three of the series "Stranger Things"—popular among contemporary youth—celebrates U.S. suburban youth mall culture of the 1980s. Today, however, U.S. covered malls are a dying breed. Even as malls are losing cachet in the United States, they are emerging as important sites of youth culture and identity in the Middle East, Asia, Africa, and Latin America, where they signify modernity and middle-classness, among other things. To provide a sense of the scale and rapidness of change, in 1999, there were three malls in India. By 2006 there were 220, and by 2015 that original number was estimated to have increased a hundredfold to more than 700. The construction of new malls in Africa has been similarly dramatic. This explosive growth is one indicator of huge social and economic changes that have transformed the lives of millions of youth rising into global middle classes. Simultaneously, omnipresent aid and development organizations are working to compel neoliberal selfhood from youth, specifically focusing on entrepreneurship. The new catchphrase of the United States Agency for International Development (USAID) is the "Journey to Self-Reliance," snappily abbreviated as "J2SR."

This push for self-reliance is confounded in a place like Qatar, home to the world's largest proportion of millionaire households. Qatari youth are, on the whole, quite wealthy: the average household income is $129,000 a year—double that of Saudi Arabia. Qatari adults have the world's lowest rate of economic activity, and when they do work, they overwhelmingly choose to participate in the public sector—that is, well-paid jobs exclusively available to Qataris in government, education, and other state-supported positions. For Qataris, labor force participation peaks in their mid-thirties, declining steadily thereafter. By their fifties, 20 percent of men have retired, while half of women are not working.[7] The bulk of Qatari youth are thus a vastly privileged, tiny minority who are wealthy enough never to work at all. Yet as Qatar moves to diversify its economy, it is investing huge amounts of resources in spurring the entrepreneurial energies of its youth, resulting in a burgeoning cohort who wield entrepreneurial consumption with a deft swipe of the touch screen.

Just as Coca-Cola has many local meanings, youth cultures of consumption are local and specific even as they are simultaneously products of global processes. In Qatar, malls are not typically middle-class spaces, but sites of extraordinary luxury. The Qatari American artist Sophia Al-Maria coined the term "Gulf futurism" as a way to capture the specific oddities of massive national oil wealth found in the Gulf that materialized as spectacular collective consumption in the form of ever-higher skyscrapers and ever-larger shopping malls.[8] Here, the neoliberal moment, rooted in enormous oil wealth, means endless free electricity, and the sense of abundance so great that in one of the world's hottest geographic locations, they even air-condition outdoor spaces.

Qatar has urbanized at a stratospheric rate, and the effects on youth have been dramatic, particularly as formerly nomadic tribes have moved cityward. Lila Abu-Lughod describes how, in the 1980s, young Bedouin women in Egypt were using notions of romance gleaned from cosmopolitan Egyptian soap operas as a way to resist arranged marriages to men they found unappealing, often because they were much older.[9] These romantic fantasies were shaped in part through watching Egyptian soap operas and materialized in underwear and lingerie, consumer objects signifying both urban sophistication and conjugal romance—neither of which were on offer in traditional marriages. Yet as Abu-Lughod points out, these love marriages were hardly an improvement. Moving to the city, these women were separated from their families and no longer had access to the freedom of roaming in expansive desert geographies.

Hemmed in by strict rules of purdah, their worlds shrank to the confines of their apartments. These young Bedouin women may have escaped being imprisoned in an unwanted marriage only to find themselves virtually imprisoned in urban homes.

This experience of living indoors takes on a different valence for today's Qatari youth, for whom tribe as both kinship and social sphere remain deeply powerful, shaping nearly the entirety of their social lives—at least offline. Qatari society is largely sex segregated, and, in addition, Qataris tend not to mix with noncitizen residents. Only Qataris may be citizens of Qatar, and citizens are a small minority of the overall population: of 2.3 million only 11.6 percent of the country is Qatari.[10] Together this results in an experience for youth where the known world is accessed through screens, social media, and video games, and where life is lived almost entirely indoors. The intensely tribal and family-focused nature of daily life for Qataris also renders their consumption less materialistic—that is, servicing individual, hedonistic goals—than it is socially embedded, with experiential aspects such as showing off, comparing what to buy, and when and how to show it.[11] The deeply social, outwardly focused aspect of youth consumption is captured in comments by one of Qatar's first fashion bloggers, Anum Bashir:

> It's such an affluent part of the world and purchasing power is so immensely high. There is a very outwardly competitive culture—if you're showing up to a dinner party and your girlfriend happens to be wearing a $1,200 pair of Manolo Blahnik slingbacks, there's this culture of, "Oh I need to go out tomorrow and buy two pairs of them."[12]

The demands of living in a sex-segregated society where family is ever present shape Qatari youth consumer lives in unique ways. Malls are especially important. The Chaloub Group, a luxury-oriented marketing and retail firm specializing in the Middle East, describes shopping malls as

> a pillar of social life, serving as "social clubs," especially for the young—being one of the few socially acceptable places for even limited mingling between the sexes. Moreover, the range of alternative leisure activities is limited and the harsh climate dictates that, for several months of the year, life is spent indoors."[13]

Destination malls in Qatar take their cues from Las Vegas and theme park designs. The Villagio, which contains 120,000 square feet of retail space, features a Venetian theme, complete with canals, bridges, and gondola rides. Not accidentally, the inside of the mall is designed as an outdoor environment, with streetscapes, streetlights, and blue sky with puffy clouds painted on the ceiling overhead.

As the Chaloub report notes, malls are one of the few spaces where young people can potentially "mingle" with those of the opposite sex. Al-Maria describes groups of same-sex youth surreptitiously passing phone numbers to one another in the mall, finding boyfriends or girlfriends who they later build relationships with through social media, as they have virtually no opportunities to physically meet. With malls as the primary public spaces available to them, this is where youth also might stage resistance to cultural norms. She describes groups of girls called "boyas" who wear men's Rolexes, cologne, and shorts beneath their abayas. In challenging gender norms through these fashion choices, boyas run serious risks; being sent to residential mental health treatment centers is one very possible result.

Qatari youth consumption is deeply influenced by cultural ideas of modesty: many popular female bloggers run anonymous feeds, featuring selfies where their faces are obscured or covered over, managing to be public while retaining appropriate feminine privacy. This sense of propriety extends so far that many youth cannot wear their on-trend fashion buys while they remain in their own country. As one manager of a luxury store noted,

> They might not really get the chance to dress up in the latest fashion/trends here in Qatar as they are usually obliged to wear the traditional dress, however they are eager to purchase the fashionable clothes to wear them when they travel; and Qataris generally speaking travel a lot.[14]

Imagine having to leave the country in order to wear your new outfit! While there is virtually no research on Qatari youth subcultures, in Iran Pardis Mahdavi has explored resistant youth sexual and fashion subcultures where engaging in proscribed behaviors including wearing revealing clothes, drinking liquor, and eating pork are forms of embodied challenge to state and generational power.[15] There are at least hints that among some Qatari youth similar consumer-based resistance is afoot.

If, for Qatari youth, luxury consumption is a display of citizenship and belonging, for the vast numbers of immigrant youth in Qatar, consumption is an equally powerful field through which a lack of citizenship is enacted and enforced. In Qatar immigrant youth are denied legal citizenship and, similarly, are virtually quarantined inside specific geographic areas. Living in geographically adjacent spaces, the consumer worlds of citizen versus immigrant youth are vastly different. If the neoliberal moment compels entrepreneurship from wealthy Qatari youth, it simultaneously produces poor, immigrant youth who have no access to the air-conditioned dream spaces described by Al-Maria; they will likely never enter the consumption cathedrals frequented by their Qatari citizen counterparts. In Qatar, class, citizenship, and consumption are layered upon each other in particularly overt and material ways. Upscale malls are available to an internationally and culturally diverse range of people; they are not, however, places where the majority of Qatar's population, who are low-paid, noncitizen guest workers, may expect to enter. Thus, the particular sort of consumer citizenship available in malls is differentially accessed depending on class and prestige. Furthermore, for immigrant youth, their immigration is the embodiment of their entrepreneurial energies. Their conditions of employment bind them to one specific employer, who usually holds their passport. Scraping their wages together to send remittances home that allow their families to consume at basic levels, these youth consume very little on their own behalf. Instead, they are consumed by their employers and facilitate the consumption of those whom they have left behind.

Even as malls have come to serve as nearly universal symbols for certain kinds of youth consumer culture, the vast majority of the world's youth may never set foot in a mall. However, this does not mean that they are not deeply caught up in consumer culture. We will examine next the ways in which rural Haitian youth and urban African youth from Côte d'Ivoire, Senegal, and Uganda dress fashionably, shop, and create consumer culture–based identities.

Finding Fashion

The fashion and shopping sensibilities of poor youth in Africa and Haiti illuminate the diverse ways that youth consumption takes place beyond the often-studied contexts of WEIRD youth cultures. Shopping, for these youth, involves a set of orientations and practices that are understudied and poorly understood. Like the ultra-luxury consumer cultures of Qatari youth, the consumer lives of the Haitian and African youth are produced by larger economic and social processes that characterize neoliberalism. In recent decades, the global production and discard of everything from clothing to furniture has mushroomed. The forces that have generated fast fashion, with its three-week turnover times, have simultaneously produced an enormous amount of used goods that flow into the global market for secondhand items; research has focused especially on secondhand clothing in Africa, but everything circulates: McDonald's toys, mattresses, underpants, cars, CD players, bedsheets, and the list goes on.

For the majority of Haitian and African youth, consumption rarely—if ever—involves malls or similar consumer dream spaces. Suzanne Scheld argues that in Dakar, "youth clothing practices keep the urban economy in motion and the city hooked into a global economy."[16] Paying attention to the larger, global systems also at work, Scheld emphasizes that overproduction in the North and growing exports from China are instrumental in creating these thriving sites. Thus, the potentials for youth consumption—and in this case, livelihoods as well—are deeply connected to patterns of consumption taking place elsewhere.

Among young men in Côte d'Ivoire, a practice called the "bluff" is central to their consumer identities and their consumer performances. Marginalized, poor, and scrambling for resources, these young men nevertheless wear name brand clothing and periodically host lavish parties where they serve fancy liquor, dance to the latest music, and live large. It's all "bluff," that is, a performance of wealth and conspicuous consumption that they can ill afford. Yet they can ill afford *not* to do the bluff if they are to maintain the web of social relationships necessary for doing daily business. Both these cases show that style is deeply important for poor youth; trends, brands, and quality remain central although the shopping and selection practices used in these contexts necessarily differ from those used in a typical mall space. These youth are discerning consumers, looking for items that fit their criteria for quality, impact, and fit. What is more difficult is finding items that possess all of these qualities together. Being able to dress well means curating relationships with vendors, having a good eye, and more than a dash of luck. And, of course, even within these cultures lies a multitude of variation. "Boy Town," "Coming Town," and "Venants" are just three consumer/cosmopolitan identities Scheld discusses, where Boy Town youth are savvy and urban, Coming Town youth are new to the city, and Venants are very high status and have the money and possessions to show for it. Each group has distinctive dressing patterns, some using their dress to communicate their disdain for others. For example, one group of Coming Town youth purposefully exaggerates their unsophisticated clothes by mismatching and, in so doing, subtly mock cosmopolitan Boy Town youth whose taste for girls and drink Venants view as a lack of correct social and moral values.[17]

The youth I came to know in Kamokwa, a slum in Kampala, Uganda, were savvy shoppers and snappy dressers. I first got to know David, in fact, because he was wearing a very striking pair of red leather shoes, and we struck up a conversation about his style. A student at university, David was always dressed impeccably. He was a member of a Christian group that performed hip-hop dance and music; most of the members had attended university, at least for a time. Just as many now could no longer afford to pay their fees and continue their education. Through the activities of the group they worked, as they said, to "give to the community," advocating for education for girls, following God, and doing good.

One morning David showed up to rehearsal with a tan-colored Coach bag slung over his shoulder. In another context, the fact that the bag was a woman's model might have signaled something faulty with his skills, or perhaps might have marked him as gender fluid. But when secondhand goods arrive in a new context, their former associations are moot. In these new settings, youth refashion items materially and ideologically, making them part of their own identity projects whose meanings are locally relevant, shared, and understood. David was visibly proud of his new bag and showed it off. When I complimented David on it, he offered to take me through Kampala's massive Owino market, saying he knew the best places and how to negotiate good prices. Here, a woman's Coach bag had no bearing on David's masculinity. Instead, its quality and value signaled his ability to spot good merchandise and to bargain well.

David, like many of his university peers, quite often bought a piece of clothing from a vendor and then had a tailor alter it to fit. In the streets near one of Makerere's back entrances, more than a dozen small tailor shops seemed to be perpetually busy. David's button-down shirts always skimmed close to his ribs, crisp and straight; this was achieved by adding darts or seams that also made the shirts' construction even more visually interesting. Time and again what I noticed was that through the work of selecting, adjusting, and even repurposing fashion items, the Ugandan and Haitian youth engaged in complex consumer and identity projects. Here the previous associations of a specific item with one gender or another, or one subculture or another, were irrelevant. In Haiti I have often seen young men wearing what in another setting would be unambiguously identified as a woman's blouse, while in this new context remaining entirely masculine, and without a whiff of gender bending.

If shopping is complex in Uganda, it is even more so in Haiti, which is a nation without a single shopping mall. The only stores selling new clothing are the few upscale boutiques in well-to-do Petionville, a suburb of the capital, Port au Prince. There are a couple of big box stores that sell a few clothing items—though hardly a wide enough selection to create a wardrobe. In the capital individual street vendors do sell new items, usually specializing in a single thing: flip flops, jeans, blankets. By far, however, the vast majority of clothes sold in Haiti are secondhand, and the same holds true for much of the world. Secondhand items in Haiti are called *pèpè*, and for decades *pèpè* have been the primary source of clothes in Haiti. "The clothes come from Miami on ships," said nineteen-year-old Gerard when I asked him to explain *pèpè* to me. *Pèpè* is part of a global system circulating secondhand goods; the Zambian version is discussed in great detail in Karen Hansen's *Salaula*.[18]

When it comes to fashion, Haitian youth—who are tremendously fashion conscious—shop in ways specific to the requirements of the sprawling street or covered markets where most things are sold. In the city, these markets and stalls can be more or less permanent. In rural areas, market sites stand empty except for the one day a week they bustle with activity. When shopping in malls and stores, consumers are met with orderly spaces where items are arranged in ways that are uniform from site to site: like items with like, sizes clearly marked, and examples of potential outfits staged throughout the space and in shop windows. In street markets, there is orderliness of a different sort. The market space itself may be laid out with stalls selling similar things grouped together: an aisle of people selling shoes, for example. Individual stall proprietors usually meticulously organize their wares, perhaps putting their items on racks, displays, or hangers. Because the vast majority of clothing items are secondhand, vendors have no way to provide a single item in a range of sizes; each item is probably unique among their offerings. That pair of sneakers you love is not available in a larger size; the pair that fits might not be the style you were hoping for. Here, youth certainly do not have the luxury of deciding to wear an item once and then discard it. On the upside, many of the items available to them in the secondhand market may be virtually new. Youth in these settings remain dedicated to style and are knowledgeable about brands, but they do not expect to find everything they want at one location or count on having a very specific item in mind and being able to find it.

The village of Matènwa lies on the island of La Gonave, itself situated in the bay of Port au Prince. Reaching Matènwa requires an hour-long trip up the coast from Port au Prince to the port at Carries to catch a ferry that takes about two hours to reach the island. Once there the trip to the village takes an hour or more along rocky, unpaved mountain roads. The rural village of Matènwa, Haiti, could be described as hugely isolated; some youth and adults have never left the island, whose population is about eighty thousand. Yet their fashion is coherent and up to date. While it takes cues from Internet trends or what's hot in Port au Prince, youths' sense of style is also very much their own. Newly adolescent boys wear sunglasses, T-shirts, and bandanas around their foreheads or wrists. In the evening they gather beneath the village's single streetlight, self-consciously trying out confident postures as they take selfies or watch others passing by. Older youth favor slim pants that hug their legs all the way down to the ankle; everything is always spic and span, wrinkle free, and color coordinated head to toe. For example, in a recent Facebook post, Gerard, a nineteen-year-old from Matènwa, showed a photo of himself wearing a T-shirt and jeans, perched atop a motorcycle. His outfit is primarily in colors of red and blue, the colors of Haiti's flag. This photo—like many in Gerard's feed—shows a mix of hope, aspiration, and a fierce love for Haiti.

Gerard himself does not have a motorcycle, and as happens so often, the photo is one showing imagined possibility: the motorcycle looks as if it is his. In the years since the 2010 earthquake, inexpensive Chinese motorcycles have become a major consumer item for Haiti's young men, who then personalize and decorate their machines with colorful zip ties and carefully applied decals, often of a Nike swoosh or an Air Jordan logo. Not only do motorcycles provide mobility, but they are also an income source. Providing rides is one of the few ways young men can earn money on the island, other than peasant farming—an increasingly untenable prospect as Haiti experiences the ravages of climate change. The motorcycles cost perhaps $300 new, an amount Gerard is never likely to see given that the gross national income per capita sits at about $800. A high school graduate, Gerard would like to go to university to study computer science, but his family cannot afford the $450 annual tuition, nor the $350 per month it would cost him for room and board in Port au Prince.

When I chatted with him about his outfit, Gerard told me that he chose the T-shirt primarily because the design incorporates the blue and red that are the colors of Haiti's flag. His shoes, red with blue laces, were a big splurge at 4,000 Haitian gourdes, about $41. Because LaGonave is not on the Haitian mainland, and because nearly everything even in Port au Prince is imported, the cost of nearly everything is inflated. Contrasted with a long set of narratives about the irresponsibility of youth who are willing to spend extraordinary amounts of money for sneakers, Gerard's splurge on these sneakers must be read in connection with his deep dedication to Haiti. All Haitians, no matter how rural or isolated, are aware of Haiti's global reputation for chaos and poverty. Like a great many Haitians, Gerard is profoundly proud of Haiti and its history. Furthermore, unlike so many from his village, he wants to remain in Haiti and work to make it better. His three older siblings have left for Chile, and his fifteen-year-old younger sister is already talking about joining them. But Gerard plans to stay.

YOUTH CONSUMERS, MIGRATION, AND ENTREPRENEURIAL SELVES

In WEIRD contexts, the development of the entrepreneurial self is exemplified in youth creating business opportunities for themselves—often through selling to other youth. For youth like Gerard and his siblings, this consumer-oriented entrepreneurialism very often takes the form of migration. Although Gerard has no plans to leave Haiti, his three older siblings are all now in Chile, sending money to their mother and the four children who still live at home. It is difficult in such a context to speak of youth consumer culture for a variety of reasons. One important reason is that our understanding of distinctive youth consumer cultures tends to assume a kind of autonomous self-interest that does not characterize the deeply family-invested lives of youth like those from Matènwa (and, as we have seen, it likely is equally awkward to apply it to rich Qatari youth).

Migration is often undertaken to get "a better life," itself understood as the ability to consume more and better things ranging from social space to education, clothing, and food. The need or desire to achieve a better standard of living fuels a significant portion of global youth migration. During my stay in Haiti in summer 2019, my seventeen-year-old goddaughter Charlene spent at least two hours each night on WhatsApp, talking to her boyfriend, who has migrated to Brazil. Meanwhile, Charlene's mother sat on the other side of the courtyard, talking to Charlene's father, who has been in Chile for the past two years. Estimates put the number of migrant youth at about thirty million globally.[19] Though data detailing precise estimates by age are absent in most low- and middle-income countries, those younger than eighteen years old represent approximately one-fourth of all migrants, and the proportion of youth as migrants is increasing. WhatsApp, owned by Facebook, has been hugely important in facilitating migration itself, and in allowing migrants to communicate with their loved ones. Thus, migration, consumption, and social media have become increasingly entwined.[20]

Youth are not just beneficiaries of migration but quite often, like Shella's boyfriend, are themselves migrants. In Matènwa, boys as young as seventeen have left to seek work in another country; their goal and responsibility goes well beyond self-support: they are sent, often with hefty investment by a family network, so that they might work and send money home. With Shella's family, remittances from abroad have supported education, the construction of houses, and the accumulation of goods. Remittances, in fact, are a major element of Haiti's economic picture, accounting for 29 percent of GDP.[21]

Remittances often pay for schooling, uniforms, and books; youth migrants often are paying for their younger siblings to be educated. Large numbers of Haitian youth are internal migrants who serve as consumer items even as their migration is spurred by the hope of consuming education. As young as three or four years old, these internal migrants, called *restavèk*, live with better-off families and do unpaid household labor in exchange for food and—hopefully—education. The lives of *restavèk* are often shockingly miserable but speak to the terrible poverty faced by their natal families, who too often face the choice of watching their children die or sending them into virtual slavery in the hopes that they might live. For the families that make use of *restavèk*, their presence is a kind of conspicuous consumption that demonstrates that the home where they live is at least not so poor that they cannot have any domestic help at all.[22]

Even as headlines focus on transnational migration that leaves African migrants piling up in Lampedusa, or at Mexico's border with the United States, it is important to remember that across Africa, the majority of migration is internal rather than external. Recalling Scheld's ethnography in Dakar, the rural youth who has become Town Boy must consume in particular ways in order to negotiate social networks. Meanwhile, his family at home expects remittances and frequently also expects him to gift them prestige items such as televisions. The entrepreneurial energies of Town Boy, then, must be demonstrated and validated by their ability to provide consumption opportunities for others. This dilemma illustrates the way in which the status of "youth" is not just chronological, but also relational. While UNICEF, for instance, defines youth in Africa as anyone up to age thirty, in many African communities, unmarried men of any age are not socially considered men in one of the ways deemed most important.

In Uganda, when I accompanied twenty-three-year-old Mike to his home village in Tororo, I got a taste of the consumer pressures faced by these migrant youth. Mike had come to Kampala several years before and, like many similar youths, was working as a security guard, a job that barely paid enough for him to eat and pay the rent on an 8-by-8-foot room he shared with his best friend. Despite being constantly broke, any visit home required Mike to bring gifts from the city. Mike could ill afford these purchases: his landlord had recently locked him out of his room because he was behind on the rent. Because this visit had been arranged for my benefit, I bought all the staples. In Kampala, where prices were lower than in Tororo, we had already bought rice, soap, Maggi, and sugar. After arriving in Tororo city, we bought white bread, fresh and soft, to complete the offerings. But it was Mike who distributed them when we arrived in his father's compound. What was crucial for Mike, and for any similar migrant, was the show of plenty, the appearance of success. In this way, these consumption moments have a certain similarity to the "bluff" performed by youth in Côte d'Ivoire. Migrant youth must maintain a sheen of urban sophistication and achievement; like other youths I knew in Uganda, Mike's Facebook account often featured photos of himself sitting at a desk or working on a computer—snaps staged late at night when offices were unoccupied and he could play the businessman.

Mike was in a situation faced by millions of heterosexual, male African youth: at an age when the obvious next step was marriage and the transition out of youthful status and into the life of an adult man, he was too poor to afford the cloth, staples, cows, and cash required by the introduction ceremony and bride price. This dilemma illustrates the intensely relational aspect of being a youth. Bureaucratic definitions of youth tend to privilege chronological age as the primary defining factor, yet as scholars have shown in the case of children and childhoods, a wide range of definitions is possible along lines of physical, social, or psychological development; passage through ritual; relationship status; etc. Chronological definitions are particularly useful in questions of crime and punishment, immigration, and rights, all of which are negotiated through complex state and national webs of policy and practice. It should be remembered, however, that such definitions are hardly universally relevant or meaningful.

In the case of Nigeria, the effects of being cut off from access to proper adult status may well feed into what she calls the "fetishization of violence" and youth extremism among male youth.[23] Among poor KwaZulu youth, the idealization of "farm girls" who have simple wants allows them to evade the pressures of town girls whose own ideas of romance are fueled by dreams of middle-class consumption.[24]

Internal migration like Mike's tends to consist of rural youth heading toward larger towns and cities. In contrast, international migration increasingly includes educational migration as a consumer and entrepreneurial strategy. Here, education itself is a consumer item while also serving as a means toward upward mobility and/or the ability to live abroad permanently. Radically different from shopping, with its impulse buys and Black Friday sales, consuming education is a long process that takes years and even decades to complete. Furthermore, when youth are engaged as migratory education consumers, they are nearly always acting on behalf of larger family units rather than as individuals. In China, young women migrate away from rural areas in numbers equal to men, yet, disproportionately, they migrate in order to pay a sibling's tuition.[25] The more well-to-do peers of these Chinese women can afford to go overseas to study, their families paying out of pocket for the full cost of tuition, room, and board that can amount to nearly $100,000 per year at top-priced institutions. Such education-oriented migration flows have many circuits and are not necessarily focused on the United States and Europe. Seeking to gain an edge in language and cultural competence, foreign students are leaving home younger and younger: in 2016 nearly 78,000 foreign students were enrolled in U.S. high schools, and 350,000 in U.S. colleges and universities.[26] Foreign-born individuals who obtain U.S. degree credentials are particularly likely to remain in the United States. Forty-five percent of foreign student graduates extend their visas to work in the same metropolitan area as their college or university. A degree from an American college or university is a consumer good with huge potential benefits aside from the obvious one of gainful employment.

Youth Consumption and Context

Anthropologists are trained to situate the specificity of culture within a broader understanding of human variability in its fullest scope. The easily accessed experiences of youth in United States and WEIRD contexts are juxtaposed with the consumer experiences of wealthy Qataris, poor Haitian youth, and poor African youth to illustrate some of the varying ways that consumption is undertaken in specific places, by specific people. In the consumer field more generally, the consumer lives of both the wealthy and the poor continue to be neglected. Their lives are worth understanding both in their own right and because any understanding that focuses on that which is most easily accessible is partial. Even within the United States and Europe, youth consumption offers nearly endless possibilities for consideration, a comprehensive view of which cannot be offered here.

The neoliberal moment, with its associated imperative for individual, entrepreneurial selfhood, has shaped youth consumption in a variety of ways. Youth in rural Haiti and urban Africa signal their personal and political aspirations through individual consumption, even as they migrate to facilitate the education of siblings, or to operate as a consumer vector for larger family networks. The nexus of family is equally foundational for wealthy Qatari youth whose consumption of extravagant, name-brand items is met with pressures to create entrepreneurially energetic selves that can move the Qatari economy into ever-greater expansion.

Globally, youth are consumers and consumed, at once freed and constrained by the identities consumption might afford them. The contexts in which their consumer selves are activated are equally complex and multifaceted, full of possibility and contradiction.

Notes

1. Xavier Livermon, "'Si-Ghetto Fabulous' ('We Are Ghetto Fabulous'): Kwaito Musical Performance and Consumption in Post-Apartheid South Africa," *Black Music Research Journal* 34, no. 2 (2014): 286, https://doi.org/10.5406/blacmusiresej.34.2.0285.
2. Elizabeth Paton, Taylor Lorenz, and Isabella Kwai, "What Do Gen Z Shoppers Want? A Cute, Cheap Outfit That Looks Great on Instagram," *The New York Times*, December 17, 2019, Style section, https://www.nytimes.com/2019/12/17/style/fast-fashion-gen-z.html.
3. Brooke Erin Duffy and Emily Hund, "'Having It All' on Social Media: Entrepreneurial Femininity and Self-Branding Among Fashion Bloggers," *Social Media + Society* 1, no. 2 (July 1, 2015): 1–11, https://doi.org/10.1177/2056305115604337; Laura Jeffries, "The Revolution Will Be Soooo Cute: YouTube 'Hauls' and the Voice of Young Female Consumers," *Studies in Popular Culture* 33, no. 2 (2011): 59–75.
4. Matthew Hale, "An Expression of Precarity: American Youth, the Creative Industries, and the Monetization of Leisure" (PhD diss., University of Indiana, 2018), 6.
5. Hanna-Mari Ikonen and Minna Nikunen, "Young Adults and the Tuning of the Entrepreneurial Mindset in Neoliberal Capitalism," *Journal of Youth Studies* 22, no. 6 (July 3, 2019): 824–838.
6. Jeffries, "The Revolution Will Be Soooo Cute," 59.
7. Philippe Fargues, "Immigration vs. Population in the Gulf," in *The Gulf Monarchies Beyond the Arab Spring: Changes and Challenges*, ed. Luigi Narbone and Martin Lestra (Florence: European University Institute, 2015), 11–17.
8. "Al Qadiri & Al-Maria on Gulf Futurism," *Dazed*, November 14, 2012, https://www.dazeddigital.com/music/article/15037/1/al-qadiri-al-maria-on-gulf-futurism; Bruce Sterling, "Gulf Futurism," *Wired*, November 11, 2012, https://www.wired.com/2012/11/gulf-futurism/.
9. Lila Abu-Lughod, "The Romance of Resistance: Tracing Transformations of Power Through Bedouin Women," *American Ethnologist* 17, no. 1 (1990): 41–55.
10. CIA, "The World Factbook," 2015. (New York: Skyhorse Publishing.)
11. Dalia Abdelrahman Farrag, "The Young Luxury Consumer in Qatar," *Young Consumers* 18, no. 4 (January 1, 2017): 393–407, https://doi.org/10.1108/YC-06-2017-00702.

12. Janelle Okwodu, "Meet the Art Insider Turned Blogger Changing the Fashion Conversation in the Middle East," *Vogue*, September 5, 2018, https://www.vogue.com/vogueworld/article/anum-bashir-desert-mannequin-fashion-in-dubai; Farrag, "The Young Luxury Consumer in Qatar."
13. Chaloub Group, "Luxury in the Middle East: An Easy Sell?" 2013, 10. https://chalhoubgroup.com/chalhoub-api/uploads/pdf/Chalhoub_Group_White_Paper_2013_English.pdf
14. Farrag, "The Young Luxury Consumer in Qatar," 398.
15. Pardis Mahdavi, *Passionate Uprisings: Iran's Sexual Revolution* (Stanford, CA: Stanford University Press, 2008).
16. Suzanne Scheld, "Youth Cosmopolitanism: Clothing, the City and Globalization in Dakar, Senegal," *City & Society* 19, no. 2 (2007): 233, https://doi.org/10.1525/city.2007.19.2.232.
17. Sasha Newell, *The Modernity Bluff: Crime, Consumption, and Citizenship in Côte d'Ivoire* (Chicago: University of Chicago Press, 2012).
18. Karen Tranberg Hansen, *Salaula: The World of Secondhand Clothing in Zambia* (Chicago: University of Chicago Press, 2000).
19. Ona Gražina Rakauskienė and Olga Ranceva, "Youth Unemployment and Emigration Trends," *MRU Repository*, March 18, 2015, https://repository.mruni.eu/handle/007/13711.
20. Jessica Heckert, "New Perspective on Youth Migration: Motives and Family Investment Patterns," *Demographic Research* 33 (2015): 765–800; Rianne Dekker, Godfried Engbersen, Hanna Vonk, and Janine Klaver, "Smart Refugees: How Syrian Asylum Migrants Use Social Media Information in Migration Decision-Making," *Social Media + Society* 4, no. 1 (January 1, 2018): 2056305118764439, https://doi.org/10.1177/2056305118764439.
21. "Haiti - Economy: Impacts of Remittances from Diaspora on the National Economy - HaitiLibre.Com: Haiti News 7/7," *Haiti Libre*, accessed December 3, 2017, http://www.haitilibre.com/en/news-20563-haiti-economy-impacts-of-remittances-from-diaspora-on-the-national-economy.html.
22. Jean-Robert Cadet, *Restavek: From Haitian Slave Child to Middle Class American* (Austin: University of Texas Press, 1998).
23. Caroline Ifeka, "Youth Cultures & the Fetishization of Violence in Nigeria," *Review of African Political Economy* 33, no. 110 (2006): 721–736.
24. Deevia Bhana and Rob Pattman, "'Girls Want Money, Boys Want Virgins': The Materiality of Love Amongst South African Township Youth in the Context of HIV and AIDS," *Culture, Health & Sexuality* 13, no. 8 (September 1, 2011): 961–972, https://doi.org/10.1080/13691058.2011.576770.
25. Yi-Lin Chiang, Emily Hannum, and Grace Kao, "It's Not Just About the Money: Gender and Youth Migration from Rural China," *Chinese Sociological Review* 47, no. 2 (April 3, 2015): 177–201, https://doi.org/10.1080/21620555.2014.990328.
26. "China Sends Most International Students to US High Schools," *Chinadaily.Com.Cn*, accessed July 23, 2019, http://usa.chinadaily.com.cn/world/2017-08/21/content_30888806.htm.

Further Reading

Aidi, Hisham. *Rebel Music: Race, Empire, and the New Muslim Youth Culture*. New York: Vintage, 2014.
Deutsch, Nancy L., and Eleni Theodorou. "Aspiring, Consuming, Becoming: Youth Identity in a Culture of Consumption." *Youth & Society* 42, no. 2 (2010): 229–254.

Khamis, Susie, Lawrence Ang, and Raymond Welling. "Self-Branding, 'Micro-Celebrity' and the Rise of Social Media Influencers." *Celebrity Studies* 8 August, 2016: 191–208.

Lam-Knott, Sonia. "Contesting Brandscapes in Hong Kong: Exploring Youth Activist Experiences of the Contemporary Consumerist Landscape." *Urban Studies* 57, no. 5 (2020): 1087–1104.

Lukács, Gabriella. 2020. *Invisibility by Design: Women and Labor in Japan's Digital Economy*. Durham: Duke University Press Books.

Miller-Idriss, Cynthia. *The Extreme Gone Mainstream: Commercialization and Far Right Youth Culture in Germany*. Reprint edition. Princeton, NJ: Princeton University Press, 2019.

Milner, Murray. *Freaks, Geeks, and Cool Kids: Teenagers in an Era of Consumerism, Standardized Tests, and Social Media*. New York: Routledge, 2015.

Nguyen, Huong. "Globalization, Consumerism, and the Emergence of Teens in Contemporary Vietnam." *Journal of Social History* 49, no. 1 (2015): 4–19.

Sugihartati, Rahma. "Youth Fans of Global Popular Culture: Between Prosumer and Free Digital Labourer." *Journal of Consumer Culture* 20, no.3 (October 2017): 305–323.

Wilson, Ara. *The Intimate Economies of Bangkok: Tomboys, Tycoons and Avon Ladies in the Global City*. Berkeley: University of California Press, 2004.

Yamanoglu, Melike Aktas. "Consumer Culture and Turkish Poor Youth's Identity: Issues of Vulnerability and Exclusion." In *Consumer Culture, Modernity and Identity*. Edited by Nita Mathur, 345–381. London: SAGE, 2020.

CHAPTER 16

YOUTH CULTURES OF ACTIVISM AND POLITICS

NAZAN MAKSUDYAN

A sizable literature stresses the transformative potential of the strong bond between youth cultures and political activism. In this constellation, young people are portrayed as rebellious, revolutionary, utopian, and idealistic. As such, they are conceived as creative producers of subcultures and new lifestyles, and carriers of revolutionary postures and politics.[1] Research on youth cultures of activism and politics has focused largely on the modern era, although youth from earlier historical periods, such as Antiquity, the Protestant Reformation, and the English and the French Revolutions, are also presented as key players in political movements.[2]

Richard and Margaret Braungart note that youth cultures, in which young people assumed political roles in an attempt "to initiate and resist change in the social order," could be first detected in the nineteenth century.[3] Politicized youth cultures can be observed first in the movements of "Young Europe (1815–1848)" in Germany, Italy, France, and Russia, which organized around the causes of "national autonomy and independence" against the absolutism of the *ancien régime*. Toward the end of the nineteenth and beginning of the twentieth centuries, there were a number of "post-Victorian youth movements," that "rejected the age of empires (British, Austro-Hungarian, Ottoman, Ch'ing, Meiji, Romanov)" and advocated for constitutional reform and nationalist politics.[4] Youth took part in this "generational movement" in a number of countries, including Bosnia, the Soviet Union, Mexico, Uruguay, Argentina, India, China, and Ottoman Turkey, and also participated in such movements as "Young Wales, Young Ireland, youthful Czechs and Poles, and the Spanish Generation of '98."[5]

One such example of advocacy for constitutional reform was the era of reforms known as the *Tanzimat* (1839–1876) in the Ottoman Empire, which ushered in a new conception of youth in Ottoman society. In this late-nineteenth-century context, educated young men were called upon to reform and "save" the Empire. The main social movements of the late Ottoman period were known as the "Young Ottoman" movement, and the new cadres ruling the country after 1908 were called the "Young Turks."[6]

In their 2014 work on youth politics, Mayssoun Sukarieh and Stuart Tannock note that even though it is possible to find much earlier examples of "generational conflict, political engagement and social activism" among the young, the appearance of organized youth and student movements and much more politicized youth cultures corresponds to a period in the early part of the twentieth century.[7] "Youth as a revolutionary subject," therefore, is usually analyzed for the course of the twentieth century. The last hundred years, with considerable engagement with other periods and eras, provides a range of different ways of youth cultures' engagement with activism and politics. *Youth culture* can be defined as "the cultural and emotional products of youths' interaction with one another and with the larger culture." During the twentieth century, nationalist youth cultures of the 1920s and 30s stressed duty, responsibility, and idealism; anti-establishment youth cultures of the 1960s and 70s aspired to *change the world* on a global scale; anarchistic and nonconformist youth subcultures of the 1980s and 1990s cultivated apathy toward traditional politics; and the globally dissenting millennials were concerned with "the commons" (cultural and natural resources theoretically owned and accessed by everyone), democratic governance, ecology, and global social justice.

IDEALISM AND NATION-BUILDING IN THE EARLY TWENTIETH CENTURY

For numerous national movements during the nineteenth century, youth were important as long as they could be manipulated and socially molded to realize a different *future*. In the early twentieth century, nation-states in the Balkans and the Middle East, and under authoritarian regimes in Europe, were engaged in efforts to build the "new man" or the "new woman" by focusing on the political socialization of young people to embrace certain new social norms.[8] Special regime-supporting organizations for youth were developed to recruit and impress upon younger generations that they were the future of the new state.[9]

In the case of Turkey in the 1920s and 1930s, "a veritable cult of youth" strongly emphasized the modernizing role of educated young people.[10] This was instrumental in building a national consciousness in the young generations of the new Turkish nation-state. In the period from the 1920s to the 1950s, educated youth came to embody the new nation within the public discussions of the political elite.[11] A significant group of young persons identified with the Kemalist transformation shaped a nationalist youth culture stressing duty toward the nation, responsibility, and idealism as its core values. These first generations of new nation-states, not only in Turkey but also in several post-imperial contexts, stressed their sacrifices (during wars, the hardships of the nation-building era, and various other crises) as definitive of their youth and as a precious badge of honor.[12]

The obsession with the "youth cult" and the formation of youth movements to embrace and cultivate the nation developed all along the political spectrum. Throughout the 1920s, the Komsomol relied on to the belief that youth would act as if "the entire purpose of their lives is to build a communist society."[13] Not only was this first generation was not only responsible for creating this society, but they were also the fortunate ones who would live in a communist society as adults. Komsomol served as a specific environment for the emergence of a distinct youth culture, as it provided an autonomous space for young people to act out and perform their "leadership." Youth were defined as the "vanguard of the proletarian revolution," because during the Russian Civil War thousands fought with the Red Guards and the Red Army. This *sacrifice* then was translated into *praise* and glorification of youth. Young people's self-image was also largely shaped by this "real shared historical conjunctive experience" that emphasized sacrifice, camaraderie, self-discipline, and heroism.[14] Young, militant veterans were the face of the Komsomol in the early 1920s, and the essential elements of the larger youth culture. Anatolii Rybakov recounted in his autobiography how impressed he was with Komsomol members in his school. One boy, "a typical komsomol'tsy," caught his attention by wearing his leather jacket in summer and his cavalry coat and sheep skin in winter, emphasizing his participation and achievements in the war.[15] The ideal of male youth was encapsulated within the identity of the soldier.

In interwar Europe, the belief in the political potential of youth also gave rise to large youth movements with intimate links to fascist, communist, and nationalist ideologies (and their imperialist and militarist undertones) and their charismatic leaders. These include the Russian Komsomol (formed in 1918), the Communist Youth International (1919), the Fascist Youth Vanguards in Italy (1919), and the Hitler Youth in Germany (1922). The economic crises of the 1930s and the dissatisfaction with the post-Versailles world order were mobilizing factors for youth demanding change and rejecting established order. Fascists created state-sponsored youth organizations, such as the well-known Hitler Jugend in Nazi Germany and Opera Nazionale Balilla in Italy. These organizations successfully directed the energies of youth into service for the totalitarian regime. Youth became "a metaphor of social change" in fascist Italy, as the leader of the movement, Benito Mussolini, considered youth as the "avant-garde of the fascist revolution."[16] In France, the interwar period was also considered as a time of youth prominence, when youth not only assumed political and social stances but also considered themselves "capable of regenerating the nation and the state."[17] In

1934, the French socialist Léon Blum declared that "we live at a time when everyone assumes the right to speak in the name of youth, when everyone, at the same time, wants to grab hold of youth, when everyone is fighting over youth."[18] It was expected that a revolutionary and rebellious youth movement would radically transform the social, economic, and political order.[19]

Youth were also celebrated for their physical vitality and bodily vigor. Many early-twentieth-century youth movements focused on developing the physical health and bodily strength of their (male) youth. The military competence and sacrifice of youth on the battlefield had also been strongly emphasized and celebrated.[20] Dynamism and transformative promise of youth were not only a European fascination; there were similar youth organizations aimed at producing dutifully nationalist and idealistic youth culture in many other new nation-states of the post–First World War era. In Iraq in the 1930s, the national youth movement, *al-Futuwwa*, defined itself largely by reference to masculinity (or "rujula"): boldness, physical fitness, chivalry, fighting spirit, self-sacrifice, and prioritizing the community over the individual.[21] The association of nature, physical activity, masculinity, and the military had appealed to youth, especially males, in Africa and the Middle East since the 1920s, and youth organizations formed along these lines were quite popular in the 1930s, as in the examples of the Jeunes Algériens, Somali Youth League, and Nigerian Youth Movement. As Peter Wien notes, "nationalist parties such as al-Kata'ib and the Syrian Social Nationalist Party in Lebanon or the Misr al-Fatat in Egypt all established paramilitary youth branches to provide training in strong nationalism and physical fitness and strength of character."[22]

Often establishing a strictly gendered division of labor, nationalist youth cultures of the early twentieth century that stressed the duty of youth to their countries dedicated the warrior role to males, and female youth were imbued with the duties of nurturing and care, as captured in the cliché of the nurse. This dichotomy was reminiscent of the imaginary of the masculine front and the feminine homeland during the First World War and immediately after. A picture that appeared in 1921 on the cover page of the *Deacon's Almanac* (*Sargavakin Daretsuytse*) encapsulates the gendered nature of the division of nationalist duties in the young Republic of Armenia. The boy in the picture wears a soldier's uniform, and the girl is dressed as a Red Cross nurse, complementing each other in defending and nurturing the nation.[23]

The reproduction of a soldiering masculinity and militarist values was part of the youth cultures of the postwar societies. The Komsomol organization was also quite masculinist and as such was unsuccessful in recruiting female members. Interestingly, the masculine culture at times crossed gender boundaries, as some female members mimicked "the male behavior, manners, and language."[24] In her analysis of girls' participation in the German youth movement from the 1900s to the 1930s, Marion E. P. de Ras highlights their construction of a "girls' culture."[25] De Ras considers the impact of the Second World War as pivotal in young women's assertion of themselves within the German youth movement. As the young men who returned from the war disapproved of the women's presence in mixed organizations, many young women supported the idea of forming autonomous girls' organizations, including the establishment of female communities and a "female culture."

ANTIESTABLISHMENT YOUTH CULTURES, 1960S AND 1970S

> ... this period [the 1960s–1970s], unlike the nineties, was a time of hope, a time of optimism. It was a period when people valued personal freedom and social equality. It was a time when *anything seemed possible*. People thought they could *change the world*—and they did.[26]

These were the words of James Henke, a central figure in American youth culture of the period, while he was opening a 1997 exhibition on the "psychedelic era." The slogan *changing the world* lay at the heart of the youth culture of the period, and young activists and their supporters proclaimed a student and youth-led revolution that was to *change the world*.[27] The confluence of various political and social transformations made it seem like everything was in motion and that change was imminent. Politicization was a defining characteristic of the youth cultures of the long 1960s, and the identity of the "activist," "militant," or "revolutionary" was highly admirable and idolized, be it in the form of a French or Greek resister, Italian partisan, Latin American guerrilla, or Palestinian fedayeen.[28] During the 1970s, various protest factions solidified and grew more radical, taking the road of "armed struggle." Countercultural sentiments became, then, the core of the "youth rebellion."[29]

The 1960s were a time of unprecedented growth and spread of global youth movements in Europe, Latin America, Africa, and the Middle East, Asia, and North America.[30] The argument that youth constituted a new revolutionary social class was embraced by the student movement leaders themselves, and by public intellectuals and social scientists. Young people strongly criticized the existing inequalities of the world; this criticism has remained an integral part of a global political culture.[31] The "anti" nature of the movements was all-encompassing, with youth taking anti-imperialist, anti-colonialist, antinuclear, anti-militarist, antiracist, and anti-authoritarian positions. Rebelliousness and dissent defined youth cultures the most. Specifically, youth mobilized over the major issues of decolonial independence struggles (such as the Palestinian liberation movement and the Algerian National Liberation Front); against racist political regimes (the Civil Rights Movement in the United States and elsewhere); the Vietnam War; the Marxist revolution and the rights of the workers; the international student movement demanding large-scale university reform and autonomy; and sexual liberation and gay rights. From Brazil to Tunisia, from Germany to Senegal, there was a global experience of dramatic social change initiated by youth.

Bayat notes that such historic events as the student revolts in Berkeley and its Free Speech Movement spreading through the U.S. campuses, youth and student rebellions in Europe, Latin America, Africa, and Asia, and especially the events during the spring of 1968 brought youth to "the forefront of revolutionary politics," "as if they possessed an inherent radical habitus."[32] Global youthful dissidence was largely related to the growth of higher education. With largely increased enrollment numbers and the changing of the profile of students from an elite privileged group to a mass model, the category of the "student," as in "student movement," became a potential mass movement. The "student movement" was able to dominate political activism in these decades in the Middle East and North Africa, as in Europe or the Americas. Revolts and social struggles were led by these young students who took to the streets. Youth were becoming more relevant, not only due to demographic developments and educational policies, but also because of political configurations and transformations in the public discourse.[33]

The principal means of political activism were demonstrations, occupations, sit-ins, strikes, and riots. Many of the radical protesters believed in the overthrow of existing society and therefore sometimes relied on violence. The view of the long 1960s as an era of violent confrontations and street violence becomes most clear in young people's clashes with the police. Activists all over the globe often accused the authorities, particularly the police, of acting with disproportional force and illegitimate violence. Despite the typical seriousness of Stalinist or Maoist versions of the Left, young activists also relied upon humorous troublemaking and pranks, as in the examples of Spaßguerilla, situationists, yippies, and the Kabouters.[34]

The consistency in goals and means of youth movements throughout the 1960s and 1970s indicated the role of mass communication technologies and rapid transportation. The political activism of youth in this period usually involved short- and long-distance travels for solidarity and support with other movements in other parts of the globe.[35] Protesting youth around the world saw themselves as part of a global rebellion and were directly inspired by the tactics and demands of movements in other countries.[36] Daniel Cohn-Bendit, one of the leaders of the student movement in France, stressed that whether in Paris or Rio or Prague, it was the "same revolt that stretched all around the globe and captured the hearts and dreams of a whole generation."[37] The International Vietnam Congress that was held in Berlin in February 1968 presented itself as an international congregation of revolutionary youth.[38] The global spirit of the 1960s created "feelings, attitudes and experiences among youth that were peculiar to time rather than place."[39]

The growing importance attached to generations and generational conflict was also at the heart of the youth culture of the period. Youth movements of the 1960s and 1970s widely employed generational rhetoric to outline their agendas and expectations. The Nazi guilt in Germany, the French collaborationist past, Britain's colonial presence, nuclear weapons, Vietnam, an authoritarianism of the postwar societies all caused legitimate hostility toward the older generation. In the case of the Global

South, the 1960s generation's coming of age coincided with the emancipation from the colonial order. They expected more from their parents, countries, and states, and from the world in general. The 1968 generation in Tunisia sought emancipation and freedom *inside* the postcolonial state, but against the postcolonial regime of autocracy.[40]

Resentment and aggression toward the older generation, seen as the "establishment," in all senses of the word, often led to challenges of traditional social rules and norms. The abundance of "new movements, new ideas, new social concerns and new forms of social participation" especially challenged conventional ways of doing things.[41] With university students as the major influences, youth cultures were strengthened by their reaction against the rest of society during these "years of contestation."[42] This becomes most clear in the case of the Youth International Party (yippies) in the United States and different groups of hippies all over the world, including the Soviet Union.[43] Yippie cofounder Jerry Rubin's manifesto, *Do it!* (1970), was a "declaration of war between generations," inviting the youth "to leave their homes, burn down their schools and create a new society upon the ashes of the old."[44]

Matters related to gender and sexuality were also central to the youth cultures of the long sixties, despite the well-grounded retrospective criticism by women activists that they were often sidelined and subjugated by male members of left-leaning organizations during this period. Women were frustrated to find out that even in radical organizations they were reduced to supportive roles such as cooking, taking care of the wounded, or preparing placards, with men taking most of the public roles. This was, for instance, the case in Turkey, where females of the student movement rarely had a say in decision-making and almost never assumed leadership roles.[45] By the same token, women's emancipation was suppressed and euphemistically postponed, until the coming of the socialist revolution.[46]

The formation of women's and feminist groups were often a response to these masculinist, if not macho, tendencies within politicized youth cultures. Women's movements, on the contrary, promised their participants the longed-for opportunity to deliberate with each other as equals and to provide mutual support and solidarity. Female activists started to revolt against traditional gender roles and family relationships and against public and private morals that entrapped them into a domestic model of virtuosity, modesty, and obedience to the authority of men. Attempts at subverting patriarchal gender regimes and heteronormativity defined feminist and queer youth cultures. Activists stressed the domestic and sexual aspects of life within the political project. The slogan "the personal is political," originally used by the women's liberation movement in the United States, was embraced by women activists in many countries.[47] In the early 1970s, there were also crucial legal developments with respect to women's rights. Thanks to creative and dedicated women's activism and women-only marches, the ratification of Abortion Law Reform of 1975 in France and similar achievements in the United States, Italy, and elsewhere opened a new era of female liberation.

The promise of liberation—political, sexual, social, personal, and otherwise—was a powerful aspect of the youth cultures. The "sexual liberation" was mostly on the discursive level and limited to the upper-class urban youth and also involved a double standard for men and for women. Nevertheless, a form of frankness and honesty in sexual matters was part of *changing the world*. At times personal and sexual freedom found expression in the wearing of miniskirts, which challenged moral codes. At other times, women found it liberating to cut their hair or to refuse makeup and feminine clothes as an anti-patriarchal strategy. The politicization of leisure and sexuality by diverse left-wing youth groups was partly under the influence of feminist and gay liberation movements, even though in large parts of the Middle East and the Mediterranean homosexuality remained a largely unspoken issue as opposed to the being under the dominance of heteronormativity.[48]

"Radically Unpolitical" Youth Cultures, Post 1980s

In their analysis of youth political activism, Mayssoun Sukarieh and Stuart Tannock note that "prior to each period of youth uprising, there had usually been widespread concern over the alleged apathy, passivity or debility of youth."[49] It would not be false to argue that most work on youth cultures in the 1980s has stressed alienation of youth from politics and their apathy toward collective activism. Jean and John Comaroff suggested as late as 2006 that youth embody the contradictions of late capitalism, constituting a new counter to or "alien-nation" outside the modern nation-state.[50] Consecutive youth generations, especially in the Global North, have been announced as "Generation Y," "Generation X," the ecstasy generation, the Internet generation, and so on, largely emphasizing their introverted postures, disinterested and desperate attitude toward societal change, and self-absorption. The allure of mobilizing in organized movements to change society slowly faded out in the early 1980s. The youth cultures of the following two decades were often defined as "cynical," because they did not have any trust in themselves or in their societies to bring about positive change.[51]

It is necessary, however, to embrace a longer-term look at the relationships of youth cultures with politics to weigh better the tenability of the claim of "radical youth." Including the periods mentioned earlier, of over-politicization, young people, whether in the Global North or South, have also exhibited passive and/or conservative orientations. Furthermore, it is usually argued that by the 1980s the majority of youth were nothing but self-absorbed and conservative young professionals, often called "Yuppies." The last two decades of the twentieth century were considered a period of hibernation for most of the younger generations. A survey carried out in Canada in 2002 to investigate the causes of the decline in voter turnout found that half of all the nonvoters were under thirty years of age. The majority of these young people expressed little interest in politics and refused to exhibit a sense of "civic duty" with respect to voting.[52]

In the case of Turkey, the September 12, 1980, military coup was an important break point. The influence of the military rule continued to shape everyday life, while the new constitution largely curbed civil rights and liberties. Young people born in the 1970s (X generation), also called "the youth of the 12 September," were raised in a harshly depoliticized environment.[53] The military regime had resolved that the key to sustaining their apoliticized society was preventing hope or aspiration for change. Thus, the younger generation had come of age in a culture of desperation and political frigidity.[54] The liberalization of the economy, privatization waves, and incorporation into the global market economy also created a consumption-oriented youth culture. The expression "turning the corner," meaning to get rich as quick as a wink, was commonly used to characterize the ethos of the post-1980 youth culture, usually called the "Özal generation."[55] Accordingly, display of "private" lives and consumption-oriented lifestyles defined apolitical youth's public appearances.

Large-scale surveys of youth politicization in the last quarter of the twentieth century often pointed to apathy and aversion to conventional politics—to political parties and to elections—because of their disenchantment with formal institutions. More specifically, economic inequalities of the neoliberal era disenfranchised an increasingly urban and youthful population from the rights of citizenship.[56] Cynicism and a strong sense of political powerlessness shaped youth cultures and determined young people's approach to politics in the 1990s in Turkey and elsewhere. Youth in Tunisia were restrained under Ben Ali's authoritarian rule from 1987 onward. In Egypt, young generations were hardly interested in civic activism during the 1990s.[57] In the affluent societies of the north, especially in the United States, new generations had come of age, feeling convinced that seeking personal well-being was a better life strategy than to aspire for common good. According to Loeb's analysis, in the age of "don't worry, be happy," wealth was celebrated more than anything; free markets and the world of finance were glorified; and the "lifestyles of the rich and famous" fuddled aspirations. In fact, the gap between the rich and poor was ever growing; the economy relied on borrowed money; bankruptcies were common; and real wages fell continuously.[58]

Young generations of the neoliberal era, working at two or more jobs, heavily indebted to banks, and scared of being unemployed, were confronted with a more precarious future than their parents. Social and economic inequalities were internalized, and youth saw little possibility of changing the world. Their personal struggles kept them so busy that they could not empathize with others who took on causes that went beyond their personal lives. Younger generations in the 1990s were not knowledgeable about other historical instances in which young people were active in bringing about change in their societies. With the past obscured, apolitical young people found it hard to imagine that their actions might have an impact on the lives of others. They were not convinced that political acts like marching or sit-ins could possibly have results. They were, in that sense, only engaged with working hard for their limited and largely individual objectives, such as having a steady job and a family.[59]

It also needs to be stressed that disenchantment with politicians and lacking confidence in established political processes might have made youth inactive, not necessarily because they were apolitical, but because they were "radically unpolitical."[60] The punk subculture's engagement with politics and activism, which also had a significant impact on the youth cultures of the 1980s and 1990s, is such a case. During the 1980s, the American mass media notoriously reduced the punk rock movement to violence and nihilism, which was actually reflective of Reagan Era conservativism that "turned any rebellion against the status quo into inexplicable nihilism."[61] Interestingly, East German State Security (Stasi) agents also defined punk youth in the early 1980s as violent, undisciplined, and aggressive; they rejected all forms of authority and projected a pessimistic and apocalyptic mood.[62] According to the Stasi, punk youth comported themselves as essentially "oppositional to society."

A growing number of *nonconformist* youth cultures generated considerable activity and controversy in the 1980s. Youth within alternative movements in both capitalist and socialist countries actually expressed their frustration with the present and complained about feelings of stagnation and having nothing to expect from the future. New youth groups were involved in several unconventional cultures such as punk rock, yoga and meditation, body building, alternative religions, and drug abuse. The global appeal of identities, pluralism, and diversity, along with human rights and greater cultural autonomy, were prominent in the post-1980s political cultures.

The subcultures of the 1980s were largely involved with the production of cultural products in conscious opposition to an increasingly corporate and one-dimensional culture. Punk youth culture, as "an oppositional form of rebellion," mostly took the form of "do it yourself" products challenging the corporate market. This was youth's *radically unpolitical* engagement with politics. There was a connection between anticorporate music and an oppositional form of politics. In GDR punk youth culture, a general "attitude of antagonism" often took the form of both direct social critique or open vulgarity.[63] Although the state and the society were seen as "restraining, controlling, and synchronizing," the GDR punk youth culture relied on an emotional state, which was "chaotic, lively and individual."[64] On the other side of the Berlin Wall, alienated German youth, or the so-called No Future Generation, lived in squatter communes in Berlin (the "Dropout capital of the world") and clashed with the police over housing rights.[65]

In their sociological assessment of the youth movements of the 1980s, Braungart and Braungart emphasized that political activity among youth had not dissipated during the 1980s; in fact, many young people around the world were politically engaged. In Western Europe, there was considerable antinuclear and environmental protest activity in the 1980s. Situated within the theater of Cold War politics, these antinuclear and peace demonstrations became, in some countries, such as the Federal Republic of Germany, England, and Denmark, quite large gatherings. Young ecological activists also took a strong "anti-authority" stand, demanding increased civil participation, political decentralization, and emancipation. In Poland and Hungary, youth supported draft resistance and formed conscientious objector movements, and they created an underground press both to support the anti-draft movement, and to make larger regime criticism. By becoming conscientious objectors, or donating to antiwar NGOs, or boycotting blacklisted corporations, or becoming vegetarians, post-1980s protest youth were turning political activism into a set of personal morals. The criticism of authority, state, corporations, and corporate culture sow the seeds of what might be called "lifestyle politics" and stylistic transgression, seeing the lived life as a manifesto of a person's protest (or support).[66] The demand for greater freedoms, democracy, and self-determination has been the main political issue of youth protests all around the world.

Either in the form of apathy or organized protest, youth cultures' engagement with politics largely relied on desperation, cynicism, and heightened individualism during the last decades of the twentieth century. Post-1980s youth produced a number of subcultures as "forms of distinction," developing also "identity, commitment, distinctiveness and a degree of autonomy with respect to spaces and networks."[67]

MILLENNIALS STRIKE BACK, POST 2000S

In the past two decades, youth cultures have stressed more and more the duties of the "global citizen," concerned with "the commons," ecology, and global social justice. From the early years of the new millennium onward, dynamic nodes of communication and linkage between the local and the transnational in global cities created a new wave of youth activism and politics. The exclusion of young people from established institutional spaces has resulted in the creation of alternative spaces and forms of political mobilization, particularly through new communication technologies. Thanks to these new spaces and means of global connectedness, in the 2010s youth activists all over the world have been in dialogue and solidarity with one another. As Doreen Massey stressed in the 1990s, in this global world, youth cultures also need to be analyzed as global hybrid cultures that need to be viewed as open systems.[68] Furthermore, the wave of youth movements after the global recession that began in 2008 also proved that both despite and due to their economic marginalization, youth have been gaining autonomy and engaging more energetically in political questions.[69]

The Global Justice Movement (GJM) that emerged at the dawn of the new century had antecedents in localized European movements, although it is best recalled for its massive demonstrations in 1999 and 2001 at Seattle and Genoa, respectively.[70] It is also possible to refer to the *color revolutions* in the former Soviet Republics that occurred between 2003 and 2005 and continued up to the "European Spring" of anti-austerity protests (in Iceland, Spain, Greece). The mass mobilizations in the Middle East, or "the Arab Spring" (which started in Tunisia in December 2010 and spread over the next year to Egypt, Yemen, Libya, Bahrain, Syria, Morocco, Saudi Arabia, and Kuwait) came about at a time when few anticipated the possibility of rebellion in the Middle East, given the strength of the region's authoritarian regimes. Sometimes referred to as the "global youth rebellion," movements of the *indignados* in Spain (2011); the *aganaktismenoi* in Greece (2010–2012); the *Geração a Rasca* (lost generation) in Portugal in 2011; student-led protests called the Chilean Winter in 2011; the Occupy movement that began in New York City in September 2011 (and spread all over the world); and the mass social unrest and riots that have erupted in England in August 2011, France in August 2012, Sweden in May 2013, and Turkey and Brazil in June 2013 generated a new political youth culture.[71] It might be necessary to highlight the presence of not-so-young demonstrators and organizations in all these movements, especially the impact of political parties, trade unions, poor people's organizations, women's groups, NGOs, ecologists, and faith-based movements. Nevertheless, the role of the youth in the outbreak and the culmination of the protests and occupations was significantly visible, as they were usually the ones who built barricades, who put tents in occupied spaces, and who resisted most strongly against the brutality of the police forces. All in all, increased levels of political engagement and activism as part of their daily lives had a remarkable impact on youth cultures.

Paul Mason argues that twenty-first-century youth movements around the world were led by "the graduate with no future," who had a high level of education, but the life chances ahead of them were not analogous to their competences, skills, and merit.[72] As waves of neoliberal policies, austerity measures, and ever-growing social and economic inequalities narrowed the everyday realities of contemporary societies, the young generation's aspirations have been constantly frustrated by the growth of precarious employment (as interns, temporary workers, independent contractors, freelancers) and a polarized labor market, where middle-class jobs disappear relative to those at the bottom, requiring few skills, and those at the top.[73] In a new zeitgeist of constant swinging between education and precarious employment, contemporary youth cultures are also defined with a prevalent mode of "waithood," a prolonged state of precariousness, dependency, uncertainty, unemployment, and underemployment, risk, and frustration.[74] Millennial youth revolted against the insignificance and emptiness of their lives in the neoliberal era.[75] One of the protesting youth groups in Spain defined the circumstances that sparked their outrage as "without a house, without work, without pension," and therefore "without fear."[76] A large literature on the Arab Spring recounts the leading role of the young and students in the revolutions. Suffering from terribly high rates of unemployment, youth in the Middle East and North Africa region were resentful. Unexpectedly, they abandoned their passive subject status to become active agents.[77]

A unique aspect of post-2000s youth cultures is their relationship with the newly developed digital technologies. Their technological prowess and connectedness have earned them the nicknames "digital natives," or "Internet youth," as those who were born in the late twentieth and early twenty-first centuries use the Internet, information technologies, and social media platforms with unprecedented scale and effectiveness in their political activism. The role of social media has been often discussed in the rapid spread of the Arab Spring, as Facebook and Twitter are said to have been crucial in drawing the initial crowds. What is also remarkable about the use of new media is that it has linked several movements across national borders with a global outlook and sensibility.[78] One of the slogans of the Gezi Park protests in Istanbul (May–June 2013) was "#OccupyGezi," while the protestors mostly shouted, "Everywhere is Taksim, resistance is everywhere." Brazilian demonstrators around the same time emphasized the global linkages: "The love is over, Turkey is right here."[79] Fifteen years after the launch of Facebook and Twitter, social media is an intrinsic part of the daily lives of youth, and the digital aspect of political activism has become central to youth culture.[80]

Ruth Milkman defines the youth of the 2000s as a "new political generation," having more progressive attitudes and beliefs than their parents on a range of issues, including refugees and migration, racism, the rights of sexual minorities, capitalism, and climate activism.[81] A growing concern over the commons, the climate, and the "right to the city," and a harsh critique of all-encompassing commodification and rising authoritarianism, drew millennial youth from their screens and into the streets. They sensed the destructive nature of capitalist development. They opposed war, they became ecologists, and they exhibited an openness toward intersectional identities—sexual, ethnic, national, religious.[82] *Addicted-to-digital* youth, often criticized for being glued to Internet and smartphones, were *en plein air* (in the open). As has recently been witnessed with the climate activism of the Fridays for Future (FFF)[83] and the political agency of children and youth in the Arab revolutions, there is a visible tendency of political activism in contemporary youth cultures. Particularly interesting in the FFF is its original conceptualization as a "school strike" and the involvement of school children as initiators, organizers, and participants on a large scale.[84]

As St. John emphasized, "the cultural politics of reclaiming (of land, culture, the internet, the commons, the streets)" became a key means to oppose and resist corporate globalization, as an alternative to neoliberalism.[85] The emphasis on urban space, real estate bubbles, and privatization and destruction of common properties constituted the central issues of protests, which often took the form of occupying public squares in the United States, Egypt, Spain, Turkey, Brazil, Israel, and Greece.[86] "Occupation" meant not only putting up tents, building barricades, and resisting the brutality of the police forces, but also living in a communal political setting. A range of communal activities in occupied/liberated common spaces became a "standard aspect of the global repertoire of protest."[87] In that respect, youth cultures engaged with the value of the commons, open discussions (and storytelling), collective decision-making, communal production, participatory democracy, and a culture of sharing. In this alternative political culture, the absence of formal leadership and hierarchical organization among youth activists was emphasized.[88] Although the criticism of inequality, racial and gender discrimination, dispossession, and ecological despoliation was obvious in many movements, often there were not formalized or programmatic demands. Instead, the performative aspects of protest enable the pursuit of the ideal (future) polity in the present through actions.[89]

In his classic work, "The Problem of Generations," Karl Mannheim noted that "nothing is more false than the usual assumption that the younger generation is 'progressive' and the older generation *eo ipso* conservative."[90] Rather, he argued, youth's potential conservative, reactionary, or progressive political stances depended on whether the existing social structure provided "opportunities for the promotion of their own social and intellectual ends." Either in progressive or conservative positions, youth, for Mannheim, were "able to re-orient any movement they embraced."[91] In other words, even though it is difficult to build a correlation between political activism and youth as a category of analysis, movements that could have recruited young people feature more prominently within the literature on social movements. In the case of most social movements in the twentieth century, youth have not only been key participants but also have often been at the vanguard of these movements.

NOTES

1. Asef Bayat, "Is There a Youth Politics?," *Middle East – Topics & Arguments* 9 (2017): 16–24.
2. For other examples of youth movements in earlier periods, see Emiel Eyben, *Restless Youth in Ancient Rome* (London: Routledge, 2003); Christian Laes and Johan Strubbe, *Youth in the Roman Empire: The Young and the Restless Years?* (Cambridge: Cambridge University Press, 2014); Herbert Moller, "Youth as a Force in the Modern World," *Comparative Studies in Society and History* 10, no. 3 (1968): 237–260; Jack Goldstone, "Population and Security: How Demographic Change Can Lead to Violent Conflict," *Journal of International Affairs*, 56/1 (2002), 3–22.
3. Richard G. Braungart and Margaret M. Braungart, "Youth Movements in the 1980s: A Global Perspective," *International Sociology* 5, no. 2 (1990): 157–181.
4. Ibid., 158.
5. Richard G. Braungart, "Historical Generations and Generation Units: A Global Pattern of Youth Movements," *Journal of Political & Military Sociology* 12 (1984): 113–135, especially 119–121, 127.
6. Leyla Neyzi, "The Construction of 'Youth' in Public Discourse in Turkey: A Generational Approach," in *Youth and Youth Culture in the Contemporary Middle East*, ed. Jørgen Bæk Simonsen (Aarhus, Denmark: Aarhus University Press, 2005), 107–115.
7. Mayssoun Sukarieh and Stuart Tannock, *Youth Rising?: The Politics of Youth in the Global Economy* (Abingdon, UK: Routledge, 2014), 82.
8. Prominent works on youth during the interwar era include Walter Laqueur, *Young Germany: A History of the German Youth Movement* (London: Routledge, 2019 [1962]); Aline Coutrot, "Youth Movements in France in the 1930s," *Journal of Contemporary History* 5.1 (1970): 23–35; Arnon Degani, "They Were Prepared: The Palestinian Arab Scout Movement 1920–1948," *British Journal of Middle Eastern Studies* 41, no. 2 (2014): 200–18; Matthias Neumann, "'Youth, It's Your Turn!': Generations and the Fate of the Russian

Revolution (1917–1932)." *Journal of Social History* 46, no. 2 (2012): 273–304; Luisa Passerini, "Youth as a Metaphor for Social Change: Fascist Italy and America in the 1950s," in *A History of Young People in the West*, vol. 1, ed. Giovanni Levi and Jean-Claude Schmitt (Cambridge: Harvard University, 1997), 281–340; Samuel Kalman, "Faisceau Visions of Physical and Moral Transformation and the Cult of Youth in Inter-War France," *European History Quarterly* 33, no. 3 (2003): 343–366.

9. Jørgen Bæk Simonsen, "Introduction: Youth, History and Change in the Modern Arab World," in *Youth and Youth Culture*, 8.
10. Neyzi, "The Construction of 'Youth,'" 109.
11. Youth became the "face" of the Turkish Republic on representative occasions. A "Youth and Sports Holiday" was introduced, which was celebrated with gymnastics performances. Ibid., 110.
12. Juliane Brauer, "'With Power and Aggression, and a Great Sadness': Emotional Clashes between Punk Culture and GDR Youth Policy in the 1980s," *Twentieth Century Communism* 4 (2012): 76–102, here 83. It is not surprising that the first president of the German Democratic Republic (GDR) also referred to the young generation as the "future," while calling the state the "Pioneers' Republic."
13. "'Youth, It's Your Turn!,'" 273–304, 275.
14. Ibid., 282.
15. Ibid., 284.
16. Passerini, "Youth as a Metaphor for Social Change 281–340.
17. Samuel Kalman, "Faisceau Visions of Physical and Moral Transformation and the Cult of Youthin Inter-War France," *European History Quarterly* 33, no. 3 (2003): 343–366.
18. Quoted in Susan Whitney, *Mobilizing Youth: Communists and Catholics in Interwar France* (Durham: Duke University Press, 2009), p. 3; Sukarieh and Tannock, *Youth Rising?*, 86.
19. Sukarieh and Tannock, *Youth Rising?*, 80–83.
20. Elizabeth Harvey, "The Cult of Youth," in *A Companion to Europe 1900–1945*, ed. Gordon Martel (Oxford: Blackwell, 2005), 66–81.
21. Peter Wien, "'Watan' and 'Rujula': The Emergence of a New Model of Youth in Interwar Iraq," in *Youth and Youth Culture*, 10–20.
22. Ibid., 11.
23. Lerna Ekmekcioglu, *Recovering Armenia: The Limits of Belonging in Post-Genocide Turkey* (Stanford, CA: Stanford University Press, 2016), 21–22.
24. Neumann, "'Youth, It's Your Turn!,'" 288.
25. Marion E. P. de Ras, *Body, Femininity and Nationalism: Girls in the German Youth Movement 1900–1934* (London: Routledge, 2008).
26. James Henke, "Introduction," in *I Want to Take You Higher: The Psychedelic Era 1969–1969*, ed. James Henke with Parke Puterbaugh (San Francisco, 1997), 11. [italics mine]
27. Prominent works on youth during the long 1960s include Axel Schildt and Detlef Siegfried, eds., *Between Marx and Coca-Cola: Youth Cultures in Changing European Societies, 1960–1980* (New York: Berghahn Books, 2005); Robert Gildea, James Mark, and Anette Warring, eds., *Europe's 1968: Voices of Revolt* (Oxford: Oxford University Press, 2013); Louie Dean Valencia-García, *Antiauthoritarian Youth Culture in Francoist Spain: Clashing with Fascism* (London: Bloomsbury, 2018); Anne Luke, *Youth and the Cuban Revolution: Youth Culture and Politics in 1960s Cuba* (Lanham, MD: Lexington, 2018); Arthur Marwick, "Youth Culture and the Cultural Revolution of the Long Sixties," in *Between Marx and Coca-Cola*, 39–58; Filip Pospíšil, "Youth

Cultures and the Disciplining of Czechoslovak Youth in the 1960s," *Social History* 37, no. 4 (2012): 477–500.
28. Robert Gildea, Gudni Jóhannesson, Chris Reynolds, and Polymeris Voglis, "Violence," in *Europe's 1968: Voices of Revolt*, ed. Robert Gildea, James Mark, and Anette Warring (Oxford: Oxford University Press, 2013), 258–279.
29. Axel Schildt and Detlef Siegfried, "Introduction: Youth, Consumption, and Politics in the Age of Radical Change," in *Between Marx and Coca-Cola*, 1–35, here 10.
30. Chen Jian, Martin Klimke, Masha Kirasirova, Mary Nolan, Marilyn Young, and Joanna Waley-Cohen, eds. *The Routledge Handbook of the Global Sixties: Between Protest and Nation-Building* (London: Routledge, 2018).
31. Simonsen, "Introduction," 8.
32. Bayat, "Is There a Youth Politics?," 18.
33. Omnia El-Shakry, "Youth as Peril and Promise: The Emergence of Adolescent Psychology in Postwar Egypt," *International Journal of Middle Eastern Studies* 43 (2011): 591–610.
34. Simon Teune, "Humour as a Guerrilla Tactic: The West German Student Movement's Mockery of the Establishment," *International Review of Social History* 52, no. 15 (2007): 115–132.
35. Sophie Lorenz, "Heroine of the Other America: The East German Solidarity Movement in Support of Angela Davis, 1970–73," in *The Routledge Handbook of the Global Sixties: Between Protest and Nation-Building*, ed. Chen Jian, Martin Klimke, Masha Kirasirova, Mary Nolan, Marilyn Young, and Joanna Waley-Cohen (London: Routledge, 2020), 548–563.
36. Victoria Langland, "Transnational Connections of the Global Sixties as Seen by a Historian of Brazil," in *The Routledge Handbook of Global Sixties*, 15–26.
37. Martin Klimke, *The Other Alliance: Student Protest in West Germany and the United States in the Global Sixties* (Princeton: Princeton University Press, 2010), 2.
38. Detlef Siegfried, "Understanding 1968: Youth Rebellion, Generational Change and Postindustrial Society," in *Between Marx and Coca-Cola*, 59–81, here 60.
39. John Davis and Juliane Fürst, "Drop-Outs," in *Europe's 1968: Voices of Revolt*, ed. Robert Gildea, James Mark, and Anette Warring (Oxford University Press, 2013), 193–210.
40. Leyla Dakhli, "The Tunisian 1960s. Coming-of-Age in a New-Born Country?" (Paper presented in *The Revolutionary Sixties in the Mediterranean and the Middle East*, Centre Marc Bloch, October 11–12, 2018, Berlin).
41. Arthur Marwick, "Youth Culture and the Cultural Revolution of the Long Sixties," in *Between Marx and Coca-Cola*, 43.
42. Genevieve Dreyfus-Armand et al., eds. *Les Annees 68: Le temps de la contestation* (Brussels: Editions Complexe, 2000).
43. Juliane Fürst, *Flowers through Concrete: Explorations in Soviet Hippieland* (Oxford: Oxford University Press, 2021).
44. Detlef Siegfried, "Understanding 1968: Youth Rebellion, Generational Change and Postindustrial Society," in *Between Marx and Coca-Cola*, 60–61.
45. A. K. Badur, *Türkiye 68'inde Kadınlar*, in *1968: İsyan, Devrim, Özgürlük*, ed. Ö. Turan (Istanbul: Tarih Vakfı Yurt Yayınları, 2019), 429–445.
46. In that respect, the feminist wave of the 1960s was not embraced by either the official socialist party of the time (Türkiye İşçi Partisi, TİP) or the radical leftist factions, which were predominantly patriarchal and militaristic anyway. Yaprak Zihnioğlu, "Türkiye'de

Solun Feminizme Yaklaşımı," in *Türkiye'de Siyasi Düşünce, Cilt 8: Sol*, ed. Tanıl Bora and Murat Gültekingil (Istanbul: İletişim, 2007), 1108–1145.
47. Rebecca Clifford, Robert Gildea, and Anette Warring, "Gender and Sexuality," in *Europe's 1968: Voices of Revolt*, 239–257.
48. Nikolaos Papadogiannis, *Militant around the Clock?: Left-Wing Youth Politics, Leisure, and Sexuality in Post-Dictatorship Greece, 1974–1981* (Oxford: Berghahn Books, 2015).
49. Sukarieh and Tannock, *Youth Rising?*, 83.
50. Jean Comaroff and John Comaroff, "Reflections on Youth, from the Past to the Postcolony," in *Frontiers of Capital: Ethnographic Reflections on the New Economy*, ed. Melissa S. Fisher and Greg Downey (Durham, NC: Duke University Press, 2006): 267–281.
51. Prominent works on youth during the 1980s include Ken Roberts, "Youth Mobilisations and Political Generations: Young Activists in Political Change Movements during and since the Twentieth Century," *Journal of Youth Studies*, 18, no. 8 (2015): 950–966; Alexei Yurchak, *Everything Was Forever, until It Was No More: The Last Soviet Generation* (Princeton, NJ: Princeton University Press, 2006); Kevin Mattson, "Did Punk Matter?: Analyzing the Practices of a Youth Subculture during the 1980s," *American Studies* 42, no. 1 (2001): 69–97; Braungart and Braungart, "Youth Movements in the 1980s," 157–181.
52. Jon H. Pammett, Lawrence LeDuc, "Confronting the Problem of Declining Voter Turnout among Youth," *Electoral Insight* 5 (2003): 3–8.
53. Neyzi, "The Construction of 'Youth,'" 111–112.
54. Nazan Maksudyan, "In den Park gehen und spielen: Eine neue öffentliche Existenz als Kinder und Jugendliche," in *Fluchtpunkt. Das Mittelmeer und die europäische Krise*, ed. Franck Hoffman and Markus Messling (Berlin: Kulturverlag Kadmos, 2017), 326–340.
55. Turgut Özal (1927–1993), Turkish prime minister (1983–1989) and president (1989–1993).
56. Neyzi, "The Construction of 'Youth,'" 111.
57. Bayat, "Is There a Youth Politics?," 18.
58. Paul Rogat Loeb, *Generation at the Crossroads: Apathy and Action on the American Campus* (New Brunswick, NJ: Rutgers University Press, 1994), 3–4.
59. Loeb, *Generation at the Crossroads*, 3–4.
60. L. McDowell, E. Rootham, and A. E. Hardgrove, "Politics, Anti-Politics, Quiescence and Radical Unpolitics: Young Men's Political Participation in an 'Ordinary' English Town," *Journal of Youth Studies* 17, no. 1 (2013): 42–62.
61. Mattson, "Did Punk Matter?," 70.
62. Brauer, "'With Power and Aggression," 86.
63. Ibid., 77.
64. Ibid., 91.
65. Braungart and Braungart, "Youth Movements in the 1980s," 166.
66. Mattson, "Did Punk Matter?," 84.
67. Paul Hodkinson, "Youth Cultures and the Rest of Life: Subcultures, Post-Subcultures and Beyond," *Journal of Youth Studies* 1, no. 5 (2016): 629–645, here 634.
68. Doreen Massey, "The Spatial Construction of Youth Cultures," in *Cool Places: Geographies of Youth Cultures*, ed. Tracey Skelton and Gill Valentine, (London: Routledge, 1998), 122–130.
69. Prominent works on youth during the post-2000s include Ruth Milkman, "A New Political Generation: Millennials and the Post-2008 Wave of Protest," *American Sociological Review* 82, no. 1 (2017) 1–31; Mavis Reimer, "'It's the Kids Who Made This Happen': The Occupy Movement as Youth Movement," *Jeunesse: Young People, Texts, Cultures* 4, no. 1 (2012): 1–14;

Asef Bayat, *Revolution without Revolutionaries: Making Sense of the Arab Spring* (Stanford, CA: Stanford University Press, 2017); Benjamin Bowman, "Imagining Future Worlds alongside Young Climate Activists: A New Framework for Research," *Fennia-International Journal of Geography* 197, no. 2 (2019): 295–305; Graham St. John, "Counter-Tribes, Global Protest and Carnivals of Reclamation," *Peace Review* 16, no. 4 (2004): 421–428; Graham St. John, "Protestival: Global Days of Action and Carnivalized Politics in the Present," *Social Movement Studies* 7, no. 2 (2008): 167–190.
70. Cristina Flesher Fominaya and Laurence Cox, eds., *Understanding European Movements: New Social Movements, Global Justice Struggles, Anti-Austerity Protest* (London: Routledge, 2013).
71. Sukarieh and Tannock, *Youth Rising?*, 80.
72. Paul Mason, *Why It's Still Kicking Off Everywhere* (New York: Verso, 2013), 63–67.
73. Milkman, "A New Political Generation," 2, 9.
74. Navtej Dhillon and Tarik Yousef, eds., *Generation in Waiting: The Unfulfilled Promise of Young People in the Middle East* (Washington, DC: Brookings Institution Press, 2011); Craig Jeffry, *Timepass: Youth, Class and the Politics of Waiting in India* (Stanford, CA: Stanford University Press, 2010).
75. Christos Memos, "Neoliberalism, Identification Process and the Dialectics of Crisis," *International Journal of Urban and Regional Research* 34, no. 1 (2010): 210–216.
76. Greig Charnock, Thomas Purcell, and Ramon Ribera-Fumaz, "Indignate!: The 2011 Popular Protests and the Limits to Democracy in Spain," *Capital & Class* 36, no. 1 (2012): 7–9.
77. Bayat, "Is There a Youth Politics?," 16–24.
78. Sukarieh and Tannock, *Youth Rising?*, 102.
79. Cihan Tuğal, "Resistance Everywhere: The Gezi Revolt in Global Perspective," *New Perspectives on Turkey* 49 (2013):147–162.
80. Perri Campbell, "Occupy, Black Lives Matter and Suspended Mediation: Young People's Battles for Recognition in/between Digital and Non-Digital Spaces." *Young* 26, no. 2 (2018): 145–160.
81. Milkman, "A New Political Generation," 1–31.
82. Maksudyan, "In den Park gehen ... "
83. FFF is a global climate strike movement that started in August 2018, when fifteen-year-old Greta Thunberg began a school strike, during which she sat outside the Swedish Parliament demanding urgent action on the climate crisis.
84. For instance, in September 2019, FFF's third Global Climate Strike mobilized six thousand protest events in 185 countries, bringing 7.6 million young people out onto the streets. See Joost de Moor, Katrin Uba, Mattias Wahlström, Magnus Wennerhag, and Michiel De Vydt, eds., "Protest for a Future II: Composition, Mobilization and Motives of the Participants in Fridays for Future Climate Protests on 20–27 September, 2019, in 19 Cities around the World," (2020). Retrieved from https://www.diva-portal.org/smash/get/diva2:1397070/FULLTEXT01.pdf.
85. Graham St. John, "Counter-Tribes," 421–428.
86. Sara Fregonese, "Mediterranean Geographies of Protest," *European Urban and Regional Studies* 20 (2013): 109–114.
87. Tuğal, "Resistance Everywhere," 152.
88. Sukarieh and Tannock, *Youth Rising?*, 83–84.
89. St. John, "Counter-Tribes," 424.

90. Karl Mannheim, "The Problem of Generations," in *Essays on the Sociology of Knowledge*, ed. Paul Kecskemeti (London: Routledge & K. Paul, 1952), 276–322, here 297.
91. Ibid.

Further Reading

Bayat, Asef. "Is There a Youth Politics?" *Middle East: Topics & Arguments* 9 (2017): 16–24.
Bayat, Asef. *Revolution without Revolutionaries: Making Sense of the Arab Spring*. Stanford, CA: Stanford University Press, 2017.
Fürst, Juliane. *Flowers through Concrete: Explorations in Soviet Hippieland*. Oxford: Oxford University Press, 2021.
Jian, Chen, et al., eds. *The Routledge Handbook of the Global Sixties: Between Protest and Nation-Building*. London: Routledge, 2018.
Kennelly, Jacqueline. *Citizen Youth: Culture, Activism and Agency in a Neoliberal Era*. New York: Palgrave Macmillan, 2011.
Kwon, Soo Ah. *Uncivil Youth: Race, Activism and Affirmative Governmentality*. Durham, NC: Duke University Press, 2013.
Levi, Giovanni, and Jean-Claude Schmitt, eds. *A History of Young People in the West*. Harvard University Press, 1997.
Papadogiannis, Nikolaos. *Militant around the Clock?: Left-Wing Youth Politics, Leisure, and Sexuality in Post-Dictatorship Greece, 1974–1981*. New York: Berghahn Books, 2015.
Passerini, Luisa. "Youth as a Metaphor for Social Change: Fascist Italy and America in the 1950s." In *A History of Young People in the West*, vol. 1. Edited by Giovanni Levi and Jean-Claude Schmitt, 281–340. Cambridge, MA: Harvard University, 1997.
Roberts, Ken. "Youth Mobilisations and Political Generations: Young Activists in Political Change Movements During and Since the Twentieth Century," *Journal of Youth Studies* 18, no. 8 (2015): 950–966.
Schildt, Axel, and Detlef Siegfried, eds. *Between Marx and Coca-Cola: Youth Cultures in Changing European Societies, 1960–1980*. New York: Berghahn Books, 2005.
Simonsen, Jørgen Bæk, ed. *Youth and Youth Culture in the Contemporary Middle East*. Aarhus: Aarhus University Press, 2005.
Skelton, Tracey, and Gill Valentine, eds. *Cool Places: Geographies of Youth Cultures*. London: Routledge, 1998.
Sukarieh, Mayssoun. "From Terrorists to Revolutionaries: The Emergence of 'Youth' in the Arab World and the Discourse of Globalization." *Interface* 4, no. 2 (2012): 424–437.
Sukarieh, Mayssoun, and Stuart Tannock. *Youth Rising?: The Politics of Youth in the Global Economy*. London: Routledge, 2014.
Taft, Jessica K. *Rebel Girls: Youth Activism and Social Change Across the Americas*. New York: New York University Press, 2011.
Valencia-García, Louie Dean. *Antiauthoritarian Youth Culture in Francoist Spain: Clashing with Fascism*. Bloomsbury Publishing, 2018.

CHAPTER 17

SEXUALITY, YOUTH CULTURES, AND THE PERSISTENCE OF THE DOUBLE STANDARD IN THE TWENTIETH-CENTURY UNITED STATES

NICHOLAS L. SYRETT

IN February of 1924, Frances Louise Fink, a University of Michigan undergraduate, received a rather extraordinary letter. Her anonymous correspondent demanded that Fink pay fifty dollars, to be left bound to the fence of her sorority house, or the correspondent would reveal just what Fink had been doing with the boys of Delta Upsilon. The letter writer threatened Fink with public exposure should she either refuse to pay or should she contact any college officials about the situation. The letter writer explained that "it has been proven by ages of trials, that in the end, the victim is not only barred from society but is also looked upon with scorn by her fellow students."[1]

Within a year, Frances Fink had dropped out of Michigan and was living at home. She eventually transferred to Syracuse University.[2]

Forty-one years later, in August of 1965, another Frances, Frances Juanita Brown, a student at the University of North Carolina at Greensboro taking summer classes at UNC-Chapel Hill, was suspended by the Woman's Council at Chapel Hill for having violated curfew by spending the night at a fraternity house with James Dickson, a member of that fraternity and president of the student body at Chapel Hill. Dickson, by contrast, was only reprimanded. The disparity in the punishments of Brown and Dickson prompted much newspaper coverage and a petition signed by between 1,500 and 2,000 students asking for Dickson's resignation as president. Brown's parents wrote to the dean of the college, and through a series of appeals, Brown was finally allowed to go back to school at Greensboro, largely because of the recognition of the unfairness evident in the disparity of the punishments.[3]

The difference between these two incidents is striking and yet considering the years separating them, not altogether surprising. In 1924, the sex that Frances Fink was presumed to be having was so scandalous that she was threatened with blackmail in order to have her secret kept. In 1965, the treatment of Frances Brown over a similar situation provoked such outrage by students that authorities lifted Brown's sentence. Jumping forward another forty years or so, twenty-first-century technologies, including numerous smartphone apps, enable, even encourage, high school and college students to "hook up," engage in casual premarital sex with no expectation for long-term commitment. Although many students say that they sanction this behavior for all their peers regardless of gender, in practice female students continue to be stigmatized for being too free with their affections, whereas young men are often rewarded with an enhanced reputation and more prestige.

The two Franceses and contemporary young people have all made decisions about sex in the context of changing youth cultures that have sanctioned, to varying degrees, sex between young people. Sex has been and remains a key part of youth culture, both in the United States and internationally, and the decision to engage in sexual activity is seen by many as a key marker of coming of age. The standards and practices have certainly changed over time, but the link between sexual experimentation, youth culture, and perceptions of emerging adulthood remains constant. How and when young people understand sex to be appropriate or inappropriate is a product of regionally variable youth cultures with regulations and mores that are linked to mainstream culture more broadly, but they also exist as their own worlds apart.

The incorporation of premarital sexual activity into the realm of youthful lives owes much to the creation of youth culture itself, a separate realm inhabited by youthful people with its own activities and mores. Modern youth culture, both in the United States and around the world, originated less with the youth themselves than with economic and demographic forces that gathered large numbers of same-aged peers together in cities and schools and workplaces, taking them out of the rural existence where they had been for centuries and where their parents had a good deal more control over courtship and marriage. This process had begun well before the dawn of the twentieth century in some locations and began later in others, but the basic pattern holds: as young people became more independent, they were able to exercise greater autonomy over their sexual and romantic selves. At the same time, by the later nineteenth century, romantic attachment itself and its relationship to marriage had undergone significant shifts in understanding; more and more people believed that marriage should be based on love and attraction between husband and wife, rather than simply economic suitability and complementarity. These beliefs trickled down to structure how young people interacted with one another in many forms of courtship, even when marriage was far from the end goal.

The general trend, in the United States and many other places, is that more and more young people had sex before they married over the course of the twentieth century, disaggregating sexual activity from marriage. Duration of courtship lengthened, as did the amount of time that a person might remain single, if they ever married at all. In part thanks to what some have called "sexual revolutions" (in the 1920s and again in the 1960s), attitudes toward premarital sex shifted, especially on the part of, and about, girls and women. The second wave of the women's movement in the 1960s and 1970s also had much to do with a growing acceptance of women's premarital sexual activity. This latter phenomenon has often been referred to as the erosion of the double standard, a standard that once sanctioned sex before marriage for men, but not women, and that continues to structure the ascribed meanings of premarital sex for boys and girls, young men and women. This decline is evident in the different responses to the actions of Fink and Brown and in the fact that today many female youth speak about their sexual relationships openly and without shame.

We know, however, that the double standard has not left us entirely. Documented here are changes in sexual behavior on the part of American young people over the course of the twentieth and twenty-first centuries; I tie these changes to the ways that a self-conscious youth culture shaped the norms for when youth might choose to have sex or be pressured into doing so. The persistence of the double standard as a way to organize and structure gender relations is demonstrated here. As it became increasingly common for girls and young women of all classes to have sex in their teens and early twenties, young men increasingly began to pressure girls to do so. And they also used a persistent double standard to enhance their own masculinity at the expense of their sexual partners' reputations. Increases in sexual permissiveness cannot be separated from the social meanings attached to sexual practices, meanings that continue to reward young men, often to the detriment of young women.

Although it should go without saying that there is no one unified "youth culture," and instead myriad variations that have developed in different regions, among varied socioeconomic classes, and among racial groups, there are (at least) two overlapping youth cultures present in most locations: one mixed-sex where young men and women share a set of expectations regarding the relationship between sex, commitment, and what constitutes exploitation; and a separate culture among some male youths, wherein young men attempt to manipulate the rules of the prior culture in order to extract sex from girls and then discuss it with their peers. Most male and female youths have participated in the former culture, whereas only a minority, although an influential minority, of male youth have been privy to the latter.

Popular culture—radio, magazines, movies, television, and eventually, the Internet—also has an enormous influence on youthful sexuality, though that role has also been dialectic. Although most youth have certainly learned about sex, dating, and romance via various forms of media, styling themselves after particular movie stars, for instance, popular culture has also responded to changes in how at least some youth have approached dating, going steady, and hooking up. Although popular culture has helped in disseminating new sexual cultures, those mores and practices are themselves derived from what at least some youthful people are already doing. That said, because the makers of television and film are interested in stories that will engage and titillate their audiences, they also sometimes select plot lines and characters on the leading edge of what only a small percentage of youth at any given time are doing. Think, for instance, of gangs, to which most young people never belong, but which see outsize media representation. Popular culture thus can represent what a minority of youth might be doing at the same time that it influences greater segments of youth to follow along.

Because youth itself is also a fuzzy category, its beginning and ending not strictly demarcated, representations of youthful sexuality on screen that depict those in their early twenties can be influential for those in their teenage years, inspiring in them behaviors that some might see as appropriate for older youth. So, too, for older youth and depictions of adult sexuality in various media. In *Where the Girls Are*, Susan Douglas has written of a generation of girls who grew up with the Shirelles, the Supremes, and other Motown groups who sang about the dangers of giving in to sexual desire—"Will You Love Me Tomorrow?"—effectively validating those feelings for their audiences.[4] So, too, movies that depicted boys and girls in love and succumbing to their desire encouraged audiences to believe that sexual feelings were natural and normal. Most youth have been consumers and not themselves producers of popular culture, and yet in the realm of fandom young people have demonstrated their affinity for particular genres and figures, and more recently zines and the Internet have allowed youth to become producers themselves. Because most youthful sexual culture produced by youth themselves is a matter of shared understandings and contested social interactions, rather than popular culture *depicting* youth, I focus primarily on those elements of a changing sexual culture for youth in the United States.

Two caveats are necessary. First, most of the sociological studies on which this work relies took high school and college students as their objects of study, and though some of those populations were multiracial, the authors of the studies did not often explicitly address racial difference in their analyses. I point out where racially distinct youth cultures might have varied from what was essentially a white, middle-class norm to augment this absence.

Second, I focus on the sexual practices and mores of youth engaged in heterosexual relationships and do not address queer youth practices, largely because for much of their history, queer youth did not constitute a separate youth culture unto themselves. Instead, queer youth mixed with their elders, both sexually and socially, and were sometimes exploited as a result of their relative lack of power in these relationships. Or they remained closeted and participated, to greater and lesser degrees, in the heterosexual youth culture that surrounded them. Queer youth cultures did emerge on college campuses by the 1970s. They were not at all common in high schools until later, only because it was atypical for youth to come out in high school until very recently. Further, much of the limited literature on queer youth from the late twentieth century to the early twenty-first century by both historians and sociologists is primarily concerned with how and when they realized their sexual identities, not the social and cultural context in which they had sex. Thus, relatively little is known about how commitment and exclusivity have structured a double or single standard for queer youth, whether male or female. Although some queer youth certainly object to casual sex, and others condone it, because sexual encounters are between people of the same sex, by definition, their repercussions for the reputations of those involved are not scripted in advance by the double standard.

The broad outlines of the U.S. account are shared by many other countries around the world, especially industrialized nations in Europe, and Canada and Australia. Many of these trends are also visible in Latin America, Asia, and parts of Africa. This is because the basic story of the emergence of youth culture and changing perceptions of the purpose of courtship and marriage also hold true elsewhere. So, too, was the emancipatory message of feminism for women's sexuality felt in other areas of the world, though in greater and lesser degrees, to be sure. Finally, American youth culture was featured in movies, music, and television shows that were also exported around the globe for consumption by youth in far-flung locations, meaning that the particular forms that youth sexuality took in the United States were influential beyond its borders.

Some changes in youthful working-class sexual culture, especially, provoked excessive handwringing on the part of middle-class observers outside the industrialized West, just as it did in the United States. In 1940s colonial Lagos, Nigeria, for instance, Abosede George shows that concerns about working-class girls' independence and the precarity of their sexual virtue took the form of a campaign to limit girl hawkers (young women who sold wares on the streets), just as girl newspaper criers were regulated in the United States. As Lagos grew and urbanized, working-class girls were sometimes endangered in their work as hawkers, and yet they also experienced greater independence and were able to make choices about their sexuality unavailable to their mothers and grandmothers. Elite reformers, however, perceived the dangers as explicitly sexual, believing that hawking would lead inexorably to prostitution. When they established a juvenile justice and welfare apparatus, girls were generally picked up for status offenses related to their girlhood: being "incorrigible," "beyond parental control," or selling on the streets after 6:30 p.m. Lagosian reformers perceived independence as sexual danger, just as American reformers did in the early part of the twentieth century.[5]

In *The English in Love*, Claire Langhamer describes a sexual culture in mid-twentieth-century England not dissimilar from that of the United States. Young courting couples met each other on the street, bus, and train, on the pier while on holiday, in schools and clubs, and in air raid shelters during the war. Wherever they met, they increasingly experimented with sex before marriage, but always in ways that were fundamentally structured by young men's greater access to money and their perceived obligation to pay for dates. This put girls and young women in the position of having to negotiate how far to go sexually, always worried about the consequences right alongside their own desires. As Langhamer puts it, "Men invested money in courtship; women invested emotion while safeguarding their sexual reputation. But the precise contours of exchange were not always transparent and it was possible to get the exchange badly wrong."[6] Sarah Fishman reports similar findings in her study of the sexual mores and behavior among French youth. In 1961 when Anita Pereire of *Elle* magazine asked twenty thousand young women (*jeunes filles*) whether a woman should be pure at the time of her marriage, 73 percent said yes. And yet Pereire so regularly received queries about whether it was proper to flirt, to approach a boy, or to go to his bedroom alone with him that Pereire published some ground rules for dating in 1960, providing advice about how forward a girl could be—not very—and when she must be exceedingly careful or else risk her safety and chastity. English and French young men and women were debating the same changed sexual landscape as Americans were, and the abiding double standard meant that although girls benefited from these changes, their reputations also bore the brunt of the consequences should they misstep.[7]

Moving forward in time, the women's and sexual liberation movements affected young women's and girls' choices around the world. In Chile by the late 1960s, various popular magazines reported that high school and college-age women no longer believed in preserving virginity until marriage. Many young women's preferred mode of sexual interaction was the *atraque*, which historian Patrick Barr-Melej describes as "sharing fleeting kisses and caresses" or "linking up." Some young women were so committed that they came up with a group called the *Movimiento Antipololeo Solo Atraque*, or No Dating, Just Linking Up Movement. Sexual behavior that, earlier in the twentieth century, might have seemed unrelated to the politics of gender, had now been linked explicitly to a feminist and revolutionist agenda. Those trends played out in the United States as well.[8]

The Loosening of Restrictions

In the United States youth in the early twentieth century paved the way for a thoroughly revised understanding of premarital sexuality. Beginning late in the prior century, a number of trends—namely, the automobile, the movies, a growing consumer culture, urbanization, the decreasing significance of religion, the increasing number of coeducational colleges, and the increase in high school attendance, among others—made it possible for young men and women to spend considerable amounts of time alone in each other's company, and away from the purview of their parents or chaperones. Beginning with the working class, youth devised new standards for sexual morality and behavior. Petting emerged as an acknowledged and discussed form of sexual intimacy, and depending upon one's standards, a girl might allow petting (that is, contact between hands and breasts and/or genitals, sometimes to the point of orgasm) or perform it herself while still maintaining her virginity (at least technically), and her reputation.

Most evidence indicates that working-class youth were always more sexually permissive than those in the middle class, precisely because sexual respectability was not a key part of working-class people's class-based identity. This was true regardless of whether they lived in rural or urban areas, were white or African American. Sexual experimentation among rural youth in the early twentieth century often began around thirteen or fourteen and could start as early as seven or eight. Part of how middle-class people performed their identity and demonstrated that they *were* middle class was by refraining from sex until marriage. There are two notable exceptions to this general rule. Some middle-class couples who were seriously enough involved as to be engaged had sex prior to marriage; the incidence of pregnant brides attested to this phenomenon. And many middle-class men and youth had sex with prostitutes and working-class women, sometimes through what working-class people called "treating," the primary innovation in courtship of this era.

A treat was a social occasion whereby a youth or man paid for a young woman's evening out on the town—dinner, drinks, perhaps a movie or admission to an amusement park—and she rewarded him via sexual favors at the end of the evening. No social stigma attached to either party, and everyone involved understood treating as different from prostitution, where cash was exchanged for sex. Historians Kathy Peiss and Elizabeth Clement explain that treating emerged among urban, working-class youth, who developed the rules that governed its acceptability. In 1914, for example, one young African American New Yorker told a vice investigator that

> she ain't out for the dollar but is as game as the rest of them and if she likes a white man, she'd go the limit with him, she wouldn't expect any pay for it but if she needs a new pair of shoes or waist she'd expect him to buy it for her.[9]

Treating was a way for underpaid working girls to enjoy nighttime amusements, and sometimes other material goods, which were paid for by boys and men who earned more than they did. Some middle-class youth, however, took advantage of this sexual system developed among the working class to satisfy their sexual desires with women who they understood as fundamentally different from them and not material for formal dating and marriage. These could be women who were of a lower socioeconomic class or of a different racial or ethnic group. Thus, early on in the development of treating, there was a double standard built in that benefited middle-class men. They courted or dated one set of women and treated others in exchange for sex. They also visited prostitutes if they wanted a more straightforward reward of sex for cash. By the same token, Clement also argues that some Black girls might have been more likely to engage in treating with wealthier or older white men, precisely because they expected to marry Black men and they may have wanted to maintain a separation between treating and the kind of courting that might lead to marriage.[10]

Some middle-class male youth also boasted about these encounters with working-class women, demonstrating to their male peers that they were masculine by virtue of their sexual encounters. As one of Robert and Helen Lynd's informants told them in *Middletown*, their 1920s study of the town of Muncie, Indiana, "'The fellows nowadays don't seem to mind being seen on the street with a fast woman, but you bet we did then!'" This informant, whom the Lynds described as having been a "young buck about town" in the 1880s, did not seem to be denying his own involvement with "fast women"; he was just decrying the openness with which some Middletown male youth carried on with them in the 1920s.[11] Although these young men may not have verbally boasted about their exploits, their openness amounted to an announcement about their sexual practices. Because middle-class men and boys were trained to believe that respectable girls would not "put out" till marriage, this kind of boasting was often framed as a tale of exploitation, the middle-class male youth having extracted from his supposedly unwilling date that which she should know better than to give. This was despite the fact that many working-class girls and women may well have been perfectly willing participants in the encounters, with little need to be coerced into having sex.

There was a great range in the agency that girls experienced in relation to their sexuality. In some instances, working-class teenage girls willingly participated in sex with casual partners, which sometimes landed them in trouble with the law. Juvenile justice authorities and social workers of this era categorized girls, but not boys, as criminal or "incorrigible" for premarital sex and sought to place them in reformatories. In other instances, girls were exploited by older men, some of them boarders in their mothers' homes. Historian Marcia Chatelain has shown that the poverty endemic to many African American households in Chicago's Great Migration often did lead to extreme vulnerability for some girls, some of whom married, had children themselves, and sometimes entered into prostitution while still teenagers. This was not "youth culture," per se, but that is only because economic circumstances did not allow for some youth to exist in a culture apart from their elders, a sobering reminder that youth culture is not equally available to all youth.[12]

Middle-class youth adapted the basic outlines of treating into what they called dating: boy pays for outing with girl, but unlike with treating, there was no explicit quid pro quo about what he was owed sexually in return for paying for the date. What this increasingly meant for middle-class boys and girls who dated was that their relations with each other were structured by a set of unwritten but widely understood rules whereby a boy attempted to get as much from a girl sexually as he was able and a girl attempted to have fun and appease the boy, while at the same time retaining her virtue and her popularity. This situation was clearly somewhat adversarial. That it proved difficult for women especially is unquestionable. Many writing on this period, and on all periods at least through the 1970s, have rightly noted that standards often varied widely from school to school and by region of the country. Different schools unofficially sanctioned different standards of sexual conduct for both their male and female students.

Although many high school and college youth were engaging in necking and petting through the 1920s (and beyond), most were *not* having sexual intercourse. A number of studies demonstrate that young women coming of age in the 1920s were much more likely to have had intercourse than prior generations, in Alfred Kinsey's study double that for women only a decade older, about 36 percent, but this number includes women who had had sex *any time prior to marriage*, not those who necessarily did so while in their teenage years or early twenties. In *Middletown*, the Lynds, writing of a sexual taboo against premarital sex, say that "there appears to be some tentative relaxing of this taboo among the younger generation, but in general it is as strong today as in the county-seat of forty years ago." Many of the youth of Middletown were engaged in petting, however, sometimes at what were called "petting parties," but most stopped short of intercourse.[13]

In 1920s Los Angeles, Nisei, or second-generation Japanese American youth, engaged in similar courtship rituals. Young men were responsible for picking up their dates, sometimes in cars borrowed from parents, and escorting them to movies or dances and socials at Japanese American youth clubs. Valerie Matsumoto reports that younger boys and girls were more likely to attend these events in same-sex groups, leaving and arriving together, whereas older teenagers were more likely to be paired off on dates. In the tight-knit Japanese American community, parents often knew the boys their daughters dated and those boys' parents as well. Girls who wanted to date interracially were careful to be discreet and do so away from Little Tokyo. In all cases, Nisei girls, like their Mexican American counterparts in Los Angeles, knew that they were held to a higher standard when it came to sex and that their sexual reputation was important in a way that was not true for their brothers.[14]

Almost all studies demonstrate that the vast majority of those middle-class young women of any racial or ethnic group who had sexual intercourse prior to marriage did so with fiancés. Young men, by contrast, were more likely to have had sex with prostitutes and working-class women. Two studies published in the mid-1920s of men who were then in college demonstrated that about 35 percent of male college students had experienced sexual intercourse in their teens or early twenties. The authors also inquired about the men's sexual partners and found that a sizable minority of those who had had intercourse had done so at least once with a prostitute.[15] Those men not having sex with prostitutes were probably engaging in coitus with women of a lower-class background than they, what men called "pickups," women and girls picked up for the express purpose of having sex. Young women were caught in a system that allowed for more sexual freedom than in previous eras but whose rules were much less clearly delineated, and thus that much more treacherous.

THE BIRTH OF GOING STEADY

Young people's rates of sexual intercourse did not rise significantly during the 1930s or early 1940s, though their attitudes toward premarital sexual permissiveness did relax. Observers also noted that there seemed to be more steady dating leading to marriage than formerly, and that sex and affection were more spontaneous, and not governed quite so strictly by the standards of conduct laid out by campus expectations in the rating and dating complex. The 1930s marks the birth, albeit in inchoate form, of "going steady." As historian John Spurlock has argued,

> If we want to assign a single cause to the lower age at which teenagers, especially girls, became sexually active in the late twentieth century, then "the pill," World War II, and the sexual openness of the 1960s all have less claim on our attention than does the shift from the ephemeral dalliance relationships of dating to the long-term involvement of going steady.[16]

Going steady, the trend whereby young people paired off into long-term couples instead of going on dates with multiple *different* people, led to increased sexual intimacy for what are probably the obvious reasons: young men and women came to care for each other and multiple social occasions with the same person also allowed for increased opportunities for sex. As couples grew more and more serious they began to think of marriage, if not actually becoming engaged, and this increased the levels of trust that young women felt toward male partners, which also contributed to their willingness to engage in more intimacy, including intercourse itself.

In their 1937 return to Muncie, Indiana, *Middletown in Transition*, the Lynds observed a loosening of strictures on public necking and affection among Middletown youth. The Lynds believed that a growing population at the local college (Ball State University) and college students' tendency to experiment with sex had led to more experimentation among local high school students as well. Their adult informants described high school students as "increasingly sophisticated," and one observed, "They've been getting more and more knowing and bold. The fellows regard necking as a taken-for-granted part of a date. We fellows used occasionally to get slapped for doing things [eight years prior], but the girls don't do that much any more." Among a group of what they describe as "two dozen young business-class persons in their twenties," 7 out of 10 men and women had had sexual relations prior to marriage. In August Hollingshead's 1949 study, *Elmtown's Youth*, for which he conducted fieldwork in 1941 and 1942 in what he described as a "Middlewestern Corn Belt community," working-class high school youth were increasingly likely to be going steady, which led, for many of them, to sexual experimentation and often to marriage at younger ages. Even in the cases of steady dating in Elmtown, those girls who had sexual experience with steady boyfriends were likely to be both younger and of a lower socioeconomic class than the boys they were dating. Hollingshead noted, "Clearly in this small sample there was a strong tendency for young Elmtown males to exploit lower class females sexually." The double standard persisted even in courtship forms that might not at first have seemed to be conducive to it.[17]

Although these two studies document towns that were almost exclusively white, similar trends in going steady prevailed among African Americans in the South as well, with increased rates of high school attendance fostering a culture that emphasized romantic pairings. This emphasis upon sexual expression within couples also led wealthier Black girls and boys to be more restrictive sexually, just as their white peers were actually becoming more permissive. Mexican American girls in California were generally raised with more strict supervision during this period, often going to dances with chaperones, but some rebelled against their parents by going steady with boys and moving out of their natal homes. There is no question that they, too, were influenced toward greater permissiveness by the changing youth culture around them.

In 1938 journalists Dorothy Dunbar Bromley and Florence Haxton Britten published a survey of over 1,300 college juniors and seniors, *Youth and Sex*, and reported that one-half of the men and one-quarter of the women had had sexual intercourse sometime in the past. This is a demonstrable increase from the 1920s for both male and female youth.[18] Among other trends, they noted the increased tolerance of sexual activity with affection, especially among their female respondents, though the women were still, predictably, quite far behind the men in terms of just how far they were willing to go before marriage. They also noted the definite persistence, despite this gradual liberalization of attitudes, in the belief in a double standard, by both their male and female respondents.

The authors divided their sample into twelve different categories, varying by their sex, attitudes, and sexual behaviors. One such category, the Hot Bloods, were those men who had had sex with between five and fifty women apiece; they constituted about 25 percent of the total men. And most of them had had sex with women of social classes lower than their own, including prostitutes. Most of these boys adhered to a double standard whereby they would have sex with a prostitute or a pickup but probably not with their girlfriends. Although the Hot Bloods were in college at the time of the study, they had been behaving like this since high school, seeking out sex wherever they could find it. As one typical boy explained of his ideal type, "She must be at least a little hard to get—but gettable."[19]

Although most of the subjects had some experience with necking and petting, many of the young women in the study had not had sexual intercourse precisely because of the effect they imagined it might have on their reputations or because of ideas about purity. As one explained about her lack of experience in petting, "mother and dad asked me not to, and the boys I went around with never seemed to expect it." This girl, and many others like her, believed that good girls only went so far before marriage.[20]

And many of them liked it this way. As Bromley and Britton explain of some of the young women in their study,

> Those who intended to wait for marriage argued that they would want to be initiated into the great and rather terrifying adventure by a man who had got beyond the fumbling stage. They would prefer that he had not been initiated by a prostitute, but they would draw the line only at a man who was diseased. Accepting the conventional moral code, they were not concerned about the exploited class of street-corner girls and prostitutes who presumably exist to teach other women's future husbands of the A B C of sex.[21]

The double standard, in other words, was not only beneficial to a certain class of young man who sought sex and courtship with different kinds of young women; some of those young women also saw themselves as benefiting from it as well.

Despite a general relaxing of strictures around necking, petting, and intercourse during the 1930s and 1940s, sexual relations among young men and women were thus still structured by the double standard: almost all parties involved seeming to be cognizant of who could be expected to do what and what that might mean for their reputations. Among middle-class high school and college students, a mixed-sex youth culture of dating and courtship prevailed in which some sexual activity was permissible under particular guidelines, and there was also a shadow youth culture among some male youth, whereby sex with working-class girls or those otherwise undesirable as long-term partners was rewarded by male peers. The systems of dating and treating were more conducive to this culture, but going steady could also accommodate it if men were willing to be disingenuous with their partners. This shadow culture was also dependent on differing tendencies toward permissiveness between working- and middle-class girls. But as more middle-class girls became more permissive over the course of the twentieth century, male youth participating in this shadow culture could increasingly turn to their same-class peers for sex.

Permissiveness with Affection

By the 1940s and 1950s, youthful Americans continued many of the practices that an earlier generation had developed. Rating and dating seem to have decreased further, as couples continued to go steady in ever-larger numbers, and there was less of a break between dating, engagement, and marriage. The age of first marriage declined precipitously, and rates of teenage birth, both within marriage and outside of it, increased exponentially. Young people's attitudes toward sex when a couple were in love or engaged continued to relax; permissiveness with affection became the single standard for many more. The adoption of this attitude was much truer, however, for women than for men. Of the girls and young women who had sex before marriage, the greatest number did so with their future spouses only; this was not the case for the men.

As a number of historians have now demonstrated, the more widespread adoption of the "permissiveness with affection" standard had many consequences for high school and college youth. In the most basic sense, many girls and boys now felt free to experiment sexually, up to and including intercourse. In an era without reliable access to birth control or much in the way of sex education, however, this sometimes resulted in pregnancy. For many thousands, this led to coerced adoption of children born to high school mothers out of wedlock, although Black girls were much more likely to keep their babies and raise them as single mothers than were their white counterparts. It also led to a huge increase in what at the time were called "forced marriages," those necessitated by the pregnancy of the bride. The increased tolerance for permissiveness with affection had other consequences: it also meant that those girls who still didn't want to have sex before marriage had lost one of the primary tools they had to resist intercourse; many were no longer able to call on possible community sanction or loss of reputation as a way to resist boyfriends' advances. And finally, there is ample evidence not only that boys knew this and used it to pressure girlfriends, but also that many took outright advantage of girlfriends via coercion or assault.

Winston Ehrmann found in his 1959 study that though for girls and young women the relation between sexual intercourse and feelings of love was directly related, "the degree of physical intimacy which the males had experienced or would permit themselves to experience is *inversely related* to the intensity of familiarity and affection existing in the male-female relationship." Boys and male youth were much more likely to have had sexual relations with what Ehrmann calls acquaintances or friends than with long-term partners; for girls the relation was exactly the opposite. The link between class and sexual partners is also striking. Young men and women were both more likely to date within their own social class; however, of those boys and men who dated above or below their social class (and they were more likely to do the latter), they were from 20 to 30 percent more likely to go further with working-class girls than they were with girls of their own class. Boys who had sex with working-class girls typically felt that they should attempt to go as far as they were able, often differentiating implicitly between pickups and good girls, as in the following: "I do have some regard for their feelings. . . . Pick-ups are, of course, another story." Another, who said that it would be wrong to do that (coitus) to "a girl," had already experienced intercourse with thirteen female people, none of them apparently girls in his mind.[22]

A Sexual Revolution?

Well before the 1960s, young women's and men's attitudes toward premarital sex had been changing gradually, with rates of young men's sexual intercourse steadily climbing, and girls' and young women's climbing, though more slowly and never keeping pace with that of men. These changes, which were really a result of the culture of going steady, came to be more openly embraced during the 1960s, when a distinct minority of young people began to openly question the morality of abstaining from premarital sex, and when many more joined them in spirit by refusing to wait until marriage. Although figures for women who had had sexual intercourse either before or during college from the 1920s onward had ranged from 13 to 25 percent (most of them closer to the lower end), by 1968, investigators were finding that as many as 41 percent of college women had had premarital sex, and this study was among a group of sophomores. As Ira Reiss put it in 1966, "What was done by a female in 1925 acting as a rebel and a deviant can be done by a female in 1965 as a conformist." This was increasingly true across racial and ethnic groups. One 1966 study, *Mexican American Youth*, found strikingly similar rates of the offense of "illegitimate sex relations," meaning sex outside of marriage, for Mexican and Anglo-American girls aged from fifteen to nineteen, 26 and 28 percent, respectively. Tellingly, the same actions for boys in both groups barely rated as "offenses" in the first place. What girls and boys must have been doing with one another was an offense for the girls and simply expected of the boys.[23]

To return to the two young women introduced earlier, what Frances Fink had been blackmailed for having done, Frances Brown did openly and eventually without punishment. The revolution in contraceptive technology—the diaphragm and the pill—also contributed to this rise in intercourse. No longer was the possibility of pregnancy as likely as it once had been. Because the double standard remained, however, there were still women reluctant to go "all the way" for fear of risking their reputations and their prospects for a husband, not to mention pregnancy and venereal disease. Rates of petting and other sexual behaviors, always far ahead of intercourse for both sexes, were also increasing. The decline, though certainly not the fall, of the double standard had brought about a sexual economy whereby more and more high school boys and college men were dating, petting, and having sex with their classmates, and not the pickups and prostitutes of earlier decades.

One incident from 1968 encapsulates many of these changes. In March of that year, the *New York Times* ran a story called "An Arrangement: Living Together for Convenience, Security, Sex," about a Barnard College student named Linda LeClair who had chosen to move out of her college dorm to live with her boyfriend, Peter Behr. LeClair and Behr explained that they had made this decision for economic and personal reasons, and though they might marry one day, they had no immediate plans to do so. As Beth Bailey explains in *Sex in the Heartland*, once Barnard officials discovered the arrangement, the college president asked LeClair to leave Barnard, which she did. More interestingly, however, the case brought widespread national attention, with hundreds of people calling and writing Barnard's administrators. Many objected to what they saw as LeClair's "flaunting" of her relationship; these were conservative Americans who believed that sex should be confined to marriage. Others worried that LeClair was being taken advantage of by Behr, that he was getting the benefits of marriage (sex) without making any commitment. LeClair and Behr explained to the *Times*, however, that they did not think about their relationship in terms of a quid pro quo of sex in exchange for commitment. Yes, they had sex with one another, but they also shared meals and expenses and were friends with one another. Bailey shows that what was significant about LeClair and Behr's relationship and the way they framed it was not as demonstrative of a sexual revolution as it was of gender. They refused the terms of the double standard, explaining that in their relationship they were equals, effectively saying that the sex they had with one another did not have a different meaning or value for Behr than it did for LeClair. The uproar about the story, however, including the support that LeClair received from her fellow classmates, demonstrates a continued divide in the United States, many clinging to a double standard that mandated the relationship be understood as exploitation. These included people who feared for LeClair *and* those who condemned her.[24]

Young people had been at the forefront not just of greater sexual permissiveness prior to marriage, but also, as in the case of LeClair and Behr, of how they understood that permissiveness. Seen from one angle, this is just the story of sexual liberation. But from another, more and more women were now pressured and coerced into having sex because it was harder to say no and use lack of birth control or fears of a bad reputation as an excuse. Gloria Steinem wrote about this in a 1962 piece in *Esquire* magazine that she called "The Moral Disarmament of Betty Coed." As sexual experience became more and more common, especially for young men, it only served to increase the pressure upon high school and college youth to have sex if they had not already done so. As greater numbers of girls and young women became more permissive, young men increasingly realized that they could obtain sex not just from pickups and prostitutes but also from their peers on campus. As sex became more accepted, and readily available, the reasons for not having had it, for men especially, dwindled. No longer could one say that it was impossible to meet a willing woman, and only the most religious and isolated men continued to insist in any public way that they would wait until marriage before having sex. Masculinity was increasingly associated with virility, and it was done so by an ever-growing percentage of the population. Testament to this is the decreasing support, if not downright scorn, for virginity in men (not to mention women in some circles). In her 1964 *Sex and the College Girl*, reporter Gael Greene only half-jokingly describes the necessity of losing one's virginity as being "... an unpleasant duty—like ROTC, only a bit more attractive." For men, especially, to be a virgin was now something of which to be ashamed.[25]

What all this meant for boys who had not abandoned the double standard was that girls of one's own class (in both senses of the word, economic and collegiate) could now be nice or bad girls, though never one and the same, at least not at the same time and for the same man. A young man would not know which kind she was until he tried his luck. As one researcher explained of a research subject and his date, "He did not approve of her going to bed with him so soon after their first meeting." In this instance, described in such a way that the man's role in the sexual encounter is almost erased, that man lost respect for his date for engaging in sex *with him*. She had proven herself too willing, even though she was presumably fulfilling his wishes as well. One of the informants in *Sex and the College Girl* put it this way: "It takes a lot of mental gymnastics to 'respect' a girl with whom you've had contact almost to the point of intercourse, then lose respect for her as soon as she goes all the way." Unfortunately, these sorts of gymnastics were actually not all that challenging for many young men during this era, as they continued to pursue both casual sex and sometimes longer-term relationships, just not with the same young women.[26]

Sociologist Eugene Kanin found that the most aggressive men were also more likely to use a greater variety of strategies to obtain sex from women than were other men: alcohol, promises of marriage and declarations of love, threats of breaking up, and physical force. Although many of these men were hesitant to admit that they would use force, they readily admitted to the other strategies:

> Erotic achievement is now evaluated by taking into account the desirability of the sex object and the nature of its acquisition. A successful "snow job" on an attractive but reluctant female who may be rendered into a relatively dependable sex outlet and socially desirable companion is considerably more enhancing than an encounter with a prostitute or a "one night stand" with a "loose" reputation.

Men sanctioned some aggression, however, when it served to bring a deviant woman back into conformity, or into the place that they had understood her to occupy: the bad girl.[27]

Thus, following the supposed sexual revolution of the 1960s, young men and women really were more permissive, largely thanks to the increase in going steady, which had actually developed in the 1930s. Both young men's and women's sexual permissiveness had increased over the course of that period, and youth cultures continued to endorse at least some version of a double standard that punished young women and girls for engaging in the behavior that was rewarded when enacted by young men and boys.

The Persistence of the Double Standard

From the late twentieth century to the early twenty-first, most of these trends continued apace. More young people have become sexually active prior to marriage. According to the Alan Guttmacher Institute, the current average age at which American youth first have sex is seventeen. In 2011–2013, among unmarried fifteen-to-nineteen-year-olds, 44 percent of girls have had sex and 49 percent of boys. These percentages have remained steady since 2002, though the percentage of teens below the age of fifteen who have had sex has actually declined somewhat. Many of these numbers document similar rates and ages for both boys and girls, a legacy of the changes in understandings of sexuality and gender that this chapter has documented.[28]

And yet remnants of gendered differences remain. Between 2006 and 2010, 73 percent of girls and 58 percent of boys reported that their first sexual experience was in the context of a relationship. Sixteen percent of girls and 28 percent of males reported that that experience was more fleeting, either with someone they had just met or with a friend. First sex was described as wanted by 62 percent of boys, but only 41 percent of girls. There is clear evidence of gender difference here that may well be explained by the persistence of the double standard: girls are more likely to be pressured into sex; boys are pursuing casual sex at higher rates than girls. If all of these encounters were wanted and consensual, then of course there would be no cause for concern, but when the Guttmacher Institute documents so many unwanted encounters, then there is clearly still a problem.[29]

Even in an era in which both young men and women themselves initiate sex in both casual encounters and long-term relationships, young women continue to be evaluated differently for their casual sexual behavior than do men, and some young women are specifically targeted for sex alone, not for longer-term relationships. In one study documenting the sexual behavior of African American teenagers in South Carolina, young men described what they called a "flip":

> The definition of a flip is when a guy talks to a girl, he usually has sexual contact with her. Then after a while you start sexting her, talking about this and that, then you have sex eventually.... You give her number, give him [a male friend] a chance to get her number, then you give him a chance to have sex with her, and then it keeps carrying on through the whole group. And eventually the girls like we call them flips 'cause they flip from one guy inside a group to another guy.[30]

Though the flips in this scenario are participating willingly, these teenage boys are bonding with one another via the flip, denigrating her sexual availability both to bolster their masculinity and solidify their friendship. Girls and young women who are called flips, or whores or sluts, are so named because they are seen to participate in sex too freely. These epithets can be harmful and carry real cultural currency. Although few people in contemporary culture would refer to a woman living in a long-term relationship with her boyfriend as a slut, as many called Linda LeClair in 1968, the fact that the flip and the slut still exist as cultural categories tells us simply that the parameters have changed, not the double standard itself. These terms are still highly gendered; when men are called sluts it is, by and large, meant in jest, precisely because most find it inconceivable that a man or boy *could* have too much sex.

It is also clear that in the realm of teenage and youth sexual culture more generally, a double standard persists around the issue of pleasure. In hookup culture, for instance, young women perform more oral sex than young men do and also have fewer orgasms. Boys' and young men's sexual pleasure is being prioritized during these encounters, so much so that some have started referring to this difference as the "orgasm gap."[31] In part this likely stems from the fact that many young men and women frame sex as something that girls agree to do *for* boys to please them, not as an act entered into enthusiastically by both partners for the purpose of mutual satisfaction. All of this tells us that though the role of sex in American youth cultures has indeed changed enormously over the last century, a residual double standard remains that influences not just how girls' and boys' deciding to have sex is perceived by their peers, but also the very experience of the act of sex itself.

Notes

1. Anonymous letter to Miss Fink, February 18, 1924, VP for Student Affairs Collection, Box 1, Folder: "Meetings, 1924–1925," Bentley Historical Library, University of Michigan.
2. Frances Louise Fink to Dean Joseph A. Bursley, January 25, 1927, and Bursley to Fink, February 1, 1927, VP for Student Affairs Collection, Box 1, Folder: "Meetings, 1926–1927," Bentley Historical Library, University of Michigan.
3. William Long, Dean of Men, to Leith Morrow, John Van MacNair, and John C. Ingram, August 26, 1965; B. J. Brown and Frances D. Brown to Dean William Long, September 13, 1965, Chancellor's Records, Chancellor Sharp Series, Subseries 10, Box 10, Folder: "Student Affairs, Aug.–Sept. 1965," University Archives, Wilson Library, University of North Carolina at Chapel Hill.
4. Susan J. Douglas, *Where the Girls Are: Growing Up Female with the Mass Media* (New York: Times Books, 1995), chap. 4.
5. Abosede George, *Making Modern Girls: A History of Girlhood, Labor, and Social Development in Colonial Lagos* (Athens: Ohio University Press, 2014), 115, 178, 183.
6. Claire Langhamer, *The English in Love: The Intimate Story of an Emotional Revolution* (Oxford: Oxford University Press, 2013), 92, 126.
7. Sarah Fishman, *From Vichy to the Sexual Revolution: Gender and Family Life in Postwar France* (Oxford: Oxford University Press, 2017), 161, 166.
8. Patrick Barr-Melej, *Psychedelic Chile: Youth, Counterculture, and the Road to Socialism and Dictatorship* (Chapel Hill: University of North Carolina Press, 2017), 77.
9. Qtd. in Elizabeth Alice Clement, *Love for Sale: Treating, Courting, and Prostitution in New York City, 1890–1945* (Chapel Hill: University of North Carolina Press, 2005), 65.
10. Ibid.
11. Robert S. Lynd and Helen Merrell Lynd, *Middletown: A Study in American Culture* (New York: Harcourt, Brace, and Company, 1929), 112.
12. Marcia Chatelain, *South Side Girls: Growing Up in the Great Migration* (Durham, NC: Duke University Press, 2015), 33–36.
13. John Spurlock, *Youth and Sexuality in the Twentieth-Century United States* (New York: Routledge, 2016), 50; Lynd and Lynd, *Middletown*, 112, 139–140.
14. Valerie Matsumoto, *City Girls: The Nisei Social World in Los Angeles, 1920–1950* (New York: Oxford University Press, 2014), 67–69.
15. M. W. Peck and F. L. Wells, "On the Psychosexuality of College Graduate Men," *Mental Hygiene* 7, no. 4 (1923), 708, 707. In their follow-up article two years later, the percentage

had risen to 37: Peck and Wells, "Further Studies in the Psychosexuality of College Graduate Men," *Mental Hygiene* 9, no. 3 (1925), 514.
16. Spurlock, *Youth and Sexuality*, 64.
17. Robert S. Lynd and Helen Merrell Lynd, *Middletown in Transition: A Study in Cultural Conflict* (New York: Harcourt, Brace and Company, 1937), 168–171; August Hollingshead, *Elmtown's Youth: The Impact of Social Classes on Adolescents* (New York: John Wiley and Sons, 1949), vii, 240.
18. Dorothy Dunbar Bromley and Florence Haxton Britten, *Youth and Sex: A Study of 1300 College Students* (New York: Harper & Brothers, 1938), 134, 4.
19. Ibid., 160.
20. Ibid., 48.
21. Ibid., 60.
22. Winston Ehrmann, *Premarital Dating Behavior* (New York: Henry Holt, 1959), 178 (italics in original), 147, 236.
23. Gilbert R. Kaats and Keith E. Davis, "The Dynamics of Sexual Behavior of College Students," *Journal of Marriage and the Family* 32, no. 3 (1970), 390; Ira L. Reiss, "The Sexual Renaissance: A Summary and an Analysis," *Journal of Social Issues* 22, no. 2 (1966), 126; Celia S. Heller, *Mexican American Youth: Forgotten Youth at the Crossroads* (New York: Random House, 1966), 71–72.
24. Beth Bailey, *Sex in the Heartland* (Cambridge, MA: Harvard University Press, 1999), 200–205.
25. Gloria Steinem, "The Moral Disarmament of Betty Coed," *Esquire*, September 1962, 97, 153–157; Gael Greene, *Sex and the College Girl* (New York: Dial, 1964), 22–23.
26. Mirra Komarovsky, *Dilemmas of Masculinity: A Study of College Youth* (New York: W. W. Norton & Company, Inc., 1976), 90; Greene, *Sex and the College Girl*, 175.
27. Eugene J. Kanin, "An Examination of Sexual Aggression as a Response to Sexual Frustration," *Journal of Marriage and the Family* 29, no. 3 (1967), 501, 502.
28. Guttmacher Institute, "Adolescent Sexual and Reproductive Health in the United States" fact sheet, September 2017, available at https://www.guttmacher.org/fact-sheet/american-teens-sexual-and-reproductive-health (accessed June 13, 2019).
29. Ibid.
30. Judith Davidson, *Sexting: Gender and Teens* (Rotterdam: Sense Publishers, 2014), 53.
31. Lisa Wade, *American Hookup: The New Culture of Sex on Campus* (New York: Norton, 2017), chap. 7.

Further Reading

Bailey, Beth. *From Front Porch to Back Seat: Courtship in Twentieth-Century America*. Baltimore: Johns Hopkins University Press, 1989.
Bailey, Beth. *Sex in the Heartland*. Cambridge, MA: Harvard University Press, 1999.
Clement, Elizabeth Alice. *Love for Sale: Treating, Courting, and Prostitution in New York City, 1890–1945*. Chapel Hill: University of North Carolina Press, 2005.
Fass, Paula. *The Damned and the Beautiful: American Youth in the 1920's*. New York: Oxford University Press, 1977.

Kordas, Ann. *Female Adolescent Sexuality in the United States, 1850–1965*. Lanham: Lexington, 2019.

Littauer, Amanda. *Bad Girls: Young Women, Sex, and Rebellion before the Sixties*. Chapel Hill: University of North Carolina Press, 2015.

Modell, John. "Dating Becomes the American Way of Life." In *Essays on the Family and Historical Change*. Edited by Leslie Page Moch and Gary D. Stark, 91–126. College Station: Texas A&M University Press, 1983.

Schrum, Kelly. *Some Wore Bobby Sox: The Emergence of Teenage Girls' Culture, 1920–1945*. New York: Palgrave Macmillan, 2004.

Spurlock, John. *Youth and Sexuality in the Twentieth-Century United States*. New York: Routledge, 2016.

Syrett, Nicholas L. *American Child Bride: A History of Minors and Marriage in the United States*. Chapel Hill: University of North Carolina Press, 2016.

Wade, Lisa. *American Hookup: The New Culture of Sex on Campus*. New York: W. W. Norton, 2017.

CHAPTER 18

CELEBRATING HOLIDAYS AND INSTILLING VALUES

Religion, Nationalism, and Youth Organization in Twentieth-Century Youth Culture

DYLAN BAUN

SCHOLARS of the historical construction of "youth" in the Global South often link the life stage to the expansion of liberal education—vis-à-vis colonialism—or global secularization more broadly. Accordingly, it is assumed that to be young in the late nineteenth and early twentieth centuries is to be secular. Yet, even as these trends in education and socialization placed young people at the center of national, secular development, this does not necessarily mean that religion, or religious affiliation, disappeared. Instead, especially in diverse, pluralistic societies, religious identity served as the backdrop for the creation of many youth organizations. Furthermore, practices central to religious identity, such as being pious and modest, are also central to youth culture, irrespective of period or locale.

Religion, religious identity, and religious practice played important roles in youth organizations in twentieth-century Lebanon. This tiny country on the Eastern Mediterranean provides a strong case study for how religion and youth interact in pluralistic societies, or what are often referred to pejoratively as "sectarian societies." While many of the youth organizations in twentieth-century Lebanon were organized according to religious denomination (e.g., Sunni Muslim, Maronite Catholic, Shi'a

Muslim, Druze), none of them were overtly religious. At the same time, religious identity and practice were central to their sense of being and their engagement in youth and popular culture.

While Lebanon is, of course, unique, it is not exceptional. As secularism became normalized and entrenched across the world, so did the presence of religious values (morality, temperance, honor) without religious doctrine in youth culture. This trend is apparent in youth organizations from Lebanon to China, as adult leaders taught young members moral citizenship and the politics of uprightness, sometimes completely devoid of religious instruction. Stated differently, even if religious doctrine were not central to youth organization in pluralistic societies across the Global South, religious identity served as the basis for group structure, discipline, and lived youth experience.

Moreover, religious and national (secular) identity was not contradictory for young people in youth organizations. Indeed, the ideal citizen, often imagined as a man, was a pious, young patriot, ready for the cause, whether that cause was national defense or spiritual activity. This was both internalized by young people and pushed upon adults by young people to constitute a hybrid youth culture, one that was national, disciplined, and religious all at the same time. Given this reality, it is necessary for historians of youth culture to consider the place of religious identity in their research, both across and beyond the Global South, and within and outside the modern world.

The concept of "youthfulness," or *futuwwa* in Arabic, has many connotations but has always been defined in relation to religion. Incorporating *futuwwa* into the history of youth culture allows for a re-evaluation of the relationship between youth culture and religion in the twentieth-century Global South. Youth organizations in Lebanon and beyond provide opportunities to "read" youth culture in two ways. The first uses a nuanced understanding of "sectarianism," or the politics of identity in pluralistic societies, to explore religious rituals and holidays within youth organizations. The second takes up scouting to analyze the teaching of religious values within youth organizations. In addition to collective rituals and rules, the sources these groups left behind allow an interpretation of individual experiences of young people and the cultures they constructed. Situating religion in youth culture and organization highlights the ways in which this form of self-expression can be both empowering and a site of disciplinary politics.

QUESTIONING THE RELIGIOUS–SECULAR YOUTH RUPTURE

In their groundbreaking *Transnational Histories of Youth in the Twentieth Century* (2015), editors Richard Jobs and David Pomfret celebrate the volume's "comparative, transnational framework for rethinking youth, the nation, mobility, and modernity." They also acknowledge that a "variety of important topics and issues in the history of youth transnationality" are absent, including "religion and spirituality."[1] Indeed, whether the work is national, regional, or transnational in thrust, there are very few historical studies that take up the relationship between youth and religion in the twentieth century (this is not the case for contemporary anthropology, sociology, or religious studies).

Haggai Erlich's *Youth & Revolution in the Changing Middle East, 1908–2014* serves as an exception. Erlich's study is the only to date to focus principally on youth and young people in the modern Middle East. Furthermore, Erlich's work stands out as one of the few books to take up youth across an entire region—rather than in a single nation-state—in all its diversity, with an emphasis on the place of religion. Therefore, Erlich's arguments can be useful for framing a broader discussion about the relationship between youth culture and religion, both in the twentieth-century Middle East, and across and beyond the Global South.

Erlich uses secularization theory to argue that the historical construction of youth in the Middle East was born in the late nineteenth century. He links youth to the development of "the modern school system [that] was not set up to train religious figures to lead a religious society . . . [but] was established to serve and contribute through their new and modern professional and practical knowledge." Erlich characterizes the effects of this educational shift as follows: "The new educated youth was seen as a new sector or class of modern students. They were viewed as free from personal, familial, or sectarian interests and as a bearing the hope of future redemption for all." Throughout the twentieth century, young people were at the forefront of the macrolevel trends of the time: from the "Ottoman 'Land of Islam'" to "a liberal age" and then "shifts as the secular and socialist 'Arab world' gave way to the political revival of Islam."[2]

Erlich is correct to focus on how the "new meaning of knowledge and how to acquire it" transformed the way young people—and adults—conceived their roles in society.[3] However, as others, including Elizabeth Thompson and Benjamin Fortna, argue, the shifts were not as much a rupture from a religious past as the product of late Ottoman reform efforts inspired by Islam and liberal education alike. Tied to this, the cyclical nature of religious identity and youth culture that Erlich lays out, from traditional and religious to secular and young to religious again, is suspect. It links with others who characterize global events and themes of the 1970s, ranging from the Iranian Revolution to evangelicalism in the United States, as part of a religious revival. While it can be argued that public and overt religiosity have been on the rise in a neoliberal, globalized world, there is much evidence that religious identity did not just go away in the early twentieth century, and come back later, but was always there.

The Arabic concept of *futuwwa* is useful to understanding Erlich's work on youth in the Middle East. This word translates to "youthfulness," a well-established term in youth studies that often refers to the state of being young, whether defined by age, race, gender, or class. Unlike the English word "youthfulness," *futuwwa* dates back to the eighth century. Similar to its English parallel, however, *futuwwa* is quite elastic with both positive and pejorative connotations, depending on the historical context. Erlich only discusses the negative connotation, writing, "In the traditional Islamic world, futuwwa (and other terms that referred to youth) . . . referred to [male] youngsters from poor neighborhoods trying to protect themselves . . . or criminals and troublemakers." In this same "traditional world," Rachel Goshgarian describes *futuwwa* as "a moral code that crystallized in an Islamic context around the notion of an 'ideal man'" and then was adapted by Christians living in the Islamic world in the thirteenth century. At the very same time, the term was associated with a set of rituals performed by young, often (but not exclusively) male, Sufi mystics and connoted their dedication to morality and spiritual learning under an elder, often male, Sufi master. Lastly, as Wilson Jacob points out in early twentieth-century Egypt, *futuwwa* was both a masculine bravado to be avoided and a "code of behavior" that was corruptible by worldly things.[4]

The complex and evolving etymology of the word serves as a metaphor for the place of religion in youth culture within and beyond the Middle East. As educational, knowledge, and power structures were transformed in the twentieth century, so was youthfulness. These changes may have marked the creation of the secular youth that Erlich pinpoints. Nevertheless, well into the twentieth century, youthfulness's reference point continued to be religious or, at least, pious. For instance, when young people are referred to as signs of youthfulness in a negative sense—rambunctious, wayward, immoral—the assumption is that they have lost their way, their values, and their religion. And when young people refer to themselves or are referred to by adults as youthful in a positive sense—drivers of their own destiny—the assumption is that they will make the right moral decisions, whatever they may be. Youth culture in the twentieth century, as observed in the histories of young people and the organizations they form, was then a way to forge a new path, but one that was inspired by previous understandings of morality.

In the context of the twentieth-century Global South, "youth" and "youthfulness" were terms often used by and ascribed to urban, middle-class young people in their teens and twenties. Even as the social construction of youth opened up to new categories of people in the latter half of the century (including women and rural men), their youth was often distinguished from the urban male ideal. At the center of this youth culture, pious, even if not zealous, masculine, even if not male, were youth organizations. In Lebanon, youth organizations of multiple religious backgrounds made up of young men practiced religious rituals publicly and actively internalized religious values such as temperance. This unfolded in the very same period in which, Erlich mistakenly claims, that religion goes away. Instead, armed with a complex understanding of *futuwwa*, so-called secular youth culture was clearly religious, and this was no coincidence. This is not exclusive to Lebanon, as evidence suggests that religious identity was essential to youth culture elsewhere in the twentieth-century Global South. What is also not unique to Lebanon is the diverse, "sectarian societies" in which this hybrid religious-national youth culture took shape.

Religious Holidays and Youth Culture in "Sectarian Societies"

Sectarianism refers to the global politics of socio-religious identity in the modern world. To be sectarian, like the so-called sectarian societies of locales like Lebanon, Northern Ireland, the Balkan States, and Sri Lanka, means one's body politic is defined by competing socio-religious groups. The emphasis on *global* as well as *modern* sectarianism is in line with those scholars who argue that the modern, universalist state, and unequal access to it, was "a necessary condition for the emergence of modern sectarianism." More specifically, sectarianism is a manifestation of modern institutions that, as Ussama Makdisi shows in the case of Ottoman Lebanon, "emphasized sectarian identity [Sunni Muslim, Maronite Catholic, etc.] as the . . . only authentic basis for political claims." Saba Mahmood adds that modern secular governance, imposed by colonial powers and practiced in the postcolonial Global South, conditioned sectarianism through legalizing "religious difference" in the form of "minority rights."[5]

While sectarianism is by no means particular to youth, youth culture, or youth organization, young people exist within this system in pluralistic societies, and sectarianism shapes the ways in which many youth groups form. In Lebanon, several of the most popular youth-centric organizations during the twentieth century were organized according to sect identity: the Najjadeh ("Helpers") Organization was Sunni Muslim, the Tala'i' ("Vanguard") Organization was Shi'a Muslim, the Kata'ib ("Phalanx") Organization was Maronite Catholic, and the Progressive Socialist Party was mostly Druze. Nevertheless, given that sectarianism is largely about competition over political power in diverse societies, and not religious differences, practicing sect identity is not the same thing as calling for the supremacy of one religion over another. In so-called sectarian contexts, groups rarely call for, nor do they practice, public, exclusivist religion. This would necessitate the state's authorization—or at least signaling—of favor to a certain religious sect, which would delegitimize their claim of being the guardian of all people and, more specifically, young people.

The paradox of non-fanatical sectarianism is not exclusive to Lebanon. It is found wherever modern secular states exist in diverse societies, particularly in the postcolonial Global South. In these cases, religious identity often plays out in terms of ritual. In other words, groups that are organized according to one religious sect may celebrate distinct religious holidays, but they are not religious per se. Religion is either placed side by side with communal or national identity or imbedded within that identity.

This, however, does not mean religion is invisible but, rather, that religious affiliation bolsters group and national identity.

Take, for example, the Najjadeh Organization of Lebanon and its annual celebrations of *Mawlid*, or the Prophet Muhammad's birthday. Mawlid is today celebrated in most countries with Muslim majorities but was in the past associated most often with Arab, Sunni Muslim communities. The Najjadeh was an Arab nationalist youth organization birthed out of the Muslim Scouts movement, and its young members were in their late teens and twenties. It formed in Lebanon and Syria during the French colonial period (1920–1946) but was active into the 1970s. Although the majority of the Najjadeh's ideologies and slogans were secular, the majority of its members were practicing Sunni Muslims, many of whom attended the Islamic Makassed College in Beirut. Therefore, it was not odd for this youth group to celebrate religious holidays central to their identity, including the holy month of Ramadan and *Mawlid*. What is interesting is how religious holidays had nationalist underpinnings. The review of the 1947 Najjadeh *Mawlid* festival, published in the Najjadeh newspaper, highlights this trend. The review is included below in its entirety:

> The Najjadeh Organization participated in big celebrations which were held in the Grand Omari Mosque on occasion of the Prophet's birthday and the unification of the Arabs and [the Najjadeh] Beirut organization teams lined up for music in front of the mosque. And the [Najjadeh] High President was surrounded by members of the high council in the mosque and they offered greetings to the Mufti of the Lebanese Republic. And the official celebrations did not finish until the High President left and paraded with leaders of the organizational teams which passed in front of him in an organized fashion to the Najjadeh home.[6]

The first thing of note in this announcement is that the actual holiday is mentioned only once, while the Najjadeh is referenced throughout. This is not meant to be a disrespect to the Prophet, as the importance of the holiday is implicit in the announcement. Yet, it is the Najjadeh who were celebrating this holiday and, hence, are the focus. Second, the Najjadeh leadership and public officials are mentioned more often than the young "teams" that were present at the event. It is clear that they were disciplined and could play music, but the announcement more so celebrates the group than young people and their youth culture. Even so, the spectacle and routine of this yearly festival placed the Prophet's birthday within the confines of the organizational culture of the Najjadeh. This youth culture, a manifestation of disciplined *futuwwa*, included playing music, marching, and ordering in rows for the sake of religious holidays like *Mawlid* or national ones like Lebanon's Independence Day.

Another important aspect of this announcement and event was the location of the celebration: the Grand Omari Mosque in Beirut. It was a Sunni mosque, which ostensibly meant a great deal to the young members of this group. At the same time, it was a national symbol, right in the middle of downtown, and close to Christian institutions, like Saint Georges Cathedral. For these reasons, the religious representative for all Sunni Muslims in Lebanon, the Grand Mufti, was present, but not only as a Sunni Muslim. As the announcement notes, he was there as a representative of the "Lebanese Republic." In addition, stressing that this holiday was meant to celebrate the "unification of Arabs" served a different role, beyond placing Islam within Najjadeh youth culture.[7] Rather, the youth that celebrated this holiday and practiced this particular sect identity were also at the forefront of forging a harmonious national identity.

This was quite similar to the case of religious festivals hosted by another Lebanese youth group, the Tala'i'. Like the Najjadeh, the Tala'i' emerged from a scouting tradition, and the two groups even held joint events and meetings early in their histories. The Tala'i' was also different from the Najjadeh, as it was founded in the 1940s, after Lebanon had technically become independent, and it was made up of Shi'a Muslims, often in their teens. Hence, in addition to festivals for all Muslims, like Mawlid, the Tala'i' sponsored celebrations for exclusively Shi'a holidays. Most notable was Ashura, a holiday that marks the martyrdom of Imam Hussein and is central to the Shi'a narrative of Islamic history. Yearly Ashura festivals were held at the 'Amiliyya school in Beirut, where the majority of Tala'i' members studied, and where Tala'i' founder Rashid Baydun served as headmaster. According to an advisor to the Tala'i', Ghassan Ahmad 'Issa, by participating in Tala'i'-sponsored events, Ashura "becomes the guide in the consciousness of the Shi'a youth towards sacrifice and redemption in order to uphold the ideals of Islam."[8]

If 'Issa stopped here, one would see how Ashura inspired religious uprightness in the Shi'a youth associated with a particular group, proving the place of religion in the youth culture of one particular group. However, 'Issa continues, Ashura also "symbolizes sacrifice in the cause of the nation." Much like the Najjadeh, Tala'i' youth practiced religious holidays, and those holidays were imbued with nationalist discourse. This was perhaps even more explicit in the case of the Tala'i' and Ashura, as, in the words of 'Issa, the "national Islamic religious holiday" that the Tala'i' sponsored is the "cause of the nation."[9] What 'Issa means by this, and what Tala'i' leaders and young members attempted to legitimize, was that Shi'a Islam and Shi'a Muslim youth were a fundamental part of the national body politic. This was not always considered to be the case, as Shi'a Muslims in the early twentieth century were severely disadvantaged in political, social, and economic resources when compared with their Sunni Muslim and Christian counterparts. Thus, young Shi'a Muslims should be on equal footing, and one way to achieve this was by recognizing the equal place of Shi'a Islamic holidays, and the role of Shi'a Muslim youth organizations and educational ventures within their holidays.

Beyond Lebanon, youth-centric movements with Shi'a majorities in the majority-Sunni Islamic Middle East practiced nationalism and their religious identity side by side. One such example is Nadi al-'Uruba or the "Arabism Club" in Bahrain. Nadi al-'Uruba was founded in 1939, when the island nation of Bahrain was still under British indirect control. Its leaders and members alike consisted mostly of young Shi'a merchants, government employees, teachers, and students (over age eighteen) in the capital of Manama. Like the Tala'i' and the Najjadeh, Nadi al-'Uruba had links to schools, specifically primary schools in Manama whose students came from the predominately Shi'a villages of Bahrain. And similar to the Tala'i', it participated in yearly Ashura festivals. Beyond the public celebration itself, another aspect of Ashura that is useful to investigate for Nadi al-'Uruba is the Shi'a mourning houses, or those institutions that organized and funded the celebration of the holiday. These houses in Bahrain, called *mat'am*, date back to the original repenters: those individuals who lamented and celebrated the martyrdom of Imam Hussein in 680 CE.

While the links between primary schools and Nadi al-'Uruba were perhaps stronger—the result of their shared investment in educating Shi'a youth—it is not implausible that the educated Shi'i merchants and government employees that founded Nadi al-'Uruba also operated *mat'am*, or at least engaged in meeting and greeting in mourning houses during the holy month of Muharram. Fuad Khuri argues these institutions "enhance[d] the religio-political consciousness of the Shi'a [sic] as a distinct polity," and, in the words of Fred Lawson, the houses represented a space in which "grievances against the regime could be aired and opposition to the authorities be mobilized."[10] The authorities were Sunni Muslims, the minority group in Bahrain. They were supported by a colonial power and were, for many Shi'a, the source of their marginalization. Nadi al-'Uruba's role in anti-colonial and antigovernment protest in the 1950s strengthened the possibility of coordination between *mat'am* and youth organization. In this case, then, religion and nationality were not just practiced side by side to create a space for a group, like with the Tala'i' or the Najjadeh. Instead, this space was then used to criticize the government for a lack of access to the reins of power. And like Ashura, youth protest around Shi'i holidays in Bahrain was a ritual. In turn, advocating for rights became central to the youth culture that groups like Nadi al-'Uruba cultivated.

Similarly, in other locales in the Middle East, religious, sect, and national identities were, and still are, inextricable parts of youth culture. In other words, where young people come from (their stories and their holidays) and what makes them religious (practices of piety) are what gives them the authority to be drivers of national development. This is slightly different from youth-centric movements in a very different sectarian society—Northern Ireland. In this case, religion appears to be imbedded fully within a communal identity, whether it be Protestant or Catholic, not a national one. According to Sean Farrell, in nineteenth-century Ulster, Protestant groups would often parade on the Twelfth Day, a holiday dedicated to William of Orange's victory against King James II in 1690, marking the beginning of Protestant Northern Ireland and the end of Catholic rule. Young "Orangemen," as they were called, would march to claim their "historical right to an ascendant position vis-à-vis Irish Catholics." On the other side, Catholic youth associations would sponsor public rituals in honor of Saint Patrick's Day, which were meant to show the growing solidarity of this marginalized group. While not a sign of unity, this is similar to the case of Bahrain, where Nadi al-'Uruba used public holidays for political action. In addition, Farrell argues that the two holidays in Northern Ireland were "not religious rites per se" but rather "ritualistic assertions of secular power and territorial control."[11] Put simply, religion was at the center of practices of youth culture, even if they were not necessarily about religion.

It must be clarified that this is not exactly the case for religious rituals and youth culture in the Middle East. Indeed, Islam, Islamic rituals, and Islamic values appear to matter a great deal in instilling positive *futuwwa*. Yet, Farrell's point is still generalizable for youth religiosity in diverse societies, Middle Eastern or otherwise. These rituals are tied to a narrative that fits within the group's religious history, whether the Prophet's day for Sunni Muslims or Ashura for Shi'a. At the same time, as noted in all examples from Lebanon and Bahrain, religious rituals were as much about legitimizing the group as part of the nation, and its access to physical space (a headquarters, an event at a famous mosque, etc.), as they were about celebrating the holiday itself. Therefore, even if the context is different, cases from Northern Ireland to Bahrain highlight that religious doctrine is not a defining feature of youth culture in sectarian societies. Rather, it is the religious ritual that links the group to the whole or one group in distinction to another.

Religious Values in Youth Culture and Organization

Even if religious doctrine did not guide youth culture in the twentieth-century Global South, religious values were of supreme importance to youth organizations. Put differently, a lack of religious doctrine does not mean that leaders, adults and youth themselves, did not use religion to harness and control negative *futuwwa*. One of the most effective ways for adults to channel youth energy toward productive activities, at least in the twentieth century, was scouting. This ideology, the crux of national youth development, was laid out by British scoutmaster Robert Baden-Powell and then spread around the world. In his 1908 *Scouting for Boys*, Baden-Powell defined what it took for a young man to become a good and pious citizen. Baden-Powell imagined this citizen as secular. At the same time, the citizen was inspired by religious values, most notably morality and temperance:

1. To be loyal to God and the King.
2. To help other people at all times.
3. To obey the scout law.[12]

This is the scout's oath, one of the first things Baden-Powell introduces in his *Scouting for Boys*. The oath stresses loyalty—religious and secular—selflessness, and obedience to the law. In regard to the latter, the scout's law is broken up into several categories, including Baden-Powell's guidance on chivalry, endurance, and patriotism. Chivalry is synonymous with honor, and Baden-Powell uses the Crusaders as metaphors for both. Scouts are literally the descendants of Crusaders in Baden-Powell's worldview. They were the ones who "made the tiny British nation into one of the best and greatest that the world has ever known," and scouts were to carry on their legacy. In his discussion of endurance, Baden-Powell remarks that a "fellow has to be strong, healthy and active," and one way to do this was to avoid any vices, including alcohol and smoking. Intemperance, in Baden-Powell's words, "makes him look like an ass." In addition to staying morally clean, as the Crusaders would have, scouts were to be modern-day patriots. Indeed, they should be proud to "belong to the Great British Empire, one of the greatest empires that has ever existed in the world."[13]

Upon reviewing the guide, one could deduce that national tropes appear to supersede religious ones. In fact, religious doctrine is not central to the Scout's law, notwithstanding a few references to reverence for God and all God's creatures. First and foremost for Baden-Powell was duty to the nation or empire. At the same time, with instructions like avoiding alcohol and remembering the Crusaders, religious values and action were everywhere in Baden-Powell's world. Even with his reference to the European, Christian Crusaders, and the greatness of British civilization and the British empire, this brand of secular but religious citizen was made modular and then spread across the Global South in the form of scouting and youth movements.

One prime example is the Muslim Scouts, the predecessor to the Najjadeh Organization. Its leader, Muhyi al-Din al-Nasuli, who was also the founder of the Najjadeh, supposedly spent time with Robert Baden-Powell at international scouting conferences, and the Muslim Scouts adapted Baden-Powell's scout's law. In the twentieth century, the Arab nation was neither an empire nor Christian, but this did not mean *Scouting for Boys* had no relevance to colonial subjects like those young men in the Muslim Scouts. In 1936, leaders and supporters of the Muslim Scouts made their case in the form of a publication on the significance of the movement. In one passage the writers wrote:

> The best way to follow in free independent education is the way of the scout, which strengthens the body, develops the mind, awakens the spirit and it returns to the origin of Islam, the generosity of creation, and after consideration [i.e., becoming a scout], accuracy in action [body] and mind.[14]

Alongside the claim that "Scouting is a movement designed to create the Arab nation in these countries and then to create humanity," the themes of chivalry, endurance, and patriotism are all on display.[15] Also, like the Tala'i', the Muslim Scouts stressed education and its connections with enriching the religious spirit of young men. Yet, this is not the focal point of the message. Rather, it is that in abiding by the "way of the scout," young men can be strong, smart, *and* pious. Stated differently, holding to the scout way achieves temperance, honors religion, and will foster national development, all at the same time.

Therefore, as with religious rituals, nation, masculine discipline, and religion are made indistinguishable from each other in youth organization. They represent a collective ethos that young men should aspire to embody. The precedent set by the Muslim Scouts carried through to the Najjadeh, the second stage of scout life. This is demonstrated in a 1944 pamphlet for leaders, an abridged Arabic adaptation of *Scouting for Boys*. The organizational center instructs leaders to make sure Najjadeh youth are moral, pious citizens with "good manners" and temperament, devoid of "outraged judgements" and irrational decisions. In addition to practicing endurance, Najjadeh members must "stick to everything that strengthens the status of masculinity."[16] If applicants to the Najjadeh exemplified these traits, they would be accepted into the group, thereafter engaging in scouting activities, playing games, and wearing uniforms, akin to Baden-Powell's scouts. Members would also don badges that read "be prepared." At first glance, it appears that this slogan was lifted directly from Baden-Powell's *Scouting for Boys*. Yet, the Arabic phrase *wa-a'iddu*, or "and prepare," is from the Quran. This melding of Baden-Powell and Islam in organizational culture is not uncommon for other youth groups in Lebanon. The Tala'i', for example, had a slogan and badge that included the religious symbol of the sword of Ali, a focal point for Shi'a Muslims, alongside calls for equality.

These are just some of the ways in which youth clubs in Lebanon adapted Baden-Powell and scouting in their own distinct ways, blending their own local and religious narratives with nationalist or universalist symbolism. Others included appropriating him as the basis to stop the British and French Empires. The Najjadeh, for instance, championed anti-colonial platforms, protested against the French throughout the late 1930s, and then were active in the independence movement that ended French colonialism in 1943. This action, in theory, would violate Baden-Powell's concept of loyalty to a higher government without question. However, in the world of the Najjadeh, chivalry, piety, and masculinity were central to building the anti-colonial project that would birth the Arab nation that was worthy of such loyalty.

Temperance, morality, and learning to embody the true man were not exclusive to groups inspired by Baden-Powell. A prime example is the Kata'ib Organization, a youth organization formed by pharmacist and sports enthusiast Pierre Gemayel, and made up almost exclusively of Maronite Christian youth in their late teens and twenties. Founded a year before the Najjadeh, in the midst of sustained French colonialism and a trip the group's founder took to the 1936 Berlin Olympics, the Kata'ib were influenced by a mix of fascist youth organizations and the French scout model under *Les Scouts du Liban*. At the same time, they fused Lebanese nationalism and Christian religious values in a way that would have made Baden-Powell proud. This is exhibited in a 1943 pamphlet written by supporters of the Kata'ib, entitled "History and Action." Following a section on "national consciousness," the writers took up "gambling, drunkenness, and moral depravity." In addition to arguing that there was no room for poor behavior in the ranks of the Kata'ib youth, the writer(s) made known that the Kata'ib was against "every mistake of good behavior in national life and every mistake of slight towards duty."[17] The concept of guided, moral duty was also enshrined in one of the Kata'ib slogans, the name of its newspaper, and a phrase included in the title of the pamphlet: *al-'Amal* or "the Action."

Even the most secular of youth-centric organizations in Lebanon during the twentieth century preached and practiced temperance. The Progressive Socialist Party, founded in 1949, was a socialist social movement with a badge that read "bread, labor, and social justice." This badge makes no reference to religion, which is in contrast to groups like the Najjadeh, the Tala'i', or the Kata'ib, whose primary slogan was "God, Family, and Nation." Yet, the Progressive Sociality Party was constructed after the horrors of World War II and the Holocaust. Consequently, the group incorporated ideals of humanitarianism into its worldview, perhaps without direct reference to religion, but nonetheless derived from religion.

Indeed, human rights discourse paired nicely with notions of spirituality and mortality, as outlined in the Progressive Socialist Party's *al-nizam al-dakhali* or "the Internal Structure." This document lays out issues ranging from logistics for routine meetings to rules on good behavior. Relating to the latter, the *nizam al-dakhali* states that to engage in activities "incompatible with aims and principles" of the party, including "spreading rumors" and "shamelessness, foulness, and naughty jokes," was strictly forbidden.[18] Violations to this honor code were assessed by the Honor Council, and punishments could be as severe as up to two years of separation from the party. The sources groups left behind, and the existence of these types of guidelines for the young, moral citizen, highlight the centrality of temperance in youth culture in Lebanon, regardless of organization. In sum, they prove that religion played a central role in youth organization, even when religion is not emphasized by the organization itself.

However, as the organizations were conceived of as masculine, with young men at the center, young women were often closed off from them. The lack of female membership was not because the groups actively blocked women from joining. Rather, it was more so a product of where youth organizations operated and recruited: mostly male, public spaces, whether the school, coffee house, mosque, church, or street. These spaces, and the groups that frequented them, did not change until the late 1940s, as youth organizations broadening their definitions of who had access to youth, even if the urban, male youth was the standard. Before this opening, Lebanese girl scout groups existed in parallel, but separate, spaces. As Nadya Sbaiti argues, these movements were associated with multiple, autonomous girl's schools, such as Ahliah, Makassed, and Collège Protestant. In women's groups, young individuals conceived of a citizenship that was not based on masculine *futuwwa*, but a mix of feminist, activist, and nationalist ideals.

This last example, where young women appear to forge their own path, signals the bottom-up construction of youth culture in youth organizations, male, female, or both. Nonetheless, whether it was an alternative, non-masculine understanding of *futuwwa*, a pamphlet that mentioned gambling is wrong, or a set of rules meant to criminalize it, leaders used these measures to control *futuwwa*, not exactly empowering youthfulness. Stated differently, the decisions of leaders should not be mistaken for the reception of young members in the group. To get at if, or how, young people received these messages, we must turn to individual experiences within youth clubs. Most contemporaneous work is filtered through the organization and, hence, can lead to the conflation of strategy and experience. While presenting similar source issues, one step removed from the specter of the organization is the individual memoirs from once young members of these organizations.

In their memoirs, individuals often highlight that they believed in the messages of their groups or at least wanted to be seen as morally upright. This is the case for even the most diverse of groups—that is, those youth organizations that were not organized or exclusive to one sect. Hisham Sharabi was a member of the Syrian Social Nationalist Party, an avidly secular social club whose members hailed from almost all religious denominations. Hisham joined the group in the late-1940s around age twenty, looking for "communal belonging" after finding the lecture series of an Arab nationalist movement at his university campus in Beirut "long and the discussion boring." He continues:

> I yearned to become part of a greater whole, an entity in which any individual identity would merge with my general communal identity, and I thought that if friendship did not have such wider bond and deeper purpose, its potentialities would remain truncated and incomplete. All this—my conversation, my loneliness, my idealist yearnings—led me in the end to join the Syrian [Social] Nationalist Party.

Being part of something bigger, more important than oneself, preoccupied Hisham. After starting to attend the meetings of the group, what struck Hisham the most about the young members of the Syrian Social Nationalist Party was their honor and dedication. He writes, "I saw dignity and pride" and "confidence and reassurance... in their looks, and the way they stood."[19] Similar to the supporters of the Kata'ib that wrote the 1943 pamphlet cited earlier, Sharabi was inspired by and wanted to feel the moral fortitude he saw in members. At the same, it must be acknowledged that the two groups' ideologies, and others that have been discussed, could not be more different. Sharabi was bored with Arab nationalism—that which was espoused by the Najjadeh—came to the Syrian Social Nationalist Party's pan-Syrian nationalism, and decried the exclusivity of the Kata'ib's Lebanese nationalism. Of course, ideology matters in describing the cultures of youth organizations, but so does practice, and Sharabi and Kata'ib members alike practiced discipline and temperance. Like the Kata'ib's focus on action, the Syrian Social Nationalist Party embodied hard work through their slogan: "Freedom, Duty, and Strong Organization."

A similar coming of age story is narrated in the memoir of a member of the Kata'ib, Antoun Jarji Jamhuri. Like Sharabi, Antoun distinguishes the organization he would join from another, lesser one. Jamhuri writes that he was from a family of communists, "But in practice, I found myself a stranger. I am a believer away from the atheists and I departed." Although the communists, like the Progressive Socialists, practiced humanitarianism, Antoun stresses that he was "a believer" and, hence, needed a group that mirrored his beliefs. As a Christian, the Kata'ib would be a top choice. But in the end, what really excited Jamhuri was "the spirit of collective discipline" in the Kata'ib.[20] Jamhuri's use of the word "spirit," or *ruh*, allows for a return to the concept of *futuwwa*. Jamhuri deliberately uses the word *ruh*, which can also be translated as "soul," to represent the spirit of youth vitality he saw and the religious values that undergirded it. And while *futuwwa* is not by definition religious, *futuwwa* has a spirit, and in the Kata'ib, that spirit sought to turn aimless youthfulness into disciplined, morally upright youthfulness.

At the same time, all of these groups, including the Kata'ib, stressed that their spirit was above all "factionalism," or *'asabiyya*, which would include overt religion, zealotry, or even worse, religious sectarianism. The Najjadeh's slogan was "Arabism above all," while the Kata'ib's 1943 pamphlet declared that the group's priority was "putting love of Lebanon above all things."[21]

The slogans from Lebanon's youth clubs reflect a global trend of publicly subsuming religious identity under a national youth culture. This includes cases as distinct as communist China and postcolonial India. In China during the Cultural Revolution, communist youth organizations "worshiped" Mao and could be found confessing their "sins" to portraits of him.[22]

There was no cult of personality on par with Mao in India, but nonetheless, Hindu nationalist youth groups like the Rashtriya Sawyamsevak Sangh, or the "National Volunteer Organization," also referred to as the RSS, embedded religion within national practices. Even as the RSS's identity was prefaced on a certain ethnic group and religious sect, against others (Muslims, Arabs, Turko-Persians, etc.), "religion and ritual [for the RSS] . . . were adapted in rather austere terms, with an emphasis on an abstract, Brahmanical conception of Hinduism."[23] While in China, one could argue that spirituality replaced religion—given that the latter was outlawed nationally in 1966—this was not the case for the RSS. At the beginning of events, for example, members of this youth group pray to the sun and the party flag at the same time. This RSS flag is saffron, a sacred color in Hinduism.

Returning to the case of Bahrain and Nadi al-'Uruba, Nelida Fuccaro discusses the absence of Shi'ism in group events. She writes:

> Although most of the club affiliates were Shi'i, the programme of public lectures and discussion forums which it organized advocated a new relationship between individual, community and society within the framework of . . . the indivisible personality of the Arab nation of Bahrain.[24]

In other words, this club, like Hisham Sharabi's Syrian Social Nationalist Party, Antoun Jarji Jamhuri's Kata'ib or India's RSS, was itself was a site for youthful togetherness. Indeed, Nadi al-'Uruba was a place for youth, predominately Shi'a youth, to practice Arab nationalism and nonsectarian belonging among like-minded individuals. Therefore, even as leaders used the basis of the group's identity (Shi'a, Maronite Christian, Sunni, Druze, humanitarian, socialist, etc.) as a way to anchor the group and discipline the young, it is misplaced to consider this a wholly nefarious act—that is, that adults in youth organizations took religious identity, stripped of actual religious doctrine, to control young people. Instead, uprightness and morality were religious values central to national development, the basis of group (often masculine) belonging, and foundational to individual experiences within youth organizations.

Problematizing Secularization and Contextualizing a Youth Religious Revival

Whether in a youth club in Lebanon, where Christians were the majority in a group, or in a Hindu nationalist organization in India, religion mattered in the twentieth century, even as it did not. In one way, this conclusion confirms the claim of secularization proponents, like Erlich, who discuss how the conception of secular youth, imagined under the universalist, totalizing framework of liberal education, subsumed the religious young person. However, when focusing on youth culture in a variety of youth organizations, the question must be raised: if youth organizations celebrated religious holidays, religious values were enshrined in group ideology, and young members believed in the moral compass of the group, was religion central to youth culture? Stated differently, should scholars explore, more critically, what the process of secularization supposedly "did" to young people in the Global South in the twentieth century?

Answering yes to both of these questions rejects the cyclical nature in which religion is characterized under secularization theory, and in particular for youth and youth organizations. As the sources of youth organizations demonstrate, religion did not disappear in the process of nation- or world-building in the early twentieth century only to return when conditions changed. Instead, and perhaps most clear in diverse, "sectarian societies," religious identity undergirds the structure, values, practices, discipline, and lived experiences within youth organizations. Furthermore, religion is only one of many identities within and beyond these societies. This chapter explored the relationship between religious identity, national identity, masculine uprightness, and youth culture, but I call others to investigate how gender and class either reinforce or defy religion. In a similar vein, I hope others will explore whether religion has ever been the exclusive form of self-expression for young people, even when it was dominant in instruction and daily life.

Nonetheless, this analysis has not accounted for how one should make sense of the religious revival in the late twentieth and early twenty-first centuries, particularly among young people. According to the recent US Pew Research Center's "Religious Landscape Study," 67 percent of youth respondents said religion was either very or somewhat important in one's life.[25] The forces of globalization, ranging from neoliberal capitalism and the retreat of the welfare state to a fear of losing oneself in a world full of individualized choices and identities, in part explain these statistics. Even in the absence of quantitative data, it is likely that the responses would be similar in the Global South. This is because the forces of globalization are even more severe, uneven, and volatile beyond Europe and the United States, rendering religion as something to hold onto in the neoliberal Global South. But again, like with the past, it is necessary to pair structural factors and quantitative data with qualitative youth experiences to add to the story. In contemporary Egypt, one young man explained his interest in an Islamic movement as follows: it was place for "The committed youth [who] has a goal and a purpose; he wants to be a servant of God."[26]

Religion may appear more manifest in this example, but that does not mean it was birthed out of thin air. In part, to consider religious rituals and values as the basis for different types of youth engagement (local to national, Christian to Muslim, Chinese to Lebanese) helps make sense of religion's persistence into the current age, even as historical circumstances change. Accordingly, religion should not be undervalued in the twentieth century, and studies that focus on the experiences of young people and their cultural production must account for the place of religious identity in youth culture.

Notes

1. Richard Ivan Jobs and David M. Pomfret, "The Transnationality of Youth," in *Transnational Histories of Youth in the Twentieth Century*, ed. Ricard Ivan Jobs and David M. Pomfret (New York: Palgrave Macmillan, 2015), 16.
2. Haggai Erlich, *Youth and Revolution in the Changing Middle East, 1908–2014* (Boulder, CO: Lynne Rienner Publishers, Inc., 2014), 14 and 17.
3. Ibid., 5.
4. Ibid., 4–5; Rachel Goshgarian, "*Futuwwa* in Thirteenth Century Rūm and Armenia: Reform Movements and the Managing of Multiple Allegiances on the Seljuk Periphery," in *The Seljuks of Anatolia: Court and Society in the Medieval Middle East*, ed. A.C.S. Peacock and Sara Nur Yıldız (London: I.B. Tauris & Co Ltd, 2013), 228; and Wilson Chacko Jacob, *Working Out Egypt: Effendi Masculinity and Subject Formation in Colonial Modernity, 1870–1940* (Durham, NC: Duke University Press, 2011), 247.
5. Michael Gasper, "Sectarianism, Minorities, and the Secular State in the Middle East," *International Journal of Middle East Studies* 48, no. 4 (2016): 772; Ussama Makdisi, *The Culture of Sectarianism: Community, History and Violence in Nineteenth Century Ottoman Lebanon* (Berkeley, CA: University of California Press, 2000), 2; and Saba Mahmood, *Religious Difference in a Secular Age: A Minority Report* (Princeton, NJ: Princeton University Press, 2016), 11.

6. *Al-Iyman*, February 10, 1947. Najjadeh Party Files, Linda Sadaqah Collection, American University of Beirut.
7. Ibid.
8. Ghassan Ahmad 'Issa, *Munathima al-Tala'i' fi Lubnan min Khilal Wath'iquha al-Asiliyya, 1944–1947* (PhD Dissertation, Lebanese University, 1992), 131–132.
9. Ibid.
10. Fuad Khuri, *Tribe and State in Bahrain: The Transformation of Social and Political Authority in an Arab State* (Chicago, IL: The University of Chicago Press, 1980), 172 and Fred Lawson, *Bahrain: The Modernization of Autocracy* (Boulder, CO: Westview Press, 1989), 58.
11. Sean Farrell, *Rituals and Riots: Sectarian Violence and Political Culture in Ulster, 1784–1886* (Lexington: University Press of Kentucky, 2009), 156, 117.
12. Robert Baden-Powell, *Scouting for Boys: The Original 1908 Edition* (Mineola, NY: Dover Publications, Inc., 2007), 20.
13. Baden-Powell, *Scouting for Boys*, 24, 27.
14. Shafiq Naqqash and 'Ali Khalifa, *Al-Haraka al-Kashshafiyya fi al-Aqtar al-'Arabiyya* (Beirut: Dar al-Kashshaf, 1936), 5.
15. Ibid (no page number), introductory letter to scout leaders from Muhyi al-Din al-Nasuli.
16. Najjadeh Party, *Al-Tanzim al-Dakhali lil-Firq* (1944), 18, Najjadeh Party Files, Linda Sadaqah Collection, American University of Beirut.
17. *Al-Kata'ib al-Lubnaniyya: Tarikh wa al-'Amal* (November 1943), 14, Lebanese Kata'ib Party Files, Linda Sadaqah Collection, American University of Beirut.
18. Progressive Socialist Party, *Al-Nizam al-Dakhali* (Beirut: Progressive Socialist Party, 1972), 58–59.
19. Hisham Sharabi, *Embers and Ashes: Memoirs of an Arab Intellectual*, trans. Issa J. Boullata (Northampton, MA: Olive Branch Press, 2008), 49, 144, and 149.
20. Antoun Jarji Jamhuri, *Thakriyat al-Mafud fi al-Quwa al-Nithamiyya al-Kata'ibiyya, Ahdath 1958* (Beirut: Manshurat dar al-'Amal, 2016), 5.
21. *Al-Kata'ib al-Lubnaniyya: Tarikh wa al-'Amal*, 9.
22. Fengang Yang, "Youth and Religion in Modern China: A Sketch of Social and Political Developments," *Annual Review of the Sociology of Religion* 1 (2010), 152.
23. Arvind Rajagopal, *Politics after Television: Hindu Nationalism and the Reshaping of the Public in India* (Cambridge: Cambridge University Press, 2004), 54.
24. Nelida Fuccaro, *Histories of City and State in the Persian Gulf: Manama since 1800* (Cambridge: Cambridge University Press, 2009), 178.
25. "Religious Landscape Study," Pew Research Center, Washington, D.C., May 30, 2014, https://www.pewforum.org/religious-landscape-study/generational-cohort/younger-millennial/
26. Carrie Rosefsky Wickham, "Interests, Ideas, and Islamist Outreach in Egypt," in *Islamic Activism: A Social Movement Theory Approach*, ed. Quintan Wiktorowicz (Indiana University Press, 2004), 237.

Further Reading

Baun, Dylan. *Winning Lebanon: Youth Politics, Populism, and the Production of Sectarian Violence, 1920–1958*. Cambridge: Cambridge University Press, 2021.
Block, Nelson R., and Tammy M. Proctor, eds. *Scouting Frontiers: Youth and the Scout Movement's First Century*. Cambridge: Cambridge Scholars Publishing, 2009.

Burke, Edmond, ed. *Islam, Politics, and Social Movements*. Berkeley: University of California Press, 1988.

Dueck, Jennifer. *The Claims of Culture at Empire's End: Syria and Lebanon under French Rule*. Oxford: Oxford University Press: 2010.

Fallaw, Ben. *Religion and State Formation in Revolutionary Mexico*. Durham, NC: Duke University Press, 2013.

Fortna, Benjamin C. *Imperial Classroom: Islam, The State, and Education in the Late Ottoman Empire*. Oxford: Oxford University Press, 2000.

Gelvin, James. *The Modern Middle East: A History*. 4th ed. Oxford: Oxford University Press, 2015.

Giordan, Giuseppe, ed. *Youth and Religion*. Leiden: Brill, 2010.

Gorsuch, Anne E. *Youth in Revolutionary Russia: Enthusiasts, Bohemians, Delinquents*. Bloomington: Indiana University Press, 2000.

Herrera, Linda, and Asaf Bayat, eds. *Being Young and Muslim: New Cultural Politics in the Global South and North*. Oxford: Oxford University Press, 2010.

Jeffrey, Craig. *Timepass: Youth, Class, and the Politics of Waiting in India*. Stanford, CA: Stanford University Press, 2010.

Meijer, Roel, ed. *Alienation or Integration of Arab Youth: Between Family, State and Street*. New York: Routledge, 2000.

Morrison, Heidi. *Childhood and Colonial Modernity in Egypt*. New York: Palgrave Macmillan, 2015.

Sbaiti, Nadya. *Gender, Education, and the Politics of Community in Mandate Lebanon*. Forthcoming.

Thompson, Elizabeth. *Colonial Citizens: Republican Rights, Paternal Privilege and Gender in French Syria and Lebanon*. New York: Columbia University Press, 2000.

Watenpaugh, Keith David. *Being Modern in the Middle East: Revolution, Nationalism, Colonialism, and the Arab Middle Class*. Princeton, NJ: Princeton University Press, 2006.

PART IV
REPRESENTATIONS OF YOUTH

CHAPTER 19

YOUTH IN THE VISUAL ARTS

ANN BARROTT WICKS

WHILE historical pictures of children are plentiful, it is difficult to establish pictures of youth as a definable category in pre-twentieth-century figural art. In many early cultures, distinguishing older children from adults in art is problematic. In some societies, especially before the eighteenth century, people were no longer children once they reached puberty. Thus, the pictorial divide would be between childhood and adulthood. From the position of our twenty-first-century outlook, it is also challenging to understand the perceptions of youth that were in the minds of the adults who commissioned and produced figural art. The adults' didactic preferences on behalf of their youth are quite clear, while the views of young people themselves hardly seem to surface no matter which specific society is studied. Despite these limitations, there *are* portrayals of adolescents in art, and their appearance and meaning in various selected cultures will be discussed.

The primary sources that inform this essay are the artworks themselves. Important secondary sources include *Imagining Childhood* by Erika Langmuir, 2001; works by historian Ann Behnke Kinney, especially *Representations of Childhood and Youth in Early China*, 2004; and *The Family Model in Chinese Art and Culture*, edited by Jerome Silbergeld and Dora C.Y. Ching, 2013. Methodological approaches to the study of youth, such as those published in Philip M. Peek (ed.), *Twins in African Art and Diasporic Culture*, 2011; Cecily Hennessy, *Images of Children in Byzantium*, 2008; and Nicholas Orme, *Medieval Children*, 2001, are also useful.

Quantitatively, depictions of figures between approximately the ages of eight to fourteen are far outweighed by representations of adults and children. The distribution among age groups in art appears to be consistent across time periods and geographical locations: mostly adults, some children, and far fewer "youth." One likely reason for this is that it is usually adults who hold the power to commission or create art. Overall, both children and youth figures in art consistently portray the ideals and mores of society's adults. Reflected through them are the adults' own ambitions and hopes. In many cases what we see are the expectations that their own progeny will fulfill the family's destiny, thus setting the framework within which youth culture developed. Select examples from China, Persia, Western Europe, and America illustrate these points.

Pictures as Wish Fulfillment

While the visual arts may not specifically depict youth, they reveal the culture within which young people lived their lives. A late seventeenth-/early eighteenth-century Chinese painting, *A Hundred Children at Play*, after Yang Jin, will serve as a case study for this idea (Fig. 19.1). It vividly portrays wishes for fertility, wealth, and prestige. The setting is a spring garden, overflowing with children, in this case all boys. The motif of plants and children together has been depicted in Chinese art since at least the third century and always represents fertility. Numerous sons ensured continuity of the connection between ancestors and descendants and increased the stability and prestige of the family clan.

The theme of "a hundred children at play" was developed pictorially around the eleventh century and continued as a meaningful subject through eight centuries of dynastic rule in China. By the Song dynasty (960–1279), the period in which this theme arose, China had a fully developed meritocracy. That is, the emperor appointed scholars educated in the Confucian classics to fill most government positions. These positions were prestigious and lucrative, but also highly competitive. Difficult imperial exams were held to identify the men most qualified to fill them. The activities of boys in private gardens, such as those owned by these scholar-officials, symbolized adult wishes for sons who could successfully compete in the exams. In this painting, the boys in the pavilion, and in the middle ground in front of it, mimic the Four Arts—painting, calligraphy, music, and chess—celebrated achievements of accomplished scholars.

In the foreground of this painting a group of children enacts a parade celebrating "the return of the scholar" to his family after passing the imperial exams held in the capital. Children with rattle, horn, drum, and other noisemakers lead the entourage. The three triumphant "scholars" wear hats and ride makeshift horses, while others hold colorful flags behind them (Fig. 19.2). One "horse" is made of little boys; another is a toy hobby horse. An unwilling deer wearing the mask of a mythical beast, pulled and pushed by additional boys, is the third child's mount. The return of sons to their families after passing the exams was joyfully celebrated, for the positions they would fill brought both economic stability and prestige to their kin.

YOUTH IN THE VISUAL ARTS 355

FIGURE 19.1. After Yang Jin (1644–1727). *A Hundred Children at Play*, late seventeenth–early eighteenth century. Hanging scroll, ink and colors on silk, 97.8 × 104.8 cm.

Miami University Art Museum, Oxford, Ohio. 2006.4.

The honor afforded an individual who passed the exams would be reason enough for the children's make-believe parade in the picture. But each detail of the procession reinforces the concept that officialdom is the best outcome for the sons of Chinese families. For example, the word for "deer" in Chinese is homophonous with the word for "emolument," specifically the salary of a government official. The mask worn by the deer is that of a *qilin*, a mythical Chinese beast who is said to have delivered a jade tablet to the future mother of Confucius, indicating that she would give birth to an exceptional scholar. The appearance of the tablet-bearing *qilin* is significant for several reasons. First, it fits in with the common Asian trope of a pre-birth sign given to the mother of a boy destined for greatness. That Confucius was the boy in the story is notable because males were required to memorize the *Five Classics*, books edited by Confucius, in order to pass the exams that qualified them for official positions.

FIGURE 19.2. *A Hundred Children at Play*. Detail of boys playing "return of the scholar."

Moreover, the jade tablet given to Confucius's mother resembled petitions, written on wood or bamboo tablets, that officials presented at court.

Another detail of the parade is the toy horse. A horse represents immediacy or speed and was in fact the transportation of scholars to and from the exams. Here it also symbolizes "quickly achieving the first rank." Many other symbols of "first place" are included in the painting. For example, one of the boys playing a successful candidate sits on top of other children. Numerous other competitions are played out in the children's games. A boy climbs a flowering plum tree, leaving others behind. Plum flowers are an apt symbol for "first place" because they are the first to bloom in spring. The blossoms are modest and can bloom even in the midst of snow. As such they were adopted by scholars as metaphors for themselves, expressing human characteristics including modesty, refinement, and resilience. Cranes are another symbol of a high-achieving scholar. Officials of the first rank were distinguished by the crane badge worn on their court robes. The depiction of cranes in the air and on the roof of the pavilion reinforces the implication of rising to the top.

Dozens of visual puns in this painting form auspicious phrases. For example, boys surrounding an osmanthus bush in front of the balustrade on the left side of the painting form the rebus *guizi*, or "noble sons." *Gui*, the name of the tree, is homophonous with "noble." The puns and symbols in this single painting are multilayered and seemingly endless, more than can be described here. The boys are playful and attractive in and of themselves, but in addition, every activity conveys a clear message of the desired outcome for sons—education, wealth, and high office. The portrayal of children as emblematic of fertility and high achievement is consistent in various Chinese media—such as ceramics, textiles, jade, and carved decoration of wood and lacquer furniture—across time, spanning more than a thousand years.

The multiplicity of symbols reinforcing success, most especially scholarly success, is playfully acted out by children in this painting. While the children in the painting frolic, however, these symbolic artworks underpin the realities of youth culture in imperial China. Parental pressure to excel in Confucian training applied to both scholarship and traditional behavior, such as filial piety. The pressure was felt among all classes, though most especially those from wealthy and educated families. Written materials, such as local history, biography, and fiction, support the evidence that the culture of youth in imperial China included anxiety, endless hours of study (or work, as the case may be), and frequent parental reproach, guidance, interference, or control.

Schools and the Education of Youth

The education of young people is a primary concern across cultures. Societies exist by forming around a common set of values and economic practices. To survive, these values must be conveyed to the generations that follow them. The ability to read is a fundamental aspect of education in literate societies. Correspondingly, youth learning to read is a subject of art in a wide variety of cultures.

Pictures of children in school is a manifestation of the importance of gaining literary skills, and in some cases, a source for images of youth. Often these pictures are visual antidotes to the serious nature of learning. Misbehaving students is a playful theme in more than one culture.

In the case of China, school scenes, like the gardens, are still the realm of small boys. The children shown are mostly too young for school. The school buildings are rendered as open-air pavilions, giving the viewer direct access to the boys and books inside. The rooms portrayed are similar to the architecture found in the gardens of elite families, where educated scholars retreated from the hubbub of the cities. Thus, the visual effect implies that the boys are protected and set in an environment specifically for learning. The behavior of the students, however, is willfully mischievous, as they variously quarrel, climb on furniture, and even poke fun at sleeping teachers. This is especially surprising given that reverence for words and writing is among the strongest and long-lasting values in Chinese civilization. These scenes offer comic relief from the actual culture that pervaded the schools. They show exactly what youth should not do and, in fact, would not dare to do. Like the hundred children playing in a garden, the pictures reinforce the high value placed on education. Thus, in China, the schoolroom scenes are another example of the pressure put on male youth to excel in their studies.

Examples outside East Asia mostly depict children of a more appropriate age for school. Nonetheless, the theme of naughty students is widespread. Examples of misbehavior in seventeenth-century Islamic miniature painting are directly related to a story in *The Gulistan* ("The Rose Garden,"), 1258, written by the beloved Persian poet, Sheik Saadi of Shiraz (ca. 1193–1291). The story describes the effect of a cruel master on "innocent boys and little maidens [who] suffered from the hand of his tyranny" that Saadi witnessed in "the Maghrib country." When the harsh teacher was replaced by a benevolent one, the students "neglected their studies, spending their time in play," and breaking their wooden tablets on each other's heads. At this point in the story a proverb by Saadi is inserted: "If the schoolmaster happens to be lenient, the children will play leapfrog in the bazar."[1]

Saadi then recounts that two weeks later he passed the same mosque and saw that the kind schoolmaster had been let go and the former cruel teacher reinstalled. Upon enquiry, Saadi writes, "An old man, experienced in the world, who had heard me, smiled and said: 'Hast thou not heard the maxim? A Padshah placed his son in a school, putting in his lap a silver tablet with this inscription in golden letters: "The severity of a teacher is better than the love of a father."' "[2]

The illustration of the story from *Gulistan* shown here depicts sons of the wealthy elite with their teacher (Fig. 19.3). The teacher's face is portrait-like, to distinguish his importance, while the faces of the boys are not individualized. Their clothing is similar to that of the teacher, but physical characteristics such as size, facial structure, and movement clearly show that the age of the figures is between childhood and adulthood. An elaborate architectural framework serves to distinguish the students indoors from the three boys playing outside. By placing a merchant selling wares on the left edge of the painting, the painter implies a bazaar, as described in the poem. Behind the merchant's stall an open door and a single stylized tree indicate a private garden. Above the garden a Chinese-style rock, plants, and bird, together with a bit of blue and clouds, suggest an entire landscape. Thus, the artist has skillfully used economy of means to delineate separate spaces within the two-dimensional painting.

One of the three boys outside the school appears to be a delinquent student playing in the bazaar with lower-class youths, whose inferior social status is indicated by their short robes. The merchant smiles privately at the boys' antics, which may have involved disturbing one of his customers, who seems to be railing in front of the merchant's stall. Meanwhile, inside the school, several of the boys are distracted by the commotion outside. While this scene is clearly an illustration of Saadi's poetry, both the poem and the painting give a glimpse of youth culture at the time. The poetic story reveals that parents preferred strict teachers. The painting provides a lesson to youth of the upper class. If they were not inside the school, included in the place set apart for them, they would ultimately be associated with the uneducated, who belonged to

FIGURE 19.3. *The Mild Teacher and the Naughty Pupils*, c. 1625. Ink, colors, and gold on paper. Illustrated page from Sadi's *Gulistan*. Isfahan, Iran.

© The David Collection, Copenhagen. 130/2006. Photo by Pernille Klemp.

a lower class. It furthermore implies that youth are not yet trusted to make good decisions on their own, and that disciplinarians were a necessary part of youth culture to squelch their inclinations toward delinquency. It may also illustrate that mischief played a part in the culture of youth.

The students in the example are all boys, yet Saadi includes girls in his poem. Paintings of the same period that include girls in school with boys are illustrations of famous love stories, such as the tragic tale of Layla and Majnun, who like Romeo and Juliet were separated by family rivalries, in this case a Christian family and an Islamic family. Parents' control over youth extended to who they were allowed to marry, thus suggesting frustration with close parental supervision as a possible element of both male and female youth culture.

Upper-class youth in schools shows the importance of education in maintaining the status of the ruling class in both imperial China and sixteenth- to seventeenth-century Persia. Depictions of schoolrooms in nineteenth-century America have a very different message, but the theme of misbehaving students also appears. In *The New England School*, circa 1852, by American painter Charles Frederick Bosworth, a young female teacher uses a stick to point to words in a book held by a young boy who scratches his head in confusion.[3] The girl next to him hides a smirk as she waits in line for her turn to read. A smaller boy sits fearfully on the bench in front of them as he looks on. Once again, the teacher is not in control of the students. Behind her back, older boys and girls flirt with one another. Another boy hides under a table in the foreground, reading his book. A girl who has discovered his hiding place smiles mischievously as the boy glares at her. Meanwhile, students seated on benches with high backs playfully toss a hat, converse, and otherwise ignore their studies.

Nineteenth-century American artists also constructed a defined space inhabited by teacher and students. The absence of one of four exterior walls in *The New England School* affords a view into a painted three-dimensional space from a Western linear perspective. In this American scene, an equal number of boys and girls of various ages are depicted in the same room. The room is simple and the children wear practical clothing. There is nothing that indicates wealth or privilege. The painting embodies the American ideals of equality and a strong middle class. A large map of both the eastern and western hemispheres provides a focal point on the back wall. Besides indicating that geography was a significant school subject, its prominence seems to illustrate the importance of and pride in the Americas.

One should point out that the American teacher is a young, unmarried female. In the previously examined societies the schoolmaster was a respected male scholar. A female teacher would automatically influence youth culture in different ways, one being the possibility of boys forming crushes on their teachers. Most importantly, women placed in a position of authority in American schools reinforced the egalitarian ideal of education for all.

A quarter of a century later, eight years after the end of the Civil War, Winslow Homer painted *Country School*, a romanticized picture of a one-room schoolhouse.[4]

YOUTH IN THE VISUAL ARTS 361

This American schoolroom scene implies that middle-class youth culture included school as a place of cooperation, friendship, learning at one's own pace, and integrated white and Black students.

The young teacher is in the center of the room, framed by the blackboard behind her and a tall wooden table in front. Two large windows on either side of the teacher afford a sunny view of the hills outside the school and bring light into the room. The teacher's pretty apron, her straw hat hanging on the wall, and a vase of flowers on her desk create a mild and pleasant atmosphere for learning. The students are casually arranged and individually engaged in their own books. The teacher appears calm and respected by her students, with none of them acting out. Nonetheless, one small boy wipes away tears, perhaps because he is the youngest and hasn't yet learned to read. Older boys with ragged trousers and dirty bare feet sit comfortably next to boys wearing jackets and shoes, concentrating on their reading. Under a window three fastidiously dressed African American girls of different ages are huddled together as if they might be sisters. There is a strong didactic message in the painting, that of equality and opportunity for all in America, wealthy or not, Black or white. Inclusion of the Black girls reflects Homer's optimism that after the end of slavery, Black and white children will unite to build the nation.

Youth and Their Mothers

The activities of mothers and children portrayed in art give specific examples of what informed youth culture as well as illustrate societal expectations of mothers. The ideal mother in China stems from apocryphal stories of Mencius and his mother, a subject that was popular in Chinese art (Fig. 19.4). The philosopher Mencius (Meng Ke 372 BCE–289 BCE) was highly revered in traditional China. His writings form part of the *Confucian Classics*, books that were memorized by scholars in preparation for the exams that would allow them access to highly sought-after jobs as government bureaucrats. The source of the stories is *Biographies of Exemplary Women* (*Lienü zhuan*), a work compiled by Liu Xiang (79 BCE–8 BCE) and presented to the emperor around 17 BCE.[5] Many of the printed editions of *Biographies of Exemplary Women* in late imperial China included woodcut illustrations of the stories.

In this example, young Mencius emerges from a building labeled *shuyuan* ("book room" or "school") in panel a. His mother, facing him from the opposite page (panel b), is threatening to cut the threads on her weaving loom, which would undo the progress she had made. Her severe reaction is a response to Mencius's seemingly lackadaisical approach to learning. The object lesson shows her determination that Mencius excel at his studies. At the same time, the composition of the picture clearly denotes separate spheres for men and women. Mencius's mother, from her designated place at home, directs his action, keeping him in the outside world of educated men. While the main intent of this illustration of the story is to instruct mothers of the late imperial

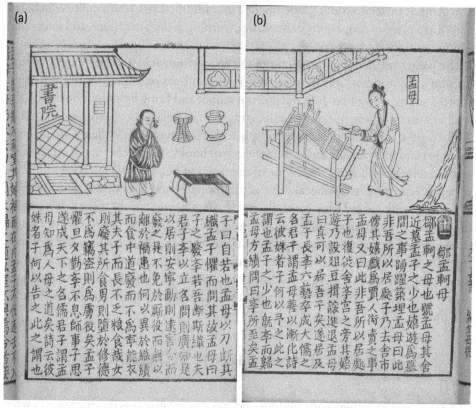

FIGURE 19.4. Illustration of Mencius and his mother. Woodblock print. From *Lienü zhuan*, Qingyoutang edition, late thirteenth–early fourteenth century. Reprinted in *Xin kan Gu Lie nü zhuan*: [8 juan]. CT3710.L5 1930 v. 1, plate 22.

Photo courtesy of Special Collections, University of Virginia, Charlottesville.

period about their role in educating their sons, the cultural milieu in which male youth go to school and female youth learn domestic arts at home is reinforced.

She Taught Her Sons While Weaving at Her Loom (Mingji kezi tu), by Gai Qi (1774-1829) and Wang Run (1756-1832) is a posthumous portrait of an early nineteenth-century official's wife and sons.[6] The mother is depicted at her loom; the two school-age boys sit at a table with candlestick and books. The painting is an obvious reference to the legendary story about Mencius's mother, as well as an illustration of the official's tribute to his spouse, "While weaving at her loom, she did not neglect the task of teaching her sons."[7] The fact that the portraits are posthumous reinforces the importance of the mother's role in that her devotion to the education of her sons becomes her tribute. This painting is also an example of Chinese portraiture that was influenced by Western techniques. Toward the end of the eighteenth century, Chinese artists began to paint three-dimensional faces in portraits so that individuals could be recognized by their physical features.

In this handscroll, the artist has captured the appearance of actual upper-class boys who are dressed in scholars' robes such as their father would have worn. Their respectful postures are similar to each other, hands folded inside the sleeves of their gowns. The difference in their body sizes and facial details are distinct, showing the physical characteristics of an older, more serious son and a younger, more childlike boy who does his best to mimic his older brother. Though the title and inscriptions on the painting praise the mother's attributes, she is depicted as a stock figure. The woman who directed the boys' learning and molded their characters is not painted as an individual, but as a model mother.

Two sympathetic colophons written on the painting are thought to have been inscribed by a woman, perhaps the poet Wang Dun (1793–1839). Other inscriptions, written on the painting by high-ranking friends of the husband whose wife died, reveal more about his prestige as a poet and an honored government official than about his consort. The wife and sons had belonged to him, and he had the means to commission the painting, which was "respectfully completed for His Honor Yingyuan, on the seventh day of the seventh month, in the autumn of the twenty-fifty year of the Jiaqing period (1820) . . ."[8] It is probably not a coincidence that the completion date given for the painting is the same day of the year as Vega and Altair, stars known in East Asia as the separated lovers Weaving Maid and Cowherd, cross each other in the Milky Way. Unmarried girls prayed on this day for the gift of excellence in sewing or weaving, reinforcing the importance of expertise in domestic arts as part of female youth culture.

Depictions of male Chinese youth are abundant but rarely depicted in any other role than aspiring Confucian scholars. Pictures of female youth are less common in Chinese art. When included, they are almost never the main subject of the painting. An elegant example is "Palace Ladies Preparing Silk," a twelfth-century copy of an eighth-century handscroll. Silk exported westward was a source of great wealth in China during the Tang dynasty (619–907). The imperial women in this painting are enacting the annual ritual of making ready the silk in order to symbolize order in the state, a metaphorical blessing on the silkworm harvest (Fig. 19.5). The painting shows the different stages of womanhood, including girlhood and childhood. The mature women, wives and concubines of the emperor, are shown as voluptuous beauties. They reflect the preferred female shape at court during the eighth century, at least in art if not in reality. The younger wives are more slender, not yet bearing the weight and prestige of the older. The two adolescent girls, identified by symmetrical hair bobs on either side of their heads, are imperial daughters. Both participate in the ritual. The small girl, also an imperial daughter, is too young to contribute and runs merrily underneath the length of silk held up for ironing. Pictures of palace women are a standard theme of Chinese figure painting. It is the women themselves who are the subjects of the paintings. As girl children were brought up with their mothers in the women's quarters of the palace, they are sometimes included, but they are never more than token additions.

FIGURE 19.5. Attributed to Emperor Huizong (1082–1135). *Ladies Preparing Newly Woven Silk in the Style of Zhou Fang*, early twelfth century. Ink and colors on silk, 37 × 147 cm.

Museum of Fine Arts, Boston, Japanese and Chinese Special Fund. 12.886.

The special attention given to boys created a male youth culture in which they assumed superiority to girls. At the same time, it cultivated loyalty to the mothers who promoted them. The culture within which female youth lived created a milieu of lesser significance, which is born out in portrayals of them in art.

They inhabited separate spheres, so that male and female youth cultures were very different from each other. Yet one aspect of youth culture they must have held in common was anxiety. Pressure to function within what was considered the norm for their gender seems to have permeated the lives of upper-class youth in imperial China.

Portrayals of the gendered experiences of youth can be found in cultures other than China. In Western art, mothers with children is a specific subcategory of both portraiture and genre scenes, built on a thousand-year tradition of depictions of Mary with the Christ Child. During the nineteenth century, intimate scenes of everyday mothers and children rose to prominence, especially among the Impressionists. In their case, both the subject matter and the composition were inspired by Japanese prints, most notably Kitagawa Utamaro (1753–1806), a prolific print designer in the third quarter of the eighteenth century.

Utamaro's prints show Japanese mothers' delight in their young sons. Yet Impressionists such as Mary Cassatt (1884–1926) and Pierre-August Renoir (1884–1919) focused on mothers with their daughters. In fact, nineteenth-century Western paintings, both portraits and genre scenes, are one of the most fertile sources for physically accurate paintings of adolescent girls. *At the Piano*, 1858–1859, by James McNeill Whistler, is a good example of a personal moment captured between a mother and her daughter (Fig. 19.6). The girl's folded arms rest on the piano, one foot casually crossed behind the other, while her mother plays. Leaning slightly toward each other, the two figures form a triangle that encloses them in a very private space. The shallow depth and the simplicity of the flat blocks of color are directly inspired by Japanese print conventions.

Scenes of girls and mothers sharing private moments, which are plentiful in nineteenth-century Western art, seem to illustrate a close bond between them. In actual life, the closeness may or may not have existed. Whether conscious or not, the artists have repeatedly created it, and the viewer wants to believe it is a genuine emotion. At this point in Western history, art has moved beyond the exclusive power of

FIGURE 19.6. James McNeill Whistler (1834–1903). *At the Piano*, 1858–1859. Oil on canvas, 26 3/8 × 35 5/8 in.

The Taft Museum, Cincinnati, Ohio. Louise Taft Semple Bequest.

the elite few who controlled commissions. Paintings were shown in public and sold in galleries. More often they were the property of the artist who created them rather than a patron who commissioned them. At the same time, paintings that reflected society's ideals were more likely to be admired and purchased, which could have influenced the artists' choice of perspective. Nineteenth-century painting styles are new and exciting. Nevertheless, the sentiments expressed reflect the Romanticism found in literature, philosophy, and the visual arts of that time. They also illustrate the belief that the activities of women are separate from those of men.

Family Portraits

Portraiture exists in a variety of symbolic forms among numerous cultures. The concept of portraits that resemble a person's physical characteristics, however, is specific to Western art, a technique that Chinese artists, following European models, began to explore in the mid-eighteenth century. Family portraits, where children of various ages are seen as a group, are not unusual in Western art. In China, however, pictures of children together with both parents were almost unknown prior to the eighteenth century and were rare even after that.

The Chinese artist Hua Guan painted the family of the well-known poet Jiang Shiquan (1725–1785) sitting in a covered pleasure boat, returning from an outing.[9] The members of Jiang's family are gazing outward from underneath the covered sections of the boat, indicating that one purpose of the painting was to capture recognizable facial features of each individual. Jiang himself is placed at the front of the boat, leaning out from inside the covered section that includes his two school-age sons. This illustrates the Chinese tradition that men move in the world outside their homes, while women are secluded on the inside. Jiang is shown as the largest of the six family members. He wears a scholar's robe and holds a scroll in his hand. The scroll signifies that he is capable of both calligraphy and painting, the marks of a well-educated and refined man. His sons also wear scholars' robes and are seated at a desk piled with books. Even though the family is shown returning from an outing, the sons represent the duty of school-aged boys to study for the imperial exams.

Jiang's wife and his mother sit in the next section of the boat with a tiny child. Their covered portion of the boat is lower, suggesting their inferior status as female as well as the belief that women should be protected from the outside world. A plate of fruit is set out on the table behind them, an obvious symbol of fertility as well as the expectation that women will bear children. This is a staged portrait of a specific family. But the presentation of the family reveals the same ambitions for boys that were demonstrated in *A Hundred Children at Play* (Fig. 19.1). It is also similar to Western family portraits in that it shows off the prestige and assets of Jiang Shiquan, the patriarch of the family, who commissioned the work.

While family portraits in traditional China are rare, portraits of Western families abound, from the seventeenth-century paintings of Anthony Van Dyck to eighteenth-century works by Francisco Goya, Charles Wilson Peale, Thomas Gainsborough, and Joshua Reynolds, and nineteenth-century artists such as John Singer Sargent and many others. Not surprisingly, Western family portraits express strong messages about the lifestyle, prestige, and even political positions of the families. They also convey expectations of their offspring, including adolescent girls and boys. The placement of girls is usually with their mothers on one side of the painting, while boys are positioned near their fathers. Generally, adolescent boys are dressed similarly to their fathers. Girls appear in dresses, though their clothing may be less elaborate than that of their mothers.

The Family of Frederick, Prince of Wales, 1751, was painted by English painter George Knapton (1698–1778) (Fig. 19.7). Augusta, wife of the Prince of Wales, commissioned the enormous painting shortly after Frederick's death. Knapton included the already deceased Frederick in the picture by placing a portrait of him in the top left of the picture, directly above his two oldest sons. Frederick is standing and pointing his finger toward the family members below, as though claiming them as his wife and children from heaven above. This clearly portrays the message that Frederick lives on through

FIGURE 19.7. George Knapton (1698–1778). *The Family of Frederick, Prince of Wales*, 1751. Oil on canvas, 350.9 × 461.2 cm.

Royal Collection Trust / © Her Majesty Queen Elizabeth II 2019. RCIN 405741.

his children. It was also a reminder to contemporaries that the family was still relevant within the royal circle. In fact, Frederick's oldest son succeeded the throne as King George III, after the death of his grandfather.

Knapton placed Augusta directly in the center of the family. Her head forms the apex of her own wide triangle, as well as the peak of the entire group, her children posed within a larger triangle around her. The overall composition presents the individuals as a close-knit and protected family. Augusta wears a black mourning veil, but it dissolves into the dark background of the lavishly decorated room while her face is lit with compassion and determination.

The artist used spotlight, bright color, and gesture to portray each person as an individual. The objects included in the portrait are clear indications of the lives of upper-class youth in eighteenth-century England, what occupied them, and what was expected. For example, the two older boys hold a map, representing plans for their inherited property. The younger boys play with a lifelike replica of a royal boat with flags of both Great Britain and the Royal Family. This could represent a future career as a naval officer, an attractive option for younger sons. Telescopes and a land survey instrument are seen in front of the male youths, symbolizing adventure and scientific progress. A lute is played by one of the girls situated on the other side of the mother. Musical skills, which could be pursued indoors, were among the important accomplishments suitable for female youth. Dogs, symbols of fidelity, are shown on the female side, a reminder to the girls to be faithful to their future husbands. The dogs also symbolize Augusta's loyalty to her deceased husband and their children.

Western Genre Painting

The cost of commissioned portraits in which youth are represented limits them to depictions of the wealthy elite. It is in genre paintings that youth from other classes are shown. When compared with Chinese works, Western genre scenes sometimes appear more straightforward and less didactic in picturing youth. When placed in the historical and cultural context in which the paintings were created, however, it is clear that these works are just as charged with societal messages as the East Asian works. For example, *Children's Games*, a sixteenth-century painting by the Flemish and Dutch artist Pieter Bruegel the Elder (1525–1569), is an allegorical painting, in which each of the seemingly innocuous games represents human folly.[10] Moreover, a close examination of the figures reveals that the bodies and clothing of the "children" are very nearly indistinguishable from those of adults.

Dutch painters are among the first to produce works describing ordinary people's lives and activities. Seventeenth-century painters Jan Steen (1626–1679), Frans Hals (1582–1666), and Jan Vermeer (1632–1675) created lively scenes of weddings, festivals, and Dutch bourgeois interiors that include young people in the mix. Eighteenth-century Spanish paintings, such as the tapestry cartoons designed by Francisco Goya (1746–1828), also portray groups of ordinary folks. In many of these genre scenes, children and youth seem to be token representatives of their age groups, while the majority of the figures portrayed are adults, thus making it difficult to determine a separate youth culture.

It is during the nineteenth century that youth themselves emerge as specific subjects of genre painting in the West. The sheer volume and multitude of artists and works makes it impossible to explore this area with just a few examples, but prominent themes will be pointed out, such as the lives and activities of working youth.

An awakening social consciousness of the plight of those living in poverty is illustrated in *The Stone Breakers*, 1849, by Gustave Courbet.[11] A young man works beside an older laborer, gathering rocks that will pave a road. The youth heaves a heavy stone while the older man doggedly pounds rocks into small pieces. The back-breaking work is portrayed in the harshly lit poses of the figures, their faces turned away from the viewer, thus representing their hopeless acceptance of unending physical labor. It is impossible to escape a visceral sense of their despair. The work was exhibited at the 1850 Paris Salon, where Courbet meant to evoke a sympathetic response among those who had the leisure to see the painting. An arousal of their feelings could lead to action on behalf of the downtrodden.

Even more heart-rending are the paintings of child laborers, such as the overly dramatic portrayal of *A Martyr: The Violet Seller* by Fernand Pelez, exhibited at the Paris Salon in 1885.[12] A ragged and dirty barefoot boy sleeps in a doorway, a small violet bunch falling from the wooden tray around his neck. The stark background, portions of a wide stone frame around a massive, closed door, emphasizes the pitiful figure of the boy, who looks to be about ten years old.

Buffalo News Boy, 1853, by Thomas Le Clear (1818–1882) gives a very different view of the adolescent worker (Fig. 19.8). It is an example showing that the concept of working-class youth culture, separate from that of adults, existed in nineteenth century America. Newsboys created a popular culture all their own, often romanticized in literature and art. Le Clear's newsboy is the main subject of the painting. Casual and confident, taking a break from his work to eat an apple, he is the embodiment of the American ideals of independence and individual industry or working for oneself. The youth is free to choose when to rest. He is not underfed, nor are his clothes shabby. He wears sturdy boots, a hat, and clothing that will protect him from the elements.

Newspapers represent literacy and a democratic approach to communication among the middle class. Advertisements and posters slapped on tall wood fences and the brick wall behind the boy speak of a thriving economy. In the painting, the news boy's elbow leads the viewer's eye directly to a notice of employment for fifty boys that one would assume are about the same age as the young man shown here. This perhaps reinforces the idea that the youth has time to eat his apple, as there are ample job opportunities. The painting reinforces the ideals that America is the land of opportunity, that youth were capable of achieving the "American dream" of prosperity through hard work.

American spirit and ideals are also evident in depictions of youths by Winslow Homer, Thomas Eakins, and numerous other painters. These works illustrate activities that engaged American youths, yet at the same time, each includes specific social messages. *Snap the Whip*, 1872, by Winslow Homer, shows a group of boisterous schoolboys playing the game as they run outdoors in the meadow, their schoolhouse in the distance behind them.[13] The messages in this painting are freedom, competition, vibrant good health, and time to play, as well as education for all youth, regardless of class.

Homer's *Watermelon Boys*, which portrays three schoolage youths splitting a watermelon, expresses Northerners' hope for amity among Black and white youth a decade after the end of the Civil War.[14] The figures, two Black and one white, are set in the forefront of an idyllic landscape bathed in the golden light of late afternoon, schoolbooks tossed on the ground. Two of them lie on their stomachs in the field eating, their legs kicked up behind them. The boys are set companionably close together and wear similar clothing. Yet there are subtle differences in their demeanors, not noticeable at first glance. One white youth unselfconsciously eats his slice; the African American

FIGURE 19.8. Thomas Le Clear (American, 1818–1882). *Buffalo Newsboy*, 1853. Oil on canvas, 24 × 20 inches (61 × 50.8 cm). Collection Albright-Knox Gallery, Buffalo, New York; Charlotte A. Watson Fund, 1942. 1942:3.

Image courtesy of Albright-Knox Gallery.

kneeling in the center of the group looks uneasily over his shoulder at the fence, as if unable to relax. The implication is that the boys are not authorized to eat the fruit. The black youth seems more wary of possible negative consequences, an unfortunate part of Black youth culture that remains to this day.

The Card Trick, painted in the 1880s by John George Brown, romanticizes the carefree life of youths who are free to work, wander the streets, and play. A group of four boys, three white and one Black, are playing on a curbside, one seated on a stool, another leaning on an upturned shoeshine box.[15] The sidewalk and street are littered with banana peels and bits of paper wrappers. All four are laughing, highly entertained by performing card tricks for each other.

Girl culture is no less common than boy culture in genre paintings of the nineteenth century, whether American or European, although generally speaking they are more often pictured in interiors. Visualization of the buoyant American spirit of freedom is mostly limited to depictions of males. While male youth gather in outdoor spaces to work, play, watch the goings-on about town, or otherwise mingle with each other, girls are shown indoors reading, sewing, and playing the piano, engaging in much quieter activities in a confined space. The exception to this would be the placement of girls in gardens. One might note, however, that albeit outdoors, a garden is also a protected space, not quite part of the larger world. In addition, the growth in gardens symbolizes fertile reproduction. Thus, pictures of adolescents in art are strongly gendered, clearly guiding young people toward choices that will fit in with what society expected.

Nineteenth-century artists do illustrate actual activities of youth, such as sons and apprentices learning a trade, or adolescent girls reading to younger siblings. They provide realistic pictures of the general physical characteristics of adolescents and a variety of their undertakings. Nevertheless, the artworks also convey a specific political view or didactic purpose, if nothing more than to direct appropriate activities by gender, thus reinforcing cultural norms for youth.

Globalism in the Twentieth and Twenty-First Centuries

Though there are continuities among traditional and contemporary pictures of youth in most cultures, the expansive content and themes of twentieth- and twenty-first-century art are beyond the scope here. Broadly speaking, when youth are depicted in Chinese art since the 1980s, artists have portrayed bewilderment, sometimes their own, as they navigate their places in a rapidly changing society, including their positions as single representatives of their families. Inner struggle and the actual feelings of individual youth seem to be more visible in contemporary art from all parts of the world. Good examples of this are found in the collection of essays published in *Depicting Canada's Children*, edited by Loren Lerner, 2009. Though the private thoughts of youth are explored in contemporary art, the messages conveyed are often a combination of individual artists' political views and the social norms of the culture around them. Contemporary artists control the meaning of their work, but it is never outside the context of previous artworks or of the society in which they live.

Summary

A historical view of works in select cultures shows a surprising consistency across time and space in the messages contained in depictions of youth culture. Yet youth do not yet form a specific category in the history of art. This is made clear by the sources in "Further Reading." Whether in past or present scholarship, images of youth are primarily included in works about children. While style and means of expression differ widely, young people portrayed in each society represent that society's ideals. Ideals held in common in different parts of the world include the education of youth to function according to the mores of society and the idea that men and women function in separate spheres. In the case of family portraiture, the works document what the leaders of the adolescents' families valued, such as lineage, moral outlook, political view, power, or wealth.

Notes

1. Sir Richard Burton, trans. Section VII, "On the Effects of Education, Story CLVII." *Tales from the Gulistan or Rose-Garden of the Sheik Sa'di of Shiraz* (London: Phillip Allan & Co. Ltd., 1928), 198.
2. Sir Richard Burton, trans. Section VII, "On the Effects of Education, Story CLVII." *Tales from the Gulistan or Rose-Garden of the Sheik Sa'di of Shiraz* (London: Phillip Allan & Co. Ltd., 1928) 199.
3. Charles Frederick Bosworth (1831–1925), *The New England School*, c. 1852. Oil on wood panel, 16.5 × 20.5 in. (41.9 × 52.07 cm). Massachusetts Historical Society, Boston. Published in Clair Perry, *Young America: Childhood in Nineteenth-Century Art and Culture* (New Haven, CT: Yale University Press; Stanford, CA: Iris & B. Gerald Cantor Center for Visual Arts, Stanford University, 2006), 189, Fig. 155.
4. Winslow Homer (1836–1910), *Country School*, 1873. Oil on canvas, 12.24 × 18.6875 in. (31.1 × 47.5 cm). Addison Gallery of American Art, Phillips Academy, Andover, Massachusetts. Published in Perry, *Young America*, 182, Fig. 152.
5. Anne Behnke Kinney, ed. and trans. *Exemplary Women of Early China: The* Lienü zhuan *of Liu Xiang* (New York: Columbia University Press, 2014), xv, xvii.
6. Gai Qi (1774–1829) and Wang Run (1756–1832), *She Taught Her Sons While Weaving at Her Loom (Mingji kezi tu)*, 1820. Handscroll; ink and colors on paper, 1 in. × 5 ft. 7 in. (31.7 × 172.5 cm). Royal Ontario Museum, Toronto. Accession number 2003.3.11. Published in Jerome Silbergeld and Dora C.Y. Ching, eds., *The Family Model in Chinese Art and Culture* (Princeton, NJ: P.Y. and Kinmay W. Tang Center for East Asian Art and Princeton University Press, 2013), 247–251, Figs. 8–13.

7. Sha Shenzi, "Mansions in Life and Death," trans. Klass Ruitenbeek, in *The Family Model in Chinese Art and Culture*, ed. Silbergeld and Ching, 247.
8. Gai Qi, "Mansions in Life and Death," trans. Klass Ruitenbeek, in *The Family Model in Chinese Art and Culture*, ed. Silbergeld and Ching, 247.
9. Hua Guan, *Sailing Back Smoothly: Portrait of Jiang Shiquan*, 1763. Handscroll, ink and colors on paper; 16 × 132.8 cm. Nanjing Museum. Illustrated in Ann Barrott Wicks, ed., *Children in Chinese Art* (Honolulu: University of Hawai'i Press, 2002), Plate 22. Also illustrated in Liang Baiquan, ed., *Selected Chinese Portrait Paintings from the Nanjing Museum.* (Hong Kong: Cultural Relics Publishing House, 1933), plate 47.
10. Sandra Hindman, "Pieter Bruegel's Children's Games, Folly, and Chance," *The Art Bulletin* 63, no. 3 (1981), 447–475; and Amy Orrock, "*Homo ludens*: Pieter Bruegel's Children's Games and the Humanist Educators," *Journal of Historians of Netherlandish Art* 4, no. 2 (Summer 2012), 1–20.
11. Gustave Courbet (1819–1877), *The Stone Breakers*, 1849. Oil on canvas, 5 ft. 3 in. × 8 ft. 6 in. (1.6 × 2.59 m.) Formerly in the Gemäldegalerie, Dresden. Destroyed in World War II. Illustrated online and featured in many art history textbooks as an example of the French Realist movement led by Courbet.
12. Fernand Pelez (1848–1913), *A Martyr: The Violet Seller*, 1885. Oil on canvas, 34.25 × 39.375 in. (87 × 100 cm). Petit Palais, inv. PPP592. Published in Champy-Vinas, Cécile. *Paris 1900: City of Entertainment* (Paris: Paris Musées Publications, 2018).
13. Winslow Homer (1836–1910), *Snap the Whip*, 1872. Oil on canvas 12 × 20 in. (30.5 × 50.8 cm). The Metropolitan Museum of Art. Gift of Christian A. Zabriskie, 1950. Accession number 50.41. Published in Perry, *Young America*, 28, Fig. 13.
14. Winslow Homer (1836–1910), *The Watermelon Boys*, 1876. Oil on canvas, 24.125 × 38.25 in. (61.3 × 96.8 cm). Cooper-Hewitt National Design Museum, Smithsonian Institution, New York. Gift of Charles Savage Homer Jr. Published in Perry, *Young America*, 97, Fig. 81.
15. John George Brown (1831–1913), *The Card Trick*, 1880–1889. Oil on canvas mounted on panel, 26 × 31 in. (66 × 78.7 cm). Joslyn Art Museum, Omaha, Nebraska. Gift of the estate of Sarah Joslyn JAM 1944.14. Published in H. Barbara Weinberg and Carrie Rebora Barratt, *American Stories: Paintings of Everyday Life 1765–1915* (New York: The Metropolitan Museum of Art; and New Haven and London: Yale University Press, 2009), 145, Fig. 136.

Further Reading

Bedaux, Jan Baptist, and Rudi Ekkart, eds. *Pride and Joy: Children's Portraits in the Netherlands, 1500–1700*. Amsterdam: Ludion Press Ghent, 2000.

Children and Youth in History. The Roy Rosenzweig Center for History and New Media (CHNM) at George Mason University and the University of Missouri-Kansas City. Web database, http://chnm.gmu.edu/cyh/. Accessed December 10, 2018.

Hennessy, Cecily. *Images of Children in Byzantium*. Farnham, UK, and Burlington, VT: Ashgate Publishing, 2008.

Kinney, Anne Behnke. *Representations of Childhood and Youth in Early China*. Stanford, CA: Stanford University Press, 2004.

Langmuir, Erika. *Imagining Childhood*. New Haven, CT, and London: Yale University Press, 2006.

Lerna, Lora, ed. *Depicting Canada's Children*. Waterloo, Canada: Wilfrid Laurier University Press, 2009.
"Mencius and His Mother: A Lesson Drawn from Weaving" [Literary Excerpt and Illustration]." *Children and Youth in History*, Item #189. Annotated by Anne Kinney. http://chnm.gmu.edu/cyh/items/show/189. Accessed January 4, 2020.
Orme, Nicholas. *Medieval Children*. New Haven, CT: Yale University Press, 2001.
Perry, Clair. *Young America: Childhood in Nineteenth-Century Art and Culture*. New Haven, CT: Yale University Press; Stanford, CA: Iris & B. Gerald Cantor Center for Visual Arts, Stanford University, 2006.
Silbergeld, Jerome, and Dora C.Y. Ching. *The Family Model in Chinese Art and Culture*. Princeton, NJ: P.Y. and Kinmay W. Tang Center for East Asian Art and Princeton University Press, 2013.
Wicks, Ann Barrott, ed. *Children in Chinese Art*. Honolulu: University of Hawai'i Press, 2002.
Wicks, Ann Barrott. "Picturing Children." In *The Family Model in Chinese Art and Culture*. Edited by Jerome Silbergeld and Dora C.Y. Ching, 301–337. Princeton, NJ: P.Y. and Kinmay W. Tang Center for East Asian Art and Princeton University Press, 2013.

CHAPTER 20

TRANSFORMING REBELLION INTO AFFIRMATION

A History of Youth Literature and Reading Cultures

PAUL RINGEL

OVER the past two and a half centuries, youth cultures and youth literature have mostly enjoyed a symbiotic relationship. The publishing industry was one of the first to market directly to young consumers, and its products, from *The Sorrows of Young Werther* in the late eighteenth century to the Harry Potter series in the twenty-first, have created international bonds among readers that outpaced noncommercial forms of connection among young people. While movies, fashion, music, and other goods forge similar global connections now, youth literature predates most of those competitors. Indeed, it largely forged the cultures that legitimized the idea of young people as consumers, and it thus facilitated the growth of these other industries.

Youth cultures and youth literature have also experienced a persistent, essential tension. Stories for young readers have traditionally been a conservative, educational instrument, emerging from adult desires to convey existing social standards to the next generation. Early producers of youth literature embraced this responsibility, which helped to validate their work for adult consumers and for critics who remained skittish about the moral and social consequences of marketing to young people. By the mid-nineteenth century, older youth who were gaining access to less proscriptive forms of entertainment began to force a change in this marketing strategy. These readers wanted stories in which young protagonists became liberated from established, age-related boundaries, and publishers striving for profit from the growing audience for youth magazines and novels had to engage with these consumer demands.

A constant struggle to balance these often-conflicting goals of education and entertainment defined this relationship throughout the publishing industry's attempts to systemize production of youth literature during the nineteenth century and diversify its voices during the twentieth. Readers of Victorian-era magazines forced their editors to endlessly refine story formulas to facilitate a stream of tales that were moral *and* fun. Audiences between and after the two world wars demanded a wider range of characters in youth fiction, which authors then mostly integrated into well-established genres and tropes.

On the surface, young readers' consumer desires seemed gradually to win this struggle (as they have in other youth-centered industries) against adults' conservative impulses. Characters from Tom Sawyer to Katniss Everdeen have achieved popularity largely because they break from traditional expectations of youth and assume more adult levels of independence and responsibility. Yet these heroines and heroes nearly always return to traditional roles and at least cautiously optimistic situations at the end of their stories; Jo March marries Professor Bhaer and opens a school for boys, just as Harry Potter marries Ginny Weasley and settles into a middle management position at the Ministry of Magic. When protagonists from Goethe's Werther to Twain's Huckleberry Finn to Walter Dean Myers's Steve Harmon (from the 1999 novel *Monster*) diverge from this pattern, adults often seek to marginalize these stories as inappropriate for young audiences or insufficiently commercial.

Whether readers embraced or even recognized this pattern amid the excitement and glamour of youthful adventure and romance stories is an open and complicated question. Still, Anglo-American youth literature has exerted global dominance by prioritizing narrative models that follow a period of adolescent rebellion with affirmation of the value of existing institutions, values, and hierarchies. This structure has persisted from seduction narratives in the early nineteenth century through series fiction at the turn of the twentieth and even post-1960 social issue novels, freeing writers to generate thrilling and romantic coming-of-age tales that might otherwise have garnered criticism as socially destabilizing. Financially, this practice has caused the genre to thrive; youth fiction currently makes up a higher percentage of publishing sales than ever before. Yet as distinct and commercialized youth cultures have become less controversial and more powerful in recent decades, continued adherence to these policies has caused youth literature to cede its position at the vanguard of these cultures to competitors less burdened by the need to deliver conventional lessons with their entertainment.

Establishing Youth Reading Cultures over a Long Nineteenth Century

While adults have produced stories to convey cultural values to young people for thousands of years, distinct youth reading cultures began to emerge alongside commercial youth literature in Europe and North America during the late eighteenth century. The early rumblings of industrialization in England birthed the novel as a literary form, and the impulse to direct this new genre toward younger readers occurred with remarkable speed. Just eight years after the 1741 appearance of Samuel Richardson's *Pamela* (which scholars widely considered the first novel), Sarah Fielding published *The Governess, or The Little Female Academy*, the earliest known English-language example written expressly for young readers. As its title suggests, the story focused on the experiences of schoolgirls rather than those of youth on the cusp of breaking free from adult control, but its appearance reveals how quickly publishers recognized the commercial and pedagogical potential of writing novels for a juvenile audience.

Two breakthrough novels affirmed the emerging power of a transatlantic culture of youth readers. Johann Wolfgang von Goethe's *The Sorrows of Young Werther*, which appeared in German in 1774 and English in 1779, and Susana Rowson's *Charlotte Temple*, which debuted in 1791 as *Charlotte: A Tale of Truth*, became international bestsellers and sparked an unprecedented scale of youth engagement. *Werther*, the story of a young man whose obsessive love for a woman engaged to another leads him to commit suicide, spawned an entire industry. Historian Georges Minios indicates "the youth of Europe learned his [Werther's] speeches as they learned Hamlet's," and the story generated countless imitations as well as products ranging from reproductions of the protagonist's trademark yellow trousers, yellow waistcoat, and blue jacket to gloves embroidered with scenes from the story to *eau de Werther* perfume. The eighteenth- and early nineteenth-century press also widely reported the occurrence of waves of copycat suicides in response to the novel; in fact, the still hotly debated theory that media coverage or depictions of suicide can influence subsequent commissions of the act remains known as "the Werther effect."[1]

In the United States, the only novel to go through more printings than *Werther* during the late eighteenth and early nineteenth century was *Charlotte Temple*. Rowson's story of a young woman corrupted morally and then physically by British officer Montraville, with the aid of her French teacher Mademoiselle La Rue, became the archetype of a seduction genre that assumed a vital role in popularizing novels in the United States. Charlotte's plight as a mistreated and then abandoned young woman made her an object of intense devotion for readers, who produced poetry and artwork within their own copies of the book and made treks to the location where they believed the fictional Charlotte was buried (a journey that continues to this day). The story spawned a sequel and a series of stage productions and remained the bestselling novel in the country until Harriet Beecher Stowe's *Uncle Tom's Cabin* dethroned it in 1850.[2]

The public attachment that young readers displayed to these characters and stories was part of what one scholar has described as a "separate semi-youth culture that . . . developed its own lifestyle and way of thinking" in response to the emerging capitalist cultures of late eighteenth-century Europe.[3] In the newly formed United States, the revolutionary rhetoric of self-determination that expanded alongside urban commercial markets in the publishing centers of the Northeast fueled a similar development. As traditional methods for regulating the conduct of adolescents and young adults became less effective, publishers perceived an opportunity to simultaneously provide a public service and achieve a commercial windfall by producing reading materials that resonated with young consumers while also reinforcing traditional social values. The consequent flood of print directed toward the youth market included sermons and advice literature as well as novels.

Werther and *Charlotte* delineate the social concerns that these products addressed. The novels share a plot trajectory and a sensibility. Both protagonists are young people newly released from their parents' direct oversight. Both display an inability to control their emotions that ultimately leads to their death. Goethe's story exemplifies the German Romantic *Sturm und Drang* literary movement, which focused on late youth and early adulthood as a time of particular emotional upheaval. Rowson's novel similarly fixates on the dangers of young people's turbulent sentimentality, and consequent abandonment of reason.

Within this template, the two stories offer quite distinct approaches to the perceived youth crisis. Werther is a complex, ambiguous figure, whose letters present him alternatively as generous and warm-hearted or selfish and delusional. He is a favorite of Charlotte's younger siblings because he plays with them unreservedly; he is also beloved by Charlotte and her fiancé Albert. Yet his vanity, pride, and lack of perspective lead to social failures, and ultimately to his own death by suicide, a choice that Goethe avoids portraying in moralistic terms. Werther is a representation of, rather than a solution to, the challenges of modern youth.

Charlotte, conversely, is a one-dimensional, didactic character. She lacks voice, individuation, and agency. The decision to meet Montraville is thrust upon her by LaRue, and Charlotte's scandalous departure from school is more kidnapping than voluntary choice. At the novel's pivotal moments, Charlotte consistently faints or sleeps rather than take action, and the narrator omits entirely the sexual encounter that ultimately leads to Charlotte's death in childbirth (a choice that contrasts with Rowson's willingness to directly present lust in other genres of writing).[4] Once she arrives in Philadelphia, Charlotte's instructor, lover, and even the narrator abandon her; Rowson shifts the story's focus onto active characters like the seducers and Charlotte's father. Throughout the novel, Charlotte remains a passive and underprepared vessel whose mistreatment serves as a cautionary tale against prematurely releasing young people from responsible adult supervision.

Most scholars recognize *The Sorrows of Young Werther* as at least a secondary literary masterpiece, whereas *Charlotte Temple* is, in the words of one commentator, a "subliterate myth" that is "hardly written at all." Even the novel's advocates argue that it "reveals Rowson's limitations as a stylist and delineator of character."[5] Yet it was *Charlotte*'s cautionary and moralistic legacy that shaped the American template for youth literature as publishers expanded and systematized their output over the course of the nineteenth century. This preference for message over quality reflected publishers' perception of youth reading cultures as communities predominantly shaped by the demands and expectations of adults.

This perception became codified in early nineteenth-century magazines. Most prominent publications of the genre—from the *Youth's Friend* and the *Youth's Companion* in the United States to the *Youth's Magazine* in England—included the word "youth" in their title; during this historical era, that broad term included children as young as seven or eight who were old enough to play without adult supervision, and it extended to young men and women in their early twenties who had not yet achieved economic independence from their parents through work or marriage. The editors' lack of concern about distinguishing among the disparate needs of this extensive audience exemplified their commercial focus on adult purchasers rather than young readers.

The magazines' foregrounding of moral instruction affirmed this focus. As their publication titles indicated, editors offered themselves in loco parentis for adults who could not always monitor their young charges as school and work outside the home replaced the traditional household economy. Early magazines pronounced their novelty to be sufficient entertainment for young readers; *The Youth's Friend* told parents that subscribing to a paper that arrives in the young person's own name will cause them to "place upon it an inestimable value," and informed readers "do not all the time be looking for something amusing or extraordinary . . . the main thing with us all in the use of books ought to be to improve our minds and to obtain good advice as to our conduct in life."[6]

Stories in these magazines offered the same type of one-dimensional, "subliterate" young characters as Charlotte. Whether they were passive, malevolent, or occasionally even benevolent, these characters were intended less to represent human experience than to convey lessons. Early tales particularly emphasized dire consequences for young people who did not adhere to strict standards of public behavior. In "The Busy Bee," a mother punishes a girl who "like a pig . . . delighted in wallowing in mire" by feeding her only garbage from the family's table. In "The Death of Francis A. Brown," a boy who strays from social expectations by pronouncing his views in public falls from a speaker's box and breaks his neck.[7] Mostly, these narratives addressed younger children, leaving the concerns and interests of older youth to novelists like Jane Austen, James Fenimore Cooper, and Charles Dickens, who wrote for a broader audience.

This marketing strategy began to change around mid-century, when older youth compelled publishers to do so. Accelerating urbanization had provided these youth with wider commercial entertainment options and (for young men, at least, who enjoyed more freedom of mobility than their female counterparts) greater opportunity to sample these products in American and Western European cities. In New York, for example, young men could enjoy sensational stories in the penny press and police magazines, and public entertainments like Bowery B'hoy comedies, blackface minstrel shows, and Barnum's American Museum. The concentrated populations that spawned these products also expanded the economic potential of the youth market. Pre-1850 magazines rarely achieved a circulation of more than 10,000, whereas the *Youth Companion* reached 100,000 during the 1870s and 500,000 in the 1880s and

1890s. Under these shifting circumstances, the entertainment demands of youth readers began to exert more influence over the content of juvenile books and magazines.[8]

Among the earliest examples of this shift was the emerging boys' book genre of the 1850s, led by English author Thomas Hughes' novel *Tom Brown's Schooldays* and the Boat Club series by New England educator William Taylor Adams, who wrote under the pseudonym Oliver Optic. Adams's stories were particularly important because they launched the series fiction format that remains foundational to youth literature almost two centuries later. These novels met the demands of youth readers by removing protagonists from the home and placing them in school or other activities at a relatively close remove from parental supervision. Early examples presented boys who were not quite ready for independence, so a paternal figure remained nearby to guide them. Gradually, in a process accelerated in the United States by the Civil War, these protagonists became older, the mentorship receded, and young characters ventured farther from home, usually to the Western borderlands or into the nation's burgeoning industrial cities.

While they retained a foundational strain of didacticism, these stories (along with the girls' books that followed) inverted the cautionary formula Rowson and other seduction narrative writers had popularized. Hughes and Adams presented boys who, despite challenges, proved capable of overcoming most obstacles that contemporary society presented. Yet as expanding commercial entertainments—particularly in the form of dime novels, which allegedly offered more dramatic adventures and abandoned didacticism—compelled authors to make their protagonists older and more independent, the anxious eighteenth-century roots of youth literature re-emerged.

In particular, *Youth's Companion* editor Daniel Sharp Ford transformed his magazine into the first national juggernaut of youth reading in part by updating the cautionary model. *Companion* stories addressed the threats of urban and peer cultures in order to titillate and instruct simultaneously young men and women who were leaving the family home. Tales like "Awkward Andy: A Story of City Life" present young migrants who lose their moral grounding in fast-paced, stranger-filled urban environments; in this case, the title character spends money impetuously, escorts disreputable women, and accrues debt, leading him to steal from his employer and go on the lam. Female-centered stories like "A Boarding-School Romance," in which a girl's novel reading causes her to perceive an itinerant man as a nobleman in disguise, highlight the threats that commercial entertainments and peer groups created for young women making life-altering, irrevocable courtship decisions.[9] These tales built upon *Charlotte Temple*'s pattern of forecasting moral and physical corruption for youth who strayed from responsible adult supervision and from genteel social expectations for their behavior. They offered more salacious details than their literary ancestors in order to attract the attention of increasingly savvy young readers, while maintaining the moralistic framework that had legitimized youth literature for adults, who remained the predominant purchasers of these products.

Despite the *Companion*'s success and the virulent warnings of late nineteenth-century vice reformers like Anthony Comstock (who described "half-dime novels" as "vermin . . . [that] germinate a harvest of death"), this return to cautionary roots proved unsustainable.[10] The expanding post–Civil War youth audience—more confident in their role as consumers—wanted optimism, and the commercial potential of that audience spurred the development of stories to feed that demand. An emerging literary genre for young readers, forged by authors like Alcott, Twain, and Thomas Bailey Aldrich, satirized the trend of focusing on young people's misbehavior. These authors also stepped away from the prevailing model of presenting youth in simple, moralistic terms. Jo March and Tom Sawyer could not be defined simply as generous or naive or naughty; they might embody all of those qualities at different times, as characters in novels for adult audiences had for generations.

Such commercially and critically successful stories fueled higher-quality magazines like *St. Nicholas*, which built upon sources ranging from Rousseau to American writer and activist Lydia Maria Child to present more confident and rounded young people in their stories. *St. Nicholas* reached a fraction of the audience of the *Youth's Companion* during the 1870s and 1880s, just as series and dime novels dwarfed the sales of even the most popular literary fiction for young readers, but the optimistic perspective of these critically admired stories increasingly filtered into better-selling genres.

Oliver Optic's late-career novels, for example, introduced more physically vigorous and geographically expansive models of the one-dimensional youths featured in his earlier books. These protagonists were nearly superheroes; they could spread American values across the globe and conquer any problem (including how to end slavery peacefully) here at home.[11] By 1890, even the *Companion* began to abandon its practice of highlighting the dangers of urban industrial societies for young men and women in favor of narratives featuring adolescents who relentlessly triumphed over hazards in schools, workplaces, and other contemporary environments.

These books were not cautionary, but they remained cautious. In addition to simplifying characters, these formulaic stories distinguished themselves from literary counterparts by adopting a less threatening justification for the emergence of this youthful power. Alcott and Twain tended to present youthful departures from community norms as internally motivated; in *Little Women* and *Tom Sawyer*, Jo and Tom were restless with social expectations of their behavior, and it was that dissatisfaction that pushed them to challenge established social boundaries. In popular fiction, young men (and less often women) broke the rules in response to external forces. Wars, crimes, and parental deaths or economic declines were among the common circumstances that compelled youthful protagonists to leave the protections of home and family and consequently display abilities that enabled them to thrive in contemporary society. Thus, while literary stories tended to perceive systemic problems with social expectations of youth, late nineteenth-century series books and magazines generally portrayed their characters as exceptions to an otherwise smooth transition from youth into adulthood.

In nearly all late nineteenth-century youth fiction, from formulaic to archetypal, young characters completed their stories in reputable positions that affirmed the social, political, and economic status quo. Just as Horatio Alger's working youths always ended on paths to prosperity, so too did Jo March abandon her plans for independence to marry Professor Bhaer and open a school. Books that did not follow this expectation—such as *The Adventures of Huckleberry Finn*, in which Huck "lights out for the territories" because of his dissatisfaction with life in antebellum Missouri—often became classified as inappropriate for young audiences, and even banned from schools and libraries.

This cautious approach to youth literature culminated in the early twentieth-century work of American author and publisher Edward Stratemeyer. A protégé of William Taylor Adams and Horatio Alger (he finished both of their final novels after they died), Stratemeyer recognized that turn-of-the-century youth cultures—fueled by expansion of American high schools, growth of extracurricular activities such as scouting and athletics, and growing attention to young consumers by retail industries—were accelerating the intellectual, if not the economic, independence of youth readers. He responded by formulating a system that enabled him to more efficiently capitalize on this trend. His mass production process, eventually known as the Stratemeyer Syndicate, generated books for this emerging audience at a rate even more prolific than that of his seemingly inexhaustible mentors. While each of those men wrote more than one hundred novels during their lifetimes, Stratemeyer's process allowed the Syndicate to generate more than twelve hundred books (an average of fifteen a year) in more than 125 series between 1905 and 1984. Between 1910 and 1930, the peak period of production, it averaged thirty-one books a year.[12]

The scale of Stratemeyer's production enabled him to dominate the industry. An American Library Association (ALA) survey taken in 1926 (taken before the appearance of the Hardy Boys and Nancy Drew, the Syndicate's most successful series) indicated that 98 percent of young readers picked Stratemeyer books as their favorite, though most of them didn't know who he was or that their choices were part of this broader system.[13] Yet his success was not only a product of this process; it also reflected his skill at subtly redefining the boundaries of youth fiction. Stratemeyer's early books innovated by building stories around current events; his novels about the Spanish-American War debuted just a few months after the fighting began. Subsequent series such as the Motor Boys and Motion Picture Boys—with girls' series on each topic following a few years later—capitalized on young readers' fascination with new technologies. Others like Ruth Fielding and Baseball Joe focused on modern youth experiences in high school and college that were becoming common for his predominant audience—white American middle-class and wealthy youth. His most popular series quickly expanded the adventures of their protagonists from the reasonable to the outlandish. Thus, the Rover Boys began their adventures at military school but subsequently sailed alone down the Hudson River to rescue a girl and traveled to Africa to save their kidnapped father. Tom Swift went from conducting experiments with his father's assistance to exploring "hidden cities" in the Andes without supervision.

While Syndicate novels generated innovative storylines for young readers, they also continued to promote established social hierarchies. Stratemeyer stories were predominantly pitched to and filled with stories of young white men. Young women who did appear as protagonists in Stratemeyer novels existed in more circumscribed environments, at least until Nancy Drew debuted in 1930 (an event that followed Edward's death and his daughter Harriet's assumption of control over the company). Nonwhite protagonists were nonexistent, and characters of color were nearly always subordinate and uneducated.

Beyond these representational choices, Stratemeyer books explicitly reinforced dominant cultural values, even as their plots potentially undercut those traditions. The hero of one of Stratemeyer's earliest series established his template for balancing outlandish tales and conservative messages. Larry Russell, the protagonist of *Under Dewey at Manila* (1898), runs away from his home in Buffalo at sixteen after his mother's death leaves him under the guardianship of a dishonest and violent step-uncle. He stows away in a railroad freight car and ends up in San Francisco and then works on a ship to the Hawaiian Islands and then another to Hong Kong. When an evil shipmate throws Larry and a friend overboard in a storm, they survive on a deserted island until a United States naval flotilla picks them up en route to invading the Philippines during the Spanish-American War. Larry enlists and becomes a hero during the bombardment of Manila.

This fantastic story coexisted with a steady stream of messages that promoted traditional standards of conduct at a time when expanding urban youth cultures were beginning to challenge these expectations. Larry was "a sturdy, conscientious American lad, of good moral character and honest Christian aim." When his ship is grounded in the Hawaiian Islands, he remains loyal to his captain but declines to ask him for a loan; "such was not his habit, and he set to work manfully to make the best of the situation." Larry attends church services on Sunday because he "thought it the proper thing to do." His commanding officer in the navy honors him as a young man "willing to do his whole duty—to do exactly what he is told to do."[14]

Along with such deferential conduct, Larry displays an unwavering faith in the current social order. His confidence in his own abilities stems from his unquestioned belief in the superiority of the American Protestant values he absorbed as a middle-class child. Through two series extending over ten books chronicling the adventures of Larry, his brothers, and their friends fighting in the Philippines, Cuba, the Boxer Rebellion, and the Russo-Japanese War, the young men embrace a willingness "to take what comes" as almost a mantra (the statement or some variation of it repeats dozens of times over the course of these novels). The young men's unrelenting faith in providence and patriotism reflected Stratemeyer's commitment to advocating a conservative worldview to his youth readers.

The Stratemeyer novels were a culmination of the system that developed to feed youth readers over the course of the nineteenth century. After 1850, publishers progressively took the entertainment interests of these readers seriously (particularly if they were white and male), but they tended to generate fantastic models of youth rather than stories that reflected the actual experiences of young people. This approach remained commercially dominant through the 1920s and 1930s in popular series like the Hardy Boys and Nancy Drew, and it was foundational to the success of youth literature throughout the twentieth century. Yet even as the Stratemeyer books reached the peak of their success, the continuing expansion and commercialization of youth cultures began to draw the attention of other voices who sought to diversify, though rarely to fundamentally change, the relationships between those cultures and literature.

DIVERSIFICATION OF YOUTH READING CULTURES

These voices started to emerge during the early twentieth century within two cultural frameworks. In countries outside of the United States and Western Europe, most of which did not have existing traditions of producing commercial literature for young readers, efforts to develop a native literature for that audience began to emerge. In nations with an existing youth literature tradition—and particularly in the United States, which was increasingly exerting commercial dominance over the field—elite institutions pushed back against the formulaic nature of series fiction and sought to create methods for providing more realistic (and eventually more socially and racially diverse) stories of youth.

Before World War II, most of the efforts to develop (or redevelop) native branches of youth literature outside the United States and United Kingdom occurred within emerging global powers that used books and magazines for young people to build allegiance to a political agenda. China was the exception to that pattern; as its Republic emerged, modernizing reformers employed literature to replace long-standing Confucian ideas about education with modern stories that emphasized inquiry rather than unquestioning loyalty. In Russia, Western-style debates over the quality of youth literature disappeared after the communist revolution of 1917, when the Soviet state sought to develop stories that facilitated its nation-building program. Nazi Germany took the political uses of such literature to frightening extremes, destroying books that did not fit the party's totalitarian agenda and promoting materials that indoctrinated young readers into the National Socialist program.[15]

Even in those authoritarian regimes, Western influences over youth literature continued to infiltrate. In the Soviet Union, a trend of translating European and American stories into Russian culminated with the work of Aleksandr Volkov, who recast *The Wonderful Wizard of Oz* for Russian youth amid the Stalinist purges of the 1930s. His original text, *Wizard of the Emerald City*, became so popular that Volkov wrote five more books in what became known as his Magic Land series, a collection that became a staple of Soviet popular culture.

The diversifying trend within twentieth-century Anglo-American literature emerged, as with Werther and Charlotte Temple, from sources outside of any system for producing youth literature. In the United States, Booth Tarkington's 1916 satirical novel *Seventeen*, which is sometimes identified as the first example of the young adult (YA) genre, and F. Scott Fitzgerald's stories and novels modernized the courtship genre through a generation of wealthy, sybaritic characters that helped to generate the popular American image of "flaming youth" during the 1920s. The mocking nature of Tarkington's story and the decidedly ungenteel public smoking, drinking, and sexuality of Fitzgerald's characters indicate that their work was not aimed directly at an adolescent audience. Yet these models dramatized the changes that were occurring in postwar American youth cultures as a result of both long-term demographic shifts (the expansion of American high schools) and more recent technological and commercial changes (including the proliferation of automobiles and movies as well as the expansion of public relations and celebrity cultures).

These changes only gradually filtered into youth literature. The initial (and less dramatic) calls for postwar change came from a growing force within the system: librarians. The ALA pushed back against the dominance of formulaic fiction in the United States through a variety of programs, including the introduction in 1922 of the Newbery Award, which was intended to help incentivize the publication of innovative original books for a youth audience. Though the Newbery has subsequently become identified predominantly with children's literature, most of the early winners, including the inaugural medalist *The Story of Mankind* (a 500+ page tome on Western history) and novels like *The Dark Frigate* and *The Trumpeter of Krakow*, targeted older youth. The 1920s Newbery committees honored new subjects—they displayed a particular fascination with international stories—but maintained many of the established preferences of popular fiction, including a focus on the experiences of white male youth as written by white men. Once the Newbery became established as a standard of critical acclaim and commercial success within the field of youth literature, the female librarians who controlled the award did use their influence to validate the work of female authors, who won every Newbery medal during the 1930s.

The ALA also helped to promote YA literature. Scholars have debated the origins of this genre, with some perceiving its emergence in the mid-nineteenth-century stories of Alcott and Twain. Modern YA, though, was a byproduct of post–World War I youth culture. The complex young characters of writers like Tarkington and Charles Boardman Hawes, and the appearance during the 1920s of specialty magazines like *The Open Road* and *American Girl* (which addressed boys who liked outdoors activities and Girl Scouts, respectively) established the potential for further growth and stratification within the youth market. Ironically, the cataclysmic economy of the Depression seemed to be the impetus that pushed sellers and critics toward exploiting this potential.

In 1930, the ALA formed its Young People's Roundtable, whose annual list for "young readers" promoted books like Will James's *Lone Cowboy* and Edna Ferber's *Cimarron*, describing the lives of young adults striking out on their own. The initial wave of books on these lists particularly focused on the Western borderlands; in addition to James and Ferber's stories, the bestselling debut novel of a Junior Book series designed explicitly to appeal to teen readers was Rose Wilder Lane's *Let the Hurricane Roar* (1933). Lane was the daughter of Laura Ingalls Wilder, who had published the first of her beloved *Little House* books the previous year. In contrast to her mother's work, Lane's book focused on an older girl, a teenaged bride who ventured out with her similarly young husband onto an unnamed frontier to establish a homestead with their infant son.

Despite the ALA's efforts to promote literary quality in stories for "young people" and "juniors," these commercial successes led to a wave of career series for YA readers. Helen Boyston's 1936 book "Sue Barton, Student Nurse" initiated this trend, which quickly expanded into a sub-genre of working-class stories about flight attendants, auto mechanics, and construction workers. John R. Tunis revitalized sports stories, which had been a staple of youth magazines since the 1890s, as formulaic YA novels beginning with *The Iron Duke* (1938).[16]

Most of these books followed the Stratemeyer formula. Caroline and Charles, the heroes of *Let the Hurricane Roar*, are one-dimensional figures who make few wrong decisions. The drama in this book comes from external, natural forces—a plague of grasshoppers, blizzards, wolves—rather than through characters' growth or conflict. Career series offered protagonists who transcended every contemporary social and economic challenge. Only a few examples offered minor deviations from this pattern; Will James's *Lone Cowboy* is a complicated figure that undercuts Western mythologies of independence and success; he survives but does not thrive at the end of his story. Tunis's books are more conventional but often provide a left-leaning subtext. His heroes in books like *Keystone Kids* and *Yea, Wildcats!* are young athletes who stand up to powerful team owners and industrialists. Still, the general pattern of the genre was to celebrate the success of young characters who thrive through the maintenance of traditional values and hard, honest work.

Hollywood also began churning out youth series during the 1930s. The most famous example is the Andy Hardy movies, which starred Mickey Rooney as a young man who progressed from high school through marriage in an idealized small American town. The courtship issues that were central to these movies (in several of them Judy Garland plays Rooney's love interest) appeared contemporaneously in youth magazines. In 1936, *Scholastic*, which traditionally had been a children's magazine, introduced an advice column called "Boy Dates Girl." These examples were harbingers of the teen romance culture that was about to explode in the United States and Western Europe.

Maureen Daly's 1942 bestselling novel *Seventeenth Summer* accelerated the commercial elevation of that culture. Daly's heroine Angie Morrow recounts the rise and fall of her first romance over a summer in Fond du Lac, Wisconsin in a narrative that is more reflective of contemporary teen experiences than Andy Hardy's. While his romances are idyllic and chaste, Angie's teen culture includes drinking, smoking, and implications of improper sexual behavior (though not by the protagonist).

Angie is still a traditionally genteel character in the Stratemeyer mold. She lives in a more contained world than most male characters; her boyfriend Jack visits family in Oklahoma, and her sisters travel back and forth to Chicago, but Angie never leaves Fond du Lac until the end of the story. She and Jack sometimes misunderstand each other, but Angie never makes immoral or ill-advised decisions. She refuses to smoke, or even go downtown at night with her friends. While she loves Jack, she gets upset by his ill-cultivated manners at dinner with her parents and ultimately chooses to go to college rather than accept Jack's marriage proposal and becoming a baker's wife.

The tensions between maintaining this genteel image of youth and selling products to this expanding audience emerged in *Seventeen* magazine, which debuted in 1944. Founding editor Helen Valentine sought to create a publication that would treat young women as "whole human beings" rather than "silly, swooning, bobby-soxers." At the same time, her publishers recognized the profits inherent in reaching "eight million teenage girls who can afford to spend $170,000,000 a year on movies" and pushed her to deliver what that audience wanted more than what Valentine thought they needed to hear.[17] The conflict embodied in *Seventeen* became inherent in the relationship between marketers and the youth cultures that exploded into prominence in the years following World War II, and publishers of books and magazines often chose different paths for their products in this rapidly changing commercial environment.

The 1950s was an era of unprecedented waves of consumer fads and more lasting products—from hula hoops to rock and roll—addressed to the newly minted teenage demographic, but for publishers of youth fiction it was largely a period of creative abeyance. One exception that highlighted the dilemma for these publishers was *The Catcher in the Rye*, J.D. Salinger's 1951 novel that was marketed as a book for adults (one critic noted at the time of publication that he found the "ugly words and images" of the story coming "from the mouths of the very young and protected . . . peculiarly offensive") and subsequently became a symbol of teen rebellion. Like the other canonical youth novel of its era that was initially targeted at adults, William Golding's *Lord of the Flies* (1954), *Catcher* featured an ambivalent ending that diverged from the established boundaries of youth literature (which is why it, like *Huckleberry Finn*, remains among the most censored books in United States schools).[18] In an era defined by intellectual caution generated largely by anticommunist crusades, book publishers seemed to cede the vanguard of marketing to youth to other mediums while focusing their attention on innovating its relationship with younger readers (through books like Dr. Seuss's *The Cat in the Hat*).

Like their nineteenth-century predecessors, magazines of the 1950s stepped into this vacuum to capitalize on the trends of a transforming youth culture. *Seventeen* cemented its status as a barometer of teenage girl culture during this decade, and specialty magazines like *Hot Rod* appealed to teenage boys. Even short-lived celebrity periodicals like *Teen Parade* and *Hep Cats* were an early recognition of the economic power of youth cultures that became widely recognized as Baby Boomers increasingly entered the teen demographic during the 1960s.

That power became manifest in nearly every medium. Hollywood, having learned from the success of Elvis Presley's movies during the late 1950s, offered beach movies in the early 1960s and counterculture movies from *The Graduate* to *Easy Rider* later in the decade. Music, from the Beatles to Woodstock, was largely defined by youth audiences. Commercial magazines like *Tiger Beat* and *Rolling Stone* flourished, and underground periodicals became a vehicle for youth to express their own anxieties and demands.

Book publishers, though, largely continued to eschew any innovations in their relationship to the youth market. Authors who resonated with this audience during the 1960s—Ken Kesey, Sylvia Plath, Malcolm X, Joan Didion, and many others—were mostly writing for adults. The innovative work taking place in the juvenile field was mostly coming from authors like Ezra Jack Keats, Maurice Sendak, and E.L. Konigsburg who were writing for younger readers (one possible exception to that rule was Madelein L'Engle, whose *A Wrinkle in Time* was a harbinger of the coming popularity of science fiction and fantasy novels among youth audiences).

Konigsburg and L'Engle particularly accelerated the trend of diverging from formula fiction by presenting complex and flawed young protagonists, though as authors explicitly targeting a youth audience, they did retain the tradition of hopeful, if not always happy, endings. When YA authors did begin to innovate near the end of the decade with a controversial approach that subsequently became known as "new realism," they followed this middle path while addressing contemporary social problems including racism, poverty, violence, and drug use.[19] The two novels that effectively launched this format in 1967 were S.E. Hinton's *The Outsiders* and Robert Lipsyte's *The Contender*.

Of the two books, *The Outsiders* had a more immediate and more sustained impact on youth culture. Hinton began writing the novel when she was sixteen and created a story about class warfare occurring between gangs at her Tulsa, Oklahoma, high school. She presents the story from the perspective of Ponyboy Curtis, a fourteen-year-old who is the youngest of three recently orphaned brothers that belong to a working-class gang known as the Greasers. This adopted family is locked in perpetual conflict with a gang of rich boys known as the Socs, and when their battles inadvertently result in Ponyboy's best friend Johnny (a quiet boy who lives with his abusive, alcoholic parents) stabbing and killing of one of the rich boys, the two friends run away to escape the law. While in hiding, the boys run into a burning church to save a group of younger children and a beam collapses on Johnny, creating injuries that eventually lead to his death. In response to Johnny's death, Dally Winston, the toughest of the Greasers, runs out and robs a store, and in the ensuing pursuit he points an unloaded weapon at the police, causing them to kill him. Despite these tragedies, the story ends with Ponyboy reunited with his brothers and determined to write about his story to help other young people who feel cast out by society.

The Outsiders is, depending on definitions of the genre, one of the bestselling YA books of all time (with approximately fifteen million copies sold as of 2017). It continues to appear on many school syllabi and became a successful movie directed by Francis Ford Coppola that helped to launch the careers of Tom Cruise, Rob Lowe, and Matt Dillon. The story was revolutionary for its time because it was written by a teenager for teenagers and was steeped in contemporary popular and literary culture.[20] These elements of the novel helped to redefine what youth fiction could be at a time when young people's world was in upheaval but when their books generally did not reflect those changes.

The Contender did not have the public impact of *The Outsiders*, but Lipsyte's novel also helped to transform the content of youth fiction. His story focuses on seventeen-year-old Albert Brooks, a high school dropout living with his aunt and three cousins in Harlem. Albert works in a grocery store and faces increased pressure to engage with drugs and gang activities; his response is to join a gym and begin to train as a boxer in order to escape the threats of his neighborhood. Though he has no skills at the beginning of the novel, he gradually develops into a competent fighter who lacks the "killer instinct" to become a great one. His trainer and mentor suggests that Alfred take the skills that he learned from his training and apply them in his community, and at the end of the novel Alfred is reaching out to his best friend James, who succumbed to the threats of the streets and is now gripped by drug addiction.

Lipsyte was a young sports reporter at the time he published this debut novel, and the initial response to his story largely focused on its power and realism as a sports story (one critic called it "the best sports novel since early Tunis"). As social commentary, the book received less praise; the *New York Times* critic wrote "If the Horatio Alger approach is to be at all relevant in a work of fiction set in the ghetto, it needs to be considerably updated and treated with much less naiveté than here," and the *Library Journal* review similarly argued that "As a sports story, this is a superior, engrossing, insider's book; but as social commentary on problems in a Negro ghetto, it is a superficial, outsider's book which doesn't increase real understanding." Yet the lack of stories about African American and other minority communities in youth fiction, and the craving for such characters within those communities, caused this book to quickly become a fixture in English classrooms across the nation.[21]

The Outsiders and *The Contender*'s adherence to the pattern of elevating traditional social norms reflects the continuing caution of youth literature at a time when the civil rights, counterculture, and antiwar movements were transforming many American youth into challengers of those norms. Other media, in contrast, were embracing that transformation. The same year these books appeared, the Beatles released *Sgt. Pepper's Lonely Hearts Club Band*, which included the song "She's Leaving Home" about a teen running away in the middle of the night, and psychedelic music introduced teens to a blossoming drug culture through songs like the Jefferson Airplane's "White Rabbit." Black musical artists like Marvin Gaye, James Brown, and Sly and the Family Stone were producing deeply politicized content that resonated with interracial audiences in a way that a "naive" young white novelist's idealistic story about Harlem could not. Hollywood presented *Bonnie and Clyde*, a story about two young gangsters that ended with their brutal deaths at the hands of law enforcement, and *The Graduate*, about a disillusioned and aimless young man who has an affair with his parents' friend and then breaks up her daughter's wedding.

This pattern of youth literature lagging behind other commercial media in its embrace of contemporary youth cultures has persisted during the late twentieth and early twenty-first centuries. One of the reasons for that trend is its continuing lack of diversity. Whereas Motown began to integrate performers of color into the commercial mainstream of popular music in the mid-1960s, a study of diversity in books for young American readers conducted in 2014–2015 found that their percentage of white characters had remained stagnant at more than 85 percent over the intervening half-century. These choices have global implications, since the dominance of a few American publishing conglomerates over the field has limited audiences for emerging post–World War II native traditions of youth literature.[22]

Even when diverse voices do appear, commercial success generally depends on highlighting the opportunities available within existing social structures. In 2017, for example, the young Black American author Angie Thomas published her celebrated debut novel *The Hate U Give*, which focused on the unjustified shooting of a Black teenaged boy by a white police officer (the story is based on the real-life shooting of Oscar Grant by the Oakland Police Department). Thomas's protagonist Starr Carter was a passenger in the car when her close friend Khalil was murdered by the police. The story explores the ramifications of this event on Starr and her community and ends with both sadness and hope. The Carter family's store is burned down during a post-shooting uprising, but they begin to rebuild and remain committed to their community and optimistic that they can exert positive change (the Black female lawyer who represents Starr during the crisis tells the young woman she has a bright future as an activist).

Books that eschew this optimism have difficulty gaining large audiences. Walter Dean Myers' 1999 novel *Monster*, about a young man who gets caught up in the criminal justice system as an alleged lookout for a robbery in which the store owner was murdered, ends with much more ambivalence than Thomas's story. Steve Harmon, the sixteen-year-old young protagonist who dreams of being a filmmaker and survives his trial by writing a screenplay of his experiences in jail, is ultimately found not guilty by the jury. Yet when he turns to hug his defense attorney after the verdict, she recoils, and Steve recognizes that she perceives him as the monster that everyone else expects him to be. The book won just about every award for which it was eligible (except for the Newbery) when it appeared in 1999 and was named by *Time Magazine* in 2020 as one of the 100 Best Young Adult Books of All Time.[23] Yet it is not canonized like *The Outsiders* or *The Hate U Give*; anecdotally, it seems to get read mostly by students of color, and the movie of the film (with its title changed to the more generic *All Rise*) was completed in 2018 but not released, in contrast to the mass-market productions of Hinton's and Thomas's novels.

This adherence to the pattern of affirming existing social hierarchies has not hampered the commerce of youth literature. Certainly, few products can match the success of the Harry Potter, Hunger Games, and Twilight series, and as a whole the genre makes up an ever-growing percentage of publishing revenues. Yet this pattern, constructed out of a nineteenth-century need to make commercial relationships with young people culturally acceptable, has mitigated literature's role in defining youth cultures over recent decades as music, fashion, television, and film have emerged with fewer concerns about interweaving education into their entertainments.

Notes

1. Georges C. Minios, *The History of Suicide: Voluntary Death in Western Culture*, trans. Lydia G. Cochrane (Baltimore: Johns Hopkins University Press, 1999), 267; Richard Bell, "In Werther's Thrall: Suicide and the Power of Sentimental Reading in Early National America," *Early American Literature* 46 (2011): 93–120.
2. Bell, 95; Cathy N. Davidson, *Revolution and the Word: The Rise of the Novel in America*, expanded ed. (New York: Oxford University Press, 2004), 144, 148; C.J. Hughes, "Buried in the Churchyard: A Good Story, at Least," *New York Times*, December 12, 2008, A19.; Ann Douglas, "Introduction," in Susanna Rowson, *Charlotte Temple* and *Lucy Temple*, ed. Ann Douglas (New York: Penguin Books, 1991), x–xv.
3. Oded Heilbrunner, "From a Culture *for* Youth to a Culture *of* Youth: Recent Trends in the Historiography of Western Youth Cultures," *Contemporary European History* 17 (2008): 575–591.
4. Marion Rust, *Prodigal Daughters: Susanna Rowson's Early American Women* (Chapel Hill: University of North Carolina Press, 2008), 57–62.
5. Douglas, Introduction, viii–ix.
6. Testimonial, *Youth's Friend* (*YF*) (1823–1824): 2; "The Beginning," *YF* 15 (January 1838): 1.
7. "The Busy Bee," *Youth's Companion* (*YC*) 5 (August 10, 1831): 47; "The Death of Francis A. Brown," *YF* 1 (January 1824): 152–153.
8. Paul Ringel, *Commercializing Childhood: Children's Magazines, Urban Gentility, and the Ideal of the Child Consumer in the United States, 1823–1918* (Amherst: University of Massachusetts Press, 2015), 1–15.
9. John Townsend Trowbridge, "Awkward Andy: A Story of City Life," *YC* 51 (August 30, 1877): 277; Ruth Chesterfield, "A Boarding-School Romance," *YC* 49 (August 5, 1875): 245.
10. Anthony Comstock, *Traps for the Young* (Whitefish, MT: Kessinger Publishers, 2005), 21, 41.

11. See, for example, Oliver Optic, *Blue and Gray on Land* series, 6 vols. (Boston: Lee and Shepard, 1894–1899).
12. Deidre Johnson, *Edward Stratemeyer and the Stratemeyer Syndicate* (New York: Twayne Publishers, 1993), 6–17.
13. Marilyn S. Greenwald, *The Secret Life of the Hardy Boys: Leslie McFarlane and the Stratemeyer Syndicate* (Athens: Ohio University Press, 2004), 39.
14. Edward Stratemeyer, *Under Dewey at Manila; or, The War Fortunes of a Castaway* (Boston: Lee & Shepard, 1898), iv, 18, 139, 216.
15. Mary Ann Farquhar, *Children's Literature in China: From Lu Xun to Mao Zedong* (New York: M.E. Sharpe, 1999); Erika Haber, *Oz Behind the Iron Curtain: Aleksandr Volkov and His Magic Land Series* (Jackson: University Press of Mississippi, 2017), 56–100; Christa Kamenetsky, *Children's Literature in Hitler's Germany: The Cultural Policy of National Socialism* (Athens: Ohio University Press, 2019).
16. Michael Cart, *Young Adult Literature: From Romance to Realism* (Chicago: Neal-Schuman, 2016), 4–11.
17. Kelley Massoni, *Fashioning Teenagers: A Cultural History of Seventeen Magazine* (Walnut Creek, CA: Left Coast Press, 2010), 40; Grace Palladino, *Teenagers: An American History* (New York: Basic Books, 1996), 193.
18. Leonard S. Marcus, *Minders of Make-Believe: Idealists, Entrepreneurs, and the Shaping of American Children's Literature* (Boston: Houghton Mifflin, 2008), 185–186.
19. Lee Rinsky and Roman Schweikert, "In Defense of the 'New Realism' for Children and Adolescents," *The Phi Delta Kappan* 58 (February 1977): 472–475.
20. Dale Peck, "The Outsiders: 40 Years Later," *New York Times*, September 23, 2007.
21. Chris Crowe, "First Opinion: Hope and Realism Offered in This Classic Sports Novel," *First Opinions, Second Reactions* 7 (May 2014): 29–31.
22. Ebony Elizabeth Thomas, "Stories Still Matter: Rethinking the Role of Diverse Children's Literature Today," *Journal of Language Arts* 94 (November 2016): 112–119; Emer O'Sullivan, "Comparative Children's Literature: Theories and Methodologies," *PMLA* 126 (January 2011): 189–196.
23. "The 100 Best Young Adult Books of All Time," *New York Times*, accessed July 29, 2021, time.com/100-best-young-adult-books/.

Further Reading

Cart, Michael. *Young Adult Literature: From Romance to Realism*. Chicago: Neal-Schuman, 2016.
Daly, Maureen. *Seventeenth Summer*. New York: Dodd, Mead, 1942.
Farquhar, Mary Ann. *Children's Literature in China: From Lu Xun to Mao Zedong*. New York: M.E. Sharpe, 1999.
Johann Wolfgang von Goethe, *The Sorrows of Young Werther*. New York: Suhrkamp Publishers, 1988.
Haber, Erika. *Oz Behind the Iron Curtain: Aleksandr Volkov and His Magic Land Series*. Jackson: University Press of Mississippi, 2017.
Hinton, S.E. *The Outsiders*. New York: Viking, 2007.

Hughes, Thomas. *Tom Brown's Schooldays*. Project Gutenberg. https://www.gutenberg.org/files/1480/1480-h/1480-h.htm. Accessed September 27, 2020.

Johnson, Deidre. *Edward Stratemeyer and the Stratemeyer Syndicate*. New York: Twayne Publishers, 1993.

Kamenetsky, Christa. *Children's Literature in Hitler's Germany: The Cultural Policy of National Socialism*. Athens: Ohio University Press, 2019.

Lipsyte, Robert. *The Contender*. New York: Harper & Row, 1967.

Marcus, Leonard S. *Minders of Make-Believe: Idealists, Entrepreneurs, and the Shaping of American Children's Literature*. Boston: Houghton Mifflin, 2008.

Myers, Walter Dean. *Monster*. New York: Harper Teen/Amistad. 2008.

Ringel, Paul. *Commercializing Childhood: Children's Magazines, Urban Gentility, and the Ideal of the Child Consumer in the United States, 1823–1918*. Amherst: University of Massachusetts Press, 2015.

Rowson, Susana, and Cathy N. Davidson, eds. *Charlotte Temple*. Oxford: Oxford University Press, 1987.

Stratemeyer, Edward. *Under Dewey at Manila; or, The War Fortunes of a Castaway*. Boston: Lee & Shepard, 1898.

Thomas, Angie. *The Hate U Give*. New York: Balzer + Bray, 2017.

CHAPTER 21

YOUTH CULTURE ON SCREENS BIG AND SMALL

HELLE STRANDGAARD JENSEN AND GARY CROSS

MOTION pictures and television have long shaped youth identity while also evoking cultural expectations and even nostalgia. After the Second World War, and particularly the 1960s, a time of youth rebellion, commercialized youth media in America has attempted to directly appeal to youth, often through fantasy and romance. By contrast, publicly funded agencies in Scandinavia and elsewhere in Europe have invited young people to use television and film to advance their own agendas and aesthetics. With the expansion of the World Wide Web, youth have been able to come together from all over the world to discuss and celebrate their favorite television series on dedicated fan pages and social media.

Boundaries between age groups have historically been hard to define, and that is reflected in the blurred boundaries between films and television for adults and youth, and even between children and youth. This lack of clear separation is sometimes the source of concerns about the impact of adult themes and images often deemed inappropriate for children or even youth. Sometimes media targeted primarily for adults or children have nevertheless been important parts of youth culture. Examples of this are the television series *Sex and the City* and the *Harry Potter* movies, which were aimed at adults and children, respectively, but had a huge fan group among youth. The same was true for earlier action and Western features and serials that might not be categorized as "youth"-specific phenomena but were a hit with them anyway.

Motion Picture Origins and American Youth: 1888–1930

The motion picture from its origins in the 1890s was adopted by youth, who, though still in their teens, often had access to small sums from earnings at work that allowed them to create their own culture and identities through attending movies. This began with short peep show films in arcades, followed from 1894 with the crowd experience of projected films on screens. Gradually, movies supplanted live theater, circuses, and soda fountains as venues of youth entertainment and escape from adult control. By 1905, nickelodeons, small movie theaters often located near public transport stops, offered youth a few minutes of cheap excitement in short silent films, which youth could attend before or after work. In particular, working-class youth enjoyed action films and slapstick comedy. Typically, as early adapters of new technologies and products, youth were attracted to the visual thrills of early cinema—working-class youth were particularly fond of action films and slapstick comedy. For instance, Biograph's irreverent "Keystone Cops" series (1912–1917) amused youth by presenting authority figures common in their lives—the police—as incompetent and foolish.[1]

Early movies included newsreels, sporting events, mild burlesque, special effects (like Georges Mèliés's famous *A Trip to the Moon* of 1902), and also action films like Edwin Porter's *The Great Train Robbery* of 1903 that used the mobility of the camera and the editing process to offer young viewers fast-paced outdoor action scenes, a heroic girl, and an exciting story of gun play.[2] From 1913, short "chapter" movies (or serials) attracted young audiences with thrilling action, often featuring beautiful women pursued or tortured by bad guys, ending in a "cliffhanger"—in some, the heroine is literally left clinging to a cliff for dear life or in some other seemingly impossible situation—to be resolved at the beginning of the next "chapter." Because of their roots in working-class pulp magazines, respectable middle-class critics attacked these chapter movies as unsuitable for children and youth. Yet they remained an important part of youth entertainment and were toned down for youth-oriented Saturday "matinees" by the 1930s.[3]

Early movie theaters became acceptable venues for groups of young females and eventually became destinations for the emerging courtship ritual of the "date," providing young unsupervised couples freedom from the Victorian courtship system that required youth to meet at home or under the watchful eye of chaperones. The movie theater also offered a setting that required little conversational skill for often inexperienced young couples. The modern movie theater emerged after 1913, when filmmakers developed feature-length films that competed with the live theater and attracted middle-class audiences, including youth. To attract a more upscale crowd, exhibitors built movie palaces, first appearing in New York in 1913. These plush auditoriums offered not only comfortable seating attractive to upscale customers, but also dark balconies that met the romantic needs of young dating couples. Another innovation was turning the lead film actor into a "star," recognizing that especially young audiences wanted to identify with featured actors such as Charlie Chaplin, Mary Pickford, and Douglas Fairbanks. These stars gained a following in fan magazines like *Photoplay* that first appeared in 1911, which attracted primarily female youth. At formative stages in life, young readers identified with the real (or manufactured) personal lives of movie stars, giving these young fans a sense of being personal friends with their idol.[4]

Movies, Youth Identity, and Adult Anxieties in the United States

Both the attraction of youth to the darkened movie houses and sometimes "lurid" themes led respectable middle-class elders to attack the cinema for corrupting youth. Even well-respected social reformers and scholars like social worker Jane Addams and psychologist Hugo Mustenberger argued that movies fostered an illusory worldview that led youth to irrational and unrealistic expectations. In 1907, the police in Chicago were authorized to censor films deemed inappropriate for youth under eighteen years of age. Soon thereafter, New York exhibitors created their own review board to forestall censorship. Fearing legal action, in 1922, the motion picture industry formed their own body to set standards under the conservative leadership of Will Hays. Not only did he impose morals contracts on actors, but he also published a list of warnings against use of profanity and depiction of attempted rape, among other offenses, designed in large part to protect youth.[5]

Despite the adoption of the restrictive Hays Production Code in 1930, the onset of the Depression and the resulting diminished crowds inspired moviemakers to step up production of sexually suggestive and mildly violent films to attract larger audiences (of which about a third were youth). In response, a group sponsored by the Payne Fund published studies of the presumably negative impact of movies on American youth. These movies, one advertisement for the book claimed, were "a monster Pied Piper . . . playing tunes irresistibly alluring to the youth of the present day." Henry Forman claimed that youth imitated the sexuality of films of Jean

Harlow and Mae West and the criminal behavior glamorized in the gangster movies of Edgar Robinson and James Cagney. All this culminated in enforcement of the Production Code in 1934 in large part to shelter youth and children from graphic violence, sexual innuendo, vulgar language, techniques of crime, and other controversial topics.[6]

One effect of the Code was that films after 1934 portrayed youth in idealistic terms that both amused and reassured adults concerned about rising generational tensions, while entertaining the young (especially females, younger teens, and children) with identifiable characters. The sweet films of child actor Shirley Temple are the best examples, but older youth were similarly shown as naive, harmless, and often comical. Most famous was the Andy Hardy series of sixteen movies between 1937 and 1946. Andy, played by the diminutive Mickey Rooney, was a small-town teen who repeatedly faced resolvable dilemmas of romance and growing up, surrounded by a doting mother and an advice-giving, white-haired judge of a father.[7]

Most of these growing-up stories were about males. But the famous female detective Nancy Drew, who was featured in book series for girls and portrayed as independent and clever, was turned into a series of movies in the late 1930s. On film, however, Nancy, played by the bubbling Bonita Granville, was comparatively less daring than in the book and relied on males for help. This image of the girl was repeated in the early roles of Judy Garland (in three Andy Hardy movies) and especially in a series of wholesome musicals about Broadway and college life (also with Rooney). These images of the docile, naive teen certainly appealed to adults, reassuring them that all was well with the next generation.[8]

However, during World War II, with many parents away at work or in uniform, concerns that youth were out of control was mirrored in the books *Where Are Your Children?* and *Youth Run Wild*. Soon after the war ended in 1945, the media publicized stories of teens racing and terrorizing citizens in their "hot rod" cars (mostly customized vehicles from the early 1930s, transformed for speed). Films such as *Devil on Wheels* (1947) exploited the hot rod theme. Cautionary short films directed toward would-be teen hot rodders like *Cool Hot Rod* of 1953 were shown to teens in high schools and at car club meetings to discourage teens from identifying with the juvenile delinquent at the wheel of the car.

In the mid-1950s, a series of cheap car movies like *Hot Rod Girls*, *Hot Rod Rumble*, and *Dragstrip Riot* attracted teens with lurid publicity posters (which also stirred up their parents). *Dragstrip Girl* suggests the powerful combination of unleashed speed and sex: "Car Crazy! Speed Crazy! Boy Crazy!" with vivid and garish images of a teen male embracing a reclined full-bosomed blonde female with racing hot rods in the background. Despite this appeal to youth, often the stories had conventionally wholesome endings with the alienated youth being reconciled with parents or adult authorities. *The Wild Ones* (1953) and *Rebel without a Cause* (1955) portrayed more realistically youth's alienation from and frustrations with adults after World War II. These films were cheaply produced and shown mostly in the expanding number of outdoor drive-in theaters that offered the young freedom from disapproving adult eyes and opportunities to "make out" (or practice foreplay) with a date in a darkened vehicle while presumably watching a movie.[9]

Filmmakers focused increasingly on the youth market after 1945 because, with the advent of television, adults tended to abandon movie theaters. Movie attendance had dropped almost by half by eight years later.[10] Filmmakers responded by offering what the seventeen-inch black-and-white TV screen could not provide: three-dimensional movies (1951), extravaganzas in widescreen CinemaScope (1953), and, especially, rock music and romance directed toward the youth and dating couples. American International Pictures (AIP), a new company that featured cheap movies mostly for drive-ins, produced *Rock All Night*. Teen idol Elvis Presley also appeared in a long string of commercially successful youth-oriented musicals starting in 1956, while AIP produced a number of "Beach Party" movies between 1963 and 1968. These films offered muted romance, drag racing, surfing, and rock music built around teens with comic relief provided by non-parental elders. While these films claimed to portray real trends in American youth culture, they usually offered a bowdlerized version—minimizing generational conflict and emphasizing the wholesomeness of modern teens.

Moviemakers also offered youth a broad range of cheap horror films, offering teens opportunities to defy adult notions of taste and propriety as well as addressing youth feelings of alienation from family and peers. Especially notable in this regard was AIP's *I Was a Teenage Werewolf* (1957). Many of these horror movies also appealed to a youthful sense of humor with their deliberate silliness and cheap special effects (for example, *Attack of the Crab Monsters*, *The Wasp Woman*, and *The Man with the X-Ray Eyes*).

In 1969, the restrictive Production Code was replaced by a film rating system that allowed for more "mature" themes, liberating adults, and also experimenting youth, from the bland fare of TV with sex, violence, and profanity in "R"-rated films, while protecting children with family-friendly films rated "G." The intermediate rating of "PG" was added in 1970 and the PG-13 rating in 1984. The latter category was for films that contained some violence and sexual suggestiveness but still were deemed acceptable for a teen audience. Realizing that teens and young adults were their most numerous customers, moviemakers began targeting this age group with PG-13 movies (the number of which rose 50 percent between 1995 and 2001 while PG movies dropped by 45 percent).[11]

Action and comedy films with "R" and, especially, "PG-13" ratings were targeted for youth audiences. Action films became more graphic with less complex plots than earlier Westerns and crime movies. Early examples are Clint Eastwood in *Dirty Harry* (1971) and Sylvester Stallone in *Rambo* (a series begun in 1981). The physiques and physicality of male leads attracted young males in particular, often insecure about their emerging bodies.[12]

Youth-oriented comedy emerged also in the early 1970s films, including *Flesh Gordon*, a sexualized spoof on the 1930s science fiction adventure *Flash Gordon*, and

Blazing Saddles, a satire on the classic Western. The youth sex comedy became common with John Belushi's *Animal House* of 1978, with its frat boy high jinks that led to a spate of high school sex comedies like *Porky's*. These comedies were followed in the 1990s by a string of movies starring Adam Sandler, including *Billy Madison*, *The Waterboy*, and *Big Daddy*, all of which celebrated perpetual youth as an alternative to growing up and maturity, presumably directed to young people rebelling against traditional markers of maturity.

The horror film also became edgier with the new rating system. *The Night of the Living Dead* (1968) became a cult film for teens and youth, breaking from old themes (as represented by classics like *Frankenstein* and *Dracula*) with a story of flesh-eating zombies. This escalated horror played especially well in youth-oriented matinees in inner-city movie houses as well as at the midnight movies shown in major city cinemas to older youth. These special viewings attracted a cult audience who repeatedly attended showings of the classic *Freaks* (1932), *The Texas Chainsaw Massacre* (1974), and especially the rock musical, *The Rocky Horror Picture Show*, in which audience members ritually acted out parts of the movie throughout its showing. A similar range of movies were regularly shown in college auditoriums through the 1970s and 1980s by several hundred college film societies.[13]

This led to a series of "slasher" films, featuring graphic murder (*A Nightmare on Elm Street* of 1984, for example). Youth seemed to be attracted to the pleasures of coping with and even laughing at frightful scenes, but, especially as the genre grew familiar, many treated horror as camp, being bemused by its exaggeration and predictability (as in Wes Craven's *Scream* of 1996).[14]

ORIGINS OF TELEVISION AND AMERICAN YOUTH

Unlike film, television was a home-based media that parents expected to offer "family" entertainment only (directed toward adults and children) and thus was slower to become a site for youth identity than movies. Because initially households contained only one TV, usually placed in the living room, and into the mid-1950s watched mostly in the evening hours, the networks created programming to meet interests of all family members. Yet, in fact, TV programming often favored adults, especially fathers, who usually controlled the TV dial.

TV became the quintessential family entertainment, even as it was slow to respond to the distinct interests of youth, as opposed to children. And teens played minor roles on sitcoms and other serials in the 1950s. Like moviemakers, television networks established a code in 1951 that prohibited profanity, religious irreverence, the mocking of family life, graphic violence or sex, and much more. Adult concern over children's exposure to violence accelerated in the 1960s with series that featured contemporary urban crime and superhero cartoon characters (reflected in the conclusions of the National Commission on the Causes and Prevention of Violence in 1969).

Gradually, as viewing hours expanded, shows were skewed toward homemakers during the day; adults, especially men, in the evening; and children in the late afternoon and Saturday morning. Cross-generational programming prevailed in the early evening, including variety shows like *The Ed Sullivan Show* from 1948 to 1971, Westerns, and features like *Walt Disney Presents*. Especially prominent were family situation comedies (or sitcoms), including *Father Knows Best* (1954–1963) and *Leave It to Beaver* (1957–1963). Responding to the multigenerational viewers of living room TVs, these series played on the relationships between parents and children, with offspring comically working out the "dilemmas" of growing up while parents benevolently provided guidance. Although youth may have watched these shows, few addressed their perspective or needs. Teens seldom had leading roles on TV, except as the perky, if somewhat ditzy, female as in *The Patty Duke Show* (1963–1966) that corresponded with the sometimes Pollyanna views of adults rather than to the actual experience or culture of youth.[15]

However, by the 1970s, after the upsurge of youthful protest in the late 1960s and building on the recognition of distinct teen music (rock and roll) and movie cultures that had emerged in the mid-1950s, the networks tried to attract the new generation of youth that advertising agencies conventionally favored. This led to more "realistic" sitcoms, especially *All in the Family* (1971–1979), which featured generational clashes between the reactionary and racist Archie Bunker and his hip young son-in-law. Other sitcoms that attracted youthful audiences, as well as adults, broke with the domestic sitcoms that had attracted older audiences in the '50s and '60s by featuring not family, but workplace interaction. These sitcoms reflected the beginnings of a major shift in American family life—from the early marriage and large families of the postwar period that produced domestic sitcoms, to a pattern of delayed marriage and childbearing, and extended youth (that favored sitcoms built around young peer and workgroups).[16]

To be sure, the 1970s also continued to produce escapist sitcoms appealing to a conservative older generation, such as *Happy Days* (1974–1984), which featured clean-cut teens and a loveable working-class youth (a "greaser"), the Fonz. This nostalgic sitcom helped adults anxious to forget rebellious youth with their rock music and hot rods in the 1950s and the youth counterculture of the 1960s even though this comedy attracted the young as well.

Still, TV turned to rock stars to win teen audiences shortly after this youth-oriented music began to challenge the multigenerational popular music of the past. As early as 1956, variety shows (like *Ed Sullivan*) featured performances by young rock idols (notably Elvis Presley). Afterschool music and dance shows, especially *American Bandstand*, which ran from 1952 to 1989, featured teenagers dancing to the current hits.

Cable TV and Recent Changes in Programming in the United States Open TV to Youth

Despite the relative neglect of youth by the networks, further innovations not only segmented viewing audiences but also made room for more youth-oriented programming and even dedicated channels. Changes included multiple TV sets per household from the 1960s and cable alternatives to conventional TV from the late 1970s. Children and youth increasingly had their own sets, breaking up family viewing and over time encouraging programming designed for narrow age, gender, and taste groups. Youth consumers were at the forefront of innovations like the VCR and DVD, and after 2008, streaming channels like YouTube.

Most important was the expansion of cable and the introduction of satellite TV. These innovations dramatically increased the number of TV channels, allowing advertisers to narrowly target audiences, especially youth on networks like MTV (1981) and VH-1 (1986), with programming that abandoned a multigenerational/mass audience. At first, MTV offered rock music videos, but soon it provided youth-oriented programming such as the irreverent cartoon *Beavis and Butt-Head* (which drove away unwanted older viewers). The cable Cartoon Network, launched in 1994 with children's animation, in 2001 added "Adult Swim," a series of cartoons shown in the evening (*American Dad*, *The Cleveland Show*, and *Family Guy*), appealing to teen and young adult viewers with their irreverent satire and suggestive themes. Late-night comedy programs (*The Daily Show* from 1996, e.g.) have been heavily oriented toward youth with their fevered pace and selection of music and guests.[17]

At the same time, on both broadcast and cable, sitcoms took a sharp turn away from domestic comedy by appealing to young audiences with programs that mocked the old formula by featuring dysfunctional, lazy, and—usually—male leads. These included *Married with Children* (1989–1999) and *The Simpsons* (1989–present). Other sitcoms offered the young a mirror of their own contemporary and future lives. They replaced the old focus on the hierarchical nuclear family with a peer group of singles. Early examples include *Seinfeld* (1990–1998), *Friends* (1994–2004), and *The Big Bang Theory* (2007–2018). In many ways, the humor in these peer sitcoms reflected both the frustrations and the fun of years of remaining single, as during the 1990s American young people often delayed marriage until their late twenties.[18]

Another TV programming trend that reflects the desire to appeal to youth is horror, represented by the hit show *The Walking Dead* (2010–2022, on AMC), featuring post-apocalyptic conflicts between zombies and human survivors based on a comic book. The small broadcast channel, The CW (launched in 2006 by CBS and Warner Brothers), similarly attracts youth with comic-derived series (*The Arrow*) and horror (*Vampire Diaries*). In a crowded market, The CW has tried to build audiences through the social media on the Internet. Youth have become at least as important to contemporary commercial American television as they were to movies in the 1950s.[19]

Youth Film in Scandinavia

The majority of scholarly work on youth film and television has centered on the United States. This can be attributed both to the vast American film industry, which has been and still is a major cultural import into countries in Western Europe and elsewhere, and to the volume of scholarship of film and television in the United States in general. The following is not an attempt to account for "the rest of the world." Rather, by focusing specifically on Scandinavia and its European context, we see one of many possible counter-narratives to the American. The Scandinavian history is not exceptional. On many accounts, it looks like that of other European countries where a focus on developing domestic programs and film for children and youth was sometimes driven by a deliberate goal to counterbalance American commercial and entertainment-focused films and television, and especially the commercial nature of American media. The European productions have to some degree, especially before the 1990s, been financed through state funding or TV licensing fees for public service broadcasting or through subsidies for films.

Before World War I European film was exported globally, but by the 1920s American film production dominated both the U.S. and the European markets. The same trajectory can be seen in Scandinavia, where Denmark had one of the biggest film industries in the world between 1900 and 1920, but after the end of the war, U.S. productions took over the market.

As in Europe more generally, the introduction of censorship in film in Scandinavia was directly related to worries about youth and their film consumption. The spread of movie theaters in Scandinavia sparked debate about their effect on children and young people, and worries about film blended with more general anxiety about the influence of such examples of popular culture as pulp fiction. When censorship of films was introduced in Sweden in 1911 and Denmark and Norway in 1913, it was directly linked to concerns about the medium's effect on children and young people. Some films were totally outlawed; others, only partially with some scenes censored or allowed for adults alone. When videocassettes became a standard household item in the 1980s and extreme violence and pornography on film extended into video, Sweden and Norway made new adjustments to their age classification systems. The Danish film authorities introduced a voluntary age classification system, rating all films 18+ if they had not been screened and classified by the Danish Media Council for Children and Young People. In television, scheduling and labeling of shows in the schedule have worked to separate "adult shows" from those directed toward children and young people. Studies of how European countries censored American movies about juvenile delinquency have shown a stricter censorship of violence in Europe than in the United States in the 1950s and early 1960s, which seems to apply to Scandinavia, too.[20]

In the 1950s, a distinct youth culture defined by youth-specific consumption patterns regarding music, clothes, and film emerged in Scandinavia, just as it had in the United States and Western Europe. In Denmark, Norway, and Sweden this culture change also drove the emergence of youth films as a distinct genre. Films that targeted youth often focused on the problems that young people experienced growing up or juvenile delinquent behavior. Dangerous lifestyles and life choices were central themes in Danish and Swedish youth film in the 1950s, such as *Dangerous Youth* (*Farlig Ungdom*, 1953), *Young Summer* (*Ung sommar*, 1954), and *Young Escape* (*Ung flukti*, 1959). These moralistic films showed the trouble that could easily befall young people if they and their parents were not careful: abortion, prostitution, alcoholism, and unemployment. American culture held an ambivalent position in these films. While Scandinavian movies portrayed American music, dance, and consumer goods as dangerous by encouraging youth to be rebellious and break with established norms, the media celebrated American actors like Marlon Brando and James Dean as cultural icons and local movie stars copied their style.

Increased focus on youth as a cultural group with a distinct identity and its own consumption patterns meant an increase in financial support for youth film from the state in the 1960s. This followed the general welfare state principle that all cultural groups should have their interests represented in the media, even if it was not commercially viable.[21] The state guaranteed plurality because it subsidized many different kinds of movies that would not necessarily be viable on a commercial market. This boost in resources for youth films led to experiments and aesthetical innovation and the creation of films that claimed to represent youth and speak directly to them (from 1982 onward, 25 percent of public film funds in Denmark have been allocated to children and youth film). The Scandinavian film tradition is inclined toward "realism," dealing with the world from young peoples' social-realistic perspectives. As Scandinavian youth began rebelling against their parents, these problem-oriented films also abandoned the moralistic tone that dominated the 1950s mainstream films. In Norway political themes were favored, whereas in Denmark and Sweden problems of identity, feelings, and complex relationships with parents and peers were featured. In general, Scandinavian youth films seem to follow the pattern of other non-U.S. youth films by focusing on politics, cultural differences, and religion.[22] This made youth films a rather small niche that could only survive because of the substantial state subsidies. Still, these youth-oriented films shared with their American counterparts an interest in issues of gender and sexuality, in particular coming-of-age identity themes including generational conflicts.[23] Often, however, the Scandinavians did not share their American counterparts' emphasis on making the audience "feel good" through the inclusion of comedy elements and happy endings.[24]

The 1968 youth rebellion heavily influenced the social realism and problem-oriented films that dominated the Scandinavian youth film market from the 1960s to the 1980s. In these films, society is often viewed through the eyes of the young protagonists, and their youthful identity problems are framed as part of larger sociocultural patterns that create frictions between peer groups and generations. Examples of this genre are the Norwegian *Lasse & Geir* (1976) and the Danish *Zappa* (1983). Both films are about teenage boys who have to adjust to the norms and values of adult society, do not get along with their parents, and have trouble with the police because of their unruly behavior in public. Both films have a lot of sympathy for the young protagonists and show their troubles with fitting in as an outcome of their parents' and other adults' emotional betrayal. Emblematic of the genre's Scandinavian outlook, no obvious solutions to generational or social conflicts are offered and no "happy endings" are reached.

When the hippies, anarchists, and communists that had driven the youth rebellion became older, the Scandinavian youth culture changed and was less overtly political, more focused on individuals. However, the social-realist genre stayed strong as filmmakers, and in particular young filmmakers, still believed that it was important to represent the lives of children and young people on screen. But the new outlook of Scandinavian youth culture was also reflected in the fact that since the 1990s, other genres were introduced and are often mixed with the realist tradition. Films such as *Nightwatch (Nattevagten,* 1994), *Midsummer (Midsommer,* 2003), and *North West (Nordvest,* 2013) represent new genres in the Scandinavian youth films such as horror and gangster movies. Often these genres draw on an American tradition, but the mixture with social realism resulted in a distinct Nordic Noir type of youth film.

Questions about gender and race politics became important topics in the Scandinavian youth culture of the late 1990s and 2000s.[25] Parallel to the broadening of the genres represented in Scandinavian youth film, distinct political themes are addressed, particularly in Swedish youth films. In the 1990s, films made for a young audience by young filmmakers portrayed the hardship of young people and their structural causes. Stories critically examine the causes of bullying, harassment, racism, and even human trafficking. In particular, sexual harassment and inequality related to gender and race were targeted in films such as *Show Me Love* (*Fucking Åmål*) (1998) and *Lilja 4-ever* (2000). In the late 1990s, Sweden began to actively support youth film with girls as the lead characters. Some of these films in the latter part of the 1990s gained international recognition. The focus on the lives, problems, and sexuality of girls can also be seen in Danish and Norwegian youth films in the 2000s. On the whole, this was part of a broader trend. The British *Bend It Like Beckham* (2002) about an 18-year-old Indian girl's dream of being a professional soccer player earned $76 million worldwide, and despite their bleak undertones, some of the Scandinavian films also were commercially successful, albeit on a much smaller scale. These Scandinavian films dwelled on troubling aspects of girlhood and the unresolved conflicts between female protagonists and their social worlds. In this, they shared themes with Anglophone youth films like *Picnic at Hanging Rock* (1975), *The Virgin Suicides* (1999), and *The Fits* (2015).[26]

Despite a European tradition of subsidizing film production to create a distinct alternative to Hollywood, American blockbusters are still favored by Scandinavian youth. As elsewhere in Europe, films series such as the *Harry Potter* series (2001–2011), *The Twilight Saga* (2008–2012), *The Hunger Games* (2012–2015), and *The Divergent Series* (2014–2016) have been big successes with the Scandinavian youth demographic. In fact, a preference for American and British films rather than European, Nordic, or national films has been directly linked to the 15–17 age group in a study from 2011.[27]

YOUTH AND TELEVISION IN SCANDINAVIA

Scandinavian broadcasting was from the beginning funded by license fees as a public service that aimed to produce information, entertainment, and education for the entire society. Organized as state monopolies until the 1980s, radio and television in Denmark, Sweden, and Norway were produced by one institution that served the whole nation. These Scandinavian organizations included the Danish Broadcasting Corporation (DR), Swedish Radio (SR) and later Swedish Television (SVT), and the Norwegian Broadcasting Corporation (NRK). From the 1980s onward, commercial and new public service channels entered the media markets.

In Denmark, Sweden, and Norway, young people were not a priority in the first years of broadcasting in the 1950s and 1960s. Programs for children were broadcasted almost every day, but youth were only targeted with their own programs once a week or even less frequently. These programs showed the life of young people as adults wished it to be. A mixture of drama and factual programs, they emphasized a healthy and responsible lifestyle and offered advice to young people, guiding them slowly and safely from childhood to adulthood.

Toward the mid-1960s this approach was no longer feasible. The youth rebellion and the cultural uproar now pressed the question of diverging interests between youth and adults to the point where it was hard to ignore. The director of the Children and Youth division in the DR said in 1968 that "It is our [journalists' and producers'] job to show the world from children's and young people's point of view; these age groups do not, contrary to adult, have any interest organizations; we need to be their spokesmen."[28] In Denmark, Sweden, and Norway, the public broadcasting institutions had a monopoly on broadcasting. Their children and youth departments covered all young people aged 0–18, and they shared this rather radical view on their role as the providers and enablers of young people's rights and voices. Many of the television producers and journalists working in the children and youth departments in Sweden and Denmark were teenagers and people in their early twenties themselves, as the expansion of broadcasting corporations in Scandinavia at the time had made room for many new hires.

The manifestation of youth as a group with separate interests and cultural needs meant more regular broadcasting of programs for youth. These programs were often produced by older teenagers and very young adults and contained a mixture of sketches, short reports on issues concerning the lives of youth, and debate in the studio. Programs often had a confrontational, direct, and critical angle when the social problems of young people were discussed. This led to a number of political controversies and formal complaints from viewer organizations. The policy also meant giving the "means of production" back to the audience. Between 1970 and 1972, the DR's children and youth department bought about forty cameras and sent them to teenagers who wanted to produce films. About six hundred films were produced during the two years, of which about a third were aired.[29]

It was not only in Scandinavia where young people's wishes and wants were high on the agenda. In inter-European settings, the role(s) of broadcasting in young people's lives became a hot topic at the end of the 1960s. In 1969, a research center connected to the European television festival Prix Jeunesse made a four-day workshop, where they asked "what do young people expect of television?" and "how can producers do justice to the expectations of young people?" The event had 132 participants with a wide representation of broadcasters from Western and Eastern Europe, the Middle East, North America, Asia, and Australia. In addition, fifteen teenagers were invited to be part of the discussions. Personal and official reports from the workshop showed great discrepancy in how young people were perceived by the adult participants. However, the final report showed the need for better representation (and participation) of youth on the small screen, and the subsequent Prix Jeunesse International Festival in June 1970 had its own youth panel that decided on the prizes in the "youth television" category.

A similar interest in the options of the teenage audience (12-to-15 years old) can be depicted in the European Broadcasting Union in 1970.[30] A five-day seminar with participants from nineteen countries was held in Stockholm in 1970 to discuss the needs of this age group with similarly ambiguous results. Even if European broadcasters could not come to an agreement on how to understand and interpret the needs and wants of young people, there was a clear interest that, at least in Scandinavia, led to a variety of programs made by young producers for young people. Just as in the youth films of the time, these programs were problem oriented and wished to confront adult authority with the challenges that young people experienced in contemporary society. One example would be the rather controversial Danish *Peberkværnen* (*the Pepper Mill*, 1968–1969), in which the young producers and journalists talked about everything from drugs to abortion, prostitution, and housing shortages.

As the strong voices of the left-wing youth rebellion died out in the 1980s, Danish youth television became less oriented toward political and social issues. Following general cultural trends in Scandinavia at that moment, creativity, irony, and the inner lives of youth came to the fore.[31] Emotional and personal empowerment tended to replace political issues, which meant a larger focus on "ordinary" youth and their identity problems. This often took the form of irony and humor to make fun of authority figures and young people themselves, not unlike *Monty Python* (which was first broadcast on the BBC in 1969).

With the rise of video in Scandinavian households in the 1980s, young people found a way around the content control by cinemas and broadcasters. Newspapers and academic reports of the time raised a great concern for young people's attachment to video film (in homes with indifferent parents). Especially in the first years of widespread distribution and little regulation (the old censorship laws only applied to public screenings), adults were concerned that young people were watching *The Texas Chainsaw Massacre* (1974), *Jaws* (1975), and other American horror movies. After the censorship laws in Sweden and Norway changed to include video and new age-based regulations appeared in Denmark, subgroups of young people started subversive VHS film collections of their own and formed alternative distribution channels for otherwise banned or 18-plus-rated films.[32] These networks were national as well as international.

The growing influence of American youth media that came with video was compounded with the introduction of commercial television in Denmark, Sweden, and Norway. The commercial channels introduced more American content, especially television series that captured a young audience. American teen soaps of the 1990s such as *Beverly Hills 90210* (1990–2000), *Melrose Place* (1992–1999), *Baywatch* (1989–2001), and *Friends* (1994–2004) were successful with the Scandinavian youth audience. The development of global reality shows like *Big Brother* (2000–) and *Survivor* (1997–), and, later, *X-factor* (2004–), were not teen or youth shows, but the often young participants dominated them as contestants, and their focus on intimacy, feelings, and relationships made teenagers and young people a primary audience, and they, too, reached Scandinavian youth.[33]

In the early 2000s the multiplatform online reality websites became a challenge to broadcasters and filmmakers. These platforms offered many possibilities for social interaction with peers alongside audiovisual output that could compete with traditional flow television, especially as streaming possibilities and infrastructure grew to an extent where it did not take hours to download a film or require technical skills to upload one's content. To keep public service television relevant to a young audience, in 2007 Norway started a public service channel for young people. In Denmark, the public service broadcaster has had a separate website for teenagers since 1999 and a television channel from 1996.

In 2015 Norwegian NRK began broadcasting *SKAM* (*Shame*, 2015–2017), which revived Scandinavian youth broadcasting. The aim was to target young Norwegian girls, specifically sixteen-year-olds. The series, however, became a big hit with viewers all over Scandinavia and the world. In 2018, international adaptions aired in eight other countries. The series has been praised for its innovative use of social media platforms, and also for reviving public service broadcasting by offering young viewers community-oriented solutions to contemporary identity problems. Drawing upon a fan community that was easy to reach and involve via online platforms, the producers created a drama that unfolded online in "real-time" and combined it with more traditional forms of broadcasting. In this programming, producers continued the long Scandinavian tradition of involving young people in the production of television made for them.

In both the United States and Scandinavia, youth-oriented films and programming have been shaped to meet adult objectives (though in different ways). Yet the contrasting roles of commercial versus public sponsorship have produced distinct historical mixes of youth-focused media. Even though the film and TV experience of the two regions are converging, they remain distinct. Though constrained by adult public pressure through industry self-censorship and repeated efforts to accommodate moralistic concerns of elites, the American film and TV industries have over time adopted a youth-oriented approach, where fantasy (sometimes romantic, sometimes violent) predominates. In Scandinavia, with strong state support for film productions and public service-oriented television, it has been possible to target the relatively limited audience of young people with distinct social realist themes even if it at times blended with American trends.

Notes

1. On the appeal of action over narrative, see Tom Gunning, "Rethinking Early Cinema: Cinema of Attraction and Narrativity," in *Cinema of Attractions Reloaded*, ed. Wanda Strauven (Amsterdam: Amsterdam University Press, 2006), 389–416.
2. Charles Musser, *The Emergence of Cinema* (Berkeley: University of California Press, 1990); Musser, *Emergence of Cinema*, 225–263; *The Great Train Robbery* (Edison, 1903).
3. Kalton Lahue, *Continued Next Week: A History of the Moving Picture Serial* (Norman: University of Oklahoma Press, 1964), 5–6, chs. 4–10; Buck Rainey, *Serials and Series: A World Filmography, 1912–1956* (Jefferson, NC: McFarland, 1999), 3–4, 92–93.
4. Samantha Barbas, *Movie Crazy: Fans, Stars, and the Cult of Celebrity* (New York: Palgrave, 2001), 1–33.
5. Hugo Munsterberg, *The Photoplay: A Psychological Study* (New York: Appleton, 1916), 95; Jane Addams, *The Spirit of Youth and City Streets* (New York: McMillan, 1909), 75–76, 86; Garth Jowett, Ian Javie, and Kathryn Fuller, *Children and the Movies: Media Influence and the Payne Fund Controversy* (New York: Cambridge University Press, 2006), 21–29.
6. Henry Forman, *Our Movie Made Children* (New York: Macmillan, 1933), 10, ch. 16; Richard Maltby, "The Production Code and the Hays Office," in *Grand Design: Hollywood as a Modern Business Enterprise, 1930–1930*, ed. Tino Balio (New York: Scribners, 1993), 37–72; Jowett, *Children and the Movies*, 29–95, quotation on 96.
7. Examples of the sixteen Andy Hardy movies include *Love Finds Andy Hardy* (1938) and *Judge Hardy and Son* (1939).
8. Ilana Nash, *American Sweethearts: Teenage Girls in Twentieth-Century Popular Culture* (Bloomington: Indiana University Press, 2006).
9. Thomas Doherty, *Teenagers and Teenpics* (Boston: Unwin, 1988), 105–10; D.M. Considine, *The Cinema of Adolescence* (New York: McFarland, 1985), 112; Catherine Driscoll, *Teen Film: A Critical Introduction* (Oxford: Burg, 2011), 66–68.

10. Cobbett Steinberg, *TV Facts* (New York: Facts on File, 1985), 86–87.
11. "Do You Know Where Your Children Are? Most Likely, They're Watching PG-13 Movies," *The Washington Post*, November 16, 2003, W12; Leo Bogart, *Over the Edge: How the Pursuit of Youth by Marketers and the Media Has Changed American Culture* (Chicago: Ivan Dee, 2005), ch. 6, esp. 160–161.
12. Eric Lichtenfeld, *Action Speaks Louder: Violence, Spectacle, and the American Action Movie* (Westport, CT: Praeger, 2004), 59; Yvonne Tasker, ed., *Action and Adventure Cinema* (New York: Routledge, 2004).
13. Kevin Heffernan, *Ghouls, Gimmicks and Gold: Horror Films and the American Movie Business* (Durham, NC: Duke University Press, 2004), 203, 207, 212; J. Hoberman and Jonathan Rosenbaum, *Midnight Movies* (New York: Harper and Row, 1983), 95, 99.
14. Robin Wood, *Hollywood: From Vietnam to Reagan . . . and Beyond* (New York: Columbia University Press, 2003), ch. 5; Reynold Humphries, *American Horror Film* (Edinburgh: Edinburgh University Press, 2002), ch. 1.
15. Nina Liebman, *Living Room Lectures: The Fifties Family in Film and Television* (Austin: University of Texas Press, 1997), 124; David Marc, *Comic Visions: Television Comedy and American Culture* (Boston: Allen Unwin, 1989), 129–139.
16. Gary Cross, *Consumed Nostalgia: Memory in the Age of Fast Capitalism* (New York: Columbia University Press, 2015), ch. 5.
17. The classic is Joseph Turow, *Breaking Up America: Advertisers and the New Media World* (Chicago: University of Chicago Press, 1998).
18. James Baker, *Teaching TV Sitcom* (London: British Film Institute, 2003), 48–49.
Michael Tuethe, *Laughter in the Living Room: Television Comedy and the American Home Audience* (New York: Peter Lang, 2005), 192.
19. Anna Aupperle, "Teen Queens and Adrenaline Dreams: A History of The CW Television Network" (PhD diss., Pennsylvania State University, 2018).
20. On censorship in United States and Europe, see Daniel Bilteryst, "American Juvenile Delinquency Movies and the European Censors: The Cross-Cultural Reception and Censorship of *The Wild One* and *Blackboard Jungle*, and *Rebel Without a Cause*," in *Youth Culture in Global Cinema*, ed. Timothy Shary and Alexandra Seibel (Austin: The University of Texas Press, 2007), 9–26.
21. For a discussion of the welfare state and representation in children's media culture see Helle Strandgaard Jensen, *From Superman to Social Realism: Children's Media and Scandinavian Childhood* (Amsterdam: John Benjamins Publishing Press, 2017).
22. Jo Sondre Moseng, "Mainstream forvirring? Norsk ungdomsfilm," in *Den andre norske filmhistorien*, ed. Eva Bakøy and Tore Helseth (Oslo: Universietetsforlaget, 2011), 152–167.
23. Caroll Driscoll. *Teen Film: A Critical Introduction* (Oxford: Berg, 2011).
24. Anne Jerslev, "Youth Film: Transforming Genre, Performing Audiences," in *The International Handbook of Children, Media and Culture*, ed. Kirsten Drotner and Sonja Livingstone (London: SAGE 2008); Anders Lysne, "Tonally Teen?" *Akademisk kvarter, Academic Quarter* (2019): 159–171.
25. Tommy Gustafsson, "Ett steg på vägen mot en ny jämlikhet: könsrelationer och stereotyper i ung svensk ungdomsfilm på 2000-tale," in *Solskenslandet. Svensk film på 2000-talet*, ed. Erik Hedling and Ann-Kristin Wallengren (Stockholm: Atlantis, 2006), 171–194; Anders Lysne, *Ungdom. Forløbimedier* (København: Lindhardtog Ringhof, 2017); Heta Mulari, "Transnational Heroines: Swedish Youth Film and Immigrant Girlhood," in *Frontiers of*

Screen History: Imagining European Borders in Cinema, 1945–2010, ed. Raita Merivirta, Heta Mulari, Kimmo Ahonen, and Rami Mähkä (Bristol: Intellect, 2013), 195–216.
26. David Buckingham, "Gender Trouble: Cinema and the Mystery of Adolescent Girlhood," *Growing Up Modern*, https://web.archive.org/web/20190331112951/https://davidbuckingham.net/growing-up-modern/gender-trouble-cinema-and-the-mystery-of-adolescent-girlhood/, accessed March 31, 2019.
27. Ib Bondebjergand and Eva Novrup Redvall, *A Small Nation in a Global World. Patterns in Scandinavian Film and Media Culture*, https://web.archive.org/web/20190331114741/https://cemes.ku.dk/research/research_literature/workingpapers/scandinavian_cinema-final_lrl_.pdf/, accessed March 15, 2021.
28. Quoted in Helle Strandgaard Jensen, "TV as Children's Spokesman: Conflicting Notions of Children and Childhood in Danish Children's Television around 1968," *The Journal of the History of Childhood and Youth* 6, no. 1 (2013): 105–128, p. 105.
29. Bayerisher Rudfunk, Internal archives of Prix Jeunesse, Binder "1969."
30. Doreen Stephens, ed., "Report of Second EBU Workshop for producers and directors of television programmes for young people" (Geneva: European Broadcasting Union, 1970).
31. Christa Lykke Christensen, "Børne-og ungdoms-tv," in *Dansk Tv's Historie*, ed. Stig Hjarvard (Frederiksberg: Samfundslitteratur, 2006), 65–105.
32. Göran Bolin, "Producing Cultures. The Construction of Forms and Contents of Contemporary Youth Cultures," *Young* 7, no. 1 (1999): 50–65.
33. Anders Lysne, *Ungdom. Forløb i medier* (København: Lindhardt og Ringhof, 2017).

Further Reading

Bailey, Beth. *From Front Porch to Back Seat: Courtship in Twentieth Century America*. Baltimore: Johns Hopkins University Press, 1988.
Barba, Samantha. *Movie Crazy: Fans, Stars and the Cult of Celebrity*. New York: Palgrave, 2001.
Bondebjerg, Ib, Tomasz Goban Klas, Michele Hilmes, Dana Mustata, Helle Strandgaard-Jensen, Isabelle Veyrat-Masson, et al. "American Television: Point of Reference or European Nightmare?" In *A European Television History*. Edited by Andreas Fickers and Jonathan Bignell, 154–183. Hoboken: Blackwell-Wiley, 2008.
Doherty, Thomas. *Teenagers and Teenpics: Juvenilization of American Movies*. Philadelphia: Temple University Press, 2010.
Driscoll, Caroll. *Teen Film: A Critical Introduction*. Oxford: Berg, 2011.
Forman, Henry. *Our Movie Made Children*. New York: Macmillan, 1933.
Jerslev, Anne. "Youth Film: Transforming Genre, Performing Audiences." In *The International Handbook of Children, Media and Culture*. Edited by Kirsten Drotner and Sonia Livingstone, 183–195. London: SAGE, 2008.
Jowett, Garth, Ian Javie, and Kathryn Fuller. *Children and the Movies: Media Influence and the Payne Fund Controversy*. New York: Cambridge University Press, 1996.
Lichtenfeld, Eric. *Action Speaks Louder: Violence, Spectacle and the American Action Movie*. Middletown, CT: Wesleyan University Press, 2007.
Marc, Gary. *Comic Visions: Television Comedy and American Culture*. Boston: Allen Unwin, 1989.

McCann, Benn. *L'Auberge espagnole: European Youth on Film*. Abingdom: Routledge, 2018.
Nash, Ilana. *American Sweethearts: Teenage Girls in Twentieth-Century Popular Culture*. Bloomington: Indiana University Press, 2006.
Schrum, Kelly. *Some Wore Bobby Sox: The Emergence of Teen Girls' Culture, 1920–1945*. New York: Palgrave, 2004.
Shary, Timothy. *Teen Movies: American Youth on Screen*. New York: Columbia University Press, 2005.
Shary, Timothy, and Alexandra Seibel, eds. *Youth Culture in Global Cinema*. Austin: The University of Texas Press, 2007.
Stanfield, Peter. *The Cool and the Crazy: Pop Fifties Cinema*. New Brunswick, NJ: Rutgers University Press, 2015.

CHAPTER 22

PARADOX AND POSSIBILITY

Youth Media Culture across the Globe

STUART R. POYNTZ

As the 2020s begin, young people's deep immersion in mediated life is the norm in societies around the world. Access to mobile phones, social media, and more traditional broadcast media has made screen-rich bedrooms and media-saturated public spaces staples of youth cultures. Bo Burnham's 2018 American film *Eighth Grade* powerfully captures this context in a series of ethnographic-like scenes about the life of an introverted teenage girl, just about to enter high school. The world of Kayla Day (played by Elsie Fisher) is awash in media involvements, including her own videos, online influencers, and social media streams that contour her self-production, including the hopes and anxieties she has about how to be a teenager. The movie is a tragic comedy and in many ways fits in with a tradition of youth films made about the traumas and emotional highs and lows of adolescence. But if the *Sturm und Drang* of this phase of life is not unusual to see on screen, what is revealing is how social media platforms and consumer culture contour and weave youth lives, providing the background environment and resources young people now use to understand themselves and who they might be.

In other parts of the globe, including China, media-saturated bedroom cultures may never have been the norm, but young people are still living deeply mediated lives that involve participation and media consumption across a range of platforms and technologies. According to a 2018 report from the China Internet Network Information Centre (CNNIC), of the 750 million Internet users in China, 169 million are under the age of 18. The Internet penetration rate is just above 93 percent among minors, and the CNNIC report indicates that 92 percent of children and youth access the Internet using smartphones and spend an average of 20.7 hours per week using the Internet.

A 2013 Guangzhou study across fifteen cities reported that 67 percent of children had household access to a tablet, 97 percent had a TV in the household, and 95.4 percent had household access to a computer. The same study notes that 70 percent of surveyed children aged 6–11 use Tencent's QQ daily for instant messaging, while 46 percent use WeChat daily for instant messaging and 51 percent of respondents blog daily.[1]

Together this data reveals that teenagers graduating from high school in 2021 across the Global North and much of the Global South are intimately connected to smartphones and social media. They have also been subject to near constant data surveillance and typically hold to the expectation that they should be able to google and Baidu facts as needed. Texting, messaging, and posting are part of the regularized rhythms of daily life, leaving the general impression that most children and youth are more involved with both media technologies and content than ever before. It is as though a whole new terrain of children's and youth media culture has emerged, a world where the Internet, mobile devices, and "television" are now consumed across multiple platforms that compete for attention alongside older media (i.e., radio, appointment TV, and movies). Regular television and radio continue to hold a place among teenagers' media choices and, along with mobile phones, are part of a primary youth media ecology through which identity is lived out.[2]

Across the history of youth media culture, issues of production, representation, circulation, and consumption have shaped the complex relationships that bind together young people, media, technology and texts. The kinds of primary relationships young people now have with media began to develop in the nineteenth century, just as the notion of youth itself was emerging in the West. New forces of mass reproduction and changes in the conditions of distance that shape youth lives were early harbingers of modern youth cultures. Developments in the United States and the United Kingdom are often taken as signposts for understanding this history; but, developments there were not universal, and the histories of media and youth culture in other countries reveal instructive differences in young people's media relationships that remain important. The recent histories of YouTube in the West and WeChat in China reveal ongoing differences in the globalization of youth cultures and yet, they also point to the persistence of a central paradox across young people's media entanglements: that is, the key media structures that shape and contour youth lives continue to be the very sites where youth navigate authentic meaning and experience and imagine their own futures. This creates tensions and risks that define youth media cultures and make young people's experiences today.

THE INVENTION OF YOUTH AND EMERGENCE OF A MEDIA CULTURE

Youth culture is now a part of popular consumer culture more generally and includes cultural practices, participants, fans, and brokers of meaning who may not be chronologically young at all. The line between youth culture as an age-specific category and youth culture, understood as a set of discourses and practices (i.e., punk music, fan communities, and cosplay, to name only a few examples), has blurred in recent decades. Even so, in the minds of many, the preoccupations of youth culture remain a primary concern of the young.

The age of transition between childhood and adulthood exists across societies; however, it wasn't until the 1940s that the term "youth culture" was first coined, and it was a series of changes in social, economic, and cultural life in the post–World War II era that proved essential in marking out a modern notion of youth. Media and consumer markets were integral to these changes.

From the start of the twentieth century mass media was among the key developments that shaped the rise of popular consumer culture and changes in youth lives. The emergence of a media culture in the West is linked to the proliferation of images in advertising and commercial photography; the rise of film (1895) and the Hollywood film industry; the emergence of popular music industries and cultures, particularly in cities; the rise of what we now call celebrity fan cultures; and pervasive changes in the accessibility of style, fashion, and mass entertainments for diverse economic groups. Together, these developments contributed to the mediatization of everyday life, a process that takes account of the deep ways that our everyday experiences have become integrated with and shaped by mass-produced and, now, digitally enabled communication.

The development of youth media cultures was first evident in Europe and North America, with the onset of industrialization and the emergence of mass consumer markets. Youth cultures (dance, music, fashion, sport, etc.) have always been mediated and shaped by the effects of mass production, wage labor relations, and the experiences of the city. Because of this, youth and the emergence of youth cultures have been closely linked to modernity. But the relationship between young people and media in modern times has been fraught.

Since the early 1900s, both youth and media have been seen as exemplars of social progress, creativity, and individual freedom. Yet over the same period, with the proliferation of images and consumerism as normative conditions of everyday life, children and youth have been thought uniquely vulnerable to media power and the risks of modernity. The resulting tensions have produced an important paradox in media cultures: youth are very often both a powerful site of hope for the future and exemplars of our deepest anxieties about contemporary social life.

The German-Jewish cultural critic Walter Benjamin offers a helpful set of resources to make sense of this condition. Benjamin was among the iconoclast group of social theorists and cultural critics connected with the Institute for Social Research (better known as the Frankfurt School that began life in Frankfurt, Germany, during the period of the Weimar Republic, 1918–1933). Influenced by the work of Karl Marx, G.W.F. Hegel, and the German Idealist tradition, theorists in the Frankfurt School, including Max Horkheimer, Theodor Adorno, and Herbert Marcuse, took up the task of examining the deep structures of Western civilization, including most importantly, how capitalism and the legacies of the Enlightenment led to profound crises in the West. Like his colleagues, Benjamin was highly critical of Western consumer culture, but he simultaneously identified new ways in which that very culture was opening spaces of freedom and opportunities for mass revolution. These ideas can be helpful for thinking about the contradictory space occupied by youth in modern times.

In Benjamin's well-known essay, "The Work of Art in the Age of Mechanical Reproduction," he draws attention to two fundamental changes in cultural experience in mass industrial societies. These changes are equally germane to postindustrial societies like our own. On one hand, with technologies like the factory assembly line, photography, movies, and advertising, mass reproducibility becomes a common feature of social life. These technologies produce multiple copies of the same thing. On a societal scale, the impact is such that mass reproduction undermines originality as a condition of cultural experience. Industrial societies produce many of the same things. Our common notion of a global youth culture, one where global kids wear the same clothes, see the same movies, and appear on the same social media platforms, anticipates this state of affairs. Benjamin interprets the loss of cultural originality as a loss in the "aura" or uniqueness historically attached to art and culture.[3] He means by this that mass reproduction and the rise of mass media cause art and culture to become mundane, common, everyday commodities. The same pop cultural things and experiences are available to anyone, anywhere, in a fashion similar to any other commodity in industrial and postindustrial societies.

On the other hand, by making art and culture available anywhere, anytime, consumer societies change how distance or space operate. Paradoxically, mass media brings culture closer to us, even as it simultaneously allows similar cultural styles, texts, industries, and technologies to reach audiences and users further afield. Radio was among the first mass technologies to enter the home, bringing new voices from afar; the television entered the living room and made the screen a new family hearth; multiple TVs eventually became common in some homes, affording different screens for all, and often in more intimate spaces; and, now mobile screens are so integrated into the habits of daily life that they (to reference Marshal McLuhan) work as extensions of our selves.[4] But media culture is not only closer to us; it also offers new connections and outlets that simultaneously pull youth away from the influence of older generations (especially parents, educators, and other adults), by providing worlds of consumption, identity, and community uniquely set to their interests. This context has fed modern anxieties and moral panics about the undue and dangerous influence of popular media on children and teenagers.

These and like developments exemplify Benjamin's contention that as consumer media culture becomes common, the dynamics of distance change. Some things are now closer than ever before, even as the distance separating some people and experiences change. In the 1930s, an emerging world of film, movie stars, popular music, and newspapers produced a new media culture, one where art and culture were increasingly detached from older auratic experiences—linked to magic or religion or the worship of beauty. In modern media societies, popular culture is instead part of everyday life, part of what Raymond Williams called our ways of living, the habits and experiences that occupy our time and make our places.[5]

Interestingly, for Benjamin these conditions free up art and culture, including popular media culture, to be refashioned for other purposes. The results are intensely paradoxical. Concentrated media industries and social media technology companies like Disney, Time Warner, Google, Facebook (owners of WhatsApp and Instagram), Alibaba (Weibo), Tencent (WeChat), and Baidu have used the profaning of culture to create vast brands, platforms, surveillance technologies, and entertainment experiences that contour youth lives (sometimes in similar ways) all around the world. At the same time, for decades, young people have used the plasticity of popular culture to reimagine the meaning and worth of popular texts, celebrities, and technologies, sometimes to lead political mobilization and social change, sometimes to negotiate and explore identities and aspirations, and sometimes just to play together or alone.

Making a Modern Youth Culture

In the postwar years in the West, youth and youth culture became a central feature of social life. The decades of the 1950s and 1960s mark a famously significant period of expansion when youth markets grew with the recovery of national economies in Europe, North America, and Asia after the global devastation of WWII. Increasing birth rates during the postwar baby boom fueled the expansion of youth markets, as did the extension of mass schooling. Importantly, the expansion of labor markets in many countries helped young people to earn disposable income, which fed the expansion of consumer markets and the development of a vast range of youth products.

Among the industries leading the charge, the music, fashion, film, magazine publishing, and television industries all developed distinctly youth sectors, with their own genres, brands, celebrities, titles, and networks. Together these developments reinforced the sense that youth had become a distinct demographic, linked together as much by common cultural practices, pastimes, and preoccupations as by biological age. The story of the emergence of youth markets is often told through the development of American popular culture and its growing influence around the world in the postwar years, largely because North America escaped the worst destruction of WWII, leaving the U.S. economy well positioned to lead economic expansion, including the rise of new industries and production centers focused on youth.

The emergence and consolidation of rock and roll as a powerful musical form and style, with its own celebrities and media outlets, was central to this transition. The roots of rock and roll originate in Black rhythm and blues, which gained popularity in American cities in the 1940s, as migration from the American South led to the rise of Black radio stations in Northern and Western U.S. cities, and eventually, crossover successes with white audiences. Rock and roll ultimately represented the "whitening" and mainstreaming of Black music and Black culture for middle-class audiences, a process of market colonization that has shaped relationships of race, popular culture, and youth markets ever since.

As a hybrid musical form, rock and roll was also quickly integrated into film with the emergence of the "teenpic" and crossover stars like Elvis Presley, Frank Sinatra, and Paul Anka. The remarkable Canadian documentary film *Lonely Boy* (Wolf Koenig and Roman Kroiter, 1962) captures Anka's stunning rise from obscurity to teen idol loved, in particular, by young women whose riotous expressions of affection caused fear among older generations wary of the new influence of mass media and sexually explicit content. Magazine publishers were equally active during this period, developing new titles for the youth market, including *Seventeen*, which launched in 1944 and by the 1950s had assumed a central role in providing fashion and relationship advice, including giving more attention to the boomer generation's increasing interest in female sexuality. Today, *Seventeen* continues to publish and has been a target of activist young women concerned with the influence the magazine has on women's body health, well-being, and self-esteem.

Teen television emerged in the 1950s in the United States, where the smaller and less established national broadcast network, ABC, targeted burgeoning youth audiences as a way to compete with the older and more established broadcasters, CBS and NBC. Like Viacom and Disney (current owner of ABC) in recent decades, ABC developed niche programming for youth markets by leveraging the success of popular music, including, most importantly, the network's new program, *American Bandstand*, which first aired in 1957 and at its height reached audiences in excess of 20 million.

The success of early youth markets was associated with other postwar developments, including the rise of the suburbs. Bill Osgerby argues that these and like changes cast teen culture "as the harbinger of a modern consumer culture in which the old boundaries of class and economic inequality were perceived as steadily disappearing."[6] Perhaps the coming of the Beatles to America in 1964 symbolized this development as much as anything else. With their arrival at John F. Kennedy Airport on the morning of February 7, and their subsequent appearance on *The Ed Sullivan Show* before a studio audience of adoring fans, the Fab Four working-class lads from Liverpool symbolized the new look and feel of youth culture: it was to be a modern culture, one deeply integrated with various media and related industries, that promised class uplift in a way that symbolized what economist J.K. Galbraith called the "affluent society."[7]

These were popular sentiments at the time, yet it quickly became apparent that youth culture was equally the site of complicated struggles over relationships of race, class, gender, and sexuality. Among the texts and events that capture these struggles, Franc Roddam's 1979 British film *Quadrophenia* is noteworthy. Set in London in the mid-1960s, the film follows the story of Jimmy (played by Phil Daniels), a young Mod, disillusioned with his parents and his dead-end job. He eventually quits the mailroom and escapes his mundane working life by turning to music, Italian-built scooters, dancing, and drugs. Jimmy and his pals represent a bored, middle-class generation of youth, escaping the bonds of an earlier time by searching out fun and frivolity while brawling with the Rockers, a gang of motorcycle-riding youth who represent working-class kids and working-class culture. The film culminates in a huge brawl at the seaside town of Brighton, a filmic event that recalls the real-life brawls between the Mods and Rockers, which were the cause of moral panics in Britain in the late 1960s.[8]

If *Quadrophenia* captured class tensions and preoccupations emerging in youth culture in the late 1960s, David Downes' study of East End youth in London and Graham Murdock and Robin McCron's study of teenagers, class, and taste in popular music and style drew attention to the ways young people were using popular culture to express class identities across Britain.[9] The work of Stuart Hall, Tony Jefferson, Dick Hebdige, and others connected with the newly influential Centre for Contemporary Cultural Studies (CCCS) at the University of Birmingham added to this work by examining how spectacular youth subcultures (i.e., punk rock) were using popular culture to express complicated forms of class-based resistance. Angela McRobbie's work added concerns for gender to early cultural studies research at the CCCS, and later Paul Gilroy, Les Back, and Sanjay Sharma and colleagues addressed the role of ethnicity and race in the negotiation of youth cultural identities. Since this pioneering work, cultural studies has emerged as a dominant framework for understanding media and youth experience around the world.

Whereas class dominated in Britain, by the 1960s the influence of race and racism rose to the fore in the United States, propelled by the growing influence of the civil rights movement and improving economic opportunities and living standards for African American communities. During the 1950s and early 1960s, youth media cultures were dominated by white audiences, as intense forms of racism and economic inequality meant that Black teenagers were largely invisible to mainstream society. But, style, fashion, and music popular among African American and Mexican American teens gained prominence and would eventually come to shape modern teen culture. The story of Motown exemplifies this development.

Founded by Berry Gordy Jr. in 1959, Motown eventually came to dominate the *Billboard* charts, featuring the sounds of African American soul and R & B artists. By the beginning of the 1970s, Motown had become a multimillion-dollar company with interests in music, motion pictures, television, and publishing for both white and Black audiences. The label's success ultimately encouraged advertisers and others to pay attention to nonwhite audiences, sometimes for the first time. This led to the launch of new programs, including *Soul Train* as a counter to *American Bandstand*, and later, ABC's *What's Happening* (1976–1979) and CBS's *Good Times* (1974–1979) and *The Jefferson's* (1975–1985), all of which took on issues of race while introducing America to the lives of Black families. These shows set the stage for later fare, including *The Cosby Show* (1984–1992), *The Fresh Prince of Bel-Air* (1990–1996), and the rise of Black Entertainment Television (BET), now the most important television network targeting Black audiences in the United States. Attention to race, gender, and class in youth popular culture made clear that youth media was no longer merely a form of entertainment. Rather, as youth came to the very center of social life in the 1960s and 1970s, youth markets, consumerism, and media emerged as powerful sites of conflict, where increasingly the most important issues of the day were addressed.

The mix of tensions in media culture has only intensified in subsequent decades, as part of the globalization of youth media. Our narrative thus far has concentrated on developments in the United States and the United Kingdom, because the vast majority of research on the emergence of youth markets in the postwar period focuses on Anglo-American contexts. Others have noted this pattern, including David Buckingham, who nonetheless highlights the work of Tora Korsvold on young people in Norway.[10] Korsvold's work offers a revealing counter-narrative to developments in the United Kingdom and the United States. In contrast to these locales, youth markets emerged much more slowly in Norway, shaped by a strong welfare state, the challenge of postwar reconstruction, and a national image of Norwegians as frugal consumers. Together, these influences strongly limited consumption until recent decades. In general, state media focused on adult entertainment and an educational mandate for youth and children's programming. In a related manner, the marketing of fashion focused on nature and physical activity in Norway, as opposed to the popular styles emerging in the United States and United Kingdom. This concern for nature and the environment continues to run though youth popular culture and has led to public suspicion of consumption in Norway, including its implications for global warming and climate change.

In China, a very different history of youth media culture has emerged. As a consequence of the profound societal upheavals produced by the civil war (ending in 1949), the turmoil of the Great Leap Forward (1958–1962), and the Cultural Revolution (1966–1976), youth media culture was much slower to develop in China. The generation of young people born after the time of Mao Zedong—called variously, the post-80s or post-90s generation(s), China's millennials, or China's me generation—are often thought of as a privileged group because they grew up in a time of stability and intense economic expansion unheard of in the nation's history. Under the leadership of Vice Chairman Deng Xiaoping, beginning in 1979, China began to open up to the rest of the world. By the early 1980s, an enormous expansion followed in all kinds of media, including newspapers, magazines, radios, televisions, telephones, and, eventually, the Internet. While still under the influence of the Communist Party and the state, the media began to compete for audiences' attention based on style and entertainment. Alongside the influx of new programming from Taiwan and Hong Kong throughout the 1980s and 1990s, and the introduction of foreign films, music, sports, and soap operas, entertainment began to dominate even state-controlled media channels, with the result that a more diverse, complex, and participatory network of communication has emerged in China over the past thirty years.

For young people, the impact of these developments has been profound. Chinese urban children and youth have experienced material well-being and prosperity unknown to previous generations. Recent generations are "media savvy, well informed about cutting-edge global trends and enamoured of cool communication gadgets."[11] They are connected to global brands, including the NBA, and have access to Hollywood movies, Japanese comic books, MP3 players and iPods, punk music, and hip-hop. Chinese media and technology companies, including Weibo, WeChat, Alibaba, and Huawei, now operate on a global stage and are increasingly recognizable brands around the world. While youth markets were slow to emerge in China, in other words, they have exploded in recent decades and now have the power to impose identities, shape the circulation of key sites of meaning, and change how families and social futures are understood.

The rise of youth media culture in China has generated excitement, but also a wave of concern about the role of media and the Internet in the lives of young people: "In an extreme version, the moral panic aroused by the Internet has led to a popular view of the Net as akin to addictive drugs, in particular, opium . . . Because of its historical connotation, associating opium with the Internet triggers an avalanche of concern and sentiments."[12] Anxieties of this sort are not wholly different from related concerns about media influence that have been common in the West since the earliest years of the twentieth century.

Most often characterized by exaggerated claims about the impact of popular media on children and youth, moral panics are a special kind of media spectacle about the influence of popular culture on vulnerable populations. Stanley Cohen's groundbreaking study of moral panics in the early 1970s focuses on popular concerns about the Mods and Rockers and shows how emerging youth media cultures have long been a target of panic.[13] Cohen's study has been criticized for simplifying the meaning of moral panics and for underestimating how complex media environments shape media panics; nonetheless, his work draws attention to the ways overwrought fears of youth and media culture can act as stand-ins for larger social crises, turning youth and youth culture into scapegoats. In other words, moral panics do not offer helpful tools for explaining the complex nexus of connections between youth, media, and social change as much as they distract parents, educators, and others from making sense of the formative conditions shaping youth lives.

Moral panics have nonetheless continued to appear around the world over the past forty years. In the 1980s in the United Kingdom, panics arose around so-called video nasties and the damage horror films and sexually explicit material newly available on videotape (VHS formats) were thought to pose for youth. Related concerns arose in the 1990s about video games and violence, the presence of dangerous and disturbing messages buried in the lyrics of popular music, and fears about fantasy board games, like *Dungeons and Dragons*. More recently, in China and other nations, anxieties have come the fore having to do with the role of the Internet and social media, including fears of stranger danger, cyberbullying, and Internet addiction, and concerns about massive changes in teenagers' online sexual lives.

Global Youth Cultures, Youth Subcultures, and Network Societies

These and like anxieties speak to the changes mediatization has wrought in everyday life. The proliferation of media culture throughout the opening decades of the postwar years reveals the impact mass reproduction had on culture. New products, new youth segments, and the exponential growth of youth media industries emerged at different stages and in varying scales around the world, but, as Walter Benjamin seemed to understand, these years marked the slow and persistent growth of consumer youth media cultures everywhere. Such cultures have since come to contour youth identities, networks, and aspirations and have become intimate sites of experience that have altered how young people learn, love, and connect. In the process, media culture has altered the conditions of distance in youth lives. Mediated communication, media technology, and media culture are now the stage, stuff, and time of youth lives. They complicate how adolescents connect with earlier generations, even while providing the symbolic and material stratum for much of their social lives.

There are, of course, vast differences in the ways young people use and are impacted by media. We have seen some of these differences already, but cultural studies research has added to our understanding of how young people's lives and transitions to adulthood have changed amid the globalization of media. Locality and place remain significant in forming youth identities, even while shared global imaginaries have become implicated in young people's future aspirations. Youth cultures and subcultures are now deeply embedded in consumer market relationships in ways that don't contest consumerism as much as they exploit and extend consumer relationships. And as we learned during the COVID-19 pandemic, screens are now places of community for many people. The upshot is to create a sense of self in a world that is increasingly unstable and shaped by risk. The result is youth identities, less bound to singular modes of subcultural expression, and more likely to shift over time.

The context for this complicated process of youth identity development is a media culture that has expanded exponentially in recent decades. From at least the 1980s onward, the quantity of media—in both content and form—has multiplied around the world, meaning more advertising, more commercial screens, more branded experiences of play, and more intensive systems of corporate surveillance and tracking have become common elements of youth experience. Two fundamental processes have driven these developments.

On one hand, the onset of a largely neoliberal policy environment has changed how media industries and companies are regulated (by states) around the world. At its core neoliberalism contends that markets are best able to provide for the well-being, development, and happiness of all. Over thirty years this idea has shaped policy and influenced thinking about families, schools, cities, work, and media, with the result that markets have been empowered as lead arbiters of the ideas, experiences, and products in kids' lives. Massive waves of government deregulation have been essential to empower markets and the companies that dominate them. In the 1980s and 1990s, the United States led the way with policies intended to curtail or eliminate government regulation of how media companies operate and target young people.[14] These conditions helped pave the way for the emergence of global media conglomerates—including the aforementioned Disney, Time Warner, Google, Viacom, and News Corp—as dominant forces in the production of media commodities, branded experiences, and the coordination of youth demographics as segmented niche markets (i.e., tweens, millennials, Generation Z, and so on).

On the other hand, this context is tied to the digitization of media and the emergence of dynamic, participatory media cultures. In the contemporary period, the miniaturization of technology and the proliferation of the computer and related digital formats have led all of us to read and write media differently. Digital media cultures are dynamic, interactive meaning spaces that afford youth with new ways to create (i.e., producing and exchanging media across platforms), circulate (i.e., blogging, podcasting, forwarding links), collaborate (i.e., working together on video and other media projects, sharing information through projects like Wikipedia), and connect (i.e., through social media sites and online communities, including game clans or fandoms) with others.[15] Digitization has allowed media conglomerates to operate across media formats, leading to the integration of historically distinct industries and the development of powerful transmedia brands and franchises (i.e., Harry Potter, the X-Men, Star Wars, etc.) that offer multiple avenues for youth engagement and connection. This leads to intensive media environments, yet digitization has also changed the nature of youth participation across everyday life. What's been called a participatory turn in media culture has enabled users (or those we used to call audiences) to become more active and involved with brands, franchises, technologies, and social media networks than ever before. This turn is evidenced by the increasing amount of time youth spend with screens, and it is also a function of how we now interact with media technology and content.

Audiences have always been involved with still and moving images, celebrities, sports, popular music, etc. Fan cultures exemplify this as do studies of how real audiences talk about and use media. But today youth (like the rest of us) are called to participate in digital media culture in new ways. Participation has become a condition that is *environmental* (a state of affairs) and *normative* (a binding principle of right action) in culture. For many of us, getting up in the morning begins with media interaction, with our mobiles. We continue participating in near constant mediated practice throughout the day. The 2016 Globe-Yconic survey of Canadian youth, for instance, indicates that 40 percent of young people say they are almost always online. The same survey indicates that many youth receive and send more than a hundred texts daily.[16]

Digital technologies and highly concentrated media industries are the architecture of this context. They allow a growing number of people to access, modify, store, circulate, and share media content in ways that have only been available to a select few in the past. This has led youth to become more involved and active as media users, but interaction with digital media has also allowed others to interact with youth in new and sometimes troubling ways. Digital media cultures allow others, including corporations, governments, and unwanted individuals to monitor, survey, coordinate, and guide activities as never before. Using data footprints, states, political parties, media, toy, and technology companies (as well as health, insurance, and a host of other industries) have become data aggregation units that map and monitor youth behavior to interact with, brand, and modify this behavior for profitable ends.[17]

Throughout the 2000s, alongside concentrated media industries, social media technology companies have created formative ties with teen experience. Companies like Google, Facebook, Alibaba, and Tencent contour youth lives in local and global contexts. They are powerful brands and companies, and at the same time, the participatory nature of social media means YouTube, Instagram, Tumblr, and WeChat are also spaces young people use to explore identities, play and meet others, and lead social change. The Internet, social media, and other digital resources are "boundary publics..., metaphorical landscapes of social interaction".[18] YouTube and WeChat exemplify these developments and highlight how social media platforms now operate as primary boundary publics, spaces of social interaction that extend an old paradox in youth culture: the key media structures that shape youth lives are also the very sites where youth navigate authentic meaning and experience and imagine their own futures.

YOUTUBE AND WECHAT

YouTube is now a primary gathering place for young people around the world. In 2020, YouTube was the second most popular website globally, behind only the site's owner, Google. It remains among the most trusted global brands, with nearly 85 percent of visitors coming to the site from outside the United States. Since its launch in 2005, YouTube has moved from a primary social media network to a mainstream media platform that operates at the uneasy juncture between community and commerce and broadcast and social media. YouTube represents the convergence between technology companies and media industries, and like WeChat in China, it has changed how cultural production, celebrity, broadcast media, data surveillance, and youth media expression operate.[19]

By 2017, YouTube accounted for 80 percent of the 12 billion hours users spent on the top ten Android video streaming apps globally, far surpassing the influence of streaming services like Netflix. YouTube has changed how young people consume music, learn just about anything, and invest in favored genres and programming.

Its popularity is unprecedented, and its impact on youth lives across much of the world (excluding China, Pakistan, Iran, Syria, North Korea, and Germany) is perhaps unmatched.

Tencent's super platform WeChat launched in 2011 and quickly took advantage of the tremendous userbase Tencent had developed through its messaging service, QQ, to become a dominant force in Chinese media. By 2017, QQ and WeChat had become overwhelmingly popular with users, numbering close to a billion for each service. Part of a wave of new platform businesses, WeChat is a *social technology* that began as a messaging service and quickly became the central point of access for media, shopping, banking, and much else in China. WeChat is a super-app that hosts and facilitates other social media services and connections. It is a social technology because it enables a vast array of interactions and because it touches people in the way of an infrastructure of social life. WeChat is a sticky platform that has become integrated, responsive to, and effective in linking together social, economic, and cultural worlds. It is now "(1) a social and visual walkie-talkie, (2) an informational and service bazaar, and (3) a scanning and messaging wallet" in China and increasingly in countries around the world.[20]

While YouTube and WeChat are not the same kind of platforms, they are helpful for mapping the contemporary context of youth media culture because both are central to and representative of participatory cultures. Each platform is a key cog that enables the kind of convergence and interaction, data mapping, and cultural production and exchange that drives participatory cultures. Because of this, each platform brings to the fore some of the fundamental challenges young people face living in contemporary participatory cultures. Again, it is worth returning to the work of Walter Benjamin and his concerns for the paradoxical ways commercial culture changes our lives to capture the impact of YouTube and WeChat today.

Recall that Benjamin draws attention to the impact the profaning of culture has had on cultural meaning and experience. In rendering culture profane, mass and digital media play on the plasticity of cultural experience, opening cultural experience to intensive forms of commodification and manipulation, even while creating possibilities for the production of new meanings and experiences. Where YouTube and youth are concerned the impact of this dynamic is profound.

While the purpose of YouTube was not always clear to its founders (former PayPal employees Chad Hurley, Steve Chen, and Jawed Karim), it quickly became a key site for the exponential growth of vernacular creativity across cultures and especially among young people.[21] Amateur media creation has a long history, and cultural expression has always been part of adolescence, but YouTube has offered a new kind of stage for everyday cultural production and expression. YouTube has become an online community of spaces that showcase a host of new and old genres, channels, and celebrities that are now the grist of popular youth media cultures. "YouTuber" is now vernacular for micro celebrities and leading lights on the site and an expression used to talk about someone who spends significant time streaming material from the site. At the same time, as YouTube has evolved, it has moved increasingly into areas previously dominated by traditional media companies. YouTube began as a site to "broadcast yourself," as the early corporate tagline proffered, but over the 2010s it evolved into a popular archive used "for everyday expression, vernacular creativity, and community formation," and an archive of professional productions and professional aesthetics that competes with, even while supporting, the influence of traditional broadcast media.[22] In this way, YouTube is now a business that hosts and enables activities on its own *while providing* the devices and software applications to support the social and cultural activities of other companies and actors.

YouTube's brand value is tied to its role in supporting co-creativity and vernacular culture, but it functions as the primary video media archive for youth cultures around the world. The very size and reach of YouTube brings media culture closer to youth. What's more, because mobile phones provide a primary point of access to the platform for most teens, relationships with YouTube are only intensified as media travel with us throughout our private and public lives. The effects of this context reflect larger tensions in youth media culture.

YouTube is both a part of and a driving force in a field of social, cultural, and technological change that has impacted youth lives. Since the ratification of the United Nations Convention on the Rights of the Child in 1990, a series of changes has focused attention on the rights and risks shaping the lives of children and youth, including the right young people have to address their own experiences. The development of youth consumer markets, with their focus on youth wants and needs, has helped to focus this interest. So, too, have changes in technology, schooling, and work, not to mention renewed concern for the way citizen learning happens among young people. All of these developments have taken diverse shape across societies, but together, they draw attention to the way youth expression, youth rights, and youth identities have become focal concerns today.

YouTube has grown up in this context and, on one hand, it has been a key cultural technology supporting youth learning, the negotiation of youth identities, and expressions of vernacular creativity. Jean Burgess and Todd Green contend that "[B]ecause so much of the symbolic material mediated via YouTube originates in the everyday lives of ordinary citizens, or is evaluated, discussed and curated by them, ... YouTube, in theory, represents a site of cosmopolitan cultural citizenship."[23] The rise of professional, commercially produced media on YouTube can mitigate this outcome, but it is worth noting that

> Far from the dizzying heights of social media entertainment stardom or trolling subcultures, the platform remains a mediator and connector of activities that might be recognized by scholars of popular culture as the practices of cultural citizenship—mundane but engaging activities that create spaces for engagement and community formation. Models of participation that function in this way range from peer-to-peer guitar lessons to "memes" based around everyday consumption ... to "coming out" videos [that] have become particularly significant social media rituals." YouTube remains

a potential enabler and amplifier of cosmopolitan cultural citizenship—a space in which individuals can represent their identities and perspectives, engage with the self-representation of others, and encounter cultural difference.[24]

The personal and intimate connections expressed and engaged on YouTube form an intimate public sphere in youth lives, a space where the local and the private concerns of everyday life are engaged, discussed, and addressed in ways that bring them into public view. As a social medium, YouTube brings cultural life into the bedrooms, the friendship circles, and the networks of young people, and in the process, it offers a platform to engage public life and potentially shape the matters of common concern that affect us all.

On the other hand, however, because of the size and reach of YouTube into the daily lives of young people, it has become a dominant tool for sophisticated data science and the active regulation of users' content and behavior through leading-edge mechanisms of sociotechnical control. Central to this control is the algorithm that enables Google and YouTube to map and coordinate young people's everyday lives in ways that previous generations would find unimaginable. Algorithms are datapoints gathered from marking all our online experiences and networks, and increasingly those when we are not intentionally online. Data aggregation enables the production of complex algorithms that produce what Wendy Chun calls "a universe of dramas" enabled by Big Data.[25] These dramas (the stories, celebrities, associations, and products we interact with) are "co-produced transnationally by corporations and states through intertwining databases of action and unique identifiers."[26] Databases and identifiers enable algorithms to target, engage, and integrate a diverse range of youth into the global imaginaries of consumer celebrity cultures and the archives of surveillance states. Not surprisingly, the results of these processes can be deeply problematic.

At the most general level, YouTube has become a curation system, a site where algorithms link youth identities to curated home pages where highly individuated video and channel suggestions are presented based on one's personal history of use on YouTube and all other activities done under a user's Google login.[27] This presents serious privacy issues for young people, who are often leading users of YouTube and other Google products. Data footprints become a resource to craft advertising, hold attention, and locate experiences on the site, typically in the service of profit. More importantly, it also leads to filter bubbles and echo chambers because YouTube's algorithms tend to expose users to things they already know and like. In large measure, YouTube curates the experience of users based on a principle of homophily, which brings like to like. What and who I have seen before, the assumption goes, is what and who I will want to see in the future. But this undermines an experience of difference for many youth. Rather than leading users to encounter ideas, images, and people that are novel or different from us, YouTube, like so many other social media sites, orients young users (and the rest of us) to sameness, to echo chambers that tell us what we already know and like. But, this is a deeply problematic pattern because different communities, different people, and different ideas are a necessary feature of everyday life in complex societies. Where homophily compromises the frequency with which young people encounter difference, then, it threatens social stability by undercutting the diversity and openness that is essential for the future well-being of democratic societies.

Data surveillance on social media, including YouTube, means that increasingly, young people are now regularly and without knowing it made accountable to corporations and governments, even as it appears these same institutions are increasingly less accountable to us.[28] In Laura Poitras's 2014 documentary, the former American military contractor and dissident Edward Snowden demonstrates how social media platforms are being used today by corporations and states to track and influence citizen behavior. The full impact of these developments on youth lives is still emerging, but the recent example provided by the company Cambridge Analytica, which illicitly used Facebook user data between 2015 and 2017 to influence voter behavior in the Brexit vote in the United Kingdom and as part of Donald Trump's 2016 election campaign in the United States, suggests how the mining of user data can lead to social conflict and political instability.

Like YouTube's influence in the West, WeChat's popularity crosses Chinese society. The platform emerged following a period of transition in China's online sphere. The early 2010s marked a period of online youth media unrest and action in a significant number of countries around the world. The Arab Spring—so-called because of the number of youth-led protest actions and revolutions happening across the Middle East and North Africa—provided powerful examples of young people demanding social, economic, and political justice, which were emulated in other countries around the world. China's Communist Party took note, and the state moved to ally more closely with media companies. In practical terms, this meant regulations compelled online companies to work with the state to regulate and oversee conduct on the Internet. WeChat arose shortly after these developments and was a rising star in China's online ecosystem by 2013.[29]

WeChat's rich functionality as a walkie-talkie, bazaar, and wallet means that, like YouTube, it is embedded in young people's everyday lives. WeChat is now a key resource to support work relationships and networking, and features like a short video clip service have made the platform key to the growth of selfies and the rise of online civic networks connected neither to work nor the state in China. The layers of close social connection embedded in WeChat have meant that while it is not a leading site to drive political movements, it is a key space where young people supplement, extend, and initiate social events and community building, beyond the bounds of the state. As noted earlier in the chapter, contemporary Chinese urban youth are engaged in media consumption and participation across a number of sites. They are connected to global media brands and are enacting new forms of social connection, communication, and community. Various challenges including housing, job markets, mobility, and access to education shape youth lives in China, and, in this context, WeChat is among the social media technologies that shape and bind youth together.

Research on how WeChat connects youth in China is emerging. The book-length study, *Super-Sticky WeChat and Chinese Society*, draws attention to the way WeChat is now being used to extend online participation by facilitating discussion of issues of public concern and creating communities and acts of online activism across the Chinese diaspora, including in response to the Covid-19 coronavirus in the Hubei province in 2019–2020. WeChat is also used by young people and others in China to mark and discuss public injustices by authorities and to discover new voices, including the literary figure Fan Yusu, a popular Internet author whose writing on WeChat about her life as a working-class woman, surviving in Beijing, has attracted attention across China. Fan Yusu has focused attention on issues of class and gender inequality and challenged how patriarchy and hypocrisy undergird a hierarchical social order.[30]

While these stories reveal the socially progressive role WeChat is having with Chinese youth (and others), like YouTube, there are also profound paradoxes in the way WeChat impacts everyday life. From its beginning, WeChat has been deeply integrated with systems of surveillance and censorship in China that aim to manage and control popular opinion and popular discontent. Specifically, WeChat has integrated keyword-filtering and keyword-sensoring systems into the platform in order to identify opposition to the state, including the way historical events (i.e., the massacre of student protesters in Tiananmen Square in 1989) deemed illegal by the Communist Party are publicly debated. The upshot of this is that while WeChat operates differently than YouTube, data aggregation and data monitoring are also used here to control populations and manage public opinion in ways that are dangerous and undemocratic.

It is likely not surprising that youth media culture continues to be the site of fundamental tensions and paradoxes. Since the early twentieth century, youth have been tied to the development of complex, mediated cultures. As workers, students, citizens, and everyday people, mediation has shaped the experiences, dreams, and networks that bind young people together. Youth and media as a consequence have become deeply tied to our conceptions of modernity. Youth media culture continues to be a site of social progress and hopes for freedom, even as it simultaneously produces profound conditions and limits that threaten our dreams for the future. This pattern has been part of modernity since the nineteenth century. The questions before us today are, how to support youth media cultures that foster plurality, difference, connection, and progressive social change.

Notes

1. CNNIC, *Statistic Report on Internet Development in China* (Beijing: China Internet Network Information Center, 2018).
2. Common Sense Media, *The Common Sense Census: Media Use by Tweens and Teens* (San Francisco, 2015); S. Livingstone et al., *EU Kids Online: Findings, Methods, Recommendations* (London: EU Kids Online, 2014).
3. W. Benjamin, "The Work of Art in the Age of Mechanical Reproduction," in *Illuminations*, ed. H. Arendt, trans. H. Zohn (New York: Schocken Books, 1986).

4. M. McLuhan, *Understanding Media: The Extensions of Man* (New York: McGraw-Hill, 1964).
5. R. Williams, *Culture and Society: Coleridge to Orwell, 1780–1950* (London: Chatto and Windus, 1958).
6. B. Osgerby, *Youth Media* (New York: Routledge), 9.
7. J. Galbraith, *The Affluent Society* (Boston and New York: Houghton Mifflin, 1958).
8. Stanley Cohen, *Folk Devils and Moral Panics: The Creation of the Mods and the Rockers* (London: MacGibbon and Kee, 1972); J. Dillabough and J. Kennelly, *Lost Youth in the Global City: Class, Culture and the Urban Imaginary* (New York: Routledge, 2010).
9. D. Downes, *The Delinquent Solution: A Study of Subcultural Theory* (London: Routledge and Keegan Paul, 1966); G. Murdock and R. McCron, "Scoobies, Skins and Contemporary Pop," *New Society* 547 (1973).
10. T. Korsvold, "Childhood and Children's Retrospective Media Consumption Experiences: The Case of Norway," *Nordicom Review* 38, no. 2 (2017): 97–122.
11. Fengshu Liu, *Urban Youth in China: Modernity, the Internet and the Self* (New York: Routledge, 2011), 59.
12. Ibid., 102; L. Tsui "Introduction: The Socio-Political Internet in China," *China Information* 19, no. 22, (2005): 181–188.
13. Stanley Cohen, *Folk Devils and Moral Panics: The Creation of the Mods and Rockers* (London: MacGibbon & Kee, 1972).
14. S. Kline, *Out of the Garden: Toys and Children's Culture in the Age of T.V. Marketing* (London: Verso Books, 1993).
15. J. Kahne, E. Middaugh, and D. Allen, "Youth, New Media and the Rise of Participatory Politics" (Youth and Participatory Politics Research Network Working Papers No. 1, 2014, 1–25, Oakland, CA).
16. See E. Anderssen, "Through the Eyes of Generation Z," *The Globe and Mail*, Published June 24, 2016, https://www.theglobeandmail.com/news/national/through-the-eyes-of-generation-z/article30571914//
17. Darin Barney, Gabriella Coleman, Christine Ross, Jonathan Sterne, and Tamar Tembeck, eds., *The Participatory Condition in the Digital Age University* (Minneapolis: University of Minnesota Press, 2016), viii.
18. M.L. Gray, *Youth, Media, and Queer Visibility in Rural America* (New York: New York University Press, 2009), 105.
19. J. Burgess and J. Green, *YouTube: Online Video and Participatory Culture*, 2nd ed. (Cambridge: Polity Press, 2018), 4.
20. Y. Chen, Z. Mao, and J.L. Qiu, *Super-Sticky WeChat and Chinese Society* (Bingley, UK: Emerald, 2018), 26, 49.
21. J. Burgess, "Hearing Ordinary Voices: Cultural Studies, Vernacular Creativity and Digital Storytelling," *Continuum: Journal of Media & Cultural Studies* 20, no. 2 (2006): 201–214.
22. Burgess and Green, *YouTube*, 12.
23. Ibid., 126.
24. Ibid., 126–129.
25. Wendy Chun, "Big Data as Drama," *EHL* 83, no. 2 (2016): 363
26. Ibid.
27. Burgess and Green, *YouTube*, 90.
28. Edward Snowden, "Big Data, Security, and Human Rights" (Keynote address for President's Dream Colloquium on Engaging Big Data, Simon Fraser University, Vancouver, BC, April 5, 2016).
29. Chen, Mao, and Qiu, *Super-Sticky WeChat*, 41–42.
30. Ibid., 94–99.

Further Reading

Back, Les. *New Ethnicities and Urban Culture: Racisms and Multiculture in Young Lives.* London: UCL Press, 1996.

Benjamin, Walter. "The Work of Art in the Age of Mechanical Reproduction." In *Illuminations.* Edited by H. Arendt. Translated by H. Zohn, 217–251. New York: Schocken Books, 1986.

Bennett, Andy. *Popular Music and Youth Culture: Music, Identity and Place.* Basingstoke: Palgrave, 2000.

Buckingham, David. *The Material Child: Growing Up in Consumer Culture.* Cambridge: Polity Press, 2011.

Burgess, Jean, and Joshua Green. *YouTube: Online Video and Participatory Culture.* 2nd ed. Cambridge: Polity Press, 2018.

Cohen, Phil. *Folk Devils and Moral Panics: The Creation of the Mods and the Rockers.* London: MacGibbon and Kee, 1972.

Dillabough, Joanne, and Jacqueline Kennelly. *Lost Youth in the Global City: Class, Culture and the Urban Imaginary.* New York: Routledge, 2010.

Drotner, Kirsten. "Dangerous Media? Panic Discourses and Dilemma of Modernity." *Paedogogica Historica* 35, no. 3 (1999): 593–619.

Gilroy, Paul. *There Ain't No Black in the Union Jack: The Cultural Politics of Race and Nation.* London: Hutchinson Group, 1987.

Hebdige, Dick. *Subculture: The Meaning of Style.* London: Meutheun, 1979.

Jenkins, Henry. *Convergence Culture: Where Old and New Media Collide.* New York: New York University Press, 2006.

Kline, Stephen. *Out of the Garden: Toys and Children's Culture in the Age of T.V. Marketing.* London: Verso Books, 1993.

Liu, Fengshu. *Urban Youth in China: Modernity, the Internet and the Self.* New York: Routledge, 2011.

McRobbie, Angela, and Trisha McCabe, eds. *Feminism for Girls: An Adventure Story.* London: Routledge and Keegan Paul, 1981.

Miles, Steven. *Youth Lifestyles in a Changing World.* Buckingham: Open University Press, 2000.

Nayak, Anoop. *Race, Place and Globalization: Youth Cultures in a Changing World.* New York: Berg, 2003.

Osgerby, Bill. *Youth Media.* London: Routledge, 2004.

Radway, Janice. *Reading the Romance: Women, Patriarchy and Popular Literature.* Chapel Hill: University of North Carolina Press, 1984.

Sharma, Sanjay, John Hutnyk, and Ashwani Sharma. *Dis-orienting Rhythms: The Politics of the New Asian Dance Music.* London: Zed Books, 1996.

Sterne, Jonathan, Gabriella Coleman, Christine Ross, Darin Barney, and Tamar Tembeck, eds. *The Participatory Condition in the Digital Age University.* Minneapolis: University of Minnesota Press, 2016.

Thornton, Sarah, *Club Cultures: Music, Media and Subcultural Capital.* Cambridge: Polity, 1995.

Index

Figures are indicated by *f* following the page number

abolition, 98–100, 103–104, 108
Abortion Law Reform (1975) (France), 299
Abu-Lughod, Lila, 280
activism and politics, 293–306. *See also* political violence
    antiestablishment movements and, 297–300
    color revolutions and, 303–304
    digital technology and, 304–305
    fascism and, 295–296
    gender and, 294, 296, 299
    global youth rebellion and, 304
    idealism and, 294–297
    millennials strike back and, 303–306
    nation-building and, 294–297
    1900s period of, 294–297
    1960s-1970s period of, 297–300
    1980s period of, 300–303
    overview of, 293–294, 306
    punk rock and, 302
    radically unpolitical youth and, 300–303
    reclaiming culture and, 305
    social justice and, 303
    social media and, 305
    Turkey and, 293–295, 299, 301, 304–305
    2000s period of, 303–306
    vitality and vigor of youth and, 296
    youth as metaphor for social change and, 295
    youth cult and, 295
Adams, William Taylor (writing as Oliver Optic), 380–381, 392
Addams, Jane, 397
Adolescence (Stanley), 5, 214
Adventures of Huckleberry Finn, The (Twain), 382
agency and the generation gap, 169–187. *See also* sexuality

    abortion and, 175–176
    age of consent and, 169
    birth control and, 183
    comic strips and, 173
    consent and, 184–186
    double standards on, 170
    education and, 171–172, 174–178
    femininity and, 170–171, 181, 186–187
    first times in trying out sexuality and, 181–182
    flirtation and, 176–178
    ignorance and, 174–176
    invisible loves and new scripts in, 178–180
    LGBTQ+ persons and, 173–174, 178–180, 185–187
    literature and, 172
    masculinity and, 170–171, 179–180, 181, 186–187
    masturbation and, 172, 181
    media coverage of youth issues and, 175
    moral panic and, 169
    oral sex and, 181–182
    overview of, 169–171, 186–187
    paternal correction and, 184
    popular culture and, 171–176
    pornography and, 173
    race and, 173, 178–180
    risks of sexuality and, 182–186
    science and, 174–176
    sentimental education and, 176–178
    sexual violence and, 185–186
    virility and, 170–171, 174–175, 179, 185–186
    youth sexual revolution and, 186–187
Aksenov, Vasilii, 202–203
ALA (American Library Association), 382, 385–386
Albarrán, Elena Jackson, 14

434 INDEX

Albarrán, Teodoro, 259
Alexander, Kristine, 14, 225
Alger, Horatio, 382
Allende, Salvador, 271
All in the Family (television show), 401
Al-Maria, Sophia, 280–282
Alvear, Marcelo Torcuato de, 256–257
American Bandstand (television show), 401, 418–419
American Broadcasting Company (ABC), 418
American International Pictures (AIP), 399
American Library Association (ALA), 382, 385–386
American Revolution, 84–85
Andy Hardy films, 386–387, 398
Anka, Paul, 418
antiestablishment movements, 297–300
Aquinas, Thomas, 31
Arab Spring, 113, 304–305
Argentina, youth organizations in, 256–257, 263–266, 269–271
Argus, The (newspaper), 156–157
Armstrong, Douglas V., 102
Arnold, Thomas, 220, 223
arts, visual. *See* visual arts
Ashby, Joseph, 222
Atlantic slavery and youth in Jamaica, 97–109
   abolition and, 98–100, 103–104, 108
   African cultural influence and, 97–99, 101–108
   battleground of youth culture and, 98–99
   Brutus and, 97–98, 103
   country marks and, 104–105
   dual identity and, 103, 107
   education and, 108
   fables and, 104
   forced adulthood of youth and, 98
   language and, 97–98, 103
   living conditions and, 106
   naming and, 102–103
   overview of, 97–99
   partial cultural freedom permitted and, 102, 107
   plantation culture and, 99–101
   psychological development and, 106
   resistance and, 103, 105–108
   runaways and, 98, 103, 105
   scarification and, 104–105
   social death and, 97, 99, 105
   tenacity of youth and, 105–106
At the Piano (Whistler, 1858-1859), 364, 364f
Augustine of Hippo, 22–24
Aurora, The (newspaper), 243–244
Austin, Joe, 2–3
Australia larrikins, 149–150, 155–160
Aymard, Maurice, 67

Babysitter (Forman-Brunell), 145
Baden-Powell, Robert, 256, 341–343
Bairon, Arkadii, 202
Baisers volés (Truffaut), 182
Baker, Josephine, 196
Balfour, Frances, 219, 223
Barbaro, Francesco, 44, 52
Barbie dolls, 276–277
Baron, Beth, 85, 116
Barthes, Roland, 161
Bashir, Anum, 281
Baun, Dylan, 15
Bayat, Asaf, 298
Bear, Gilbert, 244–245
Beatles, The, 204–206, 390, 418
Beaver, Marguerite, 247
Bee Hive, The (magazine), 213, 225–226
Behr, Peter, 326–327
Ben-Amos, Ilana, 65
Bend It Like Beckham (film), 405
Benjamin, Walter, 415–417, 422, 425
Benzaquén, Adriana, 12, 216
Berland, William, 52
Bernard of Clairvaux, 26
Betar (youth movement), 92
Big Bang Theory, The (television show), 402
Biographies of Exemplary Women (Liu), 361
Black Elk, 81–82
Black Entertainment Television (BET), 419
Blanch of Castile, 30
Blazing Saddles (film), 400
Bloom, John, 249
Blum, Léon, 296
boarding schools. *See* Indian boarding schools
Bolshevik party, 194–195
Bonjour tristesse (Sagan), 172
Book of the Knight of the Tower, The, 43–44, 51

Book of the Order of Chivalry, The (Llull), 43–44
Boomers (Brooks), 7
Borsay, Peter, 215
Bosworth, Charles Frederick, 360
boys and men. *See* agency and the generation gap; gender; sexuality
Boy Scouts, 8, 14, 193, 247, 256–259, 265, 341–342
branding, 275–279, 283, 285
Braungart, Margaret, 293, 302
Braungart, Richard, 293, 302
Brewin, Rebecca, 218, 221
Brezhnev, Leonid, 199, 203
Brickell, Chris, 156, 159
Bridges, George Wilson, 108
Brigades of the Peronist Youth, 265–266
Briggs, Laura, 237
Britten, Florence Haxton, 323
Bromley, Dorothy Dunbar, 323–324
Brooks, Victor D., 7
Brown, Frances Juanita, 313–315, 326
Browning, Elizabeth Barrett, 134–135
Brownlie, Robin Jarvis, 238
Brutus (enslaved person), 97–98, 103
Buckingham, David, 420
Buffalo News Boy (Le Cleer, 1853), 369, 369f
Burgess, Ernest, 153
Burgress, Jean, 426
Burnard, Trevor, 102–103
Burney, Fanny, 218, 224–225

Cadogan, Sarah, 217
Cagney, James, 398
Calle, Richard, 53
Cambridge Analytica, 428
Campbell, Victoria, 219
Canadian Indian, The (pamphlet), 244
Capa, Robert, 198
capoeira, 163–164
Capp, Bernard, 67
Card Trick, The (Brown), 371
Carlisle Indian Industrial School, 236
Carmina Burana, 25, 29
Carpentier, Jean, 175
Carroll, Lewis, 225
Cartoon Network, 402
Cassatt, Mary, 364

Castro, Fidel, 266–268
Catcher in the Rye (Salinger), 387
Catholic Church and Catholicism, 21, 44, 49, 257, 271
Cazes, Charles de, 243–244
CBS Broadcasting, 418
Centre for Contemporary Cultural Studies (CCCS), 419
Chaloub Group, 281–282
Chardon, Marguerite, 174
Charlotte Temple (Rowson), 377–378, 380, 385
Chatelain, Marcia, 320
Chaucer, Geoffrey, 133
Child, Brenda J., 236
Child, Lydia Maria, 381
child labor. *See* industrialization and child labor
Children's Games (Bruegel), 368
Chile, youth organizations in, 256–258, 271–272
Chilocco Indian Industrial School, 239–240, 245–246, 248
Chin, Elizabeth, 9, 14
China, youth culture in, 283, 289, 346, 354, 357–365, 384, 413–414, 420–421, 424–425, 428–429
chivalry, 43–44, 296, 342–343
Chorley, Katharine, 221
Christine de Pisan, 43, 45, 48, 50–54
Chun, Wendy, 427
Cienfuegos, Camilo, 267
Civil War (US), 85–86
Clarke, Edward, 61–63, 69
class. *See* elite coming of age; non-elite youth
Clement, Elizabeth, 319–320
Closen, Ludwig von, 85
Cohen, Stanley, 160, 421
Cohn-Bendit, Daniel, 298
Cold War, 11, 14, 171, 174, 196–198, 201–203, 209, 262–263, 266, 268–271, 302. *See also* style in the Cold War
Comaroff, Jean, 300
Comaroff, John, 300
coming of age. *See* elite coming of age
Communist Pioneers, 266–267
Communist Union of the Polish Youth, 92
Comparative Youth Culture (Brake), 1
Comstock, Anthony, 381

Confucian Classics, 361
consumer culture, 275–290
   Barbie dolls and, 276–277
   bluffing and, 283–284
   branding and, 275–279, 283, 285
   commercials and, 277
   commodification through intimacy and, 278
   entrepreneurial selves and, 278–279, 286–289
   fashion and, 283–286
   gender and, 277–278, 280–282, 285–286, 288–289
   identity and, 278–279
   malls and, 279–283
   marriage and, 288–289
   migration and, 286–289
   overview of, 275–276, 289–290
   Qatar and, 276, 280–283, 287, 289–290
   remittances and, 287
   social media and, 277–278, 281
   Uganda and, 284–285, 288
   WEIRD consumers and, 276–279
consumerism, 6, 13, 415–417, 420, 422
Consuming Work (Besen-Cassino), 145
Contender, The (Lipsyte), 388–389
Corrigan, Paul, 163
Cosby Show, The (television show), 419
Cotton, Anges, 220
Cotton, Arthur, 220
Country School (Homer), 360–361
Courbet, Gustave, 368–369
Courlander, Harold, 240
courtship practices, 4, 7, 15, 40, 50–54, 64–65, 67, 85, 116, 195, 314–319, 321, 323–324, 380, 385–386, 396
Cox, Caroline, 85
Crazy Horse, 81
Cressy, David, 50
Cross, Gary, 11, 15
"Cry of the Children, The" (Browning), 134
Cuba, youth organizations in, 266–269
Cuban Revolution, 86–87, 266, 268–269
Cultural Revolution, 11, 346, 420
CW Television Network, 402

Darrow, Joseph, 85
data surveillance, 14, 427–428
Davis, Natalie Zemon, 65–66

Dawson, Joseph, 224
De Barros, Juanita, 154, 161
de Charny, Geoffroi, 43–46
Decker, Corrie, 13
De Leeuw, Sara, 245
delinquency, 2, 6, 8, 86, 137, 142, 360, 403
Deng Xiaoping, 420
Depicting Canada's Children (Lerner), 371
Der Welsche Gast (Zirclaria), 43
Desch-Obi, T.K., 164
Destacemento Feminino of FRELIMO, 87
Devil on Wheels (film), 398
Diary of Nina Kosterina, The (Kosterina), 197
Dickson, James, 313–314
Digby, Kenelm, 48
Dirty Harry (film), 399
Disney, 401, 417–418, 423
Domination and the Arts of Resistance (Scott), 103
double standard on sexuality, 54, 64, 70, 170, 300, 315, 317–319, 323–324, 327–330
Douglass, Frederick, 99
Downes, David, 419
Doyle, Dickie, 218
Dublin, Thomas, 132, 135
Duffy, Brooke, 278
Dunton, Charles H., 140
Duodha, 23
Dyhouse, Carol, 215–217

Eales, Jacqueline, 48
Edelweiss Pirate leaders, 89–90
Ed Sullivan Show, The (television show), 401, 418
education. *See also* Indian boarding schools; monastic and university education
   Atlantic slavery and youth in Jamaica and, 108
   elite coming of age and, 42–48
   gender and, 171–172, 174–178
   holidays and values and, 335, 340
   industrialization and, 132, 138–142
   play cultures and, 221
   urbanization and, 151–152, 162
   visual arts and, 357–361, 358*f*
   Zanzibar and, 119–120, 124, 127
Egbert of Beek, 32
Ehrmann, Winston, 325
Eighth Grade (film), 413
Elisabeth, Duchess of Bouillon, 54

Elisabeth of Brunswick-Calenberg, 44
elite coming of age, 39–55. *See also* non-elite youth
    acculturation and, 45–50
    chivalry and, 43–44
    clothing and, 43
    courtship practices and, 50–54
    education and, 42–48
    gender and, 41, 43–54
    grooming and, 43
    humanism and, 48
    inheritance rights and, 40–42
    literary tropes and, 44–47
    manners and, 43
    marriage and, 50–54
    noble service and, 45–50
    overview of, 39–40, 54–55
    personal restraint and, 44–45
    play and, 50
    property and, 40–42
    responsibility and, 42–45
    training and, 45–50
    wardship and, 40–42
    young aristocrats as participants in, 54–55
Elizabeth of Hungary, 44, 50
Elmtown's Youth (Hollingshead), 322–323
El Shakry, Omnia, 115
Encyclopedia of Children and Childhood (Fass), 3
English in Love, The (Langhamer), 317
English Teddy Boys, 203
entrepreneurial selves, 278–279, 286–289. *See also* consumer culture
Equiano, Olaudah, 99, 104
Eric I of Brunswick-Calenberg, 52
Eritrean People's Liberation Front, 87
Ernaux, Annie, 185
Esenin, Sergei, 195
European Broadcasting Union, 407
Evangelical Youth Culture (Abraham), 117
Eva Perón Foundation, 264

Factory Act (1833) (Britain), 134
Fair, Laura, 124–125
Fairbanks, Douglas, 196, 397
Faith in Schools (Stambach), 117
Family of Frederick, Prince of Wales, The (Knapton, 1751), 366, 366f

family portraits, 365–368, 366f
Farrell, Sean, 340–341
Fass, Paula, 3, 8, 145
Father Knows Best (television show), 401
Felt, Jeremy, 135
femininity, 49, 114, 123, 170–171, 181–182, 186–187, 207, 296, 300
Fenchlerin, Ottilia, 51
Fernández, Osvaldo M., 265
Field, Corrine, 7, 146
film and television, 395–409. *See also* media culture across the globe
    adult anxieties and, 397–400
    cable television, 402–403
    car genre, 398
    comedy genre, 399–400
    family entertainment and, 400–401
    gender and, 398–399, 401, 405
    Hays Production Code and, 397–398
    horror genre, 399–400, 402–403
    identity and, 397–400, 404
    origins of film and, 396–397
    origins of television and, 400–401
    overview of, 395–396, 409
    race and, 405
    rating system for, 399–400
    recent changes in television programming and, 402–403
    satellite television, 402
    Scandinavian youth film, 403–406
    Scandinavian youth television, 406–409
    sex comedy genre, 400
    slasher genre, 400
    youth rebellion of 1968 and, 404–405
Fink, Frances Louise, 313–315, 326
Fitzgerald, F. Scott, 385
FitzStephen, William, 26
Five Classics, 355
Flash Gordon (film), 399–400
Flesh Gordon (film), 399–400
Foley, Alice, 223
Folk Devils and Moral Panics (Cohen), 160
Fontaine, Theodore, 240
Ford, Daniel Sharp, 380
Forman, Henry, 397–398
Fortna, Benjamin, 335
Foucault, Michel, 178

438 INDEX

Francis of Assisi, 31
Frauendienst (Liechenstein), 46
Freaks (film), 400
Free Speech Movement, 298
Fridays for Future (FFF), 305
Friends (television show), 402, 408
Frozen Deep, The (Dickens), 224
Fuccaro, Nelida, 346
Fürst, Juliane, 11, 14
Futuwwa, al- (youth movement), 296, 334–336, 338, 341, 344–345

Gainsbourg, Serge, 182
Gang, The (Thrasher), 152
Garland, Judy, 398
gender. *See also* agency and the generation gap; sexuality
  activism and politics and, 294, 296, 299
  consumer culture and, 277–278, 280–282, 285–286, 288–289
  education and, 171–172, 174–178
  elite coming of age and, 41, 43–54
  femininity, 49, 114, 123, 170–171, 181–182, 186–187, 207, 296, 300
  film and television and, 398–399, 401, 405
  holidays and values and, 336, 343, 344–345
  Indian boarding schools and, 243–246
  industrialization and, 136–140, 145
  literature and reading cultures, 377–380
  masculinity, 21, 26, 29, 31, 114, 116, 159, 170–171, 177, 179–180, 181, 186–187, 203, 207, 315, 329, 343
  media culture across the globe and, 418–419
  monastic and university education and, 25–26, 29, 34–35
  non-elite youth and, 63–64, 67–71
  play cultures and, 214–221
  political violence and, 87
  style in Cold War and, 203, 207
  tomboys and, 114, 122–123, 126, 128, 217
  urbanization and, 161–162
  visual arts and, 360–366, 371
  Zanzibar and, 116–127
generation gap. *See* agency and the generation gap
Geoffrey Le Baker of Swinbrook, 52–53
Gerald of Wales, 26–27

Gilfoyle, Timothy, 163
Gilte Legende, 44, 50
Girart of Vienne, 47
Girl Guides, 256–259
girls and women. *See* agency and the generation gap; gender; sexuality
Gleadle, Kathryn, 222
globalization, 8, 14, 128, 145, 194, 265, 275, 305, 348, 414, 420, 422
Global Justice Movement (GJM), 303
global youth rebellion, 304
Glorious Thirty, 174–175, 182–183, 186
Golden Age, The (Grahame), 214
Goldman, Emma, 171
Gooderson, Philip, 153
Good Neighbor Policy, 259–260
Good Times (television show), 419
Google, 417, 423–424, 427
Gordy, Berry, Jr., 419
Gorsky, Bradley, 203
Goshgarian, Rachel, 336
Goya, Francisco, 366, 368
Grantham, Mia, 277
Granville, Bonita, 398
Gray, Catherine, 101
Gray, Deborah, 99
Great Leap Forward, 420
Great Train Robbery, The (film), 396
Green, Todd, 426
Greene, Gael, 327
Grégoire, Ménie, 175
Grey, Louisa, 219–220
Griffith, Jane, 239, 244
Griffiths, Paul, 65
Grinspan, Jon, 137
Growing Up Amish (Stevick), 116
Guevara, Ernesto "Che," 265–267, 269
Guibert of Nogent, 24
Gulistan, 358, 358f
Gurevich, David, 205

Haiti, youth culture in, 103, 276, 283–287, 289
Hall, G. Stanley, 5, 214–215
Hanawalt, Barbara, 65
Hansen, Karen, 285
Happy Days (television show), 401
Harlow, Jean, 397–398

Hashomer Hatzair (youth movement), 91, 93
Haskell Institute, 241
Hastings, John, 53
Hate U Give, The (Thomas), 390–391
Hawes, Joseph, 16
Hays, Will, 397
Hays Production Code, 397–398
Hebdige, Dick, 161
Heeks, Jasper, 13
Helga (film), 175
Henke, James, 297
Hep Cats (magazine), 388
Hickey, William, 220
Hill, Harold, 131
Hillier, John-Joseph, 161
hippie movement, 204–209
History of Young People in the West, A
    (Levi and Schmitt), 6
Hitler Youth, 88–90, 295
Hobsbawm, Eric, 198
Hoffmann, Abbie, 204
holidays and values, 333–348
    chivalry and, 342
    coming of age narratives and, 345–346
    contextualizing youth religious revival and,
        347–348
    education and, 335, 340
    futuwwa and, 334–336, 338, 341, 344–345
    gender and, 336, 343, 344–345
    human rights and, 344
    identity and, 336
    Lebanon and, 333–339, 341, 343–348
    Mawlid, 338–339
    overview of, 333–334
    problematizing secularization and, 347–348
    questioning religious-secular youth rupture
        and, 334–337
    religious values and, 341–347
    sectarian societies and, 337–341
    Twelfth Day, 340
    youth organizations and, 337–347
Hollingshead, August, 322–323
Holloway, Joseph E., 98
Hooligans or Rebels? (Humphries), 151
Horn, Pamela, 217
Hot Rod (magazine), 388
Hua Guan, 366

Hubbard, Eleanor, 68
Hund, Emily, 278
Hunt, Mabel, 218–219, 221

idealism, 294–297
Ignatius Loyola, 33
Indian boarding schools, 235–250
    "civilizing" mission of, 237–239, 242
    domination and, 239–240
    Enlightenment thought and, 238
    gender and, 243–246
    history and historiography of, 236–239
    indigenous critiques of, 249–250
    industrial training in, 240–245
    institutional failures and, 249–250
    language and, 239–242, 248–249
    literacy and, 239–240
    memory and, 245–246
    mischief in, 245–246
    as outcome of colonialism, 236–238
    overview of, 235, 249–250
    physical culture and, 246–249
    public displays and, 240–245
    resistance to, 237–240, 244, 247–248
    student cultures and, 249–250
    team sports and, 246–249
Indian Helper (newspaper), 241
Indian Leader (newspaper), 241
industrialization and child labor, 131–146
    age of commitment and, 142
    challenge of researching, 131
    definitional fluidity and, 145
    education and, 132, 138–142
    gender and, 136–140, 145
    globalization and, 142–145
    juvenile delinquency and, 137–142
    overview of, 131–133
    preindustrial context for, 133–134
    reform movements and, 131–146
    UN and, 133, 143–145
    unemployment and, 144
    vagrancy laws and, 134
    youth culture as alternative vision of
        economic life and, 142
Industrious in Their Stations (Braslaw),
    145–146
Instagram, 275–278, 424

Institute for Social Research, 415
Instruction of a Christian, The (Vives), 44
International Boy Scout Association, 256
Inter Ocean (newspaper), 242
Iowa Juvenile Home, 142
Iranian Revolution, 335
Iron Duke, The (Tunis), 386
Iron Hawk, 81
Islam and Muslims. See holidays and values; Zanzibar
Ivaska, Andrew, 126

Jacob, Wilson, 336
Jacques de Vitry, 29
Jamaica. See Atlantic slavery and youth in Jamaica
Jamaican Assembly, 101
Jamestown Journal (journal), 242
Jamhuri, Antoun Jarji, 345–347
jazz music, 89, 197–201
Jefferson's, The (television show), 419
Jenkins, John, 108
Jensen, Helle Strandgaard, 15
Jesuit order, 33, 72
Jesus Christ Superstar (1970), 206
Jewish youth movements, 90–93
Jiang Shiquan, 366
Joachim I of Brandenburg, 52
Jobs, Richard Ivan, 7
John de Warenne, 53
John II of Brabant, 41
John of la Rochelle, 29
John Paston II, 53
Jorisdochter, Neeltje, 65
Joyce, Matthias, 218
juvenile delinquency, 2, 6, 8, 86, 137, 142, 360, 403

Kakasoo, Phoebe, 243–244
Kanin, Eugene, 328
Kata'ib Organization, 337, 343–346
Katherine of Alexandria, 50
Kellington, H.E., 140–141
Kelly, Ned, 158–159
Kelm, Mary Ellen, 238
Kennan, George, 262–263
Kett, Joseph, 7

"Keystone Cops" (films), 396
Khrushchev, Nikita, 203
Khuri, Fuad, 340
Kilvert, Henry, Rev., 219
King, Wilma, 98–99
Kinsey, Alfred, 321
Kinsey Report, 175, 321
Kirkman, Francis, 69
Kitagawa Utamaro, 364
Kitto, John, 224–225
Knabenschaften, 65
Komsomol congress, 196–197, 199, 295–296
Konadu, Kwasi, 98
Konigsburg, E.L., 388
Kopelev, Lev, 196
Korsvold, Tora, 420
Kosmodemyanskaya, Zoya, 87
Kozlov, Alexei, 202

La Ciudad Infantil, 264
La Cruzada Eucarística de los Niños, 258
Ladd, Luther, 85
Ladies Preparing Newly Woven Silk in the Style of Zhou Fang (Huizong, attributed), 364, 364f
Lal, Ruby, 121
Last of the Mohicans, The (Cooper), 223
L'Astragale (Sarrazin), 172
Latin America. See youth organizations in Latin America
Learning to Forget (Lassonde), 146
Leave It to Beaver (television show), 401
Lebanon, holidays and values in, 333–339, 341, 343–348
LeClair, Linda, 326–327, 329
Legenda Aurea (Voragine), 44
Le Moal, Paul, 178, 180
L'Engle, Madelein, 388
Lenin, Vladimir, 86
Les amitiés particulières (Peyrefitte), 178
Let the Hurricane Roar (Lane), 386
Lewis, Oscar, 268
Lewis, Ruth Behar, 268
LGBTQ+ persons, 173–174, 178–180, 185–187
literature and reading cultures, 375–391
    cautionary tales and, 377–381
    diversification of, 384–391

establishment of, 376–384
film adaptations and, 386–388
gender and, 377–380
industrialization and, 377
librarians and, 385–386
magazines and, 379–382, 386–387
overview of, 375–376
race and, 390
Romanticism and, 378
satirization of cautionary tales and, 381
social concerns and, 377–378
Stratemeyer model and, 382–384, 386–387
YA literature, 385–389
Littlefield, Alice, 248
Livermon, Xavier, 275
Lives of the Early Methodist Preachers (Jackson), 216
Llull, Ramon, 43, 46
Locke, John, 214, 217
Loeb, Paul, 301
Lomawaima, K. Tsianina, 245–246
Lone Cowboy (James), 386
Lonely Boy (film), 418
Lord of the Flies (Golding), 387
Louis François Report, 174
Lovejoy, Paul, 105
Lozee, Grace Davis, 141
Lukes, Ann, 87
Luther, Martin, 32–33
Lynd, Helen, 320–322
Lynd, Robert, 320–322
Lyttelton, Lucy, 217, 220–221

Maa peoples, 82–84
Maasai people, 83
Macaulay, Thomas, 223
MacKenzie, Clarence, 85
magazines, 225–226, 379–382, 386–387
Makdisi, Ussama, 337
Maksudyan, Nazan, 15
malls, 279–283
Mannheim, Karl, 306
March of the Penguins protest, 272
Marcuse, Herbert, 175, 415
marriage. *See also* agency and the generation gap; courtship practices; sexuality
child marriage, 121–122

consumer culture and, 288–289
elite coming of age and, 50–54
forced marriages, 325
non-elite youth and, 63–65
urbanization and, 162
visual arts and, 360
Zanzibar and, 121, 124–127
Married with Children (television show), 402
Marsh, Catherine, 225
Marten, James, 9
Martin, Joseph Plumb, 84
Martin, Mary Clare, 14
Martineau, Harriet, 222, 225
Martyr, A (Pelez), 369
masculinity, 21, 26, 29, 31, 114, 116, 159, 170–171, 177, 179–180, 181, 186–187, 203, 207, 315, 329, 343
Mason, Paul, 304
Massachusetts Nautical Reform School, 86
Massacre of Tlatelolco, 270
Massey, Doreen, 303
Masters & Johnson Report, 175
Mather, Cotton, 72
Matteson, J. Harold, 260
Mawlid, 338–339
Mayakovsky, Vladimir, 195–196
McCron, Robin, 419
McKelway, Alexander, 135
McKenzie, Parker, 240
McLeod, Jeff, 249
McRobbie, Angela, 419
media culture across the globe, 413–429. *See also* film and television
class and, 418–419
consumerism and, 415–417
cosmopolitan citizenship and, 426–427
data surveillance and, 427–428
digitization of, 423–424
emergence of, 414–417
gender and, 418–419
industrialization and, 416–417
making modern youth culture and, 417–421
moral panic and, 421
Motown and, 419
network societies and, 422–424
overview of, 413–414
postwar development of, 417–421

media culture across the globe (*cont.*)
   race and, 417–420
   rock and roll and, 417–418
   social media and, 424–429
   subcultures and, 422–424
   suburbanization and, 418
   teen television and, 418
   WeChat and, 424–425, 429
   YouTube and, 424–429
medieval education. *See* monastic and university education
Mella, Julio Antonio, 267
Melville, Herman, 85
Mémoire de fille (Ernaux), 185
men and boys. *See* agency and the generation gap; gender; sexuality
Mencius, 361–362, 361f
Mexican American Youth (1966), 326
Mexico, youth organizations in, 258, 260–262, 266, 268–270
Middletown (Lynd and Lynd), 320–321
Middletown in Transition (Lynd and Lynd), 322
Milkman, Ruth, 305
millennials, 303–306
Mills, Lowell, 145
Minios, Georges, 377
Mirguet, Paul, 185
Missing (Maira), 116
Mitterauer, Michael, 61
Mohawk Institute Indian Residential School, 247
monastic and university education, 21–35
   aristocratic university, 34–35
   arrogance of students and, 26–27
   beginnings of youth culture and, 24–27
   central middle ages and, 24–27
   challenges faced by students in, 28
   Church reform and, 24
   competition in, 30
   early middle ages and, 22–23
   early modern university and, 32–34
   friars and, 30–32
   gender and, 25–26, 29, 34–35
   hazing in, 27
   ideal of monastic youth and, 23
   identities and, 27–30

   institutions and, 27–30
   Jesuit education, 33
   late medieval countercultures and, 30–32
   material conditions for youth culture and, 24
   medieval stages of life and, 22–23
   minor orders and, 25
   ordination process and, 25
   overview of, 21–22
   reformations and, 32–34
   school to university and, 27–30
   sexuality and, 29
   social and geographic mobility and, 25–26
   student housing and, 28
   violence and, 29–30
Monster (Myers), 390
Montagu, William, 101
Montoneros, 270
Moore, Tom, 223, 225
moral panic, 2–3, 68–69, 72, 160–161, 169, 173, 196, 198, 416, 421
More, Hannah, 222
Mortimer, Roger, 53
Mosse, George, 170
mothers, 361–365, 361f, 363f, 364f
Motown, 316, 390, 419
MTV, 402
Murdock, Graham, 419
Murphy, Edgar Gardner, 135
muscular Christianity, 217
Muslim Scouts, 338, 342–343
Mustenberger, Hugo, 397

Nadi al-'Uruba (youth-centric movement), 339–340, 346–347
Najjadeh Organization of Lebanon, 337–340, 342–346
Nancy Drew books, 382–384, 398
Nasuli, Muhyi al-Din al-, 342
National Broadcasting Company (NBC), 418
National Committee to Aid Refugees (CONAR), 271
National Strike Council, 270
National Volunteer Organization, 346
nation-building, 294–297
Nazism, 88–90
Neged Hazerem, 93

neoliberalism, 14, 271–272, 275, 279–280, 282–283, 290, 301, 304–305, 335, 348, 422
Neuwirth Law (1967), 183
Nevinson, Margaret, 218–221, 224, 228
Newbery Award, 385
Nibelungenlied, The, 40, 47, 50, 52
Niget, David, 13–14
Night of the Living Dead, The (film), 400
noble service, 45–50
non-elite youth, 59–72. *See also* elite coming of age
  ambiguous status of youth and, 59–60
  apprenticeships and, 61–62
  contested territory of, 60
  fairs and festivals and, 65–68
  filles du roi and, 63
  gender and, 63–64, 67–71
  journeymen and, 62–63, 69, 71
  life-cycle service and, 61–62, 69
  literacy and, 72
  marriage and, 63–65
  middle classes and, 72
  migration and, 62–63
  moral panic and, 68–69
  orphans and, 62
  overview of, 59–60
  responding to youth culture and, 68–72
  sexuality and, 64–65, 67, 70
  tasks of youth and, 61–65
  violence and, 71
  youth groups and, 65–68, 71

O'Day, Rosemary, 48
Odlety, Nettie, 240
Ogorodnikov, Aleksandr, 206
One Hundred Children at Play, A (Yang), 354–355, 354f, 366
Optic, Oliver (pseudonym for William Taylor Adams), 380–381, 392
Organization of American States, 262
Orlova, Liubov, 197
ORTF (television station), 175
Osborne, Dorothy, 67
Outsiders, The (Hinton), 388–389, 391
overview of volume. *See* youth culture overview

Palestinian Youth Activism in the Internet Age (Dwonch), 116
Palladino, Grace, 7
Pamela (Richardson), 377
Pan American League of Miami, Florida, 260
Pan American Student Forum, 260
Pan American Union, 259, 261–262
Paris Salon, 368–369
Park, Robert, 153
Parsons, John Carmi, 39
Parzival, 41
Paston, Margery, 53
Patterson, Orlando, 97, 105
Patty Duke Show, The (television show), 401
Paul the Deacon, 23
Peiss, Kathy, 319
Pelletier, Madeleine, 171
Pepys, Samuel, 67
Pereire, Anita, 318
Perestroika, 199
Perón, Eva "Evita," 263
Perón, Juan, 263–266, 270
Peronist Youth, 265–266, 270
Peter Abelard, 25–26
Peyrefitte, Roger, 178
Phillips, Kim, 51
Photoplay (magazine), 397
Pickford, Mary, 196–197
Pilgrimage of Human Life, The (Deguileville), 45, 50
Pinochet, Augsto, 271
Pizzaro, Judith, 86
Place, Francis, 219–220
Platter, Thomas, 62, 66, 72
play cultures, 213–227
  ancient precedents of, 214
  as apprenticeship, 225–226
  boating, 220
  cricket, 221
  education and, 221
  family cultures and, 216–217
  fragmentary nature of sources on, 213–214
  gender and, 214–221
  imaginative play, 222–224
  inventiveness and, 217–221
  juvenile writing and, 225–226
  memory and, 216

play cultures (*cont.*)
   outdoor play, 217–221
   overview of, 213–216, 226–227
   periodicals and, 225–226
   riding, 218–219
   scaffolding and, 214
   sibling relationships and, 216–217
   skating, 220
   skill and, 217–221
   social worlds and, 215
   swimming, 219–220
   theatricals and, 222–224
Pocock, John, 218
political movements. *See* activism and politics
political violence, 79–93
   American Revolution and, 84–85
   Civil War and, 85–86
   definition of, 80
   fighting in the name of youth and, 86–87
   gender and, 87
   Hitler Youth and, 88–90
   Jewish youth movements and, 90–93
   limitations of youth and power and, 83–84
   mobilization for war and, 88–90
   organizing against state power and, 90–93
   overview of, 79, 93
   preindustrial world and, 81–83
   revolutions and, 86–87
   service to the state and, 88–90
   warrior culture and, 81–84
Pomfret, David, 7
Porret, Jacob, 65
Poyntz, Stuart, 16
Pratt, Richard Henry, 236
Prause, JoAnn, 86
premarital sex, 64, 117, 314–315, 320–322, 325–326
Prentice, Agnes, 141
Presley, Elvis, 388, 399, 418
Preston School of Industry, 140
Prince, Mary, 99
Private Yankee Doodle (Martin), 84
Progressive Socialist Party, 337, 344
Protestant Reformation, 21–22, 32–33, 72, 293
Providence Reform School, 86
punk rock, 208–209, 302, 415, 419, 421
Pussy Riot, 209

Qatar, consumer culture in, 276, 280–283, 287, 289–290
QQ (messaging service), 414, 425
Quadrophenia (film), 418–419

race. *See also* Atlantic slavery and youth in Jamaica; Indian boarding schools; urbanization and youth gangs
   agency and, 173, 178–180
   film and television and, 405
   literature and, 390
   media culture across the globe and, 417–420
   sexuality and, 316, 319–320, 323, 325, 326, 329
   style in Cold War and, 202
   youth organizations in Latin America and, 256–259, 262–264
Rainy Mountain Boarding School, 240
Rambo (film), 399
Ras, Merion E. P. de, 296
Rashtriya Sawyamsevak Sangh (RSS), 346
reading cultures. *See* literature and reading cultures
Rebel without a Cause (film), 398
Rees of Kingston, 106–107
Reeves, Andrew, 12
Reich, Wilhelm, 175
Reiss, Ira, 326
religion. *See* holidays and values; Zanzibar
Renoir, Pierre-August, 364
Revenin, Régis, 178–179
Revolutionary Left Movement, 271
Revolutionary Youth Work Brigades, 266
Richardson, Sarah, 219–220
Ringel, Paul, 15
Rites of Passage (Kett), 7
Robert the Devil, 47, 52–53
Robinson, Edgar, 398
rock and roll, 266, 275, 401, 417–418
Rocke, Michael, 70
Rocky Horror Picture Show, The (film), 400
Rodríguez, Aída S. de, 262
Rogers, Sidney, 247
Romero, Juan Pablo Vega, 268
Romuald of Ravenna, 24
Rook, Clarence, 155
Rooney, Mickey, 386

Roosevelt, Franklin D., 259
Rosen, David M., 9, 13
Rosner, Eddie, 197–198
Rossi, Arturo, 71, 263
Rossiaud, Jacques, 71
Rousseau, Jean-Jacques, 214, 217
Rowe, L.S., 259
Rubin, Jerry, 299
Rule of St. Benedict, 23
Russell, Mona, 116
Russian Civil War, 295
Rybakov, Anatolii, 295

Saadi of Shiraz, 358
Sagan, Françoise, 172
Salaula (Hansen), 285
Salme, 117–118, 125, 127–128
Sanderson, Maurice, 244
Sarrazin, Albertine, 172, 180
Sbaiti, Nadya, 344
Scandinavian youth film and television, 403–409
Schalbetter, Antony, 66
Scheld, Suzanne, 283–284, 288
Schindler, Nobert, 71
Schmidt, James, 13
Scholastic (magazine), 386
schooling. *See* education; Indian boarding schools; monastic and university education
Schröder, Caspar, 51
Schwartz, Marie Jenkins, 99, 132
Scott, James C., 103
Scouting for Boys (Baden-Powell), 341–343
secondary education. *See* monastic and university education
Second Sex (Beauvoir), 171
sectarianism. *See* holidays and values
Seinfeld (television show), 402
Sells, William, 105
Şenocak, Neslihan, 31
Seventeen (magazine), 387–388, 418
Seventeen (Tarkington), 385
Seventeenth Summer (Daly), 387
sex, premarital, 64, 117, 314–315, 320–322, 325–326
Sex and the College Girl (Greene), 327

sexual agency and the generation gap. *See* agency and the generation gap
sexuality, 313–330. *See also* agency and the generation gap; gender
  birth of going steady and, 322–324
  class and, 319–320
  courtship rituals and, 321
  double standard of, 315, 317–319, 323–324, 327–330
  flipping and, 329
  LGBTQ+ persons and, 316–317
  loosening of restrictions on, 318–321
  media portrayal of, 316
  necking and, 321–324
  orgasm gap and, 329–330
  overview of, 313–317, 328–330
  permissiveness with affection and, 324–325
  petting and, 319, 323
  premarital sex and, 314–315, 321–322, 325–326
  prostitution and, 319–320
  race and, 316, 319–320, 323, 325, 326, 329
  revolutions in, 315, 325–328
  treating and, 319–320
  virginity and, 319
  women's movement and, 315, 318
Sgt. Pepper's Lonely Hearts Club Band (Beatles), 205–206, 390
Shaarawi, Huda, 121
Sharabi, Hisham, 345–346
She Taught Her Sons While Weaving at Her Loom (Gai and Wang), 362
Shore, Heather, 153
Silver, Roxanne, 86
Simon Report (1972), 172, 175, 181–182
Simpsons, The (television show), 402
Sinatra, Frank, 418
SKAM (television show), 408
slavery. *See* Atlantic slavery and youth in Jamaica
Sleight, Simon, 13
Smallwood, Stephanie E., 98
Snap the Whip (Homer, 1872), 369
social justice. *See* activism and politics
social media, 277–278, 281, 305, 424–429
Solly, Henry, 218, 221
Song dynasty, 354

Sorrows of Young Werther, The (Goethe), 375–378, 385
Soul Train (television show), 419
South African War (1899-1902), 162
Southern Cone youth organizations, 269–272
Soviet Union, 87, 194–202, 205–209, 384–385
Spink, Mary A., 141
Spreat, John, 63
Spurlock, John, 322
Stalin, Josef, 196, 198–202, 205, 385
Starr, Frederick, 200
States of Delinquency (Chávez-García), 138
Steinbeck, John, 198
Steinem, Gloria, 327
Stephen, Fitzjames, 224
St. Nicholas (magazine), 381
Stolen Childhood (King), 98
Stone, Lawrence, 48
Stone Breakers, The (Courbet, 1849), 368
Story of the Kelly Gang, The (film), 159
Stratemeyer, Edward, 382–384, 386–387
Struggle of Equal Adulthood, The (Field), 146
style in the Cold War, 193–209
    Afghanistan invasion and, 206
    alcoholism and, 207–208
    androgyny and, 207
    definition of, 194–197
    gender and, 203, 207
    hippie movement and, 204–209
    jazz music and, 197–201
    overview of, 193–194
    at peace, 203–209
    post-Soviet style and, 209
    race and, 202
    slang and, 208
    stiliaga and, 199–203
    at war, 197–203
Subculture (Hebdige), 161
"Sue Barton, Student Nurse" (Boyston), 386
Sukarieh, Mayssoun, 294, 300
Swartz, Rebecca, 237
Symonds, Joan, 68
Syrett, Nicholas L., 7, 15

Tala'i' Organization, 337–340, 343–344
Talmon-Chvaicer, Maya, 164
Tang dynasty, 363

Tannock, Stuart, 294, 300
Tanzimat, 294
Tarzan (comic strip), 173
Teen Parade (magazine), 388
television. *See* film and television
Temple, Shirley, 398
Tencent, 414, 417, 424–425
Texas Chainsaw Massacre, The (film), 400, 408
Thistlewood, Thomas, 103–104
Thomas, Angie, 390
Thomas Aquinas, 31
Thompson, Elizabeth, 335
Thrasher, Frederick, 151–153
tomboys, 114, 122–123, 126, 128, 217
Tom Brown's Schooldays (Hughes), 380
Transnational Histories of Youth in the Twentieth Century (Jobs and Pomfret), 334–335
Trattner, Walter, 135
Treasure of the City of Ladies, The (Pisan), 48, 50
Trexler, Robert, 66
Trotman, David, 163
Tunis, John R., 386
Turkey, activism and politics in, 293–295, 299, 301, 304–305
Turner, Nicholas, 62
Turvey, Richard, 161
Twain, Mark, 149–150, 165, 381
Two Leggings, 81–82
Tzukunft, 92

Uganda, consumer culture in, 284–285, 288
Uncle Tom's Cabin (Stowe), 377
Under Dewey at Manila (Stratemeyer), 383
Union of Communist Youth (UJC), 267–269
United Nations, 133, 143–145
United Nations Children's Emergency Relief Fund (UNICEF), 133, 144, 288
United States Agency for International Development (USAID), 280
university education. *See* monastic and university education
Unlucky Citizen, The (Kirkman), 69
urbanization and youth gangs, 149–164
    approaches to research on, 160–162
    beyond criminalization and, 163–164

common threads and, 155–156
conditions of, 150–152
creativity and, 163
development of, 150–152
education and, 151–152, 162
gender and, 161–162
genus larrikin and, 156–160
growth and, 152–153
intersectionality and, 162–164
marriage and, 162
moral panic and, 160–161
overview of, 149–150, 164–165
slang terms and, 158
territories of youth and, 152–155
transurban phenomena and, 164–165
youthscape and, 154
Utesov, Leonid, 197–198

Vallejo, Camila, 272
Vallejo, Demetrio, 269–270
values. *See* holidays and values
Vasconcellos, Colleen A., 13
Vergerio, Pier Paolo, 44–45
VH- 1, 402
Viacom, 418, 423
violence, political. *See* political violence
visual arts, 353–372
  comic relief in, 357–358
  education and, 357–361, 358*f*
  family portraits and, 365–368, 366*f*
  gender and, 360–366, 371
  globalism and, 371–372
  hundred children at play theme in, 354
  marriage and, 360
  misbehaving youth depicted in, 358–360
  mothers and, 361–365, 361*f*, 363*f*, 364*f*
  overview of, 353–354, 372
  pictures as wish fulfillment and, 354–357, 354*f*
  Western genre painting and, 368–371, 369*f*
Volkov, Aleksandr, 385
Vygotsky, Lev, 214

Waddell, Hope Masteron, 107
Walking Dead, The (television show), 402
Wang Dun, 363
Warner, Glenn "Pop," 248

Warsaw Ghetto, 92–93
Weber, Adna, 150, 160
WeChat, 414, 417, 421, 424–425, 428–429
Weeton, Ellen, 220
West, Mae, 398
Western genre painting, 368–371, 369*f*
Where the Girls Are (Douglas), 316
White, Deborah Gray, 99
Wicks, Ann Barrott, 15
Wien, Peter, 296
Wilder, Laura Ingalls, 386
Wild Ones, The (film), 398
Wilkinson, Louise, 12
Willard, Michael Nevin, 2–3
Williams, Abigail, 222–224
Williams, Raymond, 150
Willson, Meredith, 131
Wirth, Louis, 152
Wittig, Monique, 180
women and girls. *See* agency and the generation gap; gender; sexuality
Woodman, Philip, 61, 69
Woolf, Virginia, 225
Woolford, Andrew, 236, 238, 247–248

YA literature. *See* literature and reading cultures
Yava, Albert, 239
yippies, 204, 298–299
Yonge, Charlotte, 218, 222–223, 225
Young, Frederick, 224
Young Europe (movement), 293
Young Men's Christian Association (YMCA), 115
Young Women's Christian Association (YWCA), 115
Youth and Sex (Bromley and Britten), 323–324
Youth Companion (magazine), 379–380
Youth Culture and Social Change (Gildart et al.), 7
youth culture overview, 1–16
  activism, 9–10
  adolescence, 4–5
  adults effort to shape coming of age, 3–4
  armed conflict, 9
  children and youth distinguished, 5
  complexity of youth culture, 1–2

448 INDEX

youth culture overview (cont.)
   control, 8
   definition of youth culture, 3–4
   economy, 8–9
   gender, 8, 10
   historiography, 6–8
   industrialization as key transformation for development, 6
   juvenile delinquency, 8
   moral panic, 2–3
   political awareness, 9–10
   popular culture, 11
   race, 8
   scholarship on youth culture, 1–8
   search for definition of youth culture, 4–16
   series of problems, 2–3
   spaces of their own, 11
   tension between adult culture, 5, 7
   urbanization as key transformation for development, 6
   youth and youth culture distinguished, 3
youth gangs. *See* urbanization and youth gangs
youth groups, 65–68, 71
youth organizations in Latin America, 255–272
   Argentina and, 256–257, 263–266, 269–271
   Boy Scouts and, 256–259
   Chile and, 256–258, 271–272
   contesting bureaucratic authority and, 269–272
   Cuba and, 266–269
   empire and, 259–263
   Girl Guides and, 256–259
   internationalism and, 259–263, 267–268
   Mexico and, 258, 260–262, 266, 268–270
   nationalism and, 256–259
   overview of, 255–256, 272

   Pan-Americanism exchanges and, 259–263
   populism across the ideological spectrum and, 263–269
   race and, 256–259, 262–264
   Southern Cone organizations and, 269–272
   sports and, 268
Youth & Revolution in the Changing Middle East (Erlich), 335
Youth's Companion, The (magazine), 379–381
Youth's Friend, The (magazine), 379
YouTube, 275–277, 279, 424–429
yuppies, 300

Zanzibar, 113–128
   age-of-consent laws in, 121
   change over time in, 127–128
   child marriage in, 121–122
   civilizing mission and, 115
   crossroads of religious expectations and modern influences in, 114–117
   education in, 119–120, 124, 127
   gender in, 116–127
   initiation ceremonies in, 119
   marriage in, 121, 124–127
   Muna's world and, 122–128
   overview of, 113–114, 127–128
   playfulness in, 121–122
   Salme, culture following, 119–122, 125, 127–128
   scandal in, 117–118
   sexuality in, 116–125
   socialization in, 119–120
   tomboys in, 114, 122–123, 128
Zanzibar Revolution of 1964, 126–127
Zappner, Jan, 201
Zionism, 90–92